Bernice Chesler's
BED & BREAKFAST
IN THE MID-ATLANTIC STATES

"The best [B&B] book on the market."　　　　　　**—Relax magazine**

"Chesler's guides capture the flavor of the B&B and its proprietors."
　　　　　　　　　　　　　　　　　　　　—Associated Press

"Catching the essence of a place and its hosts in such tight space is an art form."
　　　　　　　　**—Ripley Hotch, author, editor, innkeeper;
　　　　The Inn on Montford, Asheville, North Carolina**

"Guests from your book have a clear idea of what to expect, and as a result they are never disappointed. You certainly have set the standard for B&B guides."
　　　　　　**—Michele M. Schiesser, La Vista Plantation,
　　　　　　　　　　　Fredericksburg, Virginia**

"We have utilized your guide like a bible . . . each year we experience some place new . . . with the sure knowledge of your book to guide us."
　　　　　　　　—Patricia Caven, Ottawa, Canada

"To find an inn . . . check 'Bernice Chesler's Bed & Breakfast in the Mid-Atlantic States.'"　　　　　　　　　　　**—Washington Post**

"Best Bet: We recommend Bed & Breakfast in the Mid-Atlantic States."
　　—Triangle Book Shop's Grapevine, Tompkins County, New York

"Chesler's books are a valuable resource for [travel] agents interested in offering bed and breakfast as an alternative to their clients."　　　**—Travel Weekly**

"You get more detail from her books."　　　　**—Philadelphia Inquirer**

"It's one of those books you can't put down."
　　　　　　—Phyllis Long, Hershey, Pennsylvania

"Very helpful for making our vacation in the U.S. very enjoyable."
　　　　　　　　—Iris Ehgartner, Vienna, Austria

"No other author that we know of has come close to your level and quality of research."
　　　—Dane Wells, The Queen Victoria, Cape May, New Jersey

"The most detailed and extensively researched guidebooks available."
　　　　　　　　—Country Almanac magazine

By Bernice Chesler

Author
In and Out of Boston with (or without) Children
Mainstreaming through the Media
Bed & Breakfast Coast to Coast
Bed & Breakfast in the Mid-Atlantic States
Bed & Breakfast in New England

Coauthor
The Family Guide to Cape Cod

Editor and Coordinator
The ZOOM Catalog
Do a ZOOMdo
People You'd Like to Know

Bernice Chesler's *Bed & Breakfast in the Mid-Atlantic States* and *Bed & Breakfast in New England* are accessible in searchable electronic format at the Online BookStore (OBS) (e-mail address: obs@marketplace.com). For information call 508/546-7346 (fax 508/546-9807).

Bed & Breakfast in the Mid-Atlantic States

**Delaware, Maryland, New Jersey,
New York, North Carolina,
Pennsylvania, Virginia,
Washington, D.C., West Virginia**

Fourth Edition

by **Bernice Chesler**

A Voyager Book

Old Saybrook, Connecticut

Library of Congress Cataloging-in-Publication Data

Chesler, Bernice.
    Bed & breakfast in the mid-Atlantic states : Delaware, Maryland, New Jersey, New York, North Carolina, Pennsylvania, Virginia, Washington, D.C., West Virginia / by Bernice Chesler. — 4th ed.
        p.   cm.
    "A Voyager book."
    Includes index.
    ISBN 1-56440-624-5 : $16.95
    1. Bed and breakfast accommodations—Middle Atlantic States—Guidebooks.   I. Title.   II. Title: Bed and breakfast in the mid-Atlantic states
TX907.3.M53C48   1995
647.947403—dc20   94-45295
                                                                                  CIP

Editorial and production services: Editorial Inc. of Rockport, Massachusetts.
Cover design: Steven Bridges.
Cover photo: Courtesy Wadsworth Atheneum, Hartford, Connecticut. Gift of Mrs. Frederic J. Agate. Photo by E. Irving Blomstrann. Cover shows detail of quilt; entire quilt is reproduced on page 408.
Text design: Penny Darras-Maxwell.
Maps: Geoffrey Mandel.
Composition in Meridien by Cathleen Collins.

Manufactured in the United States of America
Fourth Edition / Second Printing

To David

CONTENTS

INTRODUCTION

"Those hosts would be great for a documentary film," I said to my husband. We were leaving a Vermont B&B, a genuine farmhouse, where the farmer had offered me cow salve to soothe leg muscles that ached from pedaling over the hilly terrain.

That was about 15 years ago, when I had been working as a documentary film researcher for public television—and when there weren't enough New England bed and breakfasts to fill a book! (My first B&B guide combined New England and the mid-Atlantic states.) Who would have guessed then that bed and breakfast was to become the hottest trend in American travel? The acceptance of B&Bs on this side of the ocean came at just the right time for us—just as we were to discover the joys of pedaling from B&B to B&B, and from one interesting experience to another in what is now a total of 14 states and 6 countries.

In the 1990s bed and breakfast has come to be recognized for its personalized style, for hosts who help to give a sense of place. Now many B&B hosts have plotted back-road routes for guests. With the advent of bed and breakfast reservation services, bed and breakfasts are in the city and suburbs as well as in rural areas. In addition, B&Bs have opened in restored everything—from churches to schoolhouses, from beach cottages to mansions.

To distinguish private homes from inns, this book has introduced a symbol (●) for private homes that have one, two, or three guest rooms. B&B inns are likely to be larger, are a full-time profession, and in some cases have one or more hired staffers. Other symbols—in answer to travelers' requests—will lead you (quickly) to a romantic place, a spot that is great for kids, or a B&B where your group, family, or colleagues might book the entire place. See the key to symbols that appears on the back cover and at intervals throughout the book.

In documentary film style, *Bed & Breakfast in the Mid-Atlantic States* tries to focus as much on the memorable hosts as on their homes and B&B inns. In addition, each description aims to save travelers' time by anticipating questions: Located on a main road? What time is breakfast? Sample menu? Size of bed? What floors are rooms on? Does the bath have shower *and* tub? Is smoking allowed? Any pets in residence? Is fax available? What's the difference between the $60 and the $90 room?

Now, 10 B&B books and more than 2,000 interviews later, this latest edition reflects the wide range of possibilities that fit—with rare exceptions—into my original interpretation of bed and breakfast: a home setting with an owner in residence; a maximum of about 10 rooms; a common room; breakfast included in the rate, but no public restaurant or bar on the premises.

So what's changed? New owners are in residence. Lots of new places have opened. Most have private baths. Jacuzzis have become a feature in many locations. So have fireplaces. More B&Bs offer TVs and room phones. New layers of regulations have added to costs and rates. Old-timers (more than five years in business) find themselves adding a few rooms to keep B&B economically viable. Some move across the street or next door. They learn to hire an inn-sitter now and then. And always, there is a steady stream of dreamers who see B&B—after all, it's only breakfast, they say—as a fantasy lifestyle.

And what about you, the pleasure *and* business traveler? The art of letter and card writing is alive! Throughout this book there are excerpts from the thousands of comments guests have written to me. They reinforce the concept of a people-to-people program—and make you feel good all over.

Accuracy is a hallmark of this book. Every detail was confirmed just before press time. But please keep in mind that successful hosts sometimes make *changes in rooms, beds, menu, or decor—and yes, in rates too.*

It is a joy to work with Jay Howland, my editor, who remembers everything and everyone. My thanks also go to Robert Carson and Fernando Corredor, who handled more than 30,000 pieces of paper, deciphered floor plans, and decoded hieroglyphics. Additional support and encouragement have come from my agent, Laura Fillmore, and Eugene Bailey. Quilter Sandra Keller of Needham, Massachusetts, gave much-appreciated help with cover research. And once again, David, my husband, has planned all our trips by plane, car, and bicycle. He listens, offers judgment when I solicit objectivity, and acts as my computer expert in residence.

Suggestions about people and places are welcome for consideration in the next edition. Please address them to me at The Globe Pequot Press, 6 Business Park Road, P.O. Box 833, Old Saybrook, CT 06475.

Bernice Chesler

Answers to Frequently
Asked Questions

What is bed and breakfast?

It is a package arrangement that includes overnight accommodations and breakfast. Many American B&Bs offer embellishments (amenities). Whether the B&B is a part-time endeavor or a full-time profession for the owner, the keynote is hospitality. Think of it as a varied people-to-people kind of program.

Are baths shared?

Some are—usually with just one other room. But depending on the number of guests, a shared bath could be private for you. Many American B&Bs have followed the trend to all private baths, sometimes with a shower but no tub, sometimes with a whirlpool bath and a sauna too.

How much do B&Bs cost?

Rates range from about $50 to well over $100 (including breakfast) for two people. The season, location, amenities, food, length of ownership, maintenance costs, taxes—all affect the rate. Remember: Nothing is standardized at B&Bs. In this book, check under "Rates" to see what credit cards are accepted at a particular B&B. Many small places prefer cash or traveler's checks. And it's a good idea to check on deposit requirements as well as cancellation/refund policies. Required local and/or state taxes vary from place to place and are seldom in the listed rates. Suggestion: Consider paying upon arrival. Good-byes will be that much smoother, and you really do feel as if you have visited friends.

To tip or not?

In a private home, tipping is not a usual practice, but times are changing. In a private home where B&B is rather constant, owners realize that extra help helps. Those B&B owners also know that some remembrance is appreciated by the part-time folks who contribute to your memorable stay.

In a B&B inn, treat staff as you would in a hotel. Some inns, particularly those in resort areas, add gratuities to the tab—or else they couldn't keep their help!

An interesting phenomenon: An amazing number of travelers write heartfelt thank-you notes to surprised and delighted hosts.

Is B&B like a hotel?

Not at all! It's not intended to be. You are greeted by a family member or an assistant, or occasionally by a note. A B&B may not provide the privacy—or the loneliness—of a hotel. Every room is different in size, layout, and decor. Several large properties described in this book have

cottages or outbuildings converted into very private B&B accommodations—maybe with breakfast-in-a-basket "room service."

Reminders: At a B&B there is no desk clerk. Please *call* the B&B
during reasonable hours and try to keep hosts informed of your *expected
arrival time.* If you must have things exactly as they are in the hotel
you usually go to, go to the hotel!

Is B&B for everyone?

Many B&Bs are perfect for unwinding and a change of pace, for
romantics, or for a home-away-from-home environment. If you seek
anonymity, B&B may not be for you. As one host said, "Guests who come
to B&Bs are outgoing; they want to be sociable and learn about you and
the area." Among all the wonderful guests, a few hosts can recall an
occasional "memorable" demanding guest (it's fun to see the change that
frequently takes place overnight) or a first-timer who arrived with
considerable luggage—cumbersome indeed on the narrow steep stairs to
the third floor of a historic house. Tastes and interpretations differ. Take
charm, for example. "Tell me," said the older guest, "what's so charming
about a tub on legs? I was so glad when built-ins finally became the
fashion." Recommendation: Tell the host if this is your first time at a B&B.
When making the reservation, if privacy is a real concern, say that too.
Hosts' listening skills are usually well tuned.

How do B&Bs on this side of the Atlantic differ from those in the British Isles or other countries?

The style of B&B-and-away-you-go is not necessarily the norm in
North America. Although there are B&Bs with just one room and
many where you are expected to leave for the day, guests are often
invited to spend more time after breakfast "at home"—by the pool or
fireplace, on the hiking trails, or on borrowed bicycles. Even hosts are
amazed at what they do when they get involved in others' lives! They
worry about late arrivals. They have been known to drive someone
to a job appointment or to do laundry for a businessman whose
schedule changed or to prevail upon the local auto mechanic when
the garage was closed.

Can I book through travel agents?

Many travel agents have caught on to the popularity of B&Bs. In
this book B&Bs with the ◆ in the "Rates" section pay commissions to
travel agents. And some agents will make arrangements for you,
whether or not they receive a commission from the B&B.

Do B&Bs welcome children?

In this book B&Bs with the symbol ♣ are always happy to host
children. Some B&Bs without the symbol also welcome children,
though not necessarily by the houseful! Although there are B&Bs that

provide everything from the sandbox to the high chair—and a babysitter too—some B&B hosts have been known to say (tactfully), "Children find us tiresome." Check the "Plus" section in the descriptions in this book. Consider the facilities, the room and bath arrangements, and the decor. Are your kids enticed by candlelit breakfasts? Are they used to being around "don't touch" antiques? Do they enjoy classical music? Are rooms limited to two persons? Is a crib provided? Are there lots of animals on the farm? Is there a built-in playmate, perhaps an innkeepers' child? Remember what you looked for B.C. (before children). If you do bring the kids and still wish for some private time at the B&B, please arrange for a sitter. Be fair to yourself and your children, to other guests, and to the host/chef/gardener/interior designer/historian—who really does love children.

What about facilities for physically handicapped persons?

Rooms that are handicapped accessible are noted in the detailed "Bed and bath" item of each B&B description in this book. In addition, each writeup mentions the floor locations of guest rooms.

Are there B&Bs that prohibit smoking?

Many do. (Note the ⚥ symbol in this book.) Among the relatively few B&Bs that do allow smoking, many limit it to certain areas or rooms.

If you like people and enjoy company and cooking, isn't that enough to make you a happy host?

It helps. But experienced hosts all comment on the time and work involved. Guests who ask, "Is this all you do?" would be surprised to realize that there is more to hosting than serving tea and meeting interesting people. Even I have fallen into the trap of multiplying a full house by the nightly rate, only to hear my husband say, "Never mind, that's 600 sheets!"

What do you recommend to those who dream about opening a B&B?

Stay at many. Attend one of the workshops or seminars given by adult education centers, innkeepers, B&B reservation services, or state extension services or tourism departments. Apprentice, even for a weekend; or sign up with a reservation service and host in your own home. Many prospective innkeepers attend Bill Oates and Heide Bredfeldt's seminar, "How to Purchase and Operate a Bed & Breakfast or Country Inn." Contact Oates & Bredfeldt, P.O. Box 1162, Brattleboro, VT 05302, 802/254-5931; fax 802/254-3221. For a free aspiring innkeeper's packet that includes a list of innkeeping workshops conducted in various parts of the country, contact the Professional Association of Innkeepers International, P.O. Box 90710, Santa Barbara, CA 93190, 805/569-1853; fax 805/682-1016. For a superb overview of everything from suppliers of products and services to B&B/inn publications and organizations, I recommend *Country Inns*

Yellow Pages, a thorough information resource book available at a special rate of $10 if you mention Bernice Chesler's *Bed & Breakfast in the Mid-Atlantic States.* For a copy of the *Yellow Pages* and for a free sample of *Inn Marketing* (a what's-going-on newsletter with a focus on marketing), contact Norm Strasma's Inn Marketing, P.O. Box 1789B, Kankakee, IL 60901; 815/939-3509; fax 815/933-8320.

Every host in this book enjoys what they call "the great emotional rewards of a stimulating occupation." Some remind couples who wish to make hosting a vocation that it helps to have a strong marriage. One who encourages prospective innkeeepers to "Just do it!" adds, "but be aware that you have to be more gregarious than private. You have to learn to carve time out for yourself. Hosting requires a broad range of talents (knowledge of plumbing helps), a lot of flexibility, an incredible amount of stamina, and perseverance. And did I mention you might need some capital?"

Can a host or reservation service pay to be in this book?

No. All selections are made by the author. There are no application fees. And all descriptions are written by the author; no host or service proprietor can write his or her own description. A processing fee is paid after each selected B&B and reservation service reviews its writeup. The fee offsets the extensive research that results in highly detailed writeups reflecting the individual spirit of each B&B. The processing fee for an individual B&B is $125. (For those with one or two rooms and a top rate of $50, it is $100.) The fee for a fully described reservation service is $125; for a reservation service host, $40. The author pays for all her stays.

What are some of your favorite B&Bs?

Even when you stay in hundreds, you tend to remember the hosts of each B&B more than the place. We have arrived on bicycles and been greeted with the offer of a car to go to dinner. There's the horticulturist, a septuagenarian, whom we could hardly keep up with as she toured us through her spectacular gardens. There's the couple who built their own solar house. Multifaceted retirees—some who have restored several houses. The history buffs who filled us in on the area and recommended back roads. The literary buffs who suggested good books. Hosts in a lovely residential section just minutes off the highway. Hosts we have laughed with. Yes, even some we have cried with too. Great chefs. People who are involved in their communities and trying to make this a better world. People whose home has been a labor of love and who love sharing it with others. We have enjoyed rather luxurious settings and some casual places too. It is true that each B&B is special in its own way. That's why the place to stay has become the reason to go. It's wonderful.

B&B RESERVATION SERVICES

A reservation service is in the business of matching screened hosts and guests. Although it can be a seasonal operation, in some areas the service is a full-time job for an individual, a couple, partners, or a small group. For hosts, it's a private way of going public, because the host remains anonymous until the service (agency) matches host and guest. This unique system allows hosts in private homes to have an off-and-on hosting schedule.

Listings may be in communities where there are no overnight lodging facilities, or they may provide an alternative to hotels or motels. Although most services feature private homes, some include small B&B inns. And some services now offer stays in unhosted homes.

Each service determines its own area and conducts its own inspections and interviews. A service may cover just one community, a metropolitan area, or an entire region.

Advance notice is preferred and even, with many services, required. Length-of-stay requirements vary. Some services stipulate a one-night surcharge; some require a minimum of two nights.

Rates are usually much less than at area hotels. The range may cover everything from "budget" to "luxury." Deposits are usually required. Refund policies, detailed with each reservation service description in this book, differ.

Fee arrangements vary. Many services include their commission in the quoted nightly rate. For public inns the services' quoted rate may be the same as what the inn charges, or it could be a total of the inn's rate plus a booking fee (about $5–$15).

Write for printed information or maybe, better yet, call. Before calling, think about bed and bath arrangements, parking, smoking, pets, children, air conditioning—whatever is important to you.

A reservation service acts as a clearinghouse and frequently provides an opportunity to stay at a B&B that would not be available any other way.

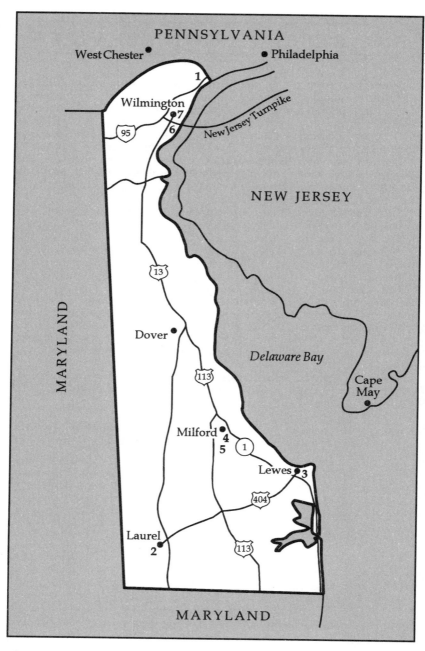

The numbers on this map indicate the locations of B&Bs described in detail in this chapter.

DELAWARE

KEY TO SYMBOLS
♥ Lots of honeymooners come here.
♣ Families with children are very welcome. (Please see page xii.)
♠ "Please emphasize that we are a private home, not an inn."
♣ Groups or private parties sometimes book the entire B&B.
♦ Travel agents' commission paid. (Please see page xii.)
✗ Sorry, no guests' pets are allowed.
✗ No smoking inside *or* no smoking at all, even on porches.

—— Delaware Reservation Service ——

Bed & Breakfast of Delaware

Box 177, 3650 Silverside Road, Wilmington, DE 19810-2211

Phone: 302/479-9500. Monday–Friday 9–5.

Fax: 302/998-7642.

Listings: Over 40. Mostly hosted private residences. Some small inns. In Pennsylvania—in Brandywine Valley, Chadds Ford, West Chester, New Hope, Landenberg, Oxford, Kennett Square. In Delaware—Wilmington, Newark, New Castle, Odessa, Dover, Bridgeville, Laurel, Milford, Lewes, Dagsboro, and Selbyville. Some are near the University of Delaware in Newark and Del-Tech campuses in Wilmington. Others are on the Eastern Shore of Maryland and Virginia's Chesapeake Bay. Directory: $2.

Reservations: 2–3 days' advance notice requested. Will try to accommodate last-minute requests.

Rates: $35–$65 single, $55–$150 double. $5 booking fee. $5 surcharge for one-night stay. Some have special rates for families, senior citizens, weekly stays. Reservations guaranteed by credit card required. For cancellations received at least 14 days prior to scheduled arrival date, deposit less a $25 processing fee refunded. No refunds for cancellation with less notice. MC, Visa. ◆

Millie D. Alford is an experienced host and reservation service owner who knows the area well. Some of her varied listings are on the National Register. "They are near beautiful museums, close to a bus line, or in suburban locations. One of those near Atlantic Ocean beaches is a Southern plantation. Some feature fireplaces, pools, and/or Jacuzzis. All feature hosts who enjoy making guests want to return soon!"

Plus: Short-term housing available. Museum discount tickets.

Delaware B&Bs

Darley Manor Inn B&B
3701 Philadelphia Pike, Claymont, DE 19703

302/792-2127
800/824-4703
fax 302/792-2127

Hosts: Ray and Judith Hester
Location: On main street next to church and across from private academy, (unoccupied) historic school, and service station. One block from I-495. Two blocks from train station. Ten to twenty minutes from Brandywine Valley attractions. Seven miles north of Wilmington; 30 minutes south of Philadelphia.
Open: Year round. Two-night minimum on major holidays.
Rates: $69 double room. $79 suites. $89 bridal suite. $10 third person. Amex, MC, VISA.
♥ ❖ ◆ ✈ ⊱

Guests wrote—and wrote: *"We loved the bridal suite and also the North/South Room with its Civil War decor . . . caring and warm hosts who make you feel special . . . breakfast is a real feast . . . this place turned us on to B&Bs . . . beautiful place . . . fantastic value . . . classical music. . . . Was seeking a refuge. Judith and Ray gave me what I needed. . . . Relaxing. . . . Perfect! . . . exceeded our expectations."*

It all began with the Hesters' B&B stay in Charleston, South Carolina. Ten years and many international travels later, Judith, a Civil War and antiques buff, and Ray, an early retiree who was a manager with DuPont, became the owners of a vacant 200-year-old Colonial house that needed everything. In 1993, after two years of renovations, this B&B opened with reproductions and refinished (by Judith) antiques throughout. Once the home of Felix O. C. Darley—a book illustrator for James Fenimore Cooper, Edgar Allan Poe, and Charles Dickens (who stayed here for two weeks in 1867)—the house is now on the National Register.

Bed and bath: Five rooms, each with queen bed, TV/VCR, private bath, phone, hair dryer, robes, toiletries. Second floor—two rooms, each with canopied bed, shower bath. Wicker-furnished bridal suite in pink with lots of lace, wood-burning fireplace, tub/shower bath. Two third-floor suites (with low and slanted 1800s ceilings), tub/shower baths, coffeemakers.
Breakfast: 8–9:30 (7–9 weekdays). Special grits presentation to first-time guests. Or omelets, pancakes or quiche, bacon or sausage, hash brown potatoes. Cereal and yogurt. Bread. Fruit. Juice. Hot beverages. In candlelit dining room. Ray serves in chef's hat and apron.
Plus: Air conditioning. Parlor, dining room, and reading room fireplaces. Player piano. Beverages, snacks, and hot/cold spring water always available. Guest refrigerator. Porch rockers. Large yard with garden, swing, fountains. Restaurant recommendations include "an inexpensive one that has good food."

Spring Garden Bed & Breakfast Inn

RD Route 1, Box 283A, Delaware Avenue Extended   **302/875-7015**
Laurel, DE 19956

Host: Gwen North
Location: Hidden from road by pine trees. Bordered by three acres of lawn, fruit trees, herb and flower gardens, and boxwood. Minutes from Route 13. Within walking or biking distance of "our friendly unspoiled National Register rural town." Four miles to state park; 30 minutes to Atlantic beaches and Chesapeake Bay.
Open: Year round.
Rates: Per room. $65 shared bath, $75 private. Suite $85. $5 one-night surcharge. Discounts for stays of five or more days.
♥ 🛏 ♣ ♦ ✄

Most of the restoration of "the house of two centuries"—a 1786 brick building and an 1800s clapboard Victorian addition—was done by Gwen's parents when they bought the property in the 1950s. After Gwen had careers in publishing, in art galleries, and as a business consultant in Europe and Mexico, she completed the restoration, keeping the original wainscoting, dentil ceiling moldings, and latch-style locks and heart pine paneling too. Her interest in the family's collectibles and 18th-century furnishings inspired her antiques shop in the barn. For her Eastern Shore inn-to-inn bicycling idea, she won Delaware's first tourism award for excellence in hospitality.

Gwen, a Realtor too, greets guests with wine and cheese and has enough "to do" suggestions (see "Plus" below) to make you wish you were staying longer.

In residence: One dog, "Boo Too, a mixed-breed enthusiastic bilingual (English and Spanish) welcomer."
Bed and bath: Five rooms. A suite, next to garden, with a four-poster double bed, private shower bath, TV, sitting room. One room with canopied double bed, fireplaced sitting area, private bath. Fireplaced Colonial room, canopied double bed, beaded heart pine paneling, wide plank floors, private whirlpool bath with views of field and trees. Twin-bedded room and one double-bedded room share one bath.
Breakfast: 8–9:30. Juice, seasonal fruits, cereals, yogurt; home-baked muffins, biscuits, or buns; Scotch eggs; coffee, tea, or milk. Served in country kitchen with wood stove or on porch overlooking garden.
Plus: Bedroom air conditioners. Fresh flowers. Fruit bowls. Fireplaced living room. TV. Library. Badminton, croquet, horseshoes. Kitchen and laundry privileges (extra charge). Will meet guests at Salisbury airport (15 miles south). Among suggestions: "the best oysters"; a place where wild ponies roam free; auctions (Gwen goes too); flea markets; wilderness canoe trips; the last remaining free cable ferry in the state; canoes and rowboats for rent; "best bass fishing in the state." Bike tours, bird-watching expeditions, antiques workshops.

Captain William Russell House
Bed and Breakfast
320 Union Street, Milton, DE 19968-1643

302/684-2504
fax 302/684-2509

Hosts: Tony and Carol Boyd-Heron
Location: In residential historic district of small town (population 1,200). Two blocks to downtown; 1½ to Broadkill River and boat launch (go downriver into Delaware Bay). Eight miles northwest of Lewes; 12 northwest of Rehoboth Beach on Atlantic Ocean. Near birding, antiquing, whale and dolphin watching, dinner train ride.
Open: Year round.
Rates: Per room. $85 Memorial Day–Labor Day. $75 May and October. $65 other times.
🛏 ✳ 🏹

From Ohio: "Hospitality is their specialty—food, accommodations, conversation . . . astutely provide information pertaining to guests' interests . . . attractively landscaped grounds with swing . . . comfort and welcome beyond compare."

It's all done in style, true British style transported across the Atlantic Ocean. Tony, a former career soldier who worked in the Ministry of Defense in London, and Carol, an American who manages a custom picture-framing and design gallery, worked for months (with Carol's parents) to undo and redo this 1850 ship captain's house. (In England they "almost" opened a B&B in a 1500s Elizabethan farmhouse.) Here they opened in 1992 with a seagoing theme—with portholes in baths and hand-painted clipper ships on antique pine headboards—and ceilings that range from 7½ to 10 feet. Eclectic furnishings include some English pieces; some floors are plank heart pine, others are carpeted.

The "English butler who serves breakfast and tea" has become a historian, chamber of commerce director, president of the Main Street Committee (new Victorian lamps installed in 1995), and a friend of the public library. Both he and Carol share their enthusiasm for this friendly "small-town America" community with guests who often request "their room" on a return visit.

In residence: Missy and Scruffy, friendly cats not allowed in guest rooms. "We Hoover our furniture every day."
Foreign languages spoken: "Schoolboy French. Limited German."
Bed and bath: Three first-floor rooms with queen bed (one is canopied); two with private terrace. All private shower (two with seats) baths; one en suite, two in hall (robes provided).
Breakfast: At guests' convenience—until 10. (Before-breakfast juice and hot beverages in sun room, or take them back to your room or terrace.) Grapefruit, fruit compote, or cereal and yogurt. "World-famous quiche" with cheese, bacon, tomato. Sundays, Belgian waffles with locally made sausages. Homemade bread and muffins served with English jam. Special diets accommodated. Served in dining room at table set with silver (napkin rings too) and damask cloth and napkins.
Plus: Classical music. Afternoon tea. Fresh fruit. Special occasions acknowledged; "we love celebrations!" Air conditioning (window units) and ceiling fans in guest rooms. No TV. Games. Small library. Turndown service. Plenty of off-street parking.

The Towers Bed and Breakfast

302/422-3814

101 Northwest Front Street, Milford, DE 19963   800/366-3814

All calls returned in evening.

Host: Dan Bond
Location: In central historic district of a quiet historic river town. Nine miles to Delaware Bay, 20 minutes to Atlantic shore, 29 miles to Rehoboth (beach resort). "Across from the best restaurant in Delaware, which is in another beautifully restored and decorated historic house."
Open: Friday and Saturday nights, year round.
Rates: $95 second-floor rooms. $125 third-floor suites. MC, Visa.
♥ ♣ ♦ ✈ ✄

A photographer's delight, this National Register Victorian mansion with extensive architectural detail was built in 1783 and remodeled in 1891 in "Steamboat Gothic" style. When, in 1992, the Bonds, former guests here, bought the Towers from an interior designer and antiques dealer, they acquired all the antique French Victorian furnishings. And they retained the exterior shades of mauve and plum—featured in *Painted Ladies: The Ultimate Celebration of Our Victorians*. One room with a 7-foot window bench overlooks the flower garden. Another has a 16-foot-ceilinged bath and porch in the tower. There's a walnut-paneled stairway; cherry woodwork in the front parlor and dining room; and a coffered sycamore ceiling in the music room, which is complete with a grand piano and working Victrola. A fountain and a swimming pool are on the grounds, a fenced yard with parklike setting.

Enthusiastic and energetic Dan, who works in Washington, D.C., as an economist for the Export Import Bank, dovetails hosting with his other interests of gardening and carpentry. "Our guests like being close to beaches, birding (Prime Hook and Bombay Hook wildlife preserves), and tax-free shopping. Most come here for a quiet, restful, and romantic weekend."

Foreign language spoken: Russian.
Bed and bath: Six large carpeted guest rooms, but no more than four (all with private bath) booked to separate parties. (If families or friends are traveling together, more than two second-floor rooms can be booked—with shared bath arrangement.) Second floor has four double-bedded rooms, two tub/shower hall baths. Third floor has two suites (one with queen bed, one with double) with private en-suite shower baths.
Breakfast: 6–11, time arranged with each guest. Ricotta cheese pancakes; seafood omelet; sausage/cheese/egg casserole; or waffles. Breakfast meats. Fruit, orange juice, tea or coffee. Served in fireplaced dining room or on gazebo porch.
Plus: Bedroom air conditioners and ceiling fans. Sherry. Bicycles to borrow.

Eli's Country Inn

302/349-4265

Route 36, Greenwood-Milford Road, P.O. Box 779   **fax 302/349-9340**
Greenwood, DE 19950-0779

Hosts: Betty, Cora, Anna, Olive, Margaret, Wanda, Sarah—seven sisters, Eli's daughters, all married, with families. "We take turns as innkeepers."
Location: On 70 acres "where you can hear the quiet." With lawns, gardens, birds, hay and small grain crops, and and a mile-long path through the fields "where, as chil-

dren, we played and helped." Near state parks and fishing. Three miles from Route 13. Eight miles south of Milford, 30 south of Dover, 30 west of Rehoboth Beach.
Open: Year round.
Rates: $55 for two. $50 single. $10 third person. Discover, MC, Visa.
♥ ♨ ❀ ✄

A real find. A memorable old-fashioned B&B. A homey family farmstead, completely redone, rebuilt really, with a great gathering spot: an enormous welcoming kitchen—"it's awesome"—with a big island, two stoves, two dishwashers, and cherry cabinets. A major attraction, dubbed "the silo" by one guest, is an always-filled two-gallon cookie jar. One dining room, with a table that seats 20, features two triple windows without curtains "so that the field views can be enjoyed." The more informal dining room, painted white, has a gas fireplace and a pump organ "that Dad had motorized." Other common rooms have fresh wallcoverings "almost identical to the ones we had in the 1930s and '40s of our childhood," with ivy and fruit and flowers. Furnishings include "our simple comfortable family pieces."

Almost every guest asks how seven women can get along so well! "Although we have our own opinions, the inn, named after our father, who died about 20 years ago, is a shared goal that we all enjoy. It fulfills his dream of keeping the home, always a haven for many, in the family. We were all born in the smaller house that was here when he bought the property in 1926. Shortly after he bought the place, he married our mother, the first graduate of the Milford Memorial Hospital School of Nursing. Five of us have become nursing professionals. When our mother died in 1989, we decided to create an inn that could, if we wished, be our own residence in the future. We removed the back half of the house and rebuilt with similar simple architecture, with larger rooms and more (small but full) baths, and with handicapped accessibility.

"Now we host business guests from near and far. Wedding guests, too, appreciate the relaxed atmosphere. So do beachgoers. And cyclists who participate in the inn-to-inn trips designed by Gwen North, page 6. Singing takes place around the organ. Coffee is often enjoyed on the decks or wraparound porch."

The warm hospitality here was summed up by Hong Kong guests who wrote: "A very extraordinary treat concocted from the following recipe: ¼ cup of Kindness and Laughter, ¼ cup of Farm House Culinary Delight, ¼ cup of Chitchat, and ¼ cup of IQ test and wit."

(Please turn page.)

Foreign language spoken: "A few of us speak some Spanish."
Bed and bath: Eight carpeted rooms, all with private new attached full baths; two handicapped-accessible rooms on first floor. Beds are king (with largest bath), queen, or double; most rooms have a single bed also.
Breakfast: Usually 8–11. "Our menu changes daily." Juice. Fresh seasonal fruit. Cold and hot cereal. Homemade muffins or banana bread. Eggs various ways or buttermilk pancakes with homemade strawberry topping. Cheese. Coffee (espresso by request), tea, milk. Eat in dining rooms or in kitchen.
Plus: Central air conditioning. Spectacular sunrises and sunsets. TV in small common room. Additional meals can be arranged. By request, literature on the family's Mennonite heritage. Sometimes, riddles from one of the fun-loving host husbands.

Bed & Breakfast of Delaware Host #32

New Castle, Delaware

Location: On the market square facing the courthouse of town founded in 1651. In historic area with 17th-century village green and 18th- and 19th-century buildings. Near fine restaurants. Five miles from Wilmington; 20 to Winterthur and Longwood Gardens.
Reservations: Available all year round through Bed & Breakfast of Delaware, page 4.
Rates: $65 single, $85 double.
♥ ♣ ✈ ⊬

Sixteen-foot ceilings and red pine floors give this 1860s Federal-style brick townhouse a very spacious feeling. In 1991 the host, a former Marriott Corporation staffer, bought the B&B from the owners/restorers who had established it eight years earlier. She decorated the house with reproduction and antique furnishings and Laura Ashley linens and comforters. "Returnees ask for specific rooms—for the one with a four-poster rice bed or maybe the canopied bed. If they are celebrating a special occasion, they are greeted with flowers and a card. Relatives of local residents come here. And corporate travelers, too, seem to appreciate the wide back verandas that face Battery Park and the river beyond."

Bed and bath: Five air-conditioned rooms with private full baths. On second floor—two large rooms with queen beds, one small room with a single. On third floor, two large queen-bedded rooms.
Breakfast: Usually 8–9. Fresh fruit, juice, cereals, homemade baked goods, coffee. In dining room at table that seats 12.
Plus: Air-conditioned guest rooms. Mints on nightstands. Menus of New Castle and Wilmington restaurants.

> From New York: *"Loved the spaciousness, cleanliness, large porch looking out on ships coming up the Delaware."*

The Boulevard Bed & Breakfast   302/656-9700
1909 Baynard Boulevard, Wilmington, DE 19802-3915

Hosts: Judy and Charles Powell
Open: Year round. Two-night minimum on holiday weekends.
Location: On a residential street in historic district. Two blocks from city park; 10 from city center. Half mile east of I-95, exit 8. Within 30 minutes of museums, Longwood Gardens, many corporations.
Rates: $55–$60 shared bath. $70 double or queen bed, private bath. $75 suite. $5–$10 extra person. Singles $5 less. Amex, MC, Visa.
♥ ♨ ⁂ ✗ ⚬

From New York: "Sumptuous breakfast. . . . My daily accounts of the B&B brought requests for Boulevard brochures from other Winterthur course participants." From Connecticut: *"Greeted with warmth and good cheer. . . . A majestic staircase that seems to draw you in. . . . Oh! And that porch, perfect for breakfast."* From Maryland: *"We had our rehearsal, wedding ceremony, and reception there . . . comfortable and elegant . . . graciousness of facility matched by graciousness of hosts."*

What Judy imagined would be a someday New England country inn evolved as a big, gracious 1913 brick house in town with, as Chuck says, some neoclassical, some Federal, some turn-of-the-century architectural features. The furnishings, too, are eclectic—with some antiques and many family pieces. Several weddings have taken place on the landing at the top of the wide red-carpeted staircase. Many a cup of warm mulled cider is enjoyed by the medieval-style library fireplace.

The Powells became innkeepers (and restorers) after 30 years of suburban living, when Chuck, an avocational flier, took early retirement from AT&T in Wilmington in 1985. Judy, an accomplished needleworker, was a bank accounting officer.

Bed and bath: Six rooms, each with air conditioning, cable TV, desk. On second floor, three with double or queen bed, all private baths (one is tub and shower, two are shower only). On third floor, honeymoon suite with queen bed, private bath with whirlpool; one twin-bedded and one single-bedded room share a tub and shower bath (robes provided). Rollaway.
Breakfast: Any time through 9. Freshly squeezed orange juice. Fresh fruit dish. Homemade muffins or fruit bread. Entree made to order—eggs, three-cheese omelet, pecan waffles, apple or yogurt pancakes, cinnamon-swirl French toast. Sausage, ham, or bacon. Cereal. In dining room or through French doors on screened porch.
Plus: Ceiling fans and phones in some rooms. Fireplace and small organ in living room. Fresh flowers. Candy. Guest refrigerator.

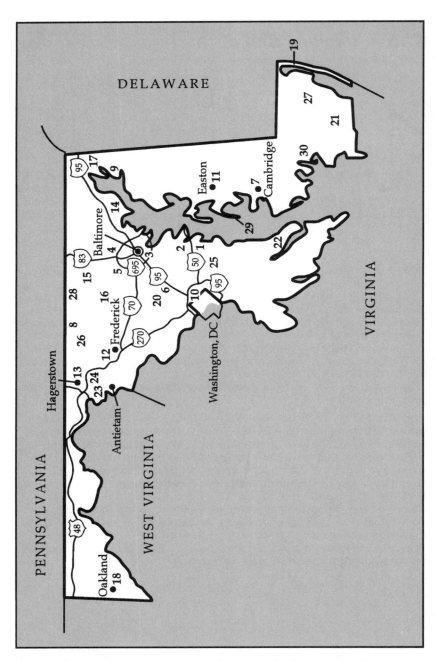

The numbers on this map indicate the locations of B&Bs described in detail in this chapter.

MARYLAND

____Maryland Reservation Services____

Amanda's Regional Reservation Service for Bed and Breakfast

1428 Park Avenue, Baltimore, MD 21217-4230

Phone: 410/225-0001 or 800/899-7533, Monday–Friday 8:30–5:30; Saturday 8:30–noon.

Fax: 410/728-8957.

Listings: 170. Private homes—historic, urban, and rural; small inns (a few with restaurant); and yachts. Many are located throughout Maryland. In Baltimore, in addition to those in downtown row houses, there are some in large older homes and several within walking distance of the new baseball park or the new light rail line to the park. Many others are in Annapolis, and some are in parts of surrounding states: Delaware; Washington, D.C.; New Jersey; Pennsylvania; Virginia; and West Virginia. Directory: $3.

Reservations: At least one week's advance notice preferred. Some hosts require a minimum stay of two nights.

Rates: $50–$75 single. $60–$295 double. Some family, senior citizen, and weekly rates available. Confirmed reservation cancellations with 10 days' notice receive refund less $25 service charge. Amex, Discover, MC, Visa; 5 percent surcharge.

Betsy Grater is an experienced host as well as reservation service owner. Her listings, visited annually, vary in size, style, and location. Some feature fireplaces, pools, and/or Jacuzzis. Most have air conditioning and private baths. All are hosted by "wonderful and helpful people."

Bed and Breakfast of Maryland/The Traveller in Maryland, Inc.

P.O. Box 2277, Annapolis, MD 21404-2277

Phone: 410/269-6232, Monday–Thursday 9–5; Friday 9–1.

Fax: 410/263-4841.

Listings: 85—in historic, urban, and rural private homes; small inns (a few with restaurant); and yachts. Located primarily in Annapolis, in Baltimore area, on the Eastern Shore, and in Civil War battlefield areas. Others are in Taneytown, Uniontown, and western Maryland. Directory: $5.

Reservations: At least 24 hours' advance notice required. Last-minute reservations sometimes possible. Two-day minimum during holidays or special events.

Rates: $50–$80 single. $55–$90 double. Deposit of one night's stay plus $5 booking fee per location. If cancellation is received at least 10 days before arrival date, deposit less $20 refunded. Amex, MC, Visa. ◆

Founded in 1982, this service annually inspects its accommodations, which vary from "the practical and central to the historic and pastoral." Hosts are "kind, concerned, well-traveled and locally knowledgeable." The service is owned and operated by Greg Page and Rob Zuchelli, Annapolis innkeepers who are active with guided city tours and bed and breakfast organizations.

Plus: Entire itineraries can be arranged with B&B reservations. Short-term (a week or more) hosted and unhosted housing available. Membership (optional for reservations) in Traveller Society is a one-time fee of $15; benefits include Maryland travel information (guidebook and maps), national listing of B&B services, special mailings, and state B&B directory.

KEY TO SYMBOLS
♥ Lots of honeymooners come here.
♣ Families with children are very welcome. (Please see page xii.)
♠ "Please emphasize that we are a private home, not an inn."
♣ Groups or private parties sometimes book the entire B&B.
◆ Travel agents' commission paid. (Please see page xii.)
✖ Sorry, no guests' pets are allowed.
✖ No smoking inside *or* no smoking at all, even on porches.

Maryland B&Bs

Amanda's Host #322
Annapolis, MD

Location: In historic district, two blocks from Naval Academy; one to City Dock; "close to everything"— historic sites, restaurants, shopping.
Reservations: Year round through Amanda's Regional Reservation Service, page 14.
Rates: $95 queen bed. $150 suite; $10 for third or fourth person.
♥ ⛵ ♣ ✖ ⌫

Wallpaper pattern numbers, paint colors, and recipes are all requested by many of the guests who enjoy their visit in this restored 1850 home. The host, a real estate agent, bought the house in 1993 and furnished it with antiques and artwork collected during her worldwide travels as a flight attendant. She and her late husband lived on a sailboat in Annapolis. "I've finally hit terra firma—and love having the world come to me!"

In residence: "The sweetest dog in the world," age 13. One cat, rarely seen by guests.
Bed and bath: Second floor—queen bed, en-suite tub/shower bath. Third floor—two-room suite with queen bed, living room with king/twins sofa bed, extra-large shower-with-seat bath.
Breakfast: 8–10. Juice. Fresh fruit. Egg dish, French toast, or pancakes. Homemade muffins—corn, blueberry, apple/walnut, cheese/herb or raisin/cinnamon breads. Hot beverages. "Served on porcelain in first-class style."
Plus: Central air conditoning. Gas log fireplace in living room. Cookies. Soft drinks. Rear garden with path, bench, flowers, birdbaths, patio. Public parking garage, 50 feet away; $8 maximum per day.

From Illinois: *"Delightful home and hostess."*

Bed and Breakfast of Maryland Host #129
Annapolis, MD

Location: In the historic district, one block from main gate of Naval Academy.
Reservations: Available all year round through Bed and Breakfast of Maryland, page 14.
Rates: $75 double bed, $80 king/twins, $85 suite plus $15 for each additional person.
♣ ⛵ ✖ ⌫

Everyone asks about the age of this Greek Revival house. Surprise! It was built in the 1930s with brick and many inside doors and beams taken from the house that had been standing here since the 1740s. Furnishings are "eclectically traditional. Our guests, including many midshipmen's families, know that this is their home away from home. They use the screened porch, patio, and fireplaced living room. And we are the best place in town for children!" The experienced hosts (12 years) keep a geographic log and photo album of all guests. The hostess is a retired registered nurse. Her husband, a retired naval officer and corporate vice president, answers lots of questions about the Academy (take a map and tour yourself or take a guided tour); the town's history and architecture (he's a tour guide); restaurants, shops, antiquing, and festivities.

Bed and bath: On second floor—room with king/twins option, working fireplace, private shower bath. Another room with double bed, private tub/shower bath. Entire third floor has a double bed and four singles, private shower bath.
Breakfast: Flexible hours. "We like to be finished by 11; most guests want to be out earlier." Fresh fruit, juice, cereals, muffins and toast. Omelets, eggs Benedict, sausage casserole, pancakes, waffles, or French toast. Served in large dining room with Queen Anne furnishings or on garden patio that has a majestic magnolia tree. Host usually joins guests.

Bed and Breakfast of Maryland Host #139
Annapolis, MD

Location: In historic district. Two blocks from Naval Academy. One block from city dock. A half block from state capitol.
Reservations: Available year round through Bed and Breakfast of Maryland, page 14.

Rates: Shared bath—$75 queen, $85 king. $95 private bath. $10 third person.
♥ ♨ ♣ ✈ ⚥

Memorable. This 70-year-old store with tin ceiling and oak display case was converted into an unusual residence—there's not a square corner in any room—by the previous owners. It was purchased in 1990 by the hosts, native Californians (and former Napa Valley part-time B&B hosts), and furnished with turn-of-the-century furnishings and fascinating collections acquired in South America and Europe. Recently, with the assistance of an architect and the historical commission, the exterior has been changed to look more residential and historic.

The host, director of a college-level international language program, and his wife, vice-principal of an elementary school, "love the three centuries of history in Annapolis, the ambiance, events, water—we're among the 10 percent of residents who are not sailors!—the walk along the dock. We are steps from a theater, within three blocks of 15 great (and different) restaurants, within 15 minutes on foot from everything. It's exciting to share all of this with travelers from all over the world."

Foreign languages spoken: French, Spanish, Portuguese.
Bed and bath: Four rooms with private baths. On first floor, king bed and sofa suitable for third person, private en-suite shower bath. On second floor, queen bed, private en-suite shower bath. One room with king bed and one with queen share a hall tub/shower bath.
Breakfast: Usually 7 or after. Buffet style. Freshly squeezed orange juice, fresh fruit, croissants, homemade nut bread, homemade granola and other cereals, coffees, teas.
Plus: Guest living and dining rooms. In every guest room, TV and coffee (and tea) maker. Two garage spaces ($5 each) available.

College House Suites

410/263-6124

One College Avenue, Annapolis, MD 21401

Hosts: Don and Jo Anne Wolfrey
Location: Quiet, historic neighborhood. On a corner overlooking Naval Academy and one block from St. John's College. A short walk to everything—city dock, Paca House and Gardens, country's oldest state capitol building in continuous use, antiques galleries, theater, restaurants, shops.
Open: Year round. Two-night minimum at all times.
Rates: $160 ($135 without breakfast). MC, Visa.
♥ ◄ ⁂ ♦ ✈ ⊬

Unusual and beautiful collections gathered by the Wolfreys from all over the world are ingeniously displayed on the walls, mirror-finished antique softwood floors, shelves, and seating in this elegant Federal-style brick townhouse with crown moldings and wainscoting. There's a mask collection from three continents, a 1770s English grandfather clock, an extensive collection of antique, silk, and wool Oriental rugs—all blended with American antiques and contemporary pieces. The terraced deck is an urban oasis fashioned with heartwood cedar, an arbor, and seating surrounded by trees and planters, vines and blossoms. Jo Anne, a volunteer for the Historic Annapolis Foundation, was an accountant for the U.S. Navy. Don, a computer systems analyst with the Justice Department, commutes to Washington. During their 17 years of living here, the Wolfreys have made all kinds of major—and wonderful—changes. B&B has been part of their sharing lifestyle since 1988.

Bed and bath: Two suites. One on ground level has private ivy-covered courtyard entrance, wet bar, antique brass double bed, shower bath, raised-hearth fireplace in sitting room that has art-covered walls. Third-level suite has a cherry four-poster double bed, window seats, sitting room, tub/shower bath with rose Italian marble floor, views of Naval Academy, and use of second-level deck.
Breakfast: 8–10. Fruit such as melon balls and raspberries with fresh mint and Grand Marnier. Strawberry-cheese croissants or iced carrot muffins. Freshly squeezed orange juice. Cereals. Perhaps yogurt. Coffee with cinnamon. Served in dining room or on that marvelous deck.
Plus: Window air conditioners. Ceiling fans. Individual heat thermostats. In each suite—phone (one with private line); remote color TV with cable (including HBO); desk. Down comforters. Fine linens. Robes. Feather beds. Fresh fruit, flowers, chocolates. Special occasions acknowledged.

Guests wrote: *"Pampered . . . stunningly beautiful, private, quiet, perfect."*

---

*B*ed and breakfast gives a sense of place.

The William Page Inn

8 Martin Street, Annapolis, MD 21401-1716

410/626-1506
800/364-4160
fax 410/263-4841

Hosts: Greg Page and Rob Zuchelli
Location: On a quiet, residential historic district street off of and two blocks from main downtown waterfront. Fifty yards from Naval Academy visitors' gate. Within minutes of restaurants and historic sites.
Open: Year round. Two-night minimum during special events.

Rates: December–March 15: $60 shared bath, $90 private bath, $110 suite. March 16–November 30: Sunday–Thursday, $85 shared, $110 private, $125 suite; weekends, $85 shared, $125 private, $150 suite. MC, Visa.
♥ ❖ ✈ ⊬

They (almost) waved a magic wand. What was to be a five-year plan took one year. What, in 1986, was to be a B&B in Montreal, Boston, or Washington, D.C., appeared in an Annapolis (Rob's hometown) real estate column: a foursquare 1908 cedar-shingled home, a Democratic Club for more than 50 years. The two young men, still in their twenties, gutted, redesigned, redecorated, and explored a tristate area for antiques. Within six months the Annapolis landmark was opened as a B&B. Soon after, Greg and Rob took on a bed and breakfast reservation service (page 14) and became B&B consultants and active community participants. They and their guests are delighted with the results.

In residence: One well-behaved dog, Rascals, "seldom seen by guests."
Bed and bath: Five antiques-furnished rooms. First floor—Victorian furnishings, queen bed, private shower bath, access to wraparound porch. Second floor—queen bed, private bath with shower/whirlpool tub. Two rooms, each with queen four-poster rice carved bed, sitting area, and armoire, share (robes provided) a tub/shower bath. Third floor—skylit dormer-style room, twice the size of any other, with queen sleigh bed, sofa in sitting area, individual climate control system, private bath with shower, and separate whirlpool room.
Breakfast: 8–10. Buffet may include juice, fresh fruit, freshly baked breads and pastries, cheeses, quiche or egg casserole, cold cereals, coffee/tea.
Plus: Central air conditioning. Fireplaced living room. Refreshments. Wet bar setup. Off-street parking (one car per room).

> From Wisconsin: *"Perfect . . . beautifully decorated . . . extremely friendly innkeepers. Highly recommended."*

Riverwatch Bed & Breakfast

410/974-8152

145 Edgewater Drive, Edgewater, MD 21037-1321

Hosts: Karen Dennis and Don Silawsky
Location: Waterfront—with spectacular river views. In a community with plenty of walkers and joggers. Ten minutes to historic Annapolis.

Open: March–November. Four-night minimum for Naval Academy commissioning week (late May) and during sailboat show (mid-October).
Rates: $65 king bed; $85 queen.
♥ ☕ ♦ ✈ ⊬

(Please turn page.)

The crystal-chandeliered dining room with river view has a mirrored wall and sliding glass doors. Comfortable furnishings in the living room of the two-storied frame house are contemporary with Oriental accents. Each guest room has access to a waterfront balcony with chairs and table and a spiral staircase that leads to the outdoor (20-by-40-foot) pool and hot tub—"our favorite seasonal suggestion."

Karen is a scientist/researcher who specializes in obesity and weight loss. When she and Don, an engineer/lawyer (environmental law) bought this too-big-for-the-two-of-us property six years ago, "the extra bedrooms and baths along with the exceptional site and our sincere enjoyment of people 'clicked.' Guests enjoy relaxing on the patio after breakfast, watching the boats go by, and solving the problems of the world. Collectively, we've solved a lot of them . . . if someone would just ask us!"

In residence: Shadow and Rina, Siamese cats.
Bed and bath: On second floor, one room with king bed, one with queen; both with private full bath.
Breakfast: 8:30–9:30. Homemade muffins and breads. Pancakes or Belgian waffles. Juice. Fresh fruits. Freshly ground coffee. Served in dining room or on patio.
Plus: Central air conditioning and heat. Fireplaced family room. Bedroom ceiling fans. Guest refrigerator. Turndown service. Beach towels. Many suggestions for Annapolis attractions. Boat dock; no charge for tie-up. Ground transportation provided for guests who arrive by boat. Off-street parking.

> From Alaska: *"We were delighted . . . spacious, impeccably clean, and very comfortable. Hosts were warm and gracious."* From California: *"GREAT! . . . What a view! . . . Manicured, beautiful grounds . . . outstanding breakfast. The Riverwatch deserves special attention as that is what you get from Don and Karen!"*

Amanda's Host #110
Baltimore, MD

Location: In a quiet historic residential area bordered by two parks: one with a lake and a bike and jogging trail; the other with golf course, tennis courts, and ball park. Five-minute walk to 15-minute bus ride to Inner Harbor. Near Johns Hopkins, seafood restaurants.

Reservations: Available all year round through Amanda's Regional Reservation Service, page 14.
Rates: $70 private bath, $65 shared bath.
🛥 🛪 ⅙

"Since our four children grew up and moved out, the house became too quiet! We enjoy hosting B&B in our three-storied Tudor-style house, where we have lived for over 30 years. It has 'gemutlichkeit,' a German word that means comfort, an all-around good feeling."

This longtime favorite B&B is hosted by a retired chemist, who plays clarinet in a band, and his wife, who teaches German and sometimes interprets for touring groups. Both are ardent sailors and classical music lovers.

In residence: "A fat lazy mostly-outside cat."

Bed and bath: Two second-floor rooms, one with twin beds and ceiling fan, the other with a queen bed and air conditioning. Private or shared modern full bath.

Breakfast: Flexible hours. Juice, fruits, hot and cold cereals, muffins with poached egg and hollandaise sauce, homemade croissants or breads—poppyseed, banana, or apricot. Option of German cold cuts and cheeses on German rye bread. "The best coffee in town." Served in breakfast room or on the secluded patio.

Plus: Arrival beverages. Fresh flowers, fruits, chocolates in guest room. TV room. Parking.

From New York: *"Friendly, welcoming, clean, comfortable . . . great cooking."*

Amanda's Host #201

Baltimore, MD

Location: On Middle River of Chesapeake Bay. Twenty minutes north of Baltimore's Inner Harbor; 10 minutes (8 miles) from I-95.

Reservations: Year round through Amanda's Regional Reservation Service, page 14.

Rates: $75–$125 for two.

♥ ⅊ ⚬⚬ ◆ ✈ ✂

A jewel. Called The Manor House by locals. Now in an area of summer-turned-year-round cottages, the four-storied historic waterfront house was built with 12-foot ceilings in the early 1900s by a local brewmaster. He and his wife, a musician, hosted summer parties here for the benefit of the Baltimore Opera. Since the B&B hosts, a CPA and his wife, a Realtor and an American Sign Language interpreter, purchased the "handyman's special" in 1987, rejuvenation has been an ongoing process and B&B has evolved. The hosts added a large in-ground pool and retained the cupola, from which you get a spectacular view (binoculars provided) of Chesapeake Bay.

The spacious rooms are filled with antiques and collectibles. There are Tiffany-style lampshades, some Art Deco items, many paintings and prints, and pewter and egg-cup collections. The dining room is Empire style with a 10-foot buffet. Some guests arrive by boat and moor at the adjacent pier. And then there are those who visit the city and love coming "home to the country," where they walk, jog, explore.

In residence: Two cats "absolutely forbidden in guest areas."

Bed and bath: Three centrally air-conditioned second-floor rooms (the smallest·is 20 by 20 feet), each with private shower/tub bath. One is a suite with king bed, working fireplace, wicker-furnished room with wet bar and water view, Jacuzzi tub. Double-bedded room overlooks the pool. One king-bedded room has shower and 6-foot claw-footed tub "that everyone loves."

Breakfast: "Almost any time." Featuring low-cholesterol recipes. Juice, fruit, egg/cheese casserole or French toast, turkey bacon, homemade muffins, coffee. In dining room or poolside.

(Please turn page.)

Plus: Many nearby seafood restaurants recommended—with the support of guests' rave reviews.

> From Wilmington, Del.: *"The house is gorgeous, beautifully decorated. . . . The host and hostess extremely friendly. . . . Would like to visit again."*

Celie's Waterfront Bed & Breakfast

1714 Thames Street, Baltimore, MD 21231   410/522-2323
800/432-0184
fax 410/522-2324

Host: Celie Ives
Location: Facing an active port. In Fell's Point Historic District. Minutes' walk to restaurants, shops, and galleries. One-quarter-block walk to water taxi ride to harbor attractions; Oriole Park at Camden Yards; aquarium; science center; Little Italy; museums; antiques row. Twelve blocks to Johns Hopkins Medical Center.
Open: Year round. Advance reservations required. Two-night weekend minimum for rooms with whirlpool and/or fireplace; for all rooms on holiday weekends.
Rates: Per room. King bed with whirlpool and fireplace $140–$175. Queen with whirlpool $120–$145. Queen without whirlpool $105–$125. Wheelchair-accessible room $90–$100. Amex, Discover, MC, Visa.

♥ ♣ ♦ ✈ ⚓

Amazing. An "instant landmark" built in 1989 with a historic-looking front, balconies, and flowering courtyards. The inviting interior features antique accents including a portrait of Celie's great-great-grandmother. In addition, there is every amenity (see "Bed and bath" below) sought by both business travelers and romantics. And then there's Celie, the Baltimore native who conceived this inn after renovating—with great imagination—a nearby 1870s townhouse. Her flair for design was recognized by Bloomingdale's when they chose her B&B as part of a *Bed & Breakfast in the Mid-Atlantic States* photo essay seen by a million people.

Bed and bath: Seven rooms (on three floors), each with private bath, desk, private phone line, modem capability, TV, refrigerator with setups and juices, coffeemaker (coffee, tea, cocoa). King-bedded rooms, facing harbor, have whirlpool tub, working fireplace, bar sink, microwave. Four queen-bedded rooms—two with whirlpool tub plus balcony overlooking rear garden; two with shower/tub baths. First-floor handicapped-accessible unit with king/twin option, shower bath, private courtyard.
Breakfast: 7–9 weekdays, 8–10 weekends. Freshly squeezed orange juice, fresh fruit, homemade breads and granola, jams and jellies, brewed coffees and teas. Serve yourself. Eat in dining room, on private balcony or rooftop deck, in garden, or in your room.
Plus: Central air conditioning. Ceiling fans. Flannel sheets. Bath sheets. Terry robes. Down comforters. Ironing facilities. Rooftop deck with built-in seating, view of harbor and skyline. Free off-street parking if needed. Van service to and from convention center by request.

*From Virginia, Pennsylvania, Florida: "A gem. . . . Heartwarming friendliness.
. . . As we curled up to the fire, the sweet smell of that day's baked breads lingered
on."*. . . *"Driving directions, coffee in room, flowers. . . . What more could you ask
for?"*

Mr. Mole Bed & Breakfast   410/728-1179
1601 Bolton Street, Baltimore, MD 21217-4347   fax 410/728-3379

Hosts: "The staff"—Paul Bragaw and Collin Clarke

Location: On historic Bolton Hill. Within walking distance of subway and light rail system, Antique Row, Meyerhoff Symphony Hall, Lyric Opera, and Walters Art Gallery. Ten-minute drive to Johns Hopkins Hospital. Two miles to Johns Hopkins University and the Baltimore Museum of Art; two miles from the Inner Harbor and Oriole Park at Camden Yards.

Open: Year round. Two-night minimum March–November and holiday weekends, and for Preakness (Triple Crown thoroughbred races) Week.

Rates: $75–$80 single, $90–95 double. Two-room suites $100–$150, depending on number of guests and bedrooms used.

♥ ❖ ◆ ✉ ✂

Decorated. Gracious. Beautiful. Acclaimed in national press. An urban B&B where guests invite Baltimorians, who are most anxious "to see"; where business travelers host clients; where getaway guests spend a lot of time; where one 73-year-old guest went up and down the three flights of steps 25 times a day for exercise.

The 1870 brick row house was on the League of Women Voters house tour even before the hosts' year-long restoration was finished in 1991. Paul is a former USAF colonel, and Collin is an antiques dealer who was a theatrical set designer in Australia, the United States, and England.

On the 14-foot-ceilinged first floor, there's a converted 1870 gasolier, original plaster moldings and marble fireplaces, and drapes made by Collin with 150 yards of Madras plaid. Throughout the spacious rooms there are 18th- and 19th-century antiques, prints and portraits, antique snuff boxes, collections of ecclesiastical antiques, and New Guinea masks—all identified by date and country of origin on a list compiled for the Maryland House and Garden Pilgrimage.

Foreign languages spoken: French, German, and Dutch.

Bed and bath: On three floors, five queen-bedded suites (two have a second room with a double bed) with sitting area, private tub/shower bath. One has private enclosed sun porch; some have canopied or four-poster bed. The street-level suite has private exterior entrance.

Breakfast: Usually 7:30–9. "Almost-famous" brown sugar/cream cheese pie or an Amish apple/walnut crumb cake. (Recipes shared/exchanged.) Fresh fruit, orange juice, Swedish crispbreads, meats, cheeses, breads (wheat ground right here). Coffees, teas, Ovaltine, milk. "We try never to repeat a menu for any guest."

Plus: Central air conditioning. Garage with automatic door opener for each suite. Private phones. Chocolates. Flowers. Hair dryer. Use of refrigerator. Tips for galleries, museums, bicycle path, antiques shops, bars and eateries, even

(Please turn page.)

an all-night diner (average meal, $6); day trips (by train) to New York too. Snack bag for guests traveling by car or train.

> From Connecticut: *"We loved it! . . . elegant, clean, and very beautiful. Paul and Collin were extremely gracious. Thanks, Bernice, for your recommendation."*

Union Square House B&B   410/233-9064
23 South Stricker Street, Baltimore, MD 21223-2423   fax 410/233-4046

Hosts: Joseph and Patrice Debes
Location: Facing a city park (appreciated by locals and guests) with fountain and gazebo. In historic district of National Register Italianate townhouses. Fifteen blocks to Inner Harbor, 12 to Oriole Park at Camden Yards, 7 to University of Maryland Hospital and downtown campus.

Open: Year round. Reservations required.
Rates: $70 single, $80 double. With fireplace—$80 single, $90 double. $115 suite. $10 additional person. Under age 18, free. Honeymoon, anniversary, and murder mystery packages. Amex, Discover, MC, Visa.
♥ ♨ ❖ ◆ ✈ ⚰

It's a getaway. A conventiongoer's haven. A baseball fan's discovery. It's just across the street from the Debeses' own residence. (Both tall-ceilinged brick houses are on this historic district's Christmas tour.) Throughout there are antique and traditional furnishings. And chintz. Designer fabrics are fashioned into swags, valences, drapes, and seat coverings. In the living room, a 10-foot year-round Christmas tree is decorated with rabbits or flags or pumpkin lights. And enjoyed from the rear deck: a water garden complete with fountain, dramatic lighting, and music.

Patrice, a former teacher, is an interior designer. Joe is a clinical nurse specialist who works in community health. They have been pampering guests since 1990, when they opened this 1868 "Millionaire's Row" house as a B&B.

In residence: In hosts' house, Elizabeth Ann, age eight; Steven Michael, age two.
Bed and bath: Two rooms and a suite; all private full tub/shower baths. Second floor—large room with queen bed, wood-burning fireplace, hall bath. Smaller rear carpeted room with canopied twin bed, hall bath. Large third-floor suite with canopied double bed, wood-burning fireplace, carpeted sitting room, en-suite bath, kitchen area. Rollaways available.
Breakfast: 8–10 (according to guests' plans); continental 6–8 by request. Belgian waffles with fruit topping and bacon or French toast casserole with sausage, cheese, and egg. Fresh fruit, juice, tea, coffee. May be served by candlelight or on wicker-furnished rear deck overlooking garden.
Plus: Air conditioning and TV in all bedrooms; ceiling fan in some. Fireplaced living room. Afternoon tea, coffee, or soft drink. Welcoming snack.

Guests come from as close as 10 minutes away or from around the world.

Twin Gates B&B Inn

410/252-3131
800/635-0370

308 Morris Avenue, Lutherville, MD 21093

Hosts: Gwen and Bob Vaughan
Location: In a quiet northern Baltimore residential suburb, 20 minutes' drive by expressway to Harborplace and Aquarium. On an acre of land with mature trees and semicircular driveway framed by twin gates. Five-minute walk to light rail service to Penn Station, BWI Airport, Inner Harbor, and Oriole Park. Fifteen minutes to Ladew Topiary Gardens and a free vineyard tour.
Open: Year round.
Rates: $85–$95 shared bath, $95–$135 private bath. Amex, MC, Visa.
♥ ♣ ♦ ✴ ⚮

From Texas: *"This is how life should be . . . sitting on porch, enjoying cool morning breezes . . . symphony of birdsong . . . beautiful gardens."* From New York: *". . . cozy quilts, antique furniture, charming teddy bears [all dressed for the season], smells of home baking. Every convenience . . . including a stocked refrigerator, microwave, and iron all set up in guest kitchen. Fluffy towels changed as soon as they are used. The hosts are warm, caring, and thoughtful."* From North Carolina: *"Lovely! Friendly, welcoming, yet privacy respected as well."*

It's no wonder that Twin Gates is a three-time "Best of Baltimore" winner! Guests come "home" to the peace and quiet of this spacious Victorian with 12-foot ceilings; to the lacy gazebo and gardens featured on a full page in *Country Inns* magazine; to a glowing fireplace; to culinary talents acclaimed by hundreds of Macy's shoppers and by the DuPont Corporation too; and to exuberant Gwen (it's worth calling just to hear her answer the phone) and helpful Bob, a hospital management consultant. The Vaughans, parents of grown twin daughters, opened Twin Gates, their seventh restoration and first inn, in 1986.

Bed and bath: Six rooms, including one two-room suite. All private baths. Second floor—four queen-bedded rooms; two with shower baths, two with tub/shower. Third floor—one room with queen bed, shower bath. Suite with king bed, sitting room with single sofa bed, tub/shower bath.
Breakfast: At 9. Entree, perhaps peach crepes or banana French toast, and a baked pear or apple such as you have never had before. Fresh fruit, homemade "muffins of the season," freshly brewed hazelnut coffee, herbal teas. All heart healthy. Presented in candlelit dining room, in fireplaced greeting room, on front porch, or in gazebo.
Plus: Guest refrigerator. Room air conditioners. Bedroom ceiling fans. Sometimes, bedtime surprises. Seasonal newsletter with B&B recommendations based on the Vaughans' travels. Free parking.

B&Bs offer the opportunity to get away without going away.

Gramercy Bed & Breakfast   410/486-2405

1400 Greenspring Valley Road, Stevenson, MD 21153-0119

Hosts: Anne Pomykala and daughter Cristin.
Location: On 45 acres with trails, streams, organic gardens. In Greenspring Valley Historic District. One and a half miles from Route 83 and Baltimore Beltway (I-695); 20 minutes to Baltimore's Inner Harbor.
Open: Year round.
Rates: $90–$175. Third person, $25 adult, $10 child; if extra single room required, $50 adult, $20 child. MC, Visa.
♥ ♦ ♦ ♣ ♦ ✗ ✂

From Philadelphia: *"This beautiful estate . . . a welcome haven of warmth and comfort."* From Maryland: *"Breakfast is elegantly prepared, graciously served, and plentiful . . . makes me feel regal. The house is secluded, huge with winding staircase, highly polished and marvelously cared for . . . I love the place!"*

"The place" is a 26-room English Tudor mansion, built at the turn of the century with baronial first-floor recessed-paneled center hall and library and enormous fireplaces. Its fascinating history includes 35 years as the home of the Koinoina Foundation, which trained mature people in literacy methods and organic gardening for service on every continent. Restoration has been continuous ever since the Pomykala family purchased the property at auction in 1985. The house became a B&B shortly after it served as the 1986 Decorators' Showhouse. Now it is decorated with many antiques, window treatments, and sculpture and other art works. Guests are welcome to swim in the pool; play tennis; explore hiking trails (map available); go bird-watching (binoculars available); and visit the orchard as well as the shiitake mushroom laying yards and the herb gardens (pick some to take home) that supply many restaurants and gourmet shops. Returnees know: Plan to spend the day right here.

Cristin is here full time. Anne owns an educational video production studio and runs (elsewhere) Girl Scouts' high adventure programs. Her husband "welcomes guests but devotes most of his time to his dental practice."

In residence: "Cookie, our collie, takes guests on hikes and tours of the property. Yasser Aracat, our king-of-the-house alley cat, summers at poolside."
Bed and bath: Ten rooms. Five (three on second floor) have private bath; five decorated second-floor single rooms share two hall baths (one has claw-footed tub; one has tub/shower combination). Extra beds and crib available. Two king-bedded rooms with fireplace, whirlpool tub, VCR, dimmer lighting, chandelier. Double-bedded suite with antique Louis XIV furniture, chandeliered and fabric-covered ceiling, sun porch facing pool, sitting room with single antique sleigh bed, fireplace, game table, tub with legs (and shower). One double modified-canopied bed, fireplace, bath with claw-footed tub (and shower). Third-floor room with double bed, bath with two shower heads, one hand-held.
Breakfast: 7–11; guest's choice. Elaborate menu includes blackberries (year round); freshly squeezed orange juice; mushroom omelet with tomato, onion, and herbs; berry pancakes; fruit compote; vegetarian platter. Special diets accommodated. On porches or by dining room fireplace with fine china, silver, and stemware.
Plus: Grand piano in living room. Fireplaced living room, center hall, dining room, parlor, library. Bedroom air conditioners. TV in all rooms. Bedroom beverage service. Bath sheets. Fresh flowers. Free Baltimore Zoo passes.

Bed and Breakfast of Maryland Host #189

Burtonsville, MD

Location: Serene. A working horse farm and equestrian center surrounded on three sides by 1,000-acre reservoir watershed. "Three very good restaurants within two miles; others in nearby (20–30 minutes) Columbia and Silver Spring." Near antiquing and dinner theaters. Via express bus, a half hour to Metro station plus a half hour on Metro into Washington, D.C. Five miles from I-95; 30 minutes to Baltimore and Annapolis.

Reservations: Available year round through Bed and Breakfast of Maryland, page 14.

Rates: $80 queen, $100 suite.

♥ ◆

Folks who come here want to get away from it all. (You can bring your horse for B&B too.) The lodgelike guest house is a rustic country home, built in 1975 with a great room that has a cathedral ceiling, exposed timbers from an old Baltimore warehouse, yellow-pine paneling, an antiques-furnished living/dining area with wide-plank flooring, Oriental rugs, cushions by the fire. A floor-to-ceiling wall of glass overlooks the deck and the stallion pasture (about 25 horses).

Grounds are beautifully manicured and landscaped (many weddings are held here) by the owner, who is on the staff of a sleeping products trade association. His wife runs the farm. The resident innkeeper gives guests a tour of the flower and herb gardens, the three barns, and the first floor of the owners' residence—an 18th-century log cabin that has a fireplace constructed with soapstone quarried on the property. When you hike through miles of wooded trails bordering the Rocky Gorge Reservoir, you might see deer and waterfowl.

Bed and bath: Two carpeted main-floor rooms. Room with queen bed, private tub/shower bath, botanical prints. Suite—Hunt Room decor with greens, red, and oranges—is one large room with king bed, double sleep sofa in sitting area, TV, private tub/shower bath. State-of-the-art beds are air mattresses with dual control (one on each side of bed) allowing for firmness adjustment.

Breakfast: Flexible hours. Fruit course. Entree such as cheese souffle with breakfast sausage. Homemade breads and muffins. Juice, coffee, tea.

Glasgow Inn Bed & Breakfast   410/228-0575

1500 Hambrooks Boulevard   (reservations only) **800/373-7890**
Cambridge, MD 21613

Hosts: Louise Lee Roche and Martha Ann Rayne

Location: Riverside setting with century-old trees; many birds; and, on the acres of "front lawn," a soon-to-be community of eight houses. Near river cruises, Blackwater National Wildlife Refuge, antiquing, outlets, canoeing, auctions, tennis, sailing.

Open: Year round. Two-day minimum on weekends, holidays, or dates of special events.

Rates: Weekends, $100 semiprivate bath, $125 private bath. Less Monday–Thursday. Corporate rate $85.

♣ ◆ ✖ ⅄

(Please turn page.)

At the head of the new gaslit village green is a wonderful National Register 18th-century brick and clapboard Georgian plantation manor with Palladian windows, spacious rooms, tall first- and second-floor ceilings, and deep window seats. It is furnished with 18th-century family heirlooms and reproductions. Often, guests—including cycling groups, wedding parties, hospital administrators and visitors, and boaters—gather in the homey kitchen—or, as of 1995, in the great room of the first of eight houses (the other seven will be privately owned) designed in 18th-century Colonial tidewater style.

(Outgoing) Louise Lee and (quiet) Martha Ann, college friends, former teachers and quilt-shop owners (who made a quilt that is hanging in the state house), established Glasgow in 1987. Since, they have met many who come for "a birder's paradise where nature's voice can still be heard."

Bed and bath: Ten rooms. Seven (three with private full baths) on three floors of manor house. One king bed. Rest are queens (one is handicapped accessible). Two third-floor rooms (slanted ceilings) share a full bath. In new house (can be booked by one party)—three queen-bedded rooms, private full baths, and that great room (kitchen/dining room/fireplaced living room).
Breakfast: At 9 Monday–Saturday; 9:30 Sunday. Country style, with juice, cider, fruit. French toast, Amish omelet, or apple pancakes with scrapple and bacon.
Plus: Air conditioning everywhere, plus ceiling fans on second floor. Lemonade and iced tea on warm afternoons. Videos of musicals by the living room fire. Pickup service at Cambridge marinas or Salisbury airport. Holiday dinners with hosts' families. Inn-to-inn biking arrangements. Innkeeping apprentice program—two, five, or ten days.

From Virginia: *"Very attractively furnished . . . gracious hosts . . . delicious breakfast."*

Bluebird on the Mountain   301/241-4161
14700 Eyler Avenue, Cascade, MD 21719   **800/362-9526**

Host: Eda Smith-Eley
Location: Among other old mansions in quiet mountain (Cacoctin) village. On two acres with lawns, large old trees, fish pond, new flower and organic vegetable gardens. Seven miles to ski resort, seven to two golf courses. Near Penn-Mar Park (summer dances with big bands) and picnic areas. One mile to Appalachian Trail. Thirty minutes to Totem Pole Playhouse.
Open: Year round. Two-night minimum on weekends.
Rates: $105 first-floor queen. $95 second-floor king. $115 or $125 suites. MC, Visa.
♥ 🛥 ♣ ♦ ✈

It's serene, peaceful, and private—intentionally. When Edie first saw the country house in 1988, it was in need of everything. Once the rehabilitation stage was completed, she brought her artistic talents (portrait photography) and sense of color to interior design. Oriental rugs are on refinished floors. Walls are soft pastel colors. Sofas and chairs were selected for comfort. "Antiques are reserved for furnishings you don't have to sit on."

Although weekends seem to bring getaway guests "who either relax here or hike, bike, golf, and/or go antiquing," some weekdays are reserved for overnight retreats with meditation and, by appointment, a clothed, seated massage. "Some wives give their husbands a session as a gift!"

In residence: Two Himalayan cats, not allowed in guest rooms, affectionately greet guests on the front walk.
Foreign language spoken: Spanish.
Bed and bath: Four very large air-conditioned rooms (two are suites); all private baths. First floor—queen bed, en-suite whirlpool bath (no shower), wood-burning fireplace. Second floor (all with ceiling fans)—king bed, private hall bath with claw-foot tub/shower. Two suites: One has queen four-poster, en-suite whirlpool tub and shower, wood-burning fireplace, French doors to heated and screened living room/porch. Other suite—king bed, hall bath, whirlpool tub, hand-held shower, sitting room with double day/trundle bed.
Breakfast: 8:30–10. Fruit cup. Home-baked zucchini, blueberry, or orange-almond bread. Apple dumplings. Served in dining room or in sitting rooms of suites.
Plus: Fireplaced living room. Large porch with rockers. Down comforters. Robes provided. Guest refrigerator. Fresh flowers.

Inn at the Canal

410/885-5995
fax 410/885-3585

104 Bohemia Avenue, P.O. Box 187
Chesapeake City, MD 21915

Hosts: Al and Mary Ioppolo
Location: On the world's busiest canal, the (lockless) Chesapeake and Delaware. In village historic district with artists' workshops, canal museum, shops, restaurants. Within two hours of Washington, Baltimore, Philadelphia. Ten miles from I-95.
Open: Year round. Two-night minimum stay on Memorial Day and Labor Day weekends.

Rates: Small double-bedded room, $75. Larger rooms, $95 queen; $115 king/twin with water view; $105 queen water view. Singles $5 less. Third person $25. December–March, excluding holidays, 50 percent less for second of two nights. Amex, Discover, MC, Visa.
♥ ❖ ◆ ✖ ⅙

During their two-year search for a country site to redo themselves, a fellow antiques dealer told the Ioppolos about this house, built by a tugboat owner in 1870 and restored as an inn in 1987. Since the Ioppolos took over in 1989, the inn and the town have been rediscovered. Al and Mary's antiques collections include blue spongeware, oil lamps, coffee mills, baskets, and, on the fireplace wall of the "gather-round-kitchen-with-island," cast-iron muffin pans. Original painted and stenciled ceilings are in the tall-windowed parlor and dining rooms. And their breakfasts have been featured in *Mid-Atlantic Country.*

Al, a Philadelphia native who worked with the Department of Energy, shares auction hints. (His latest treasure: a c. 1850 10-foot table sometimes used by small conference groups.) Mary, an Alabama-born retired occupational therapist, is active in "this great town, which has canal cruises leaving from behind the inn, a tour that leads onto private horse farms in the area, and free summer Sunday concerts—with the best view from our porch!"

(Please turn page.)

In residence: Three cats not allowed in guest rooms.
Bed and bath: Six second-floor rooms with queen, double, twins, or king beds; some with four-posters. All private en-suite baths. One queen-bedded room with shower massage; all other rooms have tub/shower with shower massage.
Breakfast: 7–9 weekdays, 8–10 weekends and holidays. Freshly squeezed orange juice, breakfast meats, maybe poached pears with raspberry sauce or French toast stuffed with cream cheese and fresh peaches, hot beverages. At intimate tables or the large one.
Plus: Individual air conditioning and heating controls. Welcoming refreshments. Wicker-furnished front and waterside porches. Brick courtyard. Croquet. Crab feasts for eight. Antiques shop in restored milking room.

Chevy Chase Bed & Breakfast   301/656-5867

6815 Connecticut Avenue, Chevy Chase, MD 20815   fax 301/656-5867

Host: S. C. Gotbaum
Location: Historic residential area. Eight miles to downtown Washington, D.C., and museums. Bus across street for 10-minute ride to Friendship Heights Metro; 20-minute subway to Washington, D.C. Less than a mile to Chevy Chase Circle/D.C. city limits; three miles to Beltway, U.S. Route 495. Ten-minute walk to Rock Creek Park and neighborhood restaurants.
Open: Year round.
Rates: $55 single, $65 double.
♥ ♨ ☜ ♣ ◆ ✈ ⊁

Tapestries, carpets, and indigenous art and crafts from around the world are part of the reason for the international flavor in this beamed-ceilinged turn-of-the-century country house. Guests from every continent find that there's a sharing of experiences, cultures, and values here. The host, a sociologist, manages a public policy consulting service specializing in consumer health and women's issues.

Bed and bath: Two spacious second-floor rooms, each with cable TV, phone, ceiling fan, adjoining private full bath. Spectacular treetop Garden Room has a double bed, cathedral ceiling, bay window with year-round flowering plants, private deck overlooking garden. Tall-ceilinged Skylight Room has two extra-long beds used as twins or one king. Adjoining large gabled room for extended party members has a single bed and a high-riser for two.
Breakfast: Usually at 8. Assorted hot breads. Breakfast cereals, juice, fruits, cheeses. Alternated with eggs, French toast, or pancakes.
Plus: Central air conditioning. Fireplaced living room. Piano in music room. Many books on travel, sociology, political science, and women's studies "for welcome use by guests." Information about theater, conferences, congressional hearings, events. Upon request, concert tickets purchased in advance.

> Guests wrote: "A restorative experience. . . . Spectacular guest room. . . . Enjoyed the hospitality as much as visits to treasures in and around D.C.! . . . Talks each morning about Chile and U.S.A, their goods and misfortunes. . . . Delectable breakfast."

Amanda's Host #137

Easton, MD

Location: In residential historic district. On a main street; three blocks to restaurants, boutiques, historical society, Academy of the Arts. Within 15-minute drive of Oxford (and ferry), St. Michaels (and Chesapeake Maritime Museum), cycling routes, cruises and sails.

Reservations: Available all year round through Amanda's Regional Reservation Service, page 14.

Rates: $75–$120.

♥ ❖ ♦ ✈

Guests admire the restored 1880 Victorian, its 14-foot ceilings, the medallions in the drawing rooms, the wraparound porch—and the innkeepers' lifestyle. The hosts, visionaries who, in 1988, took on a house that relatives thought should be torn down, agree that they have the perfect arrangement!

The hostess was formerly employed in the financial world. Her husband is a systems analyst. The "nuts about detail who enjoy making every visit special for guests" furnished with 18th- and 19th-century oak, mahogany, and walnut pieces. Oriental and rag rugs are on the refinished Georgia pine floors. Lace curtains hang in every window.

In residence: Not allowed in guest rooms—"one long-haired dachshund who wandered in a few years ago and adopted us."
Bed and bath: Five rooms (seven for group events), all with antique beds. Two rooms (maximum) share tub/shower bath; robes provided. On second floor—three double-bedded rooms, each with working fireplace and ceiling fan; the largest (17-by-28) room also has a trundle that converts to two twins. On third floor—double (with Jacuzzi) or two twin beds.
Breakfast: Usually at 8 or 9. Blueberry pancakes, two cereals (one homemade), fruit platter or bowl, fruit and nut breads, muffins, juice, coffee, tea, hot chocolate, milk.
Plus: Air-conditioned guest rooms. TV. Arrival beverages. Porch rockers. Off-street parking. Secured overnight bicycle storage. Takeaway county cycling maps. Restaurant recommendations. Free (prearranged) transportation to and from marinas and Easton Airport.

From Maryland: *"Everything was perfect. . . . An anniversary we won't forget."*

Middle Plantation Inn   301/898-7128

9549 Liberty Road, Frederick, MD 21701-3246

Hosts: Shirley and Dwight Mullican
Location: In horse country, on 26 acres surrounded by woods and a stream. In the village of Mount Pleasant, five miles east of Frederick. Within 40 minutes of Gettysburg, Pennsylvania; Antietam Battlefield, Maryland; Harpers Ferry, West Virginia. Ten minutes to New Market, the state's antiques capital.
Open: Year round.
Rates: Per room. $95 for one night. $90/night for two nights, $85/night for four or more nights. MC, Visa.

♥ ♠ ♦ ✈ ⅏

One photo album shows the 1988 "coming down" of the 1810 stone and log house that was part of the 26-acre farm purchased by Dwight's grandparents

(Please turn page.)

in 1914. Another album shows the "going up" of the new house, which tries to capture the ambiance of the old with plaster between old wood on interior walls, remilled flooring, old chimney brick in the living room fireplace, old board and batten in the log gable ends. The breakfast/keeping room features a massive stone fireplace, skylights, and stained glass windows. Every room has some stenciling. For antique furnishings the Mullicans frequented Frederick County auctions and shops. ("We still do.") The vegetable garden thrives. Fresh eggs are gathered in the henhouse.

Dwight is a bank vice president. Shirley works in the accounting department of a local power company.

Bed and bath: Four rooms, all overlooking yard, field, wooded area—and, at night, the lights of Frederick. All private full baths. First-floor room with private entrance, original flooring, extra-long double iron bed, bath with footed tub and hand-held shower. Private access to three carpeted second-floor rooms, each with antique queen bed. One has iron-and-brass bed; one has canopied bed; one has highback walnut bed, bath with claw-footed tub, stall shower.

Breakfast: At 9. Orange juice. Seasonal fruit. Freshly baked breads, muffins, or pastries. Cheese. Cereal. Tea or coffee.

Plus: Air conditioning. "Hidden" TVs in rooms. Individual thermostats. Some ceiling fans. Phone jack. Beverages. Fresh flowers. Mints.

> From Kansas: *"Accommodations were tops. Room was beautiful and delightfully private. Advice, particularly where to eat, was invaluable."*

Beaver Creek House Bed & Breakfast

20432 Beaver Creek Road, Hagerstown, MD 21740   301/797-4764

Hosts: Don and Shirley Day
Location: Country. Four miles east of town. One mile from I-70/U.S. 40 junction, 6 miles from I-81. Four miles to Appalachian Trail; 12 to Antietam; 22 to Harpers Ferry; 30 to Gettysburg. Close to many excellent restaurants.

Open: Year round.
Rates: $85 double bed, private bath. $80 twin beds, private full bath, or double bed with private half bath. $75 double bed, shared bath. Singles $10 less. Midweek (except holidays) $10 less. Amex, Discover, MC, Visa.
♥ ♣ ♦ ✠ ✄

> From *Colonial Homes* magazine staffer: *"A gem. . . . Atop a hill surrounded by horses, lush green fields, and a gorgeous view of South Mountain . . . an inviting home with an eclectic mix of classic, elegant heirlooms. . . . Hospitality is the Days' specialty."* From California: *"Felt like special guests . . . even fresh lavender to take home."* From Indiana: *"Good food and conversation."*

Dozens of guests echoed those sentiments while recounting their visits "at home" with chef Don, a former CPA with the General Accounting Office in Washington, D.C., and Shirley, a docent at the local historical society.

When Don retired in 1986, the Days, Hagerstown natives, bought this turn-of-the-century country Victorian and filled it with family pictures and Victorian pieces, a clock collection, Oriental rugs, and many quilts. The popular porch swing is the very one Shirley used while growing up. Guests include history buffs, sports enthusiasts—and memorable sisters who arrived with a picture album showing this house (and themselves) as it was when they lived here in 1915.

Bed and bath: Five rooms; some with sitting areas. First-floor room with twin beds, private tub/shower bath. On second floor, private shower bath for room with four-poster canopied bed; private tub/shower bath for room with antique double brass bed. Two double-bedded rooms, one with en-suite half bath, share (robes provided) a full hall bath. Rollaway available.

Breakfast: Usually 8–9:30; coffee earlier. Locally grown fruits and berries. Cranberry-liqueured baked apples and buttermilk pecan pancakes with pure maple syrup, locally made sausage. Juices, homemade breads, freshly brewed coffee. With fine china, crystal, silver in crystal-chandeliered dining room or on screened porch overlooking garden.

Plus: Central air conditioning with individual bedroom thermostats and ceiling fans. Fresh fruit and flowers. Freshly brewed tea, home-baked cookies and/or tea breads at 4 p.m. Mints. Fireplaced parlor. TV, games, books, magazines. Outdoor grill. Horseshoes.

Lewrene Farm B&B   301/582-1735
9738 Downsville Pike, Hagerstown, MD 21740

Hosts: Irene and Lewis Lehman
Location: On 125-acre crop farm surrounded by other farms. Four miles south of town on Route 632; ½ mile north of Maryland Route 68. Four miles to I-70 and I-81, eight to Antietam Battlefield; 90 minutes from Washington and Baltimore.

Open: Year round.
Rates: Suite $100. Private bath— $75 two double beds, $89 with whirlpool, $95 largest room. Singles $10 less. Third person $15. Shared bath— $60–$65 double, $50–$58 single.
♥ ♨ 🛏 ❄ ✈ ✄

With their six children grown (some of the 14 grandchildren help on the farm), the Lehmans added rooms in 1986 and opened a B&B in this turn-of-the-century house where they have lived for more than 40 years. Candles glow in each window. Handmade quilts are everywhere; some are for sale. In season, you can see corn being harvested with tractors. Ebony, the dog, lives in the barn. There are some chickens and peacocks, and in the woods there are deer.

Visitors from Brazil, Guatemala, Switzerland, Honduras, Italy, Germany, Argentina, and Mexico have become "family" through several organizations including Mennonite Your Way and the Experiment in International Living. The Lehmans' own travels, often with homestays and B&Bs, have taken them to Guatemala, Kenya, Iceland, Czechoslovakia, and Germany.

Foreign languages spoken: Spanish and some German.

Bed and bath: Five (one is a suite) Victorian/country antiques-furnished rooms. In 1900s part of house, one tub/shower bath shared by two double-bedded rooms and one room with a canopied queen bed. In newer part, one room with canopied queen bed, refrigerator, private bath with whirlpool tub. One room with two double beds (one canopied), private full bath. Very large third-floor room with a queen and two singles, private full bath, sitting area, refrigerator. Rollaway and crib available.

(Please turn page.)

Breakfast: Flexible timing. Juice. Homemade breads and jelly, apple crisp, applesauce. Pancakes, eggs, bacon or sausage, casseroles. Special diets accommodated. Served family style at a big kitchen table.
Plus: Large fireplaced room with piano and TV. Bedside snacks. Air-conditioned bedrooms; some with ceiling fan, individual thermostat, phone jack. Plant identification book (for walks). Gazebo. A double platform swing, Irene's lifelong dream and a favorite with guests.

> From Washington, D.C.: *"Quiet and peaceful, lovely and immaculate. . . . A perfect experience topped off by the kindness and hospitality of the Lehmans."* From New Jersey: *"Vast property for quiet walks. . . . Real country food. . . . Not only was my two-year-old welcomed, she loved romping through the grounds."*

Sunday's Bed & Breakfast   301/797-4331
39 Broadway, Hagerstown, MD 21740-4019   800/221-4828

Host: Bob Ferrino
Location: Quiet residential area. Twenty minutes to Antietam Battlefield and Whitetail Ski Resort. Within five minutes of I-70 and I-81.

Open: Year round.
Rates: $65–$75 single. $75–$95 double. Package, corporate, and long-term rates available.
♥ ♣ ✤

Bob's dream of living in an old house with the hope of one day opening a bed and breakfast became a reality when he took an early retirement in 1992 after 22 years with IBM.

The pale pink paint on this 1890 brick Queen Anne Victorian has generated much interest. Guests as well as area residents have inquired about it so that they could reproduce the same color on their own houses.

Returnees include one couple who became engaged here, wanted to return for their honeymoon, and then decided to have the wedding (50 guests) here. Another guest couldn't get over that Bob came to a theater at intermission with the glasses she had left behind.

The B&B is named after Bob's mother. "In Italian, it is Dominica. And yes, we are open seven days a week." It's the same name he had given to his part-time antiques business, "the kind of business that makes you want to keep all the wonderful pieces you have purchased to sell."

The redecorated house is immaculate, bright, and airy, with tall windows, balloon shades, scatter rugs (some Orientals, some hooked), and antiques throughout.

Bed and bath: Three second-floor rooms. Private shower bath for room with a queen and a three-quarter bed. Two rooms, each with a double bed, share a tub/shower bath.
Breakfast: 7:30–9. Could be pumpkin-raisin-walnut bread; cantaloupe with fresh raspberry garnish, orange sauce with mint; sausage spinach quiche with potatoes on the side; French brioche bread. Juice, coffee, tea. In fireplaced tea room; in breakfast room overlooking backyard; on back porch; in dining room; or in your own room.
Plus: Air conditioning, telephone jack, fruit basket, chocolates, and cordials in guest rooms. TV available. Fresh flowers. Tea (and cake) at 3 p.m.; wine and cheese at 6. Special soaps. Turndown service. Newspaper. Picnic baskets

prepared. Babysitting arranged. Local airport pickup. Dinners by advance arrangement.

> Guests wrote: *"A piece of heaven . . . felt incredibly pampered . . . comfortable . . . great attention to detail . . . beautiful . . . perfect."*

Bed and Breakfast of Delaware Host #36
Havre de Grace, Maryland

Location: In historic district, among 2,000 Victorian structures on the Chesapeake Bay at the Susquehanna River mouth. Two blocks from the water. Near fine restaurants, antiques shops, Concord Point Lighthouse, Havre de Grace Decoy Museum. Thirty minutes to Baltimore; 40 to Wilmington.

Reservations: Available all year round through Bed & Breakfast of Delaware, page 4.

Rates: $55 single, $85 double. $10 third person.

♥ ♫ ✉ ⁂ ✈

"We were overwhelmed by its beauty," say the hosts, who had experience rejuvenating another old house "not nearly this size" in town. They could see through the disrepair and the apartments that had been carved out of the 19-room turreted Victorian stone mansion. In 1987 both dovetailed their jobs—as computer programmer analyst (he still is) and as manager of an international department of a Baltimore bank—with rebuilding and restoring absolutely everything inside and out. Now guests use the grand staircase with lighted newel post lamp at base and huge stained glass window at top. The central hall, wallpapered by the hosts with Bradbury and Bradbury paper, is flanked by two parlors (one with elaborate plaster ceiling) that have large pocket doors. There are 12-foot ceilings, intricate parquet floors, Oriental rugs, and many plants. Victorian antiques, a passion for the hostess since she was 14, are everywhere—except in the fireplaced family room, which has color TV, a stereo, games, and magazines. Outside, there are extensive flower gardens, a wraparound porch with glider and wrought-iron furnishings, and even a fenced yard with swing and sandbox.

Bed and bath: Four large (two have five windows) second-floor rooms. One with queen brass bed, private tub/shower bath. Three (two unless it's all one party) double-bedded rooms share a full bath and a half bath. Extra twin bed available for any room.

Breakfast: At guests' convenience (within reason). Juices, fruit, yogurt, cereal, freshly baked breads or muffins. Entree might be apple pancakes or eggs Benedict. In dining room by working original gas fireplace.

Plus: Room air conditioners. Two parlors with wood-burning fireplace, cable TV. Fruit basket, ice bucket, and mints in each room. Turndown service. Plenty of books and places to read them. Host-guided walking tour of historic district, by request.

> From Pennsylvania: *"Room was perfect . . . town delightful . . . breakfast delicious . . . beautiful gardens . . . enjoyed conversation with the hosts. Memorable."*

Amanda's Host #209
Monkton, MD

Location: On a 60-plus-acre working farm along a country road. Two miles to a popular country restaurant; 7 to The Milton Inn, a five-star restaurant; 5 to Ladew Topiary Gardens. Two miles to tubing on the Gunpowder River and 13-mile-long hike and bike trail (bike rentals available) along old railroad line. "Antiques shops in every direction." Forty minutes north of Baltimore, off I-83.
Reservations: Year round. Available through Amanda's Regional Reservation Service, page 14.
Rate: $85.
♥ ⬛ ✈ ⚡

City folk love this "escape to the country," a 150-year-old stone house on a farm with 11 cows, 2 draft horses, 1 pig, 3 dogs (not in guests' area, but "most guests beg to meet them"), and some cats. You might see deer—sometimes in the alfalfa field with a sunset backdrop—as well as beavers, hawks, and lots of colorful birds. Many guests walk the fields—with a dog as escort. They climb the hill for a wonderful view and then go down to the dock at the pond, where you are welcome to fish and release, swim, or skate.

The host is an avocational farmer, an investment advisor who makes haying time top priority—and answers many questions about balers. He and his wife, an early childhood teacher, enjoy having the world come to their door.

Bed and bath: In a 1970s addition, a private entrance to one second-floor room with canopied double bed, working fireplace, tub/shower bath.
Breakfast: Continental on weekdays. Weekends—"Any time you'd like. It's kind of fun to spoil guests." Fresh seasonal fruit, juice, eggs, bacon or sausage; cheese omelet or French toast. Served on glassed-in porch overlooking the berry garden—and woodpile too; in winter, by fireplace in country kitchen.
Plus: A tour of the farmhouse. TV/VCR in living room. Air conditioner in guest room. Beautiful countryside.

> From Maryland: *"Gracious hospitality. . . . Charming, delightful, warm and comfortable."*

National Pike Inn   301/865-5055
9 West Main Street, P.O. Box 299, New Market, MD 21774

Hosts: Tom and Terry Rimel
Location: In historic district of a half-mile-long town known (especially on weekends) for its 30 antiques shops, old-fashioned general store, and restaurants (Mealey's is across the street). Just off I-70, exit 62. Seven miles east of historic Frederick. Near wineries, hiking, biking.
Open: Year round. Two-night minimum on New Market Days.

Rates: Monday–Thursday, doubles shared bath $75, private bath $85–$110; singles $65. Weekends, per room: shared bath $75 double bed, $90 queen; private hall bath $95 queen canopied; private en-suite bath $110 or $125 queen. Third person $15. $25 surcharge for Saturday-only bookings on holiday weekends, New Market Days, and Christmas in New Market.
♥ ⚡ ✈ ⚡

Fronted by a brick herringbone sidewalk and topped (in 1900) by a windowed widow's walk, this Colonial house built between 1796 and 1804 (you can tell the stages) fulfilled Terry's idea of B&B. "During the 15 years that we lived [with three sons] a half mile from here, we often admired this beautiful old house. There are eight fireplaces, each an architect's delight from the Federal period. Although the house had been restored 25 years before we bought it, we have strived to make it 'perfect,' keeping the worn wide-plank floors and old door hinges and locks. Room decor ranges from elegant to very country. We furnished with wonderful reproductions and some antiques."

Terry occasionally appears in period costume on Saturday evenings. Tom, a slate roof and tile specialist, joins her as cohost every evening.

Bed and bath: Five second-floor rooms. Queen four-poster, private en-suite tub/shower bath. High canopied queen bed, private hall tub/shower bath. Queen four-poster, private shower bath, twin daybed. Room with queen brass bed and one with antique carved oak double bed share a connecting full bath.
Breakfast: 9. Full. Maybe pancakes or eggs. With muffins, breads (white, wheat, or chocolate dot pumpkin), shoofly coffee cake, apple pastry. Juice. Fresh fruit. Tea and coffee. Served in Colonial dining room.
Plus: Bedroom air conditioners. Fireplace, wing chairs, and organ in living room. Complimentary Sunday paper. Bedside mints. Rear brick courtyard with gardens. Smokehouse and 1830s carriage house shown on request.

The Mill House Bed & Breakfast 410/287-3532
102 Mill Lane, North East, MD 21901

Hosts: Lucia and Nick Demond
Location: Quiet. On a tidal creek, two miles south of I-95 exit 100. One block from town center, four antiques shops. Near Day Basket Factory, where handwoven baskets have been made the same way since 1876. Short walk to waterfront town park and Upper Bay Museum. Less than an hour's drive to Baltimore's Inner Harbor, Pennsylvania Dutch country, Winterthur, Brandywine River museums. Ten minutes to designer factory outlets.
Open: March–November.
Rates: $75 canopied bed. $65 Victorian double bed. Singles $5 less. Ten percent less for stays of three or more nights. MC, Visa.
◂ ◆ ✈

The sign for this "tour house" (Maryland House and Garden Pilgrimage and Christmas fund-raiser too) is a millstone. The L-shaped antiques-furnished 1710 house is really two houses. One was built for the miller. The Dutch Colonial, built for the mill owner, has accommodated B&B guests since 1988, when the Demonds returned to the family home that had been restored "from near collapse by another generation of our family in 1950."

Now an 18th-century tall-case clock ticks in the fireplaced living room. White walls are trimmed with Colonial blue, green, or gold. Wildflowers abound along the tidal creek banks and the adjacent wooded area. Sometimes, dozens of ducks waddle onto the lawn for feeding time.

Lucia, a former docent at Winterthur Museum in Delaware and at the Valentine Museum in Richmond, Virginia, is curator for toys and dolls of the

(Please turn page.)

Historical Society Museum. Nick, a retired sales manager, is very active in several historical organizations, in scouting, and at the Fair Hill Nature Center.

Bed and bath: Two rooms, each with easy chairs and a desk, share large full bath. Larger room has high canopied double bed (step provided), walk-in closet. Victorian high double bed, walnut wardrobe in other room.
Breakfast: 7–9:30. Bacon or sausage. Scrambled eggs, omelets, or French toast. Orange juice. Fresh fruit compote. Biscuits, muffins, scones, or pecan sticky rolls. In dining room with fresh flowers, sterling silver, stemware.
Plus: Bedroom air conditioners. Use of canoe and two bikes.

From New York City: *"A charming warm house . . . Demonds are knowledgeable about the area . . . enjoyed fireplace in evening . . . different and delicious breakfast each morning."*

The Oak & Apple   301/334-9265
208 North Second Street, Oakland, MD 21550

Hosts: Jana and Ed Kight
Location: In a residential/preservation district, within walking distance of shops and restaurants. Two hours from Pittsburgh, three from Baltimore and Washington, D.C. Ten minutes from Deep Creek Lake and Wisp Ski Resort, 40 to Canaan Valley. Within 25 miles of six state parks. One hour from West Virginia University and Frostburg State University.

Open: Year round. Two-night minimum, weekends Memorial Day–November 1 and December 31–March 15, and holidays.
Rates: Private bath—large rooms $70 and $80; third floor $60, extra person $10. Shared bath $55. Singles $5 less.
♥ ♣ ♦ ✈ ⅍

From Maryland: *"The house is gorgeous . . . impeccable . . . breakfast was wonderful . . . quintessential hosts . . . even windbreakers for our bike ride during an unexpectedly chilly weekend. . . . With this glowing account it may become so popular that I might get preempted when I call for future stays."*

The Kights renovated the columned wide front porch to look like the original built around 1915. The grounds include old apple, oak, pine, cherry, and maple trees. Inside, there's a leaded-glass entrance foyer. And a big glass-enclosed sun porch. A wing chair and Sheraton sofa are by the parlor (gas) fireplace. A TV/VCR is in the informal sitting room.

Jana, an audiologist who knows basic sign language, and Ed, a realtor, were introduced to B&Bs while bicycling in Vermont. They opened here "in this area we've known all our lives" in 1992, after restoring, painting, and papering this grand old house fronted by a large lawn, a sidewalk, "and small-town ambiance."

Bed and bath: Five rooms, modern baths. Second floor—two large queen-bedded rooms, private full baths (one has jetted tub). Third floor "tucked under the eaves"—two smaller queen-bedded rooms, each with pedestal sink in room, share full bath. Room with a double and single bed, private hall shower bath.

Breakfast: Flexible hours. Fresh fruits and juices. Homemade breads, muffins, scones. Cereals. Served in formal fireplaced dining room or on sun porch.
Plus: Beverages. Flannel sheets. Guest refrigerator. Fresh flowers.

Atlantic House   410/289-2333

501 North Baltimore Avenue, Ocean City, MD 21842

Hosts: Paul Cook and Debi Thompson-Cook
Location: On a corner along main street with view of boardwalk and ocean from front porch "looking beyond the Comfort Inn located across the street." Walk to everything. Public transportation, $1 all day.

Open: Year round. Two-night minimum preferred on weekends, Memorial Day–Labor Day.
Rates: $55–$130 in season; $45 off-season. (Highest in-season rate is for room with two double beds, refrigerator, private full en-suite bath.) Discover, MC, Visa.

♥ ✿ ♦ ✈ ✄

From Massachusetts: *"Beautifully restored. Surrounded by commercial accommodations. Walk in and you're in a different world. . . . It wouldn't be out of place in a rural area. . . . Very friendly, accommodating hosts who have separate living quarters but make you feel as if you're visiting in their home. A true B&B."*

Others say it's an oasis or "just like Grandma's." That's exactly what Paul and Debi, lifelong area residents, had in mind when, in 1993, they bought this four-story dormered 1927 building that is now considered unique in this town. As Paul, a Bell Atlantic employee, says, "Returnees—including many first-time B&B guests—come back just like they did in the old days—to stay with a family. We gutted the entire lobby and redecorated throughout—not like a museum! We papered and painted, and we used a lot of wicker, quilts, and auction finds." Turn-of-the-century lobby photographs feature Debi's family, known for their Dolle's Popcorn business. In the summer, the porches are popular. On winter weekends, some guests sit, pajama-clad, in the lobby reading the Sunday paper.

In residence: Assistant innkeepers Emily, age 10; Jacob, 13; and Ethan, 17. Rusty, the cat, "receives lots of loving."
Bed and bath: Eleven air-conditioned, carpeted rooms with queen or double bed and color cable TV; five on second floor (with ceiling fans), six on third. Vary in size and number of windows. Seven private baths are en suite or in hall; one has tub, others have shower but no tub. Four top-floor rooms share a half bath and separate shower.
Breakfast: 8–10:30. Fruit, juices, yogurt, cereal, freshly baked goods and bagels. Buffet in lobby (entire front of house).
Plus: After-dinner refreshments. Color cable TV in lobby. Off-street parking. Health club privileges. Restaurant recommendations and menus. Discount coupons. Forgotten items.

*H*ospitality *is the keynote of B&B.*

The Thoroughbred Bed & Breakfast

16410 Batchellor's Forest Road, Olney, MD 20832   301/774-7649
fax 301/924-2387

Host: Helen Polinger
Location: A country road divides this estate and its new (1993) 18-hole golf course. Minutes to restaurants. Twelve miles from Washington, D.C.; six miles to subway (with parking), 40-minute ride to city; 40-minute drive to Baltimore's Inner Harbor.

Open: Year round. (Check in by 8 p.m.)
Rates: Main house $70–$95. Carriage house $95–$110. Without breakfast—farmhouse $75; slave quarters $115. Third person $35. Amex, Discover, MC, Visa.

♥ ✿ ⚘ ♦ ✗ ⚔

The Polingers built this country estate in the early 1960s. At one time they had about 150 mares here. (Helen still breeds some horses.) In 1989, with five "empty nest" rooms, Helen began B&B in the main house, which has an English country feel—with fireplaced living room, upstairs sitting room with piano, a game room with championship-sized pool table, and many reproductions. When she gutted and redid the farmhouse, interior wood trim and floors were retained; furnishings are both new and old. Antiques are throughout the guest carriage house. The pool, 20 steps from the main building, is complete with dressing room. There's a year-round outdoor hot tub. And a gazebo.

Helen has had careers as a model, a fashion show commentator, a beauty salon owner and operator, and a retailer of ski and tennis hard- and software. Now she hosts guests who come for a getaway, to visit local residents or nearby schools, or for golf (right here), and Washington visitors who prefer to stay outside the city.

Bed and bath: Fifteen air-conditioned rooms; seven with private bath. King, queen, double, or twin beds. In main house—five rooms; three have full baths; two share a bath. Carriage house—four rooms, each with private bath and deck; two have working fireplace and double whirlpool tub. Farmhouse—four rooms share two baths, each with whirlpool tub, shower, pedestal sink. Slave quarters—two bedrooms, living room, fireplace, kitchenette, wrap-around deck, one bath with steam shower.
Breakfast: 7–9 for main house rooms. Extended continental. Carriage house: continental served in your room. Farmhouse and slave quarters: Provide and prepare your own.
Plus: TV in some rooms. You are welcome to visit the barns.

Innkeepers are great sharers. One recalls the guest who arrived for a wedding only to find he'd left his dress pants at home. The innkeeper wore the same size. The guest appeared at the wedding properly dressed in borrowed pants.

Littleton's Bed and Breakfast   410/957-1645

407 Second Street   fax (phone first) **410/957-1936**
Pocomoke City, MD 21851

Hosts: Walter and Pam Eskiewicz
Location: Residential. On Eastern Shore, five minutes from Virginia border. On a corner, next to church parsonage, across from historic church. Two blocks from designated "wild and scenic" Pocomoke River, which can be seen from house. Three blocks from downtown. Four blocks from 100-km-view trail that includes very flat rural country roads. Twenty minutes southeast of Snow Hill; 35 southeast of Crisfield ferry to watermen communities of Tangier and Smith islands; 20 minutes to Chincoteague (Virginia) and Assateague (Maryland) islands. Near state parks and hiking.
Open: Year round.
Rates: $65 private bath. Ten percent less if bath shared. $60 smaller room. MC, Visa.
🕴 🛏 ❀ 🐾 🍴

> From Massachusetts: *"Fabulous. They are the ultimate in hosts. Felt like we had been friends for years. When we were leaving to continue our bicycling trip, our kids, ages 10 and 12, asked, 'Can't we stay here one more night?' House, an immaculately restored Victorian, is in a beautiful old town on the river."*

The neighbors, too, are delighted that the Eskiewiczes, experienced B&B travelers, have restored this landmark Second Empire c. 1860 house that they purchased in 1988 as a summer residence. Layers of paint were removed inside and out—even on the gingerbread. Floors were refinished. The traditional and antique furnishings include many family pieces, "the kind you can feel comfortable with." When Walter took early retirement from the New Jersey Turnpike Authority Engineering Department in 1992, the family moved to this "wonderful small town, which is rich in history, architecture, and opportunities for outdoor activities."

In residence: Two daughters—Leah is age nine; Amanda is in her twenties. "Octavious is our friendly and very clever cat."
Bed and bath: Three second-floor rooms share two full baths. One with queen bed has door to bath that also has a hall entrance. Two double-bedded rooms.
Breakfast: Usually 8–9:30. Fresh fruit. Freshly baked muffins. Blueberry-stuffed French toast, buttermilk pancakes with sausauge, granola, Belgian waffles or casseroles.
Plus: Air conditioning (window units) throughout. Spinet piano in living room. Ceiling fans in guest rooms and dining room. Italian bottled mineral water. Ice bucket. Evening dessert treats. Use of canoe (launch site in town), bicycles, fishing rods, crabbing lines (no license needed at city pier, two blocks away).

---

*T*o tip or not? (Please turn to page xi.)

Saint Michael's Manor   301/872-4025

Box 17A, Route 5, Scotland, MD 20687

Hosts: Joe and Nancy Dick
Location: On 10 acres with fruit and shade trees on a peninsula surrounded by Long Neck Creek, "which looks more like a river." Up a country lane, half a mile off Route 5. Nine miles south of Saint Mary's City, Maryland's original capital, with historic park, old state house, Trinity Church, nature center, old plantation, and museum; 17 miles southeast of Lexington Park, home of naval air research and test center. One mile from Point Lookout State Park with beach, boat rentals, visitors' center, Civil War museum, lighthouse, summer cruises to Smith Island. *Three hours from Eastern Shore and the town of Saint Michaels.* One hour and 45 minutes from Washington, D.C.

Open: February–December. Two-night minimum on holidays Memorial Day–Labor Day.

Rates: $65 Friday, Saturday, Sunday; $60 Monday–Thursday. $45 singles.
♦ ♦ ✠

From Massachusetts: *"A beautiful old manor house on an inlet . . . reasonable rates . . . powerboat, rowboat, canoe, and bicycles for guests' use . . . friendly hosts."*

Unwind. Paddle to a beautiful Chesapeake Bay beach. Sightsee. Pick and press your own grapes and take the juice home. Or, as many do, especially since a 1994 *Washington Post Magazine* article appeared, ask Joe to tell some of his ghost stories about this 1805 Federal stucco-covered brick manor house. The Dicks, parents of five and grandparents of seven, bought it in 1982 and opened as the area's first B&B a year later.

Throughout there are period pieces and collectibles. Oriental rugs are on new first-floor floors. Stenciling is by Nancy, a recently retired nurse. And those 10 varieties of table and wine grapes are grown by Joe, a retired navy captain who is now a county consultant.

In residence: Outside—two goats, three sheep, two dogs.
Foreign language spoken: Some Polish.
Bed and bath: Four air-conditioned waterview rooms. Second floor—room with queen and one with a double share a full bath. Third floor—room with king and room with two twins share a full bath. Rollaway available.
Breakfast: Usually 8:30–9. Juice. Fresh fruit. Pecan waffles topped with raspberries. Homemade crabapple and grape syrups. Local sausage. Homemade mueslix. Served in family dining room.
Plus: Welcoming beverage. Fresh flowers year round. Living/great room with spinet piano, a pump organ, original bubble glass on cupboards, fireplace at each end. Handmade bed quilts. Above-ground swimming pool. Beach towels. Birdwatching in the marsh. Wine weekends.

Innkeeping may be America's most envied profession. As one host mused, "Where else can you get a job where, every day, someone tells you how wonderful you are?"

The Inn at Antietam

220 East Main Street, P.O. Box 119
Sharpsburg, MD 21782

301/432-6601
fax 301/432-5981

Hosts: Betty and Cal Fairbourn
Location: Rural. Perfect for walking. At top of a long Main Street driveway. Surrounded by lawns with a buggy set against the horizon. Overlooking Sharpsburg, Antietam National Battlefield, and, sometimes, reenacters. Near Harpers Ferry; C&O Canal; Shepherdstown, West Virginia; Crystal Grottoes Cavern; hiking, canoeing, antiques and cottage industry craft shops, restaurants.
Open: Year round except two weeks at Christmas. Two-night minimum on weekends and holidays.
Rates: $95 Sunday–Thursday; $105 Friday–Saturday and holidays. $25 extra person. Amex.
♥ ♣ ✈

Here's "homegrown hospitality with a sophisticated touch" as seen in a *Country Inns* cover feature and in *Victoria, Mid-Atlantic Country,* and many other publications; as seen in Macy's during a cooking demonstration—part of a Meet-the-Hosts program associated with this book; and as experienced by grateful guests who comment on the "relaxed style in a beautifully restored inn run by a charming couple."

It has been that way ever since the Salt Lake City, Utah, natives—Cal, a former General Motors (Detroit) executive, and Betty, a former hospice counselor—restored the rambling Victorian in 1984. They were so good at doing their own woodwork—including new moldings and kitchen cabinets—that they now restore other properties. They are so good at "touches" that they selected elegant period antiques with an emphasis on comfort. Now, ten years later, guests meet three generations of Fairbourns who agree that "people are fabulous."

In residence: Rebok, an outdoor Maine coon cat, joins guests on porch.
Bed and bath: Four air-conditioned suites, all private baths. First floor—an 1800 queen-sized four-poster bed, sitting room, full bath. Two second-floor suites, each with full bath. One has a queen-bedded room plus a sitting room; the other, a queen bed and a dressing room. Adjoining Smoke House has loft with double bed, original massive fireplace in sitting room with beams and barnboard walls, wet bar, tub-without-shower bath.
Breakfast: 8–9:30. Freshly squeezed orange juice. Fresh fruit with Belgian waffles, blueberry pancakes, French toast, or blintzes. Country bacon.
Plus: Gorgeous gardens. Wicker-furnished solarium. Formal parlor. Wraparound porch with swing and rockers. Brick patio overlooking Blue Ridge Mountains. Arrangements made for battlefield guided tours (rave reviews).

---

*T*he place to stay has become the reason to go.

Antietam Overlook Farm

P.O. Box 30, Keedysville, MD 21756-0030

301/432-4200
800/878-4241

Hosts: John and Barbara Dreisch
Location: Tranquil. On 95 mountaintop acres with deer, turkeys, birds, and "awesome four-state views." Overlooking Antietam National Battlefield and the village of Sharpsburg (four miles); 75 minutes west of Baltimore. Near Appalachian Trail, C&O Canal, antiquing, outlet shopping, fine dining.
Open: Year round. Two-night min-

imum stay for weekends that include a Saturday or holiday reservation.
Rates: $118 Monday–Thursday, $132 Friday–Sunday. Four-state view, $132 Monday–Thursday, $152 Friday–Sunday. Without steeping tub, $108 Monday–Thursday, $118 Friday–Sunday, $35 extra person. Amex, Diners, Discover, MC, Visa.
♥ ♦ ✖ ⅄

It's plenty rustic—yet all new. What looks like a barn outside has a spacious interior with rough-sawn ceilings and walls and wide-board floors. John designed and built it in 1990, just four years after building a Cape Cod–style farmhouse on this mountaintop where there had been nothing but pastureland and trees. Connecting the two buildings is one huge great room with big stone fireplace, ceiling fans, comfortable seating, rocking chairs, and dining area. Rooms have flowered print fabrics and lace curtains.

"Shortly after we moved to the farmhouse, Shepherdstown innkeepers asked us to take their overflow. All those folks just kept coming back, so we built the barn to offer the ultimate in accommodations with a warm atmosphere and a touch of elegance."

In Baltimore, Barbara owned and operated a delicatessen. John continues to work in the construction industry.

Bed and Bath: Five spacious rooms, each with queen bed and private bath (pedestal sink in bedroom), on first and second floors. Features vary—fireplace, steeping tub (for bubble bath) in the bedroom, private screened porch, sun deck. One room can accommodate a third guest.
Breakfast: 8:30. Plentiful. Ham baked with fresh pineapple and cinnamon sugar or fried with Dijon mustard and honey glaze. Three-cheese egg casserole or cheese/vegetable/herb omelet. Battered and fried cranberry nut bread. Juice. Homemade breads, jams, curds, and chutneys. Menu never repeated during guest's stay.
Plus: Central air conditioning. Ceiling fans throughout. Large screened porch off great room. Wet bar and guest refrigerator. Complimentary beverages. European chocolates.

Bed and Breakfast of Maryland Host #185

Silver Spring, MD

Location: Secluded. Inside the Beltway on an acre of landscaped grounds overlooking Sligo Creek and woods. Ten-minute bus ride to Metro station, 30-minute drive from White House.
Reservations: Available all year

round through Bed and Breakfast of Maryland, page 14.
Rates: Per room. $70 queen bed, $55 two single beds, $45 one single bed.
♦ ✖

"The coffee is always percolating. The paper is here. A harpsichord is in the fireplaced living room. The house is yours to enjoy." Guests are treated like family in this traditionally furnished "German-looking-with-steep-slate-roof" brick house, which is surrounded by woods on three sides.

The hostess, originally from England, is an elementary school art teacher. Her husband, who grew up in Europe, works for the government on foreign affairs. He is also a violinist who sometimes plays here with a string quartet, trio, or chamber group.

Guests come from far (India and France) and near (overflow from local residents). They enjoy the quiet, the food, and conversations with the hosts—who provide a good orientation to Washington, D.C., maps, and suggestions for and menus of nearby ethnic restaurants.

In residence: One cat.
Foreign languages spoken: French, German, a little Russian.
Bed and bath: On second floor. Queen-bedded room has private tub/shower bath. Room with two single beds shares tub/shower bath with room that has one single bed.
Breakfast: Flexible hours. "A lot of wholesome food." Juices, breads, cereals, fruit, granola, porridge, no meat, tea, coffee. If very late, help yourself. Sunday feature—waffles and maple syrup. In chandeliered dining room overlooking woods; on patio in warm weather.
Plus: Off-street parking. Two patios.

Blue Bear Bed & Breakfast   301/824-2292

13810 Frank's Run Road, Smithsburg, MD 21783   800/381-2292

Hosts: Ellen Panchula and Marilyn Motter
Location: Quiet. On two acres in farm and orchard country. Five miles east of Smithsburg; 35 minutes' drive southwest to Antietam Battlefield or northeast to Gettysburg. Ten miles from Appalachian Trail, 25 to White-tail Ski Resort. Six miles to Hagerstown restaurants. Ninety minutes from Washington, D.C.
Open: Year round.
Rates: $50–$55 single, $60–$65 double. $8 child up to age 18.
♦ ♠ ✗ ✂

Three generations live in this all-new farmhouse built in 1993 from a magazine design "with a few adaptations"—a porch for rockers, a sun room and deck facing the mountains, a gazebo, and a sand volleyball court too. Mom and Dad (senior) host when Ellen is teaching school and her sister Marilyn is working as a dog groomer. (Marilyn's husband and grown son are also in residence.) For several years earlier, the sisters had B&Bs "a few miles down the road." Here they kept the name of Ellen's Blue Bear; they stenciled throughout; and they decorated with country crafts, quilts made by local Mennonite ladies, and, of course, blue bears. Guests come for hiking, cycling, antiquing, "and just to get out of the city."

In residence: Maggie is a 50-pound Border collie/husky/German shepherd. Snoopy is a beagle mix. Two parakeets.

(Please turn page.)

Bed and bath: Two second-floor rooms, en-suite baths. One with a queen bed, whirlpool bath, and separate shower. One with a double bed and a single daybed with trundle bed.
Breakfast: 7–9. Juice; fruit; Belgian waffles, quiche, baked French toast, or egg casserole; homemade rolls and breads; coffee.
Plus: Central air conditioning. Refreshments. Mints. Laundry facilities.

> From Maryland: *"Basket of fruit in the room . . . incredible breakfast at 7 a.m. . . . stimulating conversation. . . . Left with goodies in a 'Blue Bear' stenciled bag."* From Connecticut: *"Greeted us with hot tea and potato chip cookies. . . . At breakfast, keeps the food coming as long as you can eat it."*

Chanceford Hall Bed & Breakfast Inn

209 West Federal Street, Snow Hill, MD 21863   410/632-2231

Hosts: Michael and Thelma C. Driscoll
Location: On landscaped grounds with English boxwood and 200-year-old walnut trees. In historic district of residential area. Five minutes' walk to town center. Near Pocomoke River and canoeing. Three hours from Washington, D.C., and Baltimore. Half an hour to ocean, to Crisfield and boats for Smith and Tangier islands.
Open: Year round.
Rates: Per room. $120 first-floor queen. Second floor $110 double bed, $115 and $120 queens. Suite with queen and a single bed $130 for two, $145 for three.
♥ ✈

Such detailed and enthusiastic guests' letters! They comment on the personal attention, the friendliness, the exquisite craftsmanship, the food—at this restored 1759 brick Greek/Georgian, declared "a gem" by the Maryland Historic Trust and featured in *Mid-Atlantic Country.* Dan Rodricks of the *Baltimore Evening Sun* wrote, "Chanceford Hall has finally been brought back to greatness. . . . One wonders if George Washington slept there."

The Driscolls, parents of two grown daughters, had experience in graphics, real estate, market research, and sales in various parts of the country when, in 1986, they started to work on "the hulk." They scraped and sanded original crown moldings and 10 fireplace mantels; they installed a kitchen in the former ballroom, new bathrooms, and much more. Now Oriental rugs are on all the refinished floors. Throughout, there are handsome Queen Anne reproduction furnishings—some are for sale and some are made by Michael, a fine cabinetmaker (and groundskeeper). Decor done by Thelma is Williamsburg. The walls are 18 inches thick. And Chanceford Hall, on the National Register, has been part of the Maryland House and Garden Pilgrimage.

Bed and bath: Five rooms, four with working fireplaces; all private (two full, three shower) baths. First-floor room, wheelchair accessible, has queen canopy bed, working fireplace, exceptional woodwork. Four second-floor rooms have (simple) canopied beds. Most are queen-sized; one is double.
Breakfast: 7–11. Fresh fruit, eggs, bacon and sausage, potatoes O'Brian, homemade apple-cinnamon-raisin muffins. Served in crystal-chandeliered dining room with silver, cloth napkins, china.

Plus: Central air conditioning. Formal fireplaced living room. Down comforters. Beverages. Hors d'oeuvres. Bicycles. Games and TV in sun room overlooking covered covered lap pool. Dinner by reservation ($110 for two).

The River House Inn
201 East Market Street, Snow Hill, MD 21863

410/632-2722
fax 410/632-2866

Hosts: Larry and Susanne Knudsen
Location: In the center of a 300-year-old village. Set back on two acres of lawns and gardens along the Pocomoke River. Surrounded by other architectural treasures. Across street from recommended restaurant. Two doors from canoe and bike rentals. Half-hour drive to beaches.

Open: Year round. Two-night minimum on holiday weekends.
Rates: May–October $89–$129. Off-season $75 midweek, $85 weekends. Singles $20 less. Extra person in room, $10 children under 12, $20 adults. Amex, MC, Visa.
🖋 ♣ ♦ ✖ ✔

Elegant. Gracious. And comfortable. An early retirement project for Larry, who was a CEO in Ohio. A change of career for Susanne, a political activist and needlework catalog buyer who was elected mayor of Snow Hill in 1994. In 1991 they converted this 1860 Victorian–with–Gothic influence. They redecorated with striped and damask wallpapers and border treatments. Windows are draped, swagged, and lace-curtained. Furnishings are Chippendale, French, Sheraton, and Colonial. Colors are wonderful. And so are the wicker, rattan, and wrought iron–furnished porches.

And what about the guests? "Sports-oriented guests can hardly squeeze in all the activities they plan. Others intend to do more, but they find it so serene and relaxing, they just 'veg out.'"

In residence: Bonnie and Belle, black poodles, "our official greeters."
Bed and bath: Main house—five fireplaced carpeted rooms; all with queen beds (some canopied) and private tub/shower baths; all baths attached except one across the hall (robes provided). Cottages—one with twin beds, sitting room with daybed; two with queen bed, sitting room with daybed. Riverside converted carriage barn—king bed, full bath, porch. Folding cot available.
Breakfast: 8–10. Coffee ready at 7. Fresh fruit. Home-baked goodies. Bacon and sausage. Eggs (Egg Beaters available), omelet, or French toast. Cereal. In back parlor and formal dining room at tables with garden flowers.
Plus: Main house has central air conditioning downstairs, window units and ceiling fans upstairs. Cottages air-conditioned. Four fireplaced common rooms. Canoe launch. Motorboats may tie up at inn bulkhead. Lawn chairs at river's edge. Croquet. Badminton. Beach towels. "Use of our country club or eight other nearby courses for golfing." Picnic baskets ($7/person). Dinners by reservation ($30/person). Transportation to/from Salisbury airport.

B&Bs offer the ultimate concierge service.

Antrim 1844

30 Trevanion Road, Taneytown, MD 21787

410/756-6812
800/858-1844
fax 410/756-2744

Hosts: Dorothy and Richard Mollett
Location: Secluded. Off the main street on 23 acres of gardens and orchards, with sunsets and mountain views. Forty miles west of Baltimore; 60 north of Washington, D.C.; 12 south of Gettysburg.
Open: Year round. Two-night min-imum for Saturday bookings.
Rates: $175–$275 weekends. $25 less Sunday–Thursday. $50 third or fourth person in suite or for trundle. Midweek corporate rates. Five-course prix-fixe dinners (daily) by reservation, $50. Amex, MC, Visa.
♥ ❖ ◆ ✈

Getaway guests never leave this one-of-a-kind place. The media and wedding planners, too, love this antebellum working plantation; as Dort says, it "captivates historians, especially Civil War buffs." The fireplaced dining room has cobalt-blue lacquered walls, crystal chandelier, and gold leaf plaster moldings and medallions. There are yards of gorgeous fabrics (arranged by Dort—secrets shared), murals and faux marbling, high canopied feather beds, magnificent antiques (the kind that Dort couldn't bear to part with as an antiques dealer), Oriental rugs, and a late-1800s Knabe grand piano. Each outbuilding—the smokehouse (now a restaurant) with three walk-in fire-places, the distant converted barn with navy blue bath, and the former icehouse with working fireplace in bath—is extraordinary. Day and night, May through November, guests enjoy the black-bottomed pool (it retains the sun's heat) that Richard designed to look like a reflecting pool. For your playing pleasure, there's a Nova Grass tournament tennis court and a tour-nament-sized croquet lawn.

In 1988 Richard, the preservationist, first entered the boarded-up (for 60 years) Greek Revival and saw the deep plaster crown molding, 14-foot ceilings, hand-blown glass panes, and original floor plan all intact. "It was like a museum with no facilities—no plumbing nor electricity." The Molletts (who went to a garage sale on their first date) wove their magic—as they had with five Baltimore National Register houses. Now the interior designer turned innkeeper and the off-lease car broker turned multifaceted co-innkeeper live with their teenage sons on the property in a restored 1861 farmhouse that they moved through town. The acclaimed dinners, never part of the original four–guest room B&B plan, began in 1991 in response to guests' requests.

Bed and bath: Fourteen rooms or suites; all private baths. In mansion, nine (five with working fireplaces) on second and third floors with tub (some two-person)/shower baths; king, queen, or double bed; plus trundle. Two fireplaced suites in very private converted barn by a stream, and one in former icehouse by formal gardens, one in brick cottage (former plantation office), and one in 1861 frame house.
Breakfast: 8–8:30 with fresh fruit, warm muffins, coffee or tea, newspaper, and a fresh flower on silver wake-up tray outside your door. Then at 9:30 in converted smokehouse, in formal dining room, or on canopied garden veranda—fruit, maybe baked bosc pears; Belgian waffles or egg strata with veggies/bacon/cheeses.

Plus: Central air conditioning. Outside your door—afternoon tea, phone messages, extra towels, evening chocolates, a decanter of port. Fireplaced library, drawing rooms, tavern room. Complimentary tea, wine, champagne, hors d'oeuvres and cheese. Room phone jacks. View from widow's walk that was used as a Gettysburg battle lookout post. Picnic baskets. Horse and carriage rides arranged to breathtaking working farms and mills.

Glenburn
410/751-1187

3515 Runnymede Road,   (from D.C., Del., Md., Pa., Va.) **800/393-1187**
Taneytown, MD 21787

Hosts: Robert and Elizabeth Neal
Location: In the country on a 200-acre farm on Route 140 between Westminster and Taneytown. Surrounded by spacious lawns and towering trees. Fifteen miles from Gettysburg. Within 15 minutes of Catoctin Mountain State Park, Carroll County Farm Museum. Antiques shops, winery, and golf course nearby. Sixty miles from Washington, D.C., 38 from Baltimore.
Open: Year round. Usual arrival time 4–6 p.m.; departure 10:30 a.m.
Rates: Main house $60–$75 single, $80–$100 double. Guest house $85 single, $125–$150 double.
♥ ♨ ⛟ ⚶ ✕ ✂

The unique setting arouses expectations that are fulfilled at this B&B—one that is reminiscent of British B&Bs in historic homes. Cross the iron bridge that stretches over a vigorous creek and proceed along the winding drive to an imposing 1840 country Georgian home with Victorian addition that has been in Robert's family for more than 55 years. (In the 19th century it housed a boys' private school; the Neals were married 15 years before Elizabeth learned that her grandfather was a student here.) Furnished elegantly with heirlooms and American and European antiques, the house has been on several Maryland house and garden tours. And it has also served as a backdrop for a Quaker Oats commercial!

Now that all five Neal children are grown, Elizabeth, a seventh-generation area resident, and Robert, a former history professor who has always been involved with this farm, are continuing the tradition of hospitality by sharing Glenburn with travelers. It's a working farm. "Because of the farm machinery and cattle, please ask us about walking in the fields." Many guests rise early to see the deer by the creek, or to jog, bird-watch, or cycle, and then return for breakfast.

Bed and bath: Private guests' wing has three second-floor double-bedded rooms (with air conditioner and ceiling fan) and three baths. Private full bath for two rooms (one with screened porch); private or shared bath, depending upon number in party, for third room. Air-conditioned guest house has two large bedrooms—one with queen, the other with two twins—and a full bath, large living room, and kitchen/dining area.
Breakfast: 7–9:30. Orange juice, fresh country eggs, country bacon or sausage, sweet rolls, toast, coffee and tea. Graciously served in dining room that has Grandmother's china displayed on wall plate racks.
Plus: Swimming pool. Fireplaced living room. Tea and coffee always available. Tour of house. Guests' refrigerator.

> Guests wrote: *"The busy world comes to a gentle stop as you approach the serene lawns of Glenburn, a haven for the weary world."*

Chesapeake Wood Duck Inn

410/886-2070
800/956-2070
fax 410/886-2263

Gibsontown Road, P.O. Box 202
Tilghman Island, MD 21671-0202

Hosts: Dave and Stephanie Feith
Location: Serene. With back lawn overlooking harbor (spectacular sunrises) with the last working fleet of skipjacks (80- to 100-year-old sailing vessels). On an island (population: 700) in a neighborhood of watermen's residences. Steps to corner country store, shops, sailing, award-winning restaurants. Less than 15 minutes to St. Michaels.

Open: Year round. Two-night minimum on holiday and April–November weekends.
Rates: $105 single. $115–$125 double. Ten percent AARP discount. Valentine's and other special packages. MC, Visa.
♥ ♣ ♦ ✈ ✄

Guests agree with the Feiths that this *Better Homes and Gardens* "Great Escape" is a dream come true. "They come for peace, quiet, the spectacular scenery, an uncrowded noncommercial environment, time for each other, a romantic getaway. One private sunset-viewing spot has inspired several proposals! We were both in our thirties and working and traveling for competing Atlanta-based telecommunications companies when we decided to look (from Nova Scotia to Montana) for a B&B site where we could combine our interests." Dave loves to cook; Stephanie has a flair for interior design. Conversation on their very first date centered on the houses that each had restored. Here, in 1991, they bought an 1890 waterman's house, created several common rooms, and added baths and—overlooking the water—a screened porch and a deck. Window treatments, fabrics, and tradiional wallcoverings set off their collection of art, period antiques, and Oriental rugs.

Foreign languages spoken: German and Spanish; limited French.
Bed and bath: Six air-conditioned rooms (five with water view) with antique queen or double bed on second and third floors. All private new en-suite baths (some tub/shower, some shower only).
Breakfast: 8:30–10. A highlight. Maybe banana-stuffed French toast and sausage or southern grits strata. Fresh juice, fruits, and cereals. Homemade muffins or orange/cranberry coconut bread. Served in formal dining room, in the sun room, or on screened porch.
Plus: Fireplaced living room with lots of books. Late-afternoon refreshments. Evening beverage. Guest refrigerator. Croquet. Bicycles. Large TV with cable and stereo with CD player. Use of country club with golf, swimming, tennis, health club. Reservations made for a skipjack sail (hear how they dredge for oysters in the winter months) or for a crabbing trip (departure: 4:30 a.m.). Smoking permitted (by innkeeper, too) on porch deck only.

Some executives who book a meeting at an inn return on a weekend for a getaway. Some on a getaway return with colleagues for a meeting.

Tavern House   410/376-3347
111 Water Street, P.O. Box 98, Vienna, MD 21869-0098

Hosts: Harvey and Elise Altergott
Location: On the Nanticoke River (much wildlife) in historic Eastern Shore town (with walking tour) between Salisbury and Cambridge. Near Routes 331/50 intersection, antiquing, and used bookstores. Flat cycling country. Few blocks from public tennis courts and boat ramp. Fifteen miles to Blackwater Wildlife Refuge, 100 from Washington, D.C.
Open: Year round.
Rates: $65–$70. Choice, MC, Visa.
🛶 ♣ ♦ 🍴

From Washington, D.C.: *"A five-star establishment . . . charm of yesteryear and comforts of today . . . stimulating conversation. . . . Breakfasts, in themselves, worth the journey."* From Maryland: *"Everything done with artistry and taste. . . . Their knowledge of local history added to our perfect stay."* From Spokane, Washington: *"Worn steps, sloping floors . . . a sense of history. . . . We felt pampered."*

Guests keep coming. And projects continue! The plane that Harvey has been building is almost ready for takeoff.

And the Altergotts have been helping their daughter restore an old house, just a few blocks away. Their own "hidden delight" (*Baltimore* magazine), built in the early 1700s, was pretty dilapidated in 1981 when the Altergotts, not in search of any property, decided to explore this "wonderful quiet town." Harvey, a former naval officer, was a manager at the postal services headquarters in Washington, D.C. He and Elise, a Salem, Massachusetts, native who was a Girl Scouts field executive, began restoring "to elegant simplicity"—including the staircase carvings, three massive chimneys, and many windowsills. Woodwork painted in authentic colors frames white lime-sand-and-hair plaster. Colonial antiques and reproductions fit just perfectly. And so does their hosting style, one that provides for privacy or company.

In residence: Phineas Calhoon is "a not very talkative parrot." A neighbor's cat, Cricket, drops in routinely.
Foreign languages spoken: "Basic" German and Spanish.
Bed and bath: On second floor, four rooms, two with working fireplace, share two full "next-door" hall baths. Double or twin beds. "One double-bedded room has what we like to think are rum barrel stains on the floor."
Breakfast: Social; 8–noon. Flower-garnished fresh fruit. Homemade muffins and rolls. French toast, a souffle, or "something new Elise dreams up." Overlooking the river with the morning sun.
Plus: Living room with fireplace at each end. Afternoon beverage with cheese. Seasonal flowers. Air conditioners and ceiling fans in bedrooms.

No room at the inn? Ask for a suggestion! In addition to established B&Bs, there may be a new place just down the road.

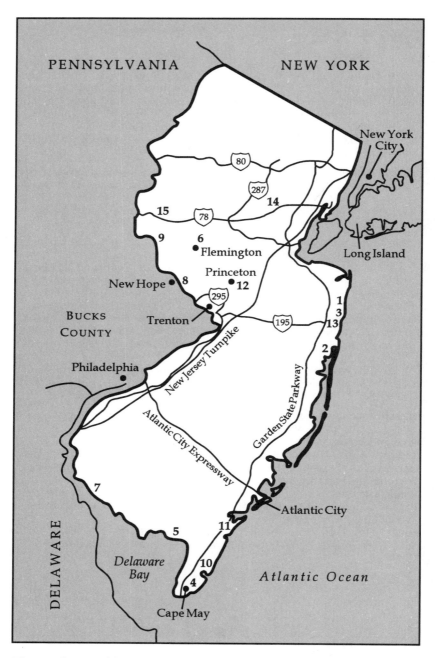

PENNSYLVANIA

NEW YORK

New York
City

80

287

14

15

78

Long Island

9

6 Flemington

Princeton

New Hope 8

12

295

1
3
13

Trenton

BUCKS
COUNTY

195

2

Philadelphia

New Jersey Turnpike

Garden State Parkway

Atlantic City Expressway

7

Atlantic City

11

5

DELAWARE

10

Delaware
Bay

4

Atlantic Ocean

Cape May

*The numbers on this map indicate the locations of B&Bs described in
detail in this chapter.*

NEW JERSEY

___New Jersey Reservation Services___

Amanda's Bed & Breakfast Reservation Service
21 South Woodland Avenue, East Brunswick, NJ 08816

Phone: 908/249-4944 Monday–Friday 8:30–5:30, Saturday 8:30–12:30 noon.

Fax: 908/246-1961.

Listings: 50. Most are inns; some hosted private residences. Located in about a dozen communities throughout New Jersey. A few are in Pennsylvania—in Center City (Philadelphia), Chalfont, Kennett Square, Manheim, and Milford.

Reservations: At least two weeks' advance notice preferred. Two-day minimum required on weekends.

Rates: $50–$100 single, $65–$145 double. Some family, senior citizen, and weekly rates available. Confirmed reservation cancellations with 10 days' notice receive refund less $25 service charge. Travel agents' commission paid for some locations. MC, Visa; 2.5 percent surcharge.

As a corporate executive secretary, Orie Barr had considerable experience arranging meetings and travel plans. After enjoying B&B as a traveler, she became first a host and then, in 1993, a reservation service owner. Her listings are B&Bs with "congenial owners who offer hospitality, privacy, and very clean accommodations." Many are historic properties. Most have private baths and air conditioning.

Bed & Breakfast Adventures
2310 Central Avenue, Suite 132, North Wildwood, NJ 08260

Phone: For information: 609/522-4000 Monday–Friday 9–5. For reservations: 800/992-2632.

Fax: 609/522-6125.

Listings: More than 200 hosts, including inns, B&Bs, and private hosted and unhosted accommodations. Located throughout New Jersey; in eastern Pennsylvania in the Lancaster, Lehigh Valley, and Reading areas; in Berks and Bucks counties and north through the Poconos and Endless Mountain regions. Also some in Florida from Orlando south to the Keys. Sixty-page directory: $5.

Reservations: Two weeks' advance notice preferred. "Every effort is made to accommodate last-minute requests."

Rates: $45–$100 single, $55–$165 double. $5–$10 booking fee. Packages include accommodations with dinner and/or murder mystery party. For cancellations received at least 14 days prior to expected arrival, deposit less $40 service fee is refunded. Cancellations received 7–14 days prior to arrival are charged one night's fee per room or 25 percent of total bill (whichever is greater). No refunds for no-shows or for notice received in less than 7 days. Amex, Discover, MC, Visa.

Paul and Diane DiFilippo, owners of this 12-year-old reservation service, have been innkeepers since 1984; they represent hosts whose accommodations range from modest to luxurious. And they conduct "How to buy, own, and operate" B&B seminars. "All hosts maintain the highest standards." Some hosts have computers and fax machines available for corporate and/or long-term guests. Some locations have appropriate space for corporate meetings and group functions.

KEY TO SYMBOLS
♥ Lots of honeymooners come here.
⚲ Families with children are very welcome. (Please see page xii.)
⚫ "Please emphasize that we are a private home, not an inn."
♣ Groups or private parties sometimes book the entire B&B.
♦ Travel agents' commission paid. (Please see page xii.)
✷ Sorry, no guests' pets are allowed.
✶ No smoking inside *or* no smoking at all, even on porches.

——————— New Jersey B&Bs ———————

Avon Manor Inn   908/774-0110

109 Sylvania Avenue, Avon-by-the-Sea, NJ 07717-1338

Hosts: Jim and Kathleen Curley
Location: A block from ocean, beach, and boardwalk; five from Main Street. Five-minute drive to restaurants; 45 minutes to Newark airport; 75 to New York City and Philadelphia. Ten miles to Monmouth College, four from Garden State Parkway and I-195.
Open: Year round. Three- or four- night minimum on holidays.

Rates: Mid-May to mid-September and holiday and special weekends: shared bath $80; private bath $100 or $110 (four-poster), smaller rooms $90–$100. Off-season: $75–$100. Some holiday packages. Amex, MC, Visa.

♥ ❖ ◆ ✗ ✠

> From New Jersey: *"Immaculate . . . quiet . . . cozy and comfortable."* From Pennsylvania: *"Every house on the street is different and meticulously cared for . . . room decorated in Laura Ashley style. . . . Kathleen and Jim make a formidable duo . . . breakfasts a delight . . . many suggestions for seeing and doing."*

It's a Colonial Revival built in 1907 as a summer residence with wraparound veranda. There are wood details throughout the house "that we continue to change. Jim and I, both born and raised in New York City, spent summer weekends and vacations at the Jersey Shore. Since [1989] we have fulfilled our dream of living here. We often meet others who met at the Shore, including one couple who met while staying at the inn 40 years ago! . . . Today this is an all-season destination." English and Irish B&B stays inspired the Curleys. Jim works for an insurance company in Manhattan. Kathleen, a former bank controller, is a library trustee.

Bed and bath: Eight air-conditioned rooms. On second floor, two rooms have queen four-poster beds, private en-suite shower baths; two smaller rooms—one queen and one with twin beds—share full hall bath. Four third-floor dormered rooms (two have skylights) with en-suite shower baths; queen (three are large rooms) or double bed.
Breakfast: 9–10. Omelets, pancakes, waffles, or eggs. Juice, cereal, rolls and muffins, coffee, tea. In chestnut-paneled dining room or on veranda.
Plus: Parlor gas fireplace. Late afternoon tea and snacks. Guest refrigerator. Backyard and 100-foot covered veranda. Transportation to/from local stations. On-site parking.

—————

Guests arrive as strangers, leave as friends.

Cashelmara Inn

908/776-8727
800/821-2976

22 Lakeside Avenue, Avon-by-the-Sea, NJ 07717

Host: Mary Wiernasz
Location: Facing a lake with swans and ducks. To the side, 100 yards away, is lifeguarded Atlantic Ocean beach. In a noncommercial one-square-mile town. Near seafood restaurants; 50 miles from New York City; 60 miles from Philadelphia.
Open: Year round. Two-night minimum March–November weekends; three nights for Memorial Day and July and August weekends; four nights July 4 and Labor Day.
Rates: Memorial Day–mid-September, $95 smaller rooms, $105 ocean view, $165 lakeside two-room suite. Off-season, $75 smaller rooms, $95 ocean view, $121 suite. Singles $10 less.

It was a blustery January afternoon in 1984 when Marty Mulligan, a technical representative for Eastman Kodak, stood on the veranda and saw the sunset over the lake and heard the ocean breaking on the beach. "After seeing the inside of this 1901 Colonial Revival home with an open center hall staircase and many fireplaces, it took me about five seconds to make an offer." Subsequently Marty had it all done over with wicker, Oriental rugs, Laura Ashley prints, and antiques that give an English country feeling—appreciated by vacationers, business travelers (for small conferences), and families (for reunions and weddings too).

In 1989 Mary, a well-traveled guest who had resort experience in her native Wisconsin, stayed in "this beautiful inn where one room is lovelier than the next" while she was working in the area for a Chicago market research company. She returned six months later to become resident innkeeper. Now, when Marty visits from Pennsylvania (page 231), he meets some of Mary's many fans.

Bed and bath: On three floors, 12 rooms and 1 suite. Many with water (lake or ocean) view. All private baths; most tubless. King, queen, or double beds. First-floor suite with canopied double bed has wood-burning fireplace. A few rooms with two beds.
Breakfast: 8–10 in summer, 8:30–10 winter. Orange juice, home-baked muffins, coffee and tea. Choice of entree including tomato/mushroom omelets; challah French toast; fruit pancakes; or house specialty of pork roll, fried egg, tomato, and melted cheese on English muffin. Served in dining room or on veranda.
Plus: Three parlors, one with working fireplace. Most bedrooms have air conditioner and ceiling fan. Fresh flowers. Individual heat control. That wraparound porch. Will meet guests at train or bus station. No parking problem. Bicycles, golf nearby.

From Pennsylvania: *"First class."*

In this book a full bath includes a shower and a tub. "Shower bath" indicates a bath that has all the essentials except a tub.

Bay Head Gables

908/892-9844

200 Main Avenue, Bay Head, NJ 08742

fax 908/295-2196

Hosts: Don Haurie and Ed Laubusch
Location: Overlooking (across the road from) dunes and private ocean beach. At the head of the barrier island. About 75 miles from New York City and Philadelphia. One and a half blocks from train station (two hours from New York City's Penn Station). Short walk to restaurants and shops.
Open: Year round; weekend only, January–March. Two-night minimum on May–October weekends. Three-night minimum on most holiday weekends.
Rates: June–August, $105–$145 weekdays, $130–$185 weekends. April–May and September–November, $95–$140. December–March, $85–$95. Amex, Discover, MC, Visa.
♥ ♣ ✗ ⚹

The community landmark, highlighted in *Mid-Atlantic Country* magazine, is a pillared and cedar-shingled three-storied Georgian Colonial built in 1913 as a private summer home in the architectural style of Stanford White. In 1983 Don, a retired teacher who is now a Bay Head planning board member, and Ed, a retired chemical industry lobbyist who has served as an environmental commissioner, "fell in love with this genteel, gracious but faded lady," which had at one time been a fine restaurant. They refurbished (and then some), making each room quite different. Art Deco is featured in the inviting tall-ceilinged living room. A six-foot impressionistic Mary Cassatt painting in the chandeliered, floral-papered Victorian bridal suite provided the perfect setting for a *Country Inns* magazine feature on a Bay Head hatmaker's workshop. Other rooms include country French and contemporary themes inspired by an extensive collection of oil paintings, serigraphs, and textiles.

Bed and bath: Eleven rooms on three floors; some with private decks, each with at least two large windows. Incredible ocean views from five Main-Avenue–facing rooms; quieter rooms—facing waterfowl sanctuary—in back. All private modern baths. King (one with private entrance on first floor), queen, double beds; some are canopied.
Breakfast: 8:30–10. Pancakes, French toast, or strata with potatoes. Breakfast meats and pastries. Fresh fruit. Juices. Home-baked bread. In atriumlike glass-enclosed porch with ocean view or (off-season) in adjoining formal dining room.
Plus: Lots of good reading material. Bedroom air conditioners. Ceiling fans in some bedrooms and common rooms. Spinet piano and TV in fireplaced living room. Guest refrigerator. Ice machine. Beach towels. Wraparound porch. Self-serve cordials. Beach and tennis passes. Outside shower. Bike rack.

From New Jersey: *"An oasis . . . peaceful . . . surrounded by good books, good artworks, and fun curios. The food is generous, plentiful, and attractively served in a leisurely, unhurried fashion—and, best of all, tasty. Bay Head Gables spells hospitality and elegance."*

Conover's Bay Head Inn

646 Main Avenue, Bay Head, NJ 08742

908/892-4664
800/956-9099

Hosts: Carl and Beverly Conover and son Timothy

Location: One block from the beach in this quiet one-square-mile town, which is still without parking meters or billboards but offers antiquing, boutiques, golf, tennis, swimming, fishing, crabbing. One hour north of Atlantic City. Seventy-five miles from New York City and east of Philadelphia.

Open: Year round. March–December 10, two-night minimum weekend stay; three or four nights on holiday weekends.

Rates: Vary according to room and bed size. Summer—$115–$195 weekends, $90–$150 weekdays. Off-season—$85–$150. Singles $10 less.
♥ ♣ ✖ ✔

The almost-legendary innkeepers have created a picture-perfect inn in this community, where they spent childhood summers. Now the 1905 residence that they bought in 1970 features a living room with Palladian window and, by the cut-stone fireplace, chintz-covered love seats. The entryway is trellised. Furnishings include turn-of-the-century pieces, family photographs, and original art. Under those matching comforters and bed ruffles are (do you remember?) line-dried and hand-ironed designer sheets. Beverly has stenciled many of the rooms. An English garden flourishes. *USAir* magazine raves.

Carl, a former structural steel erector, is an avocational steam engine restorer who is proud of his 1936 Elco wood boat. Timothy is also a full-time innkeeper. And Beverly shares her expertise with prospective innkeepers enrolled in Ocean County college courses.

In residence: One dog, Scotty. In summer, Beverly's parents and aunt.

Bed and bath: Twelve carpeted rooms (second and third floors) with double, queen (some canopied), or king bed. All private baths (shower or tub/shower). View of ocean, bay, yacht club, marina, or gardens. One room with private porch has own hall, ocean view, Laura Ashley decor, oak furnishings, sitting area.

Breakfast: Freshly squeezed Florida orange juice in season. Fresh fruit. Their own biscuits, muffins, or coffee cake. Entree such as savory egg casserole, "decadent French toast," or blueberry oven pancake. Eat in intimate dining room with crystal chandelier and wall of many-paned windows, by fireplace, or on veranda.

Plus: Air-conditioned bedrooms. Afternoon tea. Outdoor hot/cold showers. Porch rockers. Beach passes. Reserved private on-site parking. Croquet and other lawn games.

*B**reakfast is where the magic happens.*

Down the Shore Bed & Breakfast

201 Seventh Avenue, Belmar, NJ 07719-2204   **908/681-9023**
     fax 908/681-7795

Hosts: Annette and Al Bergins
Location: Residential shore community. One block to boardwalk and beach. One block to lake and sunsets. Ten-minute walk to town and restaurants. Near walking trails and shopping malls.
Open: Year round. Two-night weekend minimum in June, July, and August.
Rates: Mid-May–mid-September: $75 queen bed, $65 king, double, or twin beds. (Less Sunday–Thursday.) $20 extra bed in room. Off-season, excluding holidays, third night free. ♣ ✂

Not an inn, but a comfortably furnished new home. The guest book—fun reading—is filled with poems and laudatory comments on the breakfast—and on Sparky too. This Pennsylvania-built energy-efficient Colonial-style modular house was assembled to move-in condition in two months in 1993. The Berginses hosted for nine years in their previous residence on a New Jersey lake. Al, a food bank volunteer and former high school teacher/administrator, has a company that finds temporary accommodations for out-of-staters transferred to New Jersey. Annette, the gardener and former teacher, is a hospital volunteer.

In residence: A miniature poodle named Sparky.
Foreign language spoken: Some French.
Bed and bath: Three second-floor rooms. Southside room with queen bed, full bath en suite. Waterview room with double bed and Memories room with king/twins option share hall shower bath (robes provided).
Breakfast: 8:30–9:30. French toast, waffles, hot and cold cereals, eggs, casserole or quiche. Homemade muffins or breads. Served in the dining room with plant-filled bay window.
Plus: Central air conditioning. Guest rooms have ceiling fans. TV/VCR in living room. Afternoon refreshments. Guest refrigerator and microwave. Shaded porch. Beach passes. Picnic coolers. Transportation provided from Belmar stations. Off-street parking.

---

*B*ed and breakfast is the hottest travel trend in America.

Cape May

Known as the oldest seaside resort in America, Cape May might well be called the largest B&B community in the country. Homes, guest houses, and hotels, all with Victorian architectural detail, were built by the hundreds in the 19th century. Other resorts closer to home by way of "the machine" became more fashionable after the turn of the century. But early in the 1970s, Cape May, now a National Historic Landmark city, began to experience a renaissance. Today the streets are lined with restored Victorian homes (dozens are B&Bs) and beautiful gardens. During the summer months parking can be a problem.

The profiles of B&B owners on the following pages indicate how one has inspired another. Several hosts don appropriate hats and conduct walking tours of the historic district or of their own restored and refurbished B&Bs. There are trolley tours and horse-and-carriage tours, a boardwalk, and the main summer attraction, the beach. Some B&Bs provide bicycles, direct you to the restored Physick Estate, and note their proximity to the Washington Street Mall with its many art galleries, crafts shops, and antiques emporiums. Hiking and bird-watching opportunities are here too. Daffodils, tulips, and Victorian balls are among theme weekends in so-called off-season periods. Christmas is celebrated—starting early in December—in glorious Victorian style with many special events, decorations, and B&B tours.

Innkeeping workshops, given periodically by a group of established B&Bs, are very popular with the enormous number of guests who dream of becoming innkeepers.

The Abbey Bed and Breakfast   609/884-4506

34 Gurney Street at Columbia Avenue, Cape May, NJ 08204

Hosts: Marianne and Jay Schatz
Location: In historic district; one block from the ocean. One and a half blocks to main shopping area. Within walking distance of most restaurants and attractions.
Open: April through December. Two-, three-, or four-night minimum stay in summer and on most weekends in other seasons. Longer minimum for some rooms.
Rates: April–June and October–December $80–$165. July–September $90–$190. Rates depend on room size and availability of site parking. Ten percent discount for seven or more consecutive nights. ♥ ✵ ✖ ✂

Guests wrote: *"A picture of graciousness. Attentive hosts who make a vacation memorable. A home filled with love and laughter. Guest rooms filled with beautiful Victorian furniture, flowers, lavender soaps, lace-trimmed pillows and sheets."*

The opulent front parlor with harp was selected for the Manhattan Bloomingdale's photo essay based on *Bed & Breakfast in the Mid-Atlantic States*. Other rooms are sometimes the set for television or magazine features. Throughout this Gothic Revival home, built in 1869 as a summer retreat for coal baron

(Please turn page.)

John B. McCreary, there are exquisite antiques, chandeliers, and window treatments. In 1979 it was the fourth Schatz house restoration (and second Cape May B&B). Seven years and many delicious breakfasts later, the cottage next door, originally built by Mr. McCreary for his son, came back "into the family" with the Schatz touch.

Before becoming innkeepers, Marianne and Jay, who also has an MBA, were in chemical research and marketing in Philadelphia. Now Marianne is also a Realtor. Jay is known for his 300 period hats—which are modeled (one at a time) in the morning (see "Breakfast" below) and again in the afternoon.

In residence: Four cats restricted to first floor. (Sometimes guests coax one upstairs.)
Bed and bath: In two adjacent houses—14 rooms on three floors. All private baths. King, queen (one canopied), or double beds.
Breakfast: 8:30 and 9:30. Entree (perhaps casserole or quiches with fettuccine or fritters), muffins, fresh fruit, cereals, juice, coffee and tea. Chef Marianne and raconteur Jay (with chapeau) entertain in dining room or on veranda. "It's the best time of our day."
Plus: Air conditioning in 10 rooms; ceiling or portable fans in others; small refrigerator in all. Late-afternoon refreshments. Monday, Wednesday, and Friday at 4 p.m., tour of house followed by tea and tidbits (free for guests, charge for the public). Afternoon croquet while noncompetitors cheer from the veranda. On-site parking for Villa rooms; remote parking for next-door cottage. Beach chairs and passes in season.

Abigail Adams' Bed & Breakfast by the Sea

12 Jackson Street, Cape May, NJ 08204   **609/884-1371**

Host: Kate Emerson
Location: Just 100 feet from the beach. Half a block from Washington Street Mall. Short walk to restaurants.
Open: Year round. Two-night minimum except July–August and some holidays, when it is three nights.

Rates: July–August, $120–$150 private bath, $95–$110 shared bath. Winter, $85–$95 private bath, $65–$75 shared. Spring and fall, $110–$120 private bath, $85–$100 shared. Amex, MC, Visa.
♥ ❖ ◆ ✈ ⚕

Almost a bed and breakfast pioneer. The thought of owning a B&B first came to Kate in 1981 when she stayed in one of the then few Cape May B&Bs, at a time when she was restoring a house in Toronto, Canada. Then her position as marketing systems development director for American Express took her to London for several years. The next transfer was to New York, whence she rediscovered Cape May "and fell in love with the town all over again." In 1990 she bought the 1892 Italianate Renaissance Revival house from a couple who had established this B&B in 1983. So here she is, with a fulfilled dream and receiving rave reviews about the house, her hospitality, and breakfast. "And to think I never made a muffin until I came to Cape May! My first day here, my country Victorian antiques, old wicker, and antique quilts were being moved in through the back door while my first guests appeared at the front door!"

In residence: In hosts' quarters—daughter Jillian, age nine. "Charley is our ginger tabby."
Foreign languages spoken: Some French and Spanish.
Bed and bath: Five rooms. Second floor—private tub/shower bath for large queen-bedded room with bay window and ocean view and for queen-bedded room overlooking garden. Third floor—smaller room with double bed, private tub/shower bath. Two ocean-view double-bedded rooms share shower bath. Rollaway and crib.
Breakfast: At 9. Hot entree—maybe quiche or souffle. Homemade muffins and coffee cakes. Fresh fruit. Juices. In fireplaced, hand-stenciled dining room.
Plus: Fresh flowers. Afternoon refreshments. Bedroom air conditioning or ceiling fans. Beach towels and tags. Fireplaced living and dining rooms. Off-site permit parking May–October.

> From New York: *"A pretty house with lovely flowers, antiques, flowered wallpaper . . . helpful suggestions."* From New Jersey: *"Especially enjoyed the ocean breeze and hearing the lapping of waves at night. . . . Big delicious breakfast. At the table, the relaxation in the air could be matched only by a week at a tropical island—even though most of us had only spent one night. . . . Kate is a gentlewoman in every way. . . . Antiques created a warmth and romance."*

The Albert Stevens Inn
127 Myrtle Avenue, Cape May, NJ 08204

609/884-4717
800/890-CATS

Hosts: Curt and Diane Rangen
Location: On a quiet street across from a park. Three blocks to Washington Street Mall, four to beaches. Within walking distance of major attractions.
Open: Year round. Two-night minimum on most weekends. Three-night minimum on holiday and August weekends.

Rates (dinner is included off-season): $85, $95, $98, $120, depending on room size, decor, and bath. $155 suite; $15 third person. Ten percent discount for senior citizens and birders. Amex, Discover, MC, Visa; 4 percent surcharge.
♥ ♣ ♦ ✈ ✂

"A place with lots of space for gardening, cats, and parking." That was what the Rangens were looking for when they decided to become innkeepers in their favorite spot.

In 1989 they purchased this established B&B, originally built in 1898 by Dr. Albert Stevens for his bride, Bessie. It still has a floating staircase, an oak mantel above a gas fireplace, and the Stevenses' mother-of-pearl inlay parlor set. "And there are loads of crystal and doodads collected by Diane over the years." Now the exterior is painted in forest green and (Victorian) Perry Street Yellow, and trimmed in red. Landscaping includes a pond (complete with goldfish), a flower and herb garden, and a gazebo too. Guests sign up (September–June) for the hot tub that is in a separate building in the backyard. And you are invited to the "Cats' Garden and Tea Tour" held to raise funds for animal welfare.

(Please turn page.)

Before, Diane, the innkeeper/part-time counselor/cat fancier, had her own consulting business. Curt, an innkeeper/part-time photographer, was in corporate marketing in Philadelphia and Washington, D.C.

In residence: "The regular cast of 27 Cape May felines," stars of fund-raising teas.
Foreign language spoken: French.
Bed and bath: Seven rooms and two suites, all with Victorian beds, private baths, air conditioners, ceiling fans. First floor—three rooms with double bed, sitting area, tub/shower bath. Second floor—one room with canopied full bed, tub/shower bath; three double-bedded rooms with shower baths; two-room suite with a queen bed and a twin bed, tub/shower bath. Third floor is huge tower suite with queen bed in one room, twin and large sitting area in other, and tub/shower bath.
Breakfast: At 9. (Earlier continental buffet by request.) Perhaps Norwegian fruit, hot pumpkin bread, freshly squeezed juice, salmon strata, toasted muffins with homemade jellies. Served in formal dining rooms on china and crystal.
Plus: Off-street parking. Fireplaced parlor. Beach towels and tags. In season, "afternoon tea in the Cats' Garden." Transportation to/from airport or bus. Florida Room with TV, refrigerator, coffee and tea.

Barnard-Good House

609/884-5381

238 Perry Street, Cape May, NJ 08204

Hosts: Nan and Tom Hawkins
Location: Two blocks from main beach. Ten minutes' walk to town center.
Open: April to November. Two-night minimum April–June 15 and September 15–November 1. June 15–September 15, three- or four-night minimum.
Rates: $89 double beds. $100 or $129 king beds. $125 suites. Ten percent less for singles. MC, Visa.
♥ ✗ ⚡

> From Pennsylvania: *"Everyone should have such a first B&B experience. . . . Felt lucky to find this gem."* From New Jersey: *"Extremely well-kept. . . . Perfect hosts: down-to-earth, cordial, interesting . . . . Fantastic culinary experience. . . . Addicting!"*

We found that, indeed, the hosts love life and guests love the hosts—and their extraordinary breakfasts. It was early in the season when we visited, but it was a full house, with many in the 25 to 35 age range and others young at heart.

Before coming here in 1980, the Hawkinses had lived in central New Jersey with early American decor "complete with hanging baskets in the kitchen." About the time of their 30th wedding anniversary, when Tom was a purchasing director for a plastics manufacturing firm and Nan was marketing director for a shopping center, they were searching for a career change and found this Second Empire mansard-roofed house—empty. They did (and have continued to do) all the restoration themselves. The dining room has a gasolier made of iron, pewter, and brass. The 100-year-old organ in the living room really works if you pump hard. Each cozy guest room is quite different; the flamboyant pink, white, and green Hawkins Suite is a popular honeymooners' room. One of the bathrooms has a copper tub and pull-chain john.

Bed and bath: Five rooms on second and third floors; all private baths. Two double-bedded suites with sitting room, en-suite shower baths. One large king-bedded room, en-suite tub/shower bath. One other king-bedded room, keyed tub/shower bath across hall. One double-bedded room, en-suite half bath, assigned shower room next to room.

Breakfast: 8:30–9. Their hallmark. In dining room with fine china and silver. Maybe freshly extracted and blended juices, muffins, crepes, fruit soup, cheese bread, exotic chicken dish, chocolate-chip banana cake. Menu never repeated regardless of your length of stay. (Special diets accommodated.) Can last two hours, "depending on how much fun we are having." Cookbook —*Why Not For Breakfast*—released in 1993.

Plus: Bedroom air conditioners and ceiling fans. Living room with gas fireplace. Rockers and wicker furniture on wraparound porch. Afternoon refreshments. Off-street parking right here. Beach tags.

Bed & Breakfast Adventures Host #612

Cape May, NJ

Location: In historic district. One block to beach, mall, restaurants.

Reservations: Year round through Bed & Breakfast Adventures, page 54. Two-night minimum on weekends and in summer, three nights on summer holidays and Victorian weekends.

Rates: May–October $105–$165. Off-season $65–$95 single, $95–$125 double.

♥ ❖ ✈ ✂

The hosts, longtime inngoers, may be the only Cape May innkeepers who had never been to Cape May before they discovered (in 1992) this Carpenter Gothic Victorian. It was "nicely done but not overdone" with Bradbury and Bradbury wallcoverings, Renaissance Revival and Eastlake furnishings and original gasoliers, and a working antique pump organ. In southeastern Pennsylvania, the host was an attorney; his wife, in job development for disabled persons. For their midlife career change, they brought entertaining experience—"many Sunday brunches"—and a desire to be near the water and near family in Delaware. Here they have learned the secret (yes, they'll share) of converting antique double beds to queen beds without changing the head- and footboards. They blend iced tea with fruit juices and herbs (small garden here) and receive rave reviews for his cooking and her baking.

In residence: Two cats.

Bed and bath: Nine air-conditioned rooms on three floors. All with private baths, except two on second floor that share a bath. Some baths have tub and shower; others have shower only. Two first-floor rooms—one with queen bed, one with a double and a twin. Second floor—double or king. Third-floor suite has a queen and a twin bed in one room; other is a sitting room.

Breakfast: At 9. If more than 10 guests, at 8:30 and 9:45. Fresh fruit, juice, muffins or coffee cake. Hazelnut oatmeal pancakes; baked egg with herbs, rosemary potatoes, homemade popovers; or lemon French toast and bacon. Served in dining room on fine china, linen, and lace.

Plus: Pillared living room with fireplace. Library. Floor-to-ceiling windowed doors that open onto veranda and glassed-in sun porches. Wraparound porch

(Please turn page.)

with swing. Beach chairs, passes, towels. Outside hot/cold shower, Afternoon tea "with a sweet and a savory." Turndown service with homemade candy or cookies.

The Brass Bed Inn   609/884-8075
719 Columbia Avenue, Cape May, NJ 08204

Hosts: John and Donna Dunwoody; Angela Conran, assistant innkeeper
Location: In the historic district, two blocks from the ocean.
Open: Year round. Two- or three-night minimum (depending on accommodations) on all weekends plus July and August.
Rates: January 1–March 31, shared bath $65 midweek, $75 weekends; private bath $95 midweek, $120 weekends; private hall bath $80 midweek, $95 weekends. April 1–June 3, shared bath $75 midweek, $90 weekends; private bath $100 midweek, $130 weekends; private hall bath $85 midweek, $95 weekends. June 4–September 12, shared bath $95; private bath $125, $145, $160; private hall bath $115, $120. September 13–December 31, shared bath $90 midweek, $95 weekends; private bath $110 midweek, $125 weekends; private hall bath $95 midweek, $100 weekends.
♥ ✻ ⅄

From Pennsylvania: *"Cozy . . . romantic . . . quaint . . . entirely delightful."*

Personal touches are everywhere—family heirlooms, old photos of relatives, the 1895 upright piano that may be a gathering spot for singing, and daughter Mary's dollhouse in the foyer. (The Christmas display of the family's toy collection is almost famous.) It's like Grandma's—John's grandma did take summer boarders in her Victorian shore house—where everything is touchable and guests are treated like family. Part of the wicker-furnished veranda is screened in summer, glass-enclosed and heated in winter.

It's hard to believe now, but there were only two B&Bs in Cape May when the Dunwoodys—without a thought about innkeeping—were in search of a new place. In 1980 they "fell in love with Cape May and a 'need everything' house"; moved from Voorhees, New Jersey, and "jumped into a new lifestyle" while John, a graphic designer, continued to commute at dawn to Philadelphia.

Polished period brass beds are in every room. Many restored furnishings in the 120-year-old house are original—armoires, marble-topped tables, washstands, and dressers. There are lace curtains, period wallcoverings, and patterned Oriental carpets. Early recordings are heard on the 19th-century Graphonola, purchased in 1962 and restored by John. As the guest from Maryland wrote, "Magical."

In residence: Clancy, the dog, and feline Clarice—not in guest rooms.
Bed and bath: Eight rooms (largest is 14 by 16 feet; smallest 10 by 12 feet) with king or double bed, on second and third floors. All baths are with shower; two have tub also. Four rooms have private en-suite baths. Two have private hall baths, two on third floor share a bath; robes provided.
Breakfast: At 9 and 9:45. Fresh fruit, cereal, homemade baked goods, beverages. Eggs, pancakes, or other hot entrees. By gas fireplace in parlor.

Plus: Bedroom air conditioners and ceiling fans. Afternoon beverages. Front porch rockers. Outside hot/cold shower, dressing room. Hair dryers. Bicycle rack. Beach passes. Compiled guests' restaurant recommendations and hints in guest room logs.

Captain Mey's Inn
202 Ocean Street, Cape May, NJ 08204

609/884-7793
609/884-9637

Hosts: Kathleen and George Blinn
Location: Two blocks from the beach. A half block from the Victorian shopping mall. Within walking distance of all restaurants.
Open: Year round. Two-night minimum on weekends off season.

Three-night minimum in season.
Rates: Vary according to room location and bath arrangement. July–Labor Day, $140–$225 private bath, $105–$110 shared bath. $30 additional guest in room. Less off-season. Singles $5 less.
♥ ⋔ ⁂ ✖ �

> From New York: *"Lovely . . . furnished with true Victorian antiques . . . room was beautiful, comfortable, kept spotless . . . breakfast and afternoon tea excited our palates . . . best of all was the gracious hospitality shown by the Blinns."*

The outside warm-weather landmark: a sea of lavender and purple impatiens blossoms. In spring—hundreds of tulips. Inside there's refinished woodwork; lots of brass, copper, and silver; a Delft Blue collection; Tiffany glass; Victorian furniture; and lace curtains.

For the Blinns, it was the end of a search that began in 1986 with their first B&B stay in a Bar Harbor, Maine, Victorian. Kathleen was a newspaper office manager; George, an electrician, knows about construction and old houses. In 1994 they bought this popular established B&B named after the Dutch founder of Cape May.

In residence: Two outside-only cats.
Bed and bath: Nine rooms—all with private shower bath—on three floors. First-floor suite has queen bed and private entrance. Five second-floor double-bedded rooms. On third floor, three rooms, two with a double and a twin, the other with one double bed.
Breakfast: 8:30–9:30. Fresh fruit, homemade breads and cakes, breakfast meats. French toast, strawberry crepes, eggs Florentine, or pancakes with fruit. In candlelit dining room with classical music, or on the wraparound veranda with privacy afforded by Victorian wind curtains.
Plus: Air-conditioned bedrooms. Bedroom ceiling fans. Iced tea (with mint from the garden) and homemade goodies on the veranda in summer; sherry by fire in winter. Beach passes, chairs, and towels. Landscaped courtyard. On-site parking.

If you've been to one B&B, you haven't been to them all.

The Duke of Windsor

609/884-1355
(reservations only) **800/826-8973**

817 Washington Street
Cape May, NJ 08204

Hosts: Bruce and Fran Prichard
Location: In historic area. Four blocks from beach, "close enough, but quiet too."
Open: Year round. Three-night minimum stay, July–September and holiday weekends. Other weekends (except February and March), two-night minimum.

Rates: Vary according to room size, bath arrangement, weekdays or weekends, air conditioning. Summer $68–$105 shared bath, $85–$165 private bath. Off-season $65–$75 shared bath, $80–$95 private bath. $15 extra person.
♥ ☛ ♣ ✻ ✄

"Originally, we became enticed with the restoration process when we helped friends from home (Voorhees, New Jersey) open The Brass Bed. We soon bought this grand (in every way) 1896 house with its dramatic 45-foot tower and extended our entertaining style to new friends. We love our guests!"

The classic Queen Anne detailing includes Tiffany stained glass; a restored dining room with replica wallpaper of Queen Victoria's throne room, ornate plaster ceiling, and 1871 chandelier; original natural oak woodwork; and a three-story cantilevered stairway. Research and restoration—a labor of love by the three (the fourth is growing up) generations—are ongoing. Grandmother made the curtains. Son Bruce wallpapered. Furnishings are antiques and period pieces. A Victorian garden is in process. And there are plans for restoring the exterior.

Fran, a library/media specialist, and Bruce, a teacher of chemistry and physics, still divide their time between Voorhees and Cape May. When they are not able to be in Cape May, daughter Barbara hosts with the "assistance" of junior innkeepers, daughter Maria Frances and son Michael.

Bed and bath: Nine rooms—on second and third floors—with private baths. Four with queen or double with a twin bed; rest with double bed (including octagonal tower rooms that each have five windows). Eight baths are en suite, one bath (robes provided) is across the hall. One double-bedded room has tub and shower bath; other baths are shower only.
Breakfast: 8:30–10, but late sleepers won't go hungry. Fresh fruits, juice, freshly baked items, cereal, and an entree of the day—pancakes, scrambled eggs, or French toast, with sausage or bacon.
Plus: Afternoon tea. Beach passes. Hot/cold outside showers. Fireplaced foyer and parlor. Air conditioners (removed in mid-September) in five bedrooms. First-floor tower game room for cards, chess, and checkers. On-site off-street parking. Participant in monthlong Christmas grand tour.

Guests wrote: *"Beautiful . . . relaxing . . . festive . . . perfect antidote for long and stressful workweek . . . all the little things were special."*

The Gingerbread House

609/884-0211

28 Gurney Street, Cape May, NJ 08204

Hosts: Joan and Fred Echevarria
Location: In the historic district, half a block from the beach. Within walking distance of restaurants, shops, and homes open for tours.
Open: Year round. Three- or four-night minimum weekend stay during summer and holidays. Two- or three-night minimum weekend stay other times.
Rates: Shared bath: $88 single, $98 double. Private bath: $125 or $135 single, $140–$160 double. $15 additional person. Ten percent discount for weeklong stays. Midweek discounts September 15–June 15.

To begin with, Fred's fine craftsmanship shows in the arches and porch railings. In 1992 he made his own pattern for these missing features, which had been part of the original 1869 house. The teakwood double front doors with ornate beveled glass as well as the arched transom are also his creations—as are the teak bathroom cabinets topped with Corian counters. The parlor and dining room medallions are various shades of rose. All the wonderful watercolors—with the exception of the one of the house done by the first paying guest—were painted by Fred's mother, Jane Echevarria, an artist featured in her own book, *Victorian Interiors*. (When a guest buys a painting, Jane creates a replacement!) Antique furnishings are walnut, rosewood, wicker, and oak. There are collections—cranberry glass, animal teapots, paperweights, shells, and vases. Classical music plays all day. There's a warm, bright, airy feeling in this impeccably maintained B&B.

When the Echevarrias bought the house in 1979, many family members helped with the restoration. Until 1992 Joan commuted on weekdays to a Philadelphia investment advisory firm where she was manager of data processing. Fred is a clinical psychologist/award-winning photographer turned wood- and metalworker and cohost.

Bed and bath: Six double-bedded rooms. Three second-floor rooms (one with two double beds and private porch) have private baths. Three third-floor rooms (one with skylight, one with cathedral ceiling) share one large shower bath plus a first-floor half bath.
Breakfast: 8:30–10. Buffet includes fresh fruit, homemade coffee cake or muffins, homemade cereal, juice, coffee, tea.
Plus: Fireplace (gas) in living room. Bedroom ceiling fans. Outside enclosed shower with changing area. Wicker-furnished front porch. Afternoon tea with lemonade, tea, and sweets. Guest refrigerator. Bicycle storage (bring lock). Garden. Beach tags.

From New Jersey: *"Beautiful rooms and friendly people—all the ingredients for a wonderful stay. Highly recommended!"*

One out of five guests leaves with the dream of opening a B&B.

The Humphrey Hughes House

29 Ocean Street, Cape May, NJ 08204

609/884-4428
800/582-3634

Hosts: Lorraine and Terry Schmidt
Location: One block (five houses) from the ocean. One and a half blocks from Washington Street Mall. In historic area. On corner of Columbia Avenue.
Open: Year round. Three-night minimum May–October weekends.

Rates: May–October $110–$155 king, $105–$155 queen, $90–$120 double; November–April $90–$110 king, $85–$130 queen, $80–$105 double. Suites: May–October $165–$210; November–April $125–$150. Singles $10 less. MC, Visa.
♥ ✉ ✄

It's big and beautiful. It's a Shingle Style Colonial Revival with a huge, awninged wraparound porch, wicker-furnished sun room, stained glass windows, and, between the parlor and living room, solid carved chestnut columns. Weddings are held here. So are Christmas house tours. Returnees come to visit the Schmidts, who changed careers in 1986. Previously, Lorraine was with Merrill Lynch as vice president of banking; Terry was New Jersey Casino Control commissioner.

Built in 1903 for Dr. Humphrey Hughes, "The Doctor's House" was home to the Hughes family until 1980, when it was converted to an inn. In addition to the Hugheses' grandfather clock, dining room sideboard and table, and much silver, the inn is furnished with many museum-quality Victorian pieces, with a light touch, with peaches and blues and florals, with Lorraine's attention to detail.

In residence: "The girls"—Maggie, a standard poodle, and Elizabeth, a miniature poodle.
Bed and bath: Ten (nine are extremely large) rooms on four levels. Three are suites (two with ocean view) with bed for a third guest. TV. All private baths with tub and/or shower (en suite except for two original full baths that are a step away from room). King, queen, or double bed. Ground-level suite with king bed is handicapped accessible.
Breakfast: At 9. Fruit plate. Juice. Entree such as apple and potato frittata or cheese and bacon puff. Sour cream coffee cake, strawberry bread, bran muffins. (Newsletter includes recipes.) In candlelit dining room.
Plus: Ceiling fans in all guest rooms; air conditioning in all but the two with ocean view. Fireplaced living and dining rooms. Grand piano in parlor. Afternoon tea with home-baked goodies. Fresh flowers. Guest refrigerator. Beach towels.

According to guests (many are preservationists and/or house restorers), there ought to be a medal for the meticulous work—everything from research to labor—done by B&B owners. Indeed, many have won preservation awards.

The Mainstay Inn   609/884-8690

635 Columbia Avenue, Cape May, NJ 08204-2305

Hosts: Tom and Sue Carroll
Location: On historic, tree-lined street, within walking distance of everything.
Open: Year round. Three-day requested stay June–September. Some two-night package weekends available in spring and fall. First-time guests, in particular, should call so that the rooms and amenities can be described.
Rates: Spring/fall/winter. $100–$190. Weekends/summer $130–$195. A little more for two-night weekend packages in spring and fall. Suites: for two, $190; $135 off-season. $25 additional person. For four: $240; $185 off-season.
♥ ♣ ✈ ⚕

Elegance. Attention to detail. A visual feast that is enjoyed by "both those who want to be alone and others who seek friendship." But hardly a hidden treasure. Many major publications picture the long walnut dining room table, gas chandeliers, and ceiling-high mirrors in addition to the beautiful exterior of what was built in 1872 as an exclusive clubhouse for gamblers.

The Carrolls loved old houses, even when Tom was a Coast Guardsman (he's now a captain in the reserves) in Cape May. For postservice living, they bought their first Mainstay, which had a few rooms for summer guests. Tom worked with the planning board. Sue taught. In 1976 they acquired the current Mainstay with many of the original furnishings and fixtures. Ahead of the renewed interest in Victoriana, Sue created swag patterns (she still makes the window treatments) and wallpaper borders. Now Oriental rugs are in the 14-foot-high parlors, which feature Bradbury and Bradbury silk-screened papers. The cottage next door, where we stayed, is also furnished with choice Victorian antiques. In 1994, a World War I navy officer's house—directly across the street—became one- and two-bedroom luxury suites.

In many ways this is considered a model of the evolution of a B&B business, all the way from the hosts' struggle to overcome local opposition to the dramatic (positive) impact of B&Bs on an entire community—and the innkeepers' community involvement (Mid-Atlantic Center for the Arts, Cape May Music Festival, Cape May Point Lighthouse restoration). To this day, the Carrolls enjoy wallpapering and painting. They join guests for breakfast and tea. Tom, text writer for *Cape May: Images of a Seaside Resort*, narrates the four-times-a week Mainstay tours. This is a business run with joy, style, and personalization.

Bed and bath: Twelve large rooms with private baths on three floors (one with steep staircase). One first-floor room. Two with private porches. King, queen, double, or twin beds. Suites are handicapped accessible and have whirlpool tub, kitchenette, TV/VCR.
Breakfast: 8:15–9:45. (Coffee and tea earlier; picnic breakfast provided for early departures.) In season, light meal with homemade breads. Off-season, a full meal; could include fresh fruit dish, orange juice, strawberry French toast, bacon, dilled corn muffins, hot beverages. Option of cereals, fresh fruit, toast with sugar-free jelly, yogurt. Served on the veranda or in the dining room. Continental brought to door of suites.

(Please turn page.)

Plus: Afternoon tea. Drawing room with fireplace. Three parlors. Veranda with rockers and swing; private porches with some guest rooms. Garden for sunbathing. Ladder to cupola for ocean view. Beach passes. Outside shower. Three rooms and all suites have private parking.

Manor House   609/884-4710

612 Hughes Street, Cape May, NJ 08204-2318

Hosts: Mary and Tom Snyder
Location: On a quiet side street in historic district, 1½ blocks from the ocean. One block from shops, restaurants, and pedestrian street mall.
Open: Year round except January. Two-night minimum on weekends; three nights on holiday weekends.

Rates: Shared bath $75–$98. Private shower bath $88–$134. Private tub/shower bath $95–$146. Suite with whirlpool bath $110–$165. Higher rates in July and August, lowest on winter weekends. CB, Discover, MC, Visa.
✷ ⌁

From New Jersey: *"Special touches make us feel warm and welcome. No small detail ever overlooked for our comfort. Good food and good fun."*

Your host/barbershop quartet singer/golfer serves breakfast in bow tie, starched shirt, and colored suspenders. Mary's made-from-scratch sticky buns are signature food—a hit, too, with hundreds of Macy's shoppers who attended cooking demonstrations given by innkeepers in this book. *Gourmet* has published one recipe; many are in Manor House's own *Mary's Buns and Tom's Puns.*

When the midlife career changers bought this 1906 house, they acquired a homey place that had been completely redone in 1983 by a wood-carver who had a special appreciation for the chestnut and oak staircase, the floors and moldings. Originally a summer home, the house (without gingerbread) has bay windows, ornate radiators, a great living room fireplace, and some original as well as new stained glass. Furnishings are of the period, with each room being quite different in size and decor. Tom's postbreakfast information (performance) about doings past and present is spiced with facts and humor.

Between both hosts, there's experience in college administration, potato chip manufacturing (their own), and (for a short time) the corporate world.

Foreign language spoken: Pennsylvania Dutch.
Bed and bath: Nine rooms (some are air conditioned; ceiling fans in all) with king, queen, or double bed. On second and third floors. Most with private baths (shower only or tub and shower). Room with double bed and private half bath shares (robes provided) full hall bath with queen-bedded room that has sink en suite. Third-floor suite has queen bed, whirlpool tub, glass corner shower.
Breakfast: 8:30 and 9:30 seatings. Two entrees (you choose one) prepared from a repertoire of "more than 68." Maybe asparagus on homemade English muffin toast, poached eggs and sauce Mornay, apple-cheese pancakes, Mexican quiche, strawberry crepes, or Manor House French toast.
Plus: Punch, cider, tea, or sherry. Fireplaced gathering room. Theme weekends, including one for runners in May, a December Dickens program, and a cooking seminar. Off-premises valet parking. Garden. Beach towels, chairs,

and tags. Hot/cold outdoor shower. Hair dryers in rooms. Information about an area championship golf course where Mary and Tom have renewed an old interest.

The Mason Cottage　　　　609/884-3358
625 Columbia Avenue, Cape May, NJ 08204　　　　800/716-2766

Hosts: Dave and Joan Mason
Location: On a quiet tree-lined street in historic district. One block from beach; on horse-carriage and trolley tours route.
Open: February–December. Two-night minimum on weekends; three nights on summer and holiday weekends.
Rates: Vary according to room size, location, weekday or weekend, and season. Rooms: summer $85–$135; spring and fall $80–$110 weekends, $70–$95 weekdays. Suites: summer $145–$255; spring and fall $120–$200 weekends, $100–$155 weekdays. Ten percent less for four to six consecutive nights. Seventh night free for seven or more consecutive nights—excluding holidays. Five percent AARP discount. Special packages.
♥ ♣ ♦ ✈ ⚏

Everyone remembers the hospitality in this B&B, which has been in the Mason family since 1945. Returnees of the 1980s saw constant changes made by Joan, a registered nurse and clinical editor, and husband Dave, an electrical engineer and licensed contractor, who took over in 1981. The parlor restoration—complete with Victorian brass chandelier, plaster medallion and moldings, and floor-to-ceiling windows—has been outdone by their 1993 project: the interior connecting of the twin houses (which look like one from outside) and the addition of suites. Most of the furnishings are restored antiques that are original to the mansard-roofed house, built in 1871 as a summer residence by the Warne family of Philadelphia. To complete the picture, there are Victorian wallcoverings, restored floors, Oriental rugs, and watercolors done by local artists. One guest wrote, "The rooms and neighborhood are almost like a scene out of a movie. A prime example of the charm and hospitality this historic town has to offer."

Honeymooners receive special attention. Some weddings are held here. And, sometimes, Joan conducts tours of the inn for the Mid-Atlantic Center for the Arts.

In residence: In addition to staffers, Dave is here on all weekends; Joan, May–October weekends.
Bed and bath: In original B&B, five rooms on three floors, all private baths (some tub and shower, some shower only). In twin house, four new suites on second and third floors (two rooms with ocean views); all private baths, some with whirlpool tub. Queen or double beds.
Breakfast: 8:30–10:30. Fresh fruit. Baked apple French toast, vegetable and cheese quiche, or poached pears. Homemade breads, muffins, coffee cakes. Granola. Cereals. Juice, coffee, teas. With hosts, in dining room or on wraparound veranda.
Plus: Central air conditioning in suites. Rooms have ceiling fan or air conditioner. Afternoon tea. Private outside hot/cold shower and dressing area available after checkout. Beach passes. Bike rack. Wicker and cane porch rockers with boardwalk view.

The Queen Victoria

609/884-8702

102 Ocean Street, Cape May, NJ 08204

Hosts: Joan and Dane Wells
Location: In the historic district, 1 block from the beach and 1½ blocks from Washington Street shopping.
Open: Year round. "We never close." Holidays and weekends may require much advance notice. Weekend minimums: two nights in winter, three in spring/fall, four in summer. Two- or three-night midweek minimum stay in summer and some spring and fall periods.

Rates: Vary according to season: lowest on winter weekdays, highest on summer weekends. $160–$240 quad suite; $135–$220 double suite; $110–$180 large double; $90–$155 small double. $20 extra person. Singles $10 less. Summer, $50 off total bill for three-night stay, $100 for four; good discount for two-night winter weekday stay. MC, Visa.
♥ ♠ ✈ ⊬

From New Jersey: *"We have stayed at more than 100 inns from Maine to Florida to California. Our overall favorite is The Queen Victoria."* From Pennsylvania: *"Joan and Dane make it feel like home."*

Fit for a queen (and king), for romantics, and for families (see suite descriptions below). With classical music and handmade quilts. With period antiques, chocolates on the pillow, and innkeepers who enjoy spending time (breakfast and tea and then some) with guests. And guests who ask about Cape May (Dane was chamber of commerce president); Victoriana (Joan was executive director of the Victorian Society in America); restoration (their first building opened in 1981 after two years of researching, demolishing, and chair caning); paint colors (guests bring photos of their own home); beer judging (for American Home Brewers' Association) and barbershop quartet singing (Dane); outdoor activities and Victorian gardens (Joan); Christmas decorations, history, and folklore; benefits (the Mid-Atlantic Center for the Arts). Now the inn is located in three neighboring restored 1880s houses. Among the 15 year-round staffers is one full-time professional painter. Before becoming an innkeeper, Dane was in Main Street development in Philadelphia.

In residence: Daughter Elizabeth, age 12. Two cats—Spats and Mugsy.
Foreign languages spoken: Fluent French (Dane). Some Spanish (Joan).
Bed and bath: Twenty-three rooms with queen or double beds, all private baths (three are shower only). Seven are suites with whirlpool tub, TV, refrigerator. One suite has two bedrooms (one with gas log fireplace), each with queen bed; private bath with two-person whirlpool tub, TV; bedrooms share a parlor, pantry with refrigerator, coffeemaker, microwave, popcorn machine, sink with "hot tap," and phone. The barrier-free suite has a phone, porch, and working fireplace.
Breakfast: 8–10. Homemade granola and breads such as peach yogurt or poppyseed; Wolferman English muffins; a different egg dish each day. Baked apple or hot curried fruit compote. Eat in one of two dining rooms, in bay window of parlor, or on porch.
Plus: Air conditioner, refrigerator, and radio in each room; ceiling fans in many. Afternoon tea with homemade cookies, pates, and cheese spreads. Two parlors, one with fireplace and player piano, the other with TV and games. Library. Guest pantries with setups, mixers, coffee, tea, popcorn

maker. Dozens of porch rockers. Bicycles (free). Beach tags. Bathhouse with changing room and showers. Annotated take-away maps. Concierge and bell services. Newsletter including handyman tips and recipes.

The Summer Cottage Inn   609/884-4948
613 Columbia Avenue, Cape May, NJ 08204-2305

Hosts: Linda and Skip Loughlin
Location: On a quiet tree-lined street in historic district. One block from beach, 1½ blocks to Victorian mall. Minutes to restaurants.
Open: Year round. Two-night minimum, April–December weekends.

Rates: January–March $85–$105; April, May, October $95–$125; June–September $105–$160; November, December $90–$125. $20 third person. Singles $10 less. MC, Visa. ♥ ♠ ♣ ✈ ✔

Now the Loughlins are "everybody's favorite relatives" who live in an 1867 Italianate "cottage" that has a relaxed atmosphere, lace curtains, Victorian antiques, and collectibles. The cupola is lit at night. The front porch wicker swing has been the setting for a New Year's Eve proposal on bended knee. (She said yes.) The exterior has a fresh gold with straw trim paint job. And the Victorian garden, site of private tea parties, is often photographed by passersby.

In 1989 Skip, a contractor, and Linda, a nursing home admissions director, were honeymooners who fell in love with Cape May. Many visits later, when the Loughlins began to look for a summer home here, the Wellses of The Queen Victoria (page 74) suggested that the Loughlins look at B&Bs. The idea took; the midlife career change occurred in 1993.

In residence: Son Matthew, age 13.
Bed and bath: Eight large air-conditioned rooms. All private baths—six are en suite with shower; one on each floor is hall tub/shower bath. Second floor—queen or double bed. Third floor—double or a double and a twin.
Breakfast: 8:30–10:30. "Everything homemade by Linda; coffee is Skip's specialty." Two juices. Fresh fruit. Baked stuffed French toast, German pancake sprinkled with lemon juice and sugar, or German puff pancake. Apple crisp, apple sausage or blueberry orange bread, or muffins. Buffet in dining room or on veranda.
Plus: Teatime treats. Ceiling fans. Fireplaced sitting room. Baby grand piano. Wicker- and plant-filled porch with that swing. Enclosed outside shower and dressing room. Off-street parking. Guest bicycles. Bike storage. Nanny service arranged.

The Wooden Rabbit   609/884-7293
609 Hughes Street, Cape May, NJ 08204

Hosts: Greg and Debby Burow
Location: In historic district "on what we consider the prettiest gaslit street in town." Two blocks from beaches. One block from shops. Within easy walking distance of restaurants.
Open: Year round. Usually, three-

or four-night minimum in July and August; two nights on weekends.
Rates: June–September $175 suite, $155 other rooms. Less off-season. $15 extra person. Discover, MC, Visa for deposit only. ♠ ♣ ✈ ✔

(Please turn page.)

The country decor, very different from Cape May's featured Victoriana, follows the lead taken from the original cooking hook still in the fireplace of the house built in 1838. The rabbit theme—stuffed, painted, wooden, and stitched rabbits—started with Debby's Beatrix Potter collection. This is a B&B where children are comfortable, where adults with or without children feel relaxed. There's stenciling, baskets, comfortable seating by the fire, and interesting folk art.

The Burows stayed in B&Bs for seven years before opening here in Cape May in 1988. For a few years Debby commuted to her full-time job as art director/graphic designer in Philadelphia—while Greg was the full-time innkeeper/photographer/sticky bun baker. Recently they switched arrangements; Greg is a full-time carpenter and Debby is the primary innkeeper, greeting guests who seek a family environment.

In residence: Two school-aged sons. "Our cat, Oscar, who is not supposed to visit guest rooms, loves the fireplaces and guests' laps—and is a regular in many local shops!"

Bed and bath: Three second-floor rooms; all with private baths, TV, air conditioning. Suite with king bed, sitting room, shower bath en suite. Room with king bed, double sofa bed, shower bath. Queen-bedded room with double sofa bed, hall tub/shower bath. Please bring your own portacrib.

Breakfast: "Famous homemade granola"; homemade cinnamon buns, bread, or muffins; cold cereals; fruit or fruit dish; coffee, tea. Sometimes— bread or rice pudding, fruit crisp or tart.

Plus: Home-baked goodies at 4 p.m. tea. Chocolate treats. Guest refrigerator. Small basket of toys in common room. Outside hot/cold shower. Beach tags and chairs. Clothesline for bathing suits. Enclosed backyard. Wicker-furnished sun porch. Free parking in driveway next to inn. Nanny service recommendation (please call ahead).

Woodleigh House   609/884-7123
808 Washington Street, Cape May, NJ 08204   800/399-7123

Hosts: Buddy and Jan Wood
Location: Centrally located in the quiet historic district.
Open: Year round. Two-night minimum on weekends year round; three nights in July and August.

Rates: Weekends $145 per night year round. Midweek $100 May–October, $85 November–April. $25 additional person.
♥ 🛏 ✳ ✈ ⊬

From New Jersey, Pennsylvania, and New York City: *"The decor is authentic without being cloying. . . . Other Cape May B&Bs are fancier, but none can match the Woodleigh House when it comes to hominess and hospitality. . . . Particularly like their informal and flexible approach to breakfast. . . . A house for all seasons!"*

That's it, folks, a home away from home offered by the consummate hosts, who were "in and out" as assistants through all the years that Buddy's mother ran the guest house until she died in 1983. Since taking over, they have added their own touches (Victorian furniture, collections of glass and Royal Copenhagen), renovated (latest: all private baths), and completely redecorated. From the moment you call for a reservation, you can tell that they enjoy their role—a real balance to their other positions, where they work with "other wonderful people." In neighboring communities, Buddy is an elementary school principal and Jan is a kindergarten teacher.

Bed and bath: Four air conditioned rooms (one is on first floor); all private full baths. All queen beds; three rooms have additional single bed. Plus a one-bedroom suite with queen bed, double sleep sofa in sitting room.
Breakfast: 9–10. Fruit, cheese, granola, juice, three or four homemade pastries, bread sticks, coffee, tea. Self-serve in dining room during winter, on porch in summer.
Plus: Bedroom ceiling fans. Porches. Use of refrigerator. TV and VCR. Unscheduled—champagne sherbet, wine, or lemonade. Picnic table in garden. Courtyard lounge area. Bicycles. Beach tags. Outside shower. Off-street on-site parking.

The Henry Ludlam Inn   609/861-5847

Dennisville, NJ
Mailing address: Cape May County, 1336 Route 47, Woodbine, NJ 08270

Hosts: Ann and Marty Thurlow
Location: Rural. In Dennisville, on Route 47, a two-lane road that connects Cape May to Philadelphia. One of four houses on a 56-acre lake. Near Stone Harbor Bird Sanctuary, zoo, museums, Belle Plain State Park, antiquing. On north/south flyway. Ten miles from Garden State Parkway; 20 minutes northwest of Cape May and ferry to Delaware for outlets and dinner; 25 to Atlantic City.
Open: Year round. Two-night minimum on weekends April–November. Three-night minimum on holiday weekends.
Rates: $85–$110. $20 extra person. Amex, Discover, MC, Visa.
♥ ❖ ◆ ✖ ✄

A birder's paradise. Cyclists like the day-trip routes. Romantics, too, appreciate this award-winning "best-kept shore secret" (*Atlantic City* magazine), which has also been featured in *Country Inns* and *Mid-Atlantic Country.* In 1982 it was a "fixer-upper" that satisfied Ann's desire for a New England house by the water. She decorated with stenciling, handmade quilts, and antiques from the shop she had and from auctions. Marty, a master cabinetmaker (his touch is everywhere), duplicated an old stairway. Now the Thurlows have fans who write about the "warmth of this old house and hospitality [that] gives me a hug. . . . As if the world stopped and the inn was there just for us."

Bed and bath: Five air-conditioned rooms on three floors. All private en-suite baths. First-floor room (overlooks lake) with queen bed, wood-burning fireplace, shower bath. On second floor, one room with a single and a double bed, woodburning fireplace, tub/shower bath. Overlooking lake—queen room with wood-burning fireplace, shower bath. Two very private loft rooms (one overlooks lake), each with double bed and shower bath.
Breakfast: At 9. "Unforgettable and heart-healthy." Freshly squeezed orange juice. Entree could be cardamom French toast, poppyseed cake, baked peaches with raspberry and yogurt sauce. In candlelit dining room by fireplace.

(Please turn page.)

Plus: Welcoming beverage. Bedroom fans. Player piano. For dreaming—gazebo and swing on lake shore. Beach tags. Use of canoe and fishing equipment.

The Cabbage Rose Inn

908/788-0247
162 Main Street, Flemington, NJ 08822

Hosts: Pam Venosa and Al Scott
Location: "Typical Main Street USA" in active historic district. Five-minute walk to outlet shopping. Within 15-minute drive of countryside wineries, New Hope, and Lambertville.
Open: Year round. Two-night minimum for weekend reservations that include Saturday.
Rates: $80 detached private bath. $98 queen bed, $105 canopied; $115 with fireplace. Romance-and-roses packages; midweek and corporate rates available. Amex, MC, Visa.
♥ 👪 ✗ ⚟

With turret and third-floor open gazebo, this century-old painted lady Victorian with gingerbread has a wedding cake appearance. This is where Al and Pam were married in 1988, the day before they opened the inn, and just a few months after they discovered the house "with potential"—and with a few surprises, such as a gorgeous oak parquet entry floor and, embedded in a wall, a 1920 will (now framed for all to see).

The career changers—both were AT&T managers—based the floral decor on Pam's Aunt Rose's "cabbage rose–theme" china collection. Furnishings are eclectic—with family photographs, many Victorian pieces, Oriental and hooked rugs, and wicker. From a family reunion (of the original builder), they have learned much history about the house. From their own research they know about the town (its architecture and the courthouse where the Lindbergh kidnapping trial was held) and the area—"New Jersey's last and only covered bridge is nearby." And they have created their very own line of handmade chocolates shaped as cameos, butterflies, or fans topped with pink roses.

In residence: Two West Highland terriers, Rosie, "who sings for our guests—honest!," and Daisy.
Bed and bath: Five second-floor rooms, all private baths. One fireplaced room with four-poster queen bed, attached shower bath. Three more queen-bedded rooms; one with attached tub and shower bath, one with attached shower/no tub bath, one with shower stall in bath plus antique claw-footed tub (with shower) in the bedroom. One double-bedded room with shower bath down the hall. Rollaways available.
Breakfast: 8:30–10. "Continental plus" on weekdays. Weekends—cinnamon-raisin French toast a specialty. Fresh fruit salad, yogurt, homemade granola. Hot or cold cereals. Homemade muffins, breads, scones, and/or coffee cake (plum a specialty). In dining room, on sun porch, or, by request, on tray delivered to your room.
Plus: Air conditioning. Bedroom ceiling fans. Fireplaced living room. Baby grand piano. Robes. Private phones; some rooms with desks. Late-afternoon refreshments. Daily *New York Times.* Picnic basket ($50 for two). Refrigerator in guest pantry. Bedtime sherry. Ride to/from bus stop.

Jerica Hill Inn   908/782-8234

96 Broad Street, Flemington, NJ 08822-1604

Host: Judith S. Studer
Location: On a quiet corner in residential area of historic district. Two blocks from Main Street, near shops, outlets, restaurants. Sixty miles west of Manhattan and northeast of Philadelphia; 14 miles from New Hope, Pennsylvania.

Open: Year round. Two-night minimum on most weekends.
Rates: $105 queen or king bed. $90 and $95 double bed. $10 less midweek. Corporate rates available. $20 additional guest. Amex, MC, Visa.
♣ ♦ ✈ ⊬

Classical music. A glowing fire. Antiques without fussiness. Impeccable housekeeping. And a welcoming hostess.

"My childhood memories of this house are special. Often, I came here to visit the grandfather of a best friend. My parents ran the local hotel and I would dream of opening my own place. After buying this in 1984, I supervised the work done by a restoration firm."

Judy's creative ideas are everywhere in the antiques-filled 1901 Victorian, which features a graceful center hall staircase and individually decorated guest rooms. (Repeat guests seem to have their favorite rooms.) As you tour the house, you can tell that she enjoys books (there are baskets of them), auctions (cherry, pine, and wicker pieces), theater, gardening (plants everywhere), and hot-air ballooning (featured in *Country Inns* magazine).

Corporate and business travelers comment on the "quiet, efficient, personal service and the right price." Some come to shop at the factory outlets or for antiquing or the Delaware River sports. "They discover the architecture in this beautiful, historic town, and the area wineries."

In residence: Sometimes adult children, Jessica and Eric, visit. Two cats—Binky and Mookie, "who look almost exactly alike."
Bed and bath: Five rooms with en-suite private baths. One first-floor room with queen-sized canopied four-poster, shower bath. Upstairs, two double-bedded rooms: one with tub/shower bath, one with shower bath. One room with king bed, shower bath. One with queen bed, tub/shower bath. All antique beds—pineapple, pine, iron-and-brass. Rollaway available.
Breakfast: 8:30–9:30 weekends, earlier midweek. Juice, assorted teas and coffees, fresh fruit, homemade breads (pear a specialty), local jams, cereal, yogurt, warm pastry. Served in dining room or on screened wicker- and plant-filled porch.
Plus: Bedroom air conditioning and ceiling fans. Fireplaced living room. Flowers and fruit in rooms. Beverages including hot cider or iced tea. Guests' pantry open "all the time" with mixers, cookies, fruit, and more. The *New York Times.* Cable TV. Yard. Off-street parking. B&B&B (and ballooning) packages. Winery tour with picnic arranged. Family reunions.

Bed & Breakfast Adventures Host #533

Greenwich, NJ

Location: On 15 tranquil acres. A botanical garden with larch, oak, copper beech, cedar, hemlock, tulip magnolia, and cherry trees. Two miles from the historic village, which is on the state's scenic map.

Reservations: Year round through Bed & Breakfast Adventures, page 54.
Rates: $75 double bed. $100 king.
🏠 ⛵ 🎿 ✗

The "loved and well-maintained" 200-year-old brick Colonial (with 1930 and 1957 additions) was the 1991 answer to the hosts' search for country living complete with swimming pool and cabana. They commute 50 miles to their human resource training business and come home to this "sleepy, well-kept-rather-than-restored town, where time seems to have stopped. Many New Jerseyites are not familiar with the town, or with the 1776 tea burning that took place here in opposition to the British tax." The house has pegged floors, eight fireplaces (including a back-to-back corner one), and six-over-six windows. Furnishings—grandfather clocks, wing chairs, corner cupboards—are from the hostess's family in Kentucky and Mississippi, the host's in Georgia. The property, once owned by an Audubon Society officer and founder of New Jersey's Wetland Institute, now has, according to the hostess, "a live-in gardener, my husband, who grows tomatoes, asparagus, squash, flowers . . . all to share with our guests. They come for birding, bicycling, boating, weddings, and antiquing. Or some come just to go nowhere." For guests, both the town and this B&B are a discovery.

In residence: One black Labrador, one English setter, chickens, pygmy goats, a driving horse, kittens—"none of which live in the house."
Bed and bath: Four second-floor rooms with heirloom four-posters. Three with double bed (one is extra long) share a tub and shower bath. One with king bed, private ensuite tub/shower bath.
Breakfast: Flexible hours. Juice, bread and muffins, cereal, hot beverages. Served in keeping room, kitchen, or dining room.
Plus: Swimming pool with cabana that has kitchen, bar, changing rooms, and baths.

Chimney Hill Farm Bed and Breakfast

207 Goat Hill Road, Lambertville, NJ 08530   609/397-1516
fax 609/397-9353

Hosts: Richard and Terry Ann Anderson
Location: On a country road hilltop. An 8½-acre estate with a formal sunken garden, boxwood, lawns, deer, rabbits, birds, open space. One mile from New Hope, Pennsylvania; a half mile from Lambertville.
Open: Year round.

Rates: Vary according to fireplace and bath arrangements. April 15–January 2, $110–$145 weekends, $75–$105 weekdays. Off-season, $85–$135 weekends, $75–$89 weekdays. $20 extra person. Singles $5 less. Corporate and senior discounts. Amex, Discover, MC, Visa.
♥ 🎿 ♦ ✈ ✗

What started out in 1820 as a low-ceilinged farmhouse with 18-inch-thick walls grew in 1927 with the addition of three wings. Today it still has raised paneling and wide-plank floors, nooks and crannies, verandas, gables, and wide-silled windows. The solarium has a large stone fireplace, flagstone floor, French windows—and comfortable sofas. In 1988 the 15-room estate became a B&B (and a Designers' Showcase). In 1994 the Andersons purchased the property with guest room furnishings and most of the antiques. Now they are implementing wonderful ideas. A perennial garden has been planted. A six-person hot tub may be in the greenhouse by the time you read this. The golden raspberry plants that were part of a commercial berry farm may be ready for a berry-picking festival and/or preserving (by guests) right here. And nature paths are a possibility. It all fits into the Andersons' interest in a holistic lifestyle and their desire to provide a tranquil respite. Terry, a consultant, is also vice president of a professional women's organization. Rich is a worldwide fire protection consultant with Merck.

Bed and bath: Eight rooms; all private baths. First floor—handicapped-accessible room with canopied queen bed, wood-burning fireplace, hand-glazed walls, hall shower bath. Second floor—king bed, wood-burning fireplace, hall tub and shower bath. Faux marble room with queen bed, en-suite shower bath. Canopied king bed, en-suite shower/claw-footed tub bath. Canopied double bed, hall tub and shower bath. Canopied queen bed, hall tub/shower bath. Third floor—king bed, extra-large en-suite shower bath. "Hideaway Room" with canopied queen bed, en-suite shower bath.
Breakfast: 8:30–10. Homemade muffins, cereal, fresh fruit, Danish, coffee and teas. At banquet table in the original 1820 dining room.
Plus: Air conditioning in guest rooms and dining room. Afternoon beverage. Garden sitting areas.

Bed & Breakfast Adventures Host #610
Milford, NJ

Location: Secluded. Overlooking the river in winter; the valley in summer. On 8 private acres surrounded by another 300 with woods and fields. Near antiquing, hiking, canoeing, rafting, historic sites, bicycling (along the river to New Hope, Pennsylvania—25 miles south), fine restaurants.
Reservations: Year round through Bed & Breakfast Adventures, page 54.
Rates: $85 per room.
♥ ⬤ ⁂ ✘ ⊬

Stroll to the cliff about 200 feet above the river for a spectacular view—for miles. (Return in the winter to cross-country ski along the ridge.) Swim in the free-form pool. Or just enjoy the quiet here. Until the 1940s, the house was a stone and wood barn built with 200-year-old hand-hewn beams. Now there's a stone-walled library with fireplace, TV, stereo, and lots of gardening books; some hand-painted (by the host) furniture; a screened porch; and a terrace with trumpet-vine arbor that overlooks the pool and the extensive plantings. The host, a professional landscaper and gardener, grows organic blueberries, gold raspberries, grapes, Asian pears, Alpine strawberries—all laid out by design, with some on the contours of the slopes. There's a

(Please turn page.)

perennial garden, a water garden, and seven giant spruce. One of the projects in process is a greenhouse where mixed salad greens will be harvested.

"We came here seven years ago to grow something, but I wasn't sure what," says the host, a musician and former parking garage owner who has a degree in agronomy. "When my wife, a bank secretary, and I go to B&Bs, we prefer not to be with lots of other people. With just two guest rooms, this place is perfect for such an arrangement."

Bed and bath: In private wing of house, two second-floor rooms, each with a double bed, share a full bath plus a sitting room.
Breakfast: Time arranged with guests. Juices, fresh fruit, muffins, croissants, teas, cocoa, cappuccino. By the fire, on screened porch, or in the pool garden.

Bed & Breakfast Adventures Host #479
North Wildwood, NJ

Location: Residential. On a corner of a street with landscaped islands in the middle. Three blocks from beach and 2½-mile boardwalk. Also within walking distance of shops, restaurants, and tourist information center located in a Victorian lighthouse (on land now). Forty-five minutes south of Atlantic City; 7 miles north of Cape May.

Reservations: February–December through Bed & Breakfast Adventures, page 54. Two- or three-night minimum on July, August, and holiday weekends.
Rates: $75–$100 winter, $95–$115 summer. Rates vary according to room and bed size.
♥ ❊ ♦ ✄ ⚬

The outdoor hot tub is a feature all year long for "romantic getaway" guests. (Many are returnees.) In summer, porch sitters enjoy a breeze. New Year's Eve is booked the previous summer. There are murder mystery weekends here. And always, plenty of what-to-do information provided by the hostess, who prepares the annual chamber of commerce guidebook, and by her husband, who is active with the zoning board and the lighthouse commission.

The enthusiastic hosts, high school sweethearts, converted this turn-of-the-century Queen Anne house to a B&B in 1985. It still has some original gas lighting fixtures, pocket doors, and a built-in dining room breakfront. Lace curtains are on all the windows. Antiques include many Eastlake pieces and some from the Arts and Crafts period, Oriental rugs, an 1855 sofa, and a 1927 Estee baby grand piano (patented in 1897).

In residence: In hosts' quarters, many cats and one dog.
Foreign language spoken: "Ici on parle français."
Bed and bath: Eight rooms on ground, third, and fourth floors; all with private baths. All with ceiling fan and/or central air conditioning. Fourth floor—one room has queen bed and detached private bath with whirlpool tub and a shower. Suite has double bed, private shower bath, sitting room with TV, refrigerator, microwave, wet bar. Other rooms have king, queen, or double bed with shower baths. First floor—king-bedded room with tub and shower and queen-bedded room with shower bath share an air-conditioned and fireplaced parlor that has TV.

Breakfast: At 8:15 and 9:30. Fruit, hot or cold cereal, home-baked breads or muffins. A choice of two entrees—maybe eggs Benedict, waffles, pancakes, casseroles, or quiche. The host cooks; the hostess bakes; both join guests in the dining room.

Plus: Afternoon refreshments. Wicker-furnished porch with hammocks and swing. Sun deck and that hot tub. Beach towels. Fresh flowers. Complimentary sherry and chocolates. Gourmet dinners upon request. Special occasions acknowledged. Dinner reservations made. On-site parking.

BarnaGate Bed & Breakfast   609/391-9366
637 Wesley Avenue, Ocean City, NJ 08226

Hosts: Frank and Lois Barna
Location: On a corner in historic district; 3½ blocks to beach and boardwalk, 2 to shopping. Seven minutes from Garden State Parkway. Ten miles south of Atlantic City, 40 minutes north of Cape May. Ninety minutes from Philadelphia.

Open: Year round. Two-night minimum on holiday weekends.
Rates: $130 suite, $75 private bath, $70 with powder room, $65 shared bath. $10 extra person. Midweek discounts. MC, Visa.
✿ ✗ ⅄

B&B has made the hosts local history buffs and antiques collectors. It's all part of the fun for Lois, who often planned social functions and business seminars while assistant to a bank president, and Frank, an avid sports fan who had his own TV repair shop. Now he creates stained glass lamps. Together they host guests who come for in-house murder mystery weekends, showers, celebrations, family reunions, vacations—"and the B&B experience."

When looking for a career change, the Barnas took a B&B seminar, stayed at B&Bs, and then bought this 1895 Victorian that was a guest house. They redecorated in time for the 1988 season and moved from Somerville, New Jersey, to "America's greatest family resort, a town with a friendly atmosphere." All the beds have quilts. The furnishings are country Victorian. For special treats on holidays, the Barnas make their own ice cream.

In residence: Daughter Donna, who inn-sits occasionally.
Bed and bath: Five rooms. On second floor, private full bath for one double-bedded room. One twin-bedded room with powder room shares a tub bath with a double room. Two third-floor corner double-bedded dormer rooms (a suite when booked together) share a tub bath and a private sitting room. Rollaway available.
Breakfast: 8–9:30. Juice; fruit; sweet rolls, muffins, and breakfast cakes; coffees and teas. Extended menu in the winter—stuffed French toast or pumpkin pancakes with homemade applesauce. Buffet style in dining room that has a ceiling fan and period antiques.
Plus: Bedroom ceiling and window fans. Enclosed outside shower. Refrigerator privileges. Backyard with table and chairs. Swimsuit clothesline. Free beach tags for two-night stay. BarnaGate cookbook available.

From Pennsylvania (and echoed by several guests): *"Lois and Frank made us feel like we were old friends. . . . Animated conversations. . . . A visit with them is good for the spirit. . . . Their home is cozy and very clean, and the breakfast is*

(Please turn page.)

delicious. . . . Simple pleasures all within minutes. . . . The only thing we didn't like was leaving."

New Brighton Inn

609/399-2829

519 Fifth Street, Ocean City, NJ 08226

Hosts: Dan and Donna Hand
Location: Facing a church and Tabernacle grounds. Three blocks to beach, boardwalk, bay. Within 10 minutes' walk of shops and restaurants. Near state park with dunes.

Open: Year round. Two-night minimum on weekends.
Rates: $75–$85 private bath. $10 additional guest. Amex, Discover, MC, Visa.

♥ ⊶ ⁂ ✹ ⅄

With memories of childhood vacations in Ocean City and adult vacations at B&Bs, cabinetmaker Dan, who studied art, and quilt maker Donna, former computer programmer, transformed the turreted Queen Anne into a B&B in 1988. Along the way they made a video of this major project, which included stripping the hall woodwork (all three floors) and adding baths. Oriental rugs, brass beds, lots of rockers, and light colors give a warm ambiance. For some whimsy Dan painted the library ceiling with clouds, moon, and stars. During summer sunsets the hosts often join guests on the porch. Year round, the breakfast is remembered.

Foreign language spoken: Limited French.
Bed and bath: Six rooms. On second floor, two with queen bed (one with eight windows) and private shower bath. One double-bedded room has bath with claw-footed tub and shower. On third floor—same arrangement. Rollaway available.
Breakfast: 8–10. *Bon Appétit* recipes including fruited cheese pizza, honey lemon walnut tart, spinach frittata, quiche lorraine, strawberry tart with almond cream. Homemade sticky buns, coffee cake, or bread. Juices. Fresh fruit. Plenty of tea and coffee. On sun porch or terrace. Newspaper provided.
Plus: Air conditioner, ceiling fan, and TV in bedrooms. Sun porch with ceiling fans. Beverages on arbor-covered patio. Babysitting. Airport (10 minutes away) pickup. Hot/cold outside shower, changing stalls; for after-checkout too. Bicycles. Beach tags.

> From Pennsylvania: *"Bedrooms with country charm feature 20th-century comfort (wonderful mattresses) in a setting Grandmother would have recognized. . . . Breakfasts are copious and delicious. . . . Housekeeping met high standards of our fussy parents. . . . The Hands' friendly unaffected manner makes for a truly relaxing visit!"*

From Bernice's mail bag: "The last straw was the classmate whom I hadn't seen in 50 years, who read about us in your book. He's been here twice."

Northwood Inn Bed & Breakfast   609/399-6071

401 Wesley Avenue, Ocean City, NJ 08226

Hosts: Marj and John Loeper
Location: In historic district. Three and a half blocks to beach and boardwalk, four to town, shops, restaurants; 8 miles south of Atlantic City, 30 north of Cape May, 15 to wildlife refuge.
Open: Year round except January 2–15. Two-night minimum stay on summer weekends and most holiday weekends; three nights Memorial Day, July 4, Labor Day.
Rates: Private bath $85 or $90. En-suite bath: $95, $100 twin/king, $105 Tower Room, $145 suite. $10 less October 20–Memorial Day.
♥ ❖ ✈ ⅊

An award-winning restoration. An 1894 turreted Queen Anne Victorian that was abandoned after being gutted by the previous owner, the house was rescued just two weeks before its scheduled demolition. All thanks to John, a builder who specializes in historic restoration—and ship half models. In 1977–78 he studied wooden boat building—"a family adventure"—in Maine. Here he is chairman of the town's historic preservation commission.

Under the graceful main staircase, John built an English phone booth (with working phone). A regulation-sized oak drop pocket pool table is in the billiard room. The entire project was documented with photographs and video by Marj, the official B&B chef. Intentionally, decor is uncluttered, light and airy.

In residence: Summers, daughter Rebeca, a college student.
Bed and bath: Eight rooms on second and third floors. All private baths. Room with twin/king option has shower bath; others have queen bed, tub/shower bath—some en suite, some detached with sink in bedroom, Tower Room bath has a dressing room. Suite has double sofa bed and TV in separate sitting room.
Breakfast: Usually 8–10. Repertoire (recipes shared) includes French toast with apple syrup, two-berry pancakes, three-cheese egg puff, baked apples, apple strudel, Heath Bar crunch coffee cake (John's mother's specialty), orange or banana/sour cream muffins, cream scones. Juice, fruit, cereal, yogurt.
Plus: Central air conditioning. Bedroom ceiling fans. Hot cider or iced tea. Guest refrigerator. Outdoor hot/cold shower. Rockers on wraparound porch. Back and rooftop decks. Beach tags. Bike storage. Newspapers. Transportation to/from Ocean City bus or Atlantic City Amtrak. Murder mystery weekends in October, November, February, March.

From Pennsylvania: *"We would like to go on believing that Northwood is our secret and the Loepers our extended family. . . . It was a cold blustery February day when we discovered warm and welcoming Victorian charm . . . immaculate . . . excellent food . . . pampered us."* From Ohio: *"Five star."*

*M*any B&Bs are perfect for family reunions.

Scarborough Inn

720 Ocean Avenue, Ocean City, NJ 08226

609/399-1558
800/258-1558
fax 609/399-4472

Hosts: Gus and Carol Bruno
Location: In historic business district with some private homes, condos, and other accommodations. One and a half blocks from beach, boardwalk, and public recreation facilities. Two blocks to main (small-town) shopping district.
Open: May–mid-October; two-night minimum on weekends, three nights on holidays.

Rates: May through mid-June and post–Labor Day through mid-October $60–$80; adjoining room $70. Mid-June–mid-July $70–$100; adjoining room $85. Mid-July–Labor Day $75-$120; adjoining room $90. Additional person in room $10. Age 12 and under $5. Crib free. Amex, Discover, MC, Visa.
♥ ♨ ♦ ✖ ✂

> From Maryland: *"Clean, comfortable, friendly, excellent breakfast."* From Pennsylvania: *"Much like visiting cousins who happen to have a very large, charming seashore house."*

Since the Brunos, longtime Ocean City residents, made this 1895 four-storied landmark inn their home in 1988, they have received an award from the local historical commission. The exterior has been changed from all white to six colors, oak furnishings have been stripped of paint and refinished, and air conditioning has been installed in all guest rooms. Refurbishing and upgrading is an ongoing process. Still, the feeling of "visiting family—yet large enough to offer privacy" brings many guests back. It's just as the Brunos planned after Gus, an education major, had years of experience as a business traveler and as a boardwalk entrepreneur ("no chance really to know your customers"). Carol, an elementary school teacher of gifted and talented students, has chosen pastels for most of the bedrooms. In 1994 the redecorated Sweet Thymes—"our special occasion guest room"—won second prize in the Waverly (fabrics) Country Inn Room of the Year contest.

In residence: Sons Peter and Jason, college students.
Foreign language spoken: Italian.
Bed and bath: Twenty-six rooms (more than other entries in this book) on second, third, and fourth floors. All private baths (some with new pedestal sink); some tub and shower, some shower only. Beds (some are canopied) are queen-sized or double (some rooms with two twins or two doubles) or adjoining rooms—each with two twins or a double bed—and connecting bath.
Breakfast: 7:30–9:30. Juices. Fresh fruit. Baked goods. Coffee and tea. Buffet style in spacious double living room; in parlor with ceiling fans, upright piano, plenty of greenery; or on 100-foot wraparound porch.
Plus: All rooms have window air conditioners; some have ceiling fan also. Late-afternoon iced tea. Library. Color cable TV, VCR, and videos in lobby. Special occasions acknowledged. Room refrigerator, $3 daily. Complimentary beach tags (two per room) for two or more consecutive nights.

Red Maple Farm

908/329-3821

211 Raymond Road, Princeton, NJ 08540

Host: Roberta Churchill
Location: On 2½ acres. Four miles from Princeton University. Near Route 1 business corridor. "Road is busy during the day but quiet at night." One hour from Philadelphia or New York City.

Open: Year round.
Rates: $55 king/twin option. $65 queen, $75 with fireplace. Singles $10 less.
🛏 ✖ ✄

This National Register property, the food, and the hosts are all remembered by guests. Roberta is a former caterer and chef who had "one of the five best restaurants in New Jersey" (*New York Times*). Now she's "a passionate gardener, theatergoer, reader, and political activist." Lindsey, her husband, is a sociology professor who also teaches an adult education center wine-tasting course.

The house, built between 1740 and 1820, played a part in the Revolution and was an Underground Railroad stop during the Civil War. The Churchills bought it in 1990 complete with original latched doors that have strapped hinges. Guest rooms have been papered with small prints. One bath is stenciled. Restoration is ongoing. Furnishings are comfortable "without valuable antiques to worry about harming." As for the grounds with birds, deer, rabbits, and woodchucks: "It's like having a park of your own," said one guest. Roberta tends many flower beds and cooks with her own organic fruit, berries, and vegetables. There's a 1740 stone smokehouse; the remains of the 1740 stone barn form a great backdrop for the swimming pool, which is available to guests; and an 1850 barn built with hand-hewn beams is still in use.

In residence: One barn cat. "And one friendly German shepherd allowed in kitchen only."
Foreign language spoken: Limited French.
Bed and bath: Three second-floor rooms, two shared baths. Fireplaced room with queen brass bed connected by bath with shower stall to room with extra-long king/twins option. One room with queen four-poster shares tub/shower bath with hosts.
Breakfast: Usually 8:30. Repertoire includes johnnycakes, fruit slump, buckwheat pancakes, raised waffles, shirred eggs with asparagus, vegetable garden frittata. Local smokehouse bacon or Amish sausages. Homemade sweet breads and preserves. Served in 1820 fireplaced dining room or on patio of 1740 stone smokehouse.
Plus: Air-conditioned bedrooms. Fireplaced front parlor. Antique upright piano. Barbecue. Lawn games. Two bicycles. Tennis nearby. Pickup at Princeton train station or New York bus.

I'll just sleep in the morning," said one college-age son, until the next day when he smelled the muffins.

Ashling Cottage

908/449-3553

106 Sussex Avenue, Spring Lake, NJ 07762   800/237-1877

Hosts: Goodi and Jack Stewart
Location: On a sycamore-shaded residential street, one block to ocean, boardwalk, lake. Two blocks to shops. One hour from Philadelphia or New York.
Open: April–December. Two-night minimum on weekends in July and August.

Rates: Mid-May to mid-September: weekdays $98 shared bath, $130 private; weekends $110 shared bath, $150 private. Off-season: weekdays $75 shared, $110 private; weekends $90 shared, $125 private. Singles $5 less. Discounts for third night, off-season.
♥ ♣ ✖ ⅍

"In July 1993 we were told that our 'Anne of Green Gables' look was exactly what was needed for a Harrod's of London Christmas catalog shoot. Thank goodness for our sycamores, which provided shade for the cashmere-attired models!

"This is a wonderful storybook town with none of the frenzy often associated with beach locations. Our house was built in 1877 with lumber from the Philadelphia Bicentennial agricultural exhibit. We have blended antiques with comfort, leaning toward the 'genteel mood of yesterday' rather than formal Victorian and total authenticity. White wicker fills our screened (and glassed) solarium, which gives a peek at the ocean to the east, and to the west, the spring-fed lake with surrounding park, migrating waterfowl, and wooden bridges."

Before the Stewarts began "working together," Jack was a sales executive in Los Angeles and New York; Goodi was in the barter business in New York.

In residence: Lady Latimer, the cat, "the real mistress of Ashling Cottage," and "her nemesis, Princess Graci," an adopted stray cat.
Foreign language spoken: A little German.
Bed and bath: Ten queen-bedded rooms on three floors, each with ceiling fan and cross-ventilation. (One on first floor with private porch.) Eight with private baths; some have shower or tub only, one bathroom is sunken. Two rooms, each with sink in room, share a hall tub bath.
Breakfast: 8:30–10. Freshly ground coffee or brewed tea, two fruit juices, cold cereals, seasonal fruits, eggs (maybe in a casserole). At least two home-baked goods; might be muffins (about a dozen varieties in repertoire), Irish soda bread, sour cream pound cake, nut braid, or brioche. Served buffet style in the parlor or solarium, on porches, or in living room.
Plus: Year round, fresh flowers. Fireplaced living room with TV and VCR. Books. Games. Patio grill and picnic table. Impromptu wine gatherings. Labor Day Creative Black Tie Weenie Roast. Transportation to/from train or bus station.

Unless otherwise stated, rates in this book are per room for two and include breakfast in addition to all the amenities listed in "Plus."

Sea Crest by the Sea

908/449-9031
800/803-9031

19 Tuttle Avenue, Spring Lake, NJ 07762

Hosts: John and Carol Kirby
Location: Set back from street among other Victorian homes. Four houses from ocean and noncommercial boardwalk. Five-minute walk to village center and its 50 small shops. One-hour drive or 90-minute train ride from Manhattan.
Open: Year round. Two-night minimum July–August weekdays and off-season weekends. Three-night minimum on holiday and summer weekends.
Rates: Per room. Summer: Cozy $115, moderate $139, large $159. Suite $239. Winter: $92, $112, $129. Suite $189. Off-season packages. MC, Visa.
♥ ✈ ✄

This turreted Queen Anne Victorian, furnished with French and English antiques and period reproduction lighting, has fantasy-bent innkeepers, romantics who admit to being "more whimsical than rigid in our Victoriana." Lots of light comes through 75 big windows. Croquet and bicycles await. So do classical music, lace-trimmed Egyptian cotton sheets, and afternoon tea (mulled cider in winter) with player piano "entertainment."

Carol was a real estate agent and John, president of a medical equipment manufacturing company. In 1989, shortly after John, at age 45, decided to leave the company, "the dream happened" (a good match!). You'll probably meet many returnees. Many unwinders. Or honeymooners. Or maybe two nuns "who taught us lessons in charity, conversation, humility, and fun."

In residence: "Family members—Sneakers and Princess, affectionate cats, and Daisy, a sheltie collie mix."
Bed and bath: Twelve queen-bedded rooms on second and third floors plus second-floor two-room suite. Each with private shower bath (four also have tubs). Eight with ocean views; eight with working fireplace; four with feather beds. One with private porch. Room names include George Washington, Sleigh Ride, Yankee Clipper (with John's sailing logs from merchant marine days), and Teddy Roosevelt Suite.
Breakfast: Buffet "starts at the civilized hour of 9." Fresh fruit salad; their own granola; yogurt; muffins; Carol's buttermilk scones and John's honey walnut bread (and, "when the spirit moves," white chocolate cheesecake, cheeses, or fresh berries from the garden); featherbed eggs or quiche; freshly squeezed orange juice; Sea Crest's coffee blend (Scandinavian, half decaf), teas. Table set with family china and silver; candlelit in winter.
Plus: Central air conditioning. Fireplaced living room and library. TV in library. Rockers on wraparound and awninged porches. Handmade chocolate mints on silver tray. Tennis court passes. Down comforters. Transportation to/from train station. For those who drive—fabulous orchard stop suggestion.

---

*M*any guests write: "I hate to rave too much for fear of finding no place at the inn the next time I call."

The Whistling Swan Inn   201/347-6369
110 Main Street, Stanhope, NJ 07874-0791   fax 201/347-3391

Hosts: Paula Williams and Joe Mulay.
Location: A quiet main street of a small rural northwest New Jersey town. Near fine dining and casual restaurants, wineries, winter sports. One mile north of I-80 (exit 27), off Route 183/206; 45 miles west of George Washington Bridge; 25 miles east of Poconos.
Open: Year round. Two-night min-imum on holiday weekends.
Rates: July–October $85 small (cozy and often chosen) room, $95 large, $110 suite. November–June $10 less. $5 senior and corporate discount. Special romantic weekend and winter midweek rates. Amex, Discover, MC, Visa.
♥ ♦ ✈ ⊁

> From a Maryland architect: *"A totally renovated, stunning Victorian home, full of charm and character . . . decorated with wonderful Victorian accents . . . not too much, just enough to be refined but warm, inviting, cozy, and so comfortable . . . immaculately clean, which is vital to me as I am allergic to dust! . . . delicious, homemade full breakfast . . . hosts who are helpful, relaxed, and quite simply delightful."*

Other plaudits came from Pennsylvania, Minnesota, and Massachusetts; from business travelers; Valentine's Day guests; 30th anniversary guests—"a gift from our children we'll never forget"; antiquers; and festivalgoers (picnic dinners here and discount tickets for Waterloo Festival of the Arts).

"Our region has so much to offer!" say Paula, a former speech therapist, consultant, and corporate manager, and Joe, who was also an AT&T manager, marketer, and corporate planner. After doing most of the restoration themselves, they opened this turreted Queen Anne in 1986, "just when so many big New Jersey homes were being torn down," at a time when they had inherited Paula's grandmother's (Oklahoma) furniture. Now that the media, too, have discovered this B&B, Whistling Swan's innkeeping seminars have been featured in a *New York Times* syndicated article and the "Donahue Show" has requested a "dreams segment" interview with Paula and Joe.

Bed and bath: Ten queen-bedded rooms—each with antique radio—furnished in period themes such as Victorian, Twenties, Oriental antiques. All private baths. Second-floor rooms have shower baths. Third-floor rooms, including two-room suite, have baths with claw-footed tubs and hand-held shower. A two-tub bathroom, "our Victorian Jacuzzi," is available for all guests; robes provided. Rollaway available.
Breakfast: 7–9 weekdays, 8:30–10:30 weekends and holidays. Buffet style. Egg/fruit/cheese dishes, baked omelet, frittata, whole-kernel corn pancakes (a specialty), or waffles. Hot biscuits or muffins. Juices, fruit, yogurt, cereal, granola bars. Hosts join guests for coffee in lace-curtained dining room or on front porch.
Plus: Central air conditioning. Bedroom ceiling fans. In parlor—player piano, cable TV, cookie jar. Fireplaced dining room. Rockers, wicker, and hammocks on wraparound porch. Beverages. Bicycles. Picnic tables. Picnic baskets ($15).

The Stewart Inn

P.O. Box 6, RD 1, South Main Street
Stewartsville, NJ 08886

908/479-6060
fax 908/479-1259

Hosts: Brian and Lynne McGarry
Location: Pastoral. On 16 wooded acres with trout stream. Minutes from I-78. Five miles from Easton, Pennsylvania; 10 from Bethlehem. Near many corporate headquarters, Bucks County, historic and agricultural Warren and Hunterdon counties (with pick-your-own apples and vegetable and pumpkin places) in

New Jersey, wineries, shopping, fine restaurants. One hour from Manhattan, 75 minutes from Philadelphia.
Open: Year round.
Rates: $85 or $95; $105 with fireplace (and private hall bath). $130 larger fireplaced suite. Corporate rates Sunday–Thursday. Amex, MC, Visa.
♥ ♣ ♦ ✈ ⚵

Although many of the McGarrys' guests are business travelers from all over the world, weekend romantics, too, appreciate this gracious 1770s fieldstone manor house, which has been featured in *Country Inns* magazine. It is complete with Palladian window, working fireplaces, Oriental rugs, and early American and English antiques. Arranged flowers are throughout. The landscaped grounds include a free-form swimming pool, gorgeous gardens, horseshoes, and badminton. And then there are all those animals.

With B&B in mind, the multifaceted McGarrys—who met during a Sierra Club trail cleanup—opted for rural living in 1986, choosing a historic estate that needed "decorating only." Lynne, a licensed wildlife caretaker, has been a small-town mayor, tax collector, and kennel owner. Now she and Brian, a lawyer, design, manufacture, and market needlework kits. Here, year round, they offer "peace and solitude of our rural world."

In residence (mostly in the barns): One dog, 5 cats, 30 sheep, 3 goats, 2 peacocks, geese, chickens, ducks, raccoons, rabbits, a parrot, doves, and parakeets.
Bed and bath: Eight rooms including two suites with working fireplace. All with queen four-poster, private tub/shower bath (seven are en suite, one is a hall bath), TV, private phone, and air conditioner. First-floor room by pool. Second-floor rooms include larger suite with separate tub and shower bath, sitting area with sofa, two wing chairs, desk.
Breakfast: 7–9:30. Farm-fresh eggs, smoked bacon, pancakes, French toast, fruits, granolas. Served in fireplaced dining room.
Plus: Fireplaced living room. Use of barbecue. Needlework kits and unprocessed or processed-to-order wool for sale. Spring sheep shearing.

From New York: *"The tangible pleasures and comforts speak for themselves . . . warmth, charm, and hospitality in everything [they] say or do assures the well-being of guests."*

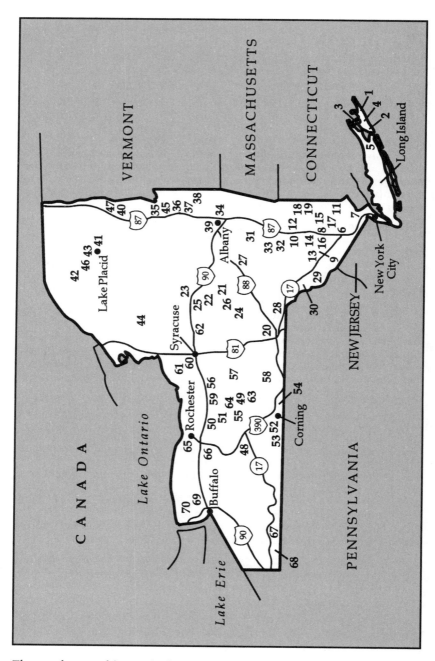

The numbers on this map indicate the locations of B&Bs described in detail in this chapter.

NEW YORK

___ Long Island Reservation Service ___

A Reasonable Alternative, Inc.

117 Spring Street, Port Jefferson, NY 11777

Phone: 516/928-4034, Monday–Friday noon–5.

Fax: 516/331-7641.

Listings: About 50 (number varies according to season) hosted private residences in Nassau and Suffolk counties, mostly along the north and south shores. Among the communities represented in Suffolk County are all of the Hamptons, South Fork, Port Jefferson, Stony Brook, and the North Fork villages (winery country). B&Bs are Colonials, Victorians, and contemporaries, and a few apartments. "Long Island is about 15 miles (north to south) by 120 miles (east to west), so almost every place is close to the water."

Reservations: Most hosts accept one-night reservations except those in the Hamptons during summer months, when there is a two-night minimum, three nights on holidays.

Rates: $44–$76 singles, $52–$80 doubles. In July and August singles and doubles $60–$125. Reservations for homes in the East End (North Fork and South Fork) must be prepaid and are nonrefundable. Some weekly rates. Deposit required—at least one night's lodging. If cancellation (East End excepted) received three days before scheduled arrival, all but a $10 service charge returned; no refund if received later. MC, Visa. ✖ ⊁

Kathleen Dexter started her reservation service in February 1981 and to this day has many of her original hosts, friendly people who enjoy sharing their homes with others. "The only reason they stop hosting is if their kids come home or they sell their house. As our guests say, 'They are wonderful people.' We take pride in operating a quality service."

KEY TO SYMBOLS
♥ Lots of honeymooners come here.
✚ Families with children are very welcome. (Please see page xii.)
● "Please emphasize that we are a private home, not an inn."
♣ Groups or private parties sometimes book the entire B&B.
♦ Travel agents' commission paid. (Please see page xii.)
✖ Sorry, no guests' pets are allowed.
⊁ No smoking inside *or* no smoking at all, even on porches.

─────── Long Island B&Bs ───────

Centennial House
13 Woods Lane, East Hampton, NY 11937

516/324-9414
fax 516/324-2681

Hosts: David Oxford and Harry Chancey, Jr.
Location: On a parklike acre with beautiful gardens, lawns, secluded pool. In historic district of country/summer estates. Within walking distance of English-style village and beach. Along the main road; 100 yards from "Currier and Ives pond" just as you enter village.
Open: Year round. Four-night minimum July 4 and Labor Day; three nights on Memorial Day and on weekends July–mid-September. Cottage: one-week minimum July 1–Labor Day.
Rates: Vary according to size of room and bed. May–October $175–$275, November–April $100–$200. Cottage (three bedrooms) $450 high season, $300 off-season. Holiday packages and corporate retreat rates. Amex, MC, Visa.

♥ ☕ ♣ ♦ ✈ ⅊

Pictured in a wonderful six-page *Country Inns* spread, this is a "passion that became a venture" only because a neighboring inn called in need of "one more room."

Built in 1876 as a family residence, the shingled Victorian had changed hands only once before David and Harry bought it in 1987. Originally from Alabama, David is a lawyer. Harry is an executive with public television station WNET.

During restoration the signature of the noted builder, Thomas E. Babcock, was uncovered. Now the hosts often share anecdotes about the acquisition of the many fine antiques and traditional furnishings. In addition to hospitality, they offer a sense of peace and quiet, privacy, and contentment.

In residence: Earl and Edwinna, two fawn-colored Lhasa apsos.
Foreign language spoken: French.
Bed and bath: Six air-conditioned rooms with king, queen (canopied or four-poster), or double beds; all with adjoining luxurious baths. Plus a three-bedroom, two-bath "fairytale cottage" (without breakfast).
Breakfast: 8:30–10. Juice. Fruit. Muffins made with homegrown herbs or scones, breads, cakes, coffees. On weekends, full menu with buttermilk pancakes, French toast, or omelets. Buffet in Georgian dining room.
Plus: Grand piano in marble-fireplaced parlor. Complimentary snacks and beverages. Bedside phones. Chocolate truffles. The Sunday *New York Times*. Terry robes. Potpourri from inn's garden. Front porch. Swim at beach or in pool right here.

From Pennsylvania: *"We have tried almost all the inns in the Hamptons in search of the perfect spot. We will look no farther!"*

The Mill House Inn

516/324-9766

33 North Main Street, East Hampton, NY 11937

Hosts: Katherine and Dan Hartnett
Location: Seven houses from shopping district with galleries, first-run movie theater, restaurants. Opposite the village green and Old Hook Windmill. Within a mile of "pristine beaches," train, bus. Short drive to wineries or whale watch excursions.
Open: Year round. Two-night weekend minimum May–October; three nights May–September holiday weekends.
Rates: Vary according to bed size and bath amenities. Late May–mid-October $150–$200. Off-season $115–$150. Amex, MC, VISA.
♥ ⚓ ✈ ✂

This 1790 Colonial house, expanded in 1878 and changed several times (Jacuzzis are the latest), is decorated with chintzes and designer fabrics, coordinating wallpaper, country pieces and hand-painted furniture, Orientals, and botanical prints.

Katherine's food is one hit. (She has extensive experience as a restaurant and hotel chef.) The house-with-character is another. The friendly Hartnetts are the clincher. Since buying this established B&B in 1994, they have purchased antique armoires from local antiques dealers. They have continued their social work as consultants on social work research projects.

In residence: Two sons—Brook is two, Sean is one.
Foreign language spoken: Spanish.
Bed and bath: Eight rooms. Some with gas fireplaces; most with sloping ceilings; all with ceiling fans. Private baths (most with shower, no tub; some with Jacuzzi) for first- and second-floor rooms. On third floor, two rooms (can be a suite) share bath that has claw-footed tub and shower. Queen (one is canopied, one with an extra twin bed in room), double, or twin beds.
Breakfast: 9–10. In season, fresh fruit. Katherine's Irish soda bread and muffins, freshly squeezed orange juice, and granola cereal. Off-season, corn-meal waffles with sausage, scrambled eggs with smoked salmon on croissants, or French toast stuffed with cream cheese and apricot preserves. In dining room or, by request, in bed.
Plus: Central air conditioning (in process as book went to press). Lemonade or tea and cookies. Fireplaced living room. Patio and backyard. Guest refrigerator. Village beach passes.

House on the Water

516/728-3560

Box 106, Hampton Bays, NY 11946-0012

Host: Ute
Location: On Shinnecock Bay. On two acres in a friendly neighborhood good for jogging. One mile from the village center and train. Two miles from bus and to ocean beaches. Seven miles from Southampton.
Open: May–December 1. Two-night weekend minimum; four nights on July 4 and Labor Day weekends.
Rates: Memorial Day–October 1, $70–$90 single, $75–$95 double. Adjoining room $40 single, $50 double. $20 extra (folding) bed. Off-season $20 less. Weekly and monthly rates.
⚓ ♦ ✈ ✂

"My home seems to appeal both to those who want to rest, relax, and hardly leave the premises, and to those who try to take in everything from discos to restaurants."

The location is one major attraction. The hostess, who definitely has a home and not an inn, is another. It's a B&B in the traditional sense. The large ranch house has a part shade/part sun 50-foot terrace where you can lounge and watch the boats go by. You are welcome to borrow a bicycle (there are four), the pedal boat, or the Windsurfers or small sailboat, all without charge.

After 20 years of owning a boutique in Acapulco for custom-made resort wear (for all ages), Ute sails, plays tennis and golf, and pursues her interests in health food, diet, and exercise. In the winter she hosts in her Acapulco beachfront condominium, which has two pools.

Foreign languages spoken: German, Spanish, and French.
Bed and bath: Three simply furnished rooms (water views from two) with two twin beds in each (one room can be a king). All private full baths. One room with private entrance can connect with another room (available only with first room). Two folding beds.
Breakfast: Generally 8–12. Fried, boiled, poached, scrambled, or Mexican eggs. French toast, Spanish tortilla, various breads, hot and cold cereals. Special diets accommodated. In living room or on the terrace.
Plus: Hot beverages always available. Kitchen privileges. Beach lounge chairs. Umbrellas. Laundry facility. Portable fans. Transportation to/from bus or train stations and beaches.

> Guests wrote: *"Very European style. Custom breakfasts, interesting conversations. A oneness with nature. A memorable visit."*

The Bayberry Bed & Breakfast   516/749-3375

36 South Menantic Road, P.O. Box 538, Shelter Island, NY 11964-0538

Hosts: Dick and Suzanne Boland
Location: Rural (Menantic Peninsula), with fields, woods, and wildlife, "but not in the middle of nowhere." (One-third of the four-by-seven-mile island is a nature conservancy.) About 3 miles from ferry landings at North (eight-minute ferry ride) or South Fork (four-minute ride). Close to dockside restaurant. "Bicycles everywhere." Two miles to tennis court. One hundred miles from Manhattan.
Open: Year round. Two-night weekend minimum; three nights on holidays.
Rates: May–October $105 twin beds. $125 king. Off-season $95 twins, $105 king.
🥾 ✖ ⅄

> From California: *"We have lodged the world over from Rio to Hong Kong, from Sydney to Stockholm. We have never enjoyed any stay more."*

This inviting antiques-furnished L-shaped ranch house, built in 1984, is deceptively small from the outside. The light-filled beamed living/dining room has Oriental rugs, wing and Windsor chairs, and sliding glass doors to a spacious deck. From the in-ground swimming pool you may see deer against a backdrop of woods—and salt marsh beyond.

Suzanne, an antiques dealer who loves to cook, spent childhood summers at her grandparents' tourist home, which was just two doors away. After Dick

(Please turn page.)

retired as a major from the New York State Police, he was a security executive for Xerox Corporation. The well-traveled hosts began B&B in 1993. They will suggest "a beach that is difficult to find unless you know the correct dirt road." They know about restaurants, island history, fishing, and beaches—and about sharing their peaceful lifestyle.

Bed and bath: Two first-floor rooms, both with ceiling fan and private bath. Larger room—king bed, en-suite bath with stall shower. Second room—two twin beds, detached tub/shower bath.

Breakfast: Usually 8:30. Egg stratas; Belgian waffles; pancakes; crepes; French toast; or eggs with bacon, ham, or sausage. Homemade breads and muffins. Cinnamon coffee cake. Fresh fruit. Presented on deck or in dining room.

Plus: Fireplaced living room with piano. Tea or cider. Down comforters. Guest refrigerator. Two hammocks under trees.

Mainstay

516/283-4375
579 Hill Street, Southampton, NY 11968   fax 516/287-6240

Host: Elizabeth Main
Location: Residential. On a corner (of Bishops Lane) one-acre lot. One and a half miles from bus stop; ¾ mile from shops. Manhattan is 80 miles.
Open: Year round. Two-night weekend minimum Memorial Day–Labor Day.
Rates: Memorial Day–Labor Day

weekends: shared bath $80–$130 double bed or twin beds, $100–$140 king; private bath $95–$145 twins, $120–$150 double, $125–$165 queen with TV, $150–$215 master suite. Monday–Thursday 20 percent less. Off-season $50–$150. Cot $20 child, $40 adult. MC, Visa.
♣ ♣

In true B&B style, the restored cedar shake 1870s Colonial has Elizabeth's imprint—with a casual flair, with wicker and English country, with iron-and-brass antique beds that can be purchased from a Manhattan shop, and with a big old-fashioned wood-ceilinged kitchen. Elizabeth, a former photo stylist, enjoys "setting a stage and atmosphere" with her own wall murals and simple white curtains. In the large backyard, a wood deck surrounds the 20-by-40-foot black-lined outdoor pool. Elizabeth bought this B&B in 1992. "It's a dream. Where else would you host a 75-year-old lady of important family background who came for three days and stayed for three weeks? B&B guests are wonderful."

In residence: "Blanche, a long-haired cat adored by guests."
Bed and bath: Eight rooms on second and third floors. Two rooms, each with double bed, and a room with two twin beds share a shower bath. One large room with queen bed, window seat, TV, en-suite tub and shower bath. Master suite (one large room that can be combined with a small room) with king bed, wood-burning fireplace, large en-suite bath with tub, no shower. Room with double bed, tub bath. Two third-floor tucked-under-eaves rooms, one with double bed, the other with a king, share a tub/shower bath.
Breakfast: 9–10:30. Homemade muffins, bread. Fruit bowl, cereal, juice, coffee, tea. Buffet in country dining room.

Plus: Off-street parking. Fresh flowers. Down comforters. Suggestions for restaurants and off-the-beaten-path beaches.

> From New York: *"A warm friendly inn. My family loved it. We'll be back. . . . Wonderful. Beautiful and comfortable. Felt right at home. . . . Breakfast was delicious."*

The Old Post House Inn   516/283-1717

136 Main Street, Southampton, NY 11968

Hosts: Cecile and Ed Courville
Location: In the village. One block from Jobs Lane boutiques, Parrish Art Museum, and Southampton Cultural Center. Two doors from Saks Fifth Avenue. Next door to Post House Restaurant. One mile to miles of ocean beaches.
Open: Year round except December 20 through January. In season, two-day weekend minimum; three days on summer holiday weekends.
Rates: Per room. May $85 weekday, $120 weekend, $160 Memorial Day weekend. June $95 weekday, $120 weekend. July–August $120 weekday, $170 weekend. September $85 weekday, $115 weekend. October–April $80 weekday, $90 weekend. $5–$10 one-night surcharge on in-season or holiday weekends. $50 late checkout (between 11 a.m. and 4 p.m.). All major credit cards accepted.
♥ ❖ ✈

Antiques, floral prints, and charm; fireplaces, private baths, and air conditioning. All wrapped up in the fantasy life of an innkeeper surrounded by history in this seaside resort just two hours from Manhattan. The ceiling beams of the common room date back to the 17th century. An archaeological dig in the basement (Ed's idea) indicated that this, the oldest privately owned and occupied English wood frame house in New York State, was part of the Underground Railroad. Now it's listed on the National Register of Historic Places.

When, in 1984, Ed retired early from his AT&T executive position, he and Cecile, a former department store buyer, searched for a New England–type inn where they could work together. What they found was a run-down boardinghouse for summer help. The added-on-to 1684 farmhouse was a guest house when the railroad came to town in 1870. "As you can well imagine, a house at this age did not have a straight wall or a level floor in it. We left them that way, of course," says Ed, a frequent visitor to the local library and historical society and a former president of the Southampton Chamber of Commerce. In addition to hostessing, Cecile has found a new career in interior design.

Bed and bath: On three floors, seven air-conditioned rooms named for "our country's founders and famous local residents." Double or twin beds; all private shower baths.
Breakfast: 9–10:30. Juice, croissant, coffee, tea, decaf. Buffet style in fireplaced common room.
Plus: Wicker-furnished and lattice-enclosed porch. Two contiguous fireplaced living rooms.

1880 Seafield House

2 Seafield Lane, P.O. Box 648
Westhampton Beach, NY 11978

516/288-1559
800/346-3290

Host: Elsie Collins
Location: "In a small village atmosphere" on a quiet lane, two blocks from Main Street shops; 15-minute brisk walk to ocean beach; 90 minutes' ride from Manhattan.
Open: Year round. Two-day minimum. Three-day minimum on holiday weekends.
Rates: Per suite. Memorial Day–Labor Day: two-night weekends $179–$200 per night; three-night weekends $175 per night; weekdays $150–$175 per night; four days, Monday–Thursday, $650; seven days, Friday–Thursday, $1,200. September–May: $100 per suite per night. $60 third or fourth person in suite.
♥ ♨ ❀ ◆ ✈ ⚞

From California: *"Elsie Collins anticipates your every need . . . lovely decor . . . tea always available in library . . . breakfast served artistically."* From Vermont: *"Have traveled in every state except Alaska. Been to England, Europe, and Japan. Accommodations and food that Elsie offers are Number One on my list."* From Michigan: *"All the warm fuzzies made our visit memorable . . . flower arrangements, apples and mints, the thirsty towels, the special shampoo and soap and the New York Times."*

Elsie's low-keyed approach is appreciated by guests who come to her comfortable century-old estate. The dining room features a 1907 Modern Glenwood potbellied stove, "the hurricane hero." Victorian, primitive, English, and Chinese antiques and Oriental rugs all blend into the ambiance of a country retreat that is complete with a 17-by-32-foot swimming pool and an all-weather tennis court. And all year round Elsie, an early childhood educator who retired early, comes up with interesting ideas—Saturday teas, senior citizens' luncheons, local bird-watching places, even family reunions. A B&B since 1982 and featured in *Country Accents* in 1993, 1880 Seafield House is considered a "hidden treasure" by many.

Bed and bath: Three suites, private baths. Two upstairs suites, each with brass double bed and sitting room; one with shower bath, one with claw-footed tub and shower. Third suite, in a rustic converted 100-year-old barn with a floor-to-ceiling window, has a brass double bed, a hi-riser that sleeps one, a shower bath, a microwave oven, a refrigerator, and, for decoration, handmade quilts on rafters.
Breakfast: 9:30–10:30. Freshly squeezed juice. Homemade muffins (rave reviews), breads, and jams. Egg dishes, pancakes, or French toast. Teas, freshly brewed coffee. Barn suite has option of breakfast there or in main house.
Plus: Welcoming beverage. Piano. Fireplaced parlor. Complimentary "take-home goodies that extend the vacation." Off-street parking.

---

*T*hink *of bed and breakfast as a people-to-people concept.*

New York City Area
_____Reservation Services_____

Abode Bed & Breakfast Ltd.
P.O. Box 20022, New York, NY 10021

Phone: 212/472-2000 or (from New York, New Jersey, Connecticut, or Pennsylvania) 800/835-8880. Year round, Monday–Friday 9–5, Saturday 11–2. Answering machine at other times.

Listings: Over 150 hosted and unhosted private residences in New York City area. All accommodations have air conditioning, and most have private baths. All are within a $5 cab ride of the center of Manhattan and have good access to public transportation. Short-term (one to three months) hosted and unhosted housing available at monthly rates.

Reservations: Two-night minimum for all hosts. Advance reservations advisable. Last-minute reservations accepted, according to availability.

Rates: $75–$85 single. $85–$100 double. $90–$300 unhosted studios to three-bedroom apartments. Discounts for extended stays. Deposit required is 25 percent of total stay. Deposit minus a $20 booking fee is refundable if cancellation notice is received at least two weeks prior to scheduled arrival date. Amex.

Shelli Leifer knows B&B from the inside out. After being a host herself for several years, she opened a personalized service, selecting hosts who "put out the welcome mat," meet guests (in both hosted and unhosted arrangements), and maintain clean residences with a warm ambiance.

At Home in New York
P.O. Box 407, New York, NY 10185

Phone: 212/956-3125; outside New York state, 800/NYC-4BNB (692-4262). Weekdays 9:30–5:30, weekends 9:30–noon.

Fax: 212/247-3294.

Listings: 300. Mostly hosted B&Bs in private apartments in large attended buildings as well as in private brownstones and townhouses. Some unhosted pieds-à-terre ranging from studios to three-bedroom flats. Most listings are in Manhattan; others are in Brooklyn, Bronxville, Queens, Roosevelt, Staten Island, and Long Island. For a sample listing of accommodations, send a self-addressed stamped business-size envelope.

Reservations: At least two-week notice suggested for best availability. Minimum two-night stay required by most hosts; some one-night reservations accepted 48 hours before arrival. Three-night minimum for all unhosted accommodations.

(Please turn page.)

Rates: $50–$80 single, $75–$100 double. $80–$260 unhosted apartments. One-night surcharge of $10 for single, $15 for double. Deposit required: 25 percent on four-night (or more) stay, or one night's rate on up to three-night stay. Deposit refunded, minus $25 cancellation fee, if cancellation notice received at least 10 days prior to arrival date; otherwise no refund made. MC, Visa for deposit.

Lois Rooks offers a personalized service that caters to out-of-towners' needs and preferences. Accommodations range from modest with a shared bath to luxury with private bath, maid service, and gourmet breakfast. Her hosts, "screened for cleanliness, convenience, security, and comfort," share their knowledge of the city's cultural events, restaurants, and shopping. (And many have told me that they appreciate the care that goes into appropriate placements.) Lois, a former professional actress and singer, often has free and discounted concert, theater, and museum tickets available to guests.

Bed & Breakfast (& Books)
35 West 92nd Street, New York, NY 10025

Phone: 212/865-8740. Year round, Monday–Friday 10–5.

Listings: 100. Mostly hosted private residences, some unhosted. All are in Manhattan. Most have air conditioning and are near public transportation. Short-term (up to a year) hosted and unhosted housing available. Send self-addressed stamped business-size envelope for directory.

Reservations: Two-night minimum stay.

Rates: $60–$75 single. $75–$85 double. $85–$130 for two in unhosted residences. $15 one-night surcharge. Some weekly rates. Deposit of one night's stay required. With 14 days' notice of cancellation, deposit minus $15 service fee refunded. ♦

"Your hosts become your guides," is the way Judith Goldberg describes her B&Bs. The range of accommodations includes an Upper West Side residence overlooking Central Park, a renovated Victorian brownstone near the Museum of Natural History, and an artist's loft in SoHo.

The service began when Judith's husband, a former bookseller who was also in the travel business, saw the need to offer Manhattan visitors a more personalized style of traveling. Now the list includes many arts-oriented hosts, several of whom have libraries in their homes.

Bed & Breakfast Network of New York
134 West 32nd Street, Suite 602, New York, NY 10001

Phone: 212/645-8134 or 800/900-8134, Monday–Friday 8–6.

Listings: 200. Most are in Manhattan. Some are in Brooklyn and Queens.

Reservations: A few weeks' notice preferred. One-night bookings made a maximum of seven nights before scheduled arrival.

Rates: $50–$70 single. $80–$90 double. $10 one-night surcharge. Unhosted apartments $80–$300. Family, weekly, and monthly rates available. Deposit of 25 percent of entire amount required. For cancellations received at least 10 days before scheduled arrival, deposit less a $20 booking fee is refunded; with less than 10 days' notice, deposit is nonrefundable. Unhosted stays of seven nights or more are nontaxable. ♦

Founded in 1986, this reservation service takes pride in making suitable matches between guest and host. The wide range of B&Bs represented by Mr. Leslie Goldberg includes lofts, brownstones, and high-rise condominiums. Most are near public transportation, shopping, and theaters.

Urban Ventures

38 West 32nd Street, Suite 1412, New York, NY 10001

Phone: 212/594-5650, Monday–Friday 8–5.

Fax: 212/947-9320.

Listings: At least 700. Residences, both hosted and unhosted, are in Manhattan, Brooklyn, and Queens. Short-term housing is available for up to three months.

Reservations: Two to three weeks' advance notice preferred. Will try to accommodate last-minute requests. Two-night minimum stay for hosted listings; three-night minimum for unhosted.

Rates: $55–75 single. $70–$125 double. $125–$160 for three or four people. Under age four, $15 per child. For two-night reservations, $5 per night booking charge. Deposit equal to cost of one night's stay (or credit card number, charged a week before arrival) is required. Deposit less $20 booking fee refunded for cancellations made at least five days before expected arrival date; with less notice, one night's fee is charged. Amex, CB, Diners, Discover, MC, Visa. ♦

This well-established service represents a wide range of accommodations, from quite simple to luxurious; all are inspected. Mary McAulay's staff books you with "achieving New Yorkers, our main stock in trade. They chat and give advice. And for business travelers as well as travelers who feel at home in New York, the apartments with no host offer the privacy of a hotel room combined with the comforts of home. Our apartments, throughout the city, range from studios to three-bedroom, two-bath homes."

——— New York City Area B&Bs ———

B&Bs are located just about everywhere, near any place you want to be. They are in townhouses, brownstones, apartments, penthouses, lofts, and other possible city spaces. Among the hosts are legal secretaries, lawyers, interior designers, social workers, executives, craftspeople, actors, teachers, writers, caterers, antiques shop owners, and scientists. And some (many) places are hostless, entirely for you. Here, as in all major cities, depending on location, parking can be an added expense.

Not always, of course, but often bed and breakfast in New York City can be quite different from any other large city in the country. It is a place where guests may be looking for a particular location at a particular rate and personal interaction may not be the top priority. But among the hundreds of Manhattan hosts there are many interesting, busy, and caring people who have comfortable to luxurious residences that they are happy to share. B&B in New York can be a home-away-from-home arrangment; and when the chemistry is right, some find that they have made new friendships and/or become repeat guests.

Please see pages 96–102 for Long Island B&Bs.

Alexander Hamilton House   914/271-6737
49 Van Wyck Street, Croton-on-Hudson, NY 10520   fax 914/271-3927

Host: Barbara Notarius
Location: In a friendly neighborhood on a cliff with view of Hudson River. A 10-minute walk to the center of town. $3 (2-mile) cab ride to 50-minute train to New York City. Twelve miles from West Point; 35 from midtown Manhattan; 20 minutes to Westchester Corporate Center along I-287. Ten-minute drive to the new Rockefeller Museum in Pocantico Hills.

Open: Year round. Two-night minimum on weekends.
Rates: $75 single, $95 double. With fireplace $75 single, $105 double. Victorian and Library suites $100 single, $130 double, $25 each additional person. Bridal and master suites $250 one night, $200 two or more nights. One-bedroom apartment $75 single, $90 double. Amex, Discover, MC, Visa.
♥ ♨ ♣ ♦ ✖ ✄

Individual phone lines, private baths, color cable TV, and suites—some with five skylights, Jacuzzi, and pink marble fireplace—are all features appreciated by romantics, corporate executives, transferees, and tourists. Since the Notarius family was inspired by a trip to England to open as a home away from home, many changes have been made to the electically furnished Victorian mansion. The latest addition was finished just in time to be featured in a 1994 issue of *Country Inns* magazine. Now B&B has become a full-time occupation for Barbara, a psychologist and world traveler who has authored *Open Your Own Bed and Breakfast*. Guests take walks in nearby woodlands and bird sanctuaries; bicycle (it's hilly); visit Hudson Valley historic houses; swim (right here); and sometimes use the home as a base for touring New York City.

In residence: Brenda, an assistant. Cydney, teenage daughter.
Foreign language spoken: A little French.
Bed and bath: On three floors—seven rooms (three are suites, one with river view), five with wood-burning fireplaces. King, queen, or double bed; all with private bath (two with Jacuzzi, five with shower only), color cable TV, private phone line, air conditioning, ceiling fan. Third-floor bridal suite has king bed, Jacuzzi for two, five skylights, pink marble working fireplace, microwave, refrigerator, entertainment center. One-bedroom apartment.
Breakfast: Flexible timing. Full. With homegrown raspberries, apples, or peaches. Served on poolside patio, in 35-foot sun room, or in bridal suite.
Plus: Air conditioning. Bedroom ceiling fans. Thirty-five-foot in-ground pool, Memorial Day–Labor Day. Free loan of bicycles. Large fireplaced living room with piano. Huge sun porch with VCR and views of orchard and, in winter, river. Transportation provided from train.

Abode Bed & Breakfast Host #77

New York, NY

Location: Upper West Side residential block. Just off Broadway. Across from Dutch church (oldest congregation in this country) with magnificent Tiffany windows. Near neighborhood shops—even a shoemaker; subway and buses; restaurants; Lincoln Center (10-minute walk); Museum of Natural History; internationally famous food emporium Zabar's. One block to Riverside Park, Hudson River, jogging and walking paths.

Reservations: Year round through Abode Bed & Breakfast, page 103.
Rates: $120 single or double. $135 for three people.
♥ ⬛ ✈

Two years in England inspired this popular host, an architect, to convert (rebuild) apartments to private B&Bs that have been decorated with attention to detail. The host or his partner, a writer—they live right here—meets travelers who appreciate the Victorian decor in one and country feeling in the others. (Some returnees want to try them all!) Forgot an umbrella? Need directions? Would you like restaurant suggestions? "I'm always trying new ones," says the host, who has seen some first-timers become "New Yorkoholics."

Bed and bath: Four studios, each with queen bed, new kitchen, and full bath; all have separate entrance off restored oak-paneled, wallpapered, and carpeted hallway. Three are quiet rear locations that have views of trees and gardens of contiguous townhouses: On second floor—high four-poster, reproduction gas chandelier, embossed burgundy paper, wooden Venetian blinds. Third floor—four-poster plus single sofa bed, wood-burning fireplace. Fourth floor—French antique sleigh bed, camelback sofa, French doors leading to terrace gazebo with hanging plants and flower boxes. Panoramic view of church from bay window of third-floor front studio, which has canopied Shaker four-poster plus twin hide-a-bed, rag-rolled walls, original mahogany woodwork, custom armoire made with 19th-century barnboards.

(Please turn page.)

Breakfast: Fruit bowl. Cereals. Milk and half-and-half. Jams. Margarine. Tea. Fresh coffee. Travelers usually buy freshly baked goods at Zabar's (four-block walk) or at bakeries that are open late and/or early.

Plus: Air conditioning, cable TV, private phone with answering machine. All new double-insulated windows. Current *New York* magazine. Maps. "Front stoop for conversations in this friendly neighborhood."

At Home in New York Host #GY-203

New York, NY

Location: On a quiet tree-lined street in the West Village. Minutes' walk to shops, clubs, restaurants, jazz clubs, bookstores, off-Broadway theater in Greenwich Village; 20 minutes to SoHo.
Reservations: September–May

through At Home in New York, page 103.
Rates: Single $50 smaller room, $60 larger room. Double $75. Two rooms, $110 for three; $130 for four guests.
🕎 🛏 ♣ ⌁

The host, an artist, "loves New York, Greenwich Village, and my house." From the stoop of her four-storied brownstone, you might view a sunset or the *QE2* passing along the river. At night, from the garden, you can see the lights of the Empire State Building. Throughout the restored antiques-furnished 1852 Greek Revival are acrylic paintings done by the host, a former interior designer who had a first solo exhibition just about the time this book was released. Now that her children are grown and gone, their rooms have become B&B rooms for guests—"including many Europeans"—who appreciate the hand-drawn map that includes subway stops, the host's favorite restaurants, "and the nicest way to walk to SoHo." Some winter guests take time to enjoy the fireplace in the large living room. And at least one couple has become engaged here.

In residence: One dog and one cat "who play together all day long and then sleep curled up together."
Foreign language spoken: Portuguese.
Bed and bath: Three second-floor rooms (two are air conditioned) share a large modern full bath. Two large rooms with nonworking fireplaces, one with two single beds and one with a queen bed. One smaller room with single bed.
Breakfast: Ready after 7:30. Juice. Muffins, Italian bread, or toast. Hot beverages. Sometimes, cheese or fruit.

At Home in New York Host #UES-89

New York, NY

Location: Upper East Side, low 90s. High up in a modern 24-hour-doorman building. Within four blocks of "museum mile," Madison Avenue, and Central Park. Bus stops in front of this building.
Reservations: Year round through

At Home in New York, page 103.
Rates: Hosted—$60 and $67 single; $75 and $85 double; $30 additional person. Unhosted—$200–$250 per diem, depending on number of guests.
🛏 ⌁

"I miss your Alice in Wonderland Bed & Breakfast," wrote one guest; she appreciated the art, the antique mirrors with cherubs, the old dollhouses, the homey eclectic furnishings (Victorian pieces and Danish too), and the studio of this communications consultant/writer/artist/seamstress. In addition to helping companies create workplaces where people work in harmony, the accommodating host, a longtime Manhattan resident, works in wood sculpture. Today's dream is a loft in SoHo where she would continue meeting travelers, "the greatest people," who appreciate her orientation, maps, and spontaneous city tours.

Bed and bath: Three rooms. Queen bed with private en-suite shower bath. Room with king/twins option and one with double bed share a hall tub/shower bath.
Breakfast: Wonderful variety of breads—cranberry, blueberry, raisin apricot; muffins, apple or orange juice, selection of herbal teas and coffee.
Plus: Air conditioner in every room. Individual heat controls. All-cotton linens. On-site garage, about $18 for 24 hours.

At Home in New York Host #MTW-10
New York, NY

Location: Mid-Manhattan. On a tree-lined block just west of 8th Avenue. Near Carnegie Hall, Broadway theaters, Lincoln Center, Museum of Modern Art.

Reservations: Year round through At Home in New York, page 103.
Rates: $60 single. $80 double.
♣ ✖ ⚰

This couture designer's apartment is in an older building that has an elevator and 24-hour doorman service. Air conditioned and located on the fourth floor with spacious rooms off a long corridor, it is bright and cheerful and has hardwood floors and some interesting antique pieces. In addition to designing for Ralph Lauren, the hostess makes custom formals and wedding gowns. Depending on her schedule, you may have more or less time for "visiting!"

Bed and bath: One room with double bed, single rollaway, radio, and plenty of closet space.
Breakfast: Fruit, juice, homemade fruit bread, cold cereal, hot beverage. (Guests also have light kitchen privileges.)

Urban Ventures Host #HAR111
New York, NY

Location: On the east side. A couple of blocks to center city with its many corporate headquarters, including Citicorp, where there's a theater, church, and frequent noontime performances. Near Bloomingdale's.
Reservations: Year round through Urban Ventures, page 105.
Rates: Studios $100 for two people, $130 for three. One-bedroom apartments $125 for two, $150 for three or four, $165 for five.
♣ ♦

(Please turn page.)

Deceiving! The outside of this six-story 1920s building is not as attractive as the inside. Completely done over, it is furnished with modern pieces. The host, a Southerner, who has decorated the entire building, lives in one of the units and has a first-floor office. A staff keeps everything shipshape, while the the host is your concierge. She welcomes you (until a reasonable hour), shares maps, and has all kinds of helpful information about her adopted city. Because of the number of units, this is a good place for groups as well as others who wish to be based in this area.

Bed and bath: Ten air-conditioned studios (all with queen bed and queen sofa bed) and 10 one-bedroom apartments. All with kitchenettes and full modern baths.
Breakfast: Provide and make your own.

Urban Ventures Host #HEC200
New York, NY

Location: On Park Avenue and 35th Street, near Morgan Library, Macy's, Grand Central Station (also home of art shows and other special events).
Reservations: Year round through Urban Ventures, page 105.
Rates: Unhosted $210 per night. Hosted $95 for two; $35 each additional person (in own bedroom).
♥ ☎ ♦ ✖ ✀

It's light and airy—with a baby grand piano in the contemporary living room, a stunning space that has a glass-roofed greenhouse extension. The Viennese host is a fashion designer who travels frequently between two continents.

Bed and bath: Up a spiral staircase to second-floor guest area with one queen-bedded room and one room with a double sleep sofa and a single bed; one full and one half bath. (First floor has master bedroom, living room, and terrace.)
Breakfast: Informal. Host "provides continental with what you wish."
Plus: Air conditioning.

Urban Ventures Host #EDW100
New York, NY

Location: Active (not quiet). On East 6th Street, in the middle of East Village. Near ethnic restaurants, discount shops, Papp's Theatre.
Reservations: Year round through Urban Ventures, page 105.
Rates: $55 single, $65 for two.
☎ ♦ ✖ ✀

Now that the family has grown, the host, a real estate broker, enjoys sharing her comfortable home (on the 16th floor) and her love of the Lower East Side. Guests are mostly young people—"many Europeans too"—who patronize the inexpensive, interesting restaurants and clubs (several showcase new music and comedy talent) that are open late.

Bed and bath: One room with queen bed shares host's tub/shower bath.
Breakfast: Continental plus. Prepared by host.
Plus: Air conditioning.

Hudson Valley B&Bs

Some Hudson Valley B&Bs are represented by The American Country Collection, page 141.

Cromwell Manor Inn 914/534-7136

Angola Road, Cornwall, NY 12518

Hosts: Dale and Barbara O'Hara
Location: A country estate setting on seven acres with extensive gardens and mountain views. Across from forest preserve (hiking and swimming). Next to working farm (and country store with gifts, frame shop, art gallery) with orchards, goats, and sheep. Five miles north of West Point; close to wineries—four miles to Brotherhood, America's oldest; 75 minutes from downtown Manhattan.
Open: Year round. April–November, two-night weekend minimum; three on holiday weekends. Five-night minimum for West Point plebe week (March) and graduation.
Rates: Suites with Jacuzzi: year round, $250 queen, $220 double. April–November: queen $135, with fireplace $150, double $120. December–March: queen $115, double $95; weekends $115–$150 with fireplace. Cottage rooms $120 winter, $150 summer. Extra person $25. For three or more rooms or nights, 5 percent gratuity. MC, Visa.

♥ ♣ ♦ ✈ ⊬

It's romantic inside and out. It's a spacious columned Greek Revival brick mansion built about 1820 by David Cromwell, a descendant of England's Oliver Cromwell. When Dale "found" it—ask him—in an ice storm, he knew this would be his eighth restoration. Over a 10-year period he matched moldings, replaced modern doors with some made in the 18th and 19th centuries, installed all new baths, used attic boards for kitchen counter tops—and got married! Barbara, who works in the insurance industry, gets credit for the decor, for the baking, for "making the inn [opened in 1993] perfect." Throughout, there are American antiques (grandfather clocks, sailing ship models, beds); marble fireplaces; chandeliers; gilded mirrors; custom-made carpets; and designer fabrics. Outside there are hundreds of blooming shrubs and plants, a goldfish pond, statuary, places to sit, a gazebo, woodlands, lawn, croquet, wildflowers, and stone walls. This property brings together Dale's interests in gardening, architecture, history, travel—and people. Before he attended college, he took a five-year round-the-world trip. In White Plains, New York, Dale had a business for 11 years.

Bed and bath: Fourteen carpeted and air-conditioned rooms with queen- or double-sized bed; all private full baths. Nine rooms (one is handicapped accessible) on first and second floors of manor house. Five in 1764 cottage. Features vary—wood-burning fireplace, Jacuzzi for two, steam room, private entrance, breakfast and sitting areas.
Breakfast: 8:30–10. French toast, apple omelet, or baked egg dish. Baked apples. Fresh fruit. Yogurt. Freshly baked goods. Served at individual tables on veranda or in country breakfast room.

(Please turn page.)

Plus: Sound of roosters crowing in the morning. Fireplaced living room. Tour of inn. Fresh flowers year round. Turndown service. Transportation to/from bus, train, Stewart International Airport. Conference room seats 30.

Point of View

914/294-6259

RR 2, Box 766H, Ridge Road, Campbell Hall, NY 10916   800/294-6259

Hosts: Bill and Elaine Frankle
Location: Quiet and rural with gorgeous views of farmland (250-acre horse farm below) and mountains. Five minutes northeast of Goshen. Within 30 minutes of West Point, spectacular and pastoral sculpture park, crafts and antiques shops, wineries, Stewart International Airport.

Near hiking and skiing. One hour from George Washington Bridge; 80-minute bus ride from Manhattan.
Open: Year round except Christmas eve and day.
Rates: $55 single. $65 double. $10 rollaway. MC, Visa.
✼

This B&B, built in 1992, has "everything"—including central air conditioning and reasonable rates—all designed from Bill's observations during his extensive travel experiences as a paper company executive. When he became a United Methodist pastor, the Frankles sold their large home, built this Cape Cod house with a private bed and breakfast wing, and furnished with a blend of old and new. Now, in addition to meeting business travelers, they host big-city folks who explore the countryside or just want to enjoy the peace of a hammock with a good book. Several newlyweds have returned for their first anniversary. And then there are some guests who go into Manhattan for a day and are happy to return to the bucolic setting.

Elaine is a social caseworker who loves to sing opera. Bill is usually the weekday morning host. As longtime area residents, they can offer a long list of "to do" suggestions.

In residence: Daughter Randi, age 18.
Foreign languages spoken: "A smattering of French, German, Swedish."
Bed and bath: Two second-floor rooms, each with queen bed, en-suite bath with large shower stall, private phone line with voice mail, cable TV, farmland views.
Breakfast: 6:30–9. Juice, coffee, fruit. Pancakes, French toast, or egg dish. Muffins and jam. Served in guests' sitting room by bay window.

Captain Schoonmaker's Bed & Breakfast

RD 2, Box 37, High Falls, NY 12440   914/687-7946

Hosts: Sam and Julia Krieg
Location: On Route 213, a state highway but a country-style road. On sloping land with grass and gardens by a trout stream, waterfall, woodlands. Half a mile from tiny High Falls village. Ten miles south of Kingston; 30 minutes to Hyde Park.

Open: Year round. Two-night minimum on weekends mid-September–Thanksgiving.
Rates: $50 single. $80 shared bath; $90 private bath, or with fireplace October–March.
♥ ✾

Such joie! You don't forget this effervescent grandmother and former elementary school teacher, who cohosts with friendly Sam, a recently retired biology professor. For a huge number of guests, one visit to this B&B is hardly enough; many return several times a year.

Woman's Day magazine, among others, has used the setting for photographs. One guest sent notepaper with a sketch of the inn, which was created by the Krieg family when their children were in college. In 1981 they bought "renovation project #8," the 1760 historically registered stone cottage with its 1800 eyebrow Colonial Greek Revival addition, which was without plumbing, electricity, water, heat, or cosmetics. Within 10 months they opened as a B&B "without fussiness" and filled with quilts, antique toys, stenciling, and collections of Americana. Soon after, the 1810 barn/carriage house was renovated to accommodate more guests. Then came the locktender's house on the Delaware-Hudson Canal, a pleasant half-mile jog or cycle to the sumptuous "expanded family" breakfast table. The last addition: Suites in an 1876 Victorian house.

Bed and bath: Fourteen rooms in four guest houses. Queen, double, or single beds. Some with private bath, canopied bed, working fireplace, private veranda, or porch overlooking stream. Suites have large rooms, canopied beds, carpeted tub and shower baths, private porch. Cots and a cradle available.

Breakfast: In main house for everyone at 9. Poached pear with raspberry sauce and whipped cream; baked apple medley with peaches, almonds, and bananas; or souffles or crepes. Home-baked bread; blueberry-walnut strudel with phyllo; rocky road fudge cake; or lemon-poppyseed cake. Juices, almond mocha coffee. By candlelight in front of original working fireplace.

Plus: Beverages and snacks at 6 p.m. in wicker-furnished solarium. Living room with Hudson Valley Dutch fireplace (6 feet high, 5½ feet wide).

American Country Collection Host #155

Katonah, NY

Location: On four acres of woods, gardens, maple sugarbush. Opposite 100-acre farm. In an upper Westchester County village, part of Bedford township. Two miles down a dirt road (or accessed from a major county road). Three miles from I-684 or Sawmill River Parkway. Near IBM and Pepsico, Caramoor Music Festival (June–August), fine art museums, gardens, historic sites (same period as B&B). Within 3–10 miles of "wonderful variety of restaurants, from very casual to elegant." Fifty miles from center of New York City, "but once you get here, it seems much farther than that."

Reservations: Year round through The American Country Collection, page 141.

Rates: $50 and $65 single. $60 and $80 double.

♥ ♨ ⛵ ⚘ ✈ ✂

One neighbor discovered the area by staying in this 1723 farmhouse, which was renovated—"while maintaining its integrity"—by the hosts in the early 1970s. It has wide-board floors, exposed beams, and eclectic furnishings—"touchable kinds of antiques, comfortable sofas to lounge on, window seat by the kitchen fire."

(Please turn page.)

Warm hospitality and memorable breakfasts are offered by the hosts, an actor whom some guests recognize and his wife, an actress who made homemaking a full-time job when the children were growing up. They delight in sharing their home with many honeymooners, who come here "on their way out of the city," and with business travelers, wedding guests, and people from all over the world who have joined the ranks of discoverers.

In residence: One cat, not allowed in guest rooms.
Foreign languages spoken: French, Greek, Russian.
Bed and bath: Up five steps to master bedroom with double bed, freestanding wood-burning Franklin fireplace/stove, en-suite private tub/shower bath. On third floor, room with double bed and one with two twin beds share tub/shower bath.
Breakfast: Flexible hours. Different every morning of your stay. Waffles, crepes, or pancakes with homemade maple syrup; homemade muffins; fruit; juice; coffee or tea. In kitchen by fire, in formal dining room, or on patio.
Plus: Fireplace in second-floor sitting room. Swimming and trout fishing in pond across the street. Benches and picnic tables.

Rondout Bed & Breakfast

914/331-2369
88 West Chester Street, Kingston, NY 12401   fax 914/331-9049

Hosts: Ralph, Adele, and Donna Calcavecchio
Location: On two acres in an old residential neighborhood. On a hill with views of Catskills. Near Hudson River, antiquing, historic sites, hiking; 25 minutes to Bard College, Vassar, and New Paltz. Ten minutes from New York State Thruway; 20 minutes to Woodstock; 40 to Hunter and Bellayre mountains.

Open: Year round. Two-night minimum on national holiday weekends.
Rates: Private bath, $65 single, $80 double midweek; $70, $85 weekends. Shared bath, $55 single, $65 double midweek; $60, $70 weekends. $10 additional person over age six. Amex, MC, Visa.
♥ ⌂ ⌂ ♣ ♦ ✈ ⊱

> Echoed by many guests: *"A genuine treasure, but guests should be warned: The Calcavecchios are both subject to bursts of enthusiasm. What a delightful weekend. . . . Food, friendliness, comfort. . . . They've got it all. . . . The rooms are fresh, airy, and pretty—and big; the breakfasts are delicious—and big! The house itself is wonderfully pleasant to sit about in, as are the porches and grounds . . . heard crickets at night. . . . An island of charm and peace."*

When theater friends asked the Calcavecchios, both thespians, to accommodate actors in 1985, they started a whole new "pleasurable lifestyle" for the hosts, whose five older children were working or in college. Daughter Donna added her artistic touches and in the early 1990s dovetailed full-time hosting with tutoring at a school for emotionally disturbed adolescents. In 1992 her well-traveled parents and teenage brother, Daniel, returned from two years in England, where Ralph was working for IBM.

Built on a grand scale with a 33-foot living room, a 20-foot dining room, and many big windows, their 1905 Federal Revival house had seen several uses when the Calcavecchios bought it in 1980. Now "loved" once again, it is furnished eclectically, with paintings and prints everywhere. Adele, a teacher, and Ralph, an engineer and pilot, share many sightseeing suggestions, including a "magnificent-in-any-weather" place that they compare to Lake Como in Italy.

In residence: Bruno, "our gentle and beautiful German short-haired pointer."
Bed and bath: Four air-conditioned rooms. On second floor, one very large queen-bedded room with private full bath. On third floor, a full bath is shared by three double-bedded carpeted rooms that have a view of the Catskills.
Breakfast: Usually at 9. Lots of fresh fruit, frittata, pastry, waffles, genuine Irish oatmeal. French toast with hosts' own maple syrup. Endless coffee or tea. Served with crystal and silver in dining room or on porch.
Plus: Fireplaced living room. Wood stove in living room and kitchen. Wicker- and rattan-furnished glassed-in porch. Paneled, gas-fireplaced library. Evening refreshments. Electrically operated player and baby grand pianos. TV. Books. Lawn furniture. Outdoor and indoor games.

American Country Collection Host #182
Montgomery, NY

Location: "Easy for new arrivals to find in the dark." On a side street lined with cherry trees. In the center of a little village with restaurants, antiques shops, and antiques auction (many dealers come) on Tuesdays; 90 minutes from New York City.

Reservations: Year round through The American Country Collection, page 141.
Rates: $85 per room, $20 third person.
♥ ♣ ♦

"It's very difficult to train with horses in Manhattan! Now my teenage son has become a riding instructor and competes as a jumper. While I was an entertainment lawyer for record companies, we had a weekend house, an old schoolhouse that we had redone, in Montgomery. This historic village is 'country'—a very pretty area—without the isolation. You walk to restaurants and little boutiques. Whether you want to go horseback riding, hiking, or skydiving, or to find a movie—or if you're looking for the *Los Angeles Times*—we manage to come up with something! Many business executives have found us too. When we moved to this added-on-to 1790 center hall Colonial in 1991, we polished the wide-board floors and furnished with many major pieces from my mother's home in France. [Three generations are now living in this 22-room house.] Guests feel very much at home here."

Indeed they do. You're welcome in the kitchen at any time. The common room is light and spacious, with sofas, piano, and fireplace. Wherever, conversations can be quite animated and extended.

In residence: One dog—allowed in kitchen only.
Foreign languages spoken: French and Spanish.
Bed and bath: Five large air-conditioned rooms on first and second floors; all with private bath, individual heat control, sitting area. Wood-burning fireplace in one room with king/twins option and in two rooms with queen bed. Two other rooms with queen bed each have a private exterior entrance.

(Please turn page.)

Breakfast: 6:30–11:30; arranged the night before. Juice. Eggs any style, pancakes, or French toast. Bacon. Muffins or croissants. Cereal. Coffee. Served on rear deck, in dining room that has a fireplace and a very large antique French armoire, or (by prior arrangement) in your room.

Plus: From barn, two miles away, opportunities for horseback riding on trails. And boarding (fee charged) for guests' horses.

Mountain Meadows Bed and Breakfast

542 Albany Post Road, New Paltz, NY 12561   **914/255-6144**

Hosts: Corinne D'Andrea and (husband) Arthur Rifenbary
Location: With panoramic mountain backdrop and no immediate neighbors. On side of driveway—hosts' getaway motor home, which "allows us to travel with our two basset hounds." On the road that connects Route 299 with Libertyville. Across from a pheasant preserve. Five minutes from extensive hiking and groomed cross-country ski trails at Lake Mohonk Mountain House and Lake Minnewaska State Park (two beautiful lakes and waterfalls too). Near biking, mountain climbing, swimming, boating, horseback riding, whitewater tubing, golfing, bird-watching, antiquing, wineries. Four and a half miles from Thruway, exit 18.

Open: Year round. Two-night minimum on weekends.
Rates: Per room. $95; $105 attached bath.
♥ ☞ ♣ ✁

From New York: "The rooms are lovely . . . warm wonderful hosts . . . meticulous . . . fine linens . . . beautiful view from sliding glass doors of great room."

"In 1990, it was love at first sight—with deer emerging from the woods in back and with the spectacular panoramic views of the mountain range and Lake Mohonk Mountain House Tower, location of *The Road to Wellville* (released in 1994)." Eighteen months later the entire first floor of this 1968 contemporary house became B&B guest quarters. At IBM, Corinne was an executive secretary. Art, a tool and die maker (now a carpenter), was in production control. Their house is the comfortable kind of place where getaway guests linger at breakfast. They lounge by the pool and enjoy the outdoor hot tub and the recreation room complete with fireplace and professional pool table. One guest calls periodically to "speak" to one of the dogs! Mountain climbers from all over the world appreciate the proximity to "the Gunks." And always—there's the view.

Bed and bath: Three stenciled first-floor rooms. Largest room has king bed, full attached bath. Two with queen bed, shower bath (one en suite, one just outside room).

Breakfast: At guests' convenience until 10:30. Freshly squeezed orange juice. Fresh fruit. Homemade breads and muffins. Strata, omelet, or quiche. Pancakes, waffles, or French toast. Freshly ground coffee or tea. Served in guest kitchen or by the pool.

Plus: Central air conditioning. TV, games, books, puzzles. Badminton, croquet, horseshoes. Patio. Gardens. Fresh flowers and chocolates. Hummingbirds at bird feeders.

Orchard House   914/883-6136

Route 44/55 at Eckert Place, P.O. Box 413, Clintondale, NY 12515

Host: Carol Surovick
Location: On two terraced acres of partially wooded land with extensive flower gardens and a Victorian three-holer painted to match the house. In a tiny village on a two-lane country highway that leads to area orchards. Ten minutes from New York State Thruway (exit 18) and SUNY at New Paltz. Two hours from New York City; one from Albany; 30 minutes to Hyde Park, Vanderbilt mansion, and Culinary Institute of America. Near Shawagunk Mountains and Minnewaska State Park.

Open: Year round. Two-night minimum May–October.

Rates: $85; $95 with balcony.

♥ ⬛ ⁂ ✈ ⊬

> From New York: *"The best choice for 50 miles around! . . . Tasteful, attractive, comfortable, warm feeling. . . . As for breakfasts—superb! . . . Surroundings were quiet, peaceful, and gorgeous . . . able to do morning yoga and tai chi exercises in back."* From Massachusetts: *"Wonderful B&B. . . . Never expected our hostess to be a tourism bureau unto herself. Our mountain hike, winery visit, and restaurant were all selected from her information. . . . Directly across the road is a postcard-size farmhouse complete with pond, ducks, horse, pony, barn, vegetable garden, and rolling hill."*

While Carol was an IBM staff communications specialist, she fell in love with this restored 1866 Queen Anne Victorian. In preparation for her 1992 early retirement—she's now a freelance editor, proofreader [art book], and technical writer—she saw B&B "as an excuse to live in a big beautiful house and decorate it to her heart's content—with needlework [many pieces are her own], art, and antiques," with a European rather than a Victorian touch. Romantics appreciate the room that is complete with enclosed balcony overlooking the plant-filled first-floor solarium. Wedding attendants like to book the entire place. Hikers, and rock climbers too, are among those who thank Carol for doing what she does.

In residence: Two cats, Squeaker and Lizzy.
Bed and bath: Three second-floor queen-bedded rooms. All private baths. One has full bath "down the hall." Other two have small en-suite shower baths.
Breakfast: 9–10. Full, varied menu with juice, fruit, homemade breads and muffins, waffles, French toasts, stratas, or other egg dishes. Served in formal dining room.
Plus: Flowering plants in solarium year round. Bedroom window fans. Front porch rockers. Fresh fruit. Access to nearby pool and golf course.

Can't find a listing for the community you are going to? Check with a reservation service described at the beginning of this chapter. Through the service you may be placed (matched) with a welcoming B&B that is near your destination.

Audrey's Farmhouse B&B   914/895-3440
2188 Brunswyck Road, Wallkill, NY 12589   fax 914/895-8114

Hosts: Don and Audrey Leff
Location: Romantic. Site of many tent weddings. On 35 acres with "golf-course-like" lawns, gardens, panoramic mountain views— "breathtaking scenery that inspires photographers." Ten miles south of New Paltz. Fifteen minutes to Minnewaska Mountain trails, Mohonk, cross-country ski rentals.

Near restaurants, antiques, wineries, hiking, biking. One hour and 45 minutes from Manhattan.
Open: Year round. Two-day minimum on weekends, three-day on holiday weekends.
Rates: $90 shared bath. $100 private bath, $110 suite. $10 third person. MC, Visa.
♥ ⬤ ⁂ ♦ ✂

"How will anyone ever find us?" Don asked Audrey in 1989 when they looked at this restored 1740 farmhouse. Audrey just knew. It's pegged, without a nail. Ceilings are beamed. There are wide-board floors and white plaster walls. Throughout, there's a lifetime collection of country antiques that blends with the Southwestern art acquired during 1980s Colorado living. There are fireplaces. An inviting library. An in-ground swimming pool. And a hostess who has entertained all her life—for her father, who had a freeze-drying corporation; for family; for the six kids' friends. What started in a smaller (New Paltz) house as "a lark" for Audrey, who has worked with relatives of intensive care patients, has become a lifestyle with an enormous extended family. The Leffs' guests (many media professionals) account for what must be one of the highest B&B returnees' rate in the country! On weekends Don, who has parking garages in Manhattan, becomes cohost, part of a team who love doing what they do.

In residence: One "very lovable" Shih Tzu. One golden retriever. Two cats.
Bed and bath: Five rooms; three with private bath. All with feather beds. Private exterior entrance for first-floor suite (pets allowed) with queen bed, large tub and shower bath. Second floor: Double four-poster with private tub and shower bath, wood stove, TV, VCR overlooks pool. Double bed and a single bed, cathedral ceiling, private stall shower bath. In a wing up steep stairs, two smaller double-bedded rooms share a stall shower bath.
Breakfast: 9:30–10. Five-course meal. Crepes, waffles, pancakes, omelets, breakfast meats, vegetable and fruit juices, homemade breads and muffins. Special diets accommodated with advance notice. Served with sterling silver and china by huge fireplace.
Plus: The house is yours as long as you are here. Fresh flowers. Turndown service. Library with electronic piano, TV, VCR, CD, games, lots of books. Window fans in bedrooms. Well-behaved dogs are welcome.

---

*I*s B&B like a hotel?
How many times have you hugged the doorman?

Empty Nest Bed and Breakfast   914/496-9263
357 Lake Road, New Windsor, NY 12553-5935

Hosts: Pat and Dick Coleman
Location: Quiet country road. On 165-acre farm with fields of clover, corn, and hay. Two miles from Stewart International Airport, 12 miles north of West Point. Within 10-minute drive of restaurants, hiking, tennis court, lake swimming, fishing, paddle and rowboats, theaters, antiques shops; 20 minutes to outlets; 60 miles from New York City.
Open: Year round. Two-night minimum on holiday weekends, four for West Point graduation.

Rates: Weekends—larger rooms $65 for two people, $60 for one. Single bed $45, plus high-riser $12. Weekdays—$61 for two, $58 for one. Single bed $43, plus high-riser $10. September, October, and West Point graduation week—$20 more. Ages 2–10 in single room, $20 for one, $30 for two. Over age 10, full room rate. Corporate rates Sunday–Thursday.
♣ ♣ ♣ ♦ ✖ ✄

From New York: *"Treated like long-lost relatives . . . interesting stories attached to the family antiques and farm tools . . . wake up to sound of birds. . . . If there's a heaven, Pat will be appointed to prepare all the breakfasts there . . . countryside is so beautiful."* From Massachusetts: *"Cheerful surroundings . . . a home away from home . . . immaculate . . . like the folk art touches."*

"We built this four-level split-level house when we got married in 1967. That's when Dick moved from the original farmhouse to this house—a matter of 300 feet. . . . Since we phased out the chickens and cows 20 years ago, Dick has been working at United Parcel Service (deliveries to West Point). . . . I worked for a company that provided postpartum care to new mothers. . . . When our daughters went off to college in 1992, we began B&B."

In residence: "Whiskers, our long-haired black cat, should have been named 'Romeo.'"
Bed and bath: Three carpeted rooms, six steps up from common room, share hall tub/shower bath. One room with queen bed and one with double, each with TV. Smaller room has single bed with single high-riser.
Breakfast: At time arranged night before with guests. Weekends—eggs, souffles, French toast, or pancakes. Ham, sausages, bacon. Fresh fruit, homemade muffins, coffee cake. Weekdays—juice, coffee, cereals, homemade muffins or coffee cake. In kitchen (if just two guests), dining room, or large screened porch overlooking countryside.
Plus: Air conditioning in two larger bedrooms and in dining, common, and family rooms. Wood stove in family room. Use of refrigerator. Playground-sized swing set. Summer and fall produce for sale. Transportation to/from bus, train, or ($5 each way) airport.

Guests come from as close as 10 minutes away or from around the world.

Veranda House Bed & Breakfast　　914/876-4133

82 Montgomery Street, Rhinebeck, NY 12572

Hosts: Linda and Ward Stanley
Location: In the village on Route 9, three blocks north of only light in town. On a one-acre corner lot with big backyard. Across from large old house on 10 parklike acres. Walk to fairgrounds, art movie theater, shops, churches. Loop bus goes to Hyde Park. Three miles to Rhinebeck Aerodrome, 15 south to Vassar College and Culinary Institute of America.
Open: Year round. Two-night minimum for October and holiday weekends and for full-house bookings.
Rates: N.Y. state tax included. First floor $100. Second floor $85 king, $95 queen, $90 double, $80 twin beds. Less on weekdays.
♥ ♨ ♣ ✈ ⊁

Linda, an artist and former medical library director, loves to cook. Ward, a college professor and architectural historian, observes that "for an Irish man to sit on the porch with guests and call it work is wonderful!"

While living in Philadelphia with their growing family, they hosted many international visitors. "For years" vacations were in this "beautiful area that has historic homes open to the public, antiques and county fairs, art galleries, hiking. . . . " (Just ask. They have a long list of see-and/or-do suggestions.) In 1993 they bought this c. 1845 Federal house and converted it to a warm, welcoming B&B. It has a comfortable at-home feeling—with Oriental rugs, modern paintings, many plants, and eclectic furnishings. During the academic year Ward continues to teach several days a week at the University of the Arts in Philadelphia.

In residence: Katerina, "our cat, who chose her former domicile, the Edgar Allan Poe House in Philadelphia."
Foreign language spoken: "A little German."
Breakfast: Presented 8–10. Fruit juice. Fresh fruit plate. Blueberry crumb or coffee cake. Onion and sweet red pepper tart; ham/mushroom/zucchini crepe with basil sauce; French toast; or pancakes. Cereal. Bagels and English muffins. (Length? "Became an ad hoc symposium when everyone, as it turned out, was born in the 'thirties.")
Bed and bath: Four rooms, all private en-suite baths. First floor in back wing—queen four-poster, bay window, shower bath. Second floor—queen four-poster, shower bath; double bed, tub/shower bath; king/twins option, shower bath. Cot available.
Plus: Central air conditioning. Fresh flowers year round. Woodburning living room fireplace. Beverages. Saturday 5:30 p.m. social hour. TV/VCR. Lots of books on art and architecture. Wicker-furnished front veranda. Transportation to/from Rhinecliff Amtrak station. Off-street parking.

*B*ed and breakfast gives a sense of place.

The Lakehouse . . . On Golden Pond

Shelley Hill Road, Stanfordville, NY 12581

914/266-8093
800/726-3323

Hosts: Judy and Rich Kohler
Location: Secluded. Without a sign. Overlooking private lake on a 22-acre wooded estate. Six miles east of Rhinebeck. Ninety minutes from New York City. Within 20 minutes' drive of Hudson River mansions, wineries, antiquing, Rhinebeck Aerodrome, restaurants.

Open: Year round. Two-night minimum on weekends, three nights on holidays.
Rates: $175–$195 queen bed. $250 king with working fireplace. $295–$450 with working fireplace, two-person Jacuzzi, private deck, color TV. $50 extra person. Amex.

Talk about getting away from it all. Here on the lake, surrounded by natural beauty, peace and quiet, sunsets, and blue heron and deer, Judy and Rich built their own house. Then Judy was inspired to design a luxurious contemporary bed and breakfast that takes advanatage of this idyllic hillside site. It has cedar exterior, huge redwood walkway, cathedral ceilings, several levels, and plenty of glass. Furnishings are a blend of original art, antiques, and modern pieces. Those decks with views await. Fireplaces do too. Boats tied up at a covered dock can be rowed to a private island. Getaway guests love this very private place. So do executives who come for meetings. And you might recognize it from a 1994 *Country Living* feature, an Avon Christmas catalog, or an Amex publication cover.

Many guests ask Judy how she happened to get into the construction business. "It was a passion, so I just did it." Rich is an engineer who is in the satellite television business.

Bed and bath: Eight rooms with king or queen bed in three buildings—lake house, boathouse, and guest house. All have views (of lake or woods). Some rooms with wood-burning fireplace, TV, refrigerator, private deck. All private full baths, several with two-person Jacuzzi and oversized shower. Rollaway available.
Breakfast: 9–10. Fresh fruit. Homemade sweet breads. Belgian waffles with sauteed apples, pecan-and-cream cheese–stuffed French toast, or omelets. Served in dining room overlooking the lake.
Plus: Central air conditioning. Ceiling fans throughout. Late-afternonoon appetizers and pastries. Swimming right here—off dock.

Many B&Bs that allow smoking restrict it to certain rooms and/or public areas. Although some of those B&Bs that have the ✂ symbol allow smoking on the porch and/or patio, others do not allow smoking anywhere on the property.

Leatherstocking/Central New York
—————— Reservation Service ——————

Bed & Breakfast Leatherstocking
Referral & Reservation Service

P.O. Box 53, Herkimer, NY 13350

Phone: 315/733-0040 or 800/941-BEDS (2337).

Listings: 26, each with two to five guest rooms. Located in central New York, within a 50-mile radius in the Utica-Cooperstown area known as Leatherstocking Country. Includes Bainbridge, Barneveld, Cleveland, Cazenovia, Durhamville, Dolgeville, Fayetteville, Fly Creek, Nelliston, Little Falls, Newport, Ilion, Mohawk, Remsen, Richfield Springs, South Otselic, Utica, Waterville, West Winfield, Vernon. All are listed in a free brochure that includes names, addresses, and phone numbers.

Reservations: "We do our best to accommodate each caller. On special events weekends, we require a minimum of two nights."

Rates: $35–$75 single. $40–$150 double. Some senior citizen and weekly rates available. $5 booking fee (charged only once when two or three reservations made at one time). Credit card number taken to hold the reservation. Payment can then be by check, cash, or, at many, MC or Visa. No credit card charge if cancellation made on or before seven days before expected arrival date.

This is a personalized and unusual service offered by a consortium of 26 private home owners who have a not-for-profit association that sets standards for their members. When you call the service telephone number, Joe Martuscello will listen carefully before making a reservation for you. "Please tell travelers to think far ahead for major college weekends!"

KEY TO SYMBOLS
♥ Lots of honeymooners come here.
♨ Families with children are very welcome. (Please see page xii.)
♨ "Please emphasize that we are a private home, not an inn."
♣ Groups or private parties sometimes book the entire B&B.
♦ Travel agents' commission paid. (Please see page xii.)
✗ Sorry, no guests' pets are allowed.
✗ No smoking inside *or* no smoking at all, even on porches.

Leatherstocking/Central New York
B&Bs

Berry Hill Farm B&B
RD 1, Box 128, Bainbridge, NY 13733

607/967-8745
fax 607/967-8745

Hosts: Jean Fowler and Cecilio Rios
Location: Quiet, secluded hilltop. On winding country road, overlooking miles of rural scenery and woods. Forty-five minutes to downhill ski areas or to Cooperstown. Seven miles from I-88, Bainbridge and Afton exit; 30 from Binghamton, 35 from Oneonta, 2⅓ miles from Route 206.

Open: Year round.
Rates: $50–$60 single. $60–$70 double. Package theme weekends— Valentine, Mexican, horse-drawn foliage tour, winter wonderland, cut-your-own Christmas tree by sleigh. MC, Visa.
♥ ♪ ♠ ❖ ✈

Away from it all. Sunrises. Sunsets. Stargazing. Fresh air. Views. A friendly informal atmosphere. Everywhere, space!—including acres of spectacular gardens. All offered by ex-Brooklynites who came for all these good things in 1982. They restored a large, comfortable 1820s farmhouse, filled it with primitive and European antiques, and opened as a B&B in 1986. Now the perennials, herbs, dryable flowers, and decorative shrubbery attract travelers and special interest groups from miles around. Cis, originally from Mexico, grew up in Texas and earned one master's degree in Oriental studies and another in history. He is a former teacher and Brooklyn antiques shop owner. Jean, a Realtor and former textile designer, makes cloth dolls and braided rugs. Their guests unwind, cross-country ski, ice skate, or go sledding right here. During warmer months they hike, pick berries, enjoy the extensive gardens, swim in the pond here, walk 15 minutes to a beaver pond, and go to auctions. And with advance arrangements they take an old-fashioned horse-drawn buggy or sleigh ride through meadows and woods.

In residence: Outdoor pets: two dogs, several cats.
Foreign languages spoken: Spanish, French, Italian, German, Latin.
Bed and bath: Four second-floor rooms share (robes provided) two full baths. Two queen-bedded rooms; one a double bed; one with two twins.
Breakfast: Until 9. (Very early for hunters.) Juice, cereals, fresh fruit. Eggs; pancakes; French toast with ham, sausage, or bacon; huevos rancheros. Homemade muffins, jellies, jams, sausage/cheese grits; baked herbed garden tomatoes.
Plus: Bedroom ceiling fans. Tea, coffee, juice always available. Flannel sheets. Down comforters. Wraparound porch. Living room wood stove. Grill, picnic table. Some ice-skating and ski equipment (no charge). Plants, flowers, and dried arrangements for sale. Workshops offered too.

From New York: *"A great getaway . . . delicious breakfast . . . wonderful hospitality"*

American Country Collection Host #128
Cooperstown, NY

Location: Quiet. On 7.5 acres with pond, sugarbush, hills and meadows. Across from local airport used by small private planes. Six miles from Cooperstown; 13 to Glimmerglass Opera House.

Reservations: Year round through The American Country Collection, page 141.
Rates: $50 single. $55–$65 double.
🏠 🛏 ♣ ♦ ✈ ⚰

"While my husband came out here to fly, I could see this derelict 17- or 18-room farmhouse across the road. The owner and real estate agent, both flyers, were here. On the spot I arranged to buy this house. With our six daughters grown, we had talked about doing B&B, but had no idea that we would sell our Schenectady house in ten days! We gutted, replumbed and rewired, and decorated eclectically. We have some English pieces—my husband, who is English, was raised in Africa—and I brought back some carpets from Iran."

Both the host, a veterinarian, and his wife, a writer, act in local theater. When the hostess played the role of a narcotics detective, one guest mentioned that he was a narcotics agency director. When she was "stuck" on the mystery she was writing, a guest encouraged her with the information that he had just had a mystery published. "B&B guests are the best!" The feeling is mutual. Joie de vivre. It's here.

Foreign languages spoken: African—Swahili, Chinyanja, Fanagalo—plus Russian, Persian (Farsi), and Spanish.
Bed and bath: Three second-floor rooms. One with a double bed and one with two twins share a tub/shower bath. Room with a double bed has a very large shower bath.
Breakfast: Flexible hours. Usually around 8. Juice, eggs, sausage, homemade blueberry muffins and honey walnut bread, hot beverages. Served in air-conditioned breakfast room.

Ängelholm Bed & Breakfast
14 Elm Street, Cooperstown, NY 13326

607/547-2483
fax 607/547-2309

Hosts: Jan and Fred Reynolds
Location: Among other early-1800s Colonials. Backyard of formal gardens abuts Historic Doubleday Baseball Field. One block from Main Street. Two blocks from National Baseball Hall of Fame. Walk to everything "in one of the most picturesque villages in America."

Open: Year round. Two-night minimum on July–September weekends; three nights on Baseball Hall of Fame (late July) weekend.
Rates: May 15–October 31: larger rooms, $95 twins or queen; smaller, $85 queen or double. Off-season, $65–$75. Singles $5 less. MC, Visa.
♥ ♣ ♦ ✈ ⚰

The place that felt "just like home" to the Reynoldses as guests became their home! "We always wanted to own a larger inn with a restaurant, but as we 'matured' we scaled back to a B&B to have more time with guests." How fortunate for travelers. In 1992, when Fred, six feet six inches of warmth and joy, retired from his international marketing position with IBM, he and just-as-personable Jan, who has considerable experience as a caterer and a real estate broker, purchased this 1805 Federal house. Comfortable furnishings include Oriental rugs, antiques, and rosewood dining room pieces from Hong Kong. The latest conversation piece is the "brighter than rose" pink carpeting—manufactured from recycled materials—installed in the 1994 addition.

Bed and bath: Five second-floor rooms overlook gardens and (one) Doubleday Field; all private tub/shower or shower baths. Three larger rooms—two with queen beds, one with twin beds—have en-suite baths. Smaller rooms—queen bed in one, double in other—have hall bath adjacent to room. **Breakfast:** 8–9:30. Fresh fruit, juice, home-baked breads, muffins, coffee cakes. Bacon, ham, or sausage. Egg souffle, French toast, casserole, or fried Shredded Wheat (Jan's specialty). Served by Fred in formal dining room with fine china and silver. **Plus:** Fireplaces in living room (with upright piano) and library. Tea and snacks, 4–5 p.m. Guest refrigerator. Veranda. Gardens for sitting or picnicking. Off-street parking. Special occasions acknowledged.

Brown-Williams House   607/547-5569
RR 1, Box 337, Cooperstown, NY 13326

Host: Deborah Bathen
Location: On Route 28, one of the main (busy) roads off the Thruway to Cooperstown. On 4½ acres with large lawn; across from a horse farm and 1888 red barn. One mile to Cooperstown trolley system; 1½ miles to village center.
Open: Year round. Three-night minimum on Baseball Hall of Fame weekend (end of July).
Rates: Late June–Labor Day and September/October weekends, $80 double or two twin beds. $90 queen and a twin. $95 two queens. $10 crib or cot. Off season, $15–$20 less; $10 for crib or cot. Year round, $35 three-quarter bed. Discover, MC, Visa.

Everyone comments on the wall finishes—stenciled, sponged, and rag-rolled. At least three guests have videoed the entire B&B in hopes of replicating some of the rooms in their own homes. The living room overstuffed (new) upholstered pieces are so comfortable that some guests fall asleep in them. Other country furnishings are locally purchased antiques. (Sources shared.) All the interior design—and exterior painting, too—has been done by Debbie, a Californian who was a professional interior designer when she lived in Philadelphia. When the house was built in the early 1820s, this was one of the largest cattle farms in the county. Today, wonderful valley views can be seen from the living and dining room picture windows.

In residence: Alexander, age nine. Ian, age six.
Bed and bath: Five rooms. First-floor wing: double bed, walk-in closet, private tub/shower bath in private attached foyer. Second floor: two twin beds, private across-hall tub/shower bath. One queen and one twin bed, private across-hall tub/shower bath. Large room with two queen beds, private

(Please turn page.)

en-suite shower bath. For families, one of these rooms and its private bath is coupled with a small room that has built-in "ship's berth" three-quarter bed. **Breakfast:** 8–10. Buffet with fresh fruit salad, homemade muffins or fruited breads, cereals, juice, coffee, teas, hot cider. Eat at dining room tables for two to four, or in the more intimate room that has French doors leading onto slate patio.

Plus: Big-screen TV in dining room. Guest refrigerator. Afternoon refreshments. Down comforters. Huge play area with playhouse and sandbox.

Creekside Bed & Breakfast   607/547-8203

RD 1, Box 206, Forkshop Road, Cooperstown, NY 13326

Hosts: Fred and Gwen Ermlich
Location: On an old stagecoach route off County Route 26. Surrounded by huge manicured lawns. Bordered by creek (for swimming and fishing). Three miles southwest of Baseball Hall of Fame in Cooperstown center, 12 miles to Glimmerglass Opera.

Open: Year round. Two-day minimum, May–November weekends; three days some holiday weekends, four on Baseball Hall of Fame weekend.

Rates: $70–$85 queen. $125 suite. $99 cottage. $10 additional person, cot, or crib.

♥ ⅱ ⅱ ⁂ ♦ ✗ ⅄

A perfect setting for a Victorian dessert buffet, an opera fund-raiser with Renaissance singers. This Colonial house—discovered by *Country Inns, Travel & Leisure*, cyclists (we were there), and many romantics—has atrium lights that twinkle all year round. Still, in true B&B style, the Ermlichs are the reason that Creekside is so popular. Even though they've been hosting—and making changes—since 1983, Gwen still gets just as excited about house decor as she did about all the opera costumes she used to make for the company she and Fred founded in 1975. During the summer you might see the multifaceted hosts perform—as they have in over 200 productions—at the acclaimed Glimmerglass Opera House built in 1987 on Otsego Lake. Before coming to Cooperstown in 1970, Gwen was an actress and singer in Manhattan. Fred is assistant dean of continuing education at SUNY Oneonta.

In residence: Sons Paul and Patrick during college vacations. Several outdoor cats.

Foreign languages spoken: French and German.

Bed and bath: Three rooms, two suites, and one cottage; all private shower baths. On second floor, two queen-bedded rooms, one with skylight. King-bedded room with 15-foot window overlooking garden, TV. Bridal suite with private entrance, canopied brass queen bed, ceiling fan, 18-by-22-foot living room with crystal chandelier, parquet floor, "Romeo and Juliet balcony." Queen-bedded third-floor suite with dining and sitting area. In three-room cottage, canopied queen bed, shower bath, living room, wet bar, deck. Rollaway and crib available.

Breakfast: 8–9:30. Fred's menu varies daily. Maybe scrambled eggs with dill, souffle, cinnamon French toast, or pancakes. Juice, bacon or ham or sausage, fruit, coffee, tea, hot chocolate. Or "scrumptious low-cholesterol menu." Served in the elegant dining room or on deck at umbrella tables.

Plus: Cable TV/HBO in each room. Two fireplaces in living room. At Christmastime, five decorated trees in the house. Beverages. Refrigerator space. Bedroom ceiling fans. Restaurant suggestions and reservations. Opera and theater tickets.

Litco Farms Bed & Breakfast   607/547-2501
P.O. Box 1048, Cooperstown, NY 13326-1048   fax 607/547-5631

Hosts: Margaret and Jim Wolff
Location: On 70 acres along New York Route 28. Three miles north of Cooperstown.
Open: April–November. Two-night minimum on weekends Memorial Day–Columbus Day.

Rates: $59 single. $79 double. $89 triple. $99 quad family suite. $109 five in suite. Package rates for quilting (workshop) weekends.

♯ ⬤ ⁂ ◆ ✈ ✂

Quilts are everywhere in this homey B&B, one of Cooperstown's originals. Two of the Wolffs' guests, an Italian sculptor and an English art critic who fell in love with the area, "bought a home around the corner and were married by Jim in our living room!"

Some guests walk the dog with Margaret and Jim at sunset to the eight-acre beaver pond, which also has ducks and geese. Some just relax, tour the area, or even get tips about refinishing floors or rearranging furniture every time a new auction treasure is acquired. Always, there's a warm welcome here.

Before Jim became Otsego town justice, he had his own imported lumber and plywood business and helped to organize the local natural food co-op. Margaret, a former home economics teacher and co-owner of a restaurant, is placement director for vocational/technical students. "And my dream has come true with Heartworks, right here at the B&B; it's a unique shop featuring fabrics and quilting supplies as well as handmade quilts that are shipped all over the country and to merry old England and Japan too."

In residence: Ruby, "the wonder dog, who is very tricky."
Bed and bath: Four rooms, all with Margaret's quilts. Two first-floor rooms (one with a double bed; one with two double beds, nonworking fireplace, and cable TV) share a bath. Upstairs suite has one room with a double bed and a double sofa bed, adjoining room with two twin beds, private full bath. Very private carriage house with double bed, bunk beds, shower bath, kitchenette, cable TV.
Breakfast: Usually 8:30 or 9. Whole-grain freshly baked breads, homemade fruit preserves and granola, farm-fresh eggs, bacon, French toast or hotcakes with pure maple syrup, freshly brewed coffee. At tables set with hand-quilted placemats and runners.
Plus: In-ground 20-by-40-foot pool. Hiking, nature, and cross-country ski trails. Deck overlooking meadows. Common room with books, magazines, and board games. Trout fishing. Bedroom ceiling fans. Picnic baskets by advance arrangement.

Thistlebrook   607/547-6093

RD 1, Box 26, Cooperstown, NY 13326

Hosts: Paula and Jim Bugonian
Location: Peaceful. On a country road with gorgeous views of valley; farm fields; meadows; and a natural pond with ducks, herons, red-winged blackbirds, deer in the eve-ning, bullfrogs at night. Three miles from center of town.
Open: May through October. Two-night minimum on weekends.
Rates: $95–$125 per room.
♥ ⁂ ◆ ✈ ⅄

One of a kind. It still looks like an old (1866) red barn from the outside. Inside, there are elegant and comfortable spaces (find your own) on several levels —with soaring ceilings, fluted columns made by Jim, welcoming fireplace, Oriental rugs over carpeting, American and European antique furnishings from several periods. Windows are many-paned, arched, and Gothic (from a local estate).

The Bugonians, who spent eight years renovating a 150-year-old farmhouse, saw the potential that the barn's previous owners had barely begun to realize. In 1992, just two years after this five–guest room B&B opened, it was the "Inn of the Month" feature in *Country Inns*. Subsequently Thistlebrook was placed on the magazine's annual "top 12" list.

Jim was a financial aid director (and golf coach) at a community college before beginning a cabinetry and carpentry business in 1986. Now he does faux finishes on interior walls, floors, and furniture. His passion for gardening and landscaping shows in the lovely lawns and gardens he is developing on the former barn grounds. Here he and Paula, who worked at IBM in the development and test areas before resigning in 1990, continue their joy of entertaining at home in a B&B that Paula calls "my absolute love!" Guests can tell.

In residence: "Kashka, our loving friendly cat; imposes only when asked!"
Bed and bath: Five spacious and very private rooms; all with private in-room full baths. On main floor, twin beds, handicapped accessible. From library, separate stairways to rooms with a queen or a double bed. Master suite on two levels (three steps) has king bed, desk, bath with double shower stall, large tub, large vanity with two sinks, and bidet.
Breakfast: 8:30–9:30. Served in crystal-chandeliered dining room, it typically includes juice, fresh fruit salad, breakfast breads, pancakes, French toast or other hot dishes, cold cereals, granola and yogurt, coffees, teas.
Plus: Intentionally without TV, but plenty of reading material. Bedroom ceiling fans, air conditioning, individual thermostats. Small indoor pool "good for a dip" (summer months only) in sun room overlooking pond and 150 acres of farm fields and meadows. Outdoor deck with chairs and tables for those views.

B&Bs offer the ultimate concierge service.

Summerwood   315/858-2024

P.O. Box 388, 72 East Main Street, Richfield Springs, NY 13439

Hosts: Lona and George Smith
Location: On three acres with huge lawns and trees. On Route 20, midway between Albany and Syracuse; 12 miles from New York State Thruway, exit 30 I-90. Fifteen miles north of Cooperstown, 7 to Glimmerglass Opera.
Open: Year round. Two-night minimum on Baseball Hall of Fame weekend.

Rates: $55–$60 shared bath, $65–$75 private. Rollaway $15 adult, $10 child. Singles $10–$15 less per room. Discount for booking of more than one room, for stays longer than three days, or for families (except July–August). Amex, MC, Visa.
♥ ♫ ⚓ ✿ ✕ ✂

Drive up to the portico, alight from your motor-driven "carriage," and enter the National Register Queen Anne Victorian. There are fireplaces in the parlor as well as in the 25-foot-wide dining room—and, as Lona says, "always, when I'm cooking, a chair at the kitchen table." The house has gables and stained glass windows, but the real hit is the authentic turn-of-the-century carousel horse in the dining room. Just imagine a chamber music retreat with trios, quartets, quintets, and sextets all playing simultaneously in several rooms. It's also a perfect setting for weddings, play readings, family reunions, and opera and theater benefits.

When the Smiths lived on the West Coast, Lona was a microbiologist and George was in computer sales and management. After coming east to take over George's family dairy farms, they bought (in 1984) and redecorated this big 1890 house "with 86 windows and a barn with wainscoting that fascinates many guests." Lona became president of the Glimmerglass Opera and a sought-after caterer. George tours guests through the farm (no cows), on hikes (acres of woods), and up to hilltops with magnificent views.

In residence: Joe, a black Lab, performs tricks (kids love them) with George.
Bed and bath: Five south-facing rooms. Second floor: two queen-bedded rooms (one with air conditioner, other with ceiling fan), each with a private full bath (one has old-fashioned deep tub). Third floor: queen-bedded room and one with two twins share a full hall bath. One room with brass double bed, private tub/shower bath tucked under eaves.
Breakfast: 8–9:30, coffee earlier. Seasonal fruit; quiche; eggs from local farms; bacon, sausage, and ham (also local); homemade coffee cakes, rolls, and muffins; sourdough pancakes with maple syrup and homemade jams. Low-cholesterol or natural-food menus available.
Plus: Air-conditioned first floor. Beverages. Sitting room with TV. Wicker-furnished porches. Yard games. Refrigerator. Ice. Assistance to guests who are seeking ancestors or guided fishing. Picnic lunches ($5–$10). By advance arrangement, opera tickets purchased and dinner ($10–$20) here.

> From New York, Michigan, Maryland, Delaware: *"Outstanding breakfasts. . . . Everything is beautiful, atmosphere is informal, thanks to Lona and George. . . . Treated royally. . . . So large, you hardly know others are there. . . . Five stars."*

Adrianna Bed & Breakfast   315/429-3249
44 Stewart Street, Dolgeville, NY 13329   800/335-4233

Host: Adrianna Naizby
Location: Five minutes from center of "quiet inviting village that has African violet greenhouses, a wildlife sanctuary, Daniel Green slipper outlet, and unusual restaurants and shops." With panoramic views of Adirondacks. Six miles north of New

York State Thruway exit 29A; 28 miles northeast of Utica.
Open: Year round except December 24 and 25.
Rates: Shared bath $45 single, $50 double. Private bath $45 single, $55 double. $10 extra person. MC.
🐾 ✈

> From Pennsylvania: *"The best . . . made me feel like it was my second home."* From Massachusetts: *"Room was charming and comfortable, the area lovely— lots to see . . . gracious hostess . . . breakfast was delicious. What more could we ask?"* From New York: *"Spent our wedding night . . . a gift on our bed and a complimentary bottle of champagne at our restaurant table."* From Massachusetts: *"Adrianna and her accommodations made me feel like queen for a day."*

One guest liked the town so much he moved here. Many find this B&B so appealing that they are inspired to open their own. Adrianna remembers guests in their nineties who were living history, honeymooners who later returned with family, and annual returnees on their way to vacation destinations.

This contemporary house looks smaller from the outside than it is. One of the very first B&Bs in the region, it is the home of a recently retired Dolgeville sixth-grade teacher who is president of the local bed and breakfast association.

In residence: Barney, a friendly cat.
Foreign language spoken: Limited Italian.
Bed and bath: On air-conditioned second floor, three large rooms (only two booked at a time) with double bed, high queen bed, or two twins share a shower bath. Plus first-floor room with canopied double bed, private tub bath, ceiling fan.
Breakfast: Usually 8–10. Orange juice, fresh fruit, or baked apple. Peaches and cream French toast and ham or pancakes and sausage. Pure local maple syrup. Homemade pumpkin bread. Cold cereals always available. Hot beverages. Served by candlelight with crystal and china in dining area.
Plus: Welcoming refreshments. Fireplaced living room with TV, VCR. Piano. Bedroom air conditioners and ceiling fans. Babysitting with prior arrangements. Kitchen privileges. Laundry. Picnic table. Terry robes, toiletries, hair dryers. Guest refrigerator with juices. Books, magazines, newspapers. Original art for sale.

No room at the inn? Ask for a suggestion! In addition to established B&Bs, there may be a new place just down the road.

The Village Green Bed & Breakfast

P.O. Box 169 Guilford, NY 13780

607/895-6211
fax 607/895-6211

Hosts: Doug Taylor and John Lynch
Location: In historic village (population: 150) with no commerce. (Well, there is one one gas pump.) With deer in the meadow and, from neighboring farms, sounds of mooing cows and gobbling wild turkeys. Thirty minutes east of Binghamton; 40 minutes to Hamilton and Colgate colleges and Cooperstown. Within seven miles of canoeing, fishing, and hiking (several state parks). Five-minute walk to 70-acre spring-fed, lifeguarded (in summer) lake.
Open: Year round.
Rates: Per room. $60–$120.
✾ ◆ ✗ ⅄

Clanggg. Cl-aangg. Your (daytime) arrival is often announced to the world as Doug pulls with all his might on the rope of the 36-inch, 450-pound bronze steeple bell. It's in the stone church set in the former town park across the street from this large 1840s Greek Revival house, a landmark complete with pillars, huge windows, and fabulous perennial and herb gardens. Doug bought the facing properties in 1991 and has converted the church to Praiseworthy Antiques—"Heaven knows you'll find it at Praiseworthy"—a shop designed with a Madison Avenue (floor is trompe l'oeil marble) rather than country-style interior. The "never-been-botched" house, less formal than the shop, is a visual treat, filled eclectically with fine antiques—all for sale—and with many Oriental rugs that John acquired during Peace Corps days in Libya, Iran, and Egypt.

Doug, who moved here from a farm, is an illustrator who has done editorial art for dozens of major magazines, including *Time* and *Newsweek* covers. "In this wonderful unspoiled hamlet," he runs his shop "after almost 20 years of buying and selling antiques as a sideline in Manhattan." He also feeds miniature horses, breeds affenpinscher and papillon dogs for shows, and cultivates espalier pear trees as well as hundreds of varieties of lilies and other magnificent flowering plants. John, who managed La Louisiana, a Manhattan restaurant, for 10 years, is full-time B&B host to guests who feel like discoverers.

In residence: Eleven miniature horses; six were pregnant when this book went to press.
Foreign languages spoken: Arabic and Persian.
Bed and bath: All with park view. Four second-floor rooms (could be a suite) with double or twin beds; one new full bath. On first floor, bath and very large custom tile shower; one guest room.
Breakfast: 8–9:30. A picture. Colonial recipes baked by local residents. Huge candlelit buffet arranged by Doug might include gingerbread and raspberry cheese coffee cakes, cranberry and banana date muffins, custard-filled corn bread, and fruit bowl. Always, freshly baked bread—maybe dill or cinnamon. Local goat cheeses. Special diets accommodated with advance notice.
Plus: Three living rooms; two with working fireplaces. Floral arrangements. Window fans in summer. Flannel sheets. Down comforters. House, park, and gardens available for private catered parties of up to 100 people.

Chesham Place

315/894-3552

317 West Main Street, Ilion, NY 13357

Hosts: Bob and Ann Dreizler
Location: On a rise of four wooded acres within walking distance of village center. Halfway between Albany and Syracuse, 1 mile south of I-90. Within 10 miles of Herkimer County, Mohawk Valley, and Utica colleges; about 30 minutes to Hamilton and Colgate colleges and Cooperstown.

Twelve miles to country's highest lift lock and Russian Orthodox monastery; 15 miles to hands-on Musical Museum.
Open: Year round.
Rates: Private bath $45 single, $50 double. Shared bath $5 less. MC, Visa.
♥ 🛏 ⚬⚬⚬ ◆ ✂

This is one of those places to stay that has become the reason to go. It's an elegant 27-room living museum—and very low-key. I felt as if I were visiting friends in their antiques-filled home decorated with many original velvets, silks, Oriental rugs, and extensive collections of china, glass, and books. (What a setting for holiday choral concerts!) History comes alive as the Dreizlers share historical anecdotes, some ghost stories, and fascinating information gathered from the original owner's grandson, who died at age 92 in 1992.

In 1983 Bob was retiring from 40 years as an executive with Aerospace Corporation of Los Angeles. Ann agreed to live in Bob's hometown if they could buy this imposing five-storied 1866 brick Italianate/Second Empire mansion, which had been unoccupied for 17 years. In 1984 the Dreizlers, parents of seven grown children, began by framing paintings found in the tower. They cleaned eight Italian marble fireplaces; put the butcher table used by Bob's grandfather in the kitchen (and installed a new parquet floor); planted hundreds of bulbs; placed the home on the National Register of Historic Places; and saved the gorgeous carriage house.

Chesham Place gives a sense of place—right up to today. Ann works with preschool handicapped children and teaches French flower beading. Bob, a village trustee, is president of the hospital foundation. They both work with hospice; the arts; and historical, preservation, and recreational groups. They make Chesham Place an experience, a find, a joy.

In residence: Francis, a 20-pound indoor tomcat. Mama, a small outdoor cat.
Bed and bath: Four rooms. Room with queen brass bed has sink in room, large shower bath. Honeymooners often request room with century-old double feather bed; working fireplace; hand-painted bird frieze; and attached Venetian tub and shower bath (the county's first) with porcelain ceiling, walls, and floors. One large room has queen canopied bed, single sleigh bed, sink, and fireplace. For families or couples traveling together, two or more rooms may share the Venetian bath.
Breakfast: At guests' convenience. Fresh fruit, juice, egg dish, meat, potatoes, dry cereals. Sometimes waffles, hot oatmeal, or popovers. In kitchen or formal dining room. Ann and Bob join guests.
Plus: Tour includes formal parlor with extraordinary Austrian crystal chandelier. Library with hundreds of first editions that captivate some guests until the wee hours. TV in den and sitting rooms. Down comforters and flannel

sheets. Candy by bedside. Spontaneous evening treats—popcorn, cider, hot chocolate, or root beer floats.

Sunrise Farm   607/847-9380

RD 3, Box 95, New Berlin, NY 13411-9614

Hosts: Janet and Fred Schmelzer
Location: On a 70-acre certified organic farm (plenty of open space). Near antiquing, several state parks for hiking, swimming, boating. Five miles to restaurants, 20 west of

Cooperstown and Oneonta; 70 west of Albany.
Open: Year round.
Rates: $35 single. $50 double. $20 third adult. Children prorated by age.
♠ ♣ ✗ ⅄

The Schmelzers needed more acreage for their "photogenic and friendly" Highland cattle, so in 1993 they moved to this new Cape Cod–style energy-efficient house, modeled after the one they had built in Pine Bush, New York. Here, too, there's a wood stove in the living room and an attached solar greenhouse. Their garden includes garlic and potato cash crops. Guests are welcome to stroll around the farm or in the adjoining woods. In winter, bring cross-country skis. "Only the docile cattle will see you fall down." Many returnees stay here on their way to and from their vacation homes.

Fred was an office supply salesman, and Janet, a native of England, did office work before they "retired" and established their very traditional B&B.

In residence: Two cats, "never in guest room."
Bed and bath: One second-floor paneled room with twins/king bed option, double sofa bed, skylight, ceiling fan, adjoining private shower bath. Crib available.
Breakfast: "We're flexible about time." Eggs with bacon or sausage. Pancakes. Cereals, toast, English muffins, juice, fruit. Home-baked goods, preserves, and "their own" honey. Homegrown berries, when available.
Plus: Evening tea and cookies. Dinner by special arrangement. Lawn chairs. "Here we have spectacular sunrises and sunsets."

> From Maryland: *"Very rural, very quiet, very clean."* From New York: *" . . . a beautiful, tranquil journey in my life and into my dream of simplicity. . . . I took some splendid pictures both mental and camera-made. Heaven was at hand! . . . Wonderful people."* From Maryland: *"Delicious and fresh breakfasts, comfortable and attractive room . . . truly a home away from home (just ask our toddler twins!)."*

Breezy Acres Farm Bed & Breakfast

RD 1, Box 191, Hobart, NY 13788   607/538-9338

Hosts: Joyce and David Barber
Location: On 300 acres of farmland and rolling hills. Five minutes to Scotch Valley ski area, 30 to Windham and Hunter ski areas, 60 to Cooperstown. Two miles south of Stamford.

Open: Year round. Two-night minimum on holiday and special weekends.
Rates: $50–$60 weekdays, $60–$70 weekend. Singles $10 less. $10 child. MC, Visa.
♥ ♣ ✗ ⅄

(Please turn page.)

Guests wrote: *"You feel as if you're visiting friends. . . . So close to country fairs, antiquing, and hiking. . . . Fresh air and scenic views are right there and through the woods. . . . A wealth of knowledge about Delaware County. . . . Joyce keeps track of what she serves, includes our favorites on return visits. . . . A good soak in hot tub [accessible to all] relaxes the body after a day in the outdoors. . . . Enjoyed candlelight on front porch overlooking the mountains. . . . Showed how they make maple syrup [in March and April] from the 8,500 trees they tap. . . . Pampered. . . . Cozy country style . . . the warm hospitality makes the difference."*

A blend of antiques (many family pieces), crafts, and contemporary furnishings are in this impeccably kept 18-room, 150-year-old rambling farmhouse, the Barbers' B&B for 10 years. Guests relax on the wide curved leather sofa in the den. Or by the fieldstone fireplace in the living room. Homegrown blueberries are served in the summer. Ninety varieties of perennials flourish. In the woods there's a private pond for swimming and fishing. Come pick your own pumpkins (from 4,000) in the fall. Cross-country ski and snowshoe here in the winter.

As for the popular hosts: Joyce, a former teacher and professional home economist, is now a voice student and the town's building inspector. For many years Dave continued the family tradition of dairy farming. Now he crop farms, hunts (and guides), taps those maple trees, sells real estate (lots right here), and sometimes builds log houses.

Bed and bath: Three second-floor rooms, all private tub/shower baths. King bed, attached bath. Double bed and daybed, attached bath. Queen-bedded room has adjoining room with queen sofa bed, unattached bath.
Breakfast: 8–9:30. A highlight. Menu changes daily with many "new favorites." Warm homemade muffins—apple/raisin/walnut or chocolate chip. Pumpkin (homegrown) pancakes with "our own" maple syrup, or layered casserole. Juice. Baked apple or fresh fruit. Hot beverages.
Plus: Joyce bakes often. Ping-Pong table. TV in den. Treats in each room. Wicker-furnished porches with rockers. Deck with umbrella table.

All the B&Bs with the ✹ symbol want you to know that they are a private home set up for paying guests, not an inn. Although definitions vary, these private home B&Bs tend to have one to three guest rooms. For the owners—people who enjoy meeting people—B&B is usually a part-time occupation.

---------- **Catskills B&Bs** ----------

The White Pillars Inn
82 Second Street, Deposit, NY 13754

607/467-4191
607/467-4189
fax 607/467-2264

Host: Najla R. Aswad
Location: Quiet. Among 19th-century Federal and Greek Revival homes in a lumbering and farming community (with well-known Americana antiques shop on old Route 17). In the Catskill Mountains; 25 minutes east of Binghamton; under three hours from Manhattan.
Open: Year round.
Rates: Single $65 (corporate rate); double $75 hall bath, $95 en-suite bath. Amex, CB, Diners, Discover, MC, Visa.
♥ ❖ ♦ ✈ ⚞

> From New York: *"An energetic gracious proprietor whose inn is in a sleepy, rural, quaint town . . . but comfortable. The rooms should be featured in* Better Homes and Gardens. *Guests are pampered."*

What a success story! At age 22, Najla decided, after college, after much experience in the food and hotel industries, and after managing a hometown (Binghamton) restaurant, that the nonstandardized world of innkeeping would allow her "to make a huge impact on a small scale." That's when she opened here, in April 1987, in the 1820 Federal Greek Revival house that had been built by the founder of the town. Najla knows how to cook (meals are created and presented here as well as at other sites) and how to bake (wedding cakes, pies, and cookies marketed in the area), and has established an inn apprenticeship program for dreamers. Some guests seek her consultation on their own home decor. Just before she got married (in 1994), Najla redecorated the entire inn and did considerable landscaping too. Always, the inn kitchen seems to be a popular gathering place. Corporate guests love this place. "But weekends belong to the romantics who start breakfast after 10, read the *Times,* and relax."

Bed and bath: Three air-conditioned rooms, all private baths. One with double and twin bed, door shower bath, sofa and love seat, desk. One with a double and a twin bed, tub/shower (hall) bath. One with a king and a twin, en-suite full bath.
Breakfast: 8–10. "As early as 6:30, with coffee at 6, on weekdays." Guests' choice—French Toast Sampler, including Grand Marnier, Flaky, and Pecan Stuffed; overstuffed Greek, vegetarian, or make-your-own omelets; eggs Benedict; baked apple wrapped in pastry with warm caramel sauce. Blended juices, fresh fruit. Homemade muffins. Specialty coffees. In dining room with heirloom Haviland Limoges, gold flatware, Waterford crystal, fresh flowers, and soft jazz. Or brought to your room.
Plus: Central air conditioning. Evening refreshments by the fire. Coffees and teas always available. *New York Times,* plus *Wall Street Journal* and CNN programming on weekdays. Fine toiletries. Pima cotton bath sheets. Bottom-

(Please turn page.)

less cookie jar. Dinner by reservation ($12.95–$26.95 for entrees); with two-day notice, for public too. Directions (in spring) to a spectacular waterfall "where the mist can be seen for half a mile," plus local hiking, bicycling, swimming, canoeing, cross-country skiing.

The Griffin House Bed & Breakfast

RD 1, Box 178, Maple Avenue, Jeffersonville, NY 12748　　**914/482-3371**

Hosts: Irene and Paul Griffin
Location: Surrounded by tall pines on almost two acres on a residential side street in a "step-back-in-time" Catskills village. Across from a church. Quarter mile from restaurants. Ten minutes to Delaware River. Three miles to horse trails. Ten miles from Liberty; 20 from Monticello. Two hours from New York City.
Open: Year round. Two-night minimum on weekends in season or holidays.
Rates: Per room. $75 shared bath, $95 private.
♥ ◀ ❖ ◆ ✈ ⅄

In 1993 PBS came here to film a segment of "Benny Goodman: Adventures in the Kingdom of Swing." Year round, some New Yorkers come for getaways. This Victorian house with chestnut paneling, intricate fretwork, stained glass windows, and herringbone oak floors was occupied by three generations of the original (Scheidell) family until the Griffins bought it in 1990. Each room, furnished with antiques and collectibles, tells a story—the history of the Scheidells; of Fred Waring (of Pennsylvanians fame), who introduced his trumpeter (Paul) to a singer (Irene) he had met in England; and of Paul's father (who lives in nearby Liberty), a trumpeter who played with Jackie Gleason and Benny Goodman. The Lancastrian Room honors Irene's English roots.

The Griffins found "the house of their dreams" in what they knew only as a pass-through town on their way to performances. Irene, who sews her own gowns, still sings in theaters and resorts—and for concerts in her own parlor. The dolls that she dresses, as well as other area-made crafts, are sold in a former chicken coop, the original settlement home.

In residence: Three cats: two 2-year-olds and one 20-year-old.
Bed and bath: Four large second-floor rooms. Antique double bed, private shower bath. Antique brass double bed, ceiling fan, private shower with seats. Room with two antique cannonball twins and one with carved antique double bed share a hall tub/bath (robes provided) plus a downstairs half bath.
Breakfast: Around 9. Juice. Fresh fruit. Cereals. Homemade muffins and preserves. Egg strata or oven-baked French toast with fruit; sausage or bacon. Tea. Gourmet coffees.
Plus: Grand piano. Fireplaced parlor and receiving room. Library with bay window. Beverages. Turndown service. Indoor or garden weddings, dinner, and catering services arranged.

The Rolling Marble Guest House 914/887-6016

P.O. Box 33, Long Eddy, NY 12760-0033

Hosts: Karen Gibbons and Peter Reich
Location: "On an acre and a half along the shore of the wild and scenic Upper Delaware River, which goes on forever." Off Route 97 in a little hamlet with historical society, freight trains passing through a couple of times a day, nearby antiquing.

Twelve miles north of Callicoon, "the dining capital of the Delaware"; 100 miles northwest of New York City.
Open: Memorial Day weekend through October.
Rates: $50 single. $70 double, $10 cot. MC, Visa.
♥ ⬛ ⁂ ✗ ⸸

> From New York: "*Great place and wonderful people . . . easygoing spirit. . . . Feel as if you're in another time . . . attention to detail . . . wraparound gingerbread porches . . . beautiful grounds with breathtaking views . . . a family canine born in Brooklyn by chance but living in God's country by choice . . . flowers . . . clean air . . . peace . . . romantic walks . . . homemade and homegrown food . . . homemade chocolate chip cookies atop the 1930s white-enameled refrigerator . . . the perfect hideaway. . . . Felt rejuvenated. . . . Like being at Grandmother's house in the country. . . . The closest you will come to unconditional love of life here on Earth. . . . P.S. Ask to see album of restoration process.*"

Urban dwellers are passionate about the hosts and their home, a five-year restoration done by Karen, a sculptor and painter, and Peter, an industrial designer. Most guests find no reason to leave—except for a 12-minute ride to dinner. Although first-timers inquire about canoeing, hiking, and horseback riding (all available), they often just enjoy the backyard, birds in the mulberry, the porches with river view, wading and swimming from the stone beach. As Peter says, "It's why we are here!"

In 1985, "by luck," Karen and Peter found this "used and abused" Italianate Victorian built by a local lumberman in 1888. Opened in 1989 as a B&B, it has a grand staircase, French doors, tall windows, curved walls, wainscoting, and—outside—flower and vegetable gardens, fruit trees, and paths through the woods to the river.

In residence: Son Luke and daughter Skylar, two-year-old twins, often "official greeters." Hector is a friendly blond shepherd mutt; Ruth, a shy black cat.
Bed and bath: Four second-floor rooms with queen or double bed share one full and one half bath upstairs and one full (with hand-held shower) downstairs bath.
Breakfast: 8:30–11. Buffet style. Homemade breads—French, oatmeal, zucchini, pumpkin. Muffins with homegrown cherries, berries, peaches. Tart apple or potato and cheese quiche. Fresh fruits, juices, cheeses. All kept warm until you get to it in upstairs common room that has antique refrigerator and outdoor deck.
Plus: Wood stove in living room. Intentionally without TV. Beach chairs to take to river. Lawn games.

The Eggery Inn

County Road 16, Tannersville, NY 12485

518/589-5363
800/785-5364
fax 518/589-5774

Hosts: Abe and Julie Abramczyk
Location: At 2,200-foot elevation; minutes to Hunter (snowmaking and innovative summer festival), Cortina Valley, and Windham alpine ski areas, and to hiking trails in Catskill Forest Preserve; 1½ miles from the village. Forty miles south of Albany; 14 northwest of I-87; 18 miles north of Woodstock; 125 from Manhattan.
Open: Year round. Two-night minimum on winter, summer, and fall weekends; three nights on holiday weekends. No meals served in April, early May, or early November.
Rates: Midweek $55–$65 single, $75–$85 double. Weekend $90–$110 per room. Additional adult $20 midweek, $25–$30 weekends. Holiday rates a little higher. Family rates when children sleep in adults' room. Amex, MC, Visa.
❖ ◆ ✈

The idea of having a ski slope in their backyard is what attracted two Long Island health care administrators (who are also jazz fans) to the then 23-room summer lodging house in 1979. "We landscaped. We refinished wainscoting, added baths and antique finds. We have redecorated several times over! And still we make changes. The parlor has a wood-burning Franklin stove, an antique player piano, Mission oak furniture—and recently added French doors (great views!) that lead to the wraparound porch. In the dining room there's a gas fireplace and picture windows that face the mountain range. This is the casual, friendly country inn we hoped to have."

In residence: Two cats, Tootsie and BoBo, "unavailable for home-taking." Babe is a black Labrador.
Bed and bath: Fifteen rooms; six rooms are handicapped accessible. All private baths: most are shower only, some are tub/shower baths. Queen, one double, two double beds, or a double and a twin bed. Cot available.
Breakfast: About 8:30. (On full-house days, 8–11.) Juice, fruit, hot and cold cereals, local jams and maple syrup, coffee, herbal teas, and hot cocoa. Eggs or omelets, French toast or pancakes, bacon, sausage, home fries. Plus heart-healthy selections.
Plus: Second- and third-floor rooms are air conditioned. Parlor games. Cable TV and table fans in each guest room. Wraparound porch. Ceiling fans in living and dining rooms. Gas fireplace in dining room. Dinner by prior arrangement for groups, family reunions, small weddings. Small fully licensed bar (for guests only) faces Hunter Mountain slopes.

From New York City: *"Greeted with warmth and care. Serene at night. Huge delicious hot breakfasts. Great dining and excursion suggestions. Two thumbs up!"*

---

*H*eard in many B&Bs: *"Most guests are surprised at all our area has to offer."*

Haus Elissa Bed & Breakfast   914/657-6277

P.O. Box 95, West Shokan, NY 12494-0095

Hosts: Helen and Gretchen Behl
Location: In a small Catskills village across the road from Ashokan Reservoir. Bordered on three sides by forests. Twenty minutes to Woodstock, 30 to Kingston, "5–30 to a veritable United Nations of restaurants," 30 to Hunter and Belleayre skiing, 10 to tubing. Two hours from Manhattan.

Open: February–December. Two-night minimum required over holidays, preferred throughout October. **Rates:** Per room. $55 or $60 shared bath. $80 private bath. $5 less for shared bath bookings made at least two weeks in advance.
♦ ✗

> From New York: *"Beautiful breakfast was almost too beautiful to eat, but I managed. . . . Genuine friendliness made my solo stay relaxing. . . . Beautiful sky without light pollution. Extensive file on restaurants . . . excellent printed directions to various hikes and towns . . . impeccably clean . . . homey, welcoming . . . accommodated special diet . . . even though house is small, plenty of privacy."* From California: *"A glimpse of deer [and bald eagles too] . . . homemade German pastries that still make our mouths water whenever they come to mind."*

Those excerpts are from a stack of mail from guests who enjoyed this almost-century-old home, brought back to life by Helen (called "Mom" by many guests), who was a USO director, and her daughter, Gretchen, a railway fan and former librarian. They decorated with local and German themes and their own handwork and opened as a B&B in 1988. Gemutlichkeit. It's here.

In residence: Katrina and Imp, "feline hostesses."
Foreign languages spoken: Fluent German; a little Dutch and French.
Bed and bath: Two second-floor rooms, each with queen bed and sloping ceilings, share hall bath with tub and Euro-style adjustable wall mount shower. Private bath arranged if room booked at least two weeks in advance.
Breakfast: Usually at 9. Home-baked German coffee cakes and pastries. In dining room or on enclosed back sun porch overlooking back garden, spruces, wildlife.
Plus: Spinet piano. Ice water carafe and homemade German cookies in each room. Window fans. Three-minute walk to town pool. (Popular) self-guided tours.

Mount Tremper Inn   914/688-5329

P.O. Box 51, Route 212 and Wittenberg Road, Mount Tremper, NY 12457

Hosts: Lou Caselli and Peter LaScala
Location: In Catskill Mountain Forest Preserve, 1.5 miles to new (1995) Catskill Mountain Interpretive Center; 20 miles west of Kingston; 8 miles west of Woodstock. Across from one well-known French restaurant, near others.

Open: Year round. Two-night minimum on weekends, three nights on holiday weekends. Reservations requested.
Rates: $65 shared bath. $80 private bath. $95 suite. MC, Visa.
♥ ♦ ⁂ ✗

(Please turn page.)

Discovered! By dreamers in 1984. And since by the *New York Times, Ski* magazine, *Victorian Homes,* and the *New York Post.* Now—with velvet parlor walls, French lace curtains, and ornate prismed lamps—it is just what the two New Yorkers, Lou, a former marketing coordinator, and Peter, a fabric importer, envisioned while they collected museum-quality antiques—everything from armoires to bedsteads—for eight years. They found the 1850 23-room summer guest house, last used as an orphanage, all boarded up and in need of everything. In five and a half months, the two men did everything all themselves. Ever since, they have been pampering guests. The innkeepers, too, love this business.

Bed and bath: Twelve rooms (furnished more simply than common rooms); every one with a sink. Private tub bath for first-floor suite that has two double beds. Private shower bath for first-floor room with two twin beds. Ten second-floor rooms (each about 10 by 12 feet) with a double or twin beds share three full hall baths.

Breakfast: 8–10. Juice, cereals (including homemade granola), "their own" baked quick breads, baked eggs with cheese and vegetable, hot beverages. Buffet style with crystal and silver in elegant dining room with classical music playing. On veranda in summer.

Plus: Bluestone fireplace in grand parlor. Full game room and library. An old music box that plays beautifully; an old organ that plays reluctantly. Croquet, badminton, shuffleboard.

> From Connecticut: *"A lovely, quiet, restful country location. Owners hospitable . . . well-deserved pride in authentic Victorian ambiance they created."* From New York: *"Breakfast was superb. Room was comfortable and homey."*

---

*U*nless *otherwise stated, rates in this book are per room for two and include breakfast in addition to all the amenities listed in "Plus."*

Albany Area to Lake George
Reservation Service

The American Country Collection

4 Greenwood Lane, Delmar, NY 12054

Phone: 518/439-7001, Monday–Friday 10–5.

Fax: 518/439-4301.

Listings: Over 120. Mostly hosted private residences; many inns and some unhosted residences and cottages. Many on the National Register. Communities represented include all of eastern New York in the Albany/Saratoga, Hudson Valley (upper and lower), Catskill, Central Leatherstocking (west to Utica, Syracuse, and Binghamton), Adirondack, Lake George, Potsdam, and St. Lawrence River Valley regions. In New England—throughout Vermont and Massachusetts and in northern New Hampshire. Also—several B&Bs on St. Thomas, Virgin Islands. Directory, 112 illustrated pages, $7.25.

Reservations: Two weeks in advance preferred. Last-minute accepted when possible. During busy seasons, some B&Bs have a two- or three-day minimum.

Rates: $35–$75 single, $40–$130+ double. Weekly and family rates at some locations. Senior citizen discounts for multinight weekday stays, excluding foliage season and Saratoga in August. Deposit of one night's lodging or one-half of total stay required, whichever is greater. During Saratoga racing season, foliage season in Vermont, and some holiday or college weekends, deposit will equal entire stay. Deposit refunded less a $20 service fee if reservation is cancelled no less than 14 days (30 days August–October) prior to scheduled arrival; for later cancellations, same refund made if room is filled. Administration charge $5–$10 on first booking; none for any bookings within next six months. Amex, MC, Visa. ◆

"When a guest walks in and says, 'This is just the way The American Country Collection described it,' we know we have done our job well," says Arthur Copeland, a reservation service owner whose inspection includes mattress testing. As one who lists customer service and satisfaction as top priorities, he selects hosts who present homemade foods, know their area, and are attentive to guests' needs while being aware of their desire for privacy.

Plus: "Ski 'n' B&B," romance packages, and short-term (up to several months) hosted and unhosted housing available. Pickup at transportation points provided by some hosts. Gift certificates available.

_ Albany Area to Lake George B&Bs _

American Country Collection Host #097
Albany, NY

Location: In residential area on a main street with bus transportation in every direction. Within two blocks of movies, restaurants, library. Minutes' ride to colleges, state office buildings. Fifteen minutes from airport. Two miles from New York State Thruway.

Reservations: Year round through The American Country Collection, page 141.
Rates: Shared bath $49 single, $64 double. Private bath $64 single, $79 double. $15 third person.
♥ ⏴ ♣ ♦ ✈ ✂

After staying at a Vermont B&B, the host, a nurse administrator, returned to look for property that would be her very own B&B. She found this "grand old house," which is now very Victorian inside—with many antiques and lots of lace and flowery prints. From auctions and estate sales came a china cabinet, a side server, iron-and-brass beds, oak dressers. "Now that I am all furnished, buys are limited to wineglasses and candlesticks!" Guests comment on the hominess, the feeling of what many call "Grandmother's house."

Bed and bath: Five second-floor rooms; four are air conditioned. All double beds; two with single bed also. Two rooms with private baths; one has jet tub/shower combination; other is a shower bath. Three rooms share a tub/shower bath and shower bath.
Breakfast: 9–10 weekends, earlier on weekdays. Juice. Fruit cup. Bagels, muffins, rolls. Cereals. Hot beverages.
Plus: Air conditioning and phone in each guest room. Fireplaced living and dining rooms. Special occasions acknowledged. TV in living room. Wicker-furnished front porch. Back porch with swing. Off-street parking.

> Guests wrote: *"We loved the Victorian atmosphere . . . I would recommend it for both personal and business trips. . . . A wonderful hostess."*

Hilltop Cottage B&B   518/644-2492
P.O. Box 186, 6883 Lakeshore Drive, Bolton Landing, NY 12814

Hosts: Anita and Charlie Richards
Location: Quiet. Eastern Adirondack region, a half mile from village center on Route 9N. On two acres across the road from Lake George. Minutes from beaches, marinas, and the Sagamore luxury resort hotel.

Eight miles from I-87 exit 22.
Open: Year round.
Rates: Shared bath $40 single, $50 double. Private bath $60. Extra person $10.
⏴ ⏴ ♣ ✈ ✂

> From Pennsylvania: *"Make you feel like part of the family . . . share wealth of information about this charming area . . . a breakfast beyond compare."* From New York: *"A charming comfortable home . . . away from touristy area—yet walking distance to swimming, restaurants, and town. . . . Remarkable ability to*

be around when we needed something, out of sight when we wanted quiet and privacy. "

The retired educators—Charlie was a guidance counselor and Anita taught German—appreciate the cycling, hiking, and cross-country ski possibilities here. They acquired this house in 1985, redecorated and updated, and opened as a B&B in 1986. Pictures reflect the estate area as it once was and the hosts' German background.

Anita had lived here with her family from the age of 8 until she was 25; at that time, this was the caretaker's house belonging to one of the estates along Millionaires' Row. (Anita's parents ran this house as a tourist home from 1950 to 1980.) The Richardses' favorite little-known place is the Marcella Sembrich Opera Museum (open summers) just 150 yards down the road. Because Anita is now executive director, out-of-season guests, too, often have the opportunity to see the memorabilia from the golden age of opera and to have a guided tour of the parklike grounds bordering the lake.

In residence: Max the dog and cats Toby and Mietze "live mostly outdoors."
Foreign language spoken: Anita is fluent in German.
Bed and bath: Three second-floor rooms. One room has a queen and a single daybed, private shower bath. Two rooms share a bath with shower; one has a queen bed, the other two twin beds. Family bath available on first floor.
Breakfast: 8–9:30. Fruits, homemade breads and coffee cakes, jams, jellies, plus standard fare, if requested; but Anita prefers to offer quiches, sausage-egg-cheese bake, German apple-and-potato pancakes, or French toast with locally produced maple syrup. In dining room or kitchen; or on screened porch shaded by lush Dutchman's-pipe vines.
Plus: Piano. Picnic table. Lawn chairs. Ample parking for boat trailers and RVs. Bedroom ceiling fans. Wood stove in living room.

The Lamplight Inn Bed & Breakfast

2129 Lake Avenue, P.O. Box 70   **518/696-5294**
Lake Luzerne, NY 12846-0070   **800/262-4668**

Hosts: Gene and Linda Merlino
Location: On Route 9N, surrounded by lawn and tall pines. Half a block to Lake Luzerne (swimming; winter carnival). Minutes to antiques shops, restaurants, outlets, horseback riding (year round), two-hour hiking trail to mountaintop, hayrides, snowmobiles (tours and trails), skiing. Ten miles from Lake George village; 17 north of Saratoga.
Open: Year round except Christmas Eve and Christmas Day. Three-

night minimum on holiday weekends and in Saratoga Race Course season; two nights on other special events weekends.
Rates: May–July and September–October $110–$125 weekends, $80–$95 weekdays. November–April $80–$95 weekends, $75–$90 weekdays. August (Saratoga Race Course season) $125–$140 weekends, $95–$110 weekdays. $25 third person. Dinner packages. Amex, MC, Visa.
♥ ⁂ ◆ ✈

From New Jersey and Massachusetts: *"I never wanted to leave! . . . Even though our room was one of the least expensive, it was nicely furnished with*

(Please turn page.)

*antiques and quilts and had a skylight that opened. . . . Extremely clean . . .
amenities galore. . . . Plentiful, absolutely delicious, beautifully presented breakfasts. . . . Although on a main road, has a quiet, peaceful ambiance. . . . We were
so impressed with the innkeepers and the inn that we returned with eight couples."*

Some whim of a purchase in 1984! A Great Room with 12-foot beamed
ceiling and chestnut wainscoting. A keyhole staircase also crafted in England.
Back-to-back fireplaces. Eight-foot doors that lead out to a wraparound porch
and lawns. And one bathroom (then). By 1993 this inn was the focus of seven
pages in *Country Inns*. In New Jersey Gene, an electrician, carpenter, and
plumber, was manager of a textile engraving business. Linda, the "comfortable Victorian" antiques expert/decorator/seamstress, was a textile artist.
Since restoring the massive Victorian that had been built by a wealthy
lumberman in 1890 as a summer Adirondack retreat, the Merlinos have
added rooms, baths, and fireplaces. And a long list of enthusiastic fans.

In residence: Never upstairs: Toto, a husky/shepherd with an almost-famous howl heard if Merlinos aren't nearby.
Bed and bath: Ten centrally air-conditioned second-floor rooms; five with
gas fireplaces. All with individual heat thermostat. All private baths; one with
tub and shower, others shower only; eight en suite, two across hall (robes
provided). Queen (five are canopied), double, or double and a twin bed.
Rollaway available.
Breakfast: 8:30–9:30. A highlight. Begin with buffet of homemade granola,
fruit, cake or muffins. Gene's entree repertoire includes crepes, Belgian
waffles, French toast, three-egg omelets, home fries and sausage; served by
Linda in sun porch dining room with mountain view.
Plus: Ceiling fans in bedrooms and Great Room. Candy. Guest refrigerator.
Perennial garden. Croquet. Badminton. Wicker-furnished wraparound porch
with swing. Hammock suspended from pine trees. Flannel sheets. Picnic
baskets. Reservations for you-name-it. March candlelit dinners. Linda's granola for sale. Wine and beer license.

American Country Collection Host #105

Saratoga Springs, NY

Location: Quiet and rural, yet just
2 miles (five minutes) from center of
town. Off a main highway, onto a
side street, through a residential
neighborhood and onto these ten
acres with woods and hayfields.

Reservations: Year round through
The American Country Collection,
page 141.
Rates: $100 single or double.
♥ ⛵ ♣ ✈

Walk or cross-country ski in the hay fields. Visit the goats; bottle feed them
in the spring. (Flat track time is the only season when it's difficult to book
children here.) Return to the big country kitchen with its wood-burning
stove, hot mulled cider, and home-baked goodies. This is home—a new/old
home, according to the hosts, who, 20 years ago, bought the abandoned 1840
farmhouse that needed everything. The kitchens and baths are modern.
Furnishings are mostly Victorian. "With the kids and both sets of grandparents, we had a full house." Ten years later they retired and became full-time

organic farmers, B&B hosts, heart-healthy gourmet cook (the hostess), and quartet musician (the host, who has played for well-known names such as Barry Manilow and Bob Hope). This immaculate B&B is casual, friendly, and very popular.

In residence: In barn, Nubian and French Alpine goats; some kittens.
Bed and bath: Seven large air-conditioned rooms; all private baths, three with tubs. First-floor handicapped-accessible room with queen bed, shower bath, private deck. Third-floor artist's garret has king bed, TV. Other rooms have king bed (built into the room), king/twins option, canopied queen, or double plus a single.
Breakfast: 8–10. Repertoire includes individual platters with five melon varieties, chocolate-dipped strawberries, fresh fig garnishes. Individual breakfast souffles, no-fat cup-shaped hash brown potato tarts stuffed with fresh vegetables. Chocolates crepes stuffed with fresh strawberries and cream. Apple strudel for dessert.
Plus: Hot tub in glassed-in Florida Room. Balloons on four-poster bed for newlyweds. Guests' refrigerator. TV in living room.

Saratoga Bed and Breakfast   518/584-0920
434 Church Street, Saratoga Springs, NY 12866   **800/584-0920**

Hosts: Noel and Kathleen Smith
Location: On a main road with rural characteristics on the outskirts of town. Within two miles of Saratoga Performing Arts Center, racetrack, shops; 200 yards to acclaimed restaurant. On seven acres with tall trees, lawn, gardens, and three buildings "including motel that came with the farmhouse." Near country lane for walkers and joggers.

Open: Year round. Two-night minimum on most weekends.
Rates: Farmhouse $65–$95; $75 June and July, $85–$135 racing season weekends. 1850 House suites $100–$135; $150–$210 racing season. Winter and arts center packages. Amex, Discover, MC, Visa.

Zest! Love for "this fabulous town." For guests (lots from Ireland and Manhattan). For family (you'll probably meet relatives). For food. And for keeping up with the times.

"Whatever has become of this fine native that she wants to take in roomers?" wondered town fathers in 1984 when Kathleen and Noel, local restaurateurs, decided to open the town's first B&B in an 1860 farmhouse. In 1991 the Smiths—who still travel to Ireland several times a year—added a tower, private baths, and some fireplaces. They also bought the adjacent 1850 Federal brick house for more upscale accommodations. Noel has a degree in hotel administration and is chef extraordinaire. Kathleen, "the social engineer," sometimes takes guests on tours that focus on architecture, culture, and history complete with stories of who married whom 40 years ago.

In residence: Daughter Ann, age 16. Bates, a 100-pound yellow Labrador, "the best dog in America." Sam is Bates's cat.
Foreign language spoken: Canadian French.

(Please turn page.)

Bed and bath: Eight air-conditioned rooms; all private baths. In Farm-house—four second-floor rooms with queen or double bed; two with working gas-log fireplace. In 1850 House—four suites (king bed in most) with gas-log fireplace, remote-control TV, private phone; one (very private) has two queen beds, two love seats, claw-footed tub and shower in bath.
Breakfast: 8:30–10. "A party." Juice. Fruit course. Blueberry-walnut pancakes or ratatouille omelets, Irish scones or corn muffins.
Plus: "Almost any request fulfilled." Upright piano in farmhouse. Babysitting. Guest refrigerator. Fresh flowers. Bathrobes. Transportation to/from local airport, train and bus stations; taxi is $3 anywhere in town.

The Six Sisters Bed and Breakfast

149 Union Avenue   **518/583-1173**
Saratoga Springs, NY 12866-3518   fax 518/587-2470

Hosts: Kate Benton and Steve Ramirez
Location: Across from racetrack and National Museum of Racing. Walk to downtown shopping, antiques, museums, restaurants.
Open: Year round. Two- to four-night minimum in racing season. Three nights during special events.

Rates: November–March $60–$80. April–mid-July and September–October $85–$100. Racing season mid-July–August $195–$225. Extra person $20. Discounts to seniors and business travelers, and for extended stays. Package rates with The Crystal Spa or Performing Arts Center.
♥ ⬛ ♣ ♦ ✖ ⚰

From New Jersey: *"The best part is when Kate opens the door and says, 'Welcome home'. . . . great home-away-from-home atmosphere . . . innkeepers sensitive to guests' needs. . . . Used to go out for brunch in Saratoga before we found the Six Sisters . . . coffee and fruit available when we go out for early golf. . . . Watch the action from porch rockers with tasty snacks served."*

The Victorian "built around 1880 with scallop-edged roof and basket weave porch added about 20 years later" was just what Kate was dreaming about in 1989 when she decided to return to her roots. For 14 years she had been in Hawaii, where she attended college, worked as a guidance counselor, and met Steve, her husband, an audiovisual teacher who has become a breakfast cook acclaimed by *Gourmet* magazine. Kate, daughter of a former mayor—and daughter and granddaughter of Saratoga Springs hoteliers (Grand Union Hotel)—grew up in a family of six sisters (hence the B&B name) and six brothers. Kate is involved with historic preservation and Steve is a tour guide "in this wonderful walking city."

In residence: Son Jared, age two. Astor and Kela, wire-haired fox terriers. "All love guests and guests love them."
Bed and bath: Four large rooms, each furnished in a different style; all private baths. First floor—king bed, full bath. Upstairs—two king-bedded rooms, one with shower bath, one with tub/shower bath and private balcony. Suite has two double beds, living room with TV, eating area, private patio, shower and tub bath.
Breakfast: 8–9:30. Fresh fruit. Thickly sliced honey oat bread French toast. Homemade peach cobbler or apple crisp. Maple sausage. Or vegetable/cheese

quiche with bacon and apple biscuits. Macadamia nut coffee. In candlelit dining room.

Plus: Air conditioners and ceiling fans in bedrooms. Complimentary beverages. Candy in rooms. Fresh flowers. Guest refrigerator. Off-street parking.

Union Gables

518/584-1558
800/398-1558

55 Union Avenue, Saratoga Springs, NY 12866

Hosts: Jody and Tom Roohan
Location: On a main street with other Victorian houses and B&Bs. Short walk to shopping, restaurants, convention center, Saratoga Race Course, and National Museum of Racing. One and a half miles from the

New York Northway (I-87) exit 14.
Open: Year round. Closed Christmas week.
Rates: $80–$90 per room; $180–$220 in August. Amex, MC, Visa.
♥ ♯ ♣ ♦

"It was like Christmas watching all the furnishings come in. They finished wallpapering the dining room ceiling at 3:30 and the grand opening began at 5 [in June 1992]."

And that's when Jody first saw the work done by a team of interior designers who, in just four months, had transformed all 10,000 square feet of this 1901 Queen Anne Victorian that is complete with octagonal tower rooms and the 1990s embellishments of an exercise room and outdoor hot tub for six. Originally a summer home, for 30 years a Skidmore College dormitory (Furness House), and for another 17 years a home for adults with developmental disabilities (who now reside in smaller group homes), it's now a popular "tour home," a B&B where guests often ask for the designer's name, for a resource, or for a method (for reproducing a glaze or lincrusta).

Tom, a Realtor whose office is across the street, oversaw the restoration and the installation of five furnaces and air-conditioning and sprinkler systems. Jody, too, is a master juggler. When Mary was an only child, this flexible couple ran a local ski area together.

In residence: Mary, 13, "assistant innkeeper." Trey, 10; Danny, 8; Kevin, 7.
Foreign language spoken: Minimal French.
Bed and bath: Ten spacious corner rooms (two are suites) with king or queen beds (suites have a queen and two twin beds) on second and third floors; all with private baths (four full, six shower only). Rollaway and crib available.
Breakfast: 8–10. Intentionally unstructured. Juice, cereals, freshly baked goods from local shops, fruit, yogurt, hot beverages. Eat on porch, in dining room, or in your own room.
Plus: Central air conditioning. Television, private phone, and refrigerator in each room. Thick bath sheets. Babysitting. Snacks. Coffee, tea, ice always available. Several bicycles (with helmets) for loan. Huge wicker-furnished porch with glider too. Restaurant recommendations and reservations.

———

*I*f you've met one B&B host, you haven't met them all.

The Westchester House B&B   518/587-7613

102 Lincoln Avenue, P.O. Box 944, Saratoga Springs, NY 12866

Hosts: Bob and Stephanie Melvin
Location: A quiet neighborhood with tree-lined streets and Victorian homes. Two blocks behind Congress Park and Broadway; three blocks from racetrack. Within walking distance of Skidmore College, Performing Arts Center, Museum of Dance, town walking tours, state park with groomed cross-country trails.
Open: February–December. Two-night minimum in July; three-night minimum on August weekends.
Rates: Per room. September–June $70–$115. July $85–$150. Racing season $175–$225.
♥ ❖ ◆ ✗ ⚰

From Maryland: *"A warm home rather than a museum . . . and plumbing, wiring, and heating that is up to snuff with the newest hotels!"* From California: *"It wasn't the beautiful home, the careful lighting next to the beds for reading and at the washbasin, or the Victorian lace curtains that made me want to return. Bob and Stephanie's personal touch made my stay all the more enjoyable."*

Stephanie still finds time to sing opera and classical music. Bob, a former computer analyst, is also delighted with their carefully selected location, which offers rich cultural and recreational opportunities. In 1987 this personable couple transformed a well-built 1885 Queen Anne Victorian that had been a rooming house for 50 years. From Washington, D.C., they brought their collections—ranging from pre–Civil War antiques to contemporary art glass. After the inn became a "painted lady" in 1991, it received local and state preservation awards. "We, too, are delighted with the interaction here. Some guests have given impromptu seminars on antique jewelry or carousel restoration. Others suggested garden ideas (hence the name of each garden). They discuss a concert or the Saratoga baths—or solve the problems of the world."

In residence: Tiger Lily, "a 35-pound, mostly Labrador retriever who shares the social responsibilities with us."
Bed and bath: Seven air-conditioned rooms with ceiling fans, all private tiled baths. On first floor, ornate Victorian brass queen bed, shower bath, signed hand-hooked rug. Second floor—corner room with Victorian iron king bed, tub/shower bath. Canopied iron king bed, bay window, shower bath. Corner room with two Louis XVI beds, oversized shower, balcony. High Eastlake Gothic queen bed, shower bath. Eastlake queen bed, shower bath. Corner room with brass queen bed, oversized shower.
Breakfast: 8–9:30. Freshly squeezed orange juice. Fresh fruit. Local freshly baked goods, tea, "our own blend of freshly ground imported coffee." A lively family-style affair in formal dining room with china and crystal by arched window overlooking century-old maple tree.
Plus: Afternoon social hour with beverages in parlor or garden or on wraparound porch. Baby grand piano. Stereo system. Extensive library. Chocolates and fresh flowers in rooms. "Our oasis in the city: old-fashioned gardens."

The Inn on Bacon Hill   518/695-3693

200 Wall Street, Schuylerville, NY
Mailing address: P.O. Box 1462, Saratoga Springs, NY 12866

Host: Andrea Collins-Breslin
Location: Surrounded by dairy and horse farms, 12 minutes east of restaurants, Saratoga's racetracks, Performing Arts Center, Battlefield. Eight miles from I-87 (Northway); 45 minutes to Albany, Lake George, and Vermont.
Open: Year round. Two-day mini-mum on weekends during August thoroughbred racing season only.
Rates: April–July and September–October, $65 shared bath, $75 private bath, $85 suite. August racing season, $50 more. November–March, $60 all rooms. MC, Visa (for balance after deposit).
♥ ♦ ✗ ⚞

From New York, Rhode Island, Virginia, California, Connecticut: "Breakfasts are best meals we've had in the area. . . . Lovingly restored and beautifully maintained. . . . Greeted by two enthusiastic women, a mother and daughter team with boundless energy and good humor. . . . Quiet and peaceful. . . . Well-loved herb and flower garden wrapped around the historic, elegant gentleman farmhouse. . . . Comfortably furnished rooms with fresh flowers, basket of toiletries, robes. . . . Enjoyed distinct absence of television. . . . Called to the dining room by Zanfir's pan flute music echoing up the stairs. . . . Felt as if we had known other guests for years. . . . From the bedroom window, the peaceful sight of waving corn stretching down the hill. . . . It was the experience more than anything that made this visit remarkable."

The fans rave on and on about this personalized B&B. It's an 1862 Victorian mansion restored and redecorated in four months by Andrea and her mother, an artist, while Mark, Andrea's husband, a consulting engineer, was out of town. It has original moldings and border paper, bay windows, a kerosene chandelier converted to electricity, and marble fireplaces. For Andrea, the career change made in 1987 is such a perfect fit that she has transferred her 18 years of corporate world (career counseling at General Electric) experience to off-season getaway/innkeeping workshop weekends held for just three couples.

A baby grand piano is in the Victorian parlor suite. The Queen Anne guest living room with gas fireplace is less formal. There are books galore. A stereo. A wicker-furnished porch. And a screened gazebo overlooking farmland and the distant Vermont hills.

In residence: Vicki, a gentle golden retriever. Muffin, a friendly cock-a-poo "similar to Benji," lives with Andrea's mother, Millie Rekdal, in the carriage house next door.
Bed and bath: Four rooms. First floor, queen-bedded room with tub and shower bath. Private adjoining shower bath for suite with spacious parlor and 10-by-10 queen-bedded room. On second floor, room with two twin beds shares a shower bath with room that has a queen four-poster bed.
Breakfast: Usually at 8:45. Different entree daily; maybe French toast and bacon, blueberry pancakes and sausage, or egg souffle with meats. Juice, fruit, homemade muffins and jams, cold cereals, coffee, tea. "Can last up to two hours!"
Plus: Central air conditioning. Welcoming refreshments.

The Widow Kendall House

518/370-5511

10 North Ferry Street
Schenectady, NY 12305

(New York state only) **800/244-0925**

fax 518/382-2640

Host: Richard Brown
Location: On quiet street in "Stockade" historic district. Near Union College, General Electric, Mohawk River parks and bike path; antiquing; 23

miles south of Saratoga Springs.
Open: Year round.
Rates: $95 per room.

♥ ⛺ ✿ ♦

From Washington, D.C., and New York: *"The house is very old and wonderfully renovated and decorated. Subtly updated. . . . Rich Brown is a warm and gracious fellow. . . . Delicious breakfasts are attractively presented. . . . Very comfortable, relaxing, quaint, and romantic. The bathrooms and kitchen are as beautiful as you would see in a magazine."*

"One room at a time" is Rich's secret to restoration. After 10 restoring years, friends suggested B&B to the host, an attorney whose partner is in theater arts. When the house was built in 1790, Widow Annie Kendall served cakes and ale here. "Modernized" in 1836 with interior Greek Revival moldings, the brick-front Colonial saltbox still has "a charmingly tipsy front door and, in the back, beautiful gardens." Richard has furnished with antiques and reproductions. He lends bicycles. He directs guests to walking tours, the gardens at Union College, or the historical society. Many write about "the perfect host."

Bed and bath: Two second-floor queen-bedded rooms (one with wood-burning fireplace) share a bath with Jacuzzi and walk-in shower plus a half bath.
Breakfast: 6:30–10:30. Fresh muffins, croissants, or bagels. Fresh fruit cup and juice. Hot or cold cereal. Cheese or mushroom omelets; sometimes pancakes or French toast. Bacon, yogurt, low-fat cottage cheese, raisins. Served in large kitchen or in dining room.
Plus: Air-conditioned bedrooms. Tea. Fresh flowers in rooms. Fireplaced parlor. Guest pickup at nearby Amtrak or bus station. Babysitting arranged. Kitchen and laundry facilities. Often, cuttings from herb garden.

Six weeks *after* one B&B opened, a neighbor inquired: "I need lodging for visiting relatives. When are you going to open?" This was the same neighbor who, during a zoning hearing, had expressed great concern about traffic and noise that a B&B would create!

__ Adirondacks Reservation Service __

Adirondack Bed & Breakfasts

10 Park Place, Saranac Lake, NY 12983-1837

Phone: Daily, 518/891-1632 or 800/552-2627.

Listings: 25. In the High Peaks, Lake George, Old Forge, Lake Champlain, and St. Lawrence Seaway regions as well as in lesser-known areas. B&Bs include rustic, elegant, and historic properties, many with lake and/or mountain views. "All feature the ample Adirondack breakfast!" Directory $2.

Reservations: Minimum of two weeks' notice preferred, but "spur-of-moment calls" often accommodated. Two-night minimum required.

Rates: $40–$85 single, $46–$95 double. Family and weekly rates available. One night's rate required as deposit. If cancellation is received at least seven days prior to scheduled arrival, deposit refunded minus $15 processing fee. MC, Visa. ◆

Entire itineraries as well as overnight stays are arranged by Nadia Korths, a chamber of commerce staffer who is fluent in French. She knows her hosts and personally inspects their properties. And she knows the Adirondacks region with its opportunities for canoeing, hiking, cross-country skiing, antiquing, and visiting galleries and museums.

—————— Adirondacks B&Bs ——————

Crown Point Bed & Breakfast 518/597-3651
Box 490, Main Street, Crown Point, NY 12928

Hosts: Hugh and Sandy Johnson; Al and Jan Hallock (managers)
Location: Quiet, rural Adirondack Park area. On 5.5 acres with wooded trails. Next to a church and a bank. Eight miles to forts—Crown Point or Ticonderoga; seven to swimming. Walk to restaurants. Forty-five-minute ride via toll-free Lake Champlain bridge to Vermont's Shelburne Museum, antiquing, Ben & Jerry's ice cream factory.
Open: Year round. Two-night minimum on holiday weekends.
Rates: $65 queen bed. $50–$60 double. $50 twins. $95 master suite for up to four. $10 extra person. No charge for crib. Some special weekend packages. AARP discount. MC, Visa.
♥ ♫ ⚘ ✈ ⊬

"If you ever want to sell it, call us," said the Johnsons about 10 years ago when they visited a friend who owned this spectacular 1887 manor house. Since their purchase in 1988, the exterior has become a painted lady of 10 different colors. Built as a banker's private home, and more recently a convent for 15 years, the interior features six different woods handcrafted by Italian craftsmen. There's an ornate and magnificent curved stair rail, paneling, pocket doors, stained and leaded glass windows, and, throughout, Victorian furnishings. Winter guests tend to sit by the fire. Summer travelers are "on the go." Year round, the Johnsons come on most weekends from New Jersey, where Sandy is research manager for a national magazine; Hugh, an account executive for an office supply company. Jan is full-time innkeeper. Al is a pilot and ham radio operator.

In residence: Gizmo, the Johnsons' friendly "would-be Shih Tzu," mostly in kitchen area.
Foreign language spoken: Spanish—weekends, by Johnsons.
Bed and bath: Five spacious carpeted second-floor rooms; each with ceiling fan, private shower bath, robes and slippers. Brass queen bed, attached tub/shower bath. Two rooms with oak double bed; tub/shower baths, one attached, one in hall. Master suite has high-back double bed, sitting room, separate small room with a daybed and pop-up child's bed, hall bath with six-foot whirlpool tub/shower, attached shower bath. Rollaways and crib available.
Breakfast: 7:30–9. German oven-puffed pancakes or stuffed French toast. Pumpkin cheese–filled, blueberry, or oatmeal date muffins. Banana, strawberry, or orange cranberry bread. Bread pudding, raspberry cake, almond scones. Juice, fruit, coffee. (Cookbook in progress.) Served in oak-paneled dining room at antique chestnut table.
Plus: Three porches. Three parlors. All those fireplaces. Wood stove in family room. Afternoon or evening tea. Croquet. Badminton. Tandem bike. Babysitting arranged. Picnic baskets, $15.

From New Jersey: *"We were in heaven . . . wonderful Victorian wallpapers and rugs . . . authentic antiques . . . immaculate . . . abundance of florals—from bedspreads to sheets to wallpaper . . . a fine decorator's eye. It was like being taken back in time."*

Trail's End

Trail's End Road, P.O. Box 793
Keene Valley, NY 12943

518/576-9860
800/281-9860

Hosts: Laura and Ray Nardelli; Erik VanderBerg and Cheri Milliman
Location: Secluded and quiet. At base of hiking and cross-country ski trails. On three acres with big lawn and mountain views. "Near all the highest peaks." Eighteen miles south of Lake Placid. Within walking distance of two restaurants.

Open: Year round.
Rates: $40 single. $65–$95 double. $110 cottage. $10–$12.50 extra person. Fifteen percent less in April, May, November, and December 1–19. MC, Visa.

"It's homey and rustic, with plenty of space inside and out. We are definitely not the crystal and silver kind of place. Our guests love the outdoors regardless of the weather. Some even hike up Marcy in mud season! There's lots of conversation about hiking and skiing trails, and rock and ice climbing too. This B&B was built in the 1900s with big brick fireplaces, French doors, Palladian windows, hardwood floors, and screened porches. When we came here in 1991, it fulfilled our dream of bringing up a family in the area where we met during ski season. We have wallpapered, kept the pedestal sinks and claw-footed tubs, added baths and a wood stove. Country antiques are enhanced with my mother's crafts—dried wreaths and flower arrangements, little dolls, quilts, and pillows. We're around much of the time, but now that we have two children, Erik and Cheri (who managed a resort) are the primary innkeepers."

Ray is a computer teacher and consultant. Laura was head track and cross-country coach at West Virginia University.

In residence: Outdoors—Miska, the cat. Poukia, a Siberian husky.
Bed and bath: Eight large rooms; five have private screened porch (sometimes enjoyed for sleeping). Private bath for four rooms. Four share two large baths. Room with working fireplace has double four-poster, sink in room, porch. Suite has king bed, living room with wood-burning fireplace, two double futons. Other rooms (most sleep three to five) have king/twins option, double, and/or single beds. Also two-bedroom cottage with kitchen, fireplace, Jacuzzi bath.
Breakfast: 7–9. (It's usually over by 9.) Intentionally hearty. Blueberry pancakes with sausage or scrambled eggs with broccoli, ham, or cheese; home fries, freshly baked biscuits, and fruit. Oatmeal and cold cereals. On glassed-in porch; parents linger while watching kids play soccer and volleyball.
Plus: Two fireplaced living rooms; fireplaced dining room; very wide front porch. Electric piano. TV, VCR, stereo. Winterized sun porch with toys and games. Guest refrigerator and microwave. Trail lunches $5. Weekend dinners by reservation $12.95/person for minimum of 10. Babysitting with advance notice.

From New York: *"A welcome antidote to New York City's normal hyper pace."*

Adirondack Bed & Breakfast Hosts #7
Lake Clear, NY

Location: In the woods, without another house in view. With lovely landscaping and trees and, 200 yards away, a canoe carry. On a cross-country ski trail too. Surrounded by state land. Twelve miles west of Saranac Lake on Route 30; minutes to restaurants or canoe rental; half mile to state boat launch on upper Saranac Lake (great old camps to explore); half mile from 18-hole golf course. In St. Regis area of Adirondack Park.

Reservations: Year round through Adirondack Bed & Breakfasts, page 151. Two-day minimum preferred on holidays.

Rates: $55–$65. $15 additional person; $10 child. Group and extended stay rates.
♥ ♦ ♣ ✗ ✄

True Adirondack style. Real B&B. Loved. For good reasons: It's away from it all, with deer passing, loons flying overhead, and warm hospitality and good food. It's a log house with the feeling of a ski chalet. A balcony overlooks the skylit main kitchen/living/dining room, which has a fireplace at each end plus a wood stove. Decor includes Indian rugs, furs, handmade quilts, dried flowers, baskets, tools, old toys, and stuffed animals (take as many as you wish to bed). Originally built in 1975 as a family home, this became a B&B in 1988 when a father and grown son in the building construction business built an adjoining house for three generations of the family. Guests canoe and hike in the summer, cross-country ski and snowshoe in the winter. And they return.

In residence: A six-year-old son in hosts' quarters. One Siberian husky. One English springer spaniel. One cat. (Any or all on loan, by request.)

Bed and bath: Four rooms. One larger loft room (only room on that level) has extra-long double bed, double sofa bed, two twin beds, skylights, private shower and tub bath. On first floor, one room with extra-long double bed and one twin has en-suite shower bath; two rooms, each with extra-long double bed, share a hall shower bath. Rollaway and crib available.

Breakfast: Usually 7:30–8:30. Orange juice, banana rum pancakes with almonds, sausage or bacon, lots of fresh fruit, hazelnut coffee. Served at huge antique oak table in main room or on screened sun porch.

Plus: Refreshments. Babysitting. Option of dinner; advance notice appreciated.

Highland House Inn
3 Highland Place, Lake Placid, NY 12946

518/523-2377
fax 518/523-1863

Hosts: Teddy and Cathy Blazer
Location: Quiet residential street. On a hillside just above Main Street. Short walk to shops, restaurants, Olympic Center, and lake too.
Open: Year round. Two-night weekend minimum, three on holiday weekends. Five-night Christmas week minimum.
Rates: Summer and winter weekends and holidays: $75 en-suite bath, $65 hall (private) bath. Weekdays: $5 less. April, May, November until Thanksgiving: $55 per night. Cottage: Sunday–Thursday $95 per night if three or less nights, $85 four or five nights; Friday or Saturday $105. Additional person: $15 adult, $10 child. Ski packages. MC, Visa.
♥ ♦ ♣ ◆ ✗ ✄

"In 1982, when we were young and naive recent college graduates, we bought this old (1910) house and rented rooms to ski racers and groups and included breakfast with the stay. Ted, now Whiteface Mountain Ski Center general manager, was a ski coach. I was a psychology major who was working as a legal secretary. Maybe B&B—it just sort of happened—was in my blood! Our whole first floor is a common area. Off the double living room, which has couches surrounding a TV and VCR, there are smaller rooms with an upright piano, a 1,000 piece puzzle, a wood stove, and games. . . . Some couples have become engaged in our spa on the large deck built between clusters of birch trees. . . . We continue to make changes—always keeping the Adirondack theme."

In residence: In hosts' quarters—son, Christian, age four. "Belle, our West Highland Terrier, loves attention. Scarlett, a very extroverted cat, acts like a dog!"
Foreign language spoken: Spanish.
Bed and bath: Eight carpeted rooms, each with extra-long bed, ceiling fan, and remote color TV. All private baths, some en-suite; if across hall, there's a sink in room. Second floor—queen bed with or without a bunk bed set; double bed and bunk bed set; double bed and adjoining room with two bunk bed sets. Third floor—double bed with and without bunk beds. Also next-door cottage with kitchen, bath, TVs, VCR, and stereo; sleeps up to five.
Breakfast: 7:30–9. Blueberry pancakes, French toast, eggs, or cheese omelets. Sausage. Hot/cold cereals. Fruit. Toast, bagels, English muffins. Juice, tea, coffee. Served at individual tables in "an indoor garden," a plant-filled glass-enclosed dining room that has a tall angled ceiling with ceiling fans.
Plus: On-site parking. Beverages always available. Guest refrigerator. Ski tuning. Bike storage and rentals. Golf and Olympic tour discounts. Lots of see-and-do ideas year round.

Hinchings Pond B&B Inn   315/376-8296

P.O. Box 426, Lowville, NY 13367

Hosts: Skip and Connie Phelps
Location: Overlooking a private 18-acre, 50-foot-deep glacial pond. One hour north of Rome; less than two hours from Syracuse; 1½ miles east of Chases Lake; 20 minutes east of Lowville; 45 southeast of Watertown/Fort Drum. "A wide range of excellent restaurants within 20 to 30 minutes' drive."

Open: Year round except during April "spring thaw."
Rates: $45–$65 weekdays. $60–65 weekends and holidays. No charge for crib. Family, business, and clergy rates available. MC, Visa.
♣ ❄ ✂

"No neighborhood" was the translation of the perfect description one Japanese exchange student gave to another when talking about this simply furnished Adirondack-style rustic house. Designed and built in 1990 by Skip, who is in the construction business, and his family, it's on 125 private acres surrounded by "millions in state park land." Guests explore some of the 45 miles of horse trails that mountain bikers consider one of the Northeast's best-kept secrets. They skate by day and night, play hockey, snowshoe, cross-country ski, and get pulled by a snow scoot on ice. During the summer there's that crystal-clear blue spring-fed pond, from which water was once bottled and sold. Swim, snorkel, fish, or canoe. Enjoy the sandy beach. A

(Please turn page.)

panoramic view of the pond is available from the living room, cathedral-ceil-inged dining room, porches, and deck.

Here the Phelpses have combined their desire to bring up a family in a backcountry environment, their love for the Adirondack Park (where they lived in a winterized camp for five years), and their memories of wonderful European pensions.

In residence: Hunter, age 18, knows the woods, marks trails, and plots routes according to guests' ability and desire. Austin, age 15, knows the art of hospitality "and has a way of making each guest feel 'special.'" Logan, age 13, is "our resident social director, who matches guests to appropriate board and card games."

Bed and bath: Six second-level rooms. Three rooms with queen beds and private shower baths. One two-bedroom family suite with connecting shower bath. Other rooms have two twin beds, private shower baths.

Breakfast: 8–9:30. Most-requested recipes—Skip's bread pudding and Connie's baked oatmeal with warm berry sauce. Other possibilities—coddled eggs, fried bread, French toast, bacon or ham, baked apples, Connie's fresh breads and pastries. Juice, fruit, hot beverages.

Plus: Huge open soapstone wood stove in dining room. Dinners ($8–$15 per person) with prior reservation. Babysitting if arranged in advance. Outdoor campfire ring. Kitchen privileges—often enjoyed by groups who book entire B&B. Driving or skiing directions to local craftsmen who practice the almost lost art of Adirondack guide boat building.

Crislip's Bed & Breakfast   518/793-6869
693 Ridge Road, Queensbury, NY 12804-9717

Hosts: Ned and Joyce Crislip
Location: On Route 9L, four miles from I-87 exit 19. About 15 minutes north of Saratoga and south of Lake George's recreation area. An hour to Albany or Killington, Vermont. Near Glens Falls summer opera performances. Ten minutes to West Moun-tain. Half mile from Warren County airport.
Open: Year round. Two-night minimum on national holidays.
Rates: $55 September–June. $65 July, $75 August. Singles $10 less. $10 per child. MC, Visa.
♥ ♨ ♨ ♣ ✄

A hitching post and carriage mount, reminders of farm days here, are in front of the early 19th-century Federal-style house. Williamsburg decor is featured in the guest rooms of this third restoration done by Ned, a vocal music teacher, and his wife, Joyce, a former teacher.

Originally the residence of the town's first doctor, the Quaker-built home was used for many years as a training center for young medical interns. The Crislips bought the property from a family that had owned it for over a century. Since opening as a B&B in 1984, the enthusiastic hosts find that business travelers appreciate the home atmosphere. Vacationing guests are interested in antiques, music, eating, and skiing. Some of them follow the hosts' suggestion and visit the Hyde Collection in Glens Falls.

In residence: Britta, a Shih Tzu. Amber is a cat.
Bed and bath: Four rooms. On first floor, one large efficiency with double four-poster bed, private shower bath. On second floor, a room with king-sized

four-poster, private shower bath. One double room with canopied double bed, private full bath. One room with three-quarter Jenny Lind bed, shared bath, for children or other family member.

Breakfast: Until 10. Juice, sausage, eggs, English muffins, or pancakes and syrup. Prepared by both hosts and served on linens in dining room, which adjoins keeping room with massive stone cooking fireplace and sun room with view of lawn, stone walls, and mountains.

Plus: Living room with grand piano. Tour of the large and interesting house. Bedroom fans. Bedroom air conditioners available. Front porch with view of mountains and, in late September, the balloon festival.

Adirondack Bed & Breakfasts Host #10
Saranac Lake, NY

Location: Way up on a hill in historic neighborhood overlooking the village "and the mountains that ring all around us." Within minutes' walk of everything—a mile-long walk around pond; a mountain hike (great view of Saranac Lakes); boat trips through locks; concerts; restaurants; shops. Near winter cross-country skiing, dogsled races, and winter carnival. Ten miles west of Lake Placid.

Reservations: Year round through Adirondack Bed & Breakfasts, page 151.

Rates: $45 single. $55 double.

♥ ⛵ ❀ ✈ ⚟

Country Living photographed and published Susan's touch—potpourri, a greenhouse porch, a drying room. Magazine staffers wrote, "We love your house—lots of magic and flowers!" in the guest book. Then, in 1989, Susan and Glenn opened their turn-of-the-century Queen Anne house as a B&B. Fans from all over the world appreciate the peaceful ambiance—not fancy, not cutesy, but filled with original furnishings, Aunt Josie's down sofa, Susan's creative dried arrangements, books, carved cherry woodwork, refinished floors, all those added-on cure porches—"a little bit like being in the clouds"—and even a ceiling with pattern recreated by squeezing plaster through a cookie cutter mold. The restoration—ongoing for more than 15 years—has been done by the acclaimed B&B chef, Glenn, an electrical contractor, a Saranac Lake native who knows every trail around. Outside he built cobblestone-walled beds that are filled with perennials and herbs. Susan, the local youth center director, who met Glenn when he had the natural food store, loves sharing this house, this "magical town," Adirondack history, driving routes, and museum suggestions. By request, she'll tell the story of early guests, cyclists in search of a wedding site, who got married in this National Register house "within an hour!" Guests and hosts refer to this B&B as a retreat, a place for rejuvenation.

In residence: One cat "who captures guests' hearts."

Foreign language spoken: "Speak French slowly and, with the aid of a translation book, it will work."

Bed and bath: Four third-floor rooms. One with double bed, private tub bath. Three share third-floor tub/shower bath and second-floor tub/shower bath. One room has queen poster bed, sun porch with sofa and rocking chair; one room has double bed, sun porch, sofa, and rocking chair; one room has single bed.

(Please turn page.)

Breakfast: 8–9. Orange juice, fresh fruit, homemade raspberry streusel muffins. Entree might be bread pudding with blueberry sauce, French toast with orange sauce, or pineapple souffle. Coffee and herbal teas. With music—maybe American Indian flute or Irish Celtic harp. In dining room.

All Tucked Inn
518/962-4400

53 South Main Street, Westport, NY 12993-0324

Hosts: Tom Haley and (wife) Claudia Ryan

Location: In village center. Across the street from Lake Champlain and a park (farmer's market in summer) that leads to swimming beach and marina (boats for rent), with Vermont's Green Mountains (15-minute ferry ride) beyond. Short walk to shops and restaurants. Near hiking, fishing, rock climbing, antiquing, golf (around corner); 45 minutes west to Lake Placid.

Open: Year round.

Rates: May–October: front rooms $85; suite $95; back rooms upstairs $75, downstairs $65–$70. November–April, $10 less. $15 third person. Weekend dinner option, $8–$15. Murder mystery weekends in fall and winter.

♥ ♣ ✈ ⚬

Excerpts from long enthusiastic letters from Connecticut, New York, Maryland, Pennsylvania, California, Texas, Montreal: *"Stayed while attending our son's wedding.... An anniversary gift from our children.... Stayed while visiting our son at camp.... Frequently stay at B&Bs; this one is at the top of our list.... Inn was filled, but given the feeling that we were their only and most important guests.... After 20 years of marriage, this was a nice getaway.... Would recommend to my clients [travel agent].... In a cozy, rural, and friendly town ... peace surrounded by quilts, creaking French doors, mountain views, and plenty of Adirondack chairs, green lawns, shady porches.... Tom even washed our car—the 'just married' (we were) in shaving cream ... charming, impeccably clean, very well maintained, nicely decorated, plus the food and service are excellent ... but Tom and Claudia make the place."*

In Albany and Washington, D.C., Tom, official chef and antiques sleuth, was a lobbyist. Claudia is still a practicing attorney. After rejuvenating this gambrel-roofed house, built in 1872 for employees of a great hotel that was across the street, they furnished in comfortable and uncluttered country style—and opened in 1993. The rave reviews continue.

In residence: Two collies, Aly and Turk, enjoy taking walks with guests.

Bed and bath: Nine rooms; all private attached baths. Five large front rooms (three with wood-burning fireplace) have lake views. King or double bed with shower bath. Double or twin beds with tub/shower bath. First-floor suite has queen bed, shower bath, private porch. Back rooms have double bed, shower bath.

Breakfast: 8–10. Homemade fruit/nut muffins and breads. Eggs; pancakes with or without fruit and Vermont maple syrup; French toast with cinnamon sugar and warm fruit. Cereal, bacon, sausage, juice, coffee, tea. In dining room, glass-enclosed porch, or front yard—all overlooking mountains and lake.

Plus: Welcoming beverages. Guest refrigerator. Cable TV, VCR, stereo. Games. Books. Adirondack chairs and umbrella tables in fenced front yard. Gardens. That starlit sky. Recipes shared.

Syracuse/Finger Lakes Area _____ Reservation Services _____

Adventures Bed & Breakfast Reservation Service

P.O. Box 83, Scottsville, NY 14546

Phone: 716/889-7190 or 800/724-1932. Monday–Friday 11 a.m.–8 p.m., Saturday 8:30–2, Sunday "by chance."

Listings: About 50. Many are small B&Bs with three or four guest rooms. A few are inns. Sometimes, unhosted cottages available. Located in the Rochester area and in 10 surrounding counties that include Canandaigua, Honeoye, the Genesee Valley region, Keuka Lake in the Finger Lakes region, and Niagara Falls.

Reservations: August–October, one to two weeks' notice suggested. Last-minute reservations sometimes accommodated.

Rates: $50–$135 single, $55–$145 double. Weekly and group discounts available. Deposit required: one night's stay. Deposit refunded minus 20 percent processing fee if cancellation received at least seven days before expected arrival date. If cancellation received with less than seven days' notice, and host is unable to rebook room, deposit may be forfeited. Diners, MC, Visa. ◆

Andrea Barnhoorn knows how to inspect and select B&Bs, and with care she matches the traveler to an appropriate place. Her extensive experience includes hosting, innkeeping, and catering. She takes the time to describe each B&B and, if you would like, to suggest highlights of the Finger Lakes/Genesee Valley region—an area known for its wineries, antiquing, parks, Erie Canal towpaths, museums, theaters, hot-air balloon rides, fishing, scenic roads, and boat rides.

Plus: Itineraries planned. Car rentals arranged. "And just about anything else (nominal fee charged), including transportation for guests and their bicycles to designated starting areas or to the next B&B."

Elaine's Bed & Breakfast Reservation Service

4987 Kingston Road, Elbridge, NY 13060-9773

Phone: 315/689-2082 after 10 a.m.

Listings: 70 hosted private residences located in about 40 New York communities in and around Syracuse, including Apulia, Auburn, Baldwinsville, Clay, Cleveland and Constantia on Oneida Lake, Conquest, DeWitt, Durhamville, Edmeston (near Cooperstown), Elbridge, Fayetteville, Geneva, Glen Haven, Gorham, Groton, Homer, Jamesville, Lafayette, Liverpool, Lyons, Marathon, Marcellus, Naples (overlooking Canandaigua Lake), Ovid, Owasco Lake, Phoenix, Pompey, Port Ontario, Pulaski, Rome, Saranac Lake, Sheldrake-on-Cayuga, Skaneateles, Sodus Bay on Lake Ontario, Tully, Vernon,

(Please turn page.)

Vesper, Waterloo, and Watertown. In addition, a few are in the Berkshires (western Massachusetts).

Reservations: At least two weeks' notice preferred; at least two months' for major college weekends. Last-minute reservations sometimes accommodated.

Rates: $35–$70 single. $45–$150 double. Senior citizen discounts for stays of seven days or more. Weekly rates available. Deposit required. Refund minus $10 processing fee if cancellation is received at least two weeks before scheduled arrival date. ◆

Elaine's inspected homes range from contemporary to historic, from urban to lakeside. Most hosts are professionals. Some are retired. Many ban smoking indoors. Some have resident pets. Breakfasts vary from simple continental to elaborate menus. "About half of my listings have private baths."

__ Syracuse/Finger Lakes Area B&Bs __

Patchwork Peace Bed & Breakfast

4279 Waterbury Hill Road, Avoca, NY 14809   **607/566-2443**

Hosts: Bill and Betty Mitchell
Location: Quiet. On 300 acres of woods, barns, and farmland, 1 mile up hill from Route 415. Four and a half miles from I-390/Route 17. About 30 miles to SUNY Alfred, Keuka College, Alfred University; 40 to SUNY Geneseo; 30 to Corning; 20 to Keuka Lake; 40 to Canandaigua Lake; 6 to new Farmers Museum and refurbished depot, train to Hammondsport.
Open: Year round.
Rates: Shared bath $30 single bed, $45 double bed, $50 queen. Private bath $65. Singles $5 less. $10 rollaway. No charge for portacrib.
♥ ♨ ⬤ ♣ ✕ ⚥

From Kansas, New York, Texas, Pennsylvania, New Jersey, Georgia, Mississippi: *"An oasis that seems to restore the balance to one's life. . . . Whiskers is the funniest dog ever. . . . The most comfortable and immaculate accommodations possible in the most beautiful countryside this side of Eden . . . genuinely warm hosts. . . . Truly wonderful . . . about 100 cows up on the hill, about a quarter mile from the house . . . huge barns and silos . . . most helpful in advising places of interest . . . enjoyed playing the piano and singing together. . . . Nicely decorated . . . eating with the hosts makes breakfast an event. . . . Books and toys to keep our three-year-old happy. . . . More like visiting family. . . . My dad was hesitant, but now he is as anxious to return as the rest of us."*

A rarity. A real working farm, with opportunities to see the milking process. Sometimes, witness a calf being born. What else? Plowing, planting, baling hay (spring and summer), corn picking and chopping (for silage), and a petting zoo. The Mitchells, both active with the historical society, purchased the 1925 clapboard farmhouse in 1983 from the great-grandson of the original family. The floors and woodwork are refinished. Bill farms, as he has for 50 years, "next door." Betty, who happily shares recipes, has experience as town clerk, bookkeeper, sales clerk, and tutor for Literacy Volunteers.

In residence: "Whiskers is a kind, vocal terrier who warms up to guests quickly."
Bed and bath: Four second-floor rooms. Private full bath for queen-bedded room that has air conditioner, ceiling fan, balcony. Three rooms—with single, double, or queen bed—share hall bath that has claw-footed tub and hand-held shower. Rollaway and portacrib available.
Breakfast: Usually 8–9. (As early as 5:30 for hunters.) Juice. Fresh fruit cup. Oven French toast with bacon; pancakes, sausage, real maple syrup; or vegetable quiche or frittata. Homemade breads, muffins, and jams. Plenty of hot beverages.
Plus: Sun-dried linens. Soft drinks. Individual heat thermostat. Picnic baskets for two (with wine) $15.

The Red House Country Inn   607/546-8566
Finger Lakes National Forest
4586 Picnic Area Road, Burdett, NY 14818-9716

Hosts: Sandy Schmanke and Joan Martin
Location: In New York State's only national forest, with 28 miles of maintained (year round) trails at the door. On the east side of Seneca Lake. Short drives to Glen Gorge, Corning Glass Center, swimming, wineries.
Open: Year round except Thanks-giving and Christmas Day. Two-night minimum on weekends and holidays.
Rates: $39 single bed. $70 double and twin bed or double bed with working fireplace. $85 queen bed. $10 extra person. Amex, Discover, MC, Visa.
♥ ♣ ✈ ⅙

Guests wrote (and wrote): *"We had some of every kind of weather—dazzling sun, brooding mists, crystalline meadows of ice—all rendered magnificent by the cozy accommodations and splendid meals. . . . Thirteen satisfied middle-age adults feel we discovered this delightful place. . . . Comfortable country atmosphere. . . . Many interesting items, each with a story. . . . Breakfast is a celebration. . . . Plenty of hot water, fresh thick towels daily, even a supply of shampoo. . . . We walked, talked, played the piano and pump organ, joked, snoozed. . . . Perfect for hiking, fishing, bird-watching, berry picking, cycling, cross-country skiing, and peace of mind. . . . Gracious hostesses who share their corner of paradise."*

One of a kind. The only private property in the forest. (The only farm not purchased by the federal government during the Great Depression.) Built in 1844, restored by owners in the 1970s, and purchased in 1981 by Sandy and Joan, who opened it as a freshly wallpapered inn in 1983. Since, they have built an addition and landscaped five acres of lawns and gardens. They have been featured in *New York Alive* and *New York* magazine and have been etched in the hearts of guests and their friends and relatives. Before becoming innkeepers, Sandy owned a media buying service and Joan, also in Rochester, New York, was in TV and radio production and business management.

In residence: In hosts' quarters only, Samoyeds Tucker, Susie, and Muffin. The goats—Annie, Sarah, Andy, and Tina—have their own quarters.
Bed and bath: Five second-floor rooms share four full baths. One room has a single bed. One with double bed, working fireplace. Two with a double and a single bed in each. Master bedroom has a queen four-poster bed plus a queen hide-a-bed. Rollaway available.
Breakfast: 8–9:30. Fresh fruit, freshly squeezed orange juice, or local grape juice. Homemade popovers or scones and jams. Fresh eggs with slab bacon or honey-glazed ham. Homemade Pilgrim's bread, apple flaps, or cinnamon crisp French toast. Freshly ground coffees, fine teas. In two dining rooms with sterling and crystal.
Plus: Afternoon tea. Candy. Bedroom fans. Huge in-ground pool with deck, cabana, and kitchen with grill. Flower-bedecked veranda. Horseshoes, darts. Picnic area. Cross-country skiing. Gift shop. November–April, option of dinner ($20 per person) with reservations.

Morgan-Samuels Inn

716/394-9232
2920 Smith Road, Canandaigua, NY 14424 　　**fax 716/394-8044**

Hosts: Julie and John Sullivan
Location: Secluded and elegant. With no sound of traffic. On 46 peaceful acres, including 5 of lawns and gardens and 30 of alfalfa fields. At the end of a very long tree-lined drive. Two miles to Canandaigua Lake and to business district; 15 minutes to Bristol Mountain ski resort; 35 miles southeast of Rochester. Near many wineries, Sonnenberg Gardens, "popular entertainment down the road—and everywhere, beauty that even year-round residents marvel at."

Open: Year round. Two-night weekend minimum May 1–November 15 and holidays.

Rates: Vary according to room size and amenities. $109, $119, $125, $135, $150, $195. Weekday business rate $69–$99. Extra person $20. Dinner ($30–$50 prix fixe) by advance arrangement. Discover, MC, Visa.

♥ ♣ ♦ ✈ ✄

Some cabin. The English country estate look-alike is an 1810 stone mansion with 1930s brick addition. Food, acclaimed in *Bon Appétit,* is a feature. And so is the decor—with detail everywhere, and with antiques and paintings that contribute to a calm ambiance. Once owned by actor/farmer Judson Morgan and later by Howard Samuels, plastic bag inventor, "the house with the perfect inn layout" became the Sullivans' six-guest-room B&B in 1989. To innkeeping Julie—the ebullient lady from Wyoming—brought her mother's sense of color and design, experience in tutoring as well as in delivering yachts all over the world, and several years' work in refugee camps. "I was seven months pregnant and ready to settle in a little cabin when we landed in this beautiful home." John, the creative chef, grew up on an area dairy farm. Today he is involved in embryo transplanting and sends eggs from about 15 cows—kept elsewhere—to many countries. Together the Sullivans share their love of life and this magnificent property with guests.

In residence: Son Jonathan is six years old. Every year a Holstein calf is raised on the grounds. And you'll find chickens, turkeys, and a couple of ducks.
Bed and bath: Six rooms on three floors. One very large suite with wood-burning fireplace, double Jacuzzi, king bed. Three large rooms with king or queen bed, French doors and balcony, wood-burning or gas fireplace, private bath (one is huge with Jacuzzi). Rope-banistered stairway to Gothic room with cathedral ceiling, king bed, stained glass, fireplace, tub/shower bath. Small room with queen four-poster bed, shower bath, Norway parlor stove in original large fireplace, private rose garden.
Breakfast: 8:30–9:30. At least a dozen, sometimes 22, kinds of fresh fruit. Breakfast meats. Entree orders individually filled. Special diets accommodated. Served on slate patio, in screened porch, in beamed and fireplaced dining room "with Mozart," or in tea room with potbellied stove and enormous windows that "bring the outside in year round."
Plus: Central air conditioning. Beverages. Guest refrigerator. Library with TV. Fireplaced living room. Tennis court.

From Virginia: *"Have stayed in B&Bs across the country and in Canada. This sets the standard of excellence."*

Sutherland House

716/396-0375

5285 Bristol Street
Canandaigua, NY 14424

(U.S./Canada) **800/396-0375**

Hosts: Cor and Diane Van Der Woude
Location: In farm country along Route 21 South. On five acres with gorgeous spreading copper beech tree in front. Surrounded by wheat fields. Two miles east of Main Street; one mile to north end (boat launch) of Canandaigua Lake; 30 minutes east of downtown Rochester; 15 minutes to Finger Lakes Performing Arts Center or to racetrack; 15 minutes north of Bristol Mountain ski Resort.
Open: Year round.
Rates: $65 double or queen. $115 queen bed with Jacuzzi. $135 suite. Bristol ski packages. Mystery weekend rates. MC, Visa.
♥ ♣ ♦ ✈ ⊱

Oohs and aahs. "Who did the stenciling? Marvelous pocket doors. And ceiling medallions. And chestnut and oak woodwork. Wainscoting. Chair rails. An entryway with faux tin ceiling that is painted a copper color. Rooms with Jacuzzis." More than 800 area residents exclaimed about everything when they came to the August 1994 open house to see what the Van Der Woudes had done to the haunted house (as it was known locally), a Second Empire-with-tower Victorian that Diane says "needed a hug." Family heirlooms "and our own treasures from 26 years of marriage" are augmented through the ongoing search for "just the right piece" at area auctions. New gardens are maturing. There are lots of red brick walks. A slate patio. And tree-shaded tables.

Diane resigned from her human resources position to become a full-time innkeeper. Cor, a talented carpenter born in the Netherlands, has a managerial position at the University of Rochester. Now that their dream of remodeling a Victorian into a B&B has come true, "we're still best friends." Their joy is shared with contented guests.

In residence: Tyson Michelle, "our blond, beautiful boxer."
Foreign language spoken: Dutch.
Bed and bath: Four carpeted second-floor rooms, all private en-suite baths. Suite has king bed, sitting room with TV/VCR, two-person Jacuzzi. Large room with queen bed, sitting area with TV/VCR, two-person Jacuzzi. One room with queen bed, tub/shower bath. One with double bed, two-person shower.
Breakfast: 8–10. (Coffee earlier in souvenir mug outside your door.) Country menu served family style. Fresh fruit. French toast, pancakes, waffles, eggs, Egg Beaters. Homemade muffins. In fireplaced dining room.
Plus: Picnic baskets prepared. On-site parking for boat trailers. Weddings, inside or out, booked.

---

*M*any guests write: "I hate to rave too much for fear of finding no place at the inn the next time I call."

Lakeview Farm Bed n' Breakfast

4761 Route 364, Rushville, NY 14544   **716/554-6973**

Hosts: Elizabeth and Howard Freese
Location: Rural. On 170 acres on both sides of the road, overlooking the east side of Canandaigua Lake. Between (five miles from) tiny Rushville and (six miles south of) Canandaigua's Sonnenburg Gardens. One mile to restaurants, public beach; 20 minutes to Naples and Widmers Winery; 45 to Rochester.
Open: Year round.
Rates: Include tax. $40–$45 single. $55–$60 double.
🛏 ◆ ✈ ⚋

"The view. That's what this place is all about. When we first got here 20 years ago, it was the only thing that didn't need fixing! Now it's a country home furnished with many interesting family antiques from the South, circa 1850s or '60s, together with other pieces that blend well. We have added a family/dining room with 20 feet of windows overlooking the lake, the pond, birds and wildlife. We love it and so do our guests. Some of our visitors walk down the ravine, a beautiful spot with a little waterfall and loads of fossils. Or they go fishing, antiquing, and wine tasting. Yes, I'm still pickling Jerusalem artichokes with our secret recipe and making jelly."

Betty, a former newspaper journalist, is a retired high school librarian. Howard is a retired engineer working with their son in his machinery business located in the red barn. The hosts, Elderhostel fans (New Zealand in 1994), live in what some travelers call "a real B&B."

In residence: Outdoors: Tobey, a mostly Gordon setter, loves to be petted. Ashley, "a friendly, fat male dog," announces arrivals.
Bed and bath: Two second-floor double-bedded rooms, both with lake views, share full bath across the hall. Cot available.
Breakfast: Early-morning coffee and tea in upstairs sitting room. Juice, homegrown fruit, eggs; bacon or sausage. Buns or interesting breads, homemade jellies. French toast or blueberry pancakes on request. Cereal available.
Plus: Central air conditioning. Welcoming beverage. Wood stove in that great family room. TV. Gardens. Trails through woods and fields for cross-country skiing. A half-hour area drive complete with history and Indian legends. The gift of a jar of jelly or Jerusalem artichoke pickle.

Guests wrote: *"Showed us Spook Hill. We'll talk about it for years to come. . . . Trusted us with Tobey for an early-morning walk. . . . Pressed cider together. . . . Superb breakfast at a lovely table. . . . Excellent books. . . . So clean. . . . Felt like extended family."*

1865 White Birch B&B   607/962-6355

69 East First Street, Corning, NY 14830

Hosts: Kathy and Joe Donahue
Location: In a quiet residential neighborhood. One block from the Rockwell Museum, two from downtown, and six from the Corning Glass Center.
Open: Year round.
Rates: Tax included. Double $71.50 shared bath, $77 private. Single $55 shared bath, $61.50 private. $20 extra person over age 10 in room. Amex, MC, Visa.
♥ 🛏 ⚊ ⚋

(Please turn page.)

Recipes, including one for lemon yogurt poppyseed bread, have traveled with guests to countries all over the world. The Donahues have been caterers for 20 years. Before becoming a full-time innkeeper, Kathy was a registered nurse for 24 years. Joe has been with the Corning Glass Works' food service department for over 30 years. In 1989 they "combined our enjoyment of people and cooking, and our love of architecture, and an old home." Their 1865 house, a former rectory, has a Federal-looking exterior and Victorian moldings and trim on the inside. It's a homey place, with country pine, oak, and wicker pieces. Among the more than 4,000 contented Donahue guests are a glass artist who comes from Holland four times a year, a retiree who grew up in the house, a Berkeley sociology professor who comes for six weeks every summer, and many first-timers too.

In residence: "Guests fall in love with Abby, our five-year-old basset hound."
Bed and bath: Up a wide winding staircase to four large second-floor rooms. Twin-bedded room has private en-suite tub and shower bath. One queen-bedded room with private shower bath. Two queen-bedded rooms share a large shower bath that has a double-sinked counter. Rollaway and crib.
Breakfast: Usually 8–9. Hot entree repertoire includes baked apple puff pancakes, fruit-filled French toast, egg-and-cheese souffle, three-layer omelet on croissants, Dutch babies. Juice. Fruit—compote, strawberry parfait, homemade applesauce. Cereals and homemade granola. Homemade muffins and bread. Served on long oak dining room table by large window overlooking yard. Hosts join guests.
Plus: Fireplaced living room with TV, VCR, tapes, radio. Babysitting. Garden flowers. Bedroom window fans. Picnic tables, umbrella tables, chairs, gas grill. Restaurant suggestions. Special holiday weekends.

From England: *"A wonderful stay. . . . Super company. . . . Wonderful food."*

Rosewood Inn 607/962-3253

134 East First Street, Corning, NY 14830

Hosts: Suzanne and Stewart Sanders
Location: On a tree-lined residential street, one block south of Route 17. Within walking distance of Corning Glass Center, museums, downtown historic district.

Open: Year round.
Rates: Single $70–$90. Double $75–$99. Suites $90–$115. $20 extra person. Amex, CB, Diners, Discover, MC, Visa.
♥ ❖ ✈ ⅊

Transferred—from their New Jersey printing business to innkeeping in Corning, "and we're never going to leave!" From, as Suzanne says, "corporate America's suit-and-briefcase world to Victorian blouses and shawls." At home, Stewart was always the official cook; here he does all the baking and cooking. In 1992, they bought the Finger Lakes' first and almost-famous bed and breakfast. Appointed with fine Victorian antiques, Oriental rugs, and lace curtains, this 1853 Greek Revival was renovated in 1915 into an English Tudor. Now the Lewis Carroll Room includes a mirror and mantel clock "as part of the looking glass scene." The Sunflower Room has Monet and Van

Gogh prints. And for a marvelous story of serendipity, ask about the Queen Elizabeth I portrait in the Royal Room.

Bed and bath: Seven rooms (six are carpeted, one has a braided rug), all private baths. Queen, double, or twin beds. Two large first-floor suites with private bath, private entrance, color TV, air conditioning; queen canopied bed and working fireplace in one suite, twin beds and a kitchen in the other. Second-floor queen-bedded rooms have tub and shower baths; shower baths in other rooms.

Breakfast: Usually 8:30–9:30. (Coffee available at 7:30.) Juice, fruit. Home-made banana or zucchini bread with Rosewood brandy/honey butter. Cereals, granola, yogurt. Entree might be challah French toast or omelet. A very sociable time in candlelit dining room.

Plus: Bedroom air conditioners. Late-afternoon tea and cookies by the fire or lemonade and cookies on porch. Sitting room with TV. In winter, flannel sheets. Dinner by reservation.

> From North Carolina: *"Elegant . . . welcomed us as if we were old friends . . . breakfast was a feast."* From Pennsylvania: *"Stewart and Suzanne truly are the definition of hospitality . . . made us feel at home . . . provided for our every need . . . allowed for privacy as well."* From Arizona: *"All six couples on our bicycling trip have stayed at many B&Bs. All agreed Rosewood was the best ever. Fantastic!"*

Addison Rose Bed and Breakfast

37 Maple Street, Addison, NY 14801   607/359-4650

Hosts: Mary Ann and Bill Peters
Location: Residential. In a valley village (five-minute walk to center) surrounded by hills and dairy farms. On a maple tree–lined street that was the childhood dream location for one guest—who was, in the 1950s, a major-league baseball player. Twelve-minute drive to downtown Corning. Near Pinnacle State Park, with golf course, picnic area, cross country ski trails.
Open: Year round. Two-night minimum on holiday weekends.
Rates: $65 twin beds, $75 double bed.
♥ 🍴 ⁂ ✗

> From Tennessee: *"Home! . . . lasting memories."* From Missouri: *"Warm hospitality . . . took our parents for their 60th anniversary, and they are still reminiscing about how special Mary Ann and Bill made it for them."* From Pennsylvania: *"Treated us like old friends."* From New Jersey: *"Treated us like family."*

That's exactly how Mary Ann and Bill pictured it would be when they searched in 1988 for a community "away from metropolitan New York; for a Victorian house that resembled the B&Bs of our own retreats; for a place that would be—as our New Jersey home was—a gathering spot with a lot of sharing going on."

Their Queen Anne, now a painted lady, was built as a doctor's office and home in 1892. After much renovation, it was opened as a B&B in 1990 with furnishings and knickknacks from auctions and local antiques shops. Bill, the backpacker/golfer/avid reader who has years of experience on Wall Street and as a pipefitter and welder, is a pipefitter for Corning. Mary Ann, an art

(Please turn page.)

major who "almost always has a needlework project in the making," cooks with herbs from the garden "here where our dream came true."

In residence: Daughters Amanda, 20, and Melanie, 17. "Sky, our well-behaved dog, who is not allowed in common rooms, 'sings' when breakfast is taking too long and she feels neglected."

Bed and bath: Three second-floor rooms, each with private claw-footed tub/shower bath. Two rooms (one with private front balcony), each with Victorian double bed, have attached bath. Room with two antique twin beds has hall bath.

Breakfast: Flexible hours. Fresh fruit. Homemade warm muffins with homemade jellies and jams. Cream cheese–filled French toast with banana/apricot sauce, or egg/meat/cheese casserole. Low-fat and low-calorie diets accommodated. Served in bay-windowed dining room.

Plus: Bedroom ceiling fans. Wicker-furnished porch. Fireplaced foyer. Beverage and homemade cookies or brownies. Fresh fruit. Addison walking tour.

Halcyon Place Bed & Breakfast   607/529-3544

197 Washington Street, P.O. Box 244, Chemung, NY 14825-0244

Hosts: Yvonne and Doug Sloan
Location: In a tiny town dubbed "the Northeast's most English-like village" by young English guests. Quiet streets with a range of architectural styles. Former blacksmith shop two doors away. "Just down the street," area's oldest one-room schoolhouse, now a private residence.

One mile off Route 17, 12 east of Elmira. Forty minutes to Ithaca, 45 to Binghamton and international racing at Watkins Glen.
Open: Year round.
Rates: Private bath $60. Shared bath $50, $55 with working fireplace. $15 extra person.
🐕 ✖ ⊱

"We felt we had discovered a secret when we stayed in B&Bs! In 1990 we bought this restored circa 1825 Greek Revival house with its wide-plank floors and six-over-six hand-blown glass windows, and furnished it with our collection of late 18th- and early 19th-century furnishings. By 1993 we became part of house tours and initiated summer garden tours with lavish teas. The name Halcyon is from the Greek myths, signifying peacefulness, tranquillity, and a healing richness. Upon departure, everyone receives a lavender wand (for a linen closet or lingerie drawer) that I make from our herb garden. It's all part of sharing our dream come true."

Yvonne, a tympanist with the Corning Philharmonic, teaches middle school instrumental music. Doug, a trained musician/avid gardener/antique furniture restorer, is an employment counselor who works with disadvantaged youths. In addition to the herb garden, the backyard has fruit-bearing trees, mature bushes, perennial beds that attract hummingbirds and butterflies, and a rose trellis with seat for stargazing.

In residence: "Tucson, our affectionate, well-traveled chocolate Labrador."
Foreign language spoken: Some German.
Bed and bath: Three second-floor rooms. Room with canopied double bed has private en-suite shower bath. Room with tall double four-poster and

working fireplace shares a full hall bath with room that has "a stunning antique tiger maple double bed."

Breakfast: Usually 8–10. Juice, freshly ground coffee, seasonal fruits. Raspberry streusel muffins with homegrown berries or popular rum sticky buns. Blueberry waffles with locally made maple syrup, omelets with herbs, quiche, or crepes. Bacon or sausages. Table set with heirloom silver on wicker-furnished screened porch overlooking garden or by candlelight in fireplaced dining room with classical music.

Plus: Afternoon tea with lemon tea bread, rose geranium cake, or lemon balm cookies; evening beverages with crackers and herb cheese. Piano. Window fans for guest rooms. Turndown service. Bicycles for guests' use. Extensive LP and CD collection of jazz and classical music. "Narrated" herb garden tour. Wednesday garden tour and tea (open to public; sells out early), $12.50; menu might include lemon verbena mousse with berries or tomato basil torte. Herb plants for sale.

> From Ontario: *"Looking out on the grape arbor and the herb garden while being serenaded by a Mozart flute concerto was a delight probably never to be duplicated."*

Another Tyme Bed & Breakfast   607/569-2747

7 Church Street, Hammondsport, NY 14840-0134

Host: Carolyn Clark
Location: A corner lot on a quiet street across from a natural, undeveloped glen (for hiking). Two blocks from historic village square; three from Keuka Lake. Thirty-minute drive to Corning Glass, Watkins Glen State Park and racetrack; 15 minutes to wineries; 21 miles to Naples.

Open: Year round. Reservations required for winter months.
Rates: Private bath $75 twins, $65 king. Shared bath $55. Rollaway $10. Crib $5. MC, Visa. Rates subject to applicable taxes.
♦ ♦ ♦ ♦ ✕ ✗

Before Carolyn was in the Peace Corps (in Africa), she was personnel manager at Cornell University's College of Veterinary Medicine. With seven children who live "all over the world," she named her B&B to represent "another time in my life." She decorated each room with mementos from Africa, furnishings from the home she and her late husband lived in, and family heirlooms and photographs. As tourist booth chairman, Carolyn is familiar with everything from wineries to "a Wizard of Clay" to "a man in Naples who makes 'living walls' from trees and plants." As hostess, she has a long list of fans who return for her breakfast and for her homey just-like-Grandmother's atmosphere.

In residence: Polly, a friendly English springer spaniel, "insists on greeting guests."
Bed and bath: Three large second-floor rooms. One with king/twins option, windows on three sides, detached private tub/shower bath. Room with queen bed and small porch shares a shower bath (robes provided) with room that has double four-poster bed. Rollaway or crib available.
Breakfast: 8:30. Shirred eggs in a basket-of-toast with cheese sauce; egg souffle or casserole; oven-baked English omelet; frittata; orange oatmeal

(Please turn page.)

custard pie; tomato quiche (for British guests); or stuffed or orange French toast. Breakfast meat, fresh fruit, orange juice, freshly ground coffee, and homemade breakfast bread.
Plus: "No TV or radio in the rooms." Cookies and tea, coffee, or cider on arrival. Parking available. Large yard (with gardens) for picnic. Lawn chairs.

> From Pennsylvania: *"Very relaxing. . . . As if we were coming to Mom's. . . . Extraordinarily clean, fresh, and friendly. Carolyn is knowledgeable and helpful. . . . Breakfast is tasty, varied, and nutritious. . . . Warm, welcome feeling."*

The Blushing Rosé B&B

11 William Street, Hammondsport, NY 14840

607/569-3402
607/569-3483
800/982-8818

Hosts: Ellen and Bucky Laufers-weiler
Location: Minutes' walk to village park bandstand, historic area, Glen Curtis Museum, shops, and free beach on Keuka Lake. Thirty minutes west of Corning; 10 minutes from Bath; two hours from Rochester, Syracuse, and Binghamton; four from Toronto. Near wineries, waterfalls, and gorges.
Open: Year round. Two-night minimum on weekends June through October.
Rates: $65–$85 per room. $15 third person.

♥ ⬗ ♣ ◆ ✂ ⊁

Quite a combination. A hostess who loves decorating, sewing, and cooking. A host who is a wood-floor specialist/refinisher. Together, a couple who, since 1986, have offered warm hospitality to grateful travelers.

Ellen and Bucky—skiers, cyclists, and boaters—"loved every minute of restoring and redecorating the entire Victorian Italianate," which was built in 1843 with a cupola, identified as "original air conditioning" by the local historical society. The exterior, painted a blushing rose color, is trimmed with a deep burgundy. Inside, the country decor is complete with handmade quilts, a spinning wheel, grapevine wreaths, and an Oriental-style rug under the dining room oak table.

In residence: Bolt, a friendly 15-year-old golden retriever, loved by guests.
Bed and bath: Four spacious second-floor rooms; three with queen bed, one with king. All private baths; two en suite, two in hall.
Breakfast: At 9. (Early-bird coffee at 8:15) Entree might be lemon yogurt poppyseed waffles, French toast, or featherbed eggs. Juice, fruit dishes, homemade granola and muesli, homemade multigrain bread, yogurt, gourmet coffees and teas.
Plus: All bedrooms are air conditioned; two have ceiling fans. Guest refrigerator. A sitting room with TV, stereo, VCR, much reading material. Traditional music. Wicker-furnished porch. Guest pickup at bus station.

> Guests wrote: *"Fond memories of friendliness, large breakfasts, country antiques. . . . Beautifully decorated. Gave me some new ideas. . . . Good advice on places to visit and to eat. . . . Clean, clean, clean! . . . Every detail was perfect."*

Elaine's Bed & Breakfast Host #1

Ovid, NY

Location: Peaceful. On Cayuga Lake. Along a country road that meanders for miles along the lake. A birder's paradise. In a glacial area with dramatic waterfalls and gorges. Within 3 miles of three award-winning wineries; 22 miles north of Ithaca.
Reservations: Year round through Elaine's Bed & Breakfast Reservation

Service, page 159. Two-night summer minimum with any Friday or Saturday reservation; three nights on graduation or holiday weekends.
Rates: $65 twin beds. $95 first-floor room and second-floor room with shower and balcony. With fireplace and Jacuzzi $115 or $125. MC, Visa.
♥ ♣ ✈ ⅄

An immediate success! A miniresort. A restored light-filled Queen Anne Victorian with big lawn and wraparound porch. Guests swim, row, and sail (boats provided) on the deep, delicious lake. They pedal the inn's bicycles, visit wineries, and enjoy food. The breakfast is prepared by the hostess, a gourmet cook. Nearby dinner recommendations include everything from a country tavern with fish and french fries to fine Victorian dining.

The host, a manufacturer's representative, lived here for 15 years before creating this soundproofed B&B in 1993. Woodwork was custom milled. Wide-board floors were refinished. Diaries and photographs of the family that lived here for 100 years have been gathered, thanks to neighbors, members of the family, who have visited and shared oral history. Furnishings include Oriental rugs and walnut, mahogany, and cherry antiques.

Bed and bath: Four rooms with lake views. First floor—handicapped-accessible room with queen bed, private porch, private tub/shower bath. Second floor—two rooms (one is air conditioned) with queen bed (one has twin sofa bed too), gas fireplace, private bath with double Jacuzzi tub/shower. Queen bed, private balcony, private shower bath.
Breakfast: 8–9:30. Large buffet with fresh fruit salad, local organic vanilla yogurt with fruit sauce and granola. Bagels and cream cheese.
Plus: Ceiling fans in all rooms. Living room wood stove.

Buttermilk Falls Bed & Breakfast

110 East Buttermilk Falls Road, Ithaca, NY 14850-8741   **607/272-6767**

Host: Margie Rumsey and granddaughters Kristen and Heather
Location: At the foot of waterfalls in adjoining Buttermilk Falls State Park; 3½ miles south of Cornell University and Ithaca College. Just off Route 13.
Open: Year round. Two-night minimum on some weekends and college graduations.

Rates: Vary according to season. $150–$195 king bed with Jacuzzi, fireplace. Second floor, $75–$120 extra-long double; $80–$135 double; $95–$140 king. $10 less for singles. MC, Visa (for holding reservations only).
♥ ♣ ✈ ⅄

(Please turn page.)

We won't ever forget our before-breakfast dip in those magnificent water-falls—followed by Margie's dramatic presentation of juice blended from fresh fruits. Her 1820 painted brick house with wide pine floorboards is decorated with antiques, family heirlooms, old Persian carpets (even on the porch), and a son's handcrafted tables and Windsor chairs. "The idea of having B&B in our family home of five generations started with a 1983 trip to England. As of 1994, the centerpiece of the house is our new AGA four-oven stove. It's like a miracle—just magic!" Margie is the innkeeper in residence—except when she sleeps in the maple tree or takes a quick getaway. A class of 1947 Cornellian, native Ithacan, and private pilot, she flies to Florida to pick calamondins for making jam. From trips to Turkey, Africa, India, Japan, New Zealand, and Australia, she brings back spices and seasonings for taste treats. All five grandchildren (two are college students) and their parents (one is a Cornell hotel school graduate), who were raised here, also assist.

Bed and bath: Five air-conditioned rooms; all private baths. "Unless there's a drought or a deep freeze, the falls can be heard from all bedrooms." On first floor, king bed, double Jacuzzi bath, shower, wood-burning fireplace, ceiling fan, TV, VCR, big comfortable chairs. On second floor, room with king bed, antique daybed, shower bath, refrigerator, windows on three walls. Room with double bed, antique daybed, shower bath, windows on three walls. Room with extra-long double hydraulic (vibrating) bed has hall tub and shower bath immediately next to bedroom door. Twins/king room has detached shower bath.

Breakfast: Usually 8:30–9:30. Full. Features fresh fruits, hot whole-grain cereals with a variety of toppings such as raisins, dates, walnuts, maple syrup, honey, yogurt, or cream. Bacon and eggs with fresh breads, "oven surprises," and apple fritters. Buffet style on busy weekends. In kitchen, in formal dining room, on screened porch with thriving plants, or under trees at picnic table at foot of waterfall.

Plus: Fireplaced living room with books, CD music, antique games. Yard swing. Beverages. Cross-country skiing from the door. Hiking and biking suggestions.

From Pennsylvania: *"A breakfast that could almost make a morning person out of me."* From New York: *"A treat to walk up the park slope before breakfast. . . . A place full of peace."*

Hanshaw House B&B   607/257-1437

15 Sapsucker Wood Road, Ithaca, NY 14850

Host: Helen Scoones
Location: Tranquil. A country setting overlooking pond (created by former owner, a Cornell-based ornithologist), woods, and a century-old apple tree. Within 10 minutes of downtown, fine restaurants, state parks, Cayuga Lake. Half a mile from Cornell's Sapsucker Woods Ornithology Laboratory and Bird Sanctuary. Less than half an hour to Greek Peak ski slopes.

Open: Year round. Two-day minimum on college graduation and parents' weekends, and on some major holidays.
Rates: $70–$105. Off-season $65–$84. Singles $8 less. Slightly higher on major holiday weekends. Extra person $25–$30. Crib $10. Corporate and educational discounts. Amex, MC, Visa.
♥ ♦ ♣ ✈ ✝

From Massachusetts and New York: "I can't think of a place that would have been as romantic for our honeymoon. Every detail was perfect! . . . Our relatives recommended this B&B for our Thanksgiving visit. We have been to many B&Bs and couldn't recommend any more highly. . . . Saw two pileated woodpeckers—simultaneously—right there in her backyard. Beautifully appointed rooms . . . spotless . . . lovely gardens . . . breakfasts are scrumptious enough to make you want to kidnap the cook . . . couldn't ask for a more gracious or helpful hostess . . . directions to a vineyard and MacKenzie-Childs pottery studios . . . suggestions for places we never had been to in four years as students."

What was, in 1988, to be a decorating studio in the 1830s Federal-style farmhouse "with a few rooms to rent occasionally" became a full-time B&B for Helen—"maybe you can tell, I am somewhat of a naturalist." Her husband, Bill, is dean at Ithaca College. The 1989 B&B addition, a perfect architectural match, was constructed from Helen's own plans drawn on graph paper. A 1993 addition includes a beautiful formal dining room that opens onto a patio and extensive perennial gardens. Throughout, decor is light and cheery country English style with antiques, wicker, dhurries, chintzes, and plants.

Foreign language spoken: "French partially understood."
Bed and bath: Four rooms with private full baths that have pedestal sink, cosmetic stand, hair dryer. One on first floor; three on second. One room with antique double bed; three with queen bed (one is a four-poster). Rollaway and crib available.
Breakfast: Flexible timing. Menu varies. Fresh fruit, baked apples, or poached pears. Juice, homemade breads and granola, bacon or sausage from local butcher, unusual coffees and teas. House specialty—Swedish pancakes with creme fraiche. Cooked before your eyes in open kitchen/dining room. Served in dining room or on garden patio.
Plus: Bedroom air conditioning and ceiling fans. Goose-down comforters and pillows. TV room. Mints on pillows. Fresh flowers. Late-afternoon lemonade or mulled cider with homemade brownies, cookies (gingerbread at Christmas), or cakes. Adirondack chairs—and, in fall, deer too—by the pond. Bluebirds at the feeder.

Rose Inn

813 Auburn Road, Route 34N
P.O. Box 6576, Ithaca, NY 14851-6576

607/533-7905
fax 607/533-7908

Hosts: Charles and Sherry Rosemann
Location: Rural. On 20 landscaped acres with lawns, gardens, terraces, and orchard. Twelve minutes from the center of Ithaca and Cornell University.
Open: Year round. Two-night minimum if stay includes Saturday night.

Three nights for holiday and special university weekends.
Rates: $110 double bed, $140 queen, $160 king or twin beds. Suites with Jacuzzi $185–$250. Additional person $25.
♥ ❖ ♦ ✖ ⅍

The ultimate. An architectural gem. For most guests, not just like home. An elegant showplace with period furnishings, artworks, flowers, attention to every detail, and service. It's personalized by professionals who began in 1983

(Please turn page.)

with five guest rooms and some shared baths. With the option of dinner, this acclaimed inn has become a destination for romantics, and with the transformed carriage house, a meeting site for groups. Weddings and receptions are held here too.

There's a fascinating story to the magnificent freestanding, self-supporting Honduran mahogany spiral staircase that extends from the main entrance hall up to the cupola with skylight in this 1851 mansion. And then there's the story of the Rosemanns, parents of two college-age children. Since Charles started his career in his native Germany in the 1950s, he has opened major Hyatt hotels in this country and managed Washington, D.C.'s Sheraton and the hotel school at Cornell. Sherry, who has lectured on American furniture, has considerable experience as an interior designer. She mastered the arts of cooking, catering, and administration after receiving an undergraduate degree in microbiology and her master's in social work. Here she supervised the construction of you-can-hardly-tell additions, duplicating the 10-foot ceilings and 8-foot French doors.

In residence: Brandi, a Labrador/Samoyed.
Foreign languages spoken: German and Spanish.
Bed and bath: Fifteen no-two-alike rooms (all private tub/shower baths), including five suites that have wood-burning fireplace and Jacuzzi for two. On first and second floors. King, queen, double, or twin beds. Three rooms can be connected with a parlor that has two sleep sofas.
Breakfast: 8–9:30; 8:30–10 Sundays. Coffee available at 7. In season, fresh apple cider from Rosemanns' orchard. German apple pancakes with apple butter, French toast, and a special house blend of coffee. Artistically presented on china, crystal, and silver in dining room.
Plus: Fireplaced parlors with ornate crystal chandeliers. Air conditioners in guest rooms and dining room. Bedroom ceiling fans and individual thermostats. In season, apples (a dozen varieties) from the inn's orchard. Turndown service with style. Candlelit dinner, Tuesday–Saturday, with advance notice ($50/person). In conference center—wide-screen TV and comfortable seating available to all inn guests.

The Fontainebleau Inn   607/594-2008
2800 State Route 228, Alpine, NY 14805

Hosts: Terri and John VanSoest
Location: Serene. On Lake Kayutah (canoeing, fishing, cross-country skiing, and swimming), with 10 acres of lawns sloping to shore, mature trees, perennial gardens, and a gazebo too. Along a rural highway, minutes' drive to Finger Lakes hiking and cross-country skiing trails. Nine miles from Watkins Glen; 15 to Seneca Lake wineries; 17 to Ithaca; 20 to Corning. Next door to county historical society–owned chapel, available for weddings.
Open: Year round. Two-night minimum on weekends April–November.
Rates: $75 per room. Singles $10 less. $15 cot. Discounts for stays over four days.
♥ ♨ ✦ ♣ ✈ ✄

From award-winning Maryland innkeepers (page 25): *"What a beautiful setting for a beautiful inn . . . spotless . . . fine innkeepers . . . breakfast was wonderful."* From New York: *"Setting reminds me of Mount Vernon . . . have*

never been treated so royally . . . relaxed atmosphere . . . old-fashioned charm. . . .
Simply but beautifully decorated. . . . Genuinely happy to share their home with
us." From North Carolina: *"Perfect in every way."*

This ideal union of place and people began in 1990, just weeks after a chance
conversation when the VanSoests, Ithaca natives, asked to use the inn's
phone because of car trouble. Terri, who handles weddings with "ease and
perfection," had experience as a chef and caterer, and as assistant innkeeper
at her mother's B&B. John is a contractor who has experience as a chef and
boat builder. Obviously, guests sense their love of spontaneity, food, and this
old house. The oldest section, a former summer residence, was built in 1814
with handsome crown and dentil moldings. The dormered bed and breakfast
wing, added about 1860, is decorated with a country theme. The fireplaced
banquet hall, added in the 1920s, was built with beams from the original barn.

In residence: Brianna, age one. "Sushi and Savannah, two wonderfully
affectionate cats."
Bed and bath: Three second-floor rooms; one with slanted ceilings, two
with lake view. All private full baths. King, queen (with space for cot), or
double bed. Crib available.
Breakfast: Memorable. Flexible hours. Raspberry streusel muffins or blueberry sour cream coffee cake. Fresh fruit sundaes with yogurt and granola,
stuffed French toast, eggs Benedict, or Mexican omelets. Fresh pork sausage
or custom-smoked and -cut bacon. On porch overlooking lake, in dining
room, or in kitchen.
Plus: Fireplaced living room and library. Piano. Bedroom ceiling fans. Plush
bathrobes. Wicker-furnished porch. Iced tea or hot cider. Garden flowers.
Babysitting. Guest refrigerator. Canoe. Barbecue. Sleds. Picnic baskets prepared. Dinners by advance reservation.

The Wagener Estate Bed & Breakfast

351 Elm Street, Penn Yan, NY 14527   315/536-4591

Hosts: Evie and Norm Worth and
daughter Connie
Location: "Away from city traffic
and hustle and bustle." On a hillside,
surrounded by four acres of lawns,
apple trees, stone walls. Five
minutes' walk to village. About an
hour from Corning, Syracuse, and
Rochester. Near many wineries, restaurants, festivals.
Open: Year round. Two-night minimum May–October weekends.
Rates: Shared bath $55 single, $60
double. Private bath $65 single, $70
double. Cot $25. Amex, MC, Visa.
♥ ♣ ⋊ ⊬

From New York: *"It's like an inn from 200 years ago, where people would stop
their journeys, sit down, eat, and talk together."*

"After our guests settle in, we usually invite them for tea. Later we sometimes
join them in their living room or our family room, the one that has wainscoting done by Norm from attic floorboards. The large pillared porch (with
wicker furniture), part of the 1830 addition to the house, is a great gathering
spot too. We gladly answer all sorts of questions about the town founder who
first owned our property and built the 1790 rooms, one of which still has the
fireplace and oven. And guests express amazement that we lived through the

(Please turn page.)

upbringing of 10 children! (There are now 19 grandchildren, ages six months to 30.) When Norm retired as director of Keuka College's physical plant and I retired from teaching, we did some traveling and realized we weren't ready for retiring. We love this house, which is filled with the country look, many crafts, usable and comfortable antiques. When we are away, our daughter Connie, mother of three including two in college, is innkeeper. After twelve years of hosting, we don't know whether the hosts or guests have more fun!"

It's a natural. It's home. A hideaway. It is recommended for a place on the National Register of Historic Places. It is recommended as a B&B.

Bed and bath: Five second-floor rooms. King bed, private shower bath, air conditioning. Queen bed, private tub and shower bath, window fan. Queen bed, private shower bath, ceiling fan. Room with two twin beds and window fan shares a shower bath with air-conditioned "small, cute" double-bedded room.

Breakfast: At 9. Juice (maybe a white grape juice blended from local vineyards), lots of seasonal fruits, homemade sticky buns, toast, or muffins. Cheese, tomato, and mushroom omelet with ham or bacon; or buckwheat (Penn Yan is the world capital) and corn pancakes; crepes with blueberries and sausages; French toast or quiche and featherbed eggs.

Plus: Fresh flowers. TV in rooms with private baths as well as in the guest living room. A great story about huge front hall mirror.

The Russell-Farrenkopf House   315/472-8001

209 Green Street, Syracuse, NY 13203   (winter phone) 910/313-1800
Winter mailing address: 218 4th Street #5, Wilmington, NC 28401

Hosts: Joan Farrenkopf, owner/innkeeper, and Tammy Waters, co-innkeeper
Location: Residential. In the Hawley–Green Street historic district. Five blocks from downtown, nine to the campus, Carrier Dome, Upstate Medical Center. Within minutes of several restaurants, and Carousel Center Shopping Center.
Open: April–November.
Rates: $65 shared bath, $75 private. Singles $10 less.
🍴 ♣ ✖ ⊬

From Washington, D.C.: *"A gem, with its beautiful chestnut-and-mahogany staircase; high ceilings with plaster cornices; large, sunny rooms; plants everywhere. . . . Proprietress who offers a homelike environment . . . tours of the city."* From Cuba (and now, Miami): *"Every time I walk through the doors, I am filled with peace."*

"This 1865 French Second Empire/Italianate house taught me how to restore," says Joan, the fine arts major (and ski instructor) whose interest in historic preservation led to her restoring several other houses on the block and many others elsewhere, including six in Wilmington, North Carolina. Some floors and doors in the eclectically furnished B&B, opened in 1988, may look like walnut or mahogany, but they are hand grained. Joan's latest project: a research and plaque program for Syracuse historic district property owners.

Tammy, who is taking a respite from being a flight attendant, dovetails innkeeping with marriage, parenthood, and baking.

Bed and bath: Four rooms. First-floor room has king/twins option, private full bath, and private entrance. On second floor, large full bath is shared by one double-bedded room, one with a queen bed, and one with a king/twins option.
Breakfast: 7:30–9:30. Fresh fruit. Juice. Gourmet coffee. Stuffed apple dumplings, oven-baked French toast with real maple syrup, or vegetable frittata. Blueberry muffins with strawberry butter or coffee hazelnut scones. Served in bay-windowed red breakfast room.
Plus: Wicker-furnished, skylit intimate solarium. Welcoming beverage. Bedroom ceiling fans. Chocolate mints. Parlor reed organ in music room. Upright piano—used by at least one musician for practicing. If you'd like, a tour. (Can you find the artist's intials in the graining?) Side porch swing. Open front piazza. Some off-street parking. Afternoon tea by request. Perennial gardens.

From New York: *"A relaxing home away from home . . . fed and bed royally."*

Elaine's Bed & Breakfast Host #2
Baldwinsville, NY

Location: Majestic. In the village. In historic district. On a hill, surrounded by two acres of sloping lawn. One block to shops and restaurants; 20 minutes northwest of Syracuse.
Reservations: Year round through Elaine's Bed & Breakfast Reservation Service, page 159.

Rates: Single $50. Double: shared bath $55; private bath $65 queen, $80 king with fireplace. Extra person $10. No charge for crib. MC, Visa.
♥ ⅋ ⅋ ⁂ ✠

Local residents book their out-of-town relatives and friends here. Many business travelers and university visitors like the short drive from the thru-way. The hostess and her husband have lived in this handsome 1845 Greek Revival National Register house for almost 10 years. It is furnished with antiques, collectibles, and made-by-the-hostess quilts, baskets, and rag dolls. There's a wide "bride's" staircase; a fireplace in the living room; and, on the porch, rockers.

Bed and bath: Four second-floor rooms. Master bedroom has king bed, private tub/shower bath, wood-burning fireplace, dressing room, color TV. Room with queen bed plus a double daybed, private hall tub/shower bath, TV. Room with double bed (and TV) and one with a three-quarter bed share a tub/shower bath. Crib available.
Breakfast: 8–10. Fresh fruit, juice, baked French toast, hot beverages. Served in formal dining room.

Innkeeping may be America's most envied profession. As one host mused, "Where else can you get a job where, every day, someone tells you how wonderful you are?"

Lavender Inn Bed & Breakfast   315/829-2440

5950 State Route 5, Vernon, NY 13476-9779

Hosts: Rose Degni and Lyn Doring
Location: Rural setting on main road. Next door to a horse farm. Seven miles from I-90, 13 west of Utica, 35 east of Syracuse, 13 south of Rome. Six miles northwest of Hamilton College; 18 miles north of Colgate University.

Open: Year round. Two-night minimum on May graduation weekends.
Rates: $90 double, $75 single. $20 extra person. $10 crib, one-time charge. Amex, Diners.
♥ ♠ ♣ ♦ ✗

From New York: *"A relaxed, comfortable atmosphere . . . immaculate. . . . Breakfasts are outstanding, substantial, delicious . . . beautiful flower gardens."* From Tennessee: *"Greeted as a member of the family."*

Tradition! One of the oldest area houses (1799) was a tourist home from 1920 to 1940. Lyn and Rose, high school counselors, bought the Federal/Greek Revival in 1988 and restored it as a B&B. They decorated eclectically—with quilts and weavings, antiques and dried flower arrangements, and artwork including watercolors done by Rose's husband.

In residence: Kit, a cat not allowed in guests' areas.
Bed and bath: Two air-conditioned rooms; each has a queen and a single bed, sitting area, desk, private en-suite full bath.
Breakfast: 8–9. Fresh fruit (in season, berries from garden). Crepes, apple or puff pancakes, phyllo rolls, or a strata. Meat. Oatmeal. Baked goods. Homemade granola. Served at antique oak table in fireplaced dining room.
Plus: Fireplaced parlor with piano, TV/VCR. Beverages and snacks. Picnic tables. Lawn chairs. Arrangements, wreaths, and dried flowers for sale.

Seneca Lake Watch Bed and Breakfast

104 Seneca Street, Watkins Glen, NY 14891   607/535-4490

Hosts: Marge and Tom Conway
Location: Quiet. On a knoll across street from and overlooking lake. Three blocks to village shops and restaurants—"and from there to the north on it's all rural." Minutes' drive to state park, swimming, lake cruises, Watkins Glen racetrack; within 30 minutes of Corning, Ithaca, Ham-

mondsport, Elmira, Geneva, many wineries.
Open: Year round. Two-night minimum on major race and holiday weekends.
Rates: Queen bed $85 overlooking lake; $75 garden view. King with private deck $95. Amex, MC, Visa.
♥ ♣ ✗ ⊁

From New York: *"Outstanding view of the lake."* From Maryland: *" . . . feel more than just welcomed . . . you feel wanted."* From Virginia: *"Prepared Egg Beaters pancakes and coffee cake for my husband's low-cholesterol diet."* From Pennsylvania: *"Breakfast is a true occasion . . . something different each morning."* From Michigan: *"Was there for two weeks on business . . . treated just as special as an overnight guest."*

"Love at first sight!" The only house the well-traveled Conways ever looked at (for a B&B) features that lake view from the rockers on a 65-foot wrap-around porch. The foyer has pocket doors, fretwork, and a detailed oak staircase. A judge's house in the early 1900s, then a guest house in the late 1940s, the large Victorian was restored as a B&B in the 1980s. When the Conways, parents of four grown children, moved in 1992 from metropolitan New York (Garden City, where Marge was chamber of commerce president), they brought their comfortable, traditional furnishings and many antiques. The landscaping is all by Tom, a marine engineer educated in Scotland, who has the perfect background for his latest career: He owned and operated a hardware, houseware, and garden supply store at the same time he ran a travel agency. And in semiretirement he sold pianos and organs. Marge, who is active with the League of Women Voters, was director of executive travel management at the world headquarters of American Express.

Foreign language spoken: French.
Bed and bath: Four large second-floor rooms; all private baths. King bed, en-suite shower bath, private deck overlooking lake. Queen beds—one with en-suite shower bath, lake view; two with hall shower baths.
Breakfast: 7:30–9:30. Fresh or baked fruit. Homemade banana bread, raspberry loaf, or sour cream coffee cake; jams. Pancakes, French toast made with baked honey bread, cream cheese with chives in scrambled eggs. Sausage or bacon. Juice. Cereal. Coffee, tea. Served in dining room with leaded glass windows overlooking fountain and gardens (often with hummingbirds).
Plus: Guests' living room with fireplace, spinet piano, TV, VCR. Guest kitchen with snacks, beverages, deck. Lawn chairs. Recipes shared.

Reading House   607/535-9785
4610 Route 14, Rock Stream, NY 14878
Mailing address: P.O. Box 321, Watkins Glen, NY 14891

Hosts: Rita and Bill Newell
Location: On a rural main road, with gardens, lawns, and expansive view of ponds, woods, and Seneca Lake in back. Across from farmland. Five miles north of Watkins Glen; 5½ miles to town center; 30 miles south of Geneva. Within 5 miles of gorge, International Auto Raceway, four wineries, golf, swimming, boating, fishing, cross-country skiing.

Within 30 miles of Corning (south-west), Ithaca (southeast), Elmira (south).
Open: Year round. Two-night minimum on major holiday and Watkins Glen raceway weekends.
Rates: $55–$60 single. $60–$65 double. $10 third person. $10 less January–April.
♥ ⬤ ❖ ✈ ⅄

From Connecticut: *"Our accommodations were so pleasant and the Newells' company so engaging that we stayed an extra night . . . beautifully and comfortably furnished . . . memorable breakfasts . . . chatting with them on spacious back lawn was delightful."* From New York: *"Friendly conversation outdoors by fish ponds . . . by fire in winter . . . helpful restaurant recommendations . . . a 'must stop' for us."*

In New York City and western New Jersey, Scottish-born Rita was a Head Start director, Bill an exporter. They moved to this rambling restored 1820 Federal house in 1989 and furnished without clutter and with a mix of

(Please turn page.)

antiques, period pieces and reproductions, many books, prints, and works by local artists. Rita, a League of Women Voters board member, has become an avid bird-watcher (bluebirds nest right here). Gardener Bill is active with the cooperative extension service and the town planning board. The Newells grow vegetables, herbs, many perennials, and fruit. In one pond there are water lilies. In another there are fish that eat from your hand. Plans call for a flowering meadow, a rock garden, and a maze "someday."

In residence: In hosts' quarters, two cats.

Bed and bath: Four second-floor rooms, each with ceiling fan. All private baths. In front of house, large room with queen bed, attached full bath; smaller room with queen bed, Indian shutters, detached full bath. In rear with lake view, king/twins option, attached shower bath; room with a double bed and a twin bed, attached shower bath.

Breakfast: 7:30–9. Buckwheat or puffed pancakes with fruit. Or French toast made with French bread. Or omelets and other main courses. Juice, fresh fruit, cereal, homemade muffins. All kinds of special diets accommodated.

Plus: Handmade quilts on beds. Beverages and cookies. Guest refrigerator. Window fans available. Picnic table, lawn chairs. Skating right here. Sometimes, great blue heron in morning, deer and rabbits at night.

Some executives who book a meeting at an inn return on a weekend for a getaway. Some on a getaway return with colleagues for a meeting.

Rochester Area B&Bs

428 Mt. Vernon—a bed & breakfast inn

428 Mount Vernon Avenue, Rochester, NY 14620   **716/271-0792**
                                                         800/836-3159

Hosts: Philip and Claire Lanzatella. **Location:** Residential. On two acres of trees, wildflowers, and birds. At Highland Park (annual Lilac Festival) entrance. One mile to downtown, University of Rochester, Medical School campus, I-390/I-490 intersection. **Open:** Year round. **Rates:** Tax included. $100.80 single. $110.88 double. Amex, MC, Visa.

♥ ♣ ♦ ✈

An elegant Irish manor house. Discovered by many business and international travelers, by wedding planners, and by Rochesterians who told me that it was "a getaway without the driving, a fulfillment of our fantasy of what a B&B should be." The heirloom-filled 40-foot-long living room has fine art, Oriental rugs, an 1859 Knabe grand piano, and huge windows that look out onto magnificent copper beech trees. I found Max, the lovable mixed Lab, on the cushioned window seat with a choice view, the place he established as his very own during the 17-month restoration period. Thanks to Claire's patience, the elaborately carved mantel no longer has layers of paint in its crevices. And all the exquisite moldings, having been marked on the back piece by piece, have been reassembled by Phil, a contractor who specializes in historic preservation. In the former chapel, added when the Sisters of St. Joseph lived here (1952–86), there's a telescope. The ambiance throughout all 10,000 square feet is comfortable and welcoming.

The Lanzatellas lived three houses away for 17 years and bought this estate—which "needed everything"—for a B&B when their children were grown. They segued quite naturally into innkeeping. I enjoyed my stay. Highly recommended!

In residence: Max, the dog, and a crow named Joe.
Bed and bath: Seven very large rooms (one handicapped accessible) on second and third floors, with antique queen, double, or twin beds. All private en-suite baths, all with showers, some with tubs. Elevator available.
Breakfast: 7–9. Six courses selected from menu the night before. Claire makes the jams and bakes the breads (including whole wheat raisin), muffins, and scones. Presented by candlelight in fireplaced dining room with 12-foot expanse of windows and bird feeders.
Plus: Guest rooms have air conditioning, individual thermostats, ceiling fan, phone, TV (and cable). A desk in several. Turndown service. Down comforters. Fresh fruit. Homemade candy and cookies. Beverages. Dinner by prearrangement.

Genesee Country Inn   716/538-2500
948 George Street, Box 340   **fax 716/538-4565**
Mumford, NY 14511-0340

Hosts: Glenda Barcklow (proprietor) and Kim Rasmussen
Location: On 8½ idyllic acres. Thirty minutes south of downtown Rochester; 20 from University of Rochester, Strong Medical Center, Rochester Institute of Technology; 10 from I-90 exit 47. Ninety minutes to Niagara Falls. Three hours from Toronto.
Open: Year round. Closed Sunday noon–Tuesday noon, November through March and Christmas week. Two-night minimum on several May–October weekends.
Rates: $80–$103 double bed, $105 queen and a single, $120–$125 with sitting room or private patio and gas fireplace. $10 additional person. Winter and romance packages.
♥ ♣ ♦ ✈

"We're really an island surrounded by water," says Glenda when describing this "escape." Built in 1833, it was a mill for one hundred years. Then a private residence. Since 1982, a haven for getaway travelers and business guests who appreciate "all the creature comforts" along with history and natural beauty.

When Glenda, a Kodak accountant for many years, and her late husband established the inn, they were experienced restorers of several Rochester area 19th-century houses. An extension of Glenda's interest in painting, needlework, and nature, the limestone inn is picture perfect inside and out. On *Country Inns* 1991–92 "top 12" list, the inn has antique and reproduction pine and maple, Williamsburg colors, and marvelous stenciling painted by Glenda and local folk artist Ruth Flowers. The grounds, often compared to a Southern bayou, are complete with millponds (for trout fishing), 16-foot waterfalls (for dreaming), gazebo, fountain, gardens, woodlands, and picnic area.

Kim, a Rochester Institute of Technology Hotel School graduate, is a Corning (nearby Finger Lakes) native. She and Glenda direct guests to Rochester; Letchworth State Park, "the Grand Canyon of the East"; back roads for cycling; outlets and antiques shops. Some spend the day less than a mile away at the fascinating Genesee Country Village Museum, which has 53 buildings plus events. "And some guests come to do 'nothing at all.'" Before dinner at nearby (less than a mile away) fine restaurants, guests relax here with tea and cheese, crackers, and cookies.

In residence: Three cats: Sylvester, Pepper, and Kati.
Bed and bath: Nine rooms (with background sound of gurgling stream) on three levels have a queen, a double, or two beds (a queen or double with a single). Some with gas fireplace. All private baths; some full, some shower only. Garden-level rooms have canopied beds and gas fireplaces; one has French doors; two have private patio.
Breakfast: 7:30–8:30 weekdays, 8:30–9:30 weekends. Daily choices vary and include fresh fruit, cheese omelets, pancakes with vanilla-cinnamon sauce, and scrambled eggs. Homemade breads and muffins. Cereals. In wood-ceilinged breakfast room with water view, gas fireplace, and morning newspaper.

Plus: Air conditioning, desks, private phone (conference-call capability), and TV in each guest room. Mints on pillows. Deck by pond, gazebo, grill.

From California: *"Beautiful pond, woods, ducks. . . . Great breakfast orchestrated with a wonderful snowfall. . . . It's a good thing Hollywood hasn't discovered this inn. We'll be back before they do."*

KEY TO SYMBOLS
♥ Lots of honeymooners come here.
♯ Families with children are very welcome. (Please see page xii.)
◖ "Please emphasize that we are a private home, not an inn."
♣ Groups or private parties sometimes book the entire B&B.
♦ Travel agents' commission paid. (Please see page xii.)
✕ Sorry, no guests' pets are allowed.
✕ No smoking inside *or* no smoking at all, even on porches.

Niagara/Buffalo/Chautauqua Area
_____ Reservation Service _____

International Bed and Breakfast Club

504 Amherst Street, Buffalo NY 14207

Phone: Live Monday–Friday, 9–9; voice mail always available. 716/873-4262. For reservations, 800/723-4262.

Fax: 716/873-4462.

Listings: Over 70 in Niagara Falls, Buffalo, Rochester, Toronto, and Lake Ontario areas. Others are in all the mid-Atlantic states in this book; many are in Pennsylvania and Washington, D.C.

Reservations: Some can be made with 24 hours' notice. Some B&Bs require a two-night minimum.

Rates: $35–$345 single, $40–$350 double; average rates $75–$185. Some weekly and family rates available. One night's rate required as deposit on fewer than three nights; for three or more nights, one-half of the total reservation is paid in advance. Nonmember booking fee $15. Annual memberships (no booking fees) $24.95 single, $39.95 double/family. Deposits, less $25 cancellation fee, are refundable if cancellation is made at least seven days prior to scheduled arrival; no refund with less than seven days' notice. Amex, Discover, MC, Visa. ♥ ♦

What began in the mid-1980s as a regional reservation service—"personalized service that matches guests to the style, rate, and location desired"—has grown and continues to grow in scope and territory. The wide range of Western New York listings include lakefront residences, Victorians, century-old farmhouses, restored historic properties, and newer homes overlooking canals and rivers. In addition, Georgia Brannan and Patrick Flanigan offer corporate B&B stays, gift certificates, B&B travel planning, and—for frequent travelers—club memberships.

Niagara/Buffalo/Chautauqua Area
B&Bs

Plumbush at Chautauqua   716/789-5309

Chautauqua-Stedman Road, P.O. Box 864, Chautauqua, NY 14722

Hosts: Sandy and George Green
Location: On 125 acres, set back from the country road. One mile from Chautauqua Institution. Opposite 36-hole golf course. One mile to lake, swimming, boating, skating; 20 minutes to wineries and antiques shops; 30 to downhill skiing. On Route 33, three miles from Route 17, less than one mile from Route 394.
Open: Year round; reservations preferred. Two-night minimum stay, sometimes three, during peak seasons and on some weekends.
Rates: $80 double bed; $85, $90, or $95 king/twins option, queen. Discover, MC, Visa.
♥ ♣ ♦ ✗ ⅄

> From New York: *"Everything is wonderful . . . from the choice of colors to the breakfasts, from the architecture to the hosts."* From North Carolina: *"A perfect 10."*

Maybe you saw this B&B in *Country Living*'s "Traveller Tips." Or in *Victorian Homes, Victoria,* or *Innsider* magazines. Or even on a Benjamin Moore paint chart!

Sandy knew this 1860s Italian villa–style house from the schoolbus window as a child. She grew up on a nearby dairy farm, three miles from where George was raised in a family that has been in the lumber industry for five generations. So when the Greens felt it was time to come back home, they sold their acclaimed Hudson Valley B&B and took on this challenge, which became a two-year restoration project. George wired throughout, installed five bathrooms, and designed a sun room with arches that echo the windows of the 11-foot-ceilinged rooms. Sandy substituted painting and papering for church organ playing. Because of the views from each window, she chose shutters rather than curtains. By the summer of 1988, the first guests climbed the beautiful circular staircase to the tower for its commanding panoramic view. Ever since, the hosts have been greeting guests, who enjoy the music room with its piano and organ, the almost-famous Green hospitality, and the country Victorian decor.

Bed and bath: Five second-floor rooms, all private shower baths. One with a double bed. One with king/twins option. Three with queen beds.
Breakfast: 8:30–9:30. Coffee ready at 7. Juice, fresh fruit, homemade muffins and breads, home-blended granola, cheese and crackers, yogurt, hot beverages. Often, extra treats on Sunday. Guests usually take breakfast into wicker-furnished enclosed sun room overlooking gardens and woods.
Plus: A real cookie jar—filled. Self-serve hot or cold drinks. Sun room with Franklin wood stove and ceiling fans. Bedroom ceiling fans. Wicker on veranda. Two-mile wooded trail for hiking, cross-country skiing, and birding right here. Bicycles available for guests' use.

Westfield House   716/326-6262

East Main Road, Route 20, P.O. Box 505, Westfield, NY 14787

Hosts: Betty and Jud Wilson
Location: Two miles east of town, between Buffalo and Erie. Near I-90 exit 60. Way back from road behind large trees. Surrounded by grape vineyards. Five minutes to Lake Erie, 15 to Lake Chautauqua, 30 to cross-country and downhill skiing. Close to

wineries and antiques shops.
Open: Year round. Two-night minimum July and August weekends.
Rates: $55 single. $60–$75 double. $95 suites. $15 third person. Midweek senior citizen discount. MC, Visa.

♥ ♣ ♦ ✈ ⅍

Guests can tell: The Wilsons love B&B. And they love their red brick Gothic Revival house, beautifully furnished with some museum-quality antiques and family heirlooms and portraits. There's a cherry staircase, lots of beveled glass, crystal-chandeliered front hall, and, in the common rooms, Gothic woodwork and windows. The house, restored by the Wilsons in 1987, was at one time the home of *Antiques Journal.*

Betty, who has a needlepoint shop here, and Jud, a salesman, have "entertained together"—as Betty says—for 44 years. As hosts they are delighted with guests who relax and enjoy their home and all the area has to offer.

Bed and bath: Seven rooms (two are suites); all private baths. All custom-made mattresses. Two adjoining first-floor rooms with shower bath; large room with queen four-poster bed and fireplace, adjoining room with double bed and telephone. On second floor, two rooms with queen beds, shower bath; one with king, shower bath; one with two double beds, full bath. Suite has two double beds, full bath, living room with TV and telephone. Rollaway.
Breakfast: At 9. Fresh fruit, homemade breads and muffins, coffee, teas, and juices. Hot entree. By candlelight in fireplaced dining room set with linen, cloth napkins, silver, fine china.
Plus: In season, bowls of grapes from the surrounding vineyards; grape juice in rooms. Evening refreshments. Fresh flowers. Down comforters. Air conditioning in three second-floor rooms. Ceiling fans in some. Guest refrigerator. Picnic tables. Lawn furniture. Walking/jogging trails in vineyards.

The William Seward Inn   716/326-4151

6645 South Portage Road (Route 394)   800/338-4151
Westfield, NY 14787   fax 716/326-4163

Hosts: Jim and Debbie Dahlberg
Location: On a high knoll with view of Lake Erie on the horizon. Minutes from the village, 20 antiques shops, five wineries. Four miles to Lake Chautauqua, 7 to Chautauqua Institution. Adjacent to cross-country skiing. Half hour to downhill ski resorts; 65 miles south of Buffalo.
Open: Year round. For some

rooms, two-night weekend minimum year round; for others, two-night weekend minimum on Saturdays in July, August, October.
Rates: Main house $90–110. Singles $10 less. $25 extra person. Carriage house $135–$155. Mystery, antiquing, and some holiday packages available. Discover, MC, Visa.

♥ ♣ ♦ ✈ ⅍

Although Chautauqua Institution is a major draw, many travelers come specifically to stay at this antiques-filled 1821 inn, which has become almost famous for Jim's cooking. (Recipes are shared—sometimes right in the kitchen.) The comfortable ambiance, created with period antiques (mid-1800s–early 1900s), wallpapers, and decor, has been acknowledged in a full-page *New York Times* travel article. Yet, as skiers, honeymooners, business guests, and antiques lovers attest, Jim and Debbie make the difference. If you'd like, they'll share the history of the inn, which was given its mansion appearance when William Seward (later governor of New York and Lincoln's secretary of state) added pillars in the 1840s. Full restoration took place in 1982, and the inn opened for business in 1983. The Dahlbergs made their career change in 1990 when they moved from Buffalo. Jim "retired" from a major commercial bank as vice president in operations. For two years Debbie continued working for a fair housing organization before becoming full-time innkeeper in 1992.

In residence: In hosts' quarters, two cats whom you might meet on the wicker-furnished patio. "Sasha, our collie, sometimes wanders the grounds."
Bed and bath: Fourteen carpeted rooms (one with fireplace), all private baths. On first and second floors in mansion, 10 rooms with king, queen (some four-posters), one or two doubles, or twin beds; some baths are tub/shower, some shower only. In carriage house (furnished with reproductions), king or queen beds, Jacuzzis for two.
Breakfast: 7:45–9:30, earlier for businesss guests and skiers. Juice, home-made muffins, fruit. Garnished hot entree choices include scrambled eggs with tarragon and four cheeses, French toast, apple cinnamon pancakes. In dining room with view of birds at feeder.
Plus: Air conditioning throughout. Fireplaced common areas. Wet bar. Late-afternoon hot chocolate, spiced cider, or lemonade and cookies. Grounds with gardens, benches, chairs, trails. Option of dinner (by advance reservation only) Thursday–Sunday, $36 per person including tax. Inquire about massages.

From Indiana: *"A native . . . returned to Westfield after 50 years . . . delighted to find such fine accommodations at the historic inn . . . friendliness makes it a must for a return visit."* From Pennsylvania: *"Superb."* From Ohio: *"Fabulous food. . . . The library with Vivaldi was a delight. . . . A wonderful hideaway."*

Manchester House   716/285-5717
653 Main Street, Niagara Falls, NY 14301-1701   716/282-2144

Hosts: Elisabeth and Carl Slenk
Location: On U.S. Route 104, main street in a commercial area. Between a Unitarian church and an accountant's offices. Ten-minute walk to the falls. Near restaurants favored by local residents.

Open: Year round.
Rates: $70 double, $50 single. Less October–April. $10 rollaway. MC, Visa.

From Maryland: *"Our family, which makes up Tale Weavers Children's Living Theater, have been guests during our performance time at Niagara Falls Kidfest.*

(Please turn page.)

We specifically asked to return to Manchester House this year. . . . Breakfasts are gorgeous and delicious." From England: *"Lovely warm comfortable atmosphere. Older style very much appreciated for its charm and character."* From Pennsylvania: *"Unhurried and friendly."*

Carl calls the brick-and-shingled house "1903 contemporary." Not a mansion, but a doctor's offices for many years, it was a two-year conversion project that culminated in the B&B opening "in the city where our three children were born" in 1991. In the 1980s the Slenks lived in England and Germany—and stayed at B&Bs—while Carl, a chemical engineer and licensed ham operator, was a Carborundum plant manager. Now retired from Carborundum, he is treasurer of a private boys' secondary school. Lis, a teacher/speech therapist/writer who now creates wearable art and crafts, is an embroiderer, silk painter, clown course graduate, and former Niagara Falls information booth manager.

In residence: "One gray Persian-type cat, Rosie or Rosie-O-Gray-dee."
Foreign language spoken: German.
Bed and bath: Four second-floor rooms, each with ceiling fan, share two tub/shower baths. Two queens, one three-quarter bed, one room with two twins and air conditioning.
Breakfast: Flexible schedule. French toast or pancakes, fresh fruit, homemade muffins or breads, and juice.
Plus: Sitting room with gas fireplace, TV, and a spinet piano. A 1900 reed organ that has been converted to electric power. TV (cable), books, board games. Off-street parking "even for your boat trailer or recreational vehicle." Transportation to/from train or bus station.

The Cameo Inns   716/754-2075
4710 Lower River Road, Lewiston, NY 14092

Hosts: Gregory and Carolyn Fisher
Location: Two properties, three minutes' drive apart. Both on the Seaway Trail, Route 18F. Victorian house, 5 miles north of Niagara Falls, is on 60-foot bluff overlooking the Niagara River and Canadian shore. Manor house, 2½ miles farther north on same road at number 3881, is on three secluded acres. Within a half hour of 14 wineries. Five minutes to Canada.

Open: Victorian house in Lewiston is open spring through fall. Manor house in Youngstown is open year round.
Rates: In Victorian house: $85 queen, $115 suite, $65 double or twins with shared bath. In manor house: suites $99, $115, $130, or $175; shared bath $75. Singles $5 less. $15 cot. No charge for crib. Discover, MC, Visa.
♥ ♣ ♦ ✕ ⊱

Guests other than romantics are welcomed by the Fishers, but romance is surely a feature of their "two-part" B&B. The 27-room manor house has a 45-foot-long living room; there's a stone fireplace at each end. And another in the hunter green–colored library. Decorated with reproductions in English country style, the mansion was brought back to life—the exterior and grounds are "to be done"—by the Fishers, native Buffalonians, in 1990. Three years earlier they had opened the original Cameo Inn, a "painted lady" Victorian house complete with period wallpapers, antiques, and Oriental rugs. I stayed in the more intimate Victorian and loved it—and wished that I had returned "home" in time to view the sunset from the swing facing the river. Breakfast companions included visiting innkeepers who invited other guests to see "their" manor house suite. Everyone had much praise for the endless buffet of gastronomic creations.

Carolyn, a registered nurse who also has a degree in fine arts, is color consultant for Greg, a professional painting and decorating contractor who recently revived his interest in vintage sports cards.

In residence: Son Aaron, a college student, is assistant innkeeper. A Gordon setter, Beauregard, "captivates guests with his beauty."

Foreign language spoken: A little French.

Bed and bath: In Victorian house, four second-floor rooms with ceiling fans. Private full bath, up on next landing, for room with brass queen bed. Private shower bath for suite with queen bed, sitting room, view of Niagara. Full hall bath shared by room with antique double oak bed and one with view of river, two twin white iron beds. In manor house, three suites (one has four rooms and one is a bridal suite) with private tub and shower baths, private sun rooms, cable TV. Plus two rooms—one with two twin beds and one with a queen bed—that share a connecting full bath.

Breakfast: 8:30–9. Guests at both houses eat in manor house dining room. Buffet with fresh orange or grapefruit juice, crepes, omelets, "Greg's eggs," or Dutch babies (oven pancakes). Homemade pastries. Hot beverages.

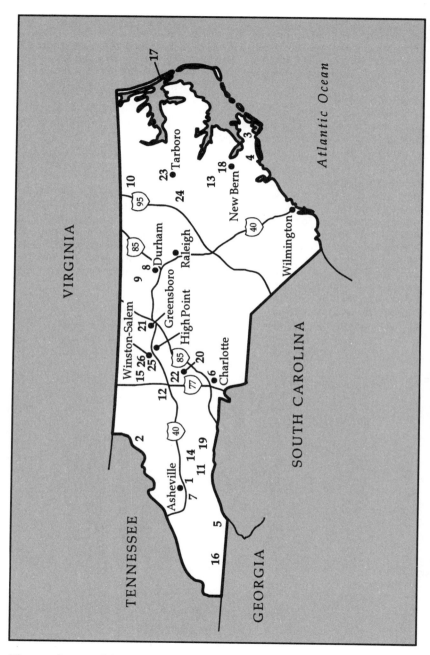

The numbers on this map indicate the locations of B&Bs described in detail in this chapter.

NORTH CAROLINA

——————— North Carolina B&Bs ———————

Albemarle Inn   704/255-0027
86 Edgemont Road, Asheville, NC 28801-1544

Hosts: Kathy and Dick Hemes
Location: Residential area with neighboring homes built in the 1920s and '30s on the acreage of this original manor house.
Open: Year round. Two-night weekend minimum, April–New Year's.

Rates: Per room. $75, $85, $90, $95, $100, $105, $110, $120, $130. Varies according to room and bed size, decor, and furnishings. Discover, MC, Visa.
♥ ◆ ✈ ⊁

From Texas: *"Style, grace, and effortless charm."* From Georgia: *"Rooms are tastefully decorated to match the style of this beautiful turn-of-the-century home. . . . Friendly and helpful innkeepers."* From Illinois: *"Best place we stayed at during our three-week vacation."* From Washington, D.C.: *"Headed for world class."*

Béla Bartók wrote his Third Concerto for Piano (Asheville Concerto) while living in this house in its 1943 rooming-house days. The setting is still grand. Featuring four 30-foot columns in front, the National Register Greek Revival mansion has high ceilings, an oak-paneled living room, and a carved oak stairway with circular landing and balcony. It's the dream of former IBMers who thought about innkeeping "through many years of entertaining and 11 years of inngoing." Dick, official omeletier, was in finance and planning for 38 years; Kathy in marketing support for almost 20. In 1992 they bought this established B&B and some of its original early 1900s furnishings. They redecorated and refurbished, adding some period pieces along with treasures they acquired during the 1980s, when they lived in Hong Kong for three years.

Bed and bath: Eleven rooms (ten are spacious), all private baths with footed tub/shower. All with TV and phone. First floor—double four-poster or queen bed. Second floor—four rooms and a suite grouped around a second living room. Queen four-poster, private balcony; queen and a double, all wicker; queen canopied; king brass and enameled iron. Suite has king bed, enclosed sun porch. Third floor—queen and, in dormer alcove, a single bed, low-ceilinged bath; queen brass bed; queen bed and, in alcove, one twin; small double-bedded room.
Breakfast: 8–9:30. Juices. Fresh fruit. Apple crisp with apple cider sauce or croissant a l'orange with smoked sausage. Stuffed French toast with cheeses, Bermuda onion, and chives, lemon dill sauce and bacon. Eggs Moonstruck—grilled egg with fresh dill and curry on black Russian butterfly-shaped bread, ham with mustard apricot sauce. Served in wicker-furnished sun room or in fireplaced dining room.
Plus: Air conditioning in nine rooms; ceiling fan in second-floor suite and third-floor rooms. Social hour at 5 p.m. with complimentary beverages and snacks on large front veranda or by living room fireplace. Lawn seating. Handmade candy. Recommendations and reservations for host-tested restaurants.

From North Carolina: *"A real treasure . . . beautifully furnished, impeccably clean . . . magnificent water views in every direction. . . . We relished the beautiful sunrises and sunsets, enjoyed the relaxing atmosphere, indulged in fantastic breakfasts . . . every detail attended to."*

Applewood Manor   704/254-2244
62 Cumberland Circle, Asheville, NC 28801-1718

Hosts: Susan Poole and Maryanne Young
Location: A quiet residential area of Montford Historic District. On two acres with trees and wildflower gardens; ¾ mile north of downtown Asheville; 3 miles from Biltmore Estate. Two blocks from Botanical Gardens.

Open: Year round. Two-night minimum on weekends.
Rates: $85 per room, $95 with balcony and fireplace. $105 with fireplace and sitting area with daybed. $115 cottage with living room and kitchen. Singles $5 less. Discover, MC, Visa.
♥ ❖ ♦ ✈ ⅄

As guests, they were two cytotechnologists from State College, Pennsylvania, when they learned that the inn was for sale. In 1991 Maryanne, a bluegrass/traditional musician/now golfer, and Susan, a basketry and fitness enthusiast/now square dancer and cookbook author, exchanged their microscopes for innkeeping hats. Here they host many guests who come for the nearby Biltmore Estate, the Blue Ridge Parkway, and Connemara (Carl Sandburg's house) too. Their turn-of-the-century Colonial Revival house, an inn since 1987, is furnished with antiques, Oriental rugs, and linens and lace.

In residence: Lucy, a calico cat, usually in hosts' quarters. During some college vacations, Susan's daughter and son.
Bed and bath: Four queen-bedded second-floor rooms. Three with working fireplace and a balcony. All with private baths (some very new); two shower only, two tub and shower. Rollaway bed. Cottage has queen bed, queen sofa bed, living room, kitchen area, bath with oversized shower.
Breakfast: 8–9:30. "Susan cooks, Maryanne serves." Blueberry sour cream pancakes, orange pecan waffles, herbed egg bake, apple brie omelets, English muffin or pear bread, cranberry orange nut or pineapple muffins. Served on wicker-furnished porch or in fireplaced dining room.
Plus: No TV. Fireplaced common areas. Air-conditioned guest rooms with ceiling fans. Afternoon beverage. Fresh fruit and flowers. Chocolates. Badminton and croquet right here. Complimentary use of nearby sports club facilities including Nautilus, sauna, aerobics. Picnic baskets, $8.50 per person. Three- and 10-speed bikes (no charge).

---

*O*ne out of five guests leaves with the dream of opening a
B&B.

Cairn Brae   704/252-9219
217 Patton Mountain Road, Asheville, NC 28804

Hosts: Milli and Ed Adams
Location: Secluded and quiet. On three wooded acres with trails, a pond, and views of Blue Ridge Mountains. Fifteen minutes from downtown.
Open: April–November. Two-day minimum in October and on holiday weekends.

Rates: $85 room with queen or room with double and single bed; $100 king with sitting room; $15 extra person. $130 family suite (maximum of four guests). MC, Visa.
♥ ◀ ♣ ♦ ✕ ✚

> From Michigan: *"I came for the Biltmore Estate. . . . [The Adamses'] gracious hospitality makes us want to return . . . a bygone way of life has a place in our hurry-scurry way of life."* From Virginia: *"The highlight of our trip."* From Florida: *"We could live there!"*

Milli and Ed fell in love with this mountain retreat when, in 1987, they were only halfway up the driveway. "And somehow the beautiful location seems to get more scenic every year." This "big wonderful three-storied house" with many floor-to-ceiling windows is furnished with wicker, antiques, and traditional pieces. The Adamses, who were in retailing and advertising in Florida, are "used to entertaining." Here they greet guests with hot cider by the fire or a beverage on the terrace-with-view.

Bed and bath: Three rooms plus two-room family suite—all with floor-to-ceiling or large picture windows. All with private baths. King bed, sitting room with queen sofa bed; queen bed; or a double and a single bed. Family suite has queen-bedded room connecting with room with bunk beds, toys, and games.
Breakfast: Usually 8–9. Homemade rolls or special breads. Casseroles, waffles, or quiche. Local fruits in season. Juice. Served at table set with fine china and crystal in dining room overlooking treetops.
Plus: Living room with stone fireplace. In each room—air conditioner, individual thermostat, phone jacks. Fresh fruit and flowers. Bedside homemade goodies.

The Inn on Montford   704/254-9569
296 Montford Avenue, Asheville, NC 28801   800/254-9569
                                          fax 704/254-9518

Hosts: Ripley Hotch and Owen Sullivan
Location: On a rise, set back from a wide street that has arched old plane trees. In Montford Historic District, surrounded by grand old homes. "We're in a comfortably sized city that seems to have a festival every other weekend—unusual botanical gardens, antiques, crafts, folk arts, foliage, Christmas . . . it goes on and on."
Open: Year round.
Rates: Per room, $90–$120 according to size of room. MC, Visa.
♦ ✕ ✚

From Georgia: *"The aroma of cookies. The sound of fine music. A palette of pleasing colors throughout. And MANY beautiful things to touch. . . . Made our lives a little bit richer."*

It's all here: Great conversation. Fireplaces. Extraordinary antiques and art collections everywhere. Comfortable beds. (Owen, now Asheville Antiques Show manager, once sold bedding.) Bath sheets. Carafes of mountain spring water in rooms. Whirlpool tubs. Soundproofing. Back garden complete with outdoor furniture. Afternoon tea. Reservations at hard-to-book restaurants. Recommendations for everything from the Blue Ridge Parkway to horseback riding, from hot-air ballooning to furniture shopping and waterfalls.

It's no wonder that returnees abound. The "Arts and Crafts interpretation of a gabled English cottage" was designed by the supervising Biltmore Estate architect with exterior shingles and pebble-dash stucco. Marine paintings and ship models, a wonderful old leather sofa, and blue-and-white porcelain are in the fireplaced den. French doors lead to the semicircular sun room, where a door opens to the big wide front porch and rockers.

Ripley is coauthor of *How to Start and Run Your Own Bed & Breakfast Inn* and technology editor of *Nation's Business* magazine. Owen is a raconteur who enjoys taking guests to antiques auctions.

In residence: Two dogs: Jefferson Davis, a collie/shepherd, "has had more offers of homes than you can imagine." Dolley Madison is an American Eskimo.
Foreign language spoken: French.
Bed and bath: Four air-conditioned second-floor queen-bedded rooms; each with gas fireplace. All private en-suite baths; three with Jacuzzis, one with claw-footed tub and full shower.
Breakfast: "A religious experience," according to one guest. About 9. Continental if earlier. Entree possibilities include puffed apple pancakes, stuffed raspberry French toast, orange croissants, frittatas, stratas. Sometimes, "Caribbean pear" in orange sauce with cinnamon stick (as a stem) and kiwi cut as the leaf. In dining room at inlaid table surrounded by collections of porcelain and china.

The Banner Elk Inn B&B   704/898-6223
Route 3, Box 1134 (P.O. Box 1953), Banner Elk, NC 28604

Host: Beverly Lait
Location: In a mountain valley village setting on a triangle of land bordered by roads; on Highway 194 north, .2 mile from town's only traffic light. Minutes to Sugar and Beech ski resorts and Grandfather Mountain. Walking distance to fine restaurants. Eight miles from Blue Ridge Parkway.

Open: Year round. Two-night minimum on weekends.
Rates: Per room. Reservations suggested. Private bath $70 weekdays, $75–$95 weekends. Families (total of four people) midweek, $120–$140 for two rooms. MC, Visa.
♥ ♫ ♣ ✄

The innkeeper is a tapestry maker, portrait artist, and real estate broker. She lives in a raspberry-pink expanded and restored 1912 farmhouse that has been a church, an inn, and a residence. When Beverly, a native of Charleston,
(Please turn page.)

South Carolina, opened her "casual, elegant, friendly, spontaneous" B&B in 1991, she filled it with carved wood furniture, stained glass, and antiques —many collected during 14 years of living in Peru, England, Uruguay, and Germany. One of her first guests was an Uruguayan architect who was amazed to find Uruguayan architectural books in her library. Many guests who come "to get away from it all" utilize the hand-drawn fun map with selected highlights including a famous general store (est. 1833), hiking and ski areas, and shops.

Foreign languages spoken: Spanish and some German.

In residence: Tati, "innkeeper kitty, a loving Maine coon cat not allowed in guest rooms."

Bed and bath: Four soundproofed second-floor rooms. One with queen bed and one with a double bed, each with large private tub/shower bath. One queen-bedded room and one with two twin beds share a tub/shower bath plus an extra hall half bath.

Breakfast: 8–10. Cottage cheese pancakes or hot baked cinnamon apples stuffed with granola or Belgian pancakes with fresh-cooked cinnamon apples, whipped cream, syrup, and sausages. Or fruit salad and Parmesan souffle omelet with cheddar sauce. Homemade whole wheat or banana nut bread. Served in wonderful Great Room at large table set with fine china, crystal, and silver.

Plus: European down comforters. Fireplaced Great Room with cable TV. Cordless phones. Fresh fruit. Restored (splashing) old stone fountain. Perennial gardens. Flower arrangements for special occasions. Handmade-sweater shop on premises.

> From North Carolina: *"Perfect . . . art, antiques, and food . . . wonderful sense of color and texture. . . . For an English assignment on the topic of a memorable meal, our 16-year-old wrote about Beverly's breakfast."*

The Langdon House Bed & Breakfast

135 Craven Street, Beaufort, NC 28516-2116   **919/728-5499**

Host: Jimm Prest

Location: Residential. "Away from tourist activity, but just a block from restaurants, museums, waterfront shops, and ferry to Cape Lookout National Seashore Park." Next door to historic homes. Across from church with c. 1731 burial ground.

Open: Year round (except for Jimm's unscheduled winter vacation). Two-night minimum on May–mid-November weekends.

Rates: Tax included. November 15– April 30: Friday and Saturday $100 per room. Sunday–Thursday, full breakfast $78 single, $90 double; continental $74/$80; coffee/tea only, $70 per room. May–November 14: Friday and Saturday $115 per room. Sunday–Thursday, full breakfast $88 single, $100 double; continental $84/$90; coffee/tea only, $75 per room.

♥ ♣ ✈ ⅙

> From North Carolina: *"As a reporter who travels 34,000 miles a year across the Tarheel state . . . nothing more refreshing than a hug from Jimm and a peaceful night in his 250-year-old house. Plus he makes the best fresh peach waffles known to man or God. . . . Even picks me up at the local airport . . . a five-star establishment.*

. . . Makes you feel like you are at home with family . . . what a B&B should be."
From a Massachusetts salesman who has been selling my guidebooks for
over 25 years: *"Jimm epitomizes real Southern hospitality in the best place I stayed
in on that long trip."*

Everyone appreciates Jimm, a former Coca-Cola Company staffer who traveled countrywide before coming in 1980 to the community he knew from
childhood summers. Since 1983 the historian/preservationist/gardener/chef
has honed "the art of innkeeping" in his "sculpture" (every detail attended
to), an added-on-to 1733 house, a three-storied Colonial/Federal that he
restored. It's comfortable, warm, and welcoming, with polished floors, country pieces, Currier & Ives prints, and several early instruments, including a
late 1800s Estes pump organ and a zither. And then there are those enticing
suggestions for things to do in historic Beaufort or (not far) beyond. "You can
'get lost'; explore the marshes in the company of wild ponies; enjoy 10 miles
of creamy white sand without a house in sight; dress for dinner and stop en
route for a sunset along a beach." I want to go—and stay.

Foreign language spoken: "Imperfect Spanish."
Bed and bath: Four first-floor rooms (back one is especially private); all
queen beds. All private baths—three with showers; one with tub/shower,
bubble bath, and rubber duckie.
Breakfast: Any time before noon. Menu never repeated during your stay.
Fresh fruit course plus entree, maybe Belgian waffles—orange pecan, ginger
bread, banana nut, or cinnamon/apple; French toast stuffed with various
fruits, meats, cheeses, and herbs; or omelets. Served in second-floor dining
room or on one of the porches. Special diets accommodated with advance
notice.
Plus: Just about anything you could wish for. The long list includes beverages, books, beach baskets and towels, bicycles, grills, hip waders, iron,
jumper cables, maps, jogging route, nautical charts, camera, porch rockers,
sun lotion, tennis rackets, shell collecting bags.

Pecan Tree Inn 　　　　919/728-6733
116 Queen Street, Beaufort, NC 28516

Hosts: Susan and Joe Johnson
Location: In historic district with
restored period homes; half a block
to waterfront. A short walk to fine
restaurants, shopping, North Carolina Maritime Museum, old burying
grounds. Close to two-minute boat
ride to Carrot Island, where wild ponies graze. Near ferry for Shackleford
Island. Fifty minutes' drive to Outer
Banks ferry.
Open: Year round.

Rates: Mid-April to mid-September: weekdays, $80 twin, $80–$95
queen, $95 king or canopy bed, $110
bridal suite; weekends, $10 more.
$15 third person in room. Mid-Sep-
tember to mid-April: weekdays, $65
twin, $65–$85 queen, $85 king or
canopy bed, $95 bridal suite; week-
ends, $5 more. $15 third person in
room. MC, Visa.
♥ ❖ ♦ ✗ ✔

From Pennsylvania: *"Enchanting."* From North Carolina: *"After visiting
B&Bs far and wide, I give Pecan Tree Inn a five-star rating in all respects."*

(Please turn page.)

Among other accolades: a restoration award from the town and a *Condé Nast Traveler* feature. Business travelers, honeymooners, and tourists, too, appreciate the freshly decorated inn, which has an uncluttered look with some antiques, refinished pine floors, and patterned carpets and Orientals. And they appreciate the Johnsons—Joe, the former New Jersey hardware store owner (a third-generation one), and Susan, who worked with AAA's insurance department. "When we found this house, an 1866 Masonic Lodge that had rooms, turrets, and gingerbread added at the turn of the century, we also fell in love with the town. Once you're here for a few days, you're on Beaufort time. So we changed our plans, spent six months renovating, and opened in 1992. When 92-year-old Howard Jones, a local resident, had breakfast with his granddaughter in our dining room, he recalled planting the two pecan trees for which the inn is named. Our most recent project is the 5,500-square-foot English flower and herb garden with a goldfish pond and more than one thousand plantings. We really enjoy B&B."

Bed and bath: Seven rooms, all private shower baths. On first floor, room with brass queen bed. Rooms on second floor (two open onto a porch) have twin, queen (one canopied), or canopied king beds. Bridal suite has king bed, two-person Jacuzzi. All rooms with canopied beds have private entrance onto porches. Rollaway available.
Breakfast: Usually 7:30–9. Homemade muffins, breads, and cakes. Fresh fruits, cereal, juices, freshly ground coffee. In dining room or on front porch.
Plus: Central air conditioning. Bedroom and living room ceiling fans. Freshly made pecan candy. Guest refrigerator with cold drinks. Beach towels and chairs. Books and games in library. Bicycles (no charge). Picnic baskets. Transportation to/from local marina and Beaufort Airport.

Harborlight Guest House   919/393-6868
332 Live Oak Drive, Cape Carteret, NC 28584   800/624-VIEW (8439)

Hosts: Bobby and Anita Gill
Location: Quiet and private. Along 530 feet of shoreline—swim, clam, and fish right here—on Bogue Sound and Intracoastal Waterway. Within minutes of five major golf courses. Within an hour of barrier island ferries. Five minutes to Swansboro for antiquing, shops, waterfront restaurants.

Open: Year round.
Rates: $140–$155 waterfront luxury suites with king bed and fireplace. Queen bed $110–$125 waterview suites; $75–$90 (without refrigerator) waterview rooms. Singles $15 less. Third person $25. Winter months $15 less excluding waterfront suites. Amex, MC, Visa.
♥ ♣ ♦ ✕ ⅄

Almost a secret getaway—because there is no highway signage. (As we go to press, *Southern Living* is scheduled to let the world know by publishing a guest's letter.) It's definitely an unusual off-the-beaten-track surprise. You pass mobile homes before coming to this tranquil peninsula. There before you is this converted big old three-storied square house, originally built as a restaurant for ferry services. "Put a paddle on the side and it would look like a steamboat," said one guest. In 1993, when the Gills gutted and rebuilt in 105 days, they created a seven-room attention-to-detail B&B with private exterior entrances, surrounding balconies, some fireplaces, and two-person

Jacuzzis too. The ambiance is Caribbean—with white siding and teal trim and lots of windows. One room is furnished in country style. Most have wicker and hand-painted furniture. Palm trees from Florida, the birds and boats, and sunrises and sunsets complete the unspoiled scene.

In Raleigh, Bobby was a landscape contractor for 25 years. Anita was an operating room nurse. Following their own B&B experiences, they researched the entire eastern seaboard before finding this secluded property.

In residence: Coco, a chocolate Lab, and Ginger, a sheltie, "our mascots, loved by guests."

Bed and bath: Seven air-conditioned and carpeted rooms (one is handicapped accessible, two are suites)—each with king or queen bed, large private full bath, in-room temperature controls, ceiling fan, coffeemaker, cable TV. Refrigerator in five rooms. Waterfront luxury suites also have two-person Jacuzzi and gas fireplace.

Breakfast: At 8:30 in dining room overlooking garden, pond with goldfish and fountain, and waterway. In suite (with fireplace) at 9. Fresh fruits or baked pineapple. Homemade breads or almost-famous cinnamon tea rolls. Egg-and-cheese strata or spinach quiche.

Plus: Special occasions acknowledged. Umbrellas (sometimes needed to get to dining room). Elevator access to second floor. Use of bicycles, and clam buckets and rakes. Intentionally, no phones in the rooms.

Innisfree Victorian Inn   704/743-2946

Lakeside Knoll, Cashiers, NC 28717

Hosts: Dottie and Henry Hoche, owners; Brenda Clickenger, innkeeper

Location: Spectacular. Overlooking Lake Glenville with its 26 miles of shoreline, waterfalls ("a major attraction"), islands, birds, no bordering highway, peace. On acres of gardens, open space, trees, and gardens with walks and seating—with view of mountain tops and not a single other structure. In Glenville, which has general store, post office, boat marina, antiquing. Shops and restaurants are six miles south in Cashiers and another six miles to Highlands.

Open: Year round. Two-day minimum preferred on weekends.

Rates: June–November: main house rooms $140 (without lake view) to $275; garden house $190–$250. Off season: main house $125–$250, garden house $175–$225. Amex, Discover, MC, Visa.
♥ ♣ ⊁

The name comes from W. B. Yeats's poem "The Lake Isle of Innisfree." When the Hoches' all-new dream Victorian house—often mistaken by guests for "a wonderful restoration" was under construction in 1989, there were so many curiosity seekers that it was changed to a B&B. There are verandas, gingerbread trim, an observatory that overlooks everything, a fantasy two-storied kitchen with fireplace (and with lake view too), an even taller great room, large rooms and closets, and everywhere treasures that are meant to be touched. One room has hats and costumes, perfect for photo opportunities. Another has a lovely jewelry box filled with a collection waiting to be examined. The garden house baths are extraordinary. Next: three gazebos and a fish pond with fountain and lilies.

(Please turn page.)

Henry, an ardent gardener, is a national dahlia-growing champion and former real estate broker. Previously he and Dottie lived in Florida.

And here's Brenda, who, as a New Hampshire innkeeper for 14 years, was described in my early B&B books. She has fallen in love with this "fabulous place" where "guests dress casually and enjoy everything—the veranda rockers, incredible gardens and tall trees, berry and grape picking, pontoon boating to see waterfalls, and area antiquing. Even the moon is gorgeous here!"

In residence: Two outdoor cats.

Bed and bath: Nine large rooms (eight face lake); all queen beds. All private baths. Main house has one with tub/shower bath; one with shower with built-in seats; two with shower only; one with Jacuzzi, plants, sculpture, huge windows overlooking lake, oversized shower, two vanities, separate room for commode and bidet. Victorian garden house built in 1993 has four rooms (two with canopied bed), each without view of another's veranda; each with private entrance, refrigerator, TV in armoire, phone, piped classical music, two-sided fireplace, garden tub that holds 110 gallons of water, and huge shower with window overlooking gardens, mountains, lake.

Breakfast: 8:30–9:30 in the inn's candlelit tower room; 9 in garden house, at bedside or on veranda. With china and crystal. Sample menu—fresh fruit; orange juice; blueberry stuffed French toast, meat, poppyseed cake or pumpkin bread. All prepared before your eyes by Brenda in that fabulous kitchen.

Plus: Turndown service; Godiva chocolate. Hospitality hour 5–7 . Beverages and freshly baked cookies always available. Late-evening port or sherry fireside in the garden house or, in the inn, Irish coffee or hot chocolate with peppermint schnapps. Hammocks. TV, VCR, movies, puzzles, books.

The Homeplace Bed & Breakfast 704/365-1936
5901 Sardis Road, Charlotte, NC 28270

Hosts: Peggy and Frank Dearien
Location: A country setting in a residential neighborhood on a 2½ acre corner property. Five miles from uptown, in southeast Charlotte. Within 15 minutes of I-77/I-85 intersection, restaurants, shopping malls; 20 to coliseum, 10 to merchandise mart and Mint Museum.
Open: Year round. Two-night minimum on holidays and special event weekends.
Rates: Queen $78 or $88; third person $20. Suite $136. Amex, MC, Visa.
♥ ⚬ ♦ ✕ ⅄

In true American B&B style, this place to stay has become the reason to go. And all because, in 1984, the Deariens, a legal secretary and an accountant/treasurer in Charlotte, purchased "on impulse" the 1902 country Victorian house they had often admired. It has a tin roof—with that special sound when it rains. There are rocking chairs on the popular wraparound porch, wooded grounds, walkways and wonderful gardens, a gazebo, and a restored barn. It is home—and now the Deariens' full-time occupation, where breakfast was made on a grill after Hurricane Hugo, and where one North Carolina resident observes: "Peggy's personality is everywhere. The Deariens give the entire B&B industry a special luster." Throughout, there are family treasures, including primitive paintings that are collectors' items done in the 1980s by John Gentry, Peggy's father, who lived to be 91.

Bed and bath: Four second-floor rooms; all private baths. Queen four-poster, ceiling fan, full bath, bay windows overlooking garden; queen four-poster and a twin, ceiling fan, shower bath; suite with a queen-bedded and a double-bedded room, adjoining full bath.
Breakfast: 7–9. Fresh fruit. Homemade breads. Egg dishes and breakfast meats. Served in intimate Victorian dining room, on wraparound porch, or—for honeymooners—in room (extra charge).
Plus: Central air conditioning. Fruit bowl and fresh flowers in season. Bedroom ceiling fans in three rooms. TV in parlor. Coffee, tea, soft drinks, and ice until 10 p.m. Mints. Bathrobes. "Garden Room" for meetings and special events.

> From Louisiana: *"I appreciate the ambiance, the Deariens, and . . . oh those break-fasts!"* From Georgia: *"We wish the Homeplace was in many places."* From North Carolina: *"Rooms that make you feel romantic and at home . . . met guests we still keep in touch with."* From Alabama: *"The home is beautiful and beautifully decorated. . . . I am a travel writer . . . have returned many times . . . the Deariens have thought of everything . . . on a 4-star rating, I give the Homeplace a 5."*

Windsong: A Mountain Inn (and llama farm)
120 Ferguson Ridge, Clyde, NC 28721

704/627-6111
fax 704/627-8080

Hosts: Donna and Gale Livengood
Location: Away. At 3,000-foot elevation on a mountainside with panoramic view of Smoky Mountains and green valley. Eight miles from U.S. Route 40. Within 40 minutes of Biltmore Estate, regional airport, Great Smoky Mountain National Park, Cherokee Indian Reservation, Appalachian Trail. Twenty minutes to antiquing and restaurants.
Open: February 15–December 15. Two-night minimum in guest house.
Rates: $85–$99. Pond House $130 for two, $150 for four. Each additional person $20. Ten percent less for singles or for five or more nights.
♥ ♣ ♦ ✈ ⊁

Romantic. Spectacular inside and out. Peaceful. Inviting. With high-beamed ceilings, Mexican tile floors, and windowed walls. Native American and Eskimo artifacts accent the spacious contemporary light-pine log home designed by Donna's architect brother. There's a heated outdoor pool (what a setting); a tennis court; grounds with ornamental grasses, flowers, huge boulders, and hemlock hedge; and a hiking trail. The lovable llamas (the youngest was weeks old when I was there) are available for day or dinner treks (featured in *Southern Living*) led by daughter Sarah.

For 35 years Gale was a Chicago-based educational film company executive. Now he imports French feature films, dreams up other exciting projects, and cohosts with chef and llama farmer Donna, who had a Round-the-World boutique in Illinois.

In residence: Katie, "the wonder dog, who deems it a pleasure and duty to accompany guests on our hiking trail." Twenty-four llamas.

(Please turn page.)

Bed and bath: Five rooms, each with phone jack, VCR player, deck or patio. Each with vanity in a separate niche. On main floor—king/twins option plus cot-sized Jenny Lind bed plus loft with twin bed; bath with deep tub, separate shower; fireplace. Fireplaced queen-bedded room has loft with twin bed, sunken tub for two, separate shower and toilet. Queen-bedded room has bath with tub and shower. On lower floor—queen bed, tub for two facing fireplace, separate room with shower and toilet. Queen bed, deep tub, fireplace, separate room with shower and toilet. *Plus* private two-bedroom guest house with skylights, wood-burning stove, bath with sunken bath for two, separate shower, deck, views.

Breakfast: 8–9:30. (Continental in guest house.) Juice, breads, and coffee available earlier. Fresh fruit, juices, home-baked sweet breads, coffee cakes, croissants. Grand Marnier orange French toast, blueberry buckwheat pancakes, omelets, quiches, egg-sausage casserole or German apple pancake. (Recipes shared.) Livengoods join guests.

Plus: Huge stone fireplace in cathedral-ceilinged living room. Upright piano, TV, refrigerator/wet bar, and hundreds of videocassettes (fine and performing arts and feature films) in guest lounge. Evening desserts. Picnic gazebo over stream.

> From North Carolina: *"Tears welled in my eyes. Quite simply, I did not want to leave."*

Arrowhead Inn, c. 1775

919/477-8430
800/528-2207
fax 919/417-8430

106 Mason Road, Durham, NC 27712

Hosts: Jerry, Barbara, and Cathy Ryan
Location: On four acres with 150-year-old magnolias, 32 varieties of birds. Seven miles north of I-85. Within 20 minutes of Duke University, Stagville Preservation Center, North Carolina Museum of Life and Science, Duke Tobacco Museum, and Research Triangle Park.

Open: Year round.
Rates: Per room. $70 shared bath. $90 private bath. $125 suite with canopy bed, private bath, patio. $150 two-room log cabin. $15 third person. Amex, Diners, Discover, MC, Visa.
♥ ⅋ ♣ ♦ ✈

> From North Carolina: *"Everything was perfect . . . personable and sensitive hosts, great food, beautiful rooms, quiet atmosphere, and affordable prices . . . a great example of what a B&B should be."*

How often, while traveling, I hear echoes of those plaudits! Everyone loves this B&B and the Ryans' story of how they were introduced to their new careers through a gift of an innkeeping seminar from two of their eight adult children. (Now their own seminars are legendary.) In 1985 Jerry, a Manhattan publisher, and Barb, a writer and needlewoman, bought and restored this historic, comfortable, inviting property. They furnished the rooms in various periods—from Colonial through Tidewater—and were written up in *USA Today, Food & Wine, House & Garden,* and *Mid-Atlantic Country.* Eventually their daughter Cathy left the world of retailing and the New York-to-Hong Kong lifestyle to assist in welcoming relocators, Duke parents, museumgoers, and sheepherders (from Utah) . . . and to help with corporate meetings, family reunions, and weddings held here. Go and experience.

In residence: Three outdoor cats. "The one in the black tux is Fred Astaire. The other two are Bartles and Jaymes."
Bed and bath: Seven rooms (plus the cabin). Two have working fireplaces. Private baths are en suite. Rollaway and crib available. In manor house, on first floor, one king, one queen-bedded room, one with private tub/shower bath, one with private shower bath; one with working fireplace and private patio. On second floor, queen, double, or twin-bedded rooms (two share a bath). Carriage house has two queen-bedded rooms, private full baths. Cabin (handicapped accessible) has king bed in sleeping loft, queen hide-a-bed in fireplaced sitting room, large full bath, porch with rockers.
Breakfast: Full served 8–9. Continental 7:30–9:30. Freshly squeezed orange juice, fruit, homemade baked goods. Chef's entree choice (endless repertoire)—ham, eggs, broiled tomatoes; banana pancakes; chicken crepes. "Our own" preserved figs. Served in dining room and keeping room.
Plus: Central air conditioning. Robes. Private phones in some rooms. Fireplaced living room and keeping room. Piano. Refreshments. Guest refrigerator. Hammock. Picnic baskets.

Old North Durham Inn   919/683-1885

922 North Mangum Street, Durham, NC 27701-2229   fax 919/682-2645

Hosts: Jim and Debbie Vickery
Location: In historic district, an older suburb where many homes have been restored. Five minutes from I-85, Duke University, Durham Civic Center, Durham Bulls Baseball Park (two reserved seats for Bulls' games available for guests). Twenty minutes from I-40, Raleigh/Durham airport, UNC-Chapel Hill.
Open: Year round.
♥ ♨ ♠ ♣ ♦ ✗ ⚞

From Massachusetts: *"Everything about it speaks 'Welcome weary traveler— enter and find rest.'"* From Missouri: *"A real haven . . . fresh towels as fast as you can use them, friendly and ultrasolicitious hosts."* From Maryland: *"Many thoughtful touches, delicious breakfast."* From Virginia: *"Comfortable, convenient. . . . Jim and Debbie enjoy what they are doing and it shows."*

Two hundred admiring people came to the grand B&B opening of this early 19th-century Colonial Revival house, an award-winning renovation of "everything" from the rebuilt roof to the removal of more than 100 telephone lines.

In Washington, D.C., Debbie, now a full-time innkeeper, was a family and youth services specialist. Jim, a Bulls fan who recently won a mascot-naming contest, worked with the Environmental Protection Agency. In 1990 the Vickerys, parents of two grown children, found Durham; the Ryans' innkeeping course (Arrowhead Inn, page 202); a local EPA agency position for Jim; and this house with 10-foot coffered ceilings. Local resident Vern Medlin did his first historic renovation job. Period wallpapers were hung. Traditional and antique furnishings completed the transformation.

In residence: Oof, a chow/retriever.
Bed and bath: Four second-floor rooms. Queen-bedded room with daybed and private bath with whirlpool. Queen high-poster bed with fireplace,

(Please turn page.)

private bath. Suite has one room with queen bed and fireplace connected by a full bath to room with double bed and TV. Rollaway and crib available.
Breakfast: Usually 8–9:30. (Busy schedules accommodated.) Fresh juice and fruit, variety of egg dishes, fruit-filled pancakes or thick homemade French toast with sausage, bacon, or ham. Muffins. Served to rave reviews in fireplaced dining room.
Plus: Central air conditioning. Bedroom ceiling fans. Fireplaced living room with piano. Extensive North Carolina reference library. Veranda with wicker rockers. Late-afternoon or evening refreshments. Turndown service. Bathrobes. Mints. Guest refrigerator.

The Hillsborough House Inn   919/644-1600

209 East Tryon Street, P.O. Box 880   fax 919/644-1600
Hillsborough, NC 27278

Host: Katherine Webb
Location: Set back from road, on seven acres of woods, gardens, ponds. In historic district of state's colonial capital (population today: 4,500). Near antiques shops and restaurants. Minutes from I-85 and I-40. Within 15 minutes of Duke University (Durham) and University of North Carolina at Chapel Hill; 30 from Raleigh International Airport, 20 to factory outlets.
Open: Year round except Christmas–New Year's.
Rates: Double occupancy. $95, $105 with porch; $165 honeymoon suite. $25 trundle. MC, Visa.
♥ ♣ ♦ ✹ ⊱

From the guest book: *"Clearly, it was upon leaving here that Shakespeare described parting being sweet sorrow. A night here is a dance of the senses; a delightful discovery at every turn. My sense of balance has been restored to me. I've remembered what I'd forgotten. Can I stay here forever?"*

That says it all! This local landmark with sweeping lawn and huge trees, with landscaped swimming pool and fish pond, is intentionally "comfortable and beautiful, elegant and gracious, eclectic and funky"—with original art (as murals and on floors too), antiques, and draped beds. Built about 1790, it became Italianate in 1853, with columned 80-foot porch added around 1900. In 1990 artist Katherine, her lawyer husband Bev, and three sons moved from Charlotte to this home, which has been in Bev's family for 150 years.

Foreign languages spoken: "Un peu français and Southern."
In residence: Katherine and Bev, her husband, live in newly built family's quarters. Outside, two dogs and three cats.
Bed and bath: Five large main house rooms with queen (two with trundles) or king/twin option. All private baths; four full, one with shower only. First-floor room has private outside entrance. Two second-floor rooms have porch overlooking pool. Brick house (former 1790 kitchen)—queen bed with canopy of poplar branches, sitting room with gas fireplace, sound system in old bread oven; full bath with whirlpool and gas fireplace.
Breakfast: 9–10 weekends; at guests' convenience on weekdays. Cereals include a special mix. Fresh fruit. Homemade baked goods. Cheeses. Juices. Custom-blended coffees. Teas. Homemade jams and spreads. From cook-

book-in-progress: Pecan Fool, Really Sticky Affairs, or equally "sinfully delicious" Willie's Apple Dapple. Buffet style. Silver service.
Plus: Central air conditioning. Bedroom ceiling fans. Fireplaces in living
room, dining room, and library. Complimentary soft and hot drinks and
snacks always available in guest kitchen. Porch rockers. Hammock. Jogging
and walking routes in historic district and countryside.

La Grange Plantation Inn   919/438-2421
State Road 1308, Route 3, Box 610, Nutbush Road, Henderson, NC 27536

Hosts: Jean and Dick Cornell
Location: Country setting. On a
bike route. On eight acres with path
through woods to Kerr Lake's southern shore. Six miles north of Henderson. Five miles from I-85, midway
between Washington, D.C., and
Charlotte, N.C. Near restaurants.

Two miles to public golf course.
Open: Year round.
Rates: $95 first night, $85 each
consecutive following night. Singles
$85 first night, then $75. Amex, MC,
Visa.
♥ ❖ ◆ ✈ ✄

From North Carolina: *"A fabulous find. . . . Pampered. . . . It was as if we entered
another time period."* From D.C.: *"Exquisite gourmet breakfast."* From Virginia:
*"Charm outdone only by that of its host and hostess, whose hospitality is generous
beyond compare."* From California: *"For our family reunion we lucked upon the
La Grange Plantation."*

Guests enter the covered and latticed breezeway for peace, quiet, and relaxation. The inn's National Historic Preservation award-winning restoration
incorporated the addition of seven baths, a kitchen, and a glassed-in dining
room. Charleston, South Carolina, B&Bs inspired the Cornells' 1985 purchase
of this "retirement project," which came with Historic Register designation
but without plumbing or landscaping. The earliest part of the house was built
in 1770. Greek Revival features were added in 1858. Recently, authentic
exterior paint colors have been restored, as have interior door faux finishes.
    In "contemporary California," Dick was in the paper industry; Jean, in
Napa Valley wine public relations. Most recently Dick, the floor refinisher and
gardener (with new greenhouse), was a North Carolina State University
professor. Jean, a native of England, is now chef, interior designer, and—for
all those window treatments and bedspreads—seamstress. The antiques are
from family and auctions—"one of our favorite forms of entertainment."

In residence: In hosts' quarters, Mai-Tai, a seal point Siamese cat.
Foreign languages spoken: "Broken French and Spanish."
Bed and bath: Five rooms with private baths; robes provided for hall baths.
Four rooms have queen beds; one on first floor has handicapped-accessible
tub/shower. Two double beds in one second-floor room.
Breakfast: 8–9. (Fresh coffee and tea await early risers.) Souffles, crepes, or
casserole. Homemade muffins and breads. Special diets accommodated. In
dining room overlooking garden.
Plus: No TV. Pool. Fireplaced parlor. Individual bedroom air condition-
ing/heat control. Turndown service. Guest refrigerator. Horseshoes. Croquet.
Hammock. Fishing equipment. Rental boats at local marina.

The Waverly Inn

783 North Main Street, Hendersonville, NC 28792-3622

704/693-9193
800/537-8195
fax 704/692-1010

Hosts: John and Diane Sheiry (pronounced Shire-ey); Darla Olmstead (Diane's sister)
Location: In town on a main street, across from tennis courts and a church. Nineteen miles south of Biltmore Estate. Two miles west of I-26. Three-minute walk to historic area, antiques shops, boutiques, restaurants; 3 miles to Flat Rock Playhouse (state theater) and Carl Sandburg National Historic Site. Within 18 miles of Chimney Rock Park, Pisgah National Forest, and Blue Ridge Parkway.
Open: Year round. Two-night minimum on all major holidays.
Rates: $89 double. $99 queen. $109 king. $165 two-room suite with canopied king bed. $65 singles. $15 third person. Crib free. Wine lovers' and mystery weekend rates include dinner. Amex, Discover, MC, Visa.
♥ ♨ ✿ ♦ ✠

From North Carolina, Georgia, Virginia, New York: *"Felt at home right away. . . . Unbelievable breakfast . . . a fantastic three-grain pancake . . . outrageous buckwheat pancakes . . . charming . . . homey yet elegant, not intimidating . . . freshly baked evening treats . . . attention to detail . . . exemplary service. . . . Help in relocation was invaluable. . . . Beautifully decorated. . . . We returned with my son, his wife, and two grandchildren. . . . Was on business. Returned for pleasure several times with my husband. . . . Provided TV for the big Duke game. . . . Charismatic innkeepers."*

Some well-known people, too, have discovered this great place to relax. It's the "direct people business" that the Sheirys sought in 1988 when they left Atlanta and 18 years (each) in the hotel and restaurant business—shortly after John, who grew up near three Franconia, New Hampshire, inns, wrote a thesis on country inns for his MBA.

A wide veranda with rocking chairs, an outstanding Eastlake staircase, the original registration desk, period furnishings, Oriental rugs, and family photographs are among the features of this National Register white wood-framed structure built as an inn in 1898.

In residence: In hosts' wing, "Christie" (Emily Christine), age 12; "Tori" (Victoria Ruth), age 2.
Bed and bath: Fourteen tall-ceilinged air-conditioned (some ceiling fans too) rooms on three floors with king, queen, double, or a queen and a twin. Some canopied beds; one two-room top-floor suite. One room has private sun porch. All private shower baths, some with claw-footed tub. Crib. Rollaways.
Breakfast: Usually 8–9. All you can eat. Cooked to order. Hot or cold all-natural cereal. Eggs or Egg Beaters. Stone-ground pancakes or French toast. Fresh fruit. Home fries or grits. Bacon or sausage. Locally baked breads. Juice. Perked coffee and decaf.
Plus: Phones in all rooms. Silver service social hour, 5–6 p.m. Freshly baked evening treats. Soft drinks. Springwater cooler. Guest refrigerator. AT&T Language Line. Suggestions for hikes, panoramic mountain views, photogenic waterfalls. Innkeeping internships.

Hidden Crystal Inn

Sulphur Springs Road, P.O. Box 58
Hiddenite, NC 28636

704/632-0063
fax 704/632-3562

Hosts: Lynn Sharpe Hill and Eileen Lackey Sharpe
Location: In a Brushy Mountains hamlet known for emeralds (mine open to public is half mile away) as well as for hiddenite, a mineral found (rarely now) only in North Carolina. Behind Hiddenite Center for Folklife and Cultural Arts (performances and classes) and Lucas Mansion Museum (antique doll and toy collections in restored Victorian mansion). An hour from Boone, Charlotte, Greensboro, and Winston-Salem; 10 minutes via new bypass from I-40 and I-77 at Statesville; 15 minutes from Hickory/Lenoir.
Open: Year round.
Rates: $95–$105 September–June, $85 July and August. $150 Topaz suite. $15 third person. MC, Visa.
♥ ✢ ♦ ✖ ✄

What one North Carolinian once reported as "a best-kept secret that belongs in your book" is now known by vacationers (great weekend getaway), business travelers (all rooms have phones), retreat planners, and shoppers. Gems and minerals are displayed throughout the inn, a restored columned manor house and adjacent garden cottage. There are antique armoires, paintings, murals, sculptures, and crafts. The carved antique self-playing European grand piano still has many of its original rolls. A gazebo garden provides a magical setting for proposals and many weddings. There is a large swimming pool, several flower-filled patios, and a Zen rock garden.

In 1981 Eileen Lackey Sharpe and her husband, the late R. Y. Sharpe, president of Pilot Freight Co., founded the cultural center and museum in their native Hiddenite. In 1989, to provide the first public lodging in town since fire destroyed the famous Sulphur Springs Hotel and Spa in the 1920s, Mrs. Sharpe and family members created this small, wonderful inn. Daughter Lynn, a former trucking executive and psychiatric hospital administrator, has worked in public relations with inns and hotels in North Carolina and Mexico. Much to guests' delight, her 86-year-old mother—"quite the story teller and a master flower arranger"—is here often.

Foreign language spoken: Lynn speaks Spanish.
Bed and bath: Twelve rooms, each quite different; all gem-named. Six are handicapped accessible. Seven rooms in manor house, five in cottage; all with remote-controlled TVs. All private baths; all with shower, some without tubs. King, queen, queen and two twins, double, or two twin beds. Working fireplace and queen bed in room with Jacuzzi. One private-exterior-entrance suite that has king/twins option in each of its two rooms. "Topaz Suite" has two-person Jacuzzi in room with canopied queen bed, Moroccan chandelier, private full bath, entertainment center with VCR and big-screen TV, stocked refrigerator. Rollaway available.
Breakfast: 6–9:30 weekdays, 7:30–9:30 weekends. Fresh fruit. Heart-healthy menu with banana/pecan buckwheat skim-milk pancakes. Yogurt. Homemade granola. Or country ham, grits, scrambled eggs, buttermilk biscuits. Served on glassed-in porch overlooking pool and patio.
Plus: Central air conditioning. Fireplaced living room in manor house and in cottage. Turndown service. Coffee and tea always available. Videotapes.

(Please turn page.)

Badminton, volleyball, croquet. Option of lunch and/or dinner in dining room, which is open (by prior reservation only) to public. Hot-air ballooning launch from nearby school.

The Bentley   919/523-BEDS (2337)

117 West Capitola Avenue, Kinston, NC 28501   fax 919/523-7211

Mailing address: P.O. Box 5111, Kinston, NC 28503

Hosts: Linda and Ward McConnell
Location: On 13 very private acres with a "resident forest." In historic district and on the only hill in town. One block from 70 Business. Twenty-five minutes south of East Carolina University.
Open: Year round.
Rates: $75 single. $85 double. Amex, MC, Visa.
♥ ⛟ ♣ ✈ ⚘

> From New Mexico: *"We've traveled the world over. This is an exquisite old home . . . something interesting to look at everywhere you turn . . . I'd like to live there permanently."*

This media secret—as of press time—has been discovered by corporate executives and wedding planners. Guests drive between pillars onto a long curving driveway and arrive at this made-for-entertaining Georgian brick mansion built in 1914. A black Rolls Royce with white linen seat covers is in front. The spacious, stunning foyer has columns, huge palms, and floor-to-ceiling mirrors that visually triple the 10-foot-wide grand staircase. An enormous Palladian window on the landing curves around onto a balcony. The (former) billiard room is furnished with tapestries and large oak pieces recently purchased in England. Without heavy window treatments and with the use of color—and a hint of whimsy too—this home is at the same time formal, elegant, and warm and welcoming. One room—decor replicated by several visitors—has deep green walls, overstuffed sofas, and white fabric with a hydrangea print. The grand piano is a French antique. The dining room has a black chinoiserie grandfather clock, a tall Chinese vase, and hardwood floors (often mistaken for marble) designed and painted by Linda. She and Ward built one floor-to-ceiling canopied bed that is draped in about 100 yards of fabric.

The well-traveled McConnells, Kinston residents since 1987 and parents of five children, opened in 1992. Ward is a manufacturer of large agricultural equipment. Linda, a former accountant, is the Bentley's fine seamstress, food shopper (in three-wheeled English car), and chef for everything from break-fast to weddings with 350 guests.

In residence: Son Marc, age 16. Bentley is a beautiful white cat.
Foreign language spoken: A little Spanish.
Bed and bath: Six second-floor rooms, all private en-suite full tile baths. King, queen, double, or twin beds.
Breakfast: Any time before 10 a.m. Menu, "as good or as bad as you'd like to be," arranged the night before. Fresh fruit, juice, homemade muffins, omelets, French toast, Southern biscuits and grits, Egg Beaters. Special diets accommodated. In plant-filled, wicker-furnished (Lloyd Loom chairs from French Riviera) sun room—"everyone's favorite"—with view of grounds.

Plus: Zoned air conditioning. Ornate fireplaces in all first-floor rooms. Wraparound porches. Welcoming wine and cheese or hot tea and cookies. Guest refrigerator with beverages and snacks. Pants pressers. Irons. Hair dryers. TV in each bedroom. Transportation to/from airport (five miles).

The Lodge on Lake Lure

704/625-2789
800/733-2785
fax 704/625-2421

Route 1, Box 529A, Lake Lure, NC 28746

Hosts: Jack and Robin Stanier
Location: On a lakeside hill with rhododendron-lined paths and a view that reminds Europeans of fjords. East side of Lake Lure, at the end of a wooded drive. Off Highway 64/74; 22 miles southeast of Asheville; 80 miles west of Charlotte.
Open: February 14–New Year's.

Two-day minimum on weekends.
Rates: Per room. April–October, $85 weekdays, $95 weekends. Suites $95 weekdays, $105 and $135 weekends. $15 third person in room. Ten percent less off-season except holidays. Amex, Discover, MC, Visa.
♥ ⚑ ⁑ ◆ ✖ ✄

What a combination! The only inn—built in the 1930s as a North Carolina Highway Patrol retreat—on what the National Geographic Society called "one of the ten most beautiful lakes in the country." A great room with vaulted ceiling, hand-hewn beams, wormy chestnut walls, and a 20-foot-tall stone fireplace. A hostess who, during 17 years abroad, collected "quantities of unusual items" for her someday inn. A (wealthy) former owner who was enamored with interesting antiques. (Guests take pictures.) An equipped boathouse with rooftop deck. Plus magnificent landscaping and gardens.

A B&B since 1985, the World War II officers' club/boarding school/foreign missionaries' retreat/private home was "found in 1990, and we have lived happily ever after," by the jeans-wearing, enthusiastic Staniers. Jack was in steel sales. Robin, a "pioneer woman in the oil industry," worked in drilling and production equipment marketing and sales. Here they offer peace, privacy, and camaraderie too.

In residence: (Blackberry) Muffin, a very friendly black Labrador.
Foreign language spoken: Spanish.
Bed and bath: Twelve rooms including two suites—one honeymoon suite and one with fireplace, soaking tub in huge bath, private deck. All with private baths (some with shower; others with tub and shower). King, queen, or double beds; some four-posters. Rollaway and portacrib available.
Breakfast: 8–9:30. An event. Juice made of blended fruits "plus." Homemade muffins, apple dumplings, or breads. Entree could be grilled peaches flambe with fresh blueberries, French toast with cardamom and currant jelly sauce, or puff pancakes with sauteed plums. On Sundays, eggs Benedict "from our New Orleans days." At round tables for four in room with The View.
Plus: Sunset lake cruise. A 6 p.m. social hour. Bedroom ceiling fans. Air conditioning in some rooms. Library with wood stove, books, games, videotapes, magazines. Guest refrigerator. Beach towels and robes. Rocking chairs and hammocks on veranda. Dock for sunning, swimming, fishing, barbecuing. Canoes and johnboat. Babysitting. Restaurant menus.

The Merritt House Bed & Breakfast

618 North Main Street
Mount Airy, NC 27030-3724

910/786-2174
800/290-6290
fax 910/786-2174

Hosts: Rich and Pat Mangels
Location: In a town sometimes dubbed "Mayberry" after the mythical "Andy Griffith Show" location. Five minutes to downtown with Snappy's Lunch (still serves pork chop sandwich) and Floyd's Barber Shop, made famous on the show. Across from visitors' center in historic district with big old turn-of-the-century houses. Thirty miles north of Winston-Salem, 20 minutes to Pilot Mountain State Park, 15 to Blue Ridge Parkway. Ten minutes from I-77 and Business 52 (borders back hedges).
Open: Year round.
Rates: $40–$55 shared bath; $65–$75 private bath. $10 extra person. Corporate rates available. MC, Visa.

The most photographed house in town is home to former Floridians who happily grant requests to tour their award-winning B&B. It's a 1901 brick Victorian that was, until Rich and Pat bought it in one day (in 1993), owned by the prominent Merritt family. Now the retired CEO of the Renfro Corporation delights in booking American and international guests at "my grandfather's house." They stay "at home" surrounded by locally purchased antiques, refinished woodwork, big floral prints, and color—peaches, greens, pinks, and burgundys. From the very low windows of the as-is 20-foot-ceilinged attic—where Merritt children used bowl and roller skate—there's a view of the Blue Ridge Mountains. A popular hot tub is in the backyard. And the Merritt House is also known for "Mrs. Wylie's tea," an annual arts council benefit in honor of Andy Griffith, who was born and raised in Mount Airy.

In Florida Pat was a bookkeeper and craftswoman. To the historic home they found after a five-year search, Rich brings extensive maintenance experience both from his own business and as school department supervisor.

Bed and bath: Four large rooms. First floor—king/twins option, private en-suite tub/shower bath. Second floor—queen bed, private en-suite shower bath. Two queen-bedded rooms share a 1920s hall tub/shower bath.
Breakfast: 8–9; earlier for business travelers. Juice or fresh fruit, sausage, bacon, quiches and stratas, muffins, scones, bread, coffee. Special diets accommodated. Served in formal dining room or on back porch.
Plus: Fireplaced living room. TV room. Wicker-furnished second-floor sitting room. Tea or wine and cheese; on wraparound porch in warm weather. Gift shop here sometimes has Pat's own patchwork Santa Claus doll, a collector's item.

In this book a full bath includes a shower and a tub. "Shower bath" indicates a bath that has all the essentials except a tub.

Huntington Hall Bed & Breakfast

500 Valley River Avenue, Murphy, NC 28906   704/837-9567
800/824-6189
fax 704/837-2527

Hosts: Bob and Kate DeLong
Location: Between home of a late senator and a church; near (daily) chiming carillon of another church. Hills behind the house. Across road, a barbecue restaurant and public school offices in a historic house. Within two hours of Atlanta, Georgia, and Asheville, North Carolina.

Within 30 miles of two major white-water rafting rivers.
Open: Year round.
Rates: $65–$85. Singles $10 less. Twenty percent less December– April. $10 third person. Family rates for two rooms. Amex, Diners, Discover, MC, Visa.

Murder mystery weekends, acclaimed in the Atlanta *Journal-Constitution,* are sometimes booked six months in advance here! It is a comfortable two-storied 1881 country Victorian, the kind of place where guests, upon leaving, often ask, "Can we take you home?" Sometimes neighbors stop in to chat with the DeLongs, avid backpackers and runners who are excited about the 1996 Olympic canoeing and kayaking coming to the nearby Ocoee River. Bob has 17 years of experience in the hotel industry—as pastry chef, baker, manager, and chief engineer. Katie, an aspiring writer of children's books, worked in the corporate world and did theatrical lighting. In 1991 they made an offer on their first visit here and became innkeepers a month later. They uncovered fireplaces and refinished heart-of-pine floors. Frequently they direct guests to Joyce Kilmer Forest—"45 miles and worth it"; to a black bear sanctuary; or to the Appalachian Trail. "And some, even those with an agenda, just unwind and do nothing."

In residence: In hosts' quarters, Elizabeth Ashley, age four.
Foreign language spoken: "Un peu French!"
Bed and bath: Five rooms with private baths. Two queen-bedded rooms on first floor. One has hall shower bath (robes provided); the other, an attached bath with tub and shower. On second floor, one queen-bedded room and one four-poster double bed have attached baths with shower and claw-footed tubs. Room with king/twins option has shower bath. Rollaway and crib.
Breakfast: 6–9:30. "Choose your own time." Crepes with peaches and apricot sauce; banana French toast with bran bread, strawberries, and whipped cream; sausages poached in apple juice. Raspberry coffee cake or bran muffins with raisins and walnuts. Served (rave reviews) in glassed-in porch at tables seating two to four.
Plus: In each guest room—heat and air-conditioning control, ceiling fan, cable TV. Desk in most rooms. Refreshments. Turndown service with hand-made chocolate truffles.

First Colony Inn

6720 South Virginia Dare Trail
Nags Head, NC 27959

919/441-2343
800/368-9390
fax 919/441-9234

Hosts: The Lawrence family— Camille and Richard; Alan, Joel, Joan, Sarah, Carolyn, Tom, and Rhoda; plus six-year-old "doorman" Rick, the oldest of the third generation
Location: Mile Post 16. Where land is less than half a mile wide. Close to ocean, via boardwalk across street to gazebo on dune. Facing the sound across a five-lane highway—to fine restaurants and miniature golf. Near Wright Brothers Memorial, Cape Hatteras National Seashore, Pea Island Wildlife Refuge, Nags Head Woods Preserve "with hiking trails that feel like mountains."

Open: Year round. Two-night minimum weekend stay, early spring to late fall; three nights on holiday weekends.
Rates: Spring and fall: first-floor rooms, no water view, $100; midsize room $110; larger room $130, $150 with king bed. Summer: $125/$150/$175/$200. November–March: $60/$75/$90/$125. $30 additional person with trundle or day bed. $10 infant in crib. Thursday night free for stays including Sunday through Thursday. Off-season and corporate rates. Honeymoon packages.
♥ ⚘ ♣ ♦ ✗ ✂

From Virginia, Rhode Island, Maryland, Illinois: *"Spent our honeymoon there . . . impeccably maintained . . . delicious afternoon tea beautifully presented . . . obvious pride of friendly staff who kept talking about how much they 'loved this place.' This pride showed up in the final product. . . . Comfort and charm of a well-run B&B with amenities of a luxury hotel . . . an endearing experience . . . belongs in your guidebook."*

Saved! Moved three miles to land that has been in the Lawrence family for more than 200 years. Gutted. Rehabilitated over a 3-year period. Furnished with English antiques and comfortable traditional furnishings. Reopened in 1991. And placed on the National Register. All thanks to the Lawrence family, whose professions include preservation, architecture, interior design, and computer systems engineering. Hence the inn's appearance in this book, which is usually limited to smaller places.

The Shingle Style inn was built in 1932 with two stories of covered verandas that encircle the building. "We have no back!" The pool has a deep wood deck with lounge chairs. Croquet is on the manicured lawn. Service is attentive. "And still, some guests choose to bring their cup and saucer into the kitchen!"

Bed and bath: On three floors, 26 air-conditioned and carpeted rooms (some connect as suites). Each has private bath (most are tub/shower; some have shower only or shower and Jacuzzi for two) with heated towel racks, TV (some with VCR), telephone, refrigerator. Rooms have king/twins option, king, or queen bed; some with a daybed and trundle bed. Amenities vary and include corner location, canopied bed, sitting room, screened porch, kitchenette with dishwasher, wet bar, microwave, ocean view with sunrise, sound view with sunset.

Breakfast: 7:30–9:30. Fresh fruit, juice cordial, juices, Danish, cake (lemon-poppyseed or banana-chocolate), croissants, English muffins, ham-and-cheese braid (whole wheat), cereals, yogurts. Buffet style in many-windowed breakfast room at tables for two or four with starched linen, flowers, silver serving pieces.

Plus: Fireplace, pump organ, and books in beamed library. Robes. Bicycle and Windsurfer storage. Picnic tables and grills. Outside shower. Games, puzzles, beach chairs and umbrellas. Chocolates. Veranda rockers.

Harmony House Inn

215 Pollock Street, New Bern, NC 28560

919/636-3810
800/636-3113
fax 919/636-3810

Hosts: Ed and Sooki Kirkpatrick
Location: In historic district of about 100 homes, museums, and sites. Four blocks from Tryon Palace, 1½ from Neuse and Trent rivers, sightseeing, and dinner cruises. "Within three blocks of everything from a deli to fancy restaurants." Seven minutes from airport.
Open: Year round.
Rates: $55 single. $85 double. $20 third person. Amex, Discover, MC, Visa.

♥ ⚘ ♣ ♦ ✗ ⅄

The small town (population: 20,000) appeals to cyclists, vacationers, people on their way to the Outer Banks (who are surprised at how much there is to do here), retirees (some move here), and business travelers. It was just what the Kirkpatricks, prospective parents and innkeepers, were looking for. "Our guests walk everywhere. They appreciate the historic district, the lack of crowds, the quiet evenings, and—maybe most of all—our front porch rockers and swings."

The inn's spacious rooms are furnished with comfortable and elegant antiques and locally made reproductions. The most interesting expansion of the 1850 house occurred in 1900, when two sons moved one half of it nine feet and filled in the space with more rooms for their "separate" residences. Hence today's two front doors and extensive hallways.

In Florida, Ed worked at Disney's Grand Floridian Beach Resort; Sooki was a cosmetologist. They purchased this established inn in 1994.

In residence: Daughter Jamie Sue, age one.
Bed and bath: Ten rooms; all private full baths. On first floor, three rooms—plus suite with queen canopied bed in one room, queen sofa bed in sitting room. Six second-floor rooms. Queen four-posters or twin beds. Rollaway and crib.
Breakfast: 7:30–9 weekdays, 8–9:30 weekends. Hot egg and meat dish, baked French toast with orange-honey butter, apple-cheese quiche, or stuffed pancake. Homemade granola and coffee cakes. Fruit. Juice, tea, freshly ground coffee. Buffet style in dining room and parlor.
Plus: Central air conditioning. In each bedroom—ceiling fan, two comfortable chairs, cable TV, electric blankets in winter. Complimentary wine, 6–7. Port and sherry after 8. Guest refrigerator with complimentary juices and soft drinks. Garage for bicycles.

Pinebrae Manor   704/286-1543

RR 5 (Highway 108), Box 479-A, Rutherfordton, NC 28139-9805

Hosts: Allen and Charlotte Perry
Location: On 10 acres with deer (sometimes) and a panoramic view (always) of woods. Three miles west of town. In foothills of the Blue Ridge Mountains. Within 30 minutes' drive of newly built Shakespearean Globe Theatre, Chimney Rock Park, Carl Sandburg home, Biltmore estate.

Open: At least March through November.
Rates: Per room. April–December: $49 shared bath, $69 private. January–March: $42 shared bath, $52 private bath, $62 with fireplace. Group and corporate discounts available. MC, Visa.
♥ ⚑ ⚑ ⁂ ♦ ✈ ⊱

> From North Carolina, Florida, Texas, Virginia: *"Wish we had known about it for our honeymoon. . . . Our first B&B stay . . . absolutely beautiful . . . spacious . . . comfortably furnished . . . spectacular view. . . . Gracious and accommodating hosts. I wish I could live there! . . . Have stayed at B&Bs all over the world . . . this is the best yet . . . made me feel as if I were part of their family . . . wonderful breakfast at beautifully set table. . . . All in all, superb. A winner."*

The local television station produced a video of the breakfast here in this Georgian Colonial, which is furnished with family heirlooms and antiques. It had been the Rutherford County Home administration building before a local builder transformed it. He added crown moldings and broken pediments, and he salvaged brick and doors from other buildings on the property for walkways, retaining walls, and wainscoting.

The well-traveled Perrys bought this "ideal for B&B" house when Allen, a chemical engineer, retired from the corporate world in 1991. Charlotte, an art instructor and craftswoman who was editor and illustrator for the Hannibal, Missouri, Bicentennial cookbook, is writing a family cookbook and a "Sailing Wife's Handbook." (Off-season allows time for Al to sail and Charlotte to cook their sea bounty—conch being a favorite.)

Bed and bath: A wide stairway leads to four second-floor rooms. Two double-bedded rooms share a full hall bath (robes provided). One room has king/twins option, wood-burning fireplace, full bath. One has king bed, private shower bath.
Breakfast: "Flexible. Have served as early as 5:30 and as late as 10:30." Juices. Hot or cold cereal. Muffins, bagels, toast. Eggs to order. Sausage casserole, French toast, eggs Benedict, or pancakes; Canadian bacon, ham, bacon, sausage. For full house, could be buffet. Just one or two couples? You might design the menu. Or it could be chef's choice with "Bon appetit" greeting. Served with fine china and heirloom silver in fireplaced and brasschandeliered dining room.
Plus: Fireplaced living room with piano. Phone and TV in each room. Refreshments. Guests have own gathering room with fireplace. Porch rockers. Horseshoes. Croquet. Game tables. Hiking right here. Half-mile nature trail; audiotape made by a friend with commentary about flora and fauna. Airport pickup arranged. For corporate guests, use of private office with fax, key telephone, extra modem jack.

Rowan Oak House

704/633-2086
800/786-0437

208 South Fulton Street, Salisbury, NC 28144-4418

Hosts: Bill and Ruth Ann Coffey
Location: Surrounded by other elegant homes in historic district. Three blocks from "turn-of-the-century business district, good restaurants, genealogical library." One mile off I-85, 35 miles to High Point, 39 to Winston-Salem, 42 to Charlotte.

Open: Year round.
Rates: $65 double-bedded room, shared hall bath; $85 twin beds; $95 honeymoon suite. $10 less for singles. Ten percent less for senior citizens or stays over four days. $15 rollaway or crib. Discover, MC, Visa.
♥ ⬛ ⁂ ♦ ✈

From New York: "A touch of class. . . . Elegance of the Victorian period, sumptuous breakfasts, warm Southern hospitality." From South Carolina: "An incredible experience . . . I was able to drop the normal stress associated with work, wander from one creative, historic room to another, and marvel at the precise detail in each. . . . Retired in true comfort, woke up 'somewhere in time' as though I had always lived there."

This house-tour Queen Anne with wraparound porch, elaborate woodwork, and original electric and gas light fixtures is in a "town that looks back in time, with its old houses that have volunteer guides, old cemeteries to browse through, an old country store, and a modern-day potter to visit." Since 1987 the Coffeys, avid antiques collectors who purchased Victorian pieces specifically for this house, have been, as guests say, "the perfect innkeepers." Flash! Just as this book went to press, the Coffeys had plans to return to Texas, where all their sons have settled. Recently retired "kindred spirits" who looked "all over" for this B&B are about to become the new owners/innkeepers.

Bed and bath: Four second-floor rooms. Wide ornate staircase leads to upstairs sitting room and porch accessible from three 17-by-17-foot rooms—as well as from back room that has a private porch overlooking gardens. One room has mahogany double bed, attached bath with double-sized Jacuzzi, French-flowered pedestal sink, working gas log fireplace. King/twin (sleigh beds) option, attached shower bath. Room with carved high-back mahogany double bed shares (robes provided) huge bath that has tub and hand-held brass shower with room that has queen-sized Victorian bed.

Breakfast: Usually 8–9. Repertoire includes baked cheese souffle, Dutch baby puff pancakes, stuffed French toast. Meats. Fresh fruit, juice, homemade breads, gourmet coffee. At table set with linen, silver, and china in dining room with original hand-painted wallpaper and large oil painting of Queen Louise of Mecklenberg/Prussia. Coffeys join guests.

Plus: Murder mystery weekends. Fireplaced living and dining rooms. Air conditioning, ceiling fan, desk, phone jack, down comforter in each guest room. Fresh fruit. Candy. Refreshments—cookies, cheese, dips, veggies.

Unless otherwise stated, rates in this book are per room for two and include breakfast in addition to all the amenities in "Plus."

Bed and Breakfast at Laurel Ridge

3188 Siler City–Snow Camp Road   919/742-6049
Siler City, NC 27344-9705   800/742-6049

Hosts: David Simmons and Lisa Reynolds
Location: Serene. On 26 beautiful acres. Down a long winding driveway to a bluff overlooking Rocky River and an enormous stand of mountain laurel. Thirty-five minutes to Chapel Hill or Greensboro, 40 to High Point (furniture markets), 30 minutes to North Carolina Zoo (largest natural zoo in the world) or to Seagrove Area Potteries (64 potters).
Open: Year round. "For arrivals after 9 p.m., prior arrangements must be made."
Rates: Private bath: $95. Shared bath: $65 queen, $50 king/twins option. $10 less for singles. Amex, MC, Visa.
♥ ⚑ ⚓ ⚘ ◆ ✈ ⚰

It's a refuge, a getaway, a home-away-from-home for international business travelers, a base for day trips. Built by craftsmen in 1984 and purchased by the Simmonses in 1990, this inviting post-and-beam country house is close to so much—with the feeling of being far away. Many mornings and evenings, deer come into the six acres of pasture. A flower-lined path leads to the English country garden with organic vegetable quadrants and wisteria-covered arbors. You may wonder if you're in the mountains if you hike along the wooded trail down to the river. And then there's David, the gardener and former Carolina Inn (Chapel Hill) executive chef who was a member of a culinary team that won gold and silver medals at the 1992 International Food Olympics. Lisa, a pediatric physical therapist, has decorated eclectically with comfortable contemporary seating and antique accessories.

In residence: All outdoors—six cats and one shy cocker spaniel.
Foreign language spoken: "A little Spanish" (Lisa).
Bed and bath: Three rooms. On second floor, master suite has queen canopied bed, ceiling fan, Jacuzzi for two, balcony overlooking river. Room with queen brass bed and ceiling fan shares (robes provided) large first-floor shower bath with first-floor Jewel Room (named for colors), which has king/twins option, TV.
Breakfast: 8–9:30. A highlight. Maybe pumpkin basil or poppyseed pancakes, frittata with sun-dried tomatoes, a creative quiche, or omelet made with organically grown vegetables. Freshly squeezed juice. David's breads. Specialty roasted coffees. Served in living/dining great room or on deck.
Plus: Central air conditioning. A tin roof (wonderful sound when it rains). Tea or—from guests' refrigerator—juices, water, sodas. Picnic baskets (extra charge) by request. Deck overlooking the mountain laurel and river.

> From Virginia: *"From the fabric-wrapped soap in our bathroom to the fresh-from-the-garden basil in our pancakes, we felt pampered. . . . Will return again for peace and rejuvenating solitude."*

---

*G*uests come from as close as 10 minutes away or from around the world.

Aunt Mae's Bed & Breakfast   704/873-9525

532 East Broad Street, Statesville, NC 28677-5331   **800/448-6862**

Hosts: Richard and Sue Rowland
Location: On nearly an acre in the middle of town. Surrounded by lawn and plantings. One mile off intersection of I-40/I-77. A short walk from historic downtown and shops. Forty- five miles north of Charlotte; 40 west of Winston-Salem.
Open: Year round.
Rates: $60 per room. $10 third person in room. MC, Visa.
♥ ♨ ♨ ♣ ♦ ✈ ⚑

From Texas: *"Two wonderful people . . . made me feel like part of their family . . . breakfast was a treat every morning."* From Ohio: *"Evening ice cream with homemade caramel sauce and nuts from their trees . . . memorabilia everywhere. . . . Spotless, quiet, comfortable rooms. . . . We awoke to coffee on a tray outside our door. Breakfast included banana-orange juice that Sue blended (I watched her) and marvelous stuffed French toast. The best part, though, was the conversation. You know, a house is just a house. The people in it make it a home."*

Pure nostalgia. As Sue says, "While growing up, I often visited Aunt Mae in this Victorian. I always wanted to snoop, but never did! Knowing our guests might feel the same way, we have encouraged browsing, even leaving some drawers, boxes, and trunks as Aunt Mae left them—with books, magazines, love letters, toys—and some notes telling of their origin or use. Guests sleep under Aunt Mae's coverlets and quilts and eat at a table set with her china and crystal. . . . We meet wonderful people from all over the world. One lady from France thought she might learn English if she stayed long enough. I told her it would certainly be with a Southern accent! . . . All this goes back to my prior vocation (mothering eight children). What a training ground! . . . Richard works in heat treatment at a local plant. . . . The house, commissioned by a cabinetmaker, was built in 1891 by workers who moonlighted while our beautiful city hall was under construction."

Bed and bath: Two second-floor rooms, each with attached private shower bath. One Victorian with double four-poster bed and single Jenny Lind daybed. One cozy country room with antique double iron bed. Rollaway and crib available.
Breakfast: Any time until 9:30. "Homemade juice concoctions." Hot or cold fruit soup, fruit sundaes, and even Swedish cream. Souffles, casseroles, omelets, or stuffed French toast. "Ends on a sweet note with homemade goodies." By candlelight. Often, complete with history of Aunt Mae's crystal, china, or linen being used.
Plus: Central air conditioning. TV and ceiling fan in bedrooms. Upstairs gathering room with homemade snacks always available. Lemonade or hot chocolate and tea. Mints on pillow. Babysitting. Kitchen and laundry privileges. Weather report and list of local events with morning coffee brought to door. Right here—Aunt Mae's Attic gift shop.

---

*H*ospitality *is the keynote of B&B.*

Little Warren Bed and Breakfast

304 East Park Avenue, Tarboro, NC 27886

919/823-1314
800/309-1314

Hosts: Patsy and Tom Miller
Location: Quiet, residential part of historic district, facing the town common. Nineteen miles off I-95 exit 138 (Rocky Mount).

Open: Year round.
Rates: Per room. $65 double, $58 single. $20 cot. Amex, Discover, MC, Visa.
♥ ♯ ❖ ◆ ✈

Twists and turns and lots of cubbies within the National Register house inspired the name of this B&B, which was built in 1913 with spacious rooms, 13-foot ceilings, and wraparound porch. Restored twice (most recently by Patsy and Tom), it has elaborate dentil work, crown molding, beams, and several knotty pine–paneled rooms. Since 1984 it has been home to the Millers, following their 24 years of living in Africa, England, the Orient, and many parts of the United States.

Kitchenalia by the thousands (much displayed on walls) represent a lifetime of collecting, dating back to the days when Tom ran a country store in his youth. Other collections include clocks, tea covers, baskets, miniatures, glassware, and furnishings—"eclectic, mostly antique, all livable and touchable." The official B&B chef, Tom, is a retired Marine colonel. Cohost Patsy, who teaches Spanish at the local high school, was raised in her family's small Virginia Beach hotel.

"Our guests are often surprised by the friendliness of this Colonial town of 11,000 people. Several guests—including a couple who ran the B&B one summer while we went to Europe—have returned to live in Tarboro."

Foreign language spoken: Spanish.
Bed and bath: Three second-floor rooms; each with desk, all with private bath. One double-bedded room with hall shower bath (robes provided). One with twin beds, adjoining shower bath. One with three-quarter bed, shower bath. Rollaway available.
Breakfast: Any time until 8:30. Full English, expanded continental, or American Southern with fried apples (a favorite). English: juice, cereal with fruit, eggs, soft bacon, sausage, toast, marmalade, grilled tomatoes, tea or coffee. Special diets accommodated. In dining room with English silver and china, crystal, and linens.
Plus: Fireplaced living room. Central zoned air conditioning. Late-afternoon beverage and snack before fire or on porch. Mints. Turndown service. Historic district walking tour map. Arrangements made for Y gym and workout facilities. Five-minute walk to the Millers' Passers-Buy Antiques Shop.

Looking for a B&B with a crib? Find a description with the ♯ symbol and then check under the "Bed and bath" description.

Miss Betty's Bed & Breakfast Inn 919/243-4447
600 Nash Street, NE, Wilson, NC 27893-3045   800/258-2058

Hosts: Betty and Fred Spitz
Location: On an acre and a half, on main street in downtown historic section, with big old trees, lawn, and gardens. About two miles to "antiques capital of North Carolina." Less than six miles from I-95. Midway between New York and Florida. Across street from Rib Room, a major restaurant. Near four well-mani-cured golf courses, many tennis courts, Olympic-sized pool.
Open: Year round.
Rates: Per room $60–$70, suite $75. Singles $10 less. Honeymoon, anniversary, or birthday package rates. Amex, CB, Diners, Discover, MC, Visa.
♥ ♣ ✗ ⅟

Business travelers from afar wish Miss Betty's were close enough so they could return for a weekend getaway. Antiques lovers feel as if they have discovered the area and this B&B. Wedding and reunion guests are among those who give rave reviews. And for their restoration work on three historic buildings (a fourth is in process), the Spitzes, who moved from New Jersey in 1989, have received a Wilson County Preservation Society award. The B&B houses—built in 1858 (National Register Italianate), 1900 (moved from two blocks away), and 1943 (with open porch and tin roof)—all feature Victorian decor and locally purchased American Victorian antiques.

Husband Fred, often called "Mr. Betty" by guests, is an engineer who was with General Dynamics. Betty, the antiques dealer, is the chef (sometimes in period dress).

Bed and bath: Ten rooms (in three buildings) with king, queen, double, or twin beds include four in main inn, one handicapped-accessible room, and three executive suites. All with phone and cable TV. All private baths (robes for the two hall baths); some shower only, some tub and shower baths. Some canopied beds.
Breakfast: Very sociable. At 7:30; on weekends at 8:30. Homemade blueberry and peach muffins; pumpkin bread or—everyone's favorite—cinnamon nut cake (locally grown pecans). "North Carolina's finest 'bacon-pressed' bacon," locally made sausage links. Sometimes grits. Fresh fruit. Freshly squeezed orange and grapefruit juice. Eggs or pancakes. Served family style in main inn's dining room.
Plus: Fireplaces in three parlors. Central air conditioning. Ceiling fans. Games. Snack crackers. Candy. Guest refrigerator with ice and cold soft drinks. Small antiques items ($8 and up) for sale. Transportation to/from airport, train, or bus station.

If you've been to one B&B, you haven't been to them all.

Lady Anne's Victorian Bed & Breakfast

612 Summit Street, Winston-Salem, NC 27101   910/724-1074

Hosts: Shelley Kirley and Steve Wishon
Location: On top of a hill in the West End, a residential historic neighborhood "with beautiful sunsets." Less than a mile from Old Salem Historic Village, Baptist Hospital/Bowman Gray Medical School, Wake Forest University, and Salem College. A few blocks to restaurants, antiques shops, Benton Convention Center. Three hours to coast; 45 minutes to Blue Ridge Parkway; 30 to Pilot Mountain for picnicking, hiking, and views.
Open: Year round.
Rates: Per room. Suite with whirlpool $85 weekdays, $120 weekends. Ground-level suites $80 weekays, $100 weekends. Queen room with private bath $55, or $65 (for three people) with twin-bedded room. Upstairs suite $110 weekdays, $140 weekends.

♥ ⬥ ⁂ ✈ ⚹

The 1890 Queen Anne, on the National Register of Historic Places, was restored in the 1980s by Steve, a contractor who renovates old homes, and Shelley, a recreation therapist who was first introduced to B&Bs in California's Napa Valley. Throughout, there are antiques—mostly Victorian— and Oriental rugs, swags, and some stained glass windows.

It's a haven for business guests, and a favorite for getaways. One couple, celebrating their tenth anniversary, both booked the same suite as a surprise (it worked) for each other! One Illinois family wrote a rave review about everything from the cleanliness to the cheerful hostess. Other guests were impressed with "this delightful Victorian home, its history as well as that of the surrounding area. We enjoyed the old-world charm, quiet atmosphere, gracious service . . . a pleasant change from the usual hotel scene."

In residence: "Chee Chee is a small, gentle Lhasa apso."
Bed and bath: Five rooms; updated baths. Two ground-level suites, each with private entrance, refrigerator, and microwave. One has private porch, elaborate Victorian double bed, private tub/shower bath, private parlor with cablevision, VCR, and stereo. The other has a queen bed, queen sofa bed, kitchenette, private parlor, two-person shower. On second floor, large suite with canopied queen bed, two-person whirlpool, private balcony. Queen-bedded room with private hall full bath. Another suite has private exterior entrance, queen bed, kitchenette with all appliances hidden, adjoining room with wall-to-wall arched window, two-person tub, shower bath.
Breakfast: 7:30–10:30. Juice. Homemade breads; bagels and muffins. Fresh fruit or apple dumplings. Yogurts. Cereals. Main dish could be waffles, French toast, omelets, or quiche. In dining room or on porch.
Plus: In each bedroom—phone, central air conditioning, ceiling fan, cable TV/HBO, poetry books, music tapes and stereo. A desk in some. Some rooms also have coffee maker, room refrigerator, and microwave. Victorian pump organ in main parlor. Fresh flowers. Tea with dessert.

MeadowHaven Bed & Breakfast   910/593-3996

N.C. Highway 8, P.O. Box 222   fax 910/593-3138
Germanton, NC 27019-0222

Hosts: Sam and Darlene Fain
Location: Peaceful. On 25 country acres along the Sauratown Mountain Range. Near major state highway; 16 miles north of Winston-Salem and Old Salem historical district. Ten minutes from Hanging Rock State Park and the Dan River; 30 to local colleges; 45 to Regional Jetport, Greensboro, and High Point.
Open: Year round. Two-night minimum for holidays and special events. In cabins, two-night minimum Friday–Monday.
Rates: Main house: iron or canopied queen $65; with whirlpool $95. Cabins: $125; $150 with steam shower/sauna. Two units as one: $200 up to four people. $25 each additional person. Business and weekly rates available. Amex, MC, Visa.
♥ ❖ ✈ ⅄

From North Carolina, Florida, West Virginia, Tennessee: *"Like stepping into another world where all your needs are anticipated and taken care of.... Close to the city, yet a world apart.... Loved the [stocked and private] bass pond, outdoor glider swing, snack sideboard. Indoor pool and hot tub are especially nice.... Casual atmosphere ... beautifully decorated ... incredibly clean.... Fresh mint extract drops to place in walk-in steam room.... Awakened on a cold winter morning to the sound of chirping birds—piped into our room via the PA system! ...Extremely personable hosts.... Breakfast was outstanding ... excellent value."*

The contemporary chalet-style house began as an A-frame built by Darlene's brother. As part of a 1981 expansion, the year-round 18-by-32-foot pool with rock border was installed. Since the Fains, who both have hotel experience, opened as a B&B in 1992, they have added many embellishments inside and out.

In residence: By indoor pool—three caged parrots and two lovebirds. Outside and 'contained'—two cocker spaniels, one 110-pound German shepherd.
Foreign language spoken: Spanish.
Bed and bath: Three main house rooms with TV/VCR, movie collection, hairdryer, phone. Plus four (new in 1994) cabins. All private baths. In house, main floor—two rooms with fully equipped kitchens with queen canopied bed; one room has shower with seat, the other has whirlpool tub, steam shower/sauna for two with dual shower heads and waterfall faucet, private patio. Second floor—queen iron bed, antique and now red claw-footed tub/shower. In each cabin—queen canopied bed with trundle, heart-shaped jetted tub for two, separate shower (one has two-person steam shower/sauna), stone fireplace and gas logs, private deck.
Breakfast: 9–9:30, earlier on weekdays by advance arrangement. (Continental plus delivered to cabins.) Waffles, quiche, or heart-shaped buttermilk pancakes. Blueberry, peach, strawberry, or lemon-nut breads; cinnamon-raisin biscuits; fresh fruit. Served in dining room or on porch or deck by Sam, the chef, who often entertains with magic tricks.
Plus: Central air conditioning. Guest pantry with microwave, refrigerator, coffee maker, snacks. Heated indoor pool, hot tub on patio, sauna, sun deck. Game room with pool table and Ping-Pong. Horseshoes. Stocked pond.

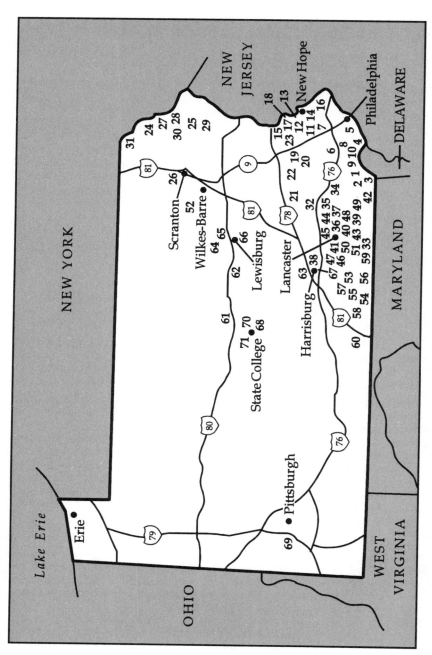

The numbers on this map indicate the locations of B&Bs described in detail in this chapter.

PENNSYLVANIA

Philadelphia and Brandywine Valley _____ Reservation Services _____

Bed & Breakfast Connections/Bed & Breakfast of Philadelphia

P.O. Box 21, Devon, PA 19333

Phone: 610/687-3565 or 800/448-3619, Monday–Friday 9–7, Saturday 9–5. Closed major holidays and Sundays.

Fax: 610/995-9524

Listings: 90. Most are private homes; 6 are inns. Located in the extended Philadelphia area, including the Center City and University, Society Hill, and Main Line suburbs. Many are located near historic sites and are convenient to public transportation. Nearby areas with listings include Valley Forge, Bucks County, Brandywine Valley, Pennsylvania Dutch country, and Poconos. Free directory available.

Reservations: Last-minute possible at some locations. For major events such as graduation, bookings made up to a year in advance.

Rates: $30–$190 single, $45–$190 double. Family and weekly rates available. $2–$5 booking fee. $5 one-night surcharge at some locations. One night or 20 percent deposit required. Deposit refunded, less a $15 service charge, if cancellation is received at least seven days prior to arrival date. No refund with less than seven days' notice. Guest can avoid deposit forfeiture by booking and staying with same host within three months from original arrival date. Amex, MC, Visa. ♦

This personalized reservation service is owned and operated by Peggy Gregg and Lucy Scribner, who have had experience as travel agent, educator, and social worker. They know their helpful and hospitable hosts well and conduct annual inspections. While booking first-time and experienced B&B guests, they explain the geography of the area and arrange for an appropriate host and location.

Guesthouses

P.O. Box 2137, West Chester, PA 19380

Phone: 215/692-4575, Monday–Friday noon–4.

Fax: 215/692-4451.

Listings: Over 200. Mostly hosted private residences. Some inns.

Reservations: At least 10 days' advance notice preferred. Last-minute accommodated if guest can receive fax.

Rates: $80–$200 double occupancy. $5 less for singles. Deposits (received within five days of request) or guarantees by credit card for the first and last nights' lodging (including tax) are required. For cancellations received five days prior to scheduled visit, full credit given as a deposit applied to any future visit within one year. To be eligible for a refund, less 5 percent bank processing fee if charged to credit card, guest must apply for cancellation insurance at the time of reservation or on receipt of confirmation. Guesthouses guarantees its accommodations; if a guest arrives but does not take occupancy, for any reason, there is no charge and any monies received are refunded in full. Amex, MC, Visa. ◆

Although many Brandywine Valley hosts are part of Janice Archbold's personalized service, her widespread listings—mostly historic—are in Philadelphia and the Main Line (Wynnewood to Paoli), Valley Forge, Lancaster, Reading, Longwood, Chadds Ford, West Chester, Gettysburg, New Hope—all in Pennsylvania. Some others are in Delaware and New Jersey and on Maryland's Chesapeake Bay. Stays on yachts (they are expensive) can be custom arranged.

"We best serve those guests who want to savor the experience of being a guest and want more than a bed to sleep in. All of our hosts want to share their part of the world and give their hospitality in return for meeting, however briefly, new friends."

KEY TO SYMBOLS
♥ Lots of honeymooners come here.
⁂ Families with children are very welcome. (Please see page xii.)
⚑ "Please emphasize that we are a private home, not an inn."
♣ Groups or private parties sometimes book the entire B&B.
◆ Travel agents' commission paid. (Please see page xii.)
✖ Sorry, no guests' pets are allowed.
✄ No smoking inside *or* no smoking at all, even on porches.

Philadelphia and Brandywine Valley
_____ B&Bs _____

Meadow Spring Farm   610/444-3903
201 East Street Road, Kennett Square, PA 19348

Hosts: Anne Hicks and daughter Debbie Axelrod
Location: On a 130-acre working farm. On Route 926, up a long lane with black-and-white cows (young stock) on one side and fields of corn and hay on the other. Five minutes from Longwood Gardens and the Brandywine River Museum.
Open: Year round. Reservations required.
Rates: Single $55. Double $75 shared bath, $85 private. $10 cot or crib.
♥ ♯ ☜ ♣ ✖

> From Virginia: *"Homey, cozy atmosphere."* From Massachusetts: *"Immaculate . . . highest quality food, deliciously prepared and generous."* From Michigan: *"The house is filled with warmth."*

Whether on Washington, D.C., TV, in the Philadelphia area Bloomingdale's (for a "Meet-the-Hosts" program based on this book), in *Country Inns* magazine, or in the *New York Times,* this B&B and Anne are big hits. Since 1983, Meadow Spring Farm has been a perfect match for travelers who come for quiet (no sound of traffic); for the cows (about 200) and calves and sheep and lambs; for the chickens (guests may gather the eggs) and rabbits too. Guests love the perennial gardens, the in-ground swimming pool, and (in winter) the hot tub in the solarium. And museum-goers, honeymooners, entire families, skiers, and canoers come again and again for Anne, the hostess who arrived as a bride (in 1948) at this antiques-filled 1836 brick farmhouse. Now her almost-famous collections include cows, dolls, and Santas of cloth, porcelain, ceramic, and wood. Three sons have taken over the farming. B&B has become so busy that daughter Debbie left her full-time job to become cohostess.

In residence: Temba, a Lab, "greets guests and accompanies you on paths around the farm." Visiting grandchildren are guides too.
Bed and bath: Seven rooms. In farmhouse, four second-floor rooms. One with canopied queen bed, working fireplace, private tub and shower bath. One with queen sleigh bed, fireplace, private bath. Room with two twin beds shares a bath with a single-bedded room. In separate building, private baths for room with twin beds and two queen-bedded rooms; first-floor room has small kitchen. Cot and crib available.
Breakfast: 7:30–9. Apple pancakes, fresh fruit, homemade breads as well as jams and jellies. Sausage, scrapple, or bacon; French toast or mushroom omelets. Homemade sticky buns on Sundays. In dining room, on glassed-in porch by the pool, or in your room.
Plus: Air-conditioned bedrooms with TVs and ceiling fans. Welcoming refreshments include home-baked goods. Fresh flowers year round. Fireplaced

living room. Wood stove in kitchen. Game room with pool table. Fresh fruit. Mints. Will meet guests at transportation points. Will plan everything from restaurant reservations to balloon rides. Babysitting. Kitchen privileges.

Scarlett House   215/444-9592
503 West State Street, Kennett Square, PA 19348-3298

Hosts: Susan Lalli-Ascosi and Andy Ascosi
Location: On main street of town, three miles south of Longwood Gardens. Short walk to shops and restaurants. Within nine miles of Winterthur, Hagley, Brandywine Battlefield and River Museum. Thirty miles from Philadelphia and Lancaster.

Open: Year round. Two-day minimum on holidays and weekends in May, June, October–December.
Rates: $65 shared bath, $85 private. $95 suite; $10 for third person in suite.
♥ ♣ ✈ ⚹

From New Jersey: *"Spectacular. . . . Perfectly appointed for aesthetics and comfort."* From Massachusetts: *". . . warm, helpful, generous."* From New York: *"Nothing (here or abroad) compares to the service and hospitality . . . a culinary treat."* From Texas: *"Magnificent."* From New York: *"A romantic (not saccharine) Victorian atmosphere. . . . Captivating . . . beautifully decorated . . . gas chandeliers that seem to have been made for the house . . . goody bag—as if Grandmother had sent us off."*

The accolades are endless for this B&B, a classic American foursquare-style granite house built in 1910 with wraparound porch, chestnut woodwork, leaded glass windows, and ornate fireplaces. The Ascosis, the first owners outside of the Scarlett family, began their "adventure," a three-year restoration phase, without plumbing! Now they host contented guests including many business travelers. And they remember the romance novelist who came with her husband for a weekend complete with flowers, champagne, chocolates, and notes pinned to the pillow. Now one parlor has red velvet settee and chairs, roses and lace; another, also fireplaced, has books and a TV and VCR. And to think "Susan's dream" all started in the 1970s with some antique hat pins and jewelry—and a memorable Nantucket B&B—before her 17 years in health care marketing. Andy is an engineer "who caught the Victorian bug. When we ran out of room, it was time to find a house of the period to go with our collection." Scarlett House opened in 1990.

In residence: In hosts' quarters, "innkeeper-in-training" Nicholas, age three.
Bed and bath: Four second-floor rooms. Suite has ornately carved queen bed, sitting area with double sofa bed, private bath with glass-enclosed shower. Another room with carved high-headboard queen bed, private shower bath. One room with spindled oak queen bed and another with double four-poster bed share a hall tub/shower bath.
Breakfast: Usually 8–8:30. Buffet may include low-fat mushroom-shaped chocolate-chip scones (a specialty), mandarin orange muffins, poppyseed lemon bread. Fresh fruits. Freshly squeezed orange juice. Bread pudding, quiche, mushroom souffle, or apple crisp. Coffee flavored with vanilla and a

(Please turn page.)

hint of chocolate. At candlelit table set with silver and lace; on porch in summer.

Plus: Bedroom air conditioning and phone jacks. Afternoon tea or lemonade with fresh fruit, homemade cookies and pastries. Evening refreshments. Turndown service with fresh flower on pillow. Upright piano in music room. Large second-floor sitting area.

Bed & Breakfast at Walnut Hill   610/444-3703

Kennett Square, PA
Mailing address: 541 Chandler's Mill Road, Avondale, PA 19311-9606

Hosts: Tom and Sandy Mills
Location: On a wooded site "along a crooked country road," facing a horse-filled meadow (that in the 1840s was site of a grist mill) with meandering creek. Seven minutes from Longwood Gardens; 15–20 minutes from Winterthur, Hagley, and Brandywine River Museum.

One hour west of Philadelphia's Center City; 40 minutes east of Lancaster; 25 minutes from Wilmington, Delaware.
Open: Year round. Two-day minimum on holiday weekends.
Rates: $70 single. $80–$85 double.
♥ ♙ ⚓ ♣ ♦ ✶

Many guests (and some who come on house tours) want to live here forever! Antiques are imaginatively displayed and used in the 1840 mill house, which has been restored by the Millses since they came here as bride and groom three decades ago. Some walls are lined with old barnboard siding. A walk-in fireplace is in the beamed den. A buggy seat is now a coffee table; a washboard, a mirror; an ironing board, a flower stand. There are dried herbs; handcrafts; fresh flowers; family photographs; braided rugs; a formal living room; designer linens—and, available to guests year round, a hot tub.

Tom works for DuPont. Sandy is a former Winterthur guide (for 10 years), caterer, and children's services social worker.

In residence: Devon, a yellow Labrador. One Persian and a tiger cat are always outside.
Foreign languages spoken: Some French and Spanish.
Bed and bath: Three second-floor rooms. (Maximum of two booked unless guests are traveling together.) One shared tub and shower bath plus a half bath. One room has four-poster canopied double bed. One with two twin beds (and space for one extra bed). One room with an antique wicker single bed.
Breakfast: Usually 7–9. Guests' choice. Cottage cheese pancakes with hot blueberry sauce; French toast (plain or stuffed with peaches and cream); mushroom omelets; or frittatas. Homemade scones, muffins, rolls, and spreads. Served in front of bay window overlooking bird feeders, picturesque meadow, and stream.
Plus: Air-conditioned bedrooms. Afternoon or evening lemonade, tea, or cider with homemade sweets. Turndown service. Mints on pillow. Down comforters. Bathrobes. Library with cable TV.

> From California: *"Like visiting someone you knew in college . . . treated our four-year-old as if they were aunt and uncle . . . told us about covered bridges . . .*

went on to a more beautiful place, but we enjoyed Walnut Hill more." From New York: *"A delightful couple who give you just the right amount of attention."* From Ohio: *"Wonderful sense of humor . . . shared recipes."* From Connecticut: *"Charming, as is the country setting."*

Cornerstone Bed and Breakfast   610/274-2143
300 Buttonwood Road, Landenberg, PA 19350   fax 610/274-0734

Hosts: Linda Chamberlin and Marty Mulligan
Location: In the rolling hills of lovely chateau country. Very close to the Delaware line. Fifteen minutes to Longwood Gardens, the University of Delaware, Brandywine River Museum. Twenty minutes to Winterthur and Amish country.

Open: Year round. Two-night minimum on weekends and holidays.
Rates: Queen $100; $125 with fireplace fall through spring. Cottages: $125 one bedroom, $250 entire cottage (with two bedrooms).
♥ ♣ ♦ ✈ ⅀

Every four years, on Chester County Day, hundreds (1,800) stand in line here to tour the spacious rooms, which are filled with still-growing collections from all over the world—fine antiques, Persian and Chinese rugs, clocks, and brasses. Built between 1704 (the oldest part) and 1820 (the date on the cornerstone), with beautiful woodwork and elaborate mantels, the house was vacant in 1980 when Linda, a chemical company executive, bought it and fulfilled her childhood dream of living in a Chester County stone house. She gained vast experience as plasterer, painter, wallpaperer, and furniture restorer. Because she created a comfortable environment that is both elegant and casual, every day a guest asks if this is the family home.

She and Marty, an Eastman Kodak technical representative turned innkeeper, have expanded the beautiful perennial, herb, and rose gardens. Put exotic fish in the pond. Renovated cottages. They host guests (many give gift certificates to relatives) who enjoy area attractions, the walks here along the miles of carriage trails, the pool with Jacuzzi, and the pampering.

In residence: Ben and Jesse are golden retrievers. Jerry is a sheltie.
Foreign languages spoken: French and German.
Bed and bath: Five rooms, two suites, and six cottages, all with period antiques, all private baths. First floor—room with canopied queen bed, sitting room, shower bath. (All other baths have tub and shower.) On second floor—canopied queen beds, two with working fireplace. Third-floor suite has king bed in one room, two double beds in the other. Each cottage has queen bed, private bath, gas fireplace, private deck, full kitchen, living/dining room, and countryside views.
Breakfast: 8–9. Juice, fresh fruit, croissants or homemade muffins, fresh toast. Egg entree, pancakes, or breakfast casserole. Special diets accommodated with advance notice.
Plus: Room air conditioners. Living room with two fireplaces. Large wicker-furnished porch. Coffee always on. Turned-down beds. Garden flowers. Plant-filled greenhouse. Bicycles to borrow.

Hamanassett

215/459-3000

P.O. Box 129, Lima, PA 19037-0129

Host: Mrs. Evelene Dohan
Location: High on a hill on 48 acres, "a 10-minute walk to nowhere, with privacy, peace, seclusion, interrupted only by sound of birds." Seven miles to Chadds Ford. Within 20 minutes of fine dining; Longwood Gardens; Winterthur, Nemours, Brandywine museums; 25 minutes to Philadelphia airport, 35 to Center City Philadelphia.

Open: Year round. Two-night minimum October–December, May, June, graduation, and holiday weekends.
Rates: $75 twin beds, shared bath. Private bath $85–$100; singles slightly less, additional person $25. Suite $120–$225 (depends on number accommodated).
♥ ⬛ ♣ ♦ ✈ ✄

Memorable. A half-mile-long horticultural extravaganza leading to an 1850 mansion (with 30-inch-thick stone walls), home to the Dohan family since 1870. Spacious and beautiful, with important heirloom antiques and collectibles, and intricate craftsmanship and architectural details throughout. Hospitality that is based on years of experience, stemming from the era when this was headquarters for the Lima Hunt, home to the Master of Hounds.

The greenhouse, filled with interesting and colorful flora from October to May, was built by Mrs. Dohan, a longtime Philadelphia Flower Show award winner, gourmet cook, and former English literature teacher. With a minimum of help, she maintains the entire house and has encouraged woodlands to minimize grounds maintenance.

Although many guests come for the area attractions, a great many just enjoy Hamanassett—its privacy, garden, fields, and country trails. Travelers from all over the country wrote long, detailed letters that recall lively conversations; gourmet breakfasts; the energetic, friendly, gracious hostess; and the "relaxed and exquisite environment." It's the perfect setting for weddings, for on-location filming (the hostess participated), and for small business meetings and retreats.

Foreign language spoken: French—"un peu, tres peu."
Bed and bath: Eight rooms (including suite), all with private full baths. On second floor, two with four-poster queen (small refrigerator in one), one with canopied king (also with small refrigerator). On third floor (all air conditioned), room with two double beds and sitting room with sofa bed; king with detached bath; room with twin beds available with either. Suite with king-bedded room, room with double bed, living room with two sofa beds, bath, small refrigerator.
Breakfast: 7:30–9:30 Monday–Saturday; 8–10 Sunday. Two fruits, juice, cereal, bacon and/or sausage and/or scrapple. Eggs cooked to order, French toast, blueberry pancakes, cheese omelet (house specialty). Homemade muffins, breads, croissants, and jams. Buffet in large dining room. Small groups sit in curve of French doors with view of lawns and woodlands.
Plus: In each room, fresh flowers arranged professionally by hostess, ice, fruit, TV. Library with over 2,000 volumes including current, classical, and first editions. Formal fireplaced living room.

Bed & Breakfast Connections/Bed & Breakfast of Philadelphia Host #B09

Philadelphia, PA

Location: Urban, yet surrounded by gardens with paths, flowering trees, and original iron fence. Ten-minute walk to University of Pennsylvania and Drexel University, Civic Center, hospitals. Ten-minute drive or 12-minute trolley ride to City Center.

Reservations: Year round through Bed & Breakfast Connections/Bed & Breakfast of Philadelphia, page 226. Two-night minimum for graduations, parents' weekends, major conventions.

Rates: Shared bath $50 single, $60 double. Private bath $$70 single, $70 double; suite 10 more.

♥ ♨ ♣ ✈ ⚷

"Believe it or not, we like working on old houses," say the hosts, two United Methodist ministers—one from New England, the other from a rural Pennsylvania town—who are often asked about the history of this Queen Anne Victorian. Once again, the former home for Jesuits has natural woodwork; its parquet floors have been restored, its wraparound porch rebuilt. All new systems have been installed. Antique furnishings include family pieces, auction finds, and some yard-sale finds too. At Christmas, every room has a tree with some of the thousands of ornaments collected by one of the host's families. This spacious house—with large entry hall and two adjoining parlors—is perfect for the many weddings that take place here. Since the hosts bought it in 1993 from friends who started the B&B a year before, they have had many opportunities to share their knowledge of the city and their appreciation for "our eclectic neighborhood, which has a sense of community within a big city." As one guest wrote, "The beauty of the house and the hospitality contributed to a memorable stay."

Bed and bath: On second and third floors—eight air-conditioned rooms, plus library sometimes used as a ninth. Some with working fireplace. One tower room on each floor. Baths have shower and tub or shower only. All private en-suite baths. Queen, double, or twin beds. Suite has queen bed, original bath with soaking tub and pedestal sink, private wicker-furnished enclosed porch. One room decorated year round for a Victorian Christmas.
Breakfast: Usually 8:30. Casserole, quiche, waffles, or pancakes. Juice, fruit, homemade muffins, croissants, cereals, gourmet coffee and teas.
Plus: Library with TV/VCR. Off-street parking.

Mrs. Ritz' Room

Philadelphia, PA

Location: Quiet. "Between the Squares" (Rittenhouse and Fittler). In neighborhood that is on the National Register of Historic Places.

Reservations: Year round through Bed & Breakfast Connections/Bed & Breakfast of Philadelphia, page 226. Two-night minimum on holiday and parents' weekends, graduations, major conventions.

Rates: $65 single. $75 double.

◀ ♦ ✈ ⚷

(Please turn page.)

While walking her dogs in 1993, the host found this treasure, a narrow Federal-style 1860s row house dubbed "one of the town's biggest surprises" during a recent historic house tour. The interior, redesigned by former owners who were architects, features a large beamed basement kitchen with glass-roofed atrium eating area that is seen from the first-floor entrance and living room. Furnishings are a blend of Art Deco, Federal, Victorian and contemporary. Everywhere there are collections: doorstops, vintage kitchenware, wire baskets, vintage suitcases—even an old steamer trunk. The host has a strong interest in decorative arts. And she is active with organizations concerned with child and animal welfare.

In residence: Two very friendly dogs.
Bed and bath: Steep winding stairs lead to second floor, all for guests—room with double bed, air-conditioned sitting room, tub and shower bath.
Breakfast: Continental. Vegetarian. Served in atrium or in guests' quarters.

Shippen Way Inn   215/627-7266
416–418 Bainbridge Street, Philadelphia, PA 19147   800/245-4873

Hosts: Ann Foringer and Raymond Rhule
Location: In rediscovered historic downtown district with Famous Deli, a Thai restaurant, a French restaurant, and a popular pastry shop close by. One block off South Street's boutiques, ethnic restaurants, shops, pubs. Two blocks from Society Hill, six to Independence Hall, Liberty Bell, Visitor Center. Walk to Penn's Landing and Hi-Speed water taxi for Camden's aquarium, and to bus for art museums and University of Pennsylvania.
Open: Year round.
Rates: $70–$80 double bed, $90 with fireplace. $90 twin beds. $90–$105 queen bed. Discounts for three or more nights. Amex, MC, Visa.
❖ ◆ ✖

Surprise! Country ambiance in the city. A wrought iron gate leads to the courtyard, the connecting link to these two 18th-century houses. One is brick; the other, frame (unusual in Philadelphia). They were restored (the facade, shutter colors, cedar-shake roof, and even type of mortar were approved by the Historic Commission) and renovated (gutted). Old beams were retained and added. Ann and her mother stenciled and decorated. They created a very comfortable, friendly environment, with country antiques and quilts, and with an open kitchen where guests can make a cup of tea and get hints for restaurants and places to see.

Raymond, resident innkeeper/restorer, paints with watercolors and oils. He and his sister Ann, full-time co-innkeeper who lives within walking distance, enjoy their role as "ambassadors for the city."

In residence: Red, a three-pawed cat.
Foreign language spoken: "A little Spanish."
Bed and bath: Nine rooms (one with working fireplace) on three floors; size ranges from large to "tiny but cozy." All private shower baths. Some are ground-floor rooms (two have private garden entrance); some on second floor are reached via steep spiral staircase; one is a third-floor dormer room. Twins, double, queen, four-posters (one with trundle bed) available.

Breakfast: 7:30–10. Freshly squeezed orange juice. Fruit. Homemade granola. Cereals. Baked goods. Buffet style in glass-enclosed breakfast room overlooking flower and herb gardens.
Plus: Central air conditioning. Ground-floor fireplaced sitting room. Private bedroom phones. TV in queen-bedded rooms. Afternoon wine and cheese in garden or by fireplace. Public parking nearby (some free, some charge). Suggestion for an Italian restaurant with opera performances.

Amsterdam B&B

610/983-9620
800/952-1580

P.O. Box 1139, Valley Forge PA 19482-1139

Hosts: Pamela and Ino Vandersteur
Location: On two-lane Route 23, the road from Valley Forge National Park (6 miles from B&B) to Pennsylvania Dutch country (20 miles). Surrounded by farms. "Within 2 miles of several great restaurants." Forty-five minutes to historic Philadelphia and to Brandywine; 20 to King of Prussia Mall.
Open: Year round.
Rates: $65 shared bath, $75 private bath. Singles $10 less. MC, Visa.
♥ ⬛ ⁂ ◆ ✈

People came from miles around to Pam's "nice little Indonesian tearoom" that seated 30 for dinner in this added-on-to 1860 general store with, in part, old 18-inch-thick stone walls. Shortly after she opened in 1989, guests who came for rijsttafel and other specialties asked to stay overnight. Thus was born the small European-style B&B. The combination was too successful! So now it's "just" a B&B, with a Jacuzzi for six, in the former greenhouse, available in the evening; with cooking influenced by Pam's training in Ino's native Holland; with Dutch tiles and warm colors; and with meticulous housekeeping.

To transform the building, a private residence when the Vandersteurs bought it, Ino took a three months' leave of absence from his pharmaceutical engineering position. Pam left her work in real estate and construction. They removed suspended ceilings, discovered original plaster under plastic brick walls, and found original latches and moldings too. The love story? Pam met Ino, who has been in this country for about 17 years, about two miles from here.

In residence: Two dogs in hosts' quarters, visited only by guest request. One Italian mastiff and one whippet.
Foreign languages spoken: French, Dutch, German.
Bed and bath: Up a steep staircase, three air-conditioned second-floor rooms, new baths with European fixtures. One queen Danish bed, private tub and shower bath, TV, plus a deck. Room with queen bed and sitting area and room with twin/king option and dressing room share (robes provided) a tub and shower bath. Across street—weekly/monthly apartment.
Breakfast: 7–8 continental; 8–9:30 choice of several entrees such as French toast, eggs any style, or the house specialty. Bacon or sausage. Fruit, orange juice, coffee, tea. "Can last for hours."
Plus: Welcoming beverage. Wood-burning stove in living room. Big front porch. Guest refrigerator stocked with beverages. TVs available. Help-yourself coffee, tea, cocoa. Guest microwave. Patio. Badminton. Picnic table. Grill.

(Please turn page.)

From Pennsylvania: *"Amiable hosts . . . interesting conversations . . . deluxe accommodations with charm and character . . . fabulous food . . . even recommended tour of a fascinating artist's studio."*

Der Stone Farmhouse   215/723-9158
82 Derstine Road, Hatfield, PA 19440

Hosts: Jim and Sylvia Derstine
Location: Quiet and rural. On 40 acres overlooking corn fields. Twenty miles east of Valley Forge; 30 north of Philadelphia; 2 miles from Pennsylvania Turnpike. Within five minutes of restaurants.

Open: Year round.
Rates: $75 shared bath. $85 private bath. Ten percent discount on stays of seven or more days.
♥ ⚓ ♣ ✈ ⚰

From Pennsylvania: *"Surrounding grounds are beautiful, but the real warmth and beauty is inside. Everything is sparkling clean. Beautiful antiques and fresh flowers abound. Our room accommodations were exceptional. . . . Breakfast was homemade, fresh . . . outstanding. All of this and gracious hosts to boot. I would recommend Der Stone and, as a travel agent, already have done so."* From another Pennsylvanian: *"Felt pampered. . . . Everything is done just right!"*

Business travelers, too, appreciate the impeccable 1857 brownstone farmhouse that the Derstines refurbished in 1992. Opening a B&B provided the perfect role for Sylvia, who loved the years of full-time homemaking, parenting (five children), and entertaining. For 30 years she and Jim, who has a trucking business, lived "just down the street."

Bed and bath: Three second-floor rooms with refinished floors, Oriental rugs. Victorian Room has high queen bed, private tub/shower bath. Carriage Room with canopied queen bed shares shower bath with Garden Room, which has brass-and-iron queen bed.
Breakfast: Flexible times. Stuffed French toast, sausage and egg casserole, ham and egg souffle, quiche, eggs Benedict, or blueberry pancakes. Homemade muffins. Served in the dining room or on the screened porch with wheat fields in view.
Plus: Central air conditioning. Fireplaced living room with cable TV in armoire. Evening beverage. Fresh flowers and fruit. Large plant-filled, wicker-furnished sun room. Anniversary or birthday cake served on pedestal plate.

Some executives who book a meeting at an inn return on a weekend for a getaway. Some on a getaway return with colleagues for a meeting.

The Great Valley House of Valley Forge

Box 110, RD 3, Malvern, PA 19355

610/644-6759
fax 610/644-7019

Host: Pattye Benson
Location: On 4 acres adjacent to 50 acres of woods with walking and jogging trails. A rural country setting, just off main road. Half a mile from Route 202, five from exit 24 (Valley Forge) of Pennsylvania Turnpike. Two miles to Valley Forge National Park. Six minutes to King of Prussia Mall; 20 to Philadelphia.

Open: Year round. Two-night weekend minimum for room with private bath.

Rates: $75 shared bath, $85 private. Singles $10 less. $10 third person in room.

♥ ♦ ♦ ♣ ♦

"Did George Washington sleep here?" is one of the most frequently asked questions at this very popular antiques-filled B&B. It was established in 1983 in the state's second-oldest house, which has an "olde kitchen" (the original 1690 house) complete with walk-in fireplace, crane, and rare stone sink. Stone walls are 27 inches thick. Hinges and brackets are hand forged. A British gramophone is in the dining room. There's a vine-covered smokehouse. A tunnel that was part of the Underground Railroad. And lots of history shared by Pattye. She is a hostess with contagious enthusiasm, a pianist who frequently entertains in the evening, an interior designer/B&B instructor/National Trust for Historic Preservation presenter/quilter who has a master's degree in political science. Her husband, Jeff, marketing director for a computer company, singlehandedly restored the "piece of American history" they found within five days after returning from living (and traveling in B&Bs) in England. This is a place that has been discovered by guests from all over the world, by business travelers who choose it over luxury hotels, by summer tourists who appreciate the pool, by families, and by honeymooners who know that Pattye rejoices in making a special breakfast for them.

In residence: Daughter Lyndsey, age 11. Whu Chi, a Shih Tzu.
Foreign languages spoken: French, German, and some Spanish.
Bed and bath: Three large rooms. All hand stenciled and air conditioned, with cable TV and radio, antique quilts. Entire third floor consists of two dormered rooms, each with a queen and a twin bed. One room has private en-suite bath with antique English footed tub and hand-held shower. The other shares a shower bath with second-floor room that has a double bed, queen sofa bed, and private phone. Rollaway and crib available.
Breakfast: Full 8–9:30. (Continental at other times.) Fruit. French toast, souffle, or quiche. Homemade breads and muffins. Freshly ground gourmet coffee. Served by fireplace in oft-photographed olde kitchen.
Plus: Grand piano. Fireplaces in kitchen and living and dining rooms. Guests have use of microwave, refrigerator, teakettle. Books and games. Down comforters. Turndown service. Picnic baskets ($15).

The Bankhouse Bed & Breakfast

875 Hillsdale Road, West Chester, PA 19382-1975   610/344-7388

Hosts: Diana and Michael Bové
Location: On a country road, across from a pond and horse farm. One mile from town and restaurants. Five miles from U.S. Route 1; 3 from Route 202; 10 from Pennsylvania Turnpike; 8 miles to Longwood Gardens and Brandywine River Mu-
seum. Twenty minutes to Valley Forge National Park; 30 to Lancaster; 45 to downtown Philadelphia.
Open: Year round.
Rates: $85 private bath suite. $65 semiprivate. Corporate rates available.
♦ ✕ ⊬

Just two guest rooms, yet close to a record number of guests' letters every year, with every one praising *everything*. A few excerpts:

> From Washington: *"The type of place that makes me want to put together another business trip to Philadelphia just so I can stay there."* From New York: *"Our first real B&B. Others had been more like small inns . . . lemonade and iced tea, good reading lamps, carrots to feed the horses and donkey . . . spotless accommodations, a peaceful and historic setting."* From Illinois: *"Charming country decor and very comfortable. . . . Best breakfast I have ever had at a B&B."* From Maryland: *"Warm and cozy . . . with shiny wood floors and stenciling . . . felt pampered."* From Massachusetts: *" . . . invited our college daughter to have breakfast with us."* From Virginia: *"Health-conscious breakfast."* From Colorado: *" . . . a wealth of information on area, especially antiques shops and sightseeing."* From California: *"Greeted us with hot cider."* From Alaska: *"Went home with luscious muffin recipe."* From Maryland: *"A quaint old house built into the bank of a hill. . . . interesting books and items by local artists and craftsmen."* From California: *"Enchanting . . . a view from balcony across a green hill with a pond and even a horse. . . . Good music with breakfast."* From Oregon: *"Perfect hosts."*

The Bovés opened in 1989 after spending 18 months renovating this 200-year-old farmhouse, after Diana had a wonderful time in Massachusetts as a substitute innkeeper, and after she decorated the Bankhouse with country antiques and folk art. Previously, she was media department coordinator at the American College in Bryn Mawr, where Michael is a production engineer and professional voice talent.

Bed and bath: Entire second floor. One double-bedded room and one with twin beds share a very large full bath, a sitting room with book-filled wall, and a balcony. Private exterior entrance.
Breakfast: 8–9:30. Repertoire of 100+ muffin recipes plus many entrees such as German apple or whole wheat pancakes or French toast with hosts' own hot orange syrup. Freshly ground gourmet coffee or tea, juice, fresh fruit. In dining room overlooking horse farm and pond.
Plus: Central air conditioning. Sitting room with desk, private phone, ceiling fan, books, games. Fresh flowers. Flannel sheets. Homemade snacks.

Lenape Springs Farm

580 West Creek Road, West Chester, PA
Mailing address: P.O. Box 176, Pocopson, PA 19366

610/793-2266
800/793-2234
fax 610/793-2272

Hosts: Bob and Sharon Currie
Location: Idyllic. Off the beaten path. On 32 acres along Brandywine Creek. With one gazebo in front and another down by spring-fed pond. Five miles northeast of Longwood Gardens; 4½ miles north of Chadds Ford; 10 miles north of Winterthur Museum. Near horseback riding, canoeing, antiquing, wine sampling. An hour to Philadelphia or Lancaster.

Open: Year round, "except the month we close for vacation" (which varies).
Rates: In carriage house, $85. Main house: second floor $70. Third floor $70 one room, $130 two rooms, $180 for three-room suite. Third person $15. Singles $5 less. Senior citizens 10 percent less. MC, Visa.
♥ ⚞ ⚘ ✕

An adventure awaits. And so it has been for the Curries, who bought this farm in 1977. Guests enjoy the restored three-storied 1847 stone "simple without ornaments" Quaker-built farmhouse; the adjoining carriage house; the deck with hot tub that faces the river and overlooks gardens and sweeping lawns; and the huge fireplaced (and air-conditioned) game room complete with pool table. Many guests appreciate the opportunity to take pretty walks; to tour the interesting early-1800s three-tiered bank barn; to talk with the owners of the boarded horses or with visiting blacksmiths or the veterinarian; and maybe to experience a truck ride or hayride with Bob, a recently retired chemical engineer who grew up on a dairy farm in Montana. Here he raises cattle and grows winter hay on this farm, which is "just about what we envisioned 17 years ago."

In residence: Much-photographed animals: beef cattle; Chinook, a white Border collie/spitz; Gizmo, Pretty Lee, and Neutron—cats frequently invited to guests' rooms.
Foreign language spoken: Dutch. (The family spent seven years in Holland.)
Bed and bath: In main house—large second-floor room has queen bed, private shower bath. Third-floor suite with two hall baths has one queen-bedded room. A larger room with king/twins option has adjoining room with two twin beds. In air-conditioned carriage house—two carpeted rooms, each with twin/king option. One with collection of bottles found on the farm, private full bath; other with Sharon's miniature doll collection, shower bath.
Breakfast: Usually 8–9:30. Fresh fruit. Fresh mushrooms in Dijon sauce over poached eggs with English muffins; scrambled eggs with homemade muffins; Bob's buttermilk waffles on weekends and holidays. In dining room, in glassed alcove, or on deck.
Plus: Window air conditioners in main house bedrooms. Beverages. Hershey kisses. Table and chairs under arbor by lily pond with goldfish. The answer to "What is that cable for?"

> From Maryland: *"Physical layout surpassed only by hospitality. . . . First time we ever booked next year's reunion at the same place . . . total relaxation . . . helpful . . . felt welcome . . . outstanding waffles."*

The Valentine

West Chester, PA

Location: Surprising. Just after many newer houses (the town) and before a 10-minute drive (the country) to Longwood Gardens. On two acres of woods, lawns, and magnificent trees and plantings including original Longwood Gardens rhododendrons, which bloom in sequence from May until July.

Reservations: Year round through Guesthouses, page 226.
Rates: $95 private hall bath. $85 semiprivate bath. $110 with fireplace and attached private bath. $65 third-floor rooms, shared bath.
♥ ♣ ✻ ✄

"There's been a wedding here every weekend for the last two months," said the hostess as we talked about her restored and inviting three-storied 1860 brick house with cupola. The detail includes carved mahogany, walnut, and chestnut; tall ceilings with plaster ornamentation; exquisite ironwork from London; tall windows that open out to a loggia and antique fountains; and a historic gazebo by the creek. There's a blend of furnishings, many ferns and palms, Victorian settees in the sun room, and maybe live goldfish swimming in vases with fresh bouquets arranged by the hostess/decorator/special events coordinator, the one who found letters from the Civil War (read them at breakfast) in a cake tin (that somehow escaped the auction) when she moved here 12 years ago. This was the home of DuPont's real estate—and Pennsylvania's first female—attorney, one of five daughters. (More discussion; pictures available.) The contemporary art on display, for sale here and in prestigious galleries nationwide, is the work of Harry Dunn, the area artist who designed the NBC peacock logo.

In residence: One five-pound peke-a-poo in hosts' quarters.
Bed and bath: Seven rooms. Second floor—one large air-conditioned room has antique brass double (feather) bed, working fireplace, private full bath. Room with brass double bed and one with large walnut double bed share large (new, but looks like it was always there) shower bath. Third floor—four antiques-furnished rooms, each with double bed, share original 1860 ceramic tile hall bath with claw-footed tub/shower bath.
Breakfast: Flexible. Usually presented at 9 on weekends. Fresh fruit or baked compote. Homemade bread, muffins, Danish, sticky buns. Croissant French toast; meat frittata and/or vegetable dish with homemade fresh salsa. Cooked cereal if you'd like. Juice, hot beverages. In fireplaced dining room. "Can last four hours on Sunday with people who never met before."
Plus: Fireplaced library. Wicker- and plant-filled wraparound porch. Evening sherry or brandy. Special occasions acknowledged.

From New York: *"We love the house and we love the hostess."*

Monument House

Dilworthtown, PA

Location: Rural. Overlooking rolling farmland. With monument to Lafayette by the tree where he was wounded. Within 10 minutes of Chadds Ford and not more than 20 minutes from any of the other Brandywine Valley attractions.

Reservations: Year round through Guesthouses, page 226.

Rates: $80 one room, private bath. $130 or $140 for entire floor ($130 three people, two rooms; $140 four people, two rooms). $25 rollaway. Singles $10 less.

♥ ♨ ⚓ ✈ ⚰

With 28 years' experience as Wedgwood's head designer in England, the host came to this country "by sheer chance" in 1979 to work for the Franklin Mint. Now he and his wife, freelance artists, design ceramics for major corporations; they also paint tile murals as private commissions. "Although we work alone in our separate (private) studios—his is up and mine is down—we switch and swap and help each other."

Since 1984 they have lived in this area. Their "comfortable, homely house, a home more than a house" has an extensive modern addition. The antiques-furnished guest rooms are in the original early 19th-century section. A wood-burning stove and TV are in a cozy living room. From the breakfast room you can see "lovely views right down to Shady Hollow, with corn or winter wheat and a farmhouse on the horizon at the far end."

In residence: One cat.

Bed and bath: For one party, the entire second (top) floor with two rooms. One with king/twin option and one with a double bed share one large shower (with seat) bath. Rollaway available.

Breakfast: 8–9. "A proper breakfast." Fruit. Eggs and bacon, tomato, sausage. French bread, homemade fruit breads, English scones, or sweet rolls. Coffee or tea.

Plus: Central air conditioning, plus freestanding fans in guest rooms. Special occasions acknowledged.

> From Virginia: *"Charming hosts. The breakfasts were magnificent! The house was delightful. A most enjoyable visit."*

---

*I*s B&B *like a hotel?*
How many times have you hugged the doorman?

—————— Bucks County B&Bs ——————

Some Bucks County B&Bs are represented by:
Amanda's Bed & Breakfast Reservation Service, page 54.
Bed & Breakfast Adventures, page 54.
Bed & Breakfast Connections/Bed & Breakfast of Philadelphia, page 226.
Guesthouses, page 226.

*Please see page 80 for Chimney Hill Farm Bed and Breakfast in Lambertville, New
Jersey, just one mile from New Hope, Bucks County.*

The Inn at Fordhook Farm   215/345-1766
105 New Britain Road, Doylestown, PA 18901   fax 215/345-1791

Hosts: Jonathan and Carole Burpee;
Elizabeth Romanella, resident innkeeper
Location: On 60 secluded acres of
meadows and woodlands. Off Route
202, 1.5 miles east of Doylestown, "a
town that is more like New England
than some in New England." Twelve
miles from New Hope. An hour from
Philadelphia by train or car.

Open: Year round. Prefer two-
night minimum on weekends; three
nights on some holiday weekends.
Rates: Main house $93 semiprivate
bath, $135 private bath, $20 third
person. ($80–$90 corporate rate for
singles, Sunday–Thursday.) Carriage
house $175 (a couple) or $250 (two
couples). Amex, MC, Visa.
♥ ♣ ♦ ✈ ⚲

Imagine strolling on the grounds of W. Atlee Burpee's estate. Or sitting at his
desk, where he wrote, by hand, the very first Burpee Seed Company catalog.
Now the spacious manor house is shared with romantics; with gardeners
(new flowers and vegetables are introduced during open house in August);
with catalog companies for photo shoots (guests can watch); with business
guests (small conference center available); with many who come to read by
the fire, to walk through the woods and meadows (maps available), or to
cross-country ski.

Members of the Burpee family (who have marvelous childhood remem-
brances to share with guests) are sometimes in residence on weekends and
during holidays. They tell Elizabeth, who was formerly with the Pennsylvania
Academy of the Fine Arts and the New-York Historical Society, that she now
works *and* lives in a museum. It is filled with family heirlooms and photographs—each with a story. Among the eight other buildings on this National
Register property is a carriage house with a B&B apartment that has a
chestnut-paneled great room, magnificent vaulted ceiling, and Palladian
windows. There's more, but you will just have to go to experience this
national treasure.

In residence: Tammy, an aging shepherd/retriever, "greets guests, sometimes leads them on walks."

Foreign languages spoken: "Elizabeth Romanella can muster up a little Italian."

Bed and bath: Seven rooms. In carriage house suite, two rooms (king and queen beds) share full bath. In main house, five rooms, three with private baths. King/twins, queen, or double bed. Some four-poster, antique, and brass beds. Rooms range from huge master bedroom with working fireplace, private balcony, and large adjoining full bath to a cozy third-floor room under the eaves. Cot available.

Breakfast: 7:30–9:30 weekdays, 8:30–10 weekends. Fordhook (old fashioned oatmeal) pancakes, cheese omelets, cream cheese–stuffed French toast, smoked bacon, local sausage, poached pears with raspberry sauce, berries from the farm, homemade jams and freshly baked muffins. Served on heirloom china in dining room that has leaded bay windows, or occasionally on the huge tiled terrace under 200-year-old linden trees and overlooking acres of meadows. "Can last for hours."

Plus: Bedroom air conditioning. Afternoon refreshments; Saturday and holiday weekend teas with baked treats and watercress "from our stream" sandwiches. Large fireplaced living room. Fireplaced study/office with phone. Butler's pantry with refrigerator and teakettle. Picnicking on lawn. Badminton. Croquet. Free tickets to March Philadelphia Flower Show. Gift of Burpee seeds.

Maplewood Farm Bed & Breakfast

P.O. Box 239, 5090 Durham Road   215/766-0477
Gardenville, PA 18926-0239

Hosts: Cindy and Dennis Marquis
Location: On five acres along Route 413 with big old maple trees, pastures, a neighboring horse farm (lessons offered), a dairy farm, and a gentleman farm with sheep and goats. Five minutes to Point Pleasant (canoeing and tubing on Delaware River). Within 15 minutes of New Hope, Peddler's Village, Doylestown.

Open: Year round. Two-night minimum on weekends; three over holidays.
Rates: Weekends and holidays: private bath $80 or $95 double bed, $100 queen bed. Suite $135. Midweek 10 percent less. Third person in room $25.
♥ ❖ ✖ ⅄

For the food, the country decor, the gardens, and the sheep and chickens (gather your own eggs, if you like) *Bon Appétit, Philadelphia* magazine, and *Glamour* have cited this B&B, a plaster-over-fieldstone farmhouse that has stenciled walls, two walk-in fireplaces in the 1792 summer kitchen/now living room, and local antiques. Down by the creek you might see the resident blue heron and, sometimes, deer.

In 1990, following two years as Bucks County inn managers, Cindy and Dennis, at age 30, bought this property. The Philadelphia area natives have become experts on area attractions as well as on cycling routes and historic covered bridges. Cindy is a former office manager of a marine construction company. Dennis, a trained biologist who worked in cardiovascular research,

(Please turn page.)

now works as a computer software engineer for Bristol-Myers Squibb. And, in season, he is an itinerant sheepshearer.

In residence: Son Benjamin, born June 24, 1994. Stinky, their house cat. Champ, a yellow Labrador. Sally, a young black Lab.

Bed and bath: Seven cozy air-conditioned rooms with queen or double beds; All private baths. Loft suite has exposed beams and natural oak and pine; living room with single pull-out couch, queen bed in loft above, private tub/shower bath.

Breakfast: 8:30–10. Fresh fruits with yogurt and "our own homemade granola." French toast with pure maple syrup, omelets stuffed with fresh vegetables, or waffles with fresh blueberry topping.

Plus: Home-baked goods in afternoon. Guest refrigerator with cold beverages. California cream sherry for nightcap. By arrangement, hot-air balloon rides depart from the inn.

From New York: *"Beautiful, charming, and quaint . . . friendly atmosphere . . . one of the most enjoyable getaways ever!"*

The Wedgwood Collection of Historic Inns

111 West Bridge Street, New Hope, PA 18938-1401   215/862-2570
or 862-2520
fax 215/862-3570

Hosts: Nadine Silnutzer and Carl Glassman
Location: In historic district, on two acres of landscaped grounds. Wedgwood House (the one with a carriage on the front lawn and a gazebo on the side) and Umpleby House are connected by brick walkways and gardens. Across the (main) residential street and three houses toward town is Aaron Burr House. One block to shops and restaurants.

Open: Year round. Two-night minimum preferred for weekends, three nights for holidays.
Rates: Weekday/weekend $70 or $80/$90 or $115 double bed or twin beds. $90/$145 queen or king; $110/$185 fireplaced suites. Singles $5 less. $20 rollaway. Corporate and long-term rates; spa and midweek "escape" packages.
♥ ⅋ ♣ ♦

"Treat all guests as royalty," Carl advises his students. Now, 14 years after he and Dinie made their dream come true, they have three 19th-century houses for "kings and queens." The story combines early (at age 30) career changes, historic preservation, community participation, and an interest in people, antiques and entrepreneurship. When Wedgwood was described in my first B&B book, Carl was still working half time as a social think-tank researcher. Dinie had just left her work in gerontology. Together they restored the 1870 frame guest house and decorated with country pieces, Dinie's aunt's artwork, and a Wedgwood collection. Guests arranged—and many still do—to be married in the gazebo. The more formal but quite comfortable next-door 1833 stone Umpleby House was added in 1985. Aaron Burr, a restored (1990) frame Victorian with in-room phones, provides enough rooms and parlor space for family reunions, business meetings, and corporate retreats. Today Carl, known for his well-established innkeeping seminars and apprentice program, is an inn consultant, Realtor specializing in inns, avocational historian, and coauthor with Ripley Hotch (The Inn on Montford, Asheville, North Carolina, page 194) of *How to Start and Run Your Own Bed & Breakfast Inn*. And in 1994 Carl and Dinie, the antiques expert/floral and interior designer, announced the arrival of Jessica Rachel, born into an enormous extended family.

Foreign languages spoken: French, Spanish, Dutch, and Hebrew.

Bed and bath: In each house, six rooms including one suite. Some with fireplace. King, queen, double, and twin beds; all private baths—tub and shower or shower only. Rollaway available.

Breakfast: 8:30–10. Freshly squeezed orange juice, fresh fruit salad, home-baked muffins and sweet breads, hot croissants, homemade granola, yogurt, freshly brewed tea and coffee. Served in each house, or in your guest room upon request. Special Passover menu.

Plus: Bedroom air conditioners. Welcoming refreshments. Saturday teatime with the hosts. Carl's almond liqueur. Fresh flowers year round. Parlors with wood-burning stoves. "By luck," free horse-drawn carriage rides to and from town. (Can be booked for a fee.) Turned-down beds. Veranda. Hammocks. Pool and tennis club privileges, croquet, and badminton. Inn-to-inn hiking and biking tours. Restaurant discounts. Courtesy bus pickup from NYC.

The Whitehall Inn

1370 Pineville Road
New Hope, PA 18938

215/598-7945
800/37WHITE (800/379-4483)

Hosts: Mike and Suella Wass
Location: On 13 secluded acres. A working dressage horse farm with walking trails, gardens, fields, majestic chestnut and maple trees. Ten minutes southwest of New Hope, five from Peddler's Village.
Open: Year round. Two-night minimum on weekends, three nights on holiday weekends. Advance reservations required.

Rates: Include extraordinary afternoon tea. Weekends, $130–$190 with private bath; $130–$190 with fireplace; $155–$190 with both; $130–$160 shared bath. Weekdays, $10 less. $30 extra per person for weekend concerts (world-class musicians). Amex, CB, Diners, Discover, MC, Visa.
♥ ♦ ✈ ✄

Style. With an afternoon tea not to be missed. With culinary talents acclaimed in major publications including *Gourmet, Food & Wine*, and the *New York Times*, and demonstrated in Bloomingdale's and Woodward & Lothrop's programs based on this book. With ultimate innkeepers who host many returnees (and romantics) in this 200-year-old stone manor house with a curved walnut staircase, wide-pine floors, Oriental rugs, family heirlooms, and other fine antiques. And still, 10 years since the two Oklahomans, a Sun Oil Company executive (Mike) and his speech therapist wife (Suella), created their fantasy inn, just six guest rooms.

Mike is the maitre d'/waiter/rose gardener who on his day off teaches B&B courses at community colleges. He is also a doctoral student. Suella's creations are now the basis of a forthcoming cookbook.

(Please turn page.)

In residence: Sarah, age 16, the King Arthur Flour Winterbake medal winner who is the cookie baker for brother Todd's (age 12) all-star baseball team.

Bed and bath: On three floors, six rooms (four with working fireplaces) with queen or double bed. Four with private baths; three with tub and shower, one shower only. Two second-floor rooms share a full bath.

Breakfast: At 9. Their own blend of coffee; 30 teas. Suella's freshly baked coffee cake, yeast bread, and muffins. Freshly squeeed juice. An unending repertoire of appetizers and entrees; may be raspberries picked that morning with chantilly cream plus herbed cheddar cheese Dijon souffle. Or cheddar cheese and corn spoon bread followed by fruit/nut/cheese crepes. And Bucks County sausage. Served by candlelight on linen with European china and crystal, heirloom silver. Suella and Mike always join guests.

Plus: Pool. Carrots for feeding the horses. Bedroom and dining room air conditioners. Four p.m. tea with pastries and tea sandwiches. Evening wine or sherry. Spacious fireplaced parlor with pump organ and piano. In rooms—fresh fruit, flowers, imported English toiletries, Wass-made bath salts, velour robes, potpourri. Turndown service with specialty chocolate truffles.

> From Pennsylvania: *"We enjoyed everything—the beautiful bedroom, all the attention and goodies . . . breakfast, none to compare!! . . . A perfect 51st anniversary celebration."*

Ash Mill Farm   215/794-5373

P.O. Box 202, Holicong, PA 18928

Hosts: Patricia and Jim Auslander
Location: On 11 acres set back from Route 202. Less than a mile from Peddler's Village. Four miles from New Hope and Doylestown. Minutes to the Delaware River "in a Cotswold-like area where there's everything except downhill skiing!"
Open: Year round. Two-night weekend minimum; three on holiday weekends.
Rates: Rooms $90, $95, $100 Monday–Thursday; $115, $125, $130 Friday, Saturday, Sunday, and holidays. Suites $105 and $115 weekdays; $135–$145 weekends, holidays. $40 third person in larger suite.
♥ ♣ ♦ ✈ ⚴

What's a Manhattan maritime litigation lawyer doing in the kitchen (many say he looks like a famous television chef); with "inherited" sheep; on a tractor/mower; and among acres of evergreens (grown for landscapers), wildflowers, and berries? What's it like for two bosses (Pat was in a major corporation) to run a small inn?

"We're having fun—and answering those questions all the time," say the Auslanders, who took an innkeeping seminar, then bought this B&B with its wide central staircase, crown moldings, and stenciling. They furnished with Colonial, Irish, and English antiques and Shaker reproductions. Since, *Victoria* magazine has taken photographs here, and the house has been used as a background setting for fashion catalogs. *Gourmet* requested recipes. And Jim has become a restaurant critic for local newspapers.

In residence: Two dogs. (The Airedale is a great guide through the property.) Three cats. And those sheep.

Foreign languages spoken: "A smattering of French and Spanish."
Bed and bath: Five air-conditioned rooms (two are suites); all private baths.
First-floor—pencil-post queen bed, shower bath. Second floor—corner room with canopied four-poster queen, two sitting areas, and tub/shower bath. One room with canopied double bed, shower bath. One suite with canopied four-poster double bed, sitting room with electric fireplace, shower bath. In third-floor suite, separate access to shower bath from room with canopied queen bed and from adjacent sitting room with double sleep sofa.
Breakfast: 8:30–9:30. Herb-cheese omelet with fresh garden herbs, sour cream or blueberry pancakes, French toast made with homemade raisin cinnamon bread, ham strata, or eggs Benedict. Jim's muffins. Breakfast meats. Fresh fruit, coffee, teas. By dining room fireplace or on stone patio overlooking gardens and meadow.
Plus: Afternoon tea. (Could be onion soup and French bread in winter; lemonade with cookies, pear cakes, maybe strawberries and cream in summer.) Down comforters. Turndown service. Nightcap by living room fireplace.

From New Hampshire: *"Excellent cooking . . . beautiful home."* From New York: *"Personable and friendly."*

Barley Sheaf Farm   215/794-5104
P.O. Box 10, Route 202, Holicong, PA 18928   **fax 215 794-5332**

Hosts: Veronika and Peter Süess
Location: Down a lane, far back from the road, on a tranquil 30-acre farm. Ten minutes from New Hope. About an hour from Philadelphia.
Open: Year round. Two-night weekend minimum preferred; three nights on holiday weekends.
Rates: $95–$175. Room with two queen beds $115–$155. Suite $135–$175. $17 additional person in appropriate rooms. Amex, MC, Visa.
♥ ♨ ♣ ✗ ⅄

There's a fascinating new chapter to the story of Bucks County's first (1979) and almost legendary B&B. In August 1994 the Süess family moved from Switzerland to this National Historic Site, a gracious antiques-filled house that was once the home of playwright and drama critic George S. Kaufman. Built in 1740 and expanded in stone in 1800, it is known for its peaceful, elegant, and warm ambiance—just what Peter and Veronika were looking for after their first B&B stays during a 1992 vacation in Maine.

As European treasurer of a Dow Chemical Company affiliate, Peter traveled extensively. In Switzerland Veronika (who lived in California for her first 14 years) taught kindergarten and her own English-speaking playgroup for three-year-olds. When the Süesses changed continents and lifestyles, they brought their collection of Swiss farm antiques, Veronika's culinary and interior design talents, Peter's passion for wines (ask about wine-tasting events), and the Swiss tradition of service along with a romantic flair.

In residence: Daughter Kristiana is eight. Her two brother cats, Pretzel and Button, also moved from Switzerland. Sheep that wear tiny Swiss bells.
Foreign languages spoken: Swiss-German, German, French.
Bed and bath: Ten air-conditioned rooms, each with private bath. Seven rooms in main house on second and third floors; three in cottage. Queen,

(Please turn page.)

double, or twin beds available. One room with two queen beds. One queen-bedded suite with woodburning fireplace overlooks pool and has adjoining room with trundle bed.

Breakfast: At 8:30 and 9:30. (Coffee and tea earlier.) Baked stuffed apple or fresh fruit with yogurt and granola. Sweet pepper-and-onion frittata or scrambled fresh farm eggs with salmon; ham or sausage. Homemade breads and jams; farm honey. Served in brick-floored sun porch (wood stove used in winter) overlooking lawns, pond, and pool.

Plus: Swimming pool, lounging chairs, hammocks. Afternoon treats; soup by the fire in winter. Soft drinks in guest refrigerator. Special occasions acknowledged. Inquire about dinner possibilities here. Converted 1820 beamed barn—featured on "CBS This Morning"—for small business meetings and conferences.

The Bucksville House   610/847-8948
4501 Durham Road, Kintnersville, PA 18930-1610

Hosts: Barbara and Joe Szollosi
Location: In pastoral countryside. Thirty minutes north of New Hope. On Route 412. One mile from Lake Nockamixon State Park with swimming, boating, fishing, hiking, and cross-country skiing.
Open: Year round. Daily July and
August. Weekends only September–June. Advance reservations required. Two-night minimum preferred; three nights on holiday weekends.
Rates: Rooms $95–$120. Suite $130. Amex, Discover, MC, Visa.
♥ ✠ ✄

What was once dubbed "one of Upper Bucks County's best-kept secrets" offers Colonial interior settings that are often photographed for magazines. It is also on the (book) cover of *A Quilter's Christmas.* Outside, there are award-winning wildflower, perennial, and vegetable gardens—now. In 1984 the former wheelwright shop, hotel, speakeasy, tavern, and private home was standing vacant when the two New Jersey teachers ended their search for an old house to renovate. Joe, a carpenter, and Barbara, who continues to teach, wove their magic—they still make changes and additions—and furnished with antiques, Joe's country reproductions, quilts, crocks, and Oriental rugs.

In residence: "Muffy is our very friendly 17-pound calico cat."
Bed and bath: Four rooms and a suite; all with air conditioning and private baths. On first floor: handicapped-accessible room with queen bed, shower bath, ceiling fan, sofa, working fireplace. Three second-floor rooms: Of two with canopied double bed and working fireplace, one has shower bath in room, the other a shower/tub bath next to room. Third room has queen bed, ceiling fan, sofa, shower bath next to room. Third-floor suite has queen bed, sitting room with sofas, two ceiling fans.
Breakfast: 8:30–10. Fresh fruit cup, bran raisin nut waffles, and sausage; or fresh pineapple with kiwi, egg casserole, and ham. Homemade sticky buns. Juice, hot beverages, and homemade breads. In screened gazebo or in dining room that has 18-inch-thick stone walls and walk-in fireplace.

Plus: Tea, coffee, cider, and homemade cookies. TV room. Fireplaced living room. Coal stove in den. Old puzzles and board games. Deck. Yard and surrounding paths. Fish pond with bass, catfish, sunfish.

> From Pennsylvania: *"Delightful, elegant, peaceful, hospitable, a gourmet's paradise . . . beautiful landscaping . . . restoration that is a labor of love . . . an out-of-the-way place but well worth the effort."* From New Jersey: *". . . shared so much of the house's colorful history. . . . As the delicious scent of ripening peaches filled the air, I knew without a doubt where I would set my next novel."*

Hollileif Bed & Breakfast Establishment

677 Durham Road, Wrightstown, PA 18940-9679   215/598-3100

Hosts: Ellen and Richard Butkus
Location: Parklike. On five acres with trees, flowers, and—over a stream—a wooden bridge. Six miles west of New Hope, five south of Peddler's Village, and four north of Newtown. On Route 413. Half mile to fine restaurant.
Open: Year round. Two-night minimum on weekends; three nights on holiday weekends.

Rates: With fireplace, $125 October–April, $115 rest of year. $130 large room. $115 third-floor room. $120 queen bed (second floor). $105 with hall bath. $20 third person on futon. Senior citizens 10 percent less. Corporate rates Monday–Thursday. Midweek rates (Monday–Thursday) $25 less. Amex, Discover, MC, Visa.
♥ ❖ ◆ ✖ ✂

> From New Jersey: *"Know how to make people feel at home. . . . Relaxed, friendly atmosphere. . . .Restaurant recommendations on the mark. . . . Richard's grounds work is miraculous."* From Texas: *"Helpful with historic points of interest."* From Pennsylvania: *"Lavish breakfasts."*

Another guest wrote about "its peaceful cozy air" and "laid-back country grace" in a long poem. It's not the Caribbean, where the Butkuses were inspired to enter the hospitality field, but this plastered stone 1700s farmhouse with 40-foot holly trees at the entrance is closer to home for the native Pennsylvanians. It was a four-year-old B&B when purchased in 1990 by Ellen, a former social worker and contract negotiator, and Richard, a supervisor of a research and development machine shop at the Naval Air Development Center. They furnished with country pieces, family artwork, and lots of lace and bows.

In residence: Two cats—"Furgy and Danielle enjoy guests' attention."
Foreign language spoken: A little Spanish.
Bed and bath: Two double-bedded rooms and three queen-bedded rooms on three floors. All private baths; four have shower; one has tub and shower. First-floor room has ceiling fan and gas fireplace that works on propane with a thermostat. Third-floor room tucked under eaves.
Breakfast: 8:30–9:30; coffee and tea at 8. Frothy fruit juice mix. Fruit—maybe peaches in butterscotch brandy sauce. Muffins—zucchini date or peanut butter banana. Entree repertoire includes asparagus turkey omelet, French toast with homemade strawberry sauce, bacon cheese puff. Home-

(Please turn page.)

made granola. Special diets accommodated. Served at individual long-skirted tables.

Plus: Central air conditioning in all common and guest rooms. Fireplaced breakfast and living rooms. Arbor-covered patio overlooking garden. After-noon beverages and home-baked items. Turndown service. Use of refrigera-tor. TV/VCR, stereo, board games, croquet, badminton, volleyball, horseshoes. Two double hammocks. Recipes shared.

Tattersall Inn   215/297-8233
P.O. Box 569, Cafferty and River Road, Point Pleasant, PA 18950-0569

Hosts: Herbert and Gerry Moss
Location: Quiet. On Route 32, sur-rounded by lawns, plantings, and century-old trees. Set a little above the village, 15 minutes north of New Hope. A few minutes' walk to tubing and canoeing on Delaware River, and to canal towpath.
Open: Year round. Two-night min-imum on weekends. Three-night minimum on holiday weekends. Reservations recommended.
Rates: $85–$94 weekends and hol-idays. $109 two-room suite and one large room with entry foyer. $15 less Monday–Thursday. $15 third per-son. Senior citizens 5 percent less weekends, 10 percent less midweek. Amex, Discover, MC, Visa.
♥ ♣ ♦ ✈

> From New York (among many): *"It is a full four-star—how about five—inn with low-keyed, warm, and helpful hosts. . . . Beautiful, homey, and romantic."*

Urbanites know they are "away" when they sit on the second-story porch and hear the nearby carillon through the tall spruce. Or when they have cheese and cider in the beamed-ceiling common room with huge hearth. Or listen to Herb's vintage phonographs in the Victorian dining room. Two rooms date back to 1740. Additions made in the 1800s resulted in a fieldstone manor house with 18-inch-thick walls. Now restored, it is furnished with family antiques and Gerry's paintings and needlework. Until the Mosses took over the inn in 1985, Gerry was editor of RCA's technical abstracting service. Even today she says, "I still can't believe that we actually own Ralph Stover's house after all the wonderful times we had—while the children were growing up—exploring in the park (once part of the property) that honors him." Herb, a part-time consultant, retired in 1988 from RCA, where he was a materials scientist.

In residence: Victoria, "a gentle cat not too sure of people."
Bed and bath: On second floor, six large air-conditioned rooms, all with private baths and queen beds. One suite with brass bed and sitting room; one with queen bed and wrought iron daybed. Cot and-futons available.
Breakfast: 8–10. Sometimes earlier, especially for 7 a.m. Tuesday flea market opening. Juice, croissants, whole wheat bread with raisins and/or walnuts, homemade muffins or cakes (maybe poppyseed or apple), jams, honey, milk, hot beverages. Selection of cereals. In Victorian dining room (hosts join guests), on one of the porches, or in your room.
Plus: Afternoon refreshments. Library. Old-fashioned pinball game. That wonderful antique phonograph collection. Jukebox. Upright piano. Choco-

lates. Apples. Book of guests' comments about area restaurants. Special occasions acknowledged.

Bridgeton House on the Delaware
P.O. Box 167, River Road, Upper Black Eddy, PA 18972   610/982-5856

Hosts: Beatrice and Charles Briggs
Location: On the Delaware River and along the river road. In a small historic village. A half block from canal towpath; 18 miles north of New Hope. Within walking distance of shops, restaurants, state park. New York City bus stops in Frenchtown, New Jersey (3½ miles south of inn).
Open: Year round. Reservations and two-night minimum weekend stays required April–December.
Rates: Weekends $75–$85 village-side room, $105–$135 river-side room with private balcony, $135–$150 fireplaced suite, $185–$200 penthouse. Monday–Thursday $10–$35 less. Mid-week hiking or biking inn-to-inn packages available. Amex, MC, Visa.

♥ ♦ ✈ ⅙

A one-of-a-kind contemporary penthouse overlooks the river and tops this transformed 1836 Federal brick house, a photographer's delight, a getaway destination. Bea has decorated with country pieces; baskets; rag, braided, and Chinese rugs; dried flowers and plants; and lots of stenciling. There are French doors; private screened balconies; suites as well as smaller rooms. And the reason for it all: those water views, captured by the Briggses when they rescued the building in 1981. They found the original fireplace behind a closet, pine floors below 17 layers of linoleum. In 1988—for something completely different—Charles, a master carpenter/professional restorer of 18th-century buildings/country furniture maker, together with his brother Jon, added the dramatic cathedral-ceilinged third-floor penthouse. (More recently they remodeled a next-door getaway cottage complete with kitchen.) Such changes to the building that was first a private residence, then a bakery, and then a general store! Before Bridgeton House, Bea and Charles had 10 years' experience in inns and restaurants. Now they dovetail innkeeping with parenting (of two).

Bed and bath: Eleven air-conditioned rooms in the main building (three are fireplaced suites) with king, queen, or double beds; some four-posters, some canopied. All are air conditioned; all have private baths. The penthouse with three large windows and contemporary furnishings has king-sized bed, fireplace, refrigerator, cable TV, a mahogany bath with oversized soaking tub, a separate shower, and a dressing room.
Breakfast: Weekdays 8:30–9:30; weekends until 10. Fresh or hot fruits, juices, homemade breads and pastries. Omelets, shirred eggs, frittata, or souffles. Eat by fireplace or riverside, or on the deck, porch, or terrace.
Plus: Afternoon tea and sherry. Oversized bath sheets and terry robes; fresh flowers and fruit in each room. Swimming or tubing off riverbank. "Finest East Coast fishing!"

___ Lehigh Valley/Reading Area B&Bs ___

Some B&Bs in this area are represented by:
Amanda's Bed & Breakfast Reservation Service, page 54.
Bed & Breakfast Adventures, page 54.

Sycamore Inn Bed & Breakfast   610/966-5177

165 East Main Street, Macungie, PA 18062

Hosts: Mark and Randie Levisky
Location: On Route 100, six miles south of I-78. Two hours to New York City, one to Philadelphia and Poconos. Ten minutes to Allentown (bus stops across from inn), Doe Mountain ski area, Velodrome at Trexlertown; 45 to Reading outlets. Macungie Memorial Park is "our backyard."

Open: Year round. Two-night minimum for Antique Truck Show in June; three nights during Das Awksht Fescht and Wheels of Time show in August.
Rates: Double occupancy. $70–$80. $10 child over 12 with parent. MC, Visa.
♥ ♣ ✈

From Maryland: *"Make you feel like old friends . . . loved the decor—mix of old and new . . . delicious food."*

It's an old stone thick-walled farmhouse—two houses in one—with "kick-off-your-shoes" comfort. It's "Mark's dream"—inspired by New England B&B stays and his love of cooking. (Randie, too, is delighted with the outcome.)

The Leviskys moved here in 1988. By the time they opened as a B&B in 1992, father and son had removed the exterior stucco covering to expose the stone. All the floors were redone. A porch was enclosed with windows that open for fresh breezes. And the quiet back house became the inn, with a common room that features original plaster walls (freshly painted) and a stone walk-in fireplace. Guest rooms are furnished by theme—Victorian, primitive, oak, and "Gentleman's Room."

Mark, a private detective, took early retirement as a criminal investigator for the Pennsylvania State Police. Randie sells antiques right here, most frequently from the inn's furnishings.

In residence: "Our doorbell, Niki, is a friendly and excitable cocker spaniel." One teenage son.
Bed and bath: Five rooms. Two first-floor double-bedded rooms have private shower baths, private porch entrance. On second floor, two queen-bedded rooms share full Victorian bath with claw-footed tub/shower. One queen-bedded room has private en-suite "outhouse" bath with Jacuzzi tub, shower, door with half moon, barn-wood walls, spider- and fly-stained glass.
Breakfast: 7–9. Fruit salad, juices, egg dishes, Levisky pancakes, Mom's Special apple dumplings, jams, muffins, and cereals. Early-bird coffee and tea. By common room fireplace or on enclosed porch.

Plus: Room air conditioning. Bedroom ceiling fans. Welcoming beverage. TV in common room. Mints on pillow. In park—pool, tennis courts, workout area, swings, basketball courts.

The Enchanted Cottage   610/845-8845
22 Deer Run Road, Boyertown, PA 19512

Hosts: Peg and Richard Groff
Location: Secluded and private. Surrounded by acres of woods. In farm country with rolling hills. Four and a half miles west of Route 100; 15 minutes to Doe Mountain ski area, 16 miles east of Reading (outlets). Nine-minute walk to fine country restaurant. Near antiques shops, auctions, crafts and flea markets, historic sites.
Open: Year round.
Rates: Friday–Sunday $80; Monday–Thursday $75. Single $70. $15 extra bed.

♥ ⬛ ◆ ✈

"It's right out of a fairy tale!" exclaim many guests when they see the romantic stone and frame ivy-covered Cotswold-like cottage built by Richard with old materials and antique tools. It is—complete with brick walk outside. Inside there's a large beamed living room with flagstone floor, primitive antiques, a Franklin fireplace flanked by comfortable checkered-covered wing chairs, and a kitchenette. Upstairs, tucked under the eaves, there's an air-conditioned bedroom with quilt-covered cannonball pine bed and Laura Ashley bathroom.

Originally the cottage was built for grandchildren. But "we can't build as fast as our daughter creates grandchildren." In addition to house building—he made the main house and all the outbuildings—Richard constructs furniture and is involved with historic preservation. Peg, who used to work in the fashion industry in Manhattan, does tole and furniture painting. In addition, she is a volunteer Literacy Workshop teacher and has hosted and directed TV talk shows in Washington, D.C., and Reading, Pennsylvania.

The Groffs enjoy serving an elaborate breakfast in the main house. Their home for more than 30 years, it has a paneled, beamed, and fireplaced living room and—everywhere—primitives and artwork. "Fax? We don't even have a typewriter!" But they do have some guests who kiss them goodbye.

In residence: In the main house—three cats. "The Dolley Lama," a Himalayan; Rufus; and Obesa (Obie).
Bed and bath: The cottage is all yours. Bedroom has double bed; bath has antique claw-and-ball-footed tub, hand-held shower. Rollaway.
Breakfast: 7:30–9:30. Fresh fruit. Popovers, homemade biscuits or muffins. Eggs Benedict or ham a la king on pastry shells; garnished with fruit or flowers. Freshly ground coffee. In dining room with wood stove or by garden. Hosts join guests.
Plus: Wine and cheese in cottage. Fresh flowers. Mints on pillow. Candy. Down comforters. Embroidered eyelet linen sheets. Dinner option ($20 per person) by prearrangement. Picnic baskets prepared.

The Loom Room   610/926-3217

RD 1, Box 1420, Leesport, PA 19533

Hosts: Gene and Mary Smith
Location: Rural. Surrounded by two and a half acres of lawn and flower and herb gardens. Two miles north of Reading Airport, just off Route 183 in Berks County. Within 25 minutes of antiques shops in Adamstown and Kutztown; 15 minutes to Reading outlets.

Open: Year round. Advance reservations requested.
Rates: $45 shared bath, $50 private. $15 extra adult. Under age 15, free. Seventh night free.
♥ ♣ ✎ ♣♣ ✕ ⊬

There's a wonderful story behind this B&B. Now the 1812 stone house with two-foot-thick walls is "comfortable and antiquey" with open-beam ceilings, five working fireplaces, and country primitives everywhere. In 1975, when Mary and Gene, teachers and area residents "for years," were looking for a country cupboard, they chanced upon the auction of the neglected house. Two hours later they owned "the perfect place for a weaving studio and shop," a 10-room center hall Colonial that had been a home, tavern, hotel, stagecoach stop, halfway house, general store, and post office. The "buy," which required all of Gene's building expertise, became the site of the Smiths' wedding—by the great summer kitchen walk-in fireplace. Gene opened a tool-sharpening business, and Mary established her enterprise for beautiful custom classic handwoven fashions (for men and women). The local conservancy awarded the Smiths a historical plaque. And then a 1985 B&B trip to Germany influenced the decision to add hosting to their activities.

This B&B has a very sharing style, with almost-famous after-dinner treats, with fireside conversations, and with tours of the reconstructed 1760 log house (another Gene job) where Mary weaves and displays the clothing she creates. And from the cupboard that *was* eventually found, for each female guest, the parting gift of a homemade sachet.

In residence: Mimi and Maytag, "guest-oriented" male tiger cats.
Bed and bath: Three second-floor rooms reached by "a stairway that is not steep at all." Two rooms, each with a double and a single bed, share a full bath. Private shower bath for room with a double bed, one twin bed, and a daybed. Rollaway and crib available.
Breakfast: Usually 8:30. (Preceded by a wake-up tray brought to your door with coffee or tea and juice.) French toast with homemade fruit sauce, local sausage or bacon, apple cinnamon pancakes. Homemade muffins, jams, and preserves. Coffee and teas. Served in kitchen, in dining room, or in Gene-built gazebo. Hosts join guests.
Plus: Air conditioning and ceiling fans in bedrooms. Evening dessert repertoire includes lemon meringue pie, Gene's "incredible sundaes and banana splits," Mary's apple dumplings or Tiramisu (complete with story of Italian chef in German restaurant, near Swiss border, who shared recipe).

From Pennsylvania: *"Felt like home and fantasyland all in one."*

Longswamp Bed and Breakfast   610/682-6197
1605 State Street, Mertztown, PA 19539   fax 610/682-4854

Hosts: Elsa and Dean Dimick
Location: On five acres in a rural village, 15 minutes southwest of Allentown, east of Kutztown. Forty minutes to Reading outlets. Within eight minutes of Route 100, Doe Mountain ski area, horseback riding. Excellent restaurant nearby. An hour northeast of Lancaster.
Open: Year round.
Rates: $60 single, $70 double, $75 in cottage, Hideaway, and barn. $30 third person in room. No charge for babies. Amex, MC, Visa.
♥ ♨ ♣ ✈ ✁

> From Indiana: *"A very special place . . . a delight for the senses . . . rolling hills are compelling and beautiful . . . an orchard, herb and vegetable gardens, extensive flower beds, berry patches . . . all find their way into the kitchen and onto the table."* From Massachusetts: *"Extraordinarily comfortable home. . . . Tastefully appointed. . . . The Dimicks obviously enjoy their enterprise and making their guests feel welcome."*

With their five children no longer at home, Elsa, a caterer and psychiatric counselor, and her husband, an endocrinologist at Lehigh Valley Hospital Center, moved in 1983 from Allentown to this lovely 200-year-old Federal house "to have a whole new challenge." Grateful comments come from business guests (some book day meetings here), vacationers, photographers, and wedding planners (gazebo is popular). They appreciate the attention to detail, the fire, the collections of books, magazines, records, and tapes. Some walk in the woods. "Most want to be part of what's going on. A few value privacy above all." Antiquers love the location—and so do sports-oriented visitors.

In residence: One loving black Lab.
Foreign language spoken: French.
Bed and bath: Ten air-conditioned rooms with Amish quilts. Six have private bath; four share two baths. In main house, six rooms on second and third floors with a queen-sized bed, a queen and a single, or a queen and a double. The cottage (1700s house that was part of Underground Railroad) has a large queen-bedded room with fireplace, an alcove with a single bed, private shower bath, and a living room with TV. Upstairs is a queen-bedded skylit room under the eaves, private shower bath. On the lower level level of cottage—The Hideaway, with a separate exterior entrance, has queen-bedded room, working fireplace, private shower bath. In part of huge old stone barn—a suite with large queen-bedded room, private shower bath, living room with television and single daybed.
Breakfast: 10:30 Sundays. 6:30–10:30 other days. Bountiful and beautiful. Repertoire includes low-fat options, fresh fruit combinations, whole-grain breads, muffins, interesting cereals, homemade granola. Dishes with polenta. French toast made with thick challah bread. By fireplace in summer kitchen overlooking lawns and fields.
Plus: Beverages before dinner. Bedroom ceiling fans. Garden flowers. Second-floor veranda rockers. Bicycles (no charge). Use of refrigerator. Horseshoe pits. Bocci court. Patio.

Classic Victorian

35 North New Street, Nazareth, PA 18064

610/759-8276
fax 610/434-1889

Hosts: Irene and Danny Sokolowski
Location: In historic district. Within 15 minutes of Abe Airport, Easton Hospital, Lehigh University, Lafayette College. Five-minute walk to center circle of town, 20 minutes from Blue Mountain ski area. Within 15 miles of antiques shops in Allentown and Kutztown.

Open: Year round. Two-night minimum on holiday weekends.
Rates: Shared bath $65 twin beds, $75 Victorian double bed. Private bath $85. $15 extra person. Ten percent less for seven days or more. Amex, MC, Visa.
♥ ♨ ♣ ✈ ✂

From New York: *"Memorable. Irene thought of everything . . . elegant breakfast. . . . Now I have a desire to run a B&B."* From Virginia: *" . . . impressed with cleanliness, charm, innovative breakfast, and genuine passion and concern for guests' comfort. . . . [Subsequently] bought out Classic Victorian for entire week of event. . . . When you walk through the door . . . it's great to be home, because that is exactly how it feels."*

High-back Victorian and 18th-century four-poster beds. Oriental rugs over carpeting. Floral and damask wallcoverings. Stained glass window on hall stairway landing. Lace. And bay windows. Hence the name of this B&B, a brick and stone 1905 Colonial Revival with huge wraparound porch overlooking a big lawn. When the Sokolowskis, who grew up in coal country, were living in Allentown (17 years), a real estate advertisement with photograph fulfilled Irene's "childhood dream house located in a small town." Together with relatives, she, a former beautician, and Dan, who runs their card and gift shop, decorated completely and opened in 1990.

In residence: "Kacey, our Keeshond, loves people, especially children, but isn't allowed run of the house."
Bed and bath: Three second-floor rooms. Private en-suite bath for room with high-board Victorian double bed. Room with pineapple four-poster twin beds shares hall tub/shower bath with room that has Colonial four-poster double bed. Rollaway available.
Breakfast: 7–9:30. French toast souffle, French cakes with apple and cinnamon filling. Broccoli-and-egg custard. Special diets accommodated with advance notice. Served in Chippendale-furnished dining room with Wedgwood china, linens, and crystal; on second-floor balcony; or, by request, in basket delivered to your door.
Plus: Central air conditioning. Afternoon tea and sweets. Down comforters and flannel sheets. Guest refrigerator.

U nless otherwise stated, rates in this book are per room for two and include breakfast in addition to all the amenities in "Plus."

Poconos B&Bs

The Beach Lake Hotel

717/729-8239
800/382-3897

Main Street and Church Road, P.O. Box 144
Beach Lake, PA 18405

Hosts: Erika and Roy Miller
Location: In a tiny country village off a main road "in the quiet part of the Poconos." Five miles to Delaware River for tubing, rafting, canoeing (pickup arranged). Three minutes' walk to Beach Lake for swimming, rowboating. Twenty minutes' drive to Lake Wallenpaupack, fishing, and ice skating. Near restored (suspension) Roebling Bridge; museums; train excursions; antiquing; ski resorts—Woodlock Pines, Mount Tone, Masthope; even a drive-in theater. 2½ hours from New York City.
Open: Year round. Two-night minimum on June–October weekends and all holiday weekends.
Rates: $95 per room. $75 for three-night reservations, Sunday–Thursday. MC, Visa.
♥ ♣ ♦ ✈

> Guests wrote: *"A fantasy fulfilled. . . . Recommended to us by friends who were impressed by the food and the decor. . . . Erika and Roy are a fount of information on local folklore and roads away from the leaf peepers. . . . Old-fashioned country charm. . . . An elegant but laid-back kind of style. . . . Clean, clean, clean. . . . Had a field day in their filled-to-the-brim country gallery. . . . Loved this place so much we thought of keeping it a secret. . . . Reflects a lot of hard work and intelligent research by an interesting couple. . . . A sense of being transplanted back in time."*

Guests' enthusiasm is matched by the Millers, two former health administrators who have fulfilled their own fantasy of combining interests in cooking, interior design, antiques, restoration, music, and theater. They followed up on a 1986 *Country Living* magazine ad and fell in love with this place, which began around 1859 as a hotel and tavern. After a year-long restoration, they furnished with "for sale" antiques of many periods—creating an ambiance appreciated by *Travel & Leisure* too. Some guests ask, "Have you always lived here?" And some inquire about sources for reproduction Victorian floral wallcoverings and lace curtains. Raspberry bushes grow. So do fruit trees, herbs, and the guest list.

In residence: In hosts' quarters, a Shih Tzu, "ten pounds of love!"
Foreign language spoken: Polish.
Bed and bath: Six rooms on second and third floors. All private baths; most are shower only, one has claw-footed tub. All double beds; two are canopied four-posters (if not sold), one requires a step stool.
Breakfast: 8–10. Entree might be apple pancakes and brandied grape sauce; eggs Benedict, eggs LeRoy (poached in artichoke bottoms and watercress hollandaise); mushroom-and-onion or cheese omelets. Homemade popovers, muffins, or coffee cakes and preserves. Juices. Hot beverages.
Plus: Air-conditioned bedrooms. Tea, wine, cheese, crackers. Fresh fruit in rooms. Bubble bath. TV in common room. Dinner ($20–$30) in dining room and gallery that seats forty.

Brookview Manor Bed & Breakfast Inn

RR 1, Box 365, Canadensis, PA 18325   717/595-2451

Hosts: Lee and Nancie Cabana
Location: On Route 447 and the Broadhead Creek, "in the heart of the Poconos." On four acres of lawns, gardens, tall hemlocks, "and trails that lead to a secret waterfall." About two hours from New York or Philadelphia. Minutes to Pocono Playhouse, Promised Land State Park, Alpine Mountain and Camelback ski areas, shopping and fine dining.
Open: Year round. Two-night minimum over holidays.
Rates: Suites $105–$115 weekdays, $125–$145 weekends and holidays. Other rooms $70–$90 weekdays. $85–$115 weekends and holidays. Amex, Discover, Diners, MC, Visa.
♥ ⚛ ◆ ✈ ⚞

When Nancie, a recreation therapist, and Lee, an American Red Cross director in Erie, Pennsylvania, decided to work together and be at home with Erin, they bought this manor house, a B&B since 1985, which had been built in 1911 as an opulent summer house. It has a light and airy feeling, with antiques and country furnishings; with views of mountains, woods, and stream from every window; with rockers and a swing for four on the wraparound porch. Wide open spaces include the front lawn, the delight of one amateur astronomer. And there have been so many requests for recipes that "a cookbook is in the works."

In residence: In hosts' quarters, Erin, age seven.
Bed and bath: Eight rooms, including three-bedroom suite; all private baths. In main house (all tub/shower baths)—two queen-bedded suites; each with sitting room, one with an enclosed sun porch. One room with king bed. One with double bed, working fireplace. In carriage house—ground-floor double-bedded room with private outside entrance and porch. On second floor—for families or couples traveling together, three-bedroom suite: two rooms with double beds, one with two twins; living room, full bath. Rollaway available.
Breakfast: 8:30–10. Juices. Fresh fruit. Homemade muffins. Hot entree could be cinnamon French toast or French toast a l'orange. Cereals including homemade granola. In sun porch, Fireplace Room, or Picture Window Room with stained glass.
Plus: Fireplace in living room, dining room, and den. Baby grand piano. Bedroom window fans. Fresh flowers. Refreshments at 5 p.m. Recreation room with darts and Ping-Pong and pool tables. Croquet, bocci, horseshoes, and badminton. Cookies and candies.

From New York: *"View of woods is hypnotizing. . . . The brook lulls you to sleep at night. . . . Lee and Nancie pampered us."* From Virginia: *"There was a feeling of privacy, and yet if you wanted to talk they were always available. . . . Enjoyed the book where guests recorded impressions of area restaurants."*

---

*M*any B&Bs are perfect for family reunions.

9 Partners Inn
717/434-2233

1 North Harmony Road, P.O. Box 300, Harford, PA 18823-0300

Hosts: Rudy Sumpter and Jim DeCoe
Location: Serene. On 24 acres, surrounded by forest, pasture, and a Christmas tree farm. "In a friendly town with historic sites, sparsely traveled roads, and trails good for cycling and hiking." Three miles southwest of I-81 (exit 65), 11 to Elk Mountain ski resort. Within 15 miles of antiques shops, weekly collectibles auction, a state park, fishing streams, many restaurants.
Open: Year round. Two-night minimum on holiday and ski weekends; three nights on Presidents' weekend.
Rates: $85 per room. (Two persons maximum per room.) Extended stay and weekday discounts available. MC, Visa.
♣ ♦ ✕ ✂

> From Pennsylvania: *"Authentic 18th-century building made us feel transported back in time. . . . Sits atop a hill with a beautiful view of the area. . . . Breathtaking sunrise was our alarm clock. . . . Welcoming, warm, and full of interesting history. . . . A weekend our family will always remember . . . hospitality warmed us after a day on nearby ski slopes."*

Rudy and Jim, who opened in 1993, think of their restored 200-year-old post-and-beam house as "a New England getaway for people who just can't drive that far! Many city folk who come with all sorts of plans seem to unwind and relax." Walls are painted in Colonial pastels; woodwork is in deeper tones. Colorful quilts are on all the beds. Doors, wide-board floors, and hardware are original. Furnishings are locally purchased antiques. "And the name comes from nine partners who were original area settlers."

In California, Rudy was in accounting and finance with a health maintenance organization. Jim works with Lexus as a computer systems support specialist.

In residence: In hosts' quarters—two cocker spaniels, Smokey and Dusty.
Bed and bath: Three second-floor rooms, all private baths. Queen-bedded and double-bedded rooms have en-suite shower bath. Room with twin beds has hall tub/shower bath.
Breakfast: 8–10. (Coffee and cereal available at 7; earlier by request.) Fresh fruit platter. Yogurt with berries. Egg dish. Muffins, caramel-nut rolls, or croissants. Cereal. Coffee, herbal tea, cocoa.
Plus: Discounted Elk Mountain Ski Resort lift passes. Fireplaced living room. Evening tea and cookies. Chocolates. Dinner-in-a-basket ($10) by request.

Academy Street Bed & Breakfast
528 Academy Street, Hawley, PA 18428
717/226-3430

Hosts: Judith and Sheldon Lazan
Location: In a quiet residential neighborhood. Five minutes from Lake Wallenpaupack's swimming and boating. Near blueberry picking, playhouse, "great restaurants." Close to Route 6 and I-84. Two hours northwest of New York City.
Open: May–October. Reservations preferred.
Rates: Include afternoon tea. $65–$70 shared bath, $75 private bath. MC, Visa.
♥ ♦ ✕

(Please turn page.)

"At our home, it sometimes feels like a family reunion, when actually no one knew each other before," says Sheldon. In 1983, after having a summer residence in Hawley for six years, the Lazans bought the Italianate-style Victorian house, which was built in 1863 with much premium oak and cherry throughout. They finished the restoration started by the previous owner, a commercial artist. Now the eclectic decor of the large, airy tall-windowed rooms is fresh and crisp with Victorian antiques, some wicker and pine pieces, vintage movie star photos, and fresh flowers and plants.

The Lazans, parents of three grown children, are from Brooklyn, New York. A trip to Europe inspired Judith—"I love to fuss" (and she does, with breakfast, high tea, and bedtime treats too)—to become a seasonal innkeeper. Sheldon, an engineering consultant, is weekend host.

Bed and bath: Seven air-conditioned rooms on first and second floors. Four with private bath; one with private half bath shares full hall bath with two other rooms. Queen, double, or twin beds. One with queen and a single. One with double and a single. Cots available.
Breakfast: 8–10. Buffet. Repertoire includes strawberry soup, baked eggs, amaretto pudding, quiche, French toast. Juices, fruit compote, homemade muffins, breads, croissants.
Plus: All rooms have cable TV. Amaretto coffee, tea, and cakes, 2–4 p.m. Lawn games. Off-street parking.

> From New York: *"Our first B&B experience was truly a pleasure . . . memorable hospitality."*

Roebling Inn on the Delaware   717/685-7900
Scenic Drive, P.O. Box 31, Lackawaxen, PA 18435-0031

Hosts: Donald (DJ) and JoAnn Jahn
Location: Facing the river in this quiet historic village. Within walking distance of National Park Service's Zane Grey Museum, Roebling's 1848 Delaware Aqueduct (restored) and Toll House (museum). Surrounded by big old maple trees. Five miles north of Barryville, New York; 15 miles west of Milford, Pennsylvania. Five minutes to Masthope Mountain; 30 to Tanglewood.
Open: Year round. Two-night min-imum May–October weekends, three-night minimum on some major holidays.
Rates: Weekdays—November–April $59 one night, $99 two nights. May–October $68 one night, $120 two. Weekends—November–April $68 one night ($120 two nights November–March); May and September $78; June, October $82; July, August $92. Third adult $10. Child $5. Amex, MC, Visa.
♥ ♣ ♦ ✈

One of 10 "Weekend Therapy" places recommended by *New York* magazine is the fulfillment of DJ's dream. In 1987 the Jahns created the only B&B in town (it still is) when they converted the untouched-for-40-years National Register Greek Revival house that was built as the home and office for the Delaware and Hudson Canal Company superintendent. "We made it inviting and comfortable—with country pieces and some reproductions.

"Just two hours from New York City and this is a different world! Honeymooners come. So do families. They all like the idea of a couple of days with beautiful scenery and water views and no driving. You can walk to restaurants, public tennis courts, canoeing, tubing, hiking, fishing, and a bait shop. Within 10 minutes there are ethnic restaurants, historic sites—even a night club!" Some guests cycle or canoe from inn to inn. They attend summer stock—or, in winter, ski. And there are those who get drawn into the simple pleasure of daydreaming from the front porch, where you can see upriver for about a mile."

As a teenager DJ worked in his family's New Jersey shore motels. Most recently he was general manager of upstate New York's (1886) Tuxedo Club, where the tuxedo originated.

In residence: Son Michael, "assistant innkeeper," age seven. Kitty/Oshkosh, an outdoor cat.

Bed and bath: Five rooms; all with private bath and TV. Queen-bedded room on first floor. On second, one room with queen plus a daybed, one with two doubles, two queen-bedded rooms. Plus one cottage with double-bedded room, living room with double futon couch, bath, kitchen (breakfast optional).

Breakfast: 8–10:30. Hot dishes—eggs and bacon, cheese omelets, or pancakes—cooked to order, plus cold buffet. Orange juice, fresh fruit, cereals, English muffins, baked dish such as peach cobbler. At individual tables set with linen and silver in dining room with large floral wallcovering.

Plus: Air conditioning and individual thermostat in each guest room. Comfortable guest living room. Beverages. Reservations made for canoeing, rafting, fly-fishing lessons. Directions to waterfalls. Eagles in winter.

Farmhouse Bed & Breakfast   717/839-0796
HCR 1, Box 6B, Mount Pocono, PA 18344-9701

Hosts: Jack and Donna Asure
Location: A quiet country road, 5 miles from two major highways. Minutes' drive to antiques shops and outlets; within walking distance of restaurants. Within 15 miles of ski areas. Ninety miles from New York City and Philadelphia.
Open: Year round. Two-night minimum on weekends and three on most holidays.

Rates: $85 second-floor master suite, $95 first-floor parlor suite, $105 caretaker's cottage and newest suites. Single $55, $65, $75. Extra person in room $25. Midweek, $15 less per night for stays over two nights. Discover, MC, Visa.
♥ ◗ ◆ ✗ ✂

"Many of our guests find that the pace here is nothing like what they are used to. Some curl up by the fire with a good book—and, when leaving, say they'll have to come back to see the attractions they saw in ads."

Once a strawberry farm, this was Jack's family home in the 1960s. In 1987, after Jack sold Memorytown USA, a honeymoon resort that had been established by his parents, the Asures restored this 1850 farmhouse—and the stone-walled icehouse—and filled them with family pieces and lots of collectibles. Donna has experience in arts management. Jack, a hunter and fisherman, was a professional chef at his resort. Both hosts, community activists, "love antiquing, flea marketing, and collecting everything!"

(Please turn page.)

In residence: Keiko, "the B&B Princess," a long-haired gray indoor kitty. Roger and Jessica, backyard rabbits.

Bed and bath: A cottage and four suites, each with private phone line. Each suite has a queen bed, private shower bath, TV, compact refrigerator, front porch entrance. Main house—large stone fireplace in first-floor suite; living room wood stove in second-floor suite. In cottage (original icehouse)—first-floor fireplace, refrigerator, shower bath, TV (second floor); small balcony leads to queen-bedded room "tucked into hillside" with ceiling fan. Ranch house—one suite has kitchen, other features a fireplace and VCR in living room and sunken tub in huge bath.

Breakfast: 8–9:30. "Jack's outlandish cooking." Maybe raisin cinnamon bread coated with granola—cooked in omelet pan; an omelet with broccoli, cheese, and hollandaise sauce; or a blueberry-stuffed French toast croissant. (And still, special diets accommodated.) Juice. Homemade muffins or cake. Different menu daily as long as you are here. Served in country kitchen overlooking hill in back of property.

Plus: In farmhouse, private air conditioning unit for each room from spring to fall. Wood stove in common area. Evening refreshments. Secluded porch. Horseshoes. Lawn furniture. Special occasions acknowledged.

> From England: *"Made welcome in this very comfortable home. . . . Their advice and guidance were faultless."* From New York: *"Clean and homey."* From Pennsylvania, New York, and New Jersey: *"Out-of-this-world breakfasts!"*

Lampost B&B   717/857-1738
HCR Box 154, Route 507, Paupack, PA 18451

Hosts: Karen and David Seagaard
Location: On two acres of tall pines and hemlocks overlooking—and just 250 feet from—Lake Wallenpaupack. Ten minutes to swimming beach. Within 20 minutes of restaurants, boat and jet ski rentals, boat launching areas, horseback riding, tennis, golf. Twenty-five minutes to Honesdale, site of country's first railroad. Nine miles south of Hawley. Two hours from Manhattan or Philadelphia.
Open: April–October weekends.
Rates: $45 single. For two, $60 shared bath, $75 private. $20 extra bed. Memorial Day, July 4, and Labor Day weekends, three-night minimum or $25 per night surcharge. MC, Visa.
♥ ♨ ⛵ ✿ ♦

The setting is a winner. David, a pharmacist and house restorer, bought the 1938 Colonial clapboard house in 1987. When he made extensive renovations, he added many skylights and, overlooking the lake, a huge deck. In the attic he found an old Lampost (tourist house) menu that inspired him to add B&B to this family lakeside home, which is located in the area where he was born. Furnishings are eclectic. The 18-by-32-foot beamed living room has a fireplace, Oriental rugs, and comfortable seating. Karen is a clothing manufacturer and president of the board of directors of a Montessori school in New Jersey.

In residence: Amanda, age 15; Samantha is 6; William, 3.
Bed and bath: Six rooms, each with queen bed and cable TV. Most have skylight; all have two tall windows, three with lake view. Largest room

accommodates four; private hall shower bath. Three rooms share two baths. The two third-floor rooms share shower (skylit) bath.

Breakfast: 8–10. Juice, Danish and other pastries, boxed cereals, hot beverages. In large country kitchen.

Plus: "Mountain air." Boat trailer parking. Advance reservations made for scenic dinner cruise.

> From Texas: *"Since we accidentally came upon this place after making a wrong turn, we have gone back each year when we drive up north to visit family. . . . It is truly 'family style' . . . feel like a visitor rather than a paying guest . . . bedrooms are well ventilated."* From New Jersey: *"Comfortable . . . clean and neat with a friendly atmosphere . . . area stimulates the artistic imagination."*

The Nethercott Inn Bed and Breakfast

P.O. Box 26, Main Street, Starrucca, PA 18462   717/727-2211

Hosts: Ned and Ginny Nethercott
Location: In a tiny Endless Mountains borough with a population of about 150 people. Ten miles from the Starrucca Viaduct (150-year-old stone railroad bridge still in use); 35 from Binghamton, New York; 45 from Scranton, Pennsylvania; 19 to Elk Mountain and Mount Tone ski areas; 10–15 minutes to cross-country skiing. Near streams for fishing.
Open: Year round.
Rates: For one or two guests, $75 per room. $15 extra bed. Amex, Discover, MC, Visa.

The sign on the front lawn came with Ned and Ginny in 1986 when they moved from their ranch house B&B in California. "We love old houses, so when Ned retired from the Air Force, we searched for one in a quiet town. This Victorian—in what was once a thriving tannery and lumber community—seemed right for our dream of a B&B with an antiques shop." For a hint of the complete renovation, see the before-and-after photo album. The house is carpeted throughout, and "furnishings are in the style of 1893, with hands-on antiques so you aren't afraid to touch anything. Our style of hosting means that all our guests are like family when they leave."

In 1992 the Nethercotts published *Klondike Tenderfoot*, edited versions of Ginny's great-grandmother's 1898–1902 diaries. That spunky lady went to Alaska at age 40, bought two gold mines, worked in a millinery shop that is there to this day—and more. Inquire!

Bed and bath: Five second-floor rooms—all with mountain views. Four with queen beds. One with a queen bed plus adjoining room with two twins and a youth bed. Three rooms with tub/shower; two with stall shower.

Breakfast: 8–9:30. Fruit compote, orange juice, homemade sweet breads, egg souffle, special blend of coffees. In dining room on crystal and china.

Plus: Use of sleds. Wraparound veranda.

In this book a full bath includes a shower and a tub. "Shower bath" indicates a bath that has all the essentials except a tub.

Pennsylvania Dutch Country
_____ Reservation Service _____

Hershey Bed & Breakfast Reservation Service

P.O. Box 208, Hershey, PA 17033

Phone: 717/533-2928. Monday–Friday 10–4. Answering machine at other times.

Listings: Most are private homes; four are inns and four are farms. Located throughout southeastern Pennsylvania, including Hershey, Middletown, Harrisburg, Lancaster, Lebanon, New Cumberland, and Gettysburg. Send a self-addressed stamped envelope for a directory.

Reservations: Two-week advance notice preferred. Last-minute requests filled if possible.

Rates: $50–$55 single, $55–$100 double. Deposit required is 25 percent of total cost of stay. Refunds less $10 service charge made if cancellation is received at least 48 hours prior to arrival date. ♦

Renee Deutel knows her hosts and their homes—and she is fussy! She has places that are perfect for honeymooners, places where kids can milk a cow, places where you can gather your own eggs or just enjoy country living in an atmosphere of friendliness with easy access to many recreational facilities. She accommodates bridal parties, family reunions, and corporate retreats, and arranges "anything you need to make your trip special," including reservations for a memorable experience, a bountiful dinner at a long table in the Brethren home of the Meyer family.

Some B&Bs in Pennsylvania Dutch Country are also represented by:
Bed & Breakfast Adventures, page 54.
Bed & Breakfast Connections/Bed & Breakfast of Philadelphia, page 226.
Guesthouses, page 226.

_ Pennsylvania Dutch Country B&Bs _

Adamstown Inn

717/484-0800
800/594-4808

62 West Main Street, P.O. Box 938
Adamstown, PA 19501-0938

Hosts: Tom and Wanda Berman
Location: In a small (population 1,100) Dutch country town, known for 2,500 antiques dealers within a three-mile radius. Next door to church. Ten minutes to "outlet capital" Reading, 20 to Lancaster. Minutes to restaurants.

Open: Year round. Two-day minimum on April–December weekends.
Rates: $65 double bed. $70 canopied queen. $90 queen bed, Jacuzzi. $105 king bed, Jacuzzi. MC, Visa.
♥ ♣ ♦ ✈

The innkeepers/restorers/antiques collectors have fans from all over the country who write: *"The Bermans clearly love what they are doing. . . . A treat away from the 'real world' . . . well cared for. . . . Friendly, relaxed . . . felt pampered . . . good restaurant suggestions . . . convenient for antiquing. . . . Our 81-year-old mother loved it as much as we did. . . . Had interesting information about the area, good bike-tour maps . . . new bathrooms . . . comfortable, lovely old-fashioned atmosphere."*

Newly planted perennials and more than 5,000 bulbs are the latest embellishments to this 1989 restoration. It's a large early 1800s yellow brick Victorian that had major 1920s additions—chestnut woodwork, leaded glass doors and windows, and a columned wraparound porch. The Bermans painted the exterior trim—with seven colors on the house, four on the garage. They furnished the fireplaced living room without clutter, with lots of comfortable seating, and with a working 1850 Estey pump organ, one of the many antiques refinished by Tom. Formerly a banker in Baltimore, now Tom is the inn's high-place painter. Wanda, a former mortgage banker, became the low-place painter, seamstress (41 window treatments), and baker. And for crafts shows, she makes folk art items, tole paintings, and dried flower arrangements (some blossoms are microwave dried) and wreaths.

In residence: Magic, a Brittany spaniel.
Foreign language spoken: A little German.
Bed and bath: Four second-floor rooms, all private baths. Master bedroom with canopied king bed, two-person Jacuzzi tub, shower. One queen-bedded room, two-person Jacuzzi. One room with canopied queen bed, shower bath. One double-bedded room (with seven windows overlooking garden), shower bath.
Breakfast: 7–9 coffee, tea, or hot chocolate brought to your room. Tom serves, 7:30–9:30, at dining room table set with antique china and crystal. Fresh fruit salad, juices, cheese plate or sausage balls, muffins, sweet breads, and cereal.
Plus: Air-conditioned bedrooms; all have ceiling fans. Beverage. Robes. Mints on pillows. Off-street parking.

Spring House   717/927-6906
Muddy Creek Forks, Airville, PA 17302

Host: Ray Constance Hearne
Location: Over a running spring in a tiny (population: 17) pre-Revolutionary village on the National Register. Very rural and scenic, off the beaten track (detailed directions are useful). Five miles from shops; 30 minutes southeast of York; 45 minutes southwest of Lancaster.

Open: Year round. Two-night weekend stays preferred; required for cottage.
Rates: Per room. $60 shared bath, $85 private bath. $95 cottage. $10 surcharge for one-night weekend stay.
♥ ♨ ⚓ ♣ ♦ ✗ ⚷

> From Brazil: *"In this house I could enjoy deeply the serenity of the Pennsylvania countryside, and from [Ray's] sensitivity I could also enjoy the rest of the world, especially through the Basque music and the frittatas."*

Almost a B&B pioneer! Since the spring of 1981, visitors have asked lots of questions about the plastered, whitewashed, and stenciled walls; floor cloths, country antiques, and Oriental rugs; pottery (some done by the hostess and fired in a kiln she made while a student at Antioch College); paintings (some her own) of local scenes; and herb garden too. She lives here "in the way I grew up—with wood heat, cookstoves, cool bedrooms, and good pure food and water." Ray, a dairy-farm girl who became a York County historic preservationist, turned B&B host after a 3½-month backpacking trip in England that followed 10 years of restoring this 18th-century stone house to its "simple strong character." Both *Country Home* and *Country Decorating* (by *Woman's Day*) have featured this "genuine country inn."

In residence: Ulysses, "a cozy entertaining St. Bernard." Tashi and Tundrup, "purring companions."
Foreign language spoken: Spanish.
Bed and bath: Four rooms plus cottage. Large first-floor room with double bed, French stove, grand piano, private shower bath. On second floor, private shower bath in large room with antique three-quarter bed and a double bed. Two double-bedded rooms, one with stove, share a bath with tub, no shower. Cottage, decorated in Japanese/French mode, has queen futon in sleeping loft, first-floor shower bath, antique wood cookstove, daybed, antique clay tile floor.
Breakfast: By 9; hour arranged night before. Made with locally produced ingredients including organically grown wheat flour. Usually two main courses. Maybe wineberries on buttered buckwheat pancakes with maple syrup or honey from Ray's bees. Or a clafouti with ginger and pears; or a Basque piperade with peppers, onions, garlic, eggs, and smoked sausage. Jams, jellies (Ray makes her own pectin from green apples), and syrups from fruits she has picked and preserved. Served in dining room or on the porch.
Plus: Popcorn at just the right time. Local Amish cheese. Wine from award-winning winery three miles away. Porch swing. Feather beds, down puffs, and flannel sheets. Bicycle routes. Trout-stocked Muddy Creek. Swimming, canoeing, horseback riding, cross-country skiing. River trails and unused Ma and Pa railroad bed for hiking. In process—restored Maryland & Pennsylvania line for an eight-mile scenic train trip.

Churchtown Inn   717/445-7794
2100 Main Street, Churchtown, PA 17555

Hosts: Stuart and Hermine Smith, and Jim Kent
Location: On Route 23W with Amish buggies going by front door (and patio). Across from historic church. Views of hundreds of acres of farmland and Welsh Mountains in back. Five miles from Pennsylvania Turnpike; 20 miles east of Lancaster; 45 minutes from Philadelphia and Hershey. Two and a half hours from Manhattan and Washington, D.C.
Open: Year round. Two-night minimum on weekends, three on holiday and special weekends.
Rates: Semiprivate bath $49 and $55. Private $75–$95; skylit room $85–$105. Singles $5 less. Honeymoon suite in carriage house $125. Special holiday packages. MC, Visa.
♥ ♣ ✸ ⚲

This inn, now on the National Register, is worth a cover feature. And that's exactly what I wrote for *Innsider* magazine after experiencing Saturday dinner at an Amish home. Back at the inn there was a fun treasure hunt "award ceremony" with guests' tales of the day's discoveries (places and people).

This "favorite B&B"—according to dozens of guests' letters written to me—has ambiance, art, European and American antiques, handmade quilts, and its very own cookbook (and to think Stu took basic cooking lessons before opening). Since Stu and Jim restored the 18th-century fieldstone mansion in 1987, Amish neighbors have built additions: a lovely garden breakfast room, a carriage house/honeymoon suite from a 1735 springhouse, and a ballroom.

For 20 years Stu directed singers—150 adults, 100 children, and two handbell choirs—in the northeast (in Carnegie Hall too) and in Europe. In New Jersey, Hermine, Stu's wife, was a health food retailer. Jim, who teaches ballroom dancing, was an accountant. Here they are active with the Lancaster Shelter for Women. At the inn they plan an amazing array of theme weekends, including murder mysteries, walking tours, formal Victorian balls, country dances, and barbecues with accordion music.

Foreign languages spoken: Limited German and Italian.
Bed and bath: Eight queen-bedded rooms; all private baths except for two third-floor rooms that share a bath. One third-floor room has a queen and a single bed, cathedral ceiling, skylights, private full bath. In carriage house, first-floor honeymoon suite has elaborate shower bath.
Breakfast: At 9. Five-course meal beginning with freshly squeezed orange juice. Entree might be buttermilk pancakes with fruit, French toast made with Grand Marnier, Scottish oatmeal custard, or egg souffle. Homemade breads and jams. Coffee cake.
Plus: Air conditioning. Often, evening tea or wine in the Victorian parlor; maybe a sing-along with Stu at the baby grand piano and/or the sounds of antique organ, phonograph, and music boxes. Game room. Den. Courtyard. Garden swing (what a view). Lavish Christmas decorations. By advance arrangement, dinners ($12.50) in Amish home Tuesdays and Thursdays (June–October) and Saturdays.

Clearview Farm Bed & Breakfast

355 Clearview Road, Ephrata, PA 17522   717/733-6333

Hosts: Glenn and Mildred Wissler
Location: A 200-acre farm in easy-to-find countryside. Three miles west of Ephrata; half mile off Route 322; 15 minutes from Pennsylvania Turnpike; 20 minutes to Lancaster and Reading outlets; 25 minutes to Hershey.

Open: Year round. Two-night minimum on holidays and during special events.
Rates: $95–$110 per room. $25 rollaway. MC, Visa
♥ ❀ ✗ ⅄

Whether guests come for the wide-open farmland, for warm hospitality, and/or for attractions in the area, they are inspired to take a tour of this 1814 limestone farmhouse, restored over three decades by Mildred, the daughter of an antiques dealer, and Glenn, a farmer and (creative) master craftman. There's an aptly named French Room. And a Royal Room. A Princess Room with a lace-covered four-poster. A wicker carriage with parasol and dolls. A sink set into an old bureau. A dining room with Victorian print paper and formal draperies. And an inviting living room that overlooks the manicured lawns and the pond with swans. Everywhere, you see Glenn's sense of color combined with Mildred's displays (lots of collectibles) and her wallpapering and sewing (all the curtains, drapes, and canopies)—a style of making things come together without a sense of clutter. Since 1989 this family home has been a B&B. "Our son is married. We were not ready to retire from farming and thought it would be fun—it is!—to share this large house that we continue to find treasures for."

Bed and bath: Five rooms, each with sitting area and private bath. On second floor—one with carved Victorian double bed, claw-footed tub and shower bath. Two queen-bedded rooms; one with shower bath, one with tub/shower bath. On third floor—two with canopied queen bed, sink en suite, private shower bath, exposed stone walls, hand-pegged beams. Rollaway.
Breakfast: 8:30. Fresh fruit. Homemade muffins. Ham-and-cheese souffle, peaches-and-cream French toast, or Belgian waffles. At dining room table set with china, crystal, and fresh linens, or on screened and awninged porch.
Plus: Central air conditioning. Fresh flowers. Mints on pillows. Fireplace and wood stove in beamed den. Lawn furniture.

Springhouse Inn B&B   717/859-4202

806 New St., Akron, PA 17501-1325

Hosts: Ray and Shirley Smith
Open: Year round.
Location: Surrounded by an acre of lawn on a quiet street in a small town. Nine miles north of Lancaster; two miles south of Ephrata; seven to antiques markets. Close to restau-

rants; historic sites; back roads past Amish farms, one-room schoolhouses, and covered bridges.
Rates: Shared bath $55. Private bath $65; with canopied bed $75. Single $10 less. Cot $15. MC, Visa.
♥ ❀ ✗ ⅄

After selling a B&B in Ephrata, Shirley, a former teacher, and Ray, an avid sailor, restored this 1790 farmhouse, stenciled interior steps and walls, and furnished with antiques and traditional pieces. Guest rooms each have a literary theme such as poetry, Dickens, or Gatsby. On the grounds are the age-old spring, a massive willow tree (big enough to shade an entire reunion picnic), and flower and herb gardens. The Smiths, lifelong area residents, share lots of hints, including back roads, quilt shops, and—"our specialty"—auctions.

In residence: Mrs. Kitty, a cat; four hand-fed mallard ducks.
Bed and bath: Four rooms, all with wide pine floors and deep windowsills. All new baths with pedestal sinks. First floor—very large room with queen canopied bed, private en-suite shower bath, sitting area, classic literature collection. Second floor—queen bed, private shower bath. Smaller corner room with queen bed shares a hall shower bath with room with twin beds.
Breakfast: 8:30–9:30. Thick French toast, eggs Benedict, pancakes and scrapple, or scrambled eggs. Juices, fruit cup, homemade coffee cake, freshly ground coffee, herbal teas. Served at individual tables in room with stone walls, walk-in fireplace. Or in library/sitting room.
Plus: Air conditioning in guest rooms. Fresh springwater (hence the B&B name). Afternoon herbal (homegrown) tea. Pavilion with gas grill and fireplace. Picnic table. Mints on pillows. Special occasions acknowledged.

The Osceola Mill House   717/768-3758
313 Osceola Mill Road, Gordonville, PA 17529

Hosts: Robin and Sterling Schoen
Location: In Old Order Amish community without a power or telephone line in view. "With heavy buggy traffic year round." Approached via a little bridge over a creek with a gristmill on one side and the miller's house on the other. On a bend in the road along the banks of Pequea Creek. About a mile north of Intercourse; 15 miles east of Lancaster.
Open: Year round except Christmas–New Year's. Two-night minimum on weekends.
Rates: $100 per room.
♥ ♣ ✻ ✿

Country Living featured this large 225-year-old stone house just before the Schoens moved in in 1989. Their extensive research, discoveries, and restoration resulted in the place seen in *Vogue* and *Modern Bride* the same year (1993) that Sterling was filmed right here for a BBC segment. Photographers, too, like the idea of having more buggy than car traffic, along with barns, horses and plows, and winding lanes. Now that the Victorian touches are gone, the Georgian house has 12-over-12 windows complete with 18th-century glass. There's a beehive oven and four working fireplaces. An 18th-century herb garden. And Williamsburg whitewash walls with period and local colors for accents. The 18th- and 19th-century antiques were moved from New Hampshire, where, in the 1980s, Robin had been an antiques dealer and interior designer. Sterling, the gourmet cook, is a fly-fishing expert/former Philadelphia litigation lawyer who was administrator of a computer-related company in New Hampshire. Here he is active in preserving this unique pocket of the country, where guests from all over the world take walks and meet Amish neighbors along the road and "where there's a glorious morning mist and spectacular sunsets."

(Please turn page.)

In residence: One Newfoundland dog named Oliver.
Bed and bath: Four second-floor rooms. Three with canopied queen bed; one of these has high bed, working fireplace. One with pencil-post queen bed, working fireplace. Three detached baths; one (private for one of the rooms) located downstairs. One new bath has enormous footed tub, hand-held shower; another bath has tub, hand-held shower; third is a shower (no tub) bath.
Breakfast: Usually 8:30. Specialties include German apple pancakes or French toast that some guests say are "alone worth the trip." In fireplaced keeping room or in dining room with those 12-over-12 windows.
Plus: Air-conditioned bedrooms, June–September. Handmade quilts. Directions to small step-back-in-time country stores. Shared tips about 18th-century restoration—here they found the original door nailed as a patch on a neighbor's barn—and Pennsylvania antiquing. Walk to dinner at farm of Amish neighbors.

Pinehurst Inn Hershey

50 Northeast Drive, Hershey, PA 17033

717/533-2603
800/743-9140
fax 717/534-2639

Hosts: Roger and Phyllis (Long) Ingold.
Location: Surrounded by lawns and (through the night) the sound of the passing train. Abutting a new (1995) 65-store outlet mall. Within a mile of the Sports Arena, Hersheypark, Chocolate World, Hershey Museum, Golf Courses, and Rose Garden. One hour's drive to Gettysburg and Lancaster.
Open: Year round.
Rates: $59 shared bath; $69 private bath. $5 extra person. MC, Visa.
♥ ♨ ⛵ ⁂ ♦ ✈ ⊁

This sprawling brick B&B was built by Mr. Hershey as a home—not a dormitory—for orphaned boys who attended the Milton Hershey School (which has a current coed enrollment of 1,200). There is a comfortable, welcoming many-windowed living room. The guest rooms have built-in bureaus and are decorated minimally as a reminder of their origin.

Phyllis, a substitute teacher at the school in the 1970s, lived here as a young child when her parents were Pinehurst house parents. "As a teenager I entertained some dates on the porch swing, the same one on which my mother read to her grandchildren. After our own four children grew up—in a Cape house right in town—my late husband and I bought this property and established the B&B. While at a work camp in Nigeria, I met Roger, a former chemistry teacher, retired missionary administrator, and ordained minister. Since our marriage (Christmas 1993) he has conducted weddings here—and then switched roles and worn an apron at the reception!"

In residence: Nickolas, a gentle Maine coon cat.
Bed and bath: Fifteen rooms on first and second floors. Three have private shower bath; 12 share five full baths. Queen, double, or twin beds and rollaway.
Breakfast: Usually 8:30–9:30. Juice or fruit, homemade coffee cakes, teas, coffee. Scrambled eggs, pancakes, or stuffed French toast.

Plus: Air conditioning. Bedroom ceiling fans. Chocolate kiss on each pillow. That swing is on the porch.

From New York: *"We like the stenciling . . . and the long tables at breakfast."* From Massachusetts: *"Treated as visitors at a private home."* From Virginia: *"Great for 19 of us, ages 6 to 78, who gathered for a family reunion."*

Carriage Corner Bed & Breakfast

3705 East Newport Road, P.O. Box 371   **717/768-3059**
Intercourse, PA 17534   **800/209-3059**

Hosts: Gordon and Gwen Schuit
Location: On an acre of lawn, set back from the road where horse-drawn sleighs and wagons pass. Across from Stoltzfus Farm Restaurant, and fenced pastures with black Angus cattle, sheep, and horses. Five-minute walk to Intercourse and shops. Nine miles east of Lancaster.

Open: Year round. Two-night minimum on holiday weekends.
Rates: January–March shared bath $45, private $55. April–December shared bath $55; private $65 one queen bed, $70 two queens. Extra person $10; under age 12, $6. MC, Visa.

From New Jersey, North Carolina, California, Pennsylvania, Alabama, Michigan: *"Warm and friendly hosts . . . delicious breakfast . . . welcoming atmosphere . . . immaculate . . . short walk to quaint Amish town. . . . Went to a local park and had a wonderful visit with some Amish folks . . . beautiful scenery in heart of Amish country. . . . Clip-clop of carriages going by. . . . Genuine feeling of home away from home . . . made me feel special. . . . Made us feel as if we were the only guests . . . reasonable rates. . . . Highly recommended."*

Others call this "a real B&B," a visit with a sharing family. It's a homey contemporary Colonial, built in 1980 to be a B&B, and furnished comfortably with reproductions and quilts. The Schuits, who came here in 1992, were introduced to B&Bs during their own travels in Ireland and New Zealand. In Bergen County, New Jersey, Gordon was a pastor of youth and Christian education. Gwen is a nursing instructor at Brandywine School of Nursing.

In residence: Daughter Katie, age 11. Buffy, a friendly golden retriever.
Bed and bath: Four first-floor partially paneled rooms with radio and cable TV. Private shower baths for room with two queen beds and another with one queen bed. Two rooms, one with a double bed and another with two double beds, share (robes provided) a shower bath.
Breakfast: 8:30. Egg dishes or French toast with meats. "Whenever we serve baked oatmeal or oatmeal pancakes, recipes are requested—and shared." Homemade muffins. Served in L-shaped dining area with view of neighboring farm.
Plus: Central air conditioning. Wood-burning stove, spinet piano, and TV in living room. Beverages. Guest refrigerator. Bicycling suggestions. Weekend dinner reservations at Amish home.

Gardens of Eden   717/393-5179
1894 Eden Road, Lancaster, PA 17601

Hosts: Marilyn and Bill Ebel
Location: Tranquil. Overlooking the Conestoga River, "where the water still runs over the millrace falls." On 3½ acres with terraced gardens and woodsy trails; all just 10 minutes from downtown. Walk across bridge to fine (Austrian) dining.

Open: Year round. Two-night minimum, April–November for guest house and main-house room with private bath. **Rates:** Shared bath $65; $75 king bed. Private bath $85. Guest cottage $110; extra person over age six $10.
♥ ♯ ◄ ⁂ ◆ ✘ ⅄

A joy. Grounds with wildflowers in the woods and extensive perennial and herb gardens. After-breakfast walks offered in spring, tours in summer. Songbirds. Bird feeders. A canoe. A rowboat. Fishing on the river. Custom-designed driving or cycling tours. Arranged meals in a young Amish couple's home. All in an 1867 brick ironmaster's house that is filled with primitives, handmade quilts, woven (by Marilyn's mother) woolen coverlets, needlework, plants, and dried flower arrangements. All hosted by Bill, an environmental activist who was a corporate business manager (Ford/New Holland) for over three decades, and Marilyn, a third-generation floral designer/lecturer/demonstrator who is happy to show you her basement workshop—complete with original furnace! Since opening as a B&B in 1987, they have converted the former summer kitchen into a guest cottage, a photographer's delight.

Foreign languages spoken: A little French and Spanish.
Bed and bath: Three main-house second-floor rooms plus cottage. Private en-suite tub/shower bath for large room with canopied queen bed, river view. One double and one with king/twins option share (robes provided) a tub/shower hall bath. Guest cottage (children very welcome here)—second floor has double platform bed, TV, and private shower bath; on first floor, sitting/dining area with walk-in wood-burning fireplace, foldout double sofa, efficiency kitchen. Crib available.
Breakfast: 7:30–9. Bill's baked eggs. Flower syrup and toppings. Herb butters and garnishes. In dining room with family needlework and window bird feeder, or on screened porch with river view.
Plus: Central air conditioning. Grand piano in fireplaced living room. Welcoming beverage. Chocolates. Bike storage. Requests for violet jelly recipe filled. Recommendations for personalized tours of Amish and Mennonite communities. Saturday dinners arranged in Amish home.

Hollinger House Bed & Breakfast   717/464-3050
2336 Hollinger Road, Lancaster, 17602-4728

Hosts: Gina and Jeffrey Trost
Location: On 5½ acres of pastures and woods along an old road below and parallel to Route 222. Three miles to Lancaster center.
Open: Year round; two-night minimum preferred on holiday weekends.
Rates: Per room. $85–$100 Febru-

ary–November. $70–$90 December and January. $20 rollaway. Corporate rates available. Discounts for senior citizens and groups and for five or more nights. Mystery and theme weekends. Discover, MC, Visa.
♥ ⁂ ✘ ⅄

"A cure for two tired souls," wrote one guest from Montreal. The "cure" begins with welcoming hors d'oeuvres. "I was raised in an Italian family where food meant friendship and comfort," declares enthusiastic Gina, a caterer who started collecting antiques for her "someday B&B" long before she and Jeff, a local physician, bought this Adams period brick house in 1994. They added baths and updated systems. Ornate moldings and walls are painted in soft colors. Furnishings are light wood, wrought iron, and primitives—"nothing heavy or frilly." Fabrics are Ralph Lauren florals, paisleys, and ginghams. The spacious house has high ceilings, plenty of comfortable seating, French doors, refinished hardwood floors, balconies, a wraparound porch with a swing and rockers, lots of land, and innkeepers who truly love doing what they do.

Foreign languages spoken: A little French and Italian.
Bed and bath: Six large bedrooms; one with king canopied bed; five with queens (one has a twin bed also, another a sofabed, too). All private tub/shower baths; five en suite, one in hall.
Breakfast: Usually 8:30–9; determined night before with guests. "Healthy menu." Peach or berry soup. Country casserole, poached eggs with herbal sauce, potato/onion/low-fat cheese pie, fruit-stuffed French toast, berry-nut hotcakes, or vegetarian dish. Pastries—"more than muffins." Turkey sausage and other meats. Juices. Cereals. Hot beverages. Special diets accommodated with advance notice. Served in dining room at individual tables that can be arranged as one large table or on balcony.
Plus: Window air conditioners in summer. Bedtime snack. Fireplaces. TV, VCR. Robes. Use of bicycles. Picnic lunches (charges vary). Transportation to/from local stations.

Lincoln Haus Inn Bed & Breakfast

1687 Lincoln Highway East, Lancaster, PA 17602-2609   **717/392-9412**

Host: Mary K. Zook
Location: On main road, within walking distance of some restaurants. Bus and tourist trolley go by the house. Two miles off Route 30. Minutes to several colleges and many attractions. Five minutes to Pennsylvania Dutch Visitors Information Bureau.

Open: Year round. Two- or three-day minimum during holidays.
Rates: $48–$65. Suite $70–$75. Singles $2 less. Rollaway $10. One-night surcharge $5–$10. Off-season, 10 percent less, excluding holidays from December until March 15.
♥ ♨ ♣ ♦ ✖ ⚄

From Pennsylvania: *". . . the next best thing to staying with family . . . have returned 'home' after a long working day to find Mary making applesauce from fruit of tree outside, or canning peaches, or pickling beets . . . foods that often turn up on the breakfast table. No shrinking violets at this table! Mary coaxes introductions and conversation. . . . House is set back from the highway behind a well-tended lawn complete with swing and shade trees. Inside and out, it is unmistakably the new identity of what was once an elegant private home, with handsome woodwork, pleasant rooms, and a now-modernized (but nonelectric) roomy kitchen."*

(Please turn page.)

Mary, a Lancaster native and member of the Old Order Amish church, grew up without electricity. A B&B hostess since 1989, she lights the living room with gaslights—and, for safety reasons, provides electric lights in the bedrooms (which also have air conditioners). Often, guests ask her about Amish ways, about restaurant recommendations, about hidden places, and about having dinner (reservations made) with her Amish cousin or friends.

Foreign language spoken: German.
Bed and bath: Six rooms with a queen, a double, or a double and a twin bed. All private baths; one with shower only, others with tub and shower. Suite has two double beds, double sofa bed, exposed beams, skylight, kitchenette. Rollaway and crib. Across street—two apartments, breakfast optional.
Breakfast: (None on Sunday; gift certificate for restaurant within walking distance.) Served family (Amish) style in dining room. Menu varies according to season. Breads. Pumpkin, raisin bran, or whole wheat carrot muffins. Maybe zucchini pie, fresh fruit, or home-canned peaches with mandarin oranges. Blueberry or whole wheat/banana potato pancakes; waffles or ham quiche. Sausages, ring bologna, or scrapple. Juice could be papaya/orange. Herbal teas, coffee blends.
Plus: "In cooler months, goodness of basement wood-burning stove can be smelled throughout the house."

Maison Rouge Bed and Breakfast

2236 Marietta Avenue, P.O. Box 6243   717/399-3033
Lancaster, PA 17607-6243   800/309-3033

Hosts: Rodney J. Petrocci and William L. Stromski
Location: In small community of Rohrestown, 3 miles west of downtown Lancaster; 2½ miles west of Franklin and Marshall College; 2 miles west of Wheatland, home of President James Buchanan. Next to a church; across from two other Victorian homes. Two blocks from Route 30, Route 741 exit.
Open: Year round. Two-night minimum on holiday weekends.
Rates: Shared bath $80. Private bath $100; Senator's Room $120. MC, Visa.
♥ 🛥 ❖ ✗ ✔

From Pennsylvania: *"Felt pampered. . . . Even outdoor gardens were lovely."* From Maryland: *"Charming atmosphere . . . wallpaper fresh and elegant. . . . Out-of-this-world breakfasts. . . . Wonderfully restored Victorian home enhanced by the friendliness of owners."* From Florida: *"Clean and neat, not hodgepodged. Taste and thought is evident. . . . Clincher is the breakfast."* From Colorado: *"Highly recommended."*

Selected: to showcase a new (1994) line of Eisenhart wallcoverings and fabrics from London's Victoria and Albert Museum. Featured: in *Traditional Home* magazine. All within two years after Rod, the gardener and floral arranger, and Bill, a Lutheran pastor who also designs church interiors, purchased (in 1992) the 1882 Second Empire red-painted brick house. For a century it was a doctor's residence; most recently it was the home and show house of an interior design business. Pocket doors, gilded mirrors, a porcelain dog collection, chandeliers, and marble (nonworking) fireplaces form the backdrop for antiques and period furnishings in this formal but comfortable Victorian B&B.

Bed and bath: Four air-conditioned second-floor rooms, each with queen bed and sitting area. One with private en-suite modern shower bath plus in-room sink. One room with canopied bed, private hall bath with large footed tub, hand-held shower; marble sink and floor, original Minton porcelain wall tile. Room with paisley wallcovering, four-poster bed, marble-topped in-room sink and adjoining room decorated in florals and lace share connecting tile shower bath.

Breakfast: 8:30 spring and summer; 9 fall and winter. Fresh fruit or fruit soup. Muffins. Stuffed French toast with orange sauce and Lancaster County smoked bacon. Dessert—a cobbler, strudel, or pumpkin custard. Served in crystal-chandeliered dining room with classical music.

Plus: Welcoming refreshments. Room air conditioners. Turn down service. Day-trip planning. Gardens and grove (sometimes for weddings or marriage renewal). Formal tea by arrangement. Open porches. Robes. Small library. Room for cards or board games. For sale—Rod's dried flower and wreath arrangements; some silk ones too.

O'Flaherty's Dingeldein House   717/293-1723

1105 East King Street, Lancaster, PA 17602   800/779-7765
fax 717/293-1947

Hosts: Jack and Sue Flatley
Location: On a main road. Ten minutes to historic Central Market in downtown, and to train and bus stations, discount shopping malls, amusement park.
Open: Year round. Two-night min-
imum on July–October weekends.
Rates: Tax included. $63.60 twins or double bed, shared bath. $74.20 double or queen bed, private bath. $15 extra bed. No charge for playpen. Discover, MC, Visa.
♥ ♠ ♣ ❀ ♦ ✈ ⅄

From Netherlands: *"Beautiful house. Good breakfast. Relaxed atmosphere. A great discovery."* From New Jersey: *"Our first B&B. My husband was doubtful. We loved it so much that I took my mother the next time. My in-laws went for a weekend, and now I can't wait to go again."* From California: *". . . sent us to the best bargain shops and local attractions. . . . We often stay in family settings, but none as 'family friendly' as this."* From Maryland: *"Even made special dinosaur pancakes for our four-year-old."*

Absolute naturals. Born innkeepers. The Flatleys got the idea "for our retirement" from a B&B trip in Ireland. In 1989 they bought this B&B, a traditionally furnished Dutch Colonial that was once the home of the Armstrong (floor tile) family and for 50 years was in the Leath (Strasburg Railroad and Museum) family. The colorful and profuse gardens are tended by Sue, who is also a fine craftsperson. The goldfish and koi pond is Jack's pride and joy. Formerly a manager with Boeing Helicopters, he is co-chef and tour planner, the one who explored side roads and found Amish friends—a toymaker who lives on a farm and loves to meet guests; a cabinetmaker who shows you around a shop with air power, no electricity; and a family that may have you to dinner.

(Please turn page.)

In residence: "Our Lhasa-poo, McTuffy, a great people dog."
Bed and bath: Four rooms. Private full baths for two third-floor rooms, one with queen and one with double bed. On second floor, room with double bed and one with two twins share a full bath. Rollaway available.
Breakfast: 8–10. Fresh fruit or poached pears in strawberry sauce, home-made breads and muffins. Heart-shaped blueberry or cinnamon oat pancakes with brandied apples, "world-renowned omelets," or quiche. Potato pie.
Plus: Fully air conditioned. Fireplaced living room and study. Afternoon beverages. Bicycle storage. Use of refrigerator. Porch swing, chairs, game table. Transportation to/from Lancaster airport, bus or train station. Custom-marked map of Amish country.

Patchwork Inn
2319 Old Philadelphia Pike, Lancaster, PA 17602

717/293-9078
800/584-5776

Hosts: Lee and Anne Martin
Location: On a main road, adjacent to an Amish farm. Three miles east of Lancaster, near the village of Smoke-town. Two miles from Bird-in-Hand farmers' market and craft shops.

Open: Year round. Two-night min-imum on major holiday weekends.
Rates: $70 private bath, $60 shared. $80 suite. $15 per extra per-son in room. Discover, MC, Visa.
♥ ✲ ✖ ⅄

> From Michigan: *"Lee and Anne helped with off-the- beaten-path suggestions . . . inn is shiny clean and charming."* From Maryland: *"Home is warm and inviting. Collection of quilts is huge and fun."* From Canada: *"A superb collection of books on the Amish and Mennonites and on quilting."* From New Jersey: *" . . . told my wife about a remote Amish fabric store where she was finally able to find some specific quilting material. . . . Everybody wanted breakfast recipes."*

Hospitality is the feature of this updated and well-maintained 1800s farm-house, where you'll find a collection of more than 70 handmade quilts, country antiques, and old telephones (including a booth with working sign and fan).

It just so happened that B&B was taking hold in Lancaster when Lee was retiring in 1987 as a colonel from the Marine Corps. That's when he and his late wife, Joanne, opened the inn. They ran it together until she died in 1989.

Lee and Anne, married in 1991, have put their varied talents and antiques together—and have participated in a barn raising with Amish friends. Anne, who has worked in high school media services, has a degree in foods and nutrition. In response to guests' requests, the Martins have produced a cookbook.

In residence: "Precious, our 15-year-old cat, knows who the cat lovers are."
Bed and bath: On second floor, three rooms and one suite, all with quilt-covered antique queen beds. One room has private full bath. Two rooms share one large full bath with double sinks. Suite has bedroom, living room with queen sofa bed, full bath, kitchen, and private entrance.
Breakfast: Usually 8:30. "Wholesome." Juice. Fresh fruit. Breakfast pizza, Dutch babies, or souffles. Homemade breads. Coffee and teas.

Plus: Central air conditioning. Bedroom ceiling fans. Amish-made wood glider on front porch. Guest refrigerator. Flannel sheets in winter; line-dried sheets in summer. Bicycle storage and tour maps.

The Columbian
360 Chestnut Street, Columbia, PA 17512

717/684-5869
800/422-5869

Hosts: Becky and Chris Will
Location: "In a small town where almost everyone has friendship lights in house windows." On a side street, on the last corner of the commercial district (with restaurants and antiques shops); next to two neighboring "gorgeous restored mansions." Three blocks to one-mile bridge (for walking or jogging) over Susquehanna River. Eight miles from Lancaster city line; 45 minutes to Hershey or Gettysburg.
Open: Year round. Two-night minimum on holiday weekends.
Rates: $70, $80 with fireplace or for very large room, $85 with balcony. $10 each additional person. November–March, 10 percent less. MC, Visa.

♥ ♨ ♣ ✗ ✂

Everyone exclaims when they see the dramatic and beautiful staircase featuring an enormous stained glass window. And they find it hard to believe that it took a lot of time "playing detective" in order to reassemble the stairway, which had been dismantled when the imposing brick Colonial Revival mansion was turned into apartments and a video store. The restoration was complete when Chris, a computer programmer/video game creator, and Becky, a former nurse, purchased this B&B and its Victorian and country furnishings in 1994. Their own stays at B&Bs inspired them to become innkeepers in a big old house in a small town. Now they meet travelers who come for the clock museum (two blocks away), which is the international headquarters for the National Association of Watch and Clock Collectors. Many come for sightseeing. And more than one returnee says that Becky's breakfast is the major draw.

In residence: Katie, "our outgoing two-year-old daughter."
Bed and bath: Six queen-bedded rooms (some with a twin bed too) with air conditioning (some with ceiling fan too), sitting area, private tub/shower bath. Gas fireplace in first-floor room. Second-floor suite has a queen-bedded room, a twin-bedded room, private porch; some other rooms have a queen and a twin bed. Third-floor room has two dormered windows. Rollaway available.
Breakfast: Flexible hours. Usually by 10. Half a grapefruit. Homemade granola. Quiche Lorraine, waffles, egg casserole, blueberry or apple pancakes, or French toast strata. Fresh fruit. Homemade breads and muffins. Hot fruit dish. Juices, teas, coffee. "No need for lunch." (Recipes shared.)
Plus: Central air conditioning in common rooms. Fireplaced living and dining rooms. Welcoming refreshments. Evening tea. All rooms have TV. Some have individual thermostat. Wraparound porches. Dinner reservations made at restaurants or in an Amish home. Off-street parking. Transportation to/from Harrisburg airport or Lancaster train station.

From Florida: *"Truly a home away from home."*

Early American
Oxford, PA

Location: A working dairy farm (95 cows) surrounded by Amish farms—and in back, an 18-hole Scottish golf course. Within 20 minutes of Strasburg, Longwood Gardens, Winterthur Museum, Brandywine River Museum, Chadds Ford, Lancaster outlets. Within 10 minutes of fine dining, Herr's Potato Chips, Eldreth Pottery.

Reservations: Available year round through Bed & Breakfast Connections/Bed & Breakfast of Philadelphia, page 226.
Rates: Single $50. Double $60; double with guaranteed private bath $80. Third person in room $15.
♦ ♣ ♦ ✄

Welcome—in the herb garden with May wine made with sweet woodruff and fresh strawberries, or with sun tea with mint and lemon verbena; or in winter with hot cider by the working fireplace in the kitchen. Other herbs from the host's gardens flavor the full country breakfast featured at this B&B, which has been discovered by travelers from all over the world.

It's a restored 1793 brick farmhouse that was once a stagecoach stop, general store, and post office. Stucco, added in the early 1930s, was removed with hammer and chisel by the host—"yes, it was a big project"—in 1986. Furnished with many collectibles and antiques, the house is well located for exploring the area; for hearing the clip-clopping of Amish buggies; and, depending on the season, for seeing calves being born.

In residence: Two dogs. Numerous cats in the barn. Teenage daughter and 12-year-old son, "very busy with their own activities."
Bed and bath: On second floor, two (three available for one party) air-conditioned, antiques-furnished rooms. All double beds; one room has a double and a single. One pullout cot available. One shared tub/shower bath.
Breakfast: 8–9. Full country start to the day. Fresh fruit; home fries, sausage; apples sauteed in garlic, rosemary, and sage from the herb garden, with scrambled eggs and fresh dill. Blueberry muffins with lemon verbena and homemade sticky buns. In fireplaced breakfast room.
Plus: Air-conditioned guest rooms. Welcoming beverage served in herb garden or in front of the fireplace. An old toolbox filled with brochures of attractions and guests' impressions.

From Colorado: *"Our first B&B. . . . A delight!"*

The Apple Bin Inn   717/464-5881
2835 Willow Street Pike, Willow Street, PA 17584   800/338-4296

Hosts: Barry and Debbie Hershey
Location: On a main road, in center of village, near restaurants and shops. Two minutes to oldest house in Pennsylvania Dutch country. Four miles south of Lancaster. An hour north of Baltimore.

Open: Year round. Three-day minimum on holiday weekends.
Rates: Shared bath $60; suite $65. Private bath $75–$85. Additional person $15. Amex, MC, Visa.
♥ ♣ ✄ ✂

"Take our county maps and get lost for an hour or two. That's what we tell our guests. And in minutes they are off the beaten track into beautiful countryside with farms and one-room schoolhouses. We know these roads from cycling." (When their children were younger, the Hersheys, Lancaster Bicycle Club members, took an 1,100-mile cycling trip to Florida.) "As area residents, we knew this 120-year-old house, a local landmark that was originally a grocery store and then a private residence with many additions built on through the years."

In 1986 the family started the B&B here. Now Barry makes apple checkerboards with three-dimensional apple playing pieces. Debbie, who has become proficient in sign language, quilts and cross-stitches. The Hersheys have filled the house with folk art and crafts—and with contentment for both hosts and travelers.

In residence: Lauren, age 15. Two outdoor dogs, Cocoa and Buttons.

Bed and bath: Four double-bedded (pencil- or acorn-post) rooms. On first floor—private exterior entrance, cathedral ceiling, barn siding on walls, private shower bath. On second floor—room with pencil-post bed, wing chair, love seat, balcony overlooking yard, private tub and shower bath. Room with wicker and oak furnishings shares a bath with suite that has a sitting room. Cot available.

Breakfast: 8–9:30. Fresh fruits, homemade bread and muffins, French toast/pecan sauce or German apple pancake. Served in country dining room or on one of two shaded patios.

Plus: Air conditioning and color cable TV in each room. Evening refreshments. Dinner offered occasionally. Will meet guests at Lancaster airport, train, or bus. Piano in living room. Hershey candy kisses. Secure bicycle storage. Custom packages for ice hockey games and dinner, for theater, and for walking or cycling tours. Picnic lunches prepared.

From Maryland: *"Beautiful . . . little touches in each room appreciated. . . . Food was great and the hospitality topped it. They helped us to find attractions and even a truly romantic anniversary restaurant."* From New Jersey: *"Cozy, comfortable, and clean. . . . Now I understand why B&Bs have become so popular."*

Swiss Woods Bed & Breakfast

500 Blantz Road, Lititz, PA 17543-9997

717/627-3358
800/594-8018
fax 717/627-3483

Hosts: Werner and Debrah Mosimann

Location: Off the beaten path, among rolling fields and country scenes. On the edge of woods that surround Speedwell Forge Lake (hiking and fishing). Three miles north of Lititz and pretzel factory; 20 minutes to downtown Lancaster; 25 to Hershey.

Open: Year round. Two-night minimum on weekends; three nights on holidays.

Rates: Double occupancy. Downstairs $75 woodland view, $85 south-facing lakeview rooms. Suites $105 or $115; $125 lake view (with Jacuzzi). Ten percent less January–March, Monday–Thursday. $15 extra person in room. Children under age one, free (crib available). MC, Visa.

♥ ❖ ◆ ✈ ✂

(Please turn page.)

From New Jersey: *"When you walk through the door, a sense of comfort and peace wraps around you. . . . An uncanny touch with detail that is surpassed only by warm kindness."* From Massachusetts: *"Suggested great bike routes . . . places that weren't on tourist maps . . . light and airy rooms . . . breakfasts spectacular."*

There are some weeks when I think that every Swiss Woods guest writes to me about their wonderful visit.

This is a Swiss-style house with natural woodwork and a contemporary country feeling—hosted by a Lancaster County native and her Swiss husband, whom she met in Austria while working with an interdenominational group. Debrah explains, "Wherever we lived, it seemed that we had visitors who had come a long way. B&B seemed like something I could do at home. While still in Switzerland we drew our own plans for this house to be built—with Werner's help—on land that has been in my family."

Since opening in June 1986, they have added a huge beamed common room with a floor-to-ceiling stone fireplace at one end. Thousands of daffodils bloom in the spring. Asparagus and red raspberries flourish. And the orchard produces peaches, nectarines, apples, walnuts, plums, cherries, and quinces that enhance breakfast for vacationers from all over the world.

In residence: In hosts' quarters—Mirjam Anne, age 13; Esther, age 12; Lukas, age 10; and Jason is 7. Outdoors—five cats. Two golden retrievers, Gretel and Heidi.

Foreign languages spoken: German and Swiss German.

Bed and bath: Seven rooms. On first floor, three queen-bedded rooms and one with two twins; each with private exterior entrance, sitting area, tub/shower bath. Two second-floor beamed cathedral-ceilinged rooms—each with a queen bed (one is a four-poster), balcony, private bath with Jacuzzi and hand-held shower. Second-floor suite with outside entrance, queen and one twin sleigh bed in one room, queen sofa bed in living room, large full bath, private deck with table and chairs. Crib available.

Breakfast: 8:30–9:00. (Coffee available from 7:30 on.) Strawberry gratin or maybe a peach raspberry cream. Birchemuesli, an original Swiss recipe, is all-time favorite. Entrees might include cinnamon raisin French toast stuffed with wild berry cream cheese, granola apple pancakes, or egg-sausage souffle. Homemade breads, buttermilk raised biscuits, chocolate chip/macadamia scones, or sour cream bran muffins. Homemade jams such as pear-cranberry. Juice. Their own coffee blend. (Cookbook is available). In breakast room or on patio.

Plus: Central air conditioning. Always-full cookie jar. Instant hot water spigot in fully equipped guest kitchenette. Bedside Swiss chocolates. Goose-down covers. Binoculars. Bird book. Games. TV. Coffee, tea, sweets, 4–6 p.m. Gift shop with cowbells "depending on when we were last in Switzerland."

Looking for a B&B with a crib? Find a description with the ♯ symbol and then check under the "Bed and bath" description.

Herr Farmhouse Inn

2256 Huber Drive, Manheim, PA 17545

717/653-9852
800/584-0743

Host: Barry A. Herr
Location: Pastoral. An 11-acre pocket with panoramic view of farmland bordered by Routes 283 and 230, major highways just east of Mount Joy. Nine miles west of Lancaster.
Open: Year round.

Rates: Double occupancy. April–October $75 and $80 shared bath, $90 private bath, $100 suite. Ten percent less off-season for two-night stay (holidays excluded). $15 extra person in room. MC, Visa.

Now this wonderful limestone federal Colonial, the fourth Herr restoration, is picture-perfect with chair rails, four-poster beds, Williamsburg colors, 22-inch-thick walls, and six working fireplaces. When Barry gives the guided tour requested by most guests, you hear about how he and his late wife found this gem—the oldest part dates back to 1737—which had not been remodeled. A tenant house for almost a hundred years, it had been vacant for at least 10 when the Herrs returned to their native Lancaster County. Even though there was much to be done (see the before-and-after pictures), all the architectural details, including moldings, floors, and even the beehive oven, were intact.

The first Herr restoration was in 1969 in Connecticut, where Barry was in engineering and a building contractor. Here he cut cherry, walnut, and pear wood for the fireplaces. And he restored outbuildings that "should be good for another 50 years." Adding to the bucolic scene is the red (former dairy) barn; the chicken house, which is now a woodworking shop; two corncribs; and tobacco sheds (which are rented by a farmer who cures tobacco in them). The gazebo is used for picnic lunches. There are country roads for jogging. And, for every winter guest, a flannel nightshirt.

In residence: Clyde, "a friendly gray mostly-outside tiger cat."
Bed and bath: Three second-floor rooms plus a third-floor suite. Private full bath for room with canopied double bed and working fireplace. One room with canopied queen bed and one with double four-poster (with working fireplace) share a full bath. Up a steep stairway to suite with private full bath, two twin beds, sitting room with king-size bed. Rollaway available.
Breakfast: At 9. Fresh fruit, cereal, assorted breads, English muffins, homemade jelly, apple butter. Juice, coffee, tea, milk. In country kitchen with walk-in fireplace, in fireplaced dining room, or on sun porch.
Plus: Central air conditioning. Bedroom ceiling fans. Fireplaced common room. Game room with player piano. Wicker-furnished sun room. Lawn furniture, porch rockers, picnic table and grill. Indoor storage for bicycles.

Can't find a listing for the community you are going to? Check with a reservation service described at the beginning of this chapter. Through the service you may be placed (matched) with a welcoming B&B that is near your destination.

The Noble House
717/426-4389

113 West Market Street, Marietta, PA 17547-1411

Hosts: Elissa and Paul Noble
Location: On main street of the historic district. "Some guests, too, fall under the charm of this town and spend hours walking around." Thirty minutes west of Lancaster and east of Hershey. Less than an hour from Baltimore, Maryland. Minutes to antiquing, outlet shopping, museums, theaters.

Minutes' walk to new Le Petit Museum of Musical Boxes. Two blocks from trains (sound and nostalgia).
Open: Year round.
Rates: $75 suite. King/twins $75 shared bath, $95 private. Queen $55 shared bath, $75 private. Sofa bed $30.
♥ ✈ ⊁

How often Elissa would say, "Some day we will find a little corner of the world—near trains for Paul and a B&B for me!" In 1992, two years after they found Marietta, the Nobles opened this B&B in an 1820 Federal brick townhouse that had been restored as an antiques and art gallery. It has 12-foot first-floor ceilings and huge windows, and it is furnished with a blend of pieces that date from the 1850s to the 1930s.

In Yorktown Heights, New York, Paul was an art director who also had a home-based Lionel train business. (Here he has built a working Lionel train layout.) Elissa, who now teaches part time at a Waldorf School, was a child-care specialist.

In residence: Fred the dog. Crash and Baby, the cats.
Bed and bath: Three rooms. Two large, carpeted second-floor front rooms: One with king/twins option and gas fireplace sometimes shares (robes provided) large full bath with room that has queen four-poster. Plus—for same party—double sofa bed in common room (with refrigerator) that overlooks river and gardens. Private exterior entrance to first-floor suite (1950s railroad sleeper car theme) with double bed, shower bath, kitchenette, cable TV; breakfast with hosts or self-serve food provided.
Breakfast: 6–10. Wake-up basket of muffins followed by meal in candlelit dining room or on porch. Fresh fruit and juice. Choice of egg dish or French toast. Home fries and breads. Freshly ground and locally roasted coffee.
Plus: Fireplaced living room with upright piano and color cable TV. Room air conditioners. Welcoming refreshments. Turndown service. Fresh flowers.

From New York, Maryland, Pennsylvania: *"Had never stayed in a B&B before. Was hesitant. I am sold! I loved the Victorian ambiance, the special treats. . . . Charming, exquisite antiques, spotlessly kept. . . . Two breakfasts—first with morning paper . . . followed by brunch on antique china. . . . A lending library (really!) . . . congenial hosts. . . . I am British . . . felt transported to a genteel Victorian home in England."*

*T*o tip or not? (Please turn to page xi.)

Vogt Farm Bed & Breakfast

717/653-4810
800/854-0399

1225 Colebrook Road, Marietta, PA 17547

Hosts: Kathy and Keith Vogt
Location: On a quiet country road. A 30-acre farm with barns, a small pond, cows in the pasture, and a garden. "Within six miles of all types of dining." Fifteen miles west of Lancaster. Within 30 minutes of Harrisburg and Hershey.
Open: Year round.
Rates: $45 single, $55 for two; $10 each additional person in same room.
🏠 🛏 ✈ ✂

"Our brick home was a real showplace, so we are told, when it was built in 1865. We like to say it is decorated in 'Early Vogt,' the kind of place where guests often gather in the kitchen. Through the years we have had guests from around the world. Now that the older kids are married, we have official empty (redecorated) rooms, some of which were featured in *Weekends* as well as *Country Decorating* magazine. When guests ask about our country elevator, I am happy to explain the process of storing corn, wheat, and soybeans in the big bins. . . . Kathy, an excellent cook, seamstress, quilter, company gofer, garden supervisor (teaching grandson to weed), farm emergency management coordinator, and wife, has lived within five miles of here all her life. I have my pilot's license and we have our own plane [for travels as far away as Prince Edward Island or Puerto Rico]. Our fun-loving family hosts with the motto, 'Backdoor guests are best.'"

In residence: Two teenage daughters, Jennie and Rebecca. Several outdoor barn cats. A small flock of sheep.
Foreign language spoken: A little Spanish.
Bed and bath: Three second-floor rooms—with king/twins option, queen, or double bed—share (robes provided) a full bath (tub plus hand-held shower) and a half bath. Crib available.
Breakfast: At 8 on Sundays. Other days, 8:30. Early tea or coffee with wake-up call, if you'd like. Home-baked bread, rolls, coffee cakes, casseroles, and fruit. In large farm kitchen. Hosts join guests.
Plus: Bedroom air conditioners. Refreshing drink. Use of refrigerator. Living room with baby grand piano. Fireplaced basement family room with TV. Maps. Tips for things to see and do. Mints. Ice water in rooms. Dinner can be arranged with Amish family.

From Maryland: *"Kathy Vogt is simply exceptional! . . . huge breakfasts. . . . Immaculate. . . . You are instantly part of the family . . . a perfect getaway where you can smell the roses or watch the strawberries grow (and pick)."* From New York: *"Our daughters, ages 11 and 13, wanted to bring their room home with them. . . . Great hosts, great place."* From Pennsylvania: *"Relaxing. . . . Our children loved the kittens."* From Arizona: *"Evening 'serenade' of sheep made for a memorable stay."*

Breakfast is where the magic happens.

Cedar Hill Farm   717/653-4655

305 Longenecker Road, Mount Joy, PA 17552-9300

Hosts: Russel and Gladys Swarr
Location: Rural and quiet. A 51-acre farm on a hill, across Chiques (pronounced "chickies") Creek via a steel bridge. Surrounded by meadows, trees, a martin house, even a dinner bell mounted on a tall post. One-quarter mile drive from Route 230. Midway (12 miles) between Lancaster and Hershey.
Open: Year round. Two-night minimum on holiday weekends.
Rates: $65–$70 per room. $20 third person. Amex, Discover, MC, Visa.
♥ ♨ 🍳 ♣ ✈ ✄

What *Philadelphia* magazine dubbed "the creme de la Lancaster" for "weekend luxury" is a stone farmhouse, the birthplace of Russel, a third-generation farmer who now raises 56,000 chicks to laying age. The house's original 1817 side is simpler than the mid-1800s Victorian addition, which features a graceful winding stairway, high ceilings, and elaborate moldings. In 1987, when the Swarrs' son and daughter were grown, central air conditioning and private baths were added. A carved walnut bedroom suite with marble-topped dresser and washstand, made by Russel's cabinetmaker grandfather, provided pieces for two of the bedrooms. (The bed's footboard became the headboard for the other room.) Gladys left her 17-year office job at NCR Corporation, worked with an interior designer to coordinate family heirlooms with period wallpapers and swags, and became a full-time innkeeper. Now they're waiting for "Idaho," the only state missing from their guest list—which also includes many international travelers.

Bed and bath: Five second-floor rooms. All private baths. Queen bed (high headboard), tub and shower bath. Queen bed (ceiling canopy), large sit-down shower, private wicker-furnished balcony. Double bed, shower bath. Two double beds, tub/shower bath. Twins/king option, claw-footed tub and shower bath. Rollaway and crib available.
Breakfast: 8–9. Homemade muffins, coffee cakes, and breads. Fresh fruit and cheeses. Individual cereal boxes with low-fat milk. Orange juice, coffee, decaf, tea, hot chocolate. In guests' favorite room, the kitchen with walk-in fireplace, hanging herbs and baskets.
Plus: "I-could-sit-here-all-day" porches overlooking creek. Upright piano. Ice bucket. Use of refrigerator. Separate guest entrance. TV room with stereo, VCR, computer games. Sleds in winter. Croquet in summer. Hershey kisses. "Directions to our favorite road, where an Amish lady sells quilts in her home."

> From New Jersey, Ohio, Pennsylvania, New York: Virginia: *"Decorated beautifully. . . . Perfect. Far exceeded our expectations. . . . Sensational food . . . lemon bread and cherry crumb to die for. . . . Friendly, quiet, unpretentious, delightful. . . . A quick escape by train from Philadelphia. . . . Awoke to birdsong. . . . Just what I imagined a B&B to be."*

The Country Stay   717/367-5167
2285 Bull Moose Road, Mount Joy, PA 17552-9767

Hosts: Lester and Darlene Landis
Location: Rural. "Where the silence and sounds of nature can be heard—the songs of birds, locusts, bullfrogs, and crickets." On a working farm. Minutes from Routes 743, 441, and 30. Within half an hour of Hershey, Lancaster, York, and Harrisburg. Within 15 minutes of fine dining and family restaurants.
Open: April–November. Two-night minimum for rooms on holiday weekends. Advance reservations required.
Rates: $55 single, $60 double, $100 suite. MC, Visa.
◆ ✗ ✄

From England, California, Georgia, Maryland, Virginia, Ohio, New York, South Carolina (and more!): *"An atmosphere of welcome, care, and attention to detail. . . . A little piece of paradise tucked among rolling farmlands. . . . Wonderfully decorated with antiques. . . . The grounds are as impressive as the inside. . . . Meticulously kept . . . ironed sheets. . . . Took a midnight walk under a full harvest moon when rows of corn gleamed like silver . . . delicious food on a beautifully prepared table . . . served by Darlene in Colonial dress . . . joined them for an evening bicycle ride . . . accompanied them to church on Sunday. . . . Booked us for dinner with Amish family. . . . Seem to know when guests need privacy. . . . Traveled alone. Found warmth and friendship . . . detailed map custom marked for our interests. . . . Shared facts about their home, their life, the area. . . . Shared information on quilts (my love) and sang around the [restored player] piano. . . . Exceeded expectations. . . . We arrived as strangers and left feeling like family."*

Williamsburg and Victorian colors enhance the magnificent woodwork, the wide staircase to the second floor, the marble-topped furnishings, the comfortable living room chairs, the bay windows, and the bedrooms in this 1880 brick Victorian farmhouse, home to the Landis family for 25 years—and featured in both *Country Extra* and *Country Almanac*. Windows, each with a lighted candle, are decorated with graceful swags or ruffled curtains. In season, the window boxes overflow with blossoms. It's serene and welcoming. I, too, felt richer for my brief stop here.

In residence: Douglas, 18; Katie Joy, 10.
Bed and bath: One suite plus two rooms. First-floor Victorian honeymoon suite with private tub/shower bath, high queen four-poster, sitting room. Private guest entrance to second-floor rooms—carpeted double-bedded room with handmade Amish quilt shares a full hallway bath with room that has canopied queen bed, Amish quilt. Extra mattresses available.
Breakfast: 8:15 Monday–Saturday; at 8 on Sundays. A brunch. Baked cinnamon oatmeal (a major hit) topped with fresh fruit; homemade granola; apple dumplings. Fruit dish. Heart-shaped waffles with blueberry sauce, sausage and English muffin, or meat and potato quiche. Homemade breads, coffee cake, muffins, sticky buns or streusel.
Plus: Bedroom air conditioners and ceiling fans. Use of refrigerator. Porch rockers. Because guests asked, some of Darlene's handcrafts are for sale.

Hillside Farm Bed & Breakfast   717/653-6697

607 Eby Chiques Road, Mount Joy, PA 17552-8819   fax 717/653-6697

Hosts: Gary and Deb Lintner, nights and weekends; Gary's parents, Bob and Wilma, weekdays
Location: On two "middle-of-no-where" acres surrounded by dairy farms. Overlooking Chiques Creek, dam, and a mill house. Ten miles west of Lancaster; 35 east of Harrisburg.
Open: Year round.
Rates: $62.50 private bath, $50 shared. $10 each additional person over age 10.

> From New York, South Carolina, Pennsylvania, Louisiana, Virginia, Massachusetts, Connecticut (and many more): *"Friendly and homey atmosphere. . . . Comfortable. . . . Immaculate . . . good food . . . relaxing."* From dozens of others: *"The entire farm exuded warmth and real living. . . . Recommendations for what to see and do were on the money. . . . Went out of their way to make reservations for us. . . . Daughter enjoyed tour of next-door milking parlor. . . . Wrote to us with an answer about a quilt question. They are nice nice people who like people. I'm going back."*

Enter via the kitchen, the most popular gathering place in this home-away-from-home 1863 red brick farmhouse. When the dairy went out of business in 1957, apartments went in. Since the Lintners opened as a B&B in 1989, they have continued to make changes, still decorating eclectically—with hundreds of milk bottles, ceramic and wooden cows, milk cans, and other country items. Gary, a Lancaster County native, and Deb, "a transplant from Erie," work for the same construction company. He is project superintendent; she, an executive secretary, writer, and B&B event coordinator.

In residence: In hosts' quarters—two indoor cats. Several outdoor cats.
Bed and bath: Five rooms, all with air conditioning and four with ceiling fans. Third-floor carpeted loft has a double bed, king/twins option, space for rollaway, exposed beams, private shower bath. On second floor, two queen-bedded rooms; one has private shower/tub bath, other has canopied bed, private shower bath. One room with king/twins option shares tub/shower bath (robes provided) with room that has queen four-poster.
Breakfast: At 8:30. Fruit cup or cobblers. Orange juice, coffee, decaf, tea, herbal tea, milk. Casserole, French toast, waffles, or eggs. Ham, sausage, or bacon. Muffins or sweet breads. Homemade jams and jellies. By candlelight; can last for hours.
Plus: Central air conditioning on second floor; window unit on third floor and ground level. Individual heat thermostats. (Note: Windows, hard to move, are kept closed at all times.) Guest refrigerator. Color TV/VCR in living room. Movie library. Grand piano. Special occasions acknowledged. Suggested bicycling routes.

Innkeeping may be America's most envied profession. As one host mused, "Where else can you get a job where, every day, someone tells you how wonderful you are?"

Maple Lane Guest House   717/687-7479

505 Paradise Lane, Paradise, PA 17562

Hosts: Marion and Edwin Rohrer
Location: Pretty. Set back from the highway, surrounded by acres of lawn and rolling meadows with winding stream. One mile to Pennsylvania Railroad Museum of Strasburg.
Open: Year round. Two-night minimum on summer weekends.
Rates: Private bath $55 single, $65 double. Semiprivate bath $50 single, $58 double. $40–$50 off-season. $8 cot. Crib, free.
♥ ◀ ♣ ✖ ✄

> From Massachusetts: *"Our beautiful accommodations included a bedroom hand stenciled by Mrs. Rohrer, with a handmade quilt and other homemade crafts. . . . Mr. Rohrer gave us a tour of the farm with a full explanation of the milking machinery."* From New York: *"Well away from traffic of other tourists and curiosity seekers . . . spotlessly clean."* From Connecticut: *"As we took our morning walk before breakfast, could see Amish children walking to school . . . could hear horses and buggies coming down the road."* From Washington, D.C.: *"We, a German family living here for a year, enjoyed very much the cozy atmosphere and the hospitality."*

This is home! Marion was born just a mile down the road in one direction; Ed, a mile in the other. They have been sharing their lifestyle with travelers for over 25 years. Until 1980, when they built this Colonial-style brick home, they lived next door in the 200-year-old fieldstone house that is now occupied by their married son (whom you are likely to meet when you tour the farm). This newer house is filled with family heirlooms and with Marion's handwork, including quilting, painting, sewing, pierced lampshades, and counted cross-stitch—all pictured in a *Country Almanac* feature. For back roads, unadvertised Amish shops, or covered bridge locations, you have the experts here.

Bed and bath: On second floor, four double-bedded rooms; two baths, which can be private depending on reservation arrangements. Cot and crib available.
Breakfast: 8–9. Juice, fresh fruits, several kinds of breakfast rolls, cereal, cheese and meat tray, homemade pecan rolls and/or cheese pastry, coffee, tea. A time when Marion answers a lot of questions.
Plus: Central air conditioning. TV in each guest room. Refrigerator. Organ in guests' Victorian parlor. Picnic table. Large front porch.

The Decoy   717/687-8585
958 Eisenberger Road, Strasburg, PA 17479   800/726-2287
fax 717/687-8585

Hosts: Debby and Hap Joy
Location: Just off a main road, seven miles south of Lancaster. "At night you can hear the clip-clopping of buggies in the distance." Surrounded by views of Amish farms. Forty-five minutes to Longwood Gardens.
Open: Year round. Two-night minimum on holiday weekends.
Rates: Memorial Day weekend–November $70 king, $65 queen, $60 double bed. Off-season $10 less. $10 over age 12; $5 ages 4–12; free under age 4.
♥ ♦ ◀ ♣ ✖ ✄

(Please turn page.)

"Few antiques. We cater to kids. And we have a wonderful time!" That about sums up the Joys' style, which they adapted from their British B&B stays. "In 1985 we were caterers in Washington, D.C., when we found the perfect 'escape,' a farmhouse built for an Amish family in 1979 with large rooms and a huge all-purpose kitchen. We added electricity and heat, plus four more baths. Often, our guests enjoy going up the hill to watch the evening milking at our Amish neighbors' farm. We help plan day trips, reminding guests that many shops, farmers' markets, and local restaurants are closed on Sundays."

Hap is a Metropolitan Life B&B insurance consultant and financial estate planner. Debby is a quilter. The grandparents of five worked as volunteers in Florida after Hurricane Andrew.

In residence: Two cats; one is a blue-eyed Siamese, Cattiva (Italian for "mischievous"); Orphan is a calico cat.
Bed and bath: Five rooms; all private shower (no tub) baths. First floor—double bed. Four second-floor rooms with king/twins, queen, or double bed, plus two single daybeds in each.
Breakfast: 8:30 (wake-up call is at 8). Meat and potato quiche; baked oatmeal; sausage/grits and cheese casserole; or pancakes and waffles with real maple syrup. Homemade jellies, jams, and fruit syrups. "Family-raised bacon and sausage. Eggs from Amish neighbor's chickens." Served in long narrow dining room at two large tables.
Plus: Bedroom air conditioners. Tea or wine. Kitchen privileges. Option of lunch and dinner for groups only. Several quilting seminars.

Limestone Inn   717/687-8392

33 East Main Street, Strasburg, PA 17579

Hosts: Janet and Dick Kennell
Location: In historic district on Route 896 "where the clatter of horses and buggies awakes you in the morning." Eight miles east and south of Lancaster city. Short walk to shops and walking tour of historic Strasburg. Minutes' drive to Railroad Mu-seum, antiques shops, outlet malls, Amish attractions, and quilt shop.
Open: Year round. Two-night minimum on weekends and holidays.
Rates: $75 double or twin beds, $95 queen. Amex.
♥ 🛏 ♣ ✈ ⅍

Shy? Not really, but Dick wasn't all that sure—in 1985—about B&B as the next step after retiring from 30 years as a forester with the federal government. For their fourteenth move—this time without six growing children—the grandparents of nine chose this handsome National Register 1786 limestone five-bay Georgian, considered one of Lancaster County's most important historic buildings. They restored and decorated with Williamsburg colors, primitive antiques, and period curtains. And they became co-chefs, who frequently wear Colonial outfits during breakfast. Jan's dates back to her days as a costumed guide in Annapolis. Dick's brings out the actor in him—as well as his love of people.

In residence: Betsy, "our miniature schnauzer, who loves stroking."
Foreign languages spoken: A little French and German.

Bed and bath: Five rooms. Three large queen-bedded second-floor rooms, one with gas fireplace, all private full baths; two en-suite baths, one across hall. Up steep staircase with display of Amish wall hangings are two third-floor double- or twin-bedded rooms "partially tucked under the roofline." From 1839 to 1860 they were Strasburg Academy dormitory rooms; now each has a private shower bath down or across the hall.

Breakfast: At 8:30; 9 on weekends. A five-course meal. Entree might be sourdough pancakes, French toast, or egg souffle. Bran and blueberry muffins.

Plus: Central air conditioning. Keeping room with fireplace flanked by wing chairs and spinning wheel. Family's player piano in living room. Individual thermostats in third-floor rooms only. Occasional afternoon wine and cheese. Courtyard. Chocolates. Special occasions acknowledged. Suggestions for best buys, eating, biking. Ample bike storage. Dinner with Amish arranged with prior reservations.

From Maryland: *"A beautifully restored distinguished-looking inn, but it was really Jan and Dick who made this B&B stand out."* From New Jersey: *". . . accommodating and interesting, warm and friendly but not intrusive . . . culinary talent is imaginative and substantial."*

Smyser-Bair House Bed and Breakfast

30 South Beaver Street, York, PA 17401   717/854-3411

Hosts: The King family—Bob and Hilda, Tom and Nancy

Location: On a corner in downtown historic district. Walk to shops and restaurants. Twenty-eight miles west of Lancaster, 31 east of Gettysburg.

Open: Year round. (Note that most bookings are made in advance.)

Rates: Double bed $60, queen $65. Suite $80 for two people. Singles $5 less. $10 each additional person. MC, Visa; cash or check preferred.

Tom and Nancy were inspired by their stay at The Queen Victoria in Cape May, New Jersey. In 1989, while looking for a big old house in the country, they found this urban location and decided to do B&B on a smaller scale right here. This is a well-maintained, beautiful old Italianate brick townhouse that has stained glass windows, parquet floors, and ceiling medallions. In the handsome living room there's an original crystal chandelier reflected in the floor-to-ceiling gold-leaf mirrors, and, for fun, a player piano. Throughout, there are elegant-but-comfortable Victorian pieces purchased at area antiques shops.

The official (in-residence) hosts are two "retirees"—Tom's brother Bob, who worked in the restaurant supply business, and Hilda, Bob's wife, who has considerable experience as a cook.

Bed and bath: On second floor, two rooms and a suite. Room with double bed and one with queen bed share a shower bath. Suite has one room with double bed, smaller room with two single beds, private balcony off adjoining hallway, shower bath.

(Please turn page.)

Breakfast: Flexible. Usually 7:30–9. Full country breakfast. Juice. Fruit. Eggs with bacon or ham or sausage. Toast. Hot beverages. Served in dining room.
Plus: Central air conditioning. Welcoming beverage. York peppermint patties. Late-afternoon tea and cookies. Some off-street parking.

> From California: *"What a lovely experience."* From Pennsylvania: *"Our first B&B but definitely not our last."* From Maryland: *"Beautiful home and gracious hospitality."*

Bed & Breakfast Connections/Bed & Breakfast of Philadelphia Host #H11

Brogue, PA

Location: Serene, rustic setting. On a country road. Good bicycling and jogging area. One mile to Susquehanna River for boating and fishing. Near fine restaurants and a winery; 17 miles southeast of York. Ninety minutes from Philadelphia and Baltimore.

Reservations: Year round through Bed & Breakfast Connections/Bed & Breakfast of Philadelphia, page 226. Two-night minimum on holiday weekends.
Rates: $95 one couple. Family rates available.
♥ ♨ ♦ ✈ ✂

Bordered by woods (for hiking) and a stocked stream that has an old-fashioned swimming hole. Perfect for a small family reunion or business retreat or for your own private getaway. Meet the hosts—and their cat and dog—in the 1700s farmhouse that, they say, once belonged to a grandson of Ben Franklin. (The hosts use the former gristmill for their offices.) Then cross over the creek to your private accommodations in the former miller's house. Built in the late 1800s, it was recently restored "with love"—and with all new baths and kitchen appliances and counters. The eclectically furnished first floor has a living room, dining room, and kitchen. The screened porch, too, has wonderful countryside views. It's idyllic. Enjoy.

Bed and bath: Up narrow winding staircase (with Oriental runner) to three second-floor rooms booked for one couple or up to six people in same party. King bed, en-suite bath with Jacuzzi and shower. Room with king/twins option shares tub/shower bath with room that has a double bed.
Breakfast: Flexible hours. Full country breakfast served in guest cottage dining room, or stocked groceries if you submit requests before arrival.
Plus: Central air conditioning. Fax, phone, and VCR available.

The tradition of paying to stay in a private home—with breakfast included in the overnight lodging rate—was revived in time to save wonderful old houses, schools, churches, and barns all over the country from the wrecking ball or commercial development.

Central Pennsylvania
_____ Reservation Service _____

Rest & Repast Bed & Breakfast Reservation Service
P.O. Box 126, Pine Grove Mills, PA 16868

Phone: 814/238-1484, Monday–Friday 8:30– 11:30 a.m. Answering machine at other times. Open peak Penn State weekends. Closed December 15–January 15.

Listings: 60. Four are inns. Four are cottages or guest houses on hosts' property. Most are private residences. Some available April–November only. Located in Centre, Blair, Huntington, and Clearfield counties—in and around Aaronsburg, Bellefonte, Boalsburg, Clearfield, Centre Hall, McAlevy's Fort, Pine Grove Mills, State College, Spruce Creek, Tyrone (near famous Grier private girls' school).

Reservations: One week's advance notice usually needed. For big weekends, five months' advance notice recommended.

Rates: $40–$50 single, when available. $40–$80 double. Peak weekends $50–$85. $15 surcharge on peak weekends for one-night stay, where permitted. Family and weekly rates. Deposit of $25 per night required except for peak weekends, when $50 per room per night is required. All cancellations subject to $25 processing fee. Given at least 7 days' notice, balance of deposit is refunded; for peak weekends, at least 14 days' notice required.

Linda Feltman and Brent Peters started the reservation service in 1982 to provide needed lodging during peak times in the Penn State area. Because travelers also come for history, culture, and recreation, the service has become active year round. More than 50 percent of the hosts have been on the roster for more than two years. "More than 90 percent attend our summer ice-cream social. Some have received a plaque acknowledging 10 years of football weekend hosting. They are a bunch of friendly folks, that's for sure!"

Plus: Some B&Bs available for up to 14 days. For short-term (4–20 days) housing in private apartments in hosts' homes, breakfast may or may not be included.

Central and Western
_____ Pennsylvania B&Bs _____

Ponda-Rowland Bed & Breakfast Inn

Beaumont, PA   717/639-3245
Mailing address: RR 1, Box 349   800/854-3286
Dallas, PA 18612-9604   fax 717/639-5531

Hosts: Jeanette and Cliff Rowland
Location: Serene. On 129 acres (with wildlife sanctuary and incredible night skies) "where the pavement ends" in the Endless Mountain region. Four hours from Washington, D.C.; 3 from New York City, 2½ from Philadelphia. Ten minutes from Wilkes-Barre.
Open: Year round. Two-day minimum Memorial Day–Labor Day, on holiday weekends, Christmas, New Year's.

Rates: First floor—$75 king/twins and twin; $65 double, bunk beds, youth bed; $85 king/twins and youth bed/settee. Second floor—$70 king/twins, $65 double bed. $30 one-night surcharge on holiday weekends and in October. $15 child in room; crib free. $30 third adult. Amex, Discover, MC, Visa.
♥ ♨ ♣ ♦ ✄

Found—by families, and by drummers who played from different points on the mountain. By artists, photographers, business travelers, antiquers, nature and animal lovers, a group on a yoga retreat, and romantics too. The Rowlands moved to this former dairy farm from New Jersey, where they had hosted paying guests in an 18-room antiques-filled house, in 1988. That's when Cliff retired from his positions in the U.S. Postal Service (preceded by many years in labor relations with Grace Line). Here, trails were cut. On the largest of six developed ponds an open pavilion was built for canoeists, picnickers, "fisherpeople," and skaters. A changing house was built for swimmers who use the sandy beach, diving board, and slide at another pond. The "simple 150-year-old farmhouse" was changed by the Rowlands' son, a timber-frame builder, to a picture-perfect setting—with solid oak beams, some wood ceilings, and plank walls—for the museumlike collection of Colonial antiques. Deer appear at dusk for feeding. There are mallards, great blue heron, doves, swans, partridge, geese, feeding stations. A treasure.

In residence: Matt, a greyhound; Beau, a white shepherd; Sam, a retriever. At last count—sheep, horses, foals; one cat, a big turkey, a ferret, a potbellied pig, a rabbit; some chickens.
Bed and bath: Five carpeted rooms, all private shower baths. First floor—room with king/twins option and one twin bed and room with king/twins option plus youth bed (each room has gas fireplace and shower bath). Both rooms connected by center room that has a double bed, bunk beds, and a youth bed; also microwave, sitting area, tub/hand-held shower bath. Crib available. Second floor—two rooms with king/twins option, one with double bed.
Breakfast: Guests' choice of hour. Eggs with bacon, sausage, or ham; casseroles; or pan (corn) cakes—a specialty. Juices, fruit platter, homemade

and English muffins, jellies. Special diets and vegetarians accommodated. In candlelit dining room, on porch, in great room, or on patio.
Plus: Fireplaced great room. Bedroom ceiling fans. Refreshments. Binoculars. Volleyball. Horseshoes. Toboggan. Cross-country skiing. Off-site horseback riding arranged. Pony rides ($15). Hayrides—horse-drawn ($35) or by antique tractor (free). Explorers: bring boots or old shoes.

> From Pennsylvania: "... *a place apart, created of warm hearts and gentle spirit. If there is a five-star B&B designation, we give Ponda-Rowland six!*" From New Jersey: "*Even an antique high chair for our little one, baby silverware, a special place mat. ... Enjoyed canoeing on the pond and the nature walk where we encountered several deer.*" From New York: "*Went for one day and stayed for four. ... Have been back two times within two months! ... Rooms are lovely, food delightful, Rowlands are great, antiques a pleasure to peruse ... plenty to do.*"

The Bechtel Mansion Inn   717/259-7760
400 West King Street, East Berlin, PA 17316   800/331-1108

Hosts: Charles and Mariam Bechtel; Ruth Spangler, innkeeper
Location: In Pennsylvania Dutch country. In the center of East Berlin on Route 234. Near fine restaurants, antiques shops, wineries, major weaving center. Eighteen miles east of Gettysburg; 40 west of Lancaster; 100 from Washington, D.C., and Philadelphia; 58 from Baltimore.
Open: Year round. Two-night min-imum on holiday weekends and all of October.
Rates: April–November $65–$115 single, $105–$115 double. December–March $65–$100 single, $75–$100 double. Suites $135 and $145 year round. $20 rollaway. All rates plus 7 percent service charge. Amex, Diners, Discover, MC, Visa.
♥ ♨ ♣ ♦ ✕ ✂

For honeymooners and anniversary couples, for architecture and history buffs, for arts and crafts–oriented travelers, and for skiers too, here's a magnificent 28-room 1897 Queen Anne Victorian that the Bechtels have restored and furnished with museum-quality antiques. The mansion has original etched glass windows, gold leaf wallpaper, brass chandeliers, beautiful woodwork, and handwoven Chinese carpets. On the National Register of Historic Places, it is also in a National Historic District that includes 18th-century homes, a restored gristmill, an 18th-century school, an 1820 log house, and shops located in period buildings.

Charles's grandparents and great-grandparents were Virginia innkeepers. His father grew up in a Pennsylvania Dutch family here in East Berlin. Charles has led Smithsonian groups on walking tours and spearheaded the 40-mile Historic Conewago Tour, which includes German farmland, Victorian New Oxford, and early American East Berlin. Ruth, an area resident, is also quite knowledgeable about the Amish, Brethren, and local history.

The well-traveled Bechtels are "sometimes" weekend hosts. Charles is a consultant who retired from Bell Atlantic managership in 1994. Mariam, a member of Senator Robert Dole's staff, is from Kansas.

Bed and bath: Nine rooms. All private baths; some tub/shower, some with shower only. Private parlor in first- and second-floor suites. Other rooms are

(Please turn page.)

on second floor. Twin, double, and queen beds; rollaway and portacrib available.

Breakfast: 8:30–9:30. Fruit ambrosia; orange juice; egg dishes or French toast; coffee cake or home-baked biscuits, muffins, or breads; coffee or tea. Served family style.

Plus: Air conditioning in all guest areas. Beverages. Porches. Living room with oak sliding shutters. Breakfast room (original cooking kitchen) with exhibits by local artists. For sale in carriage house shop—German nutcrackers and smokers, handmade Amish-made children's and doll furniture.

Baladerry Inn   717/337-1342
40 Hospital Road, Gettysburg, PA 17325

Hosts: Tom and Caryl O'Gara
Location: On four secluded acres, at the edge of Gettysburg Battlefield National Park. Two miles south of the park's visitor center, restaurants, and town. Near golf courses, skiing, antiquing, orchards, summer stock, bike routes.
Open: Year round. Two-night minimum on holidays or special events.
Rates: $78–$95. Singles $10 less. Amex, Diners, MC, Visa.
♥ ♣ ✕

One guest expressed appreciation for lodging recommendations for her horse! Others wrote about the snow-cleared car, the directions to romantic sunset views, the family feeling, and the attention to detail in this traditionally furnished 1812 brick house. The gathering place is the 1977 two-storied great room with wood stove, library, piano, and dining area. The recently converted carriage house offers a conference room with gas fireplace, sun porch, and brick patio. On the grounds are a tennis court and a gazebo. Tom, who worked in the insurance industry, and Caryl, who was with a New Jersey actuarial firm, are the parents of six grown children. With fond memories of their own extensive B&B travels, they purchased this historic property in 1991. The name? Tom remembers his mother talking about her birthplace, Ballaghadereen, Ireland. "She always pronounced it 'Baladerry Inn'!"

Bed and bath: Eight carpeted rooms, all private baths. Main inn—first floor, two queen-bedded rooms with shower baths. Second floor, one queen-bedded room with shower and Jacuzzi tub; one room with two extra-long twin beds/king option, shower bath. Carriage house (converted in 1994)—four rooms, each with queen bed, shower bath; two are on first floor with French doors to brick patio. Gas fireplace in second-floor rooms.

Breakfast: 8–10. Juice. Fresh fruit. Hot and cold cereals. Entree possibilities include poached eggs with bacon or pancakes with sausage. Served at individual tables in great room.

Plus: Air conditioning throughout; five separate zones. Fireplaced living room. Individual heat thermostats. Tennis racquets. Guest refrigerator. Fresh flowers. Spacious brick terrace with wisteria arbor.

---

*D*id you hear about the salesman who left a B&B breakfast
with five good leads?

The Brafferton Inn
717/337-3423
44 York Street, Gettysburg, PA 17325

Hosts: Jane and Sam Back
Location: In downtown Gettysburg, within walking distance of Battlefield, shops, restaurants, college, and theater. Fifteen minutes to Liberty ski area.
Open: Year round. Two-night minimum on holiday weekends and college events.
Rates: $70–$85 single, $80–$95 double. $100–$125 suites. $10 extra person. MC, Visa.
🏠 ❀ ♦ ✈ ✁

When the "Today" TV crew was in town to record the sunrise on the Battlefield, they stayed in this National Register building, which is flanked by a stained glass shop and a bookstore. This B&B with magnificent copies of 18th-century stencils on whitewashed walls consists of the original 1786 stone house (Gettysburg's first residence) and, across the skylit atrium, an 1860 brick addition. Furnishings include 200-year-old family heirlooms and portraits, wing chairs, and brass and Colonial beds.

Following renovations and the addition of more baths, the Backs opened in 1993—during the blizzard of the century! The lifelong Connecticut residents were preparatory school administrators at Choate Rosemary Hall. Their friendship with the former owners, the Agards (page 296), led to this midlife career change "in an area beautiful beyond compare, where the lifestyle is laid back. . . . For us and our guests, it feels like home."

Foreign language spoken: French.
Bed and bath: Ten air-conditioned rooms; vary in size from The Nook to large third-floor beamed cathedral-ceilinged suite. Queen, double, or twin beds. All private baths. Some tub/shower baths, some shower only; most are en suite, three are detached.
Breakfast: Usually 8–9. Peaches and cream French toast or apple cinnamon pancakes. Orange juice. Fresh fruit. Hot beverages. Served in the dining room, which features a painted primitve mural of 18 Gettysburg historic buildings.
Plus: Air-conditioned guest rooms; two with TV. Secured bicycle storage. Afternoon beverages. Intimate garden and deck. Arrangements for high tea in farmhouse ten miles from here. Suggestions for pottery, woodworking, and antiques shops.

> From Pennsylvania: *"Comfortable and inviting—the perfect balance of traditional and convenient. The Backs were the perfect balance of discreet and welcoming. . . . Breakfast was delicious. Helped plan our day . . . arranged the most romantic dinner!"*

Keystone Inn
717/337-3888
231 Hanover Street, Gettysburg, PA 17325

Hosts: Wilmer and Doris Martin
Location: Residential. Two blocks to Battlefield, five to Lincoln Square. Nine miles to Ski Liberty.
Open: Year round. Two-night minimum on holidays and special events.
Rates: $59 shared bath; $75 private. Suite $100. Singles $5 less. $15 rollaway. Weekday package rates (four nights for price of three) available. MC, Visa.
♥ 🏠 ❀ ✈ ✁

(Please turn page.)

One guest room is called "Grandpa's." Another, "Aunt Fay's." Intentionally, this is your home away from home, with "some fine antiques, but most are comfortable and practical." The three-storied brick house, built in 1913 by a furniture maker, has a wide, columned, wicker-furnished porch, much natural wood, and a grand chestnut staircase. Doris, who had worked in nursing for many years, thought it "cried B&B" in 1987, when Wilmer, an owner/operator of a farm in western New York for 20 years, accepted a job as crop farmer for a major operation here. Since the Martins converted the property back from five apartments, they have added a suite with complete kitchen and private phone.

Bed and bath: Five rooms. On third floor—room with king/twins option and room with brass queen bed each have private en-suite tub/shower bath. Two rooms, each with antique double bed, share hall bath with claw-footed tub and shower. On second floor—suite with antique hand-carved oak queen bed, full bath, living/dining room with queen sleep sofa, TV, private phone, full kitchen complete with popcorn popper and popcorn. Rollaway available. **Breakfast:** 7–9:30. Choose from a full menu with juice, oatmeal or raisin muffins, entree—cinnamon-apple or blueberry pancakes, waffles, French toast, creamed eggs and toast; scrapple, ham, bacon, or sausage. Coffee, tea, milk. **Plus:** Air conditioning in rooms. Upright piano. Afternoon coffee, tea, lemonade. A before-and-after restoration photo album.

> From Arizona: *"What a wonderful experience! We could feel the warmth and friendliness everywhere . . . pleasant surprise to be able to make selections for the marvelous breakfast."* From California: *"Comfortable, clean (spotless) . . . quiet."*

Mulberry Farm Bed & Breakfast 717/334-5827
616 Flohrs Church Road, Biglerville, PA 17307-9556

Hosts: Mimi and Jim Agard
Location: In peaceful apple orchard country "exceptional for jogging, bicycling and walking." House, close to road, has more than three acres of lawn; spectacular views of adjacent farm, fields, and, to the east, an early Mennonite cemetery. Near-

by church with chimes (full tunefest at 6 p.m.). Eight minutes from Gettysburg. Half mile to fine dining.
Open: Year round.
Rates: $95 per room. $10 third person. MC, Visa.
♯ ♦ ✗ ✁

And for his tenth gorgeous restoration (in 1994), Jim, studio art professor at Gettysburg College, chose this 1817 brick Georgian Colonial with seven fireplaces, a big beautiful bank barn, five acres with established perennial gardens and, yes, mulberry trees. Stenciling is on walls and floor coverings. Floors are satin pine. Baskets, paintings, a mask and hat collection, and pewter accent country antiques. And then there's Mimi, primary innkeeeper, who was in public relations at CBS before she and Jim created the Brafferton Inn in Gettysburg. Now that their youngest of five is in college, they have located at this "retreat that has an absolutely breathtaking walk from our door past ponds, stream, unique barns, beef cattle, and orchards." In addition to suggesting ways to experience Gettysburg, they offer directions to their own favorite antiques haunts, crafts centers, and summer theaters.

In residence: Quincy, "our sweet seven-year-old white poodle."
Bed and bath: Four air-conditioned rooms; all private baths. On third floor, two large rooms, each with slanted ceilings, queen bed (one is handmade), sofa (one is a sleep sofa), tub/shower bath. On second floor, suite with canopied queen bed, shower bath, sitting room, and small library with wood-burning fireplace. In cottage, queen bed, shower bath, private deck.
Breakfast: Entree might be waffles with applesauce or French toast with mulberries (in season). Served in candlelit dining room or on brick terrace. Or, by request, breakfast in bed.
Plus: Living room/library with two fireplaces and entertainment center. Video collection with Ted Turner's "Gettysburg"; Jim was an extra. Information about the Agards' unhosted Caribbean house.

Beechmont Inn
315 Broadway, Hanover, PA 17331

717/632-3013
800/553-7009

Hosts: Susan and William Day
Location: On a tree-lined residential street. Near intersection of Routes 194, 94, and 116; 15 minutes east of Gettysburg Battlefield; 45 from Baltimore. Near wineries, restaurants, farmers' market, state park, skiing, antiques shops, and outlet shopping. Two hours from Washington and Philadelphia.

Open: Year round. Two-night minimum for suites on weekends.
Rates: Per room, $80–$95. Suites $115 with kitchenette; $115 with fireplace; $135 with fireplace and whirlpool. Getaway, golf, and horse-and-carriage-ride weekend packages. Amex, Discover, MC, Visa.
♥ ♣ ♦ ✦

From England: *"Warm and welcoming. We stayed one night on the way to visit friends. We enjoyed it so much that we stayed for three nights on the way back."* From Pennsylvania: *"Close attention to detail. Friendly. Great breakfast. It's marvelous!"* From Washington, D.C. *"Great getaway."* From Ohio: *"I loved it. . . . The inn is gorgeous. . . . Sue helped me into my Civil War gown . . . fastening the corset and tying my shoes."*

"This elegant but comfortable home, decorated in Federal period colors and furnishings, is a great place to unwind. Gardens and even an old-fashioned glider swing are in the landscaped courtyard. It appeals to romantics. Some come to visit Gettysburg or for antiquing. Business guests return as tourists. For many years we lived just a block away and I worked here—sometimes as substitute innkeeper—with the Hormel family who created this B&B in 1986. When, in 1994, they decided to sell, I said, 'Wait until I speak to my husband!' Now it is my dream come true." Susan is a former tax preparer. Bill operates and monitors quarry equipment.

In residence: Sons Eric and Jeremy, in their twenties.
Bed and bath: Seven rooms (three are large queen-bedded suites) with queen or double bed; all private baths. Of the two first-floor suites, one has a fireplace; one, a fireplace and whirlpool. Second-floor rooms, including

(Please turn page.)

fireplaced suite with kitchenette and balcony, are reached by a wide spiral staircase. Extra bed in some rooms.

Breakfast: Memorable. Monday–Saturday at 8, Sundays at 9. Could be apricot puff pancakes with bacon, shirred eggs in bread basket with pumpkin souffle, or herbed cheese tart with corn souffle. French country eggs. Freshly baked muffins or sweet breads. Fruit, coffee, teas, juice. York County Fair prizewinning homemade granola. In dining room, outside under the trumpet vine trellis, or in bed.

Plus: Afternoon and evening refreshments. Air-conditioned guest and common rooms. Formal parlor and library. Wicker-furnished back porch. Vine-covered veranda. Flagstone patio with park bench under a 130-year-old magnolia tree. Off-street parking.

Conewago House

New Oxford, PA

Location: Gorgeous. On a ridge, on ½ mile of river frontage. Eight miles east of Gettysburg. Within 20 minutes of Ski Liberty and Ski Roundtop. Close to Caledonia State Park. "Great area for history, antiquing, the outdoors, Amish country." Fifty-eight miles from Baltimore Harbor, 90 minutes from D.C. Beltway.
Reservations: Year round through Guesthouses, page 226. Two-night minimum for guest house accommodations.
Rates: $95. Second-floor riverview room $115, third-floor suite $135; whole house $1,800 per week. Guest house $200 (two to four people), two-night minimum; $1,200 per week.
♥ ♣ ◀ ✗ ⅓

One of a kind. When, in 1989, the prominent Baltimore architect finished redoing the National Register property, "B&B just seemed a natural outgrowth." Maples arch over the long driveway of this 1908 Arts and Crafts brown Shingle Style house. A wonderful Palladian window frames the stairway. In the stone-fireplaced living room, and in the dining room too, there is 6-foot-high wainscoting. Furnishings include pottery collections, antiques, some 1940s and '50s collectibles, and some ultramodern pieces. A large glass sun room looks onto the river. The entire tall-ceilinged guest house, formerly the stables, now has cedar walls, ceilings, and floors. Enormous glass garage doors give a view of the 50-by-25-foot brick swimming pool—what a setting—on a two-acre landscaped "island" surrounded by old sugar maples. From here you can see the rustic Adirondack-style gazebo up on a knoll. On most weekends the owner/architect is in residence and happy to give tours of his private museum, which has one of the country's largest collections of contemporary artist-designed furniture. If this all sounds familiar, you have been reading *Mid-Atlantic Country, Baltimore* magazine, the *Baltimore Sun,* or *Country Home.*

In residence: Mighty Dog, a Jack Russell terrier. On weekends, Aalto, a cocker/Gordon setter mix. ("Everyone wants to buy one.")
Bed and bath: Three rooms and one suite in main house. Two bedrooms in guest house. Luxurious baths. Main house: on second floor, one huge riverview room (used to be two) with queen bed, elaborate bath with separate area for each fixture. Room with queen bed, full bath. Room with twin bed,

shared full bath. Third-floor suite has queen-bedded room, large living room, bath with tub and shower. Guest house: two second-floor rooms, each with queen bed, large vanity. Downstairs, full bath, large dining room/sitting room, and small full kitchen.

Breakfast: Self-serve continental with bagels, muffins, breads, juices, cheeses, jams, coffee, tea.

Plus: Central air conditioning. Laundry in each building. Screened porch off huge kitchen of main house. Use of canoe and life vest. Ice skating when river freezes.

Hickory Bridge Farm   717/642-5261

96 Hickory Bridge Road, Orrtanna, PA 17353

Hosts: Nancy Jean Hammett and Mary Lynn Martin

Location: Quiet. On 100 acres in Appalachian Mountain foothills. Trout fishing (bring license) in meandering stream right here. Eight miles west of Gettysburg, 60 to Baltimore. Five miles to Ski Liberty.

Open: Year round. Closed Christmas–New Year's. Two-night minimum on weekends; exception when one-night opening is available one week prior to date requested. Reservations required. (Restaurant open to public weekends, to private groups weekdays; see below.)

Rates: Monday–Thursday: $79 cottage; in farmhouse, $79 room with private bath, $110 (three people) or $135 (four people) two rooms with one bath; $150 (five people) or $195 (six people) three rooms with two baths. Weekends: $89 cottage; $89 one farmhouse room with private bath; $195 (five people) or $225 (six people) three rooms, two baths. Crib $10. MC, Visa.
♥ ❖ ✈

This well-known, rather unusual B&B evolved from Mrs. Hammett's research of the area during the 1960s. When she found that a franchise was going to buy an old stagecoach stop, the family bought and restored it as an inn. In 1977 they sold that property and bought Hickory Bridge—with B&B in the farmhouse (great for families) and in the cottages on the wooded hill. In the restaurant, located in the old barn across the street from the farmhouse, they displayed many farm-related antiques and began their tradition of farm-style meals with a set menu.

Daughter Mary Lynn, in college then, has become restaurant manager. Her children have 4-H projects on the property, and her husband farms. Jeans-clad dad, "a real country doctor" (for more than 40 years) is around. Mom Hammett still cooks breakfasts and greets "a long list of friends and friends of friends."

Bed and bath: Seven air-conditioned rooms. In farmhouse, private shower bath for one room with queen bed. One room with queen and one with a double bed share a full bath. Four country-decorated cottages, each with a queen or two double beds, private shower bath, working Franklin fireplace.

Breakfast: 8:30–9. Farm style. Pancakes, sausage, eggs, bacon, homegrown fruits, homemade jams, apple butter, and potato bread. In farmhouse dining room or on deck.

Plus: Fireplaced farmhouse living room. Porches. Use of bicycles. On the farm—covered bridge over stream; swing set; antique fire engine. Next to

(Please turn page.)

washhouse, a country store/museum that has jams and penny candy for sale, enormous collection of items—from boots and lace to tobacco bags and cash register—for display. Dinner (bring your own wine): Friday–Saturday dinner starts at 5, last seating at 8; Sunday dinner 12–3; $16.95 per person.

Dogwood House at Spoutwood Farm

RD 3, Box 66, Glen Rock, PA 17327   717/235-6610

Hosts: Rob and Lucy Wood
Location: Enchanting. In York County on Maryland/Pennsylvania line. On 26 acres with two streams, pastures with sheep and cows, herb and flower gardens. Close to restaurants (one gives culinary workshops here), wineries, antiques shops, state park, golf courses. Forty-five minutes north of Baltimore; 25 minutes to York; 45 minutes to Gettysburg or Lancaster.
Open: Year round.
Rates: $70 first night. $60 each additional night. $5–$20 each additional person. MC, Visa.
♥ ⚥ ✗ ⚰

From Virginia: *"As close to heaven as I have ever been . . . aroma of herbs encircled us, as did the quiet friendliness of Rob Wood. . . . Gathered fresh herbs in one of their baskets, made a wreath . . . read poetry in the porch rocker . . . soaked in the view of antebellum house and farm. . . . We reveled in the delicious privacy of the small cottage. . . . Fresh whole-grain muffins and breads delivered while we were at dinner. . . . Rob and Lucy's reverence for 'every seed-bearing plant' is evident . . . tasteful and simple furnishings . . . I could have stayed all year!"*

One Canadian guest enrolled for a single workshop and then took three—in one day. A German couple brought pieces of the Berlin wall. Many come for the "the sense of peace amidst nature" on the farm that Rob and Lucy bought in 1983 when they lived in Baltimore and wanted a garden. Their herb gardens, featured in *Country Home,* are the basis for workshops—everything from growing to storytelling, from wreath-making to culinary and medicinal uses. "Visiting time (with guests) is usually upon arrival—and sometimes in the morning."

Rob is a Yale art history major who was in the Peace Corps in India before becoming an educator and then arts coordinator (for the Council on Aging). Lucy is a pastoral counselor and Towson State University professor of art. They have written two editions of *The Art of Dried Flowers.*

In residence: McKeever and St. Lucie are thoroughbreds. Three cats. Pip, "a ragamuffin eight-pound rascal and self-appointed CEO of Spoutwood Farm, heads a canine brigade of five dogs."
Bed and bath: The guest cottage sleeps up to five persons of the same party. Two air-conditioned bedrooms—large one with double bed; small room has "hired-hand" bed for one. Fold-out futon for two in dramatic L-shaped living area with soaring ceiling. Full bath. Well-equipped kitchen.
Breakfast: "Bountiful breakfast basket of country baked breads, fresh country eggs, several kinds of locally grown fruit, granolas, milk, orange juice, jam, butter, honey, and fresh cream." All brought to cottage night before.
Plus: On-premises shop, open Wednesday–Saturday, "whenever, for guests."

Welsh Run Inn Bed and Breakfast

11299 Welsh Run Road, Greencastle, PA 17225   **717/328-9506**

Hosts: Bob and Ellie Neff
Location: Quiet. Rural—with silos, pastures, farmhouses, historic steepled church, and panoramic views Tuscarora Mountain range and ski runs. Five miles to Mercersburg (boyhood home of James Buchanan), seven to Whitetail ski resort, eight to Greencastle Greens Golf Course. Ten minutes to Routes I-81 and I-70.
Open: Year round.
Rates: $65 queen. $55 double bed. $60 twin beds. $10 third person. Amex, MC, Visa.
⚓ 🛏 ⁂ ♦ ✈

"We're home!" announce the skiers as they return from the slopes—and then as they return again in the summer. There's privacy, if you wish, but often there's interesting conversation with foreign guests about similarities and differences. Or the kitchen table becomes the game room. Or Ellie, by request, gives a minilesson in stenciling.

Ellie was a floral designer and shop owner and Bob worked in management and sales before they moved in 1993 to this Victorian farmhouse. It has oak and chestnut woodwork and pocket doors. Furnishings are traditional—with family pieces from Pennsylvania and New England. The garden thrives with fruits and vegetables that are savored all year round at the memorable candlelit breakfasts. Guests can tell that the Neffs, parents of seven grown children, enjoy doing what they do.

In residence: "Mandy is our friendly and entertaining springer spaniel."
Bed and bath: Three second-floor rooms. Room with queen bed, en-suite shower bath. Large room with two twin beds shares a tub/shower bath with smaller room that has canopied Victorian double bed.
Breakfast: Usually 7:30–9. Fresh fruit. Juices. Homemade rolls, breads, preserves, and jellies. Chef's choice—waffles, pancakes, egg dishes, or casserole; sausages or bacon. Served on fine china and crystal in hand-stenciled Colonial dining room. Classical music.
Plus: Spontaneous snacks. Flannel sheets. TV, VCR, games, puzzles, books. Open wraparound porch. Directions to long covered bridge and beautiful state park. Reservations made at a "wonderful little pub with fantastic food."

> From New Hampshire: *"Tastefully furnished inn . . . warm, caring innkeepers . . . share recipes . . . feel as if we are visiting family."*

Curtinview

Howard, PA

Location: Secluded. On 20 wooded acres. Up a gravel lane, high on a hill overlooking historic village. Six miles north of Bellefonte. Within walking distance of Curtin Village. Two miles off I-80, exit 23, Milesburg. Twenty-five minutes to Penn State.
Reservations: Year round through Rest & Repast, page 291. Two-night minimum on major events weekends.
Rates: $60–$75 per room. Suite $75 for two, $130 for four. $15 one-night surcharge per room on peak weekends. $25 sofa bed if entire suite is booked by one party. $15 rollaway.
♥ 🛏 ⁂ ✈ ⤢

(Please turn page.)

A complete turnabout by the couple who made mid-1980s headlines—"Operatic Soprano Gets Practice Raising Roof"—when they rebuilt a Bellefonte Victorian home that was, like this house, high on a hill. In 1989 the consulting engineer (who is also known for the award-winning 1947 Stinson fabric-covered plane that he restored) and his wife, a well-known performer/music teacher, built this brand-new log home. In 1990 they planted a vineyard,now they make their own wine. Guests enjoy the wide front deck overlooking the Allegheny foothills and Curtin Village, the community with a dominating mansion built by Richard Curtin of iron industry fame. In the evening you may see deer, bear, or other wildlife at this quiet getaway.

In residence: "Our geriatric pets": two cats, Wooly and Tabatha, and two dogs, cocker spaniel Velvet and Brittany Duchess.
Bed and bath: On private second-floor loft, two cathedral-ceilinged rooms—one with an antique spool double bed and one with two twin beds; a common sitting area with TV and, if entire suite booked by one party, a double sofa bed. One tub/shower bath. Rollaway available. Ground-level suite—private entrance, bedroom with queen water bed, queen sofa bed in living room, private hall shower bath.
Breakfast: 7–9. Juice, fresh fruit, yogurt, cereal, muffins or French toast, coffee and tea.
Plus: Air conditioning and ceiling fans in guest rooms. Welcoming beverage. Hiking and cross-country skiing right here and/or in nearby state parklands. In-ground 20-by-40-foot pool surrounded by wooden decks.

Webb Farm Bed & Breakfast　717/725-3591

RR 1, Box 441, Spruce Run Road, Loganton, PA 17747

Hosts: Bud Webb and Sharon Maurer
Location: Quiet. Three miles from exit 27, I-80. On top of Central Pennsylvania mountains. "A great place for hunting." Within an hour's drive of Penn State, Williamsport (home of the Little League Museum), Woolrich Outlet Store and Bald Eagle Outlet Mall; 14 miles to Ravensburg State Park.
Open: Year round.
Rates: Shared bath $45 double, $35 single. Private bath $65 double, $55 single. $10 crib.
🛏 ⛵ ✈ ✂

"Bed and breakfast is something we had thought about. In 1991, with our children grown and married, we bought this large 1940s two-storied frame house that just seemed perfect. It's located on the Old Florida Fruit Farm, named for a man from Florida who planted 100 acres of apple trees more than 100 years ago. It's surrounded by a white fence enclosing 1½ acres. Outside the fence are fields of grain and woodlands. Furnishings are nothing fancy, but they are comfortable. There's a double waterfall hidden atop the mountain about a half mile from here. And we tell guests about the covered bridge at Logan Mills."

Bud is a fertilizer dealer and farmer. Sharon is an office clerk and greenhouse operator.

Bed and bath: Four second-floor corner rooms overlook fields and old apple trees. Two rooms, each with two double beds, share a hall shower/tub

bath. One room has king bed, private shower bath. One has a queen bed and a queen water bed, private shower bath. Crib available.
Breakfast: At 7. Orange or tomato juice. Fruit salad. Bananas and cold cereal. Fruit-of-the-season muffins. Freshly brewed coffee. Buffet style in dining room.
Plus: Window fans. Refreshments. Guest kitchenette. Large outdoor deck. Glasses, ice bucket, ice. TV in living room.

From Illinois: *"Warm hospitality . . . immaculately clean . . . nicely prepared and good food."* From Virginia: *"Location in mountains is beautiful. . . . We actually saw a group of deer just across the street from the Webb's home."* From Pennsylvania: *"Even in summer, we used a light sheet blanket. . . . Spring was beautiful with apple blossoms. . . . Enjoyed the countryside and walking along the country road."*

Victorian Manor Inn   717/692-3511
312 Market Street, Millersburg, PA 17061

Hosts: Donald and Suzanne Wingard
Location: On Route 147, a tree-lined street in a small town "with streets to stroll"; 28 miles north of Harrisburg. One block from Market Square Park, bandstand, shops, restaurants. Walk to historic Millers-burg Ferry (runs April–October) and riverfront park on Susquehanna River.
Open: Year round.
Rates: $60 shared bath. $70 private bath. $25 third person. Singles $10 less. Amex, MC, Visa.
♥ ♣ ✈

From Pennsylvania: *"Delightful . . . stayed while on a golfing trip . . . felt so welcomed . . . great food . . . everywhere something interesting to look at."* From New York: *"Like stepping back in time . . . decor is breathtaking . . . immaculate."* From Virginia: *"Invited exploration and explore we did! . . . wandered from room to room and admired all the treasures . . . gourmet breakfasts. . . . We manage a B&B ourselves; this is one of our absolute favorites."*

Victoriana through and through—with lamps, lace, shawls, authentic furnishings including high-board beds and armoires, china, prints, dolls, bows, claw-footed tubs, plants, wallcoverings . . . all in this Second Empire mansard-roofed brick house just across the street from where Sue grew up. With inspiration from annual visits to Cape May, Sue and Skip, an analyst who commutes to Harrisburg, spent four years restoring before they opened in 1990. Their courtyard is an attraction for camera-carrying tourists, who sometimes ask if they may enter for a better view of the brick walk that borders a wicker-filled porch on the way to garden, shade trees, and a latticed gazebo with hanging plants.

Bed and bath: Three air-conditioned second-floor rooms, all with ceiling fans, antique beds. Two rooms share a tub/shower bath. Suite has sitting room with daybed, private tub/shower bath with reproduction pull-chain water closet, private wicker-furnished porch overlooking courtyard.
Breakfast: 7–9. Fresh fruit. Juice. Sometimes, cold soup. French toast, frittata, souffle, or waffles. Homemade muffins. Breakfast desserts. Served in dining room or on the patio.

(Please turn page.)

Plus: Tea, coffee, and baked goodies. Chocolates. Robes. Toiletries. Fresh fruit. Coins for parking meters in front. Elaborate Christmas decorations.

The Carriage House at Stonegate

RD 1, Box 11A, Montoursville, PA 17754   717/433-4340
                                                fax 717/433-4563

Hosts: Harold and Dena Mesaris
Location: On 30 wooded acres along Mill Creek banks. On Route 87, a minute from I-180. Within 30 minutes of Lycoming, Bucknell, and Bloomsburg. Six miles east of Williamsport; two miles from Williamsport/Lycoming County airport. Close to new performing arts center, hiking, fishing, hunting, Crystal Lake Cross-Country Ski Center.
Open: Year round.
Rates: $50 one room, $70 two rooms. $10 rollaway.
♥ ♯ ⬛ ♣ ♦

> From Virginia: *"Private, comfortable, and roomy. . . . Breakfast was great. . . .woods a miniadventure at every turn. . . . Gracious . . . helpful with area information."*

A haven at the end of the road—even in a winter's storm! Your own home away from home, a 1,400-square-foot getaway, is in a converted carriage house located just 30 yards from the main house, one of the oldest farmhouses in the lower Loyasock Creek Valley. Remodeled in 1985, the two-storied B&B has wide-board floors, hand-hewn beams, some country antiques, and some modern pieces. Harold and Dena usually book one party—could be a couple or up to 10 guests (for a wedding)—at a time.

If you'd like, there are opportunities to meet the family—Harold, a pilot and aircraft accident investigator; Dena, a teacher who is active in the community; their grown daughters; and all the farm animals. For a little history, the hosts will tell you about the early valley settlement. Lots of guests follow Harold's self-guided tour to several state parks (one has 20 waterfalls) and three covered bridges.

In residence: In main house, teenagers—Allison, Meghan, Darcey, and Judd. One Newfoundland, several Persian cats, two ducks, three geese, eight chickens—all with names.
Foreign languages spoken: Some Spanish and German.
Bed and bath: Two second-level rooms—one with a double bed and one with a four-poster queen bed—share a full and a half bath. Rollaway and crib available.
Breakfast: 7:30–10. Homemade muffins. French toast, cheese/bacon/potato quiche, or ham-and-cheese pudding. Fruit, juice, coffee, tea. Harold cooks breakfast and brings it to you in a basket.
Plus: On first floor, large sitting room with cable TV, dining area, fully equipped kitchen, refrigerator stocked with snacks. Window and floor fans in summer. Babysitting. Swing set. Electric blankets. Accessible old logging roads for "moderately difficult exercise." Record for wildlife seen by early-morning walkers: six turkeys, three deer, and several bears.

The Bodine House 717/546-8949

307 South Main Street, Muncy, PA 17756

Hosts: David and Marie Louise Smith
Location: On a tree-lined street in a National Historic District, three blocks from center of Muncy. Ten minutes from I-80 and U.S. Route 15. Bucknell University and the city of Williamsport 15 minutes away. Within 30 minutes of sports, wineries, two state parks in Endless Mountains, summer theater.
Open: Year round.
Rates: Per room. $50 double bed. $60 canopied double bed. $65 two single beds, fireplace. Singles $5 less. $15 rollaway.
♣ ✈ ⊬

From Maryland: *"Beautifully kept and elegant home in a lovely small town. . . . We enjoyed walking . . . and coming back to the candlelit sitting room for refreshments."*

Colonial Homes, in a glorious four-page spread, pictured this National Register restored Federal townhouse, which was occupied by the same family for about 165 years. It has been home to the Smiths since 1978, when they moved from Washington, D.C., for a quieter pace. They had always admired this small town as they drove through on their way to visit relatives. Throughout, there are 18th- and 19th-century antiques. The fireplaced living room, lit by candles and furnished as a typical Philadelphia townhouse in Marie Louise's home city, includes a baby grand piano that has been enjoyed by several talented guests. A portrait, painted by a German itinerant artist, is of the hostess's great-great-grandmother at about age 90. A dining room bureau was David's great-grandmother's.

In Washington, David was a marketing manager; here he is host/chef/gift and picture-framing shop owner. Marie Louise is business manager in a physician's office.

Bed and bath: Four second-floor rooms, each with individual heat control and air conditioner. All private baths. Two rooms with canopied double bed, one with tub and shower bath, one with shower only. One with two single beds, working fireplace, bath with shower. One with double bed, full hall bath.
Breakfast: 7:30–8:30. Hot and cold cereal, bacon and eggs, toast, muffins, coffee, tea, milk, juices. Served by candlelight; in winter, by the dining room fireplace.
Plus: Refreshments 5–7 p.m. Line-dried sheets. Free use of bicycles—for viewing three centuries of architecture in town. Brick garden patio. Second-floor study/library. Off-street parking.

If you've been to one B&B, you haven't been to them all. If you have met one B&B host, you haven't met them all.

The Inn at Olde New Berlin

717/966-0321

321 Market Street, New Berlin, PA 17855-0390   fax 717/966-9557

Hosts: John and Nancy Showers
Location: Rural and quiet, with panoramic mountain views. Within 15 minutes of Bucknell and Susquehanna universities. Less than an hour to Penn State, Bloomsburg, and Lycoming colleges; 55 minutes to Harrisburg.

Open: Year round. Two-night minimum on some college weekends and graduations, and on New Berlin's Heritage Day (August) weekend.
Rates: $75–$85. $15 additional person (cot). $5 crib. MC, Visa.

From Pennsylvania: "Made a reservation for one night, stayed four. Have planned another. 'Bed' is wonderful, 'breakfast' is fantastic." *From Maryland:* "We flew in by private plane . . . John picked us up . . . he and Nancy continued to show special care and attention throughout our stay." *From Pennsylvania:* "I left inspired and relaxed. . . . There's no stone unturned. . . . Our first B&B and we're sold!"

Now the Showerses' three older children, ages 17–23, know the answer to their "Who will come to little ol' New Berlin?" Together, John, a former state representative, and Nancy, who was a school psychologist, chose all the deep-colored wallcoverings; the Amish quilts; every candlestick, sconce, marble-topped table, and antique armoire too. The idea began in 1988 when John and Nancy were guests in another lovely inn. In 1991 their family grew when they adopted four-month-old Michael from Peru. And in 1992 this neighboring Victorian home became available. Meanwhile, John enrolled in culinary school "just to be informed." The inn, opened in 1993, is fully staffed, allowing Nancy and/or John to meet just about every guest at what has become a destination known for its food—they come from miles around for Gabriel's, the first-floor restaurant in two dining rooms—and for the service and the Victorian ambiance.

Bed and bath: Five second-floor air-conditioned and carpeted rooms, each with queen antique bed. All private baths, three en-suite; all with showers, two with tub also.
Breakfast: "Almost any time." French toast with strawberry sauce; Walnut Acres 12-grain pancakes with blueberries; orange-pecan waffle with maple syrup; fruit crepes; or omelets. Served in dining room; option of romantic meal in turreted area of one guest room.
Plus: Grand piano in the living room. Welcoming refreshments. Directions to nearby mountain gorge for walk or picnic. Wednesday–Sunday, 4:30–8:30 dinner option (plus brunch 10–2) in public dining rooms that together seat 55.

According to guests (many are preservationists and/or house restorers), there ought to be a medal for the meticulous work—everything from research to labor—done by B&B owners. Indeed, many have won preservation awards.

Farm Fortune   717/774-2683

204 Limekiln Road, New Cumberland, PA 17070

Hosts: Chad and Phyllis Combs
Location: On a three-acre wooded hill overlooking (path leads to) a popular trout stream. Close (¼ mile) to Route 83 and Pennsylvania Turnpike. Ten minutes to Harrisburg; 20 to Hershey or Ski Roundtop, 40 to Lancaster and Gettysburg.

Open: Year round.
Rates: $65–$75 shared bath. $85 private bath. Singles $10 less. Extra person $15. Business rates. Amex, Diners, Discover, MC, Visa.
♥ ♣ ◆ ✈ ⅄

"Do you have another one in your hip pocket?" Chad asked when inquiring about an 18th-century stone farmhouse that had just been sold. That's how, in 1976, after being twice flooded out of their own custom-built home along the creek, the Combs family came to settle (for the first six months) in a part of this light-filled limestone farmhouse while heating, plumbing, and wiring were added. Today there are still nine exterior doors, four interior stairways, and three porches. Legend has it that this was on the Underground Railway. The name is the same that Peter Hursh gave the land when he purchased it for three of his sons. In 1988 *Early American Life* produced a marvelous seven-page story with photographs of the wide-board floors, deep window-sills, Williamsburg blue and Sturbridge accents—and, everywhere, antiques: Sheraton and Hepplewhite pieces; primitives; brass ladles; pewter; pottery; blue spongeware; and Oriental, rag, and braided rugs. It's a lovely setting for small weddings. (Chad is a Presbyterian clergyman.) Now the Combses' children are grown and gone, but the extended family of B&B returnees includes business travelers in addition to those who come for celebrations, sightseeing, or even, as one couple did, to make a folk-art snowman.

In residence: Kitty, a friendly cat.
Bed and bath: Five rooms, all with private phones. Third floor—two dormered rooms, one with a double and a daybed, the other with two twin beds; one booked with private tub/shower bath or both rooms by same party. Second floor—room with double bed, private full bath, porch with swing and rocking chairs. One room with double bed shares a tub/shower bath with room that has twin canopied beds, private stairway, and a large porch with rockers.
Breakfast: Flexible timing. Fresh fruit. Juice. Homemade muffins or coffee cake. Blueberry pancakes, egg dishes, or waffles with apricot sauce. Served in dining room, by walk-in kitchen fireplace, on patio, in bed, or with tray outside your door!
Plus: Central air conditioning. Grand piano. Fireplaced keeping room. Welcoming beverage. Fresh fruit. Guest microwave and refrigerator. Ironed sheets and pillow cases. Porch swing. Patio overlooking creek. Antiques shop in former summer kitchen.

Split-Pine Farmhouse B&B   814/238-2028
P.O. Box 326, Pine Grove Mills, PA 16868   (U.S./Canada) **800/257-2028**

Host: Mae McQuade
Location: Quiet and rural. Five miles to Penn State University. Close to restaurants. Thirty minutes off I-80; four from Philadelphia or Pittsburgh.
Open: Year round. Two-night minimum stay in high season.
Rates: High season (football, arts fes-

tival, Valentine's Blue/White game, commencements): private bath $100 double, $80 single; shared bath $85; $15 one-night weekend surcharge. Off-season: private bath $85, semi-private bath $70; single $55. Third person $25. Discover, MC, Visa.
♥ ♣ ♦ ✻ ✂

> From Maryland, Wyoming, Pennsylvania, New Jersey: " . . . *in the finest tradition of hospitality, privacy, and comfort . . . beautiful farmhouse . . . a barometer for hospitality everywhere.*" From Washington, D.C.: "*Truly an oasis. My husband and I (and sometimes our teenage son) have spent many rejuvenating weekends with 'the world's best' innkeeper/B&B hostess . . . an artist in her breakfasts and service. Pampers each guest and makes you feel special.*"

When Mae lived on two continents with her late army officer husband, she often entertained. And she collected treasures (some are whimsical), antiques, and traditional furnishings. Since 1986 she has been sharing her home, decorating hints, and recipes too—for benefits and with a long list of well-traveled fans.

In residence: Two cats—Pippin, a short-haired brindle; Winkie, a long-haired marmalade.
Foreign languages spoken: "Rusty Spanish and Portuguese."
Bed and bath: Five very large rooms. Three second-floor rooms; one has king bed, private en-suite shower bath; other two have queen bed and share one hall shower bath. Two third-floor slanted-ceiling air-conditioned rooms, one with king bed and one with two twins, can be very private suite; one shower bath.
Breakfast: 8 or 8:30. (Juice and coffee earlier.) Ham timbales, kabobs, mushroom strudel. Fruit course, hot breads, sweet coffee cake. Juice. Hot beverages. In formal dining room.
Plus: Fireplaced living room. Robes. Floor fans on second floor. Tea or coffee always available. Glasses, ice, sodas. Patio tables. Robes. Suggestions for bicycling routes, cross-country skiing, "swimming just over Tussey in Stone Valley."

Country Road Bed & Breakfast   412/899-2528
Moody Road, Box 265, Clinton, PA 15026

Hosts: David and Jan Cornell
Location: On 10 rural and peaceful acres. Great countryside for walking, jogging, bicycling. Walk to public golf course. Twenty minutes west of downtown Pittsburgh, five from Greater Pittsburgh Airport.

Open: Year round.
Rates: Queen $55. Suite or cottage $75 for two, $35 additional person. Ten percent family discount. Extra for hayride or plane ride. MC, Visa.
♥ ♯ ✦

Rare. A historic red barn—used for Thanksgiving dinner and meetings—that houses an antique sleigh, a buggy, and old farm tools. A cornfield that forms a backdrop for the in-ground swimming pool and plank deck. Ducks and geese in the stocked trout pond to be seen from every guest room. Country crafts in the 1868 farmhouse. All so close to the airport and city. For more than 20 years it has been the Cornells' farm and home. (Three children are married.) The well-traveled hosts began to "share their blessings" with B&B guests in 1993. Since retiring as an airline pilot (USAir), David has had more time to "restore everything." The latest project is the 200-year-old log cabin that they moved—complete with found 1700s newspapers—from a nearby property. Hayrides can be arranged. From a vintage 1940s aircraft that seats two or five, you can get an overview of the area. And if you're coming overnight from the Pittsburgh airport, Jan is likely to chauffeur you (in good weather) in a gleaming black 1956 Ford T-Bird convertible. Country Road is a getaway, a jogger's delight, a retreat, a haven.

In residence: Son Daniel, age 15, sells corn on Route 30 in the summer. Maverick, the family dog, is usually outside.

Bed and bath: Three rooms; all private baths. On second floor—queen four-poster, hall claw-footed tub bath. Suite with separate entrance and balcony has queen sleigh bed and two twin beds, pullout love seat in sitting room, Jacuzzi tub for two plus shower. In handicapped-accessible cottage—double bed, Jacuzzi tub plus shower. In log cabin (ideal for families)—double bed, loft twin beds; wood-burning fireplace, shower bath.

Breakfast: 8–9. (Flexible; coffee tray earlier.) Blueberry pancakes or quiche. (Fresh farm eggs right here.) Homemade buns and pastries. Served in dining room or on sun porch; basket option for cottage.

Plus: Fireplaced living room. Wood-burning stove in kitchen. Welcoming refreshments. Fresh fruit. Use of refrigerator and barbecue grill.

General Potter Farm

Potters Mills, PA

Location: Down a long lane off of Route 322. On pretty acreage (for walks) with Sinking Creek at the bottom of the property. Thirteen miles east of Penn State. Near Amish country, caves, museums, and state recreational areas.

Reservations: Year round through Rest & Repast, page 291. Two-night minimum on major events weekends.
Rates: $65–$75 shared bath, $75–$85 private bath. $15 one-night surcharge on peak weekends.
♥ ⁂ ✖ ⅄

The search for an old house ended in 1990 with this B&B, which had been restored in part by previous owners. It's a 17-room red brick farmhouse—the oldest part was built in 1820—that is on the National Register of Historic Places. A large fireplaced living room overlooks the pasture, where the boarded horses—eight are draft, two are thoroughbreds—add to the scene. Sometimes, former guests who cannot get a booking drop by to visit the folks who love sharing their country home.

What a combination! The host's (three-generation) furniture store, which sells reproductions, has decorators who assisted with the selection of paint and wallcoverings for the guest rooms. Because the hostess's father, an

(Please turn page.)

antiques dealer, imports English scrubbed pine (farm) pieces, some here may change from time to time. Others are accent pieces in the host's store, located in an 1880s barn in State College. Recently completed landscaping includes walkways, fencing, plants, and herb garden.

In residence: In hosts' quarters, two preschoolers, one golden retriever, and one black Lab. In the barn, two cats.
Bed and bath: Three second-floor rooms. One with two antique twin beds shares shower bath with room that has queen sleigh bed. Room with queen pencil-post bed has private en-suite shower/bath.
Breakfast: Usually 8–9:30. Fruit, juice, baked goods, yogurt and granola, coffee and tea. Plus, on weekends, stuffed French toast, Belgian waffles, quiche, or strata. In fireplaced formal dining room or on deck overlooking creek.
Plus: Homemade cookies for evening snacks.

The John Thompson House B&B
Stormstown, PA

Location: On 26 scenic acres with cornfield, paths, woods, pond. At the foot of Bald Eagle Mountain. In the village of Stormstown, on a road shared by farm equipment. Eight miles west of Penn State.
Reservations: Year round through

Rest & Repast, page 291. Two-night minimum on major events weekends.
Rates: $60–$75 shared bath, $70–$85 private bath. $15 one-night surcharge on peak weekends.
♥ ⚑ ❖ ✕ ⚗

"In 1990 we left our jobs in the human resources department of a company. My husband was in the training and development department (he consults now), and I was in recruiting and employee services. We moved from the Philadelphia area to this 1817 Georgian stucco house with random-width pine floors, nine-over-six bubble glass windows, and all this glorious land complete with a meandering stream. We painted, replastered, and added a bath. Furnishings include some reproductions, anything we happen to find that we like, and antiques including a lock display case (everyone asks about it) that is filled with redware. There's a welcoming electric candle in every front window. Oil lamps are in all the rooms. Beyond B&B, we weren't sure what we would do, but we have become small-scale farmers with organic tomatoes, pumpkins, and herbs. Depending on the season, some guests wiggle toes in the pond or cross-country ski (we do too) on the trails. Some accompany our son to the pond while he points out the fish and blue heron or talks about the woodchuck seen yesterday. We're meeting many who come for Penn State events—and business travelers too."

Guests leave this B&B with the feeling that they have visited with friends.

In residence: Son Doug, "our official guide." Herman, a friendly chocolate Lab; Fric and Fran, two cats who tend to hide when guests arrive.
Foreign language spoken: Some Spanish. "Please speak slowly."
Bed and bath: Three second-floor rooms. Master bedroom with double bed with feather bed, private tub and shower bath. At other end of hallway, one room with a double bed with feather bed and a queen sofa bed and a room

with two twin beds share a bath that has separate shower and an unusual tub—"even shower lovers use it"—with an oil light on one wide rim.

Breakfast: At guests' convenience. (Caution: Those who sleep on feather beds tend to oversleep.) Juice, fruit, homemade muffins or banana bread, pancakes with apple cider syrup and sausage or omelet, coffee or tea. In spacious dining room or on screened deck with view of meadows and stream.

Plus: Fruit basket. Fresh flowers. Forgotten items. Screened porch with view of meadows and stream. Volleyball and croquet.

From Pennsylvania: *"Beautiful people. . . . Everything was perfect. . . . Take a walk in the field and woods before breakfast. It's great!"*

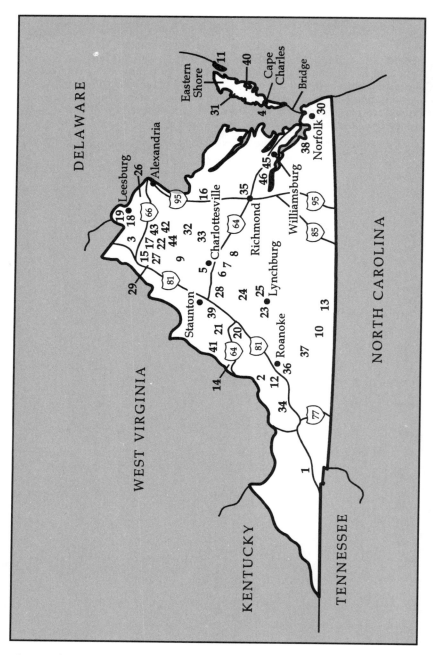

The numbers on this map indicate the locations of B&Bs described in detail in this chapter.

VIRGINIA

_____Virginia Reservation Services_____

Guesthouses

P.O. Box 5737, Charlottesville, VA 22905

Phone: 804/979-7264. Monday–Friday 12–5; emergency call forwarding on weekends. Closed weekends, major holidays, and Christmas week.

Fax: 804/293-7791.

Listings: 60 regular hosts. More than 150 for major University of Virginia weekends. Almost all listings are hosted private residences or guest cottages. Five are inns. Directory is $1.

Reservations: Two weeks' advance notice preferred.

Rates: $48–$100 single, $52–$200 double. $4 surcharge for one-night weekend stay in spring and fall. Some weekly rates available. Deposit of 25 percent of total fee plus state and local tax required. With seven days' advance notice of cancellation, deposit less $15 service fee refunded. Amex, MC, Visa for deposits only. ♦

Originally established for America's bicentennial year, Mary Hill Caperton's service has many experienced hosts in the Charlottesville/Albemarle County area. Most are within 20–30 minutes of Monticello, Ash Lawn, and University of Virginia. The wide range of properties (and rates) includes luxurious estates, antebellum homes, and modest comfortable residences. Some homes are on the National Register and have been on the annual "Historic Garden Week in Virginia" tour.

Plus: Short-term (one week to three months) housing available in apartments or efficiency suites and in guest cottages with host nearby.

Princely Bed & Breakfast, Ltd.

819 Prince Street, Alexandria, VA 22314

Phone: 540/683-2159. Monday–Friday 10–6.

Listings: 30. Mostly hosted private residences. A few unhosted apartments.

Reservations: One week's advance notice and two-day minimum stay preferred.

Rates: $80–$95 per room. $15 surcharge for a one-night stay. Monthly rates available. Deposit required is equal to one night's stay. With more than 14 days' notice of cancellation, full refund will be made, minus $20 service charge. ♥ ↰ ⌂ ♦ ✈

"Deluxe accommodations and beautifully served breakfasts" have been offered by E. J. Mansmann's Alexandria hosts since he established the service in 1981 on retiring from the State Department. All have private baths and air conditioning. Most hosts live in Old Town in historically significant and

(Please turn page.)

antiques-furnished houses (many are part of benefit tours) near fast, frequent transportation to Washington, D.C. The oldest house owned by a host was built in 1770. (Alexandria is eight miles from George Washington's Mount Vernon.) One 1820 house is in the cobblestoned Captains' Row block.

Plus: Some hosts take guests sightseeing.

KEY TO SYMBOLS
♥ Lots of honeymooners come here.
♠ Families with children are very welcome. (Please see page xii.)
♣ "Please emphasize that we are a private home, not an inn."
♣ Groups or private parties sometimes book the entire B&B.
♦ Travel agents' commission paid. (Please see page xii.)
✕ Sorry, no guests' pets are allowed.
✕ No smoking inside *or* no smoking at all, even on porches.

_____ Virginia B&Bs _____

Summerfield Inn   540/628-5905
101 West Valley Street, Abingdon, VA 24201

Hosts: Champe and Don Hyatt
Location: In historic district of a town with "five excellent restaurants" and mountain views. One block from Barter Theatre, the country's oldest continuously running repertory theater. Three blocks from start of 34-mile Virginia Creeper rails-to-trail hiking and biking trail; 20-minute shuttle to midpoint (Appalachian Trail) or to end (on border of North Carolina) at Whitetop Mountain base. One hour west of Blue Ridge Parkway, two from Roanoke. One-half mile from I-81, exit 17.
Open: March–November. Reservations recommended April–October; required other months. Two-night minimum on special weekends.
Rates: Tax included. $70 single; $85 or $90 double. Ten percent discount on stays of three or more nights. Amex, MC, Visa.
♥ ♦ ✈

> From half a dozen states: *"Elegant . . . charming . . . hospitable hosts. . . . A pleasant experience for a woman traveling alone. . . . The stay was the highlight of our trip. . . . A marvelous blend of yesterday and today. . . . Breathtaking antiques. . . . Breakfast served with china, sterling, and crystal. . . . A jewel!"*

Those comments hint at the praise heaped on the home environment created by the Hyatts, hosts who enjoyed B&Bs during their own travels in California. They thought about Don's retirement from dentistry and bought a grand 1920s house in Abingdon, the town where Champe's parents lived for 25 years while her father was manager and president of the Martha Washington Inn. After extensive renovations the Hyatts opened in 1987, with color schemes—soft pinks and greens—chosen from a living room portrait of their children, who are now grown. The paneled dining room with Oriental decor, the tall king four-poster, the wraparound veranda with welcoming flags, popular porch rockers, and family treasures have all been highlighted in glorious magazine features. A jewel indeed.

In residence: "Pepper, our resident miniature schnauzer, the perfect pet, has been called 'the little square dog.'"
Bed and bath: Four spacious second-floor rooms, all with fans on 10-foot ceilings, private full baths (robes provided for those that are unattached). King, double, or twin beds.
Breakfast: 7–9:30. Juice, fruit, quiche, muffins or pastries, coffee, milk. In elegant dining room or on porch.
Plus: Sun room with plenty of plants, wicker furnishings. Guest pantry with refrigerator, ice, soft drinks, setups. Phone jacks in rooms.

> From Marilou Awiakta, Cherokee/Appalachian poet: *"A road-weary poet looks for a place with good vibes. Warm, quiet, private, hospitable—and interesting. Hosts Champe and Don Hyatt create the vibes. Summerfield Inn is the place."*

Brush Mountain Inn Bed & Breakfast

3030 Mount Tabor Road
Blacksburg, VA 24060-8928   540/951-7530

Host: Mode A. Johnson
Location: Secluded. In the woods, on 20 acres. Adjacent to Jefferson National Forest. Fifteen minutes to Blacksburg and Virginia Tech; 30 from I-81 and Roanoke.

Open: Year round.
Rates: Per room. $60 weekdays. $70 weekends. $15 third person. MC, Visa.
♥ ♻ ⬛ ♦ ⅄

Fantasy—for many. A rustic but comfortable place to get away from it all. With deer and birds and peace and quiet. With a 20-foot stone fireplace in the timber frame great room, a wood stove in a sitting area, cathedral ceilings, knotty pine walls, and many decks. Mode, a Virginia Tech administrator for almost two decades, based the design on the plans of a Puget Sound (Washington) island house. (Although he has been in all 50 states, it was a magazine photograph that led him to the architect.) Cedar and pine logs came from Montana, oak from Maryland. In 1992, Mode acted as general contractor, did much of the finish work, furnished with Scandinavian pieces, planted 500 pine trees and a wildflower field, and put out birdhouses and feeders. It's a haven enjoyed by visiting Virginia Tech parents as well as by tourists; guests write about "meticulous attention to thoughtful detail . . . easy-to-be-with host . . . beautiful home, wonderful books, delicious food."

As we were going to press, Mode, an award-winning skier and experienced mountain climber "in my youth," was planning a hiking and fishing trip for an expected English guest. For others, he has many suggestions for "unmarked but obvious" trails here and in the surrounding national forest.

Bed and bath: First floor—large carpeted room with private entrance, queen bed and a sofa bed, private tub/shower bath. Cathedral-ceilinged second floor—double bed, private bath with Jacuzzi and a glass shower for two, two pedestal sinks, balcony.
Breakfast: 8–9:30. Belgian waffles, pancakes, French toast, eggs and biscuits, or—by request—Southern country ham and grits. Special diets accommodated with advance notice.
Plus: Down comforters. Robes. Coffeemaker in each guest room. Snacks. Bottled water. Deck rocking chairs. Horseshoes. Use of orange vests in hunting season. A reminder to bring a sweater or jacket, even in summer. Restaurant suggestions. Short cuts to Blue Ridge Parkway (45 minutes).

In this book a full bath includes a shower and a tub. "Shower bath" indicates a bath that has all the essentials except a tub.

The River House

540/837-1476
fax 540/837-2399

Route 1, Box 135, Boyce, VA 22620

Hosts: Cornelia and Don Niemann
Location: On corner of Route 50 and Shenandoah River; on 17 acres, 100 yards from 2-mile-long walking and cycling dirt road that borders the Shenandoah River. Three miles to Appalachian Trail; 14 east of I-81 and Winchester; 16 west of Middleburg; 60 to Washington, D.C.
Open: Year round. Two-night minimum on holiday weekends.

Rates: Ground floor: $105 queen, $115 king/twins. Second floor: $80 double bed, small bath; $85 or $105 king/twins, full bath. Singles $15 less. Saturday night–only reservations, $25 surcharge. Scheduled "Enter Laughing" and murder mystery weekend packages include superb dinner. $15 rollaway or crib. MC, Visa.
♥ ♨ ♨ ⁂ ◆ ✈

Known nationwide for their winter play-reading weekends for closet thespians, the Niemanns, former Manhattanites, met on stage ("Don was a fabulous actor"). The oldest part of their large seven-fireplaced fieldstone house, their home for more than 25 years, dates back to 1780. "Through five major overhaulings we have furnished in stage-set style with Chinese, French Provincial, some so-called treasures, and some beautiful and unusual pieces, including Don's grandfather's 150-year-old cathedral chime clock."

Cornelia, a fireball who calls herself "a woman of an uncertain age," is a former professional actress/teacher of French ("my first language")/community theater director. She shares recipes—with the caveat that she never measures. Don (just as lovable), a former radio announcer who became an independent school headmaster at age 28, is now headmaster emeritus of the country day school he founded in 1982, a year after he had a serious automobile accident.

Foreign languages spoken: French (fluently) and Spanish (household).
Bed and bath: Five large air-conditioned rooms, each with private bath, phone, wood-burning fireplace. On ground floor, private exterior entrance for two bed/sitting rooms, each with shower and soaking-tub bath. One is beamed, has a queen and a double sofa bed; the other has five-foot fireplace, king/twins option, double sofa bed. Stair lift available to 1820 second floor with one king/twins option room, en-suite tub/shower bath. Another king/twins option, shower bath/dressing room. Double bed, small shower bath. Rollaways and cribs.
Breakfast: Four-course brunch at 10. (For early risers, continental self-serve kitchenettes.) Juice, fruit, meat, egg dish, two vegetables, hot breads. Special diets accommodated. Menu never repeated regardless of length of stay. Family style with antique silver and china. Up to two hours, "maybe more!"
Plus: Fruit and mineral water in rooms. On each floor, kitchenette with snacks. Fireplaced living and dining rooms. Piano. Huge collection of plays. Cycling maps. Games. Books. Grandchildren's swings, sandbox, toys. Private house parties with readings, mysteries, cooking classes, or seminars.

From Virginia: *"Don and Cornelia are the most charming couple we have ever met . . . a relaxing visit in the countryside. . . . We hiked . . . visited caverns. . . . Excellent food is beautiful, atmosphere very romantic."*

Nottingham Ridge

804/331-1010
804/442-5011

28184 Nottingham Ridge lane, Cape Charles, VA 23310

Hosts: Bonnie Nottingham and M. S. Scott
Location: Secluded. Through woods and farmland with long stretches of beach beyond. Four miles north of Bay Bridge Tunnel, midway between (one hour from) Williamsburg and Chincoteague.

Near to golf, tennis, charter fishing boats, harbor cruises, antiquing.
Open: Year round. Two-night minimum on weekends April–October.
Rates: $60–$70 single. $80–$120 double. $20 extra person. Family rates available.
♥ 🏠 ⛵ ♣ ✈ ⚱

Excerpts from many guests' letters: *"The most peaceful beach I have ever been to. . . . A quiet place with a wonderful view of the bay, in lovely pine woods, well off the beaten track. . . . I travel all over the world and would rate this B&B the best . . . a beautifully appointed, comfortable home . . . unbelievable breakfasts. . . . Shared flavor of the community, information about local activities and eating places. . . . Breathtaking sunsets."*

A whole different world. A retreat. Still, virtually undeveloped. No wonder many guests, enchanted with this unique spot, ask if there might be nearby property for sale.

In 1975, when the family was younger, the Nottinghams had the two-storied brick Colonial house built by a local craftsman on 100 acres of family-owned land. It has raised panels and heavy woodwork and is furnished with antiques, reproductions, and collectibles. A welcoming fire glows in the family room during chilly months. As guests attest, Bonnie, who loves to cook, knows the art of hospitality. Cohost Scotty's family has lived in the area for several generations; he loves the outdoors and local history.

In residence: Outside pets—Mutt, a bird dog; Boo-Boo, a cat.
Bed and bath: Four rooms with private baths. First-floor—canopied queen bed, full bath, bay view, private porch entrance. Second floor—antique double sleigh bed, full bath; queen bed, shower bath. Queen-bedded suite with shower bath, TV, sitting room with one twin and one rollaway.
Breakfast: 6–9. Maybe Virginia baked ham, sweet potato biscuit, bacon quiche, waffles, homemade bread and (sometimes hot) jam. Plenty of fruit. In country kitchen or on porch.
Plus: Central air conditioning. Evening wine and cheese. Suggestions for "safe flat cycling roads" and walking tours.

Pickett's Harbor

804/331-2212

Box 97AA, 28288 Goffigon Lane, Cape Charles, VA 23310

Hosts: Sara and Cooke Goffigon
Location: Rural. On 27 Chesapeake Bay acres of private beach directly across from Virginia Beach. Four miles north of Chesapeake Bay Bridge Tunnel. Two miles from Route 13, on Virginia's Eastern Shore.

Open: Year round. Best times to call are 6–7:30 a.m. and 5–10 p.m. Two-night minimum during holidays.
Rates: $65–$75 shared bath. $85–$95 private bath. $125 suite.
♥ ♣ ⚱

A real find: on a secluded and marvelous wide private beach "for family, guests, seagulls, brown pelicans, and sandpipers" with spectacular sunsets. A Colonial home that has a kitchen with cupboards, doors, and floor made from old barn lumber. It's decorated with antiques, reproductions, and country pieces, and in season there are wildflower arrangements in every room.

Cooke, an avocational pilot who "retired from the ABC Commission and manicures the yard," and Sara, a secondary school teacher, built the home on family land. (Sara grew up on the farm, just a half mile away down a country lane.) Now that all five Goffigon children are grown and gone, the world comes to this wonderful doorstep. Guests come for a retreat, for auctions, for nearby nature tours. Some beachcomb (acres), swim, fish, or crab (a skill Sara has taught to many, including an anthropologist who was with a camel caravan in the Sudan for about a decade). Others come to research old homes or to take day trips to Norfolk, Williamsburg, or Virginia Beach. *Mid-Atlantic Country* came in the winter and produced a glorious five-page spread.

Bed and bath: Six rooms, all with views of Chesapeake Bay. First-floor queen-bedded room shares a full bath. Second floor: two cozy dormer rooms—one with double bed, other with three-quarter bed—share a full bath. Queen-bedded room has private shower bath. Double-bedded room and one with queen (together can be a suite) share full bath and a dressing room. Cot. Sleeping bags.
Breakfast: 6–9. Juice or fresh fruit, sweet potato biscuits, popovers, rolls, cinnamon buns, bran muffins, ham, sausage, cheese-egg-sausage casserole, scrapple, eggs, and, in season, fish. In the kitchen, in Williamsburg-style dining room, or on the porch overlooking bay.
Plus: Central air conditioning. Fireplaced living room. Dining room with open fireplace. Ceiling fan in bedrooms and on porch. Beverages. Use of refrigerator. Dinner sometimes available by advance arrangement. Paths through woods "where deer, squirrel, quail, foxes, and rabbits roam freely."

Sea Gate Bed & Breakfast   804/331-2206
9 Tazewell Avenue, Cape Charles, VA 23310-1345

Hosts: Chris Bannon and Jim Wells
Location: Two houses from beach in small (population 1,500) Victorian Eastern Shore town, a designated historic district. Walk to shops, restaurants, golf course, dock (from which to fish and crab), marina, fishing charters. Six miles north of new (1992) state park with nature trails and seven miles of beach. Ten miles north of Chesapeake Bay Bridge and Tunnel, and from Federal Wildlife Preserve; 35 northeast of Virginia Beach and Norfolk; 35 south of Tangier Island ferry.
Open: Year round. Two-night minimum on holiday weekends.
Rates: Per room. Queen bed with private bath $80; private half bath $70 or $75 (with porch). King bed $70.
♥ 🛏 ⚶ ♦ ✈

From Maryland: *"A 'step back in time' to a lifestyle that many of us have lost touch with."* From Washington, D.C.: *"Flair for decorating."* From Virginia: *"Enchanting . . . lovely breakfast, enthusiastic conversation, masters at what they do."*

(Please turn page.)

That has been the reaction from the day the hosts opened in what they call Camelot, "the perfect place to live, where the beach is never crowded, where it's quaint and quiet, true no-glitz 1950 Americana. In addition, this area is a birder's paradise." Several guests have returned to buy property in the recently rediscovered—it's becoming gentrified—waterfront town.

The *Los Angeles Times, International Getaways,* and *The Washingtonian* have covered Sea Gate. The restored/rebuilt/redesigned (with new bathrooms and porches) 1910 house is furnished eclectically with French, English, and American antiques together with some Persian and Chinese rugs. The exceptional rag-rolled (faux finish) and raised relief painting was done by Jim, an interior designer, a Manhattanite who searched the entire East Coast for what was to be a personal shore getaway. Since he and Chris, a manager of conference centers and small retreat houses, opened in 1988, they have become very involved in the community. In summer, breezes come on cue. Year round, there are sunsets too.

In residence: Albert, the cat.

Bed and bath: Four second-floor rooms, all with custom handmade quilts, color TV. Private full bath for room with queen antique brass bed, semiprivate enclosed porch overlooking bay. One queen, full bath. One queen four-poster, private half bath, semiprivate porch. One king bed, private half bath.

Breakfast: Usually 8–10. Maybe French toast made with homemade bread, a variety of omelets with garden herbs. Bacon, country scrapple, and regional sweet potato biscuits. Fresh fruit, cottage cheese, cereals, juices, hot beverages. Served in dining room with gas-burning fireplace, or on year-round enclosed or screened porch.

Plus: Afternoon tea. Central air conditioning plus, for an option, guest room ceiling fans and window air conditioners. Fireplaced living room. Beach chairs. Outdoor hot/cold shower. Bicycles. No parking problems. Pickup service arranged from marinas.

Alderman House
Charlottesville, VA

Location: Just a mile from the university.
Reservations: Year round except December 15–February 1 through Guesthouses, page 315.

Rates: $80 per room. $4 one-night surcharge spring and fall weekends.
♥ ⬛ ◆ ✕ ⊱

Elegance. Southern hospitality. And history. The *Washington Post* and *Country* magazine have featured this formal Georgian house, which was built in the early 1900s as the retirement home of the first University of Virginia president. It is now the residence of a gracious hostess and her physician husband, parents of a grown family. Seminar leaders, international visitors, and students' parents are among those who have appreciated their hospitality, the flower-filled brick-walled terrace, and a delightful balcony with pink awnings, lounge chairs, and hanging plants.

In residence: One grown daughter. One black poodle.
Bed and bath: Two second-floor rooms, each with private full bath. One with canopied double four-poster bed. One with twin beds.
Breakfast: 7:30–9:30. Cheese souffle. English muffins, homemade preserves, fresh fruit, coffee or tea. Served in crystal-chandeliered dining room or on the terrace.
Plus: Central air conditioning. Today's papers. Beverages.

From California: *"Wonderful hosts and house. Superb!"* From Virginia: *"A jewel."* From Washington, D.C.: *"Grateful for all the extras."*

Bollingwood
Charlottesville, VA

Location: In a convenient neighborhood, within walking distance of the university.
Reservations: Year round through Guesthouses, page 315.

Rates: $72 and $68 per room. $4 one-night surcharge on spring and fall weekends.
🦆 ⚘ ♦ ✈ ✂

The fence-enclosed city gardens and slate terrace of this handsome Colonial have been featured during Historic Garden Week. Built in 1927 with many windows, the house is furnished with antiques throughout.
    Word has it that Albemarle County natives are rare in Charlottesville. Here you have one, a woman returned after living in New Orleans, New York, and Washington, D.C. She has experience as a stockbroker and as a presidential personnel staffer. Several of her guests have been journalists who wrote articles about area gardens, starting right here.

In residence: Bear, a very friendly terrier who loves guests.
Bed and bath: Two second-floor rooms, each with private full bath. One with two twin beds. Another room with a canopied double and, in a connected room, a three-quarter bed.
Breakfast: Flexible hours. Homemade breads and muffins. Raisin bread French toast. Served in formal dining room or on terrace.
Plus: Bedroom air conditioners and ceiling fans. Tea or wine. Tour of house. TV. Fireplace in lovely living room. Extensive library/sun room.

From New York: *"A wonderful way to introduce our son to the UVA community."*

Recoletta
Charlottesville, VA

Location: Within walking distance of University of Virginia, restaurants, theaters, and shops. Ten-minute bus ride to downtown.
Reservations: Year round through Guesthouses, page 315.

Rates: $72 single or double. $4 one-night surcharge on spring and fall weekends.
♥ ⚘ ♦ ✈

By the time most guests rise for breakfast, this hostess has probably walked many laps around the university track. Guests feel very much at home in this

(Please turn page.)

Mediterranean-style villa built with flair and imagination, with a red tile roof and a walled garden complete with pools. The comfortable and rather elegant living room filled with books gives the feeling of an Italian library. There are American antiques and many from Central America as well as from Europe. The effervescent and welcoming hostess, an administrator in education, is active in the Society for the Prevention of Cruelty to Animals. (For an epitaph, she once chose "Born a dog, died a gentleman.") Many seasoned travelers write that this is their favorite B&B.

In residence: One English bulldog.
Bed and bath: One second-floor room with brass double bed, adjoining private tub/shower bath.
Breakfast: Until 9:30. Juice, fruit, eggs, bacon or sausage, muffins, gourmet jams, yogurt, cereals, coffee, tea.
Plus: Air conditioning. Beverages. Fireplaced living room.

> From Boston, Massachusetts: *"One of the very best places we have ever stayed."* From California: *"House is one discovery after another."* From Canada: *"I want to move in."*

Boxwood Lane Farm
Batesville, VA

Location: Wonderful. On extensive grounds with gardens. And terraces. And mountain views. Some ponds have koi fish and water lilies. Fifteen miles south of Charlottesville.

Reservations: Year round through Guesthouses, page 315.
Rates: $80 single. $80 double.
♥ ⬤ ✄ ✂

An oasis. A country getaway. A delight to the senses. The hosts, an artist who exhibits and teaches, and an architect who has a passion for spectacular gardening, have lived in this gracious Victorian manor house since 1983. In 1990 they added a complementary gold-colored living room with Palladian windows and doors that open onto a stone terrace with pond beyond. Contemporary paintings are in blues, turquoise, purples, and reds. The library walls are a muted coral. Everywhere there are strong colors, beautiful Oriental rugs, and a combination of interesting furnishings. The hosts, who "feel fortunate to be here," enjoy hosting. It's no wonder that most guests wish they could stay longer.

> From California: *"Best B&B ever ... breakfast is truly 'full' and very good."* From Illinois: *"Great hosts who are very interesting ... beautiful home."*

In residence: One very welcoming, very large English mastiff.
Bed and bath: Two large air-conditioned second-floor rooms, one with queen bed, wood-burning fireplace, private hall shower and tub bath. Room with double four-poster bed has adjoining private shower and tub bath.
Breakfast: Usually around 9. Fruits. Fresh breads. Hot entree. Served in dining room or on stone terrace.

Ammonett Farm

North Garden, VA

Location: Pastoral. On a small farm with beautiful views. Twenty minutes south of University of Virginia, 30 to Wintergreen ski resort.
Reservations: Year round through Guesthouses, page 315.

Rates: $60 single. $68 double. $4 one-night surcharge on spring and fall weekends.
🏠 🛏 ✿ ♦ ✗ ⅀

"I might be feeding a calf or two when you arrive. We serve home-cooked homegrown foods in our green room, so called because it was added to the house for lots of plants—and people."

It's a century-old, meticulously restored farmhouse. Home to the host family for more than a decade, it is filled with family pieces and a country feel. "Some guests feed the calves. Others just relax. This is a very low-key place."

In residence: One yóung adult. Inside, a cockatiel. Outside, cats, dogs, rabbits, a small herd of beef cattle.
Bed and bath: Three second-floor rooms. One double-bedded with private full bath. One with a double and one with two twins share a full bath. Rollaway and crib available.
Breakfast: Flexible hours. Home style. Fruit or juice, homemade bread and jelly, eggs and bacon; cereal. Hostess joins guests.
Plus: Tea or wine. Bedroom window fans. Tour of house and farm. Hiking on more than 50 acres of woodlands and pasture.

From Virginia: *"A wonderful memory. . . . Spectacular; our daughters were treated like queens."*

Ingleside

North Garden, VA

Location: "Away." On a hill overlooking grazing animals, sweeping fields, valleys, woods, and steep mountains. A working farm on 1,250 acres. Twenty miles south of Charlottesville.

Reservations: Year round through Guesthouses, page 315.
Rates: $72 per night. $4 surcharge on spring and fall weekends.
♥ 🛏 ♦ ✗ ⅀

Turn off the main road for a mile of paved road and another that is unpaved onto the half-mile-long gravel road. Drive "straight up" to this early Victorian house, which was built by the hostess's great-great-grandfather with big square rooms, 10-foot ceilings, and huge windows. Most guests seem to gravitate to the recently added big country kitchen with, of course, those views. They enjoy meeting the well-traveled hosts—a British-born landscape architect and his wife—who maintain a breeding herd of cattle. At last count they had about 60 cows and calves. In addition, the hosts speak of their "retirement home for horses." You'll see about 25 equines that are "cared for and loved." Although some Charlottesville-oriented guests come just to stay outside—albeit close to—the city, many enjoy the walks (short or hours long)

(Please turn page.)

through open fields, along a stream, or down into and up out of the valleys. (Bring hiking boots.) Some "discover" foundations of old cabins or a family cemetery. And they comment: "Wonderful people . . . an exceptional B&B experience. . . . We want to return."

In residence: Outside dogs—"a mixture and two basset hounds who love to escort guests on walks."
Bed and bath: One first-floor double-bedded room with working fireplace, adjoining tub/shower bath.
Breakfast: Flexible hours. Juice. Fruit course. Cereals, including various granolas. Pancakes or sweet rolls and homemade breads. In fireplaced dining room.
Plus: Window air conditioner. Tennis court. In October, sight of newborn calves in addition to spectacular foliage.

From North Carolina: *"In the most beautiful spot imaginable . . . wonderful hosts."*

Chester   804/286-3960
2783 James River Road, Route 726, Scottsville, VA 24590

Hosts: Gordon Anderson and Richard Shaffer
Location: On a seven-acre estate with more than 50 varieties of trees and shrubs, each identified with botanical and common name. Just off Route 20. Within half an hour of Monticello, Ash Lawn, Charlottesville; 45 minutes from Skyline Drive, Montpelier.
Open: Year round. Two-day minimum during UVA graduation and parents' weekends, July 4, and December 22–January 2.
Rates: Per room. Private bath $115. Shared bath—$65 double bed; $75 king bed with fireplace; $95 queen bed with fireplace and adjoining sitting room. $30 sofa bed (one or two people).
♥ 🏠 ❖ ◆

From New Jersey, New Hampshire, Illinois: *"Superb. . . . Memorable and elegant meals . . . tastefully decorated . . . spotless . . . lingered over specially brewed coffee . . . hosts joined us for drinks on the front porch . . . suggested routes . . . marked maps. . . . The conversation was animated, to put it mildly. . . . Grounds bring one back to a more leisurely lifestyle. . . . A single overnight yielded more relaxation than the time invested would warrant."*

Gordon was a Wall Street investment banker (for 23 years) and Dick a legal administrator in Manhattan before they spent a year restoring the gracious 1847 Greek Revival frame house built by a landscape architect from England. Since opening in 1986, this B&B has been acclaimed by James Yenckel in the *Washington Post,* and the hosts have appeared twice in Woodward & Lothrop's cooking demonstrations given by *Bed & Breakfast in the Mid-Atlantic States* innkeepers. Featured on Historic Garden Week in 1991, Chester has a columned portico, four porches, eight wood-burning fireplaces, expansive lawns, and large stands of English boxwood. Many of the furnishings were acquired during the hosts' own extensive travels. This is "home" with Oriental rugs, comfortable chairs, traditional pieces, classical music, and artwork.

In residence: "We breed and show borzoi (Russian wolfhounds) who love people and often are visited by guests." Johnny Weismuller is an outside cat.
Bed and bath: Five rooms; all with heated towel racks. Private full bath for first-floor room that has four-poster double bed, wood-burning fireplace. On second floor, suite with queen four-poster bed, pedestal sink, wood-burning fireplace, sitting room with double sofa bed shares a tub-and-shower bath with room that has a double bed, pedestal sink, wood-burning fireplace. Guests in room with king bed and wood-burning fireplace walk through library to tub-and-shower bath shared with smaller room that has a double bed.
Breakfast: 7–9:30. Fresh fruit. Eggs (maybe sherried) or omelets, or Swedish oven pancakes; local sausage or bacon. Homemade breads. Cereals. Juices. Coffees, teas. Served with fine china, crystal, and silver on large screened porch or by dining room fireplace.
Plus: Central air conditioning. Beverages. Flowers. Bicycles. Library with satellite TV, stereo, books. Croquet. Laundry room with ironing facilities. Tour of house, kennels, greenhouse. Picnic baskets prepared. Sociable dinner party ($30 per person includes wine; advance reservation required) at table set with fine china, sterling silver, and Waterford crystal; hosts join guests. Complimentary take-home recipe booklets. Cigarettes provided in living room. "Guests' dogs allowed in our kennel."

Edgewood Farm Bed & Breakfast

RR 2, Box 303, Stanardsville, VA 22973-9405   **804/985-3782**
                                                      fax 804/985-3782

Hosts: Eleanor and Norman Schwartz
Location: Off the beaten track on a 130-acre farm with woods (hiking), a river, streams, many birds. Five miles from town. Twenty-five miles north of Charlottesville; 15 to Swift Run Gap entrance of Shenandoah National Park/Appalachian Trail. Within 20 minutes of crafts shops, antiquing, wineries, pick-your-own strawberries, apple orchard and cider mill. Two hours from Washington, D.C., or Richmond, Virginia.
Open: Year round except Christmas, Easter, and Thanksgiving. Two-night minimum holiday weekends and October.
Rates: Shared bath $70 double bed, $75 queen bed. Private bath and queen bed $85. Singles $5 less. Rollaway $15. MC, Visa.
♥ ⅁ ♣ ♦ ✗ ⅃

From many Virginians: *"Greeted with sparkling cider, fruit, and cheese. . . . Beautiful mountain views from all the rooms . . . elegance, a sense of authenticity, and comfort. . . . Privacy. . . . Grounds, too, are beautifully maintained. . . . What makes it a special place are the people who run it. . . . Breakfast is sumptuous. . . . Received your B&B book and a gift certificate as a Christmas gift from our daughter. From initial contact with Eleanor Schwartz until the last goodbye we were enchanted . . . surpassed your description."*

In 1986, the first B&B guests were members of one of the many families who had owned this 1790 Virginia Colonial farmhouse with 1860 addition. Since, the Schwartzes have heard others share some oral history about the property and the plantation overseer's house. The extensive restoration took place

(Please turn page.)

with the help of a historic preservationist and a professional decorator. Furnishings are period antiques—"some from our home state of Texas"—and reproductions. Every room has a wood-burning fireplace. Norman, a retired air force officer, and Robert Cary, a son-in-law, have established a nursery here with the state's largest selection of herbs and unusual perennials. Eleanor, a former writer/editor with the air force at the Pentagon, retired to "enjoy the country life."

In residence: "Buddy, our sweet farm dog, will love you to death if you let him. Garfield is our cat."
Bed and bath: Three second-floor rooms. One with queen Victorian. One with four-poster. Steep staircase leads to one with double brass-and-iron bed. Two full baths; can be private or shared depending on number of rooms booked. Rollaway and crib available.
Breakfast: 6:30–10. Early coffee. Entree in dining room set with china, silver, and fresh flowers might be breakfast casserole with ham or sausage, eggs, cheese, cream sauce. Four or five homemade sweet breads, muffins, or coffee cakes. Juice, fruit, hot beverages. "Constantly trying new recipes. Cookbook is planned."
Plus: Central air conditioning. Bedroom ceiling fans. Complimentary Virginia-made goats' milk toiletries. Morning newspapers. Horseshoes. Croquet. Maybe a Carolina wren nesting in front porch grapevine heart wreath. Patio. Transportation to/from Charlottesville Amtrak station and/or Shenandoah National Park. Picnic baskets, $25 for two.

House of Laird   804/432-2523

335 South Main Street, Chatham, VA 24531-1131

Hosts: Ed and Cecil Laird
Location: On a street lined with other big old lovely homes. Two-minute walk to bucolic village. "Five minutes to just about every place, including Chatham Hall School for Girls, Hargrave Military School, excellent restaurant." One hour to Appomattox, 45 minutes to Blue Ridge Parkway, 20 to Danville (last Confederate capital). Two hours south of Charlottesville and north of Raleigh-Durham, North Carolina.
Open: Year round.
Rates: (Include tax.) $75 per room; less for business travel Sunday–Thursday. Library suite $109 at all times. Amex, MC, Visa.
♥ ◂ ♣ ♦ ✈ ⊁

> From Virginia: *"The quintessential experience. . . . Exquisite. . . . Detail includes heated towel bars and plush robes. . . . In a small town rich in history and architectural heritage. . . . Have stayed several times; look forward to returning again. . . . The crowning touch is breakfast."*

A best-kept secret, maybe. Affordable luxury, surely. And romantic. Professionally decorated in 1988 with fine antiques, Oriental rugs, and imported wallcoverings and fabrics, the century-old Greek Revival with original moldings and glass had been in one family until the Lairds bought it "to create a personalized B&B"—after seeing a *Country Living* ad, and after they found Chatham on the map! The magnificent floor-to-ceiling dining room mirror is reputed to have been in Washington, D.C.'s Willard Hotel (Abraham Lincoln's era). The handsome 1830 Empire four-poster has been in Cecil's family "for years." The teddy bear collection started during the hosts' mid-1980s courtship. Kentucky-born Cecil was in banking in Richmond when her neighbor introduced her to his college roommate, Georgia-born Ed, who was in real estate in California. Here, "in this one-traffic-light town," two happy people "host [pamper] wonderful [and contented] travelers from near and far."

In residence: Tonk, a Siamese/Burmese cat, in hosts' quarters.

Bed and bath: Three rooms and library suite; each with working (pressed wood logs) fireplace, adjoining (new) private bath, cable TV. First floor—handicapped-accessible suite with queen tester bed, a queen Murphy bed, bath with tub and hand-held shower. Second floor—three rooms (two with queen beds, one with king canopied bed), each with shower bath.

Breakfast: Early coffee or tea outside your door. Continental at 7, full at 8:30. Breakfast roulade, quiche, sausage, crepes, fresh fruit. "Ed's smoothie," a fruit drink. Freshly baked breads and muffins. In formal dining room with cloth napkins, antique china, and period silver.

Plus: Fireplaced guests' sitting room. Central air conditioning. Beverages and snacks. Fresh fruit and flowers. Turndown service. Schedule for recommended antiques auction one hour away. Upon departure, "a care package."

The Watson House

804/336-1564

4240 Main Street, P.O. Box 905, Chincoteague, VA 23336   **800/336-6787**

Hosts: Tom and Jacque Derrickson; David and Jo Anne Snead
Location: On a corner of Main Street, across the street from Chincoteague Bay, ¼ mile from the heart of town. One mile to the Chincoteague National Wildlife Refuge, 2 to beach.

Open: March–November. Two- or three-night minimum on many weekends.
Rates: Double bed $75–$85 weekends, $65–$85 midweek. Queen room $85–$105 weekends, $85–$105 midweek. MC, Visa.
♥ ⁂ ◆ ✈ ⅊

"This B&B was my father's idea. He's always wanted one, and wanted it to be here on the island where we've always lived. In 1991 he, together with my husband, put a bid on this turn-of-the-century house, and then they told my mother and me about their plan. It was fun to redo the entire house and to add the friendly and welcoming wraparound porch complete with gingerbread, inspired by Cape May B&Bs. Half of the Victorian and country furnishings came from local residents who wanted us to have Chincoteague pieces. The other half we bought at auctions. Since opening in 1992 it seems that we have become known for our food—both breakfast and teatime. And we have been on the Learning Channel's 'Romantic Escapes'!"

Jackie used to work for NASA. She and husband Tom, an electronic technician, take turns as hosts along with co-chef Jo Anne (Jackie's mom) and David (Jackie's dad), a plumber.

Bed and bath: Six rooms; one on first floor, five on second. All attached private baths; one has claw-footed tub and shower, rest have shower without tub. Queen iron-and-brass beds or double high-back oak beds. Two rooms have their own attached private sitting room. Rollaway available.

(Please turn page.)

Breakfast: 8–9:30. Buffet includes French toast or egg-and-meat casserole, hot or cold fruit dish, homemade pastries/breads/muffins, cold cereals. In dining room or on side porch.
Plus: Air conditioning. Bedroom ceiling fans. Individual thermostats. Tea-time with cakes and cookies at 4 p.m. Complimentary use of bicycles, beach towels, and beach chairs. Fresh flowers on special occasions.

The Oaks Bed & Breakfast Country Inn
311 East Main, Christiansburg, VA 24073   540/381-1500

Hosts: Margaret and Tom Ray
Location: Massive oak trees on grounds. In historic district, three blocks from downtown. Two miles from I-81, 8 from Virginia Tech and Radford University; ½ to antiques shops. Half hour to Blue Ridge Parkway, Roanoke, winery. Close to new rails-to-trails cycling path, hiking, cruise boat. Near restaurants—one at a mountain vineyard, another fea-turing Southern home cooking, Brazilian international cuisine.
Open: Year round. Designated minimum stays for university special events weekends.
Rates: $95–$115 ($75 for single business traveler) Sunday–Thursday; $105–$130 Friday and Saturday. Singles $10 less. Amex, Discover, MC, Visa.
♥ ❖ ♦ ✈ ✂

It's a photographer's delight seen on the cover of many publications. One of *Country Inns* magazine's 1991 "top 12" list, it's a turreted National Register yellow 1889 Victorian with wraparound porch. Fireplaces are in two parlors and in the sun room. Furnishings are a blend of contemporary and antiques. French doors open onto a large terrace by a perennial garden, a gazebo, and a fish pond with fountain. The monthlong Victorian Christmas celebration includes 10-foot trees that are a major attraction (and community fund-raiser).

Margaret, a former corporate executive who had her own public relations agency, is a fine seamstress and cook. Tom, a multifaceted architect, is almost famous for his coffee. They lived in Royal Oak, Michigan, for 28 years before moving to Washington, D.C., and then, in 1989, to The Oaks—their restoration "experienced" to date by guests from 48 states and 20 countries.

In residence: "Miss Lulu, a Scottie, our social director; precocious Westie Kaile Bonnie Faire. Sidney, a beautiful and lazy Persian."
Bed and bath: Five air-conditioned rooms, private baths. First floor: very quiet room with canopied queen bed, tub/shower bath. Second floor: canopied king, gas fireplace, refrigerator, his and her baths with claw-footed tub. Five-windowed turret with queen bed, gas fireplace, refrigerator, bath with dressing area, Jacuzzi for two, shower. Canopied queen, gas fireplace, refrigerator, private tub and shower hall bath. Third floor: canopied king bed, tall ceiling with skylight, gas fireplace, shower bath, TV.
Breakfast: A hallmark. Flexible weekday hours. Weekends, at 9. Perhaps curried eggs with shiitake mushrooms in white wine sauce or apricot-walnut pancakes with ice cream and orange syrup. Fresh breads and fruit. French service in candlelit dining room with antique china and sterling silver.
Plus: In all bedrooms—ceiling fans, private phones, turndown service. Beverages. TV and VCR in sun room. Library. Games. Porch rockers. Sun deck.

Oak Grove Plantation   804/575-7137

Highway 658, Cluster Springs, VA   (winter) **703/527-6985**
Mailing address: P.O. Box 45, Cluster Springs, VA 24535

Host: Pickett Craddock
Location: On a 400-acre tree farm with great hiking, biking, and bird-watching. Five miles south of South Boston, Virginia. Antiquing locally. Thirty minutes from Buggs Island Lake (fishing, boating, swimming, quilt store, 18th-century mansion); Appomatox; and Danville, Virginia (where you tour last capital of Confederacy and Victorian homes on Millionaires' Row). One hour north of Durham, North Carolina.
Open: Daily Memorial Day weekend through Labor Day and on weekends and during special events in May and September.
Rates: Per room. $50 double, $45 single. $5 children over six. Three-day midweek and weeklong family packages include all meals and supervised activities for children.
🏕 🏠 ☂ ♦ 🐾

> From New York: *"A strong sense of another time . . . walked for hours through woods and meadows . . . service on family china was gracious and elegant."* From North Carolina: *"Charming rooms. . . . Comfortable bringing our two-year-old."* From Washington, D.C.: *"Picked us up at train station . . . delicious home-cooked breakfast and special vegetarian dinner . . . played croquet on front lawn . . . a gracious hostess who knew when to be affable and when to allow privacy."*

You, too, can discover this off-the-beaten-path haven—thanks to Pickett's desire to share the Classical Revival house built by her great-great-grandfather on a tobacco plantation. Three-foot-high wainscoting carved with stars and bars, floor-to-ceiling parlor windows, an antique box grand piano, and a Korean Buddha are all part of the family history. Adults unwind. Kids climb magnolia and oak trees. From a trestle they count the boxcars of a passing train. And they find turtles and frogs in the creek.

Pickett is a Washington, D.C., preschool teacher and director (for 22 years) and caterer. She continued her B&B dream—still with grace—through one summer with a broken leg, the result of an accident when she and husband Mike Doan, an editor for *Kiplinger Washington Newsletter,* went to Honduras to meet newborn Sara.

In residence: Daughter Sara is five. "Tara is our people-loving dalmatian."
Foreign language spoken: Spanish.
Bed and bath: Two air-conditioned second-floor rooms share a 1980s crystal-chandeliered full bath that has a private porch. Additional bath with tub is on first floor; robes provided. Room with wood-burning fireplace has canopied double four-poster bed made for Pickett when she was seven. Other room has king/twins option. One crib and sleeping bags for children available.
Breakfast: At guests' convenience. Egg dish, waffles, or pancakes. Bacon or sausage. Fresh fruit. Homemade breads. In bay-windowed dining room.
Plus: Area events calendar. Glassed-in sun porch. Iced tea or lemonade whenever. Kitchen and laundry facilities. Use of two adult bicycles and baby jogger. Babysitting. High chair, swings, games. Dinner, $12 per person, by reservation. No television. Line-dried sheets.

Milton Hall Bed and Breakfast Inn

207 Thorny Lane   540/965-0196
Covington, VA 24426-9803

Hosts: John and Vera Eckert
Location: A rural mountain set-
ting. On 44 acres next to George
Washington National Forest. In
Callaghan, five miles west of Coving-
ton. One mile from I-64, exit 10.
With "sweeping lawns" much as they
were when the house was built.
Thirty minutes south of the Home-
stead in Hot Springs, 20 minutes east
of the Greenbrier in White Sulphur
Springs, West Virginia.
Open: Year round.
Rates: $140 suite. $95 master bed-
room. $75 or $85 queen bed. MC,
Visa.
♥ ♨ ◀ ♣ ♦

Come to breakfast when you want. Unwind. And beware: Many who come
with plans to attend theater, go horseback riding, or visit the baths in Warm
Springs "do" as little as possible. As John, the retired naval officer who was
for nine years a computer corporation analyst and manager, says, "Our guests
enjoy the scenery, good restaurants, small villages, the hike from our back
door into the national forest, and comfortable fireplaced rooms."

The rather imposing brick exterior with gables, buttressed porch towers,
and Gothic trimming gives way to a plainer interior, as intended by one of
England's oldest families when they built the house in 1874. The Eckerts
decorated the Virginia Historic Landmark, which is also on the National
Register, with muted bird- and floral-patterned wallpapers and with reproductions and some antiques. Their player piano, purchased in England, has
been restored. Tea at four is very English. Before B&B, Vera, as a Washington,
D.C., sales associate, specialized in fine English china. Here, the Eckerts'
hospitality is influenced by their 26 years of travel with the United States
Navy.

In residence: Heather, 20. Sassy, a 9-year-old Brittany.
Bed and bath: Six rooms, all with four-poster beds, private baths, wood-
burning fireplaces. First-floor suite has two rooms with fireplaces—one
queen-bedded room and a parlor with queen sofa bed—both with French
doors leading to garden; shower bath. On second floor—master bedroom with
queen four-poster and a twin, sitting area with sleep sofa, antique tub/shower
bath. One queen with shower only. One queen with antique tub/shower
bath. One queen with modern tub and shower. One queen with private bath
suite at opposite end of hall with whirlpool tub, exercise bike.
Breakfast: At guests' convenience. Juice, fresh fruit, eggs, local meat or fish
(sausage, bacon, rainbow trout), baked cheese grits or sliced baby red potatoes
browned in butter, fresh-baked biscuits or muffins, milk and cereal, coffee or
tea. In fireplaced dining room overlooking gardens.
Plus: Air-conditioned bedrooms. Fireplaced living room with TV and that
1916 player piano. Welcoming beverages. Turndown service. Bedtime snack.
Flannel sheets. Fresh flowers. Unlimited firewood. Use of bicycles. Picnic
baskets ($6 per person) and suggestions for picnic sites. With advance
arrangement, informal country supper ($10 per person) or full dinner for
groups of 10 or more ($25 with wine). Croquet. Option of TV in room.

Edinburg Inn Bed & Breakfast Ltd.

218 South Main Street, Edinburg, VA 22824 **540/984-8286**

Hosts: Judy and Clyde Beachy
Location: On spacious grounds in Shenandoah Valley, just off Route 81, 90 minutes from Washington, D.C. Next to historic Edinburg Mill (now a restaurant) and creek with ducks and geese. Near "easy access to an absolutely awesome view of the Seven Bends of the Shenandoah."
Open: Year round.
Rates: $65 single, $75 double. $10 rollaway. $85 for three or four in suite. $10 less for two or more nights.
⚐ ⚑ ✿ ✈ ✂

"Grandma's house of storybooks" is the feeling enjoyed by guests who come for hiking, biking, fishing, or hunting in the nearby George Washington National Forest. Some come for the caverns, museums, Civil War battlefields, Skyline Drive, flea markets, and antiques and crafts shops. "We used to read your book, Bernice, and picture ourselves in it—in an old house in a small town. When, in 1993, our friends [previous owners] decided to sell, our dream came true. From 1850 to 1982 this was a miller's house. The massive Jeffersonian French doors leading to a wraparound porch were added in 1890."

And so, fellow traveler, here they are—Judy, the "plant lady," who worked in a school health clinic, and Clyde, the Central Intelligence Agency staffer of 30 years, who loves woodworking (furniture making).

In residence: "Jopa, our friendly beagle, spends much time outdoors."
Bed and bath: Three air-conditioned rooms with ceiling fans; all private baths. First floor—double bed in large handicapped-accessible room, full bath. Second floor—one large room with double bed, private tub/shower hall bath. Suite (great for a family)—double bed in one room, two twins in other; large shower bath with dressing/sitting area. For a group with more than eight, small room with double bed. Rollaways. Portacrib.
Breakfast: Usually 8–10 (earlier if prearranged). Chef's choice of casserole, pancakes, French toast, or eggs and local ham, bacon, or sausage. Cereal. Sweet breads. Fresh fruit, juices, hot beverage, milk. Served family style in dining room; may be taken to porch.
Plus: Plants everywhere. Common room with wood-burning stove, player piano, vintage magazines, games. Porch swing and rockers. Snacks; hot or cold beverages; use of refrigerator. Bocci. Croquet. Badminton. Food to feed ducks and geese.

B&Bs offer the ultimate concierge service.

La Vista Plantation

4420 Guinea Station Road
Fredericksburg, VA 22408-8850

540/898-8444
fax 540/898-1041

Hosts: Michele and Edward Schiesser
Location: Surrounded by farm fields; herb and vegetable gardens; pond for fishing; woods with paths for walks, cycling, bird-watching. Eight miles south of Fredericksburg, just off Route 1. Five miles from I-95. On the East Coast bicycle trail. Near Civil War battlefields, antiques shops, pick-your-own farms. An hour to Monticello and Mount Vernon.
Open: Year round.
Rates: $65 single. $85 double. Children 12 and under, free. Additional person $5 ages 12–17; $10 age 18 and older. Seventh night free. MC, Visa.
♥ ♨ ✐ ✿ ♦ ✈ ✄

> From Massachusetts: *"A warm welcome. Plenty of space and privacy. Lovely antiques and artworks. Morning brought the rooster's crow, sunlight streaming in from all sides, and a delicious hot breakfast. . . . A feeling for the period of the lovely house."* From California: *"Ken Burns's 'Civil War' series brought us here, but La Vista will bring us back."*

Romantics wrote about sitting by the fire. Some guests see their first lightning bugs here. They enjoy the opportunity to gather eggs and explore 10 acres. Business guests, too, appreciate hearing some history and anecdotes about the 1838 Greek Revival manor house, which was occupied by both armies during the Civil War. Since 1983, when the Schiessers moved from the Victorian house they renovated in Maryland, this has been a restoration-in-progress for Mickey, a historic preservation activist and former junior high school teacher, and Ed, Hirshhorn Museum chief of exhibits and design.

They made the sunny English basement (with cathedral-type windows) into one of the area's first B&Bs by updating the former winter kitchen and furnishing the spacious rooms with antiques, Ed's limestone sculptures, and many books. This arrangement of a home-within-a-home provides as much privacy or company as you wish. The more formal first-floor guest room has wide heart pine floors, Empire furniture, and an antique clock collection.

In residence: William, age 15; Julia, 13. Emily, "beautiful, well-behaved, quiet English setter." Chickens and rabbits.
Bed and bath: Rooms on two floors. A four-room ground-level suite with private shower bath, double bed in huge room, living room with queen-sized sofa bed, fireplace, large fireplaced kitchen, two private entrances. On first floor, a huge fireplaced room with king four-poster bed, large private full bath. Crib available.
Breakfast: 7–9:30. Danish with coffee or tea, La Vista's fresh brown farm eggs, toast, bacon, homemade jams from fruit trees here, orange juice, milk. Varied menu for extended stays. Served in main-floor dining room or in guests' rooms.
Plus: Central air conditioning (window unit in suite). In-room TV, radio, phone. Beverages. Fresh flowers. Plenty of wood in hearths. The family's living room. Today's newspaper. Use of two bicycles, rowboat, and fishing tackle. Option of dinner (no charge) to those arriving on bicycles. Babysitting if arranged in advance. In December, pick-your-own Christmas trees.

Chester House Inn

43 Chester Street, Front Royal, VA 22630

540/635-3937
800/621-0441

Hosts: Bill and Ann Wilson
Location: On two acres in historic residential district. One block from renovated Main Street with its old-time general store, and antiques and craft shops; summer evening concerts at village common gazebo. Within minutes of Shenandoah National Park; Skyline Drive and caverns; George Washington National Forest; winery tours; recreational activities including horseback riding, canoeing, fishing, golf. Three miles south of I-66, exit 6; 70 miles west of Washington, D.C.
Open: Year round. Two-night minimum on some September, October, and holiday weekends.
Rates: $110 suite. $105 large king. $95 queen. $85 king/twins option. Twenty percent business travelers' discount, Sunday–Thursday. Amex, MC, Visa.

♥ ⬛ ⁂ ♦ ✈

From Maryland: *"A relaxed and gracious home away from home."* From New Hampshire: *"We felt like house guests—friends of Ann and Bill—in their very elegant home."* From Florida: *"Panache and '50s music with breakfast. What more could one ask for?"* From Virginia: *"A wonderful honeymoon spot."*

The simple bronze "Chester House" plaque on the wrought iron fence symbolizes the Wilsons' low-key approach to B&B, Bill's seventh career. He has worked in labor relations and as a stockbroker, manufacturer, conference center manager, and educational administrator. A chance conversation, a single B&B stay, and timing led to innkeeping in 1989. Bill, the chef, a New Englander by birth, and Ann, a former veterinary technician who is now official gardener, were enthusiastic Front Royal residents when they moved to "Ann's dream," this stately 1905 Georgian mansion, always a private home. Distinctive dentil molding is in the living room. Furnishings are antique and traditional. The extensive gardens include a formal boxwood maze, a fountain, wisteria arbors, shade trees, and benches. Small groups and nonprofit community organizations also enjoy the opportunity to have fund-raisers and small dinner parties here.

In residence: Spice, an English springer spaniel; Slater, the cat.
Bed and bath: Five second-floor rooms vary in size; all private full baths. Honeymoon suite with waist-high queen four-poster, wood-burning fireplace, separate sitting room. Large king-bedded room and a queen-bedded room overlook gardens. Queen four-poster, wood-burning fireplace. King/twins option in corner room has bath just outside door, which is shared only when same party books small adjacent double-bedded room.
Breakfast: 8–10. Freshly squeezed orange juice or apple cider. Homemade popovers or muffins. Fresh fruit. Cold cereals. Hot beverages. In formal dining room at table set with silver and crystal. Can last up to two hours.
Plus: Central air conditioning. Wood-burning fireplace and upright piano in living room. Fireplaced TV/smoking lounge. Card and game room. Porch and lawn games. Complimentary beverages. Guest refrigerator. Turndown service. Champagne tray for special occasions.

The Norris House Inn

108 Loudoun Street S.W., Leesburg, VA 22075

540/777-1806
800/644-1806
fax 540/771-8051

Hosts: Pamela and Donald McMurray
Location: In historic district, on main street. Walk to fine dining including restaurant across the street. Near bicycle trails: W&OD, 45 miles long, is 200 yards from inn; shuttle service provided for 5 miles to C&O Towpath (runs from Cumberland, Pa., to Washington, D.C., along Potomac River); if you'd like, luggage transported to next B&B booked. One-hour drive northwest of Wash-ington, D.C.; 16 miles from Dulles International Airport.
Open: Year round. Two-night minimum on weekends in April, May, June, September, and October and on three-day holiday weekends.
Rates: Weekdays, double bed $80 or $85 (overlooking garden); queen $100. On Friday and Saturday, $90 or $100; queen $120. Singles $15 less. Additional person $25. Less for off-season. Amex, Diners, MC, Visa.
♥ ✤ ◆ ⅙ ✈

"When we both traveled extensively during our careers as business executives, we would pick a location for weekends and fly home to California on Monday. After staying in or visiting more than 200 B&Bs, we bought this established B&B, a Federal-style brick house, in 1991. Built in 1806, it was added to in the mid-1800s by the Norris brothers, architects who built—with attention to detailed woodwork—every major building in town. For the feeling of a lovely Virginia country home, we have decorated with Federal colors, antiques, and reproductions. Pat's home economics major has inspired handmade candies for turndown service, Thanksgiving and Christmas dinners, and, next door, a public tearoom in another historic building."

In residence: Klaus (as in Santa), a handsome Persian cat, and Miss Lily, a pretty Himalayan cat, visit, often by guests' requests, in common areas.
Bed and bath: Six large rooms (all with sitting areas and antique bedspreads or quilts; some with feather beds) share three full baths (two rooms per bath) that are between rooms or in hall adjacent to room. Rooms have queen bed (one is canopied) with wood-burning fireplace, or double bed (one is canopied). Two third-floor dormer rooms, each with windows on three walls.
Breakfast: 7:30–9:30 (coffee and paper earlier) or weekdays as requested. Freshly squeezed orange juice. Fresh melon. Home-baked quick breads. Entree possibilties include French toast casserole with chicken/apple sausage or oven pancakes with fresh fruit or cooked apples and ham. Herbs from inn's garden used in season. Special diets accommodated. Served in fireplaced dining room with china, crystal, and silver, or on wicker-furnished 40-foot-long veranda that has three ceiling fans.
Plus: Individual room thermostats. Afternoon tea. Complimentary juice bar, fruit bowls, evening wine and hors d'oeuvres in fireplaced library. CD collection. Elaborate gardens with miniamphitheater. Croquet. Computer, fax, telephone mailbox, and audiovisual equipment available.

Springdale Country Inn
Lincoln, VA 22078

540/338-1833
800/388-1832
fax 540/338-1839

Hosts: Nancy and Roger Fones
Location: On a main artery surrounded by countryside, in historic district. On six acres with terraced gardens; walking bridges; brook; paths; original spring-, smoke-, and henhouses still here. Minutes to country store. Two miles to antiquing, restaurants, bicycle trail; 5 to golf and vineyard towns. Ten miles west of Leesburg, 45 west of Washington, D.C.; 18 to Dulles airport, 20 to Harpers Ferry.

Open: Year round.
Rates: Per room (vary according to private baths and working fireplaces). $95–$125. $200 three-room Victorian Suite (up to six people). Group ($35.50 and up for 25 or more), corporate, and government rates and packages available. MC, Visa.
♥ ❊ ◆ ✕ ⅄

"Little Girls' School Would Make Great B&B" read the newspaper advertisement photograph caption. Fast forward through five years of restoration/discovery, zoning hearings, research, and refurbishing, and you arrive at a 28-room Federal frame building "all back to the way it was in the 1830s." What was first a boarding school for high school girls, and later a Civil War hospital as well as a stop on the Underground Railroad, now has period wallcoverings, authentic antiques, refinished wide-board floors, and a (hidden) sprinkler system too. The Foneses show guests the dining room lamp under which Sam Rayburn and Lyndon Johnson played poker with their weekend retreat host, Dr. Walter Splawn, the then head of the Interstate Commerce Commission. To 200-year-old recipes, Nancy, who has developed an in-house catering company, adds native herbs and wildflowers that she has planted here. Weddings (inside or out), family reunions, and business meetings utilize the open spaces and formal ballroom (with piano). Many bicycling groups use the inn as a base for trips. "Interluders find us on weekends."

Nancy is a part-time IBM software trainer; Roger, a lawyer with the U.S. Justice Department.

Bed and bath: Eight rooms (two can be a suite) with double or twin beds; three with working fireplace. Six unattached full baths; three are private, three are shared. One room on first floor with Murphy bed is handicapped accessible. All rooms have desks and sofas. Office space and equipment available; TV and private phone may be arranged.
Breakfast: 7–noon. Homemade granola bars, Scottish shortbreads, hazelnut biscotti, Bavarian "quark" (a compote with yogurt and fruit), deep-dish apple pancakes, country baked eggs, frittata, pecan waffles, mini–eggs Benedict, country puff pastries. Eat in dining room, on sun porch, or in room.
Plus: Central air conditioning. Fireplaces in parlor, living and dining rooms, and three bedrooms. Five p.m. tea or wine and cheese hour. Complimentary recipe booklets. Oversized towels. Guest refrigerator. Homemade sweets. Overhead projector. VCR. Slide projector. Fax. Computer. Parking for 60 cars.

Fassifern Bed & Breakfast

Route 5, Box 87, Lexington, VA 24450   540/463-1013

Hosts: Mrs. Frances Smith and daughter Ann Carol Perry
Location: A parklike setting. On a country road. Two miles from town center. Three-quarters of a mile from I-64. Half mile from Virginia Horse Center; 15 miles from Blue Ridge Parkway; 11 from Natural Bridge.
Open: Year round.
Rates: $70 single. $84 double. $92 queen. MC, Visa.
♥ ⚓ ❀ ✈ ⚬

From an experienced Rhode Island innkeeper: *"Perfect in every detail—from decor to food to hospitality."*

Perfect, too, in enthusiasm. When Frances Smith's daughter, a Lexington Visitors' Center staffer, told her in 1988 that this established B&B, an 1867 Victorian home, was for sale, she "just knew" that it was time to leave the New Jersey drive-in theater business and return to her native Virginia, "which is filled with so much history." To the furnishings—such as an Austrian burled walnut bedroom set and Korean windows—that were owned by the previous innkeeper, a retired colonel, Frances has added her own Oriental rugs, antiques, charcoal portraits of grandparents—"and, in 1994, a Yamaha digital piano that makes every sound in the world! It's in the parlor with the wonderful 1894 pump organ that my brother, who is in the piano business, restored completely."

The entire inn is redecorated. Guests enjoy everything: the living and dining room fireplaces, the front porch with hanging plants, the accommodations, the century-old trees, the pond with fountain—and the hosts.

In residence: Everyone's favorite cat, T.C.—"tough cat"—loves everyone.
Bed and bath: Five rooms, all private baths. On second floor, queen, double, or twin beds with full bath. In cottage, queen with full bath, double bed with shower bath.
Breakfast: Usually 8–9:30. Coffee earlier for judges and others going to horse center. Choices include herb omelets, Virginia ham pate with melba toast and rye bread, bread pudding with fresh raspberry sauce, cheese grits with fried apples, strata with homemade salsa. Homemade rolls, sticky cinnamon buns, muffins, jellies and jams. Colombian coffee—decaf or regular. Served in dining room, on patio, or front porch.
Plus: Central air conditioning. Floor fans in guest rooms. No TV.

Llewellyn Lodge

603 South Main Street, Lexington, VA 24450   540/463-3235
800/882-1145

Hosts: Ellen and John Roberts
Location: In a lovely old residential neighborhood of this historic Shenandoah Valley community, "a New England town in Virginia." Ten minutes' walk to downtown historic area. Five-minute drive to Virginia Horse Center; three to Washington & Lee University or Virginia Military Institute.
Open: Year round. Two-night minimum in October.
Rates: Queen $75 or $80. Two double beds $75 (for two); additional person $15. Twin beds $75. King with TV $85. Singles $5 less. Amex, MC, Visa.
♥ ❀ ♦ ✈

Ellen says, "I've been in the hospitality business for more than 25 years, working in New York City for Pan Am and Finnair, and in Washington, D.C., with Finnair, Washington Circle Inn, and Fourways Restaurant. From all my worldwide travels, I fell in love with the concept of B&B, and in 1985 bought this half-century-old brick Colonial. Now it has just been freshly painted and papered (again). Furnishings include antiques, period pieces, and things I collected from different parts of the world. In 1989 I married John. An area native, he is now a Realtor and co-innkeeper who enjoys taking guests on fishing adventures."

Bed and bath: Six rooms, all private baths; three shower, three with tub and shower. Five second-floor rooms—king with sitting area and TV, three with queen beds, one with two brass double beds. First-floor room has two four-poster twin beds.
Breakfast: 8–9:30. Juice. Farm-fresh eggs with ham and sausage or bacon; French toast; or Belgian waffles. Homemade muffins or biscuits with home-made jellies. Garnished with fruit of the season. Hot beverages. Served in dining room.
Plus: Central air conditioning. Bedroom ceiling fans. Beverages and cana-pes. TV. Telephone room. Will meet guests at Greyhound bus stop.

> From Maryland: *"Hospitality is fantastic; the house is a home; the rooms are appointed quite nicely; the breakfast is a gourmet's delight and tailored to each guest; the price for all of this is quite reasonable. What more could one ask?"*

Seven Hills Inn

540/463-4715
fax 540/463-6526

408 South Main Street
Lexington, VA 24450

Hosts: Jane Grigsby Daniel; Jeanne Tomlinson
Location: On landscaped grounds. In a residential area (no trucks al-lowed) of downtown historic district. Five-minute walk to town center; 10 to campuses and visitor center. "His-tory, recreation, and education are the draw here!"

Open: Year round. Two-night min-imum on some college or special weekends.
Rates: $75–$95. Suite $145. Third person $15. Less in January and Feb-ruary. MC, Visa.
♥ ♠ ❖ ✈ ⅄

The classic white-columned brick Southern Colonial, built in 1928 as a fraternity house and most recently a Presbyterian children's home, was purchased in 1989 by Jane's son and daughter-in-law, who are currently living in England. (Grigsby ancestors built many area houses—now re-stored—in the late 1700s.) After the second and third floors were redesigned with all private baths, the Grigsbys, together with an interior designer, decorated with traditional colors and fabrics and antiques and hand-crafted reproductions. Co-innkeeper Jeanne hails from Ithaca, New York, where she had her own B&B for many years.

Bed and bath: Seven rooms, including one suite; all tub/shower baths. On second floor: one double-bedded room, private bath. Queen-bedded room and bath with Jacuzzi tub and double sinks can be a suite with another

(Please turn page.)

queen-bedded room, bath, parlor with porch. Third floor: two rooms, each with double bed and private bath. One room with two antique three-quarter beds shares huge bath with large room with canopied queen bed.
Breakfast: 8–9:30 or by request. Juice. Fresh or baked fruit. Homemade breads and muffins. Crepes or casserole. Served in large dining room at skirted round tables.
Plus: Central air conditioning. Guest refrigerator. Fireplaced living room. Big inviting porch. Basement lounge—only room where smoking is allowed—with fireplace, games, cable TV/VCR.

> From England: *"Impressed by the beautiful house and the hospitality."* From New Jersey: *"Friends in Lexington gave it a very high recommendation, and they were right. Excellent accommodations, hearty breakfast, congenial hostess."*

The Hummingbird Inn
Wood Lane, P.O. Box 147, Goshen, VA 24439-0147

540/997-9065
800/397-3214
fax 540/997-9065

Hosts: Jeremy and Diana M. Robinson
Location: On a quiet cul-de-sac "in this quaint Shenandoah Valley country town of 300 people." On an acre of landscaped grounds with picket fence in front, old red barn by trout stream in back. Near golf, swimming, skiing, canoeing, tubing, fishing, hunting. Five minutes to hiking (Goshen Pass), fishing, kayaking; 25 minutes to Warm Springs; 30 to Hot Springs; 40 to Natural Bridge; 35 to Staunton; 23 to Lexington.

Open: Year round. Two-night minimum on holiday weekends, graduation and parents' weekends.
Rates: April–October "Abigail" $80, "Eleanor" $70, "Franklin" $80, "Martha" $95. November–March $60/$70/$70/$85. Third person $15. Sunday–Thursday, third night free. Ten percent AARP discount. Mystery and art workshop weekend packages. Amex, MC, Visa.
♥ ❖ ♦ ⅍

> From many guests' long letters: *"A charmed visit . . . warm and cordial innkeepers . . . so beautiful . . . a relaxing cocoon from outside world . . . extensive book and music library . . . served hot gingerbread and coffee and tea by the fire . . . knowledgeable about the area and history of the house [Eleanor Roosevelt stayed here. Latin classes and Greek dancing once taught on third floor] . . . vistas from every window. . . . Flowers everywhere, even in the dead of winter. . . . By far the best B&B breakfast ever . . . all served on exquisite china . . . everything is special . . . felt like king and queen!"*

The Victorian Carpenter Gothic villa with wide-board floors, rustic beamed den, and solarium (now wicker-furnished) was just what the Robinsons hoped to find when they decided to leave New York City, where Diana was a registered nurse; Jeremy, a publisher of technical books. Since arriving "in this beautiful area with wonderful neighbors" in 1992, Jeremy has done much restoration; the house, originally built in 1780, has been an inn "on and off" since 1853. Diana, the acclaimed chef who grew up on a farm in England, has established a perennial garden.

In residence: "Lettie, our gentle and affectionate collie."
Bed and bath: Four named second-floor rooms; all private baths. Abigail—queen bed, roomy stall shower bath, private veranda. Eleanor—double bed, footed tub with brass shower; connecting double doors to Franklin room, which has queen four-poster and antique twin bed, modern tub/shower bath, access to wraparound veranda. Martha—pencil-post canopied queen bed, large full bath.
Breakfast: 8–9. Fruit compote or fresh fruit. Oven-baked honey-cinnamon French toast or omelets. Raisin-filled scones, rose geranium and lemon cake-breads. Freshly blended and brewed coffee.
Plus: Bedroom air conditioners and ceiling fans. Tea or lemonade and shortbread on arrival. Picnic baskets, $18. Lawn games. Candlelit dinner ($22.50 per person) with 24 hours' notice.

Shenandoah Countryside

Route 2, Box 370, Luray, VA 22835   540/743-6434

Hosts: Phel and Bob Jacobsen
Location: On a hilltop, surrounded by 45 acres with panoramic views of the Shenandoah Valley and Blue Ridge Mountains; 20 minutes from Shenandoah National Park entrance and Shenandoah River canoeing and tubing; 10 minutes from Luray Caverns; two miles from swimming beach; two hours from Washington, D.C.
Open: Year round. Reservations required. Two-night minimum on holiday and October weekends.
Rates: $60 single, $65 double.
♥ ⊶ ⁂ ⋊ ⋊

After a friend said, "I could have stayed there forever," we had the opportunity to pedal up the winding lane, see the chimney smoke from the Finnish sauna, and meet Phel, Bob, and the dogs. They were waiting for us outside of the dream (brick) house that the Jacobsens designed and built—with some help—in 1980. After enjoying a refreshing drink on the screened porch, which overlooks Luray in the distance, we visited in the keeping room with wood-burning stove. Somehow theater, music, family, and environmental concerns became part of the unfinished conversation.

The spacious and gracious home has enough decorative and imaginative touches (all Phel's), blending country and traditional themes, to fill many magazine pages. Bob, now retired superintendent of the Shenandoah National Park, and Phel tend an extensive organic garden. They host guests who savor the view (selected by Bloomingdale's to represent Virginia B&Bs in a Manhattan photography exhibit based on this book), the food, the sauna—and the hospitality.

In residence: Miss Kathryn, an outside cat.
Foreign language spoken: Limited Finnish.
Bed and bath: Three rooms. First-floor room with queen bed, private shower bath. Two large second-floor rooms share one full and one half bath and sauna shower. One has a brass double bed (Phel's grandmother's) and a balcony; the other has king/twins, dressing room.
Breakfast: 8–10. Homegrown berries in season. Homemade breads, jams, and jellies. Sausage or bacon. Entree might be eggs Benedict, Finnish pancake, or fruit waffles. Sweet rolls or coffee cake. Phel and Bob usually join guests

(Please turn page.)

at beautifully set harvest table or on huge cathedral-ceilinged screened porch. Views everywhere.

Plus: Beverages. Often, evening dessert. Bedroom ceiling fans. Robes for sauna bath. Three five-speed bicycles; one tandem.

Langhorne Manor

804/846-4667
313 Washington Street   (guest line) 800/851-1466
Lynchburg, VA 24504-4619   804/845-8419

Hosts: Jaime (Hi-Mee) and Jaynee Acevedo

Location: On historic Diamond Hill in a quiet downtown neighborhood of large old homes. "Our architecturally unmatched downtown area has an antiques mall, a family restaurant, museums, and gardens." Three blocks from Lynchburg Expressway and Visitors' Information Center.

Open: Year round. Two-night minimum on some weekends.

Rates: $95 two double beds. $80 one double bed. $90 queen. $105 suite. $15 extra person. Corporate rates available. Option of light suppers. Package rates with area dining, theaters, museums, massage. Amex, Discover, MC, Visa.
🛥 ❖ ♦ ✈ ✂

> From Washington, D.C.: *"A nice escape."* From Australia: *"The hosts are special. . . . House is a delight."* From Texas: *"Most creative and delicious breakfasts I've ever had . . . wonderful accommodations . . . they enjoy what they do and make everyone feel at home in their home."*

And to think the Acevedos, who met while working for the same Washington, D.C., catering company (now they have their own), started in 1987 with an 1850s tall-ceilinged brick tobacco mansion that had become a vacant 13-apartment building. Now, while appreciating the relaxed atmosphere, guests catch the Acevedos' contagious enthusiasm for this "forever-in-progress" 27-room property and for "charming Lynchburg with picturesque rolling hills and riverfront now being revitalized." Here there is zest for food (and its presentation), for family, for life! Horseshoe-shaped exterior steps lead to a huge crystal-chandeliered reception hall. Eclectic antique furnishings include Louis XIV gilt parlor pieces. A trompe l'oeil sky is on the ceiling of the oak-paneled dining room. An art gallery is in the enormous second-floor hall. And Jaime's Colombian heritage is seen in many shared ancestral traditions.

In residence: Concierge Jimmy, age 10. Bellhop William, age 6. Arizona is a long-haired cat, age 4.

Foreign language spoken: Jaime speaks Spanish.

Bed and bath: Four very large second-floor (19 steps from first floor) rooms with air conditioning, ceiling fan, phone. All private baths. Room with two double beds, sofa, gas fireplace. Queen bed, gas fireplace, claw-footed tub bath; can be a suite with double-bedded room that has private hall shower bath. Suite has two double beds, gas fireplace, sitting room, claw-footed tub and shower bath.

Breakfast: "Almost any time." Among favorites "rarely made with recipes": gingerbread waffles with lemon or orange-cranberry ice cream; cottage cheese pancakes; egg roulade; garlic potatoes; fruit strudels; unusual muffins; scones. Most special diets accommodated.

Plus: Evening beverages—*agua aromatica, panela* (Spanish raw sugar and lime drink), sun teas. Cookies baked by the boys. Mixers and bar fruits. Babysitting. Turndown service. Ironed bed linens! Off-street parking. Maps for "getting lost." Small conferences booked.

Lynchburg Mansion Inn Bed and Breakfast

804/528-5400
800/352-1199

405 Madison Street, Lynchburg, VA 24504-2435

Hosts: Bob and Mauranna Sherman
Location: In residential National Register district with other restored mansions (tours arranged). On street with turn-of-the-century brick and Belgian block.

Open: Year round.
Rates: $84 single, $89 double. $119 suites. $20 third person. Amex, Diners, MC, Visa.
♥ ♣ ♦ ✈ ✕

Drive through the gates of the 6-foot iron fence that surrounds the stucco Spanish Georgian mansion and carriage house. Continue under the columned porte cochere. When you enter the 50-foot grand hall—pictured in *Country Inns* magazine and viewed by thousands during Historic Garden Week—you see magnificent cherry woodwork everywhere, photos from the original owner's family, and a three-storied spindled staircase. Decor is classic, elegant, and comfortable. Doorknobs are cut glass. The 105-foot wicker- and plant-filled wraparound veranda, truly an outdoor living space, is terra-cotta tiled. Azaleas, hydrangeas, boxwood, hollies, flowering trees, and wisteria too have been planted on the grounds, which were once known for their elaborate gardens.

The Shermans, Realtors in northern Virginia for more than 20 years, "decided to open a B&B (never having stayed in one) at the suggestion of several Realtors we talked to while house hunting up and down the East Coast. We knew nothing about Lynchburg when we saw the *Washington Post* ad for this house (which had those cherry columns hidden behind sheet rock). Now we have the joy of seeing brides toss bouquets from the Juliet balcony. Guests unwind, explore this luxurious B&B, sip iced tea or hot chocolate, relax in the five-person porch spa, and enjoy the city's history and culture."

In residence: In hosts' quarters—two miniature schnauzers.
Bed and bath: Five rooms with private en-suite tub/shower baths. First-floor suite has private veranda entrance, king-bedded room, solarium with queen sleep sofa, space for three-quarter rollaway, working fireplace; solarium with refrigerator (with beverages), popcorn maker. High king four-poster, 16 pillows, lots of lace, working fireplace, large original tub in bath. Country French room has queen four-poster. The Nantucket king-bedded room has shells "and gifts from friends who know we love the water." Garden suite with private entrance, high king bed, claw-footed tub bath, fireplaced beamed living room, dining room, kitchen.
Breakfast: Upstairs, early coffee and juice on a silver tray. Flexible hours for meal. Orange juice and ice water in crystal. Hot or cold fruit dishes. Peach French toast, quiche, sausage-and-egg casserole, or Belgian waffles with

(Please turn page.)

country ham. Butter shaped in roses and leaves on crushed ice. All presented in formal dining room with silver, antique china, background music. **Plus:** Room phones. Central two-zone air conditioning. Fireplaced living room with piano. Fireplaced library with period books. Turndown service. Beverages, goodies, and fruit always available. Color TV with remote control, free HBO, ESPN, and other channels. Morning newspaper at your door. Robes for spa.

From Texas: *"Five-star accommodations."*

Dulwich Manor Bed & Breakfast   804/946-7207

Route 5, Box 173-A, Amherst, VA 24521

Hosts: Bob and Judy Reilly
Location: "In lush countryside" at the end of a winding country lane. On 85 acres of woodland and meadows with mountain views and lots of wildlife. Fifteen miles north of Lynchburg, 3 from Sweet Briar College; 22 from Blue Ridge Parkway; 20 to spectacular Crabtree Falls, 45 to Natural Bridge, 25 to Wintergreen ski resort.
Open: Year round.
Rates: $69 shared bath. $79 private bath and working fireplace. $89 with Jacuzzi. Honeymoon packages available. Third person in room: $20 adult, $5 under age 12, $10 ages 12–17.
♥ ♨ ❀ ◆ ✈

The perfect match began in 1988 when the hosts ended their year-long search for a new lifestyle. In the metropolitan New York area Bob was an actor who had lead roles in *The King and I* and *Evita.* He also sang with the Buddy Rich Orchestra and Ray Charles Singers. Judy worked in public relations and advertising. They bought this imposing 22-room English-style brick manor house, which has a columned veranda (spectacular sunsets), a third-floor ballroom, a large oak central staircase, five acres of lawn, and, in the spring, "a sea of lace from dogwoods." They did all the papering and painting, added baths, and furnished with antiques, reproductions, modern art, and comfortable family pieces. Now they are the official gardeners/wedding coordinators/historic preservationists whose guests from New Jersey, Maryland, North Carolina, Pennsylvania, Virginia, Florida, California, and Massachusetts wrote to me about "the best"—referring to everything, including the decor, food, and accommodations; the outdoor hot tub in the Victorian gazebo; and the hospitality.

In residence: Two "woodland guides"—one mixed breed and one cocker spaniel. Two lap cats—not allowed in guests' areas.
Bed and bath: Six air-conditioned rooms; two also have ceiling fans. All with cedar-lined closets. Second floor—five very large queen-bedded rooms. One with canopied bed, large bath with whirlpool tub and separate shower. Two rooms—one with private shower bath, one with private tub/shower bath—have working fireplaces and window seats. One with Shaker-style canopied bed shares a full bath with room that has a queen and a twin bed. Third-floor "treehouse room" has antique double bed, country furnishings, private tucked-under-eaves shower bath. Rollaway, crib, and high chair available.

Breakfast: 8:30–9:30 weekends; weekday time set by guests. Cheese-and-egg souffle, baked stuffed French toast, blueberry or apple pancakes. Side dish may be corn or apple fritters, potato pancakes, quiche. Bacon, ham, or sausage. Fruit in season. Orange juice, fresh-brewed teas, coffees (decaf).
Plus: Parlor with fireplace, upright piano. Study with fireplace, TV. Refreshments. Hammock. Badminton. Double swing. Transportation to/from bus, train, or airport. Planned tour routes.

Winridge Bed & Breakfast   804/384-7220
Route 1, Box 362, Winridge Drive, Madison Heights, VA 24572-9781

Hosts: LoisAnn and Ed Pfister
Location: On 14 acres—3 are lawn—with panoramic views of Blue Ridge Mountains. Six miles north of Lynchburg, 14 east of Blue Ridge Parkway.

Open: Year round.
Rates: Per room. $65 shared bath; $79 private. Family rate: second room is 50 percent less for under age 18.
♠ ♣ ⁂ ◆ ✗ ✂

From Virginia, Pennsylvania, Florida, California, North Carolina, Massachusetts, Indiana, Minnesota: *"Unique blend of elegance from a bygone era and the warmth of a modern-day family . . . great suggestions for places to eat and visit. . . . Lovely and relaxing . . . even provided a crib and toys for our eight-month-old. . . . Able to conduct my business during the day and actually look forward to return to my evening 'digs.' . . . Simple elegance. . . . Breakfasts are beautiful and delicious. . . . The bed was so-o-o comfortable that we came home and bought a similar mattress. . . . Meticulously clean . . . chocolates before bedtime. . . . The house is absolutely grand. . . . Out in the country. Nice and quiet. . . . You would have thought we were friends for years. . . . Wish we could have stayed longer."*

Those excerpts are from dozens of ecstatic letters written to me. A family atmosphere is exactly what the Pfisters had in mind when they decided to move from the Lynchburg house that they had restored to this 1910 white frame Southern Colonial with mesmerizing view from its full-width second-story porch. Restoration here included four new 20-foot Corinthian columns. Ed, a former food service executive who plays percussion with the Lynchburg Symphony, has become known for his greenhouse business specializing in perennials, unique annuals, and container gardening. (Bring your site plans and he'll consult on gardening design.) LoisAnn retired from her 10-year catering position "to be home with our daughters, to cook, and to meet people."

In residence: Frances, age nine; Elizabeth, age seven. Outdoors, horses Blaze and Chrissy; Charlie, a German shepherd; Bitzie, a Bernese mountain dog. Three outdoor cats; one indoor cat (can be confined to hosts' quarters).
Bed and bath: Three second-floor rooms. One with queen four-poster, three large bay windows, private shower bath. Room with queen bed and another with two twins share a full bath with footed tub and brass/porcelain shower.
Breakfast: 6:30–8:30. Fresh fruit. Juice. Oven-baked French toast with pecan topping, bacon-and-cheese frittata, or stuffed French toast with fresh

(Please turn page.)

blueberry sauce. Strawberry cream cheese Danish, blueberry patch muffins, or coffee cakes. Hot beverages. Served in dining room with tall bay windows. **Plus:** Bedroom air conditioning (window units) and ceiling fans. Individual thermostats. Fireplaced library and living room. Cranberry cooler or mint tea. Homemade treats. Turndown service. Line-dried sheets. Books. Games. Swing. Hammock. Picnic table. Bluebird houses. Pick-your-own strawberries for snacks or picnics. Gather chestnuts to take home. Plants for sale.

Middleburg Country Inn

109 East Washington Street
Middleburg, VA 22117

540/687-6082
800/262-6082
fax 540/687-5603

Hosts: John and Susan Pettibone
Location: On Route 50, the main street of a historic one-light town (population: 550) in fox-hunting country. Walk to shops, galleries, restaurants. Forty miles west of Washington, D.C.; 50 to Skyline Drive. Two miles to three wineries that offer tours. Ten-minute drive to Oatlands, National Trust mansion with formal gardens.
Open: Year round.

Rates: Rooms: Sunday–Thursday $89 (corporate rates available); Friday–Saturday $109 queen, $139 king. For overnight guests only—dinner option(reserve by noon, please) $18 per person, wine extra. Suites: $225 includes dinner for two, Jacuzzi, flowers, champagne, hors d'oeuvres. Extra person $10. No charge for children. Amex, Discover, MC, Visa.
♥ ♠ ❀ ♦ ✈

Welcome! Upon arrival, you will be served a beverage and baked goods—and an invitation to make yourself at home. Susan learned the art of innkeeping from her mother, who was still running a North Carolina inn—in Nag's Head—at age 90. Together, in the late 1980s, Susan and John, a Middleburg native, planned and directed the two-year conversion of this red brick building, a parsonage for 150 years. They tunneled through one 18-inch brick wall (guests love to hear "what was"); opened and refurbished fireplaces; and furnished with canopied beds, antiques, and yards and yards of fabric. Romantics, international visitors, and wedding and reunion planners too all appreciate the food, the terrace's 8-by-10-foot hot tub, and the rear balcony that offers a wonderful view of the countryside.

In residence: Jason Ferguson, innkeeper
Foreign languages spoken: French, Spanish, and "Southern English."
Bed and bath: Eight rooms (include two suites) on three floors; all have king or queen canopied bed, wood-burning fireplace, private full bath, cable TV, VCR (lending library of movies right here). Suites—they are large—have two-person Jacuzzi and kitchenette. Sofa bed in some rooms. Cots and cribs available.
Breakfast: 8:30–11. "A brunch." Fresh fruits. Waffles (blueberry, apple spice, or chocolate chip with maple syrup, honey, and peanut butter), eggs Benedict; hot maple oatmeal, Southern grits, and cold cereals. Almost-famous warm glazed coffee cake, homemade breads, muffins, jams, jellies, apple butter. In dining room at table for eight or at small tables with umbrellas on open veranda overlooking countryside.

Plus: Central air conditioning. Fireplaced living room. Off-street parking. Transportation to/from Dulles International Airport.

Widow Kip's Shenandoah Inn

355 Orchard Drive   **540/477-2400**
Mount Jackson, VA 22842

Hosts: Betty and Bob Luse
Location: Rural setting. House is visible from I-81. Shenandoah River is 50 yards away. Short walk to village (population: 1,100) center with craft shop, art gallery, four antiques shops. Four fine restaurants within 10 miles; 90 minutes from Washington, D.C.

Open: Year round.
Rates: In main house—$55 single, $65 or $70 double. Courtyard efficiency cottages—$75 and $85. $12 per extra person. MC, Visa.
♥ ⭐ ❀ ◆

The restored 1830 home, once part of a huge farm, has picture-perfect guest rooms—featured in *Country Magazine*—with wonderful wallcoverings in shades of burgundy, mauves, yellow, Wiliamsburg blue, or peach and green. Guests come for all the area offers—hiking, canoeing, downhill skiing, golf, antiquing, caverns, and restaurants. And they enjoy the pool right here.

This is not a coast-to-coast-search or even a lifelong-dream story. It all began with a "You'd make great B&B hosts" comment from the Luses' daughter-in-law in Virginia. It continues with Bob, retired from the world of marketing in Manhattan, seeing a *New York Times* ad about this B&B for sale. One trip is all it took. By Christmas 1991 the Luses moved their Victorian furnishings into this established B&B. Now their "forest" (it will be) of 800 newly planted trees is growing. And the hosts, who are very active with local arts organizations, say, "B&B is like having company 24 hours a day and we love it."

In residence: Cali, a calico cat. "Kip is a love bird loved by guests."
Bed and bath: Seven air-conditioned rooms with private baths. In main house, working fireplace in each guest room. First-floor room has eight-foot-high Lincoln double bed, shower bath. Four second-floor rooms, one with canopied queen, tub and shower bath; one canopied queen, shower bath; two double-bedded rooms, shower bath. In one cottage is a double-bedded room, sitting room with trundle bed for two, cable TV, tub and shower bath, kitchenette, porch. Second cottage has a double-bedded room, cable TV, shower bath, porch.
Breakfast: At 8 and at 9 (can last for a couple of hours). Stuffed French toast and award-winning apple dapple cake are favorites. Shenandoah apple juice; fruit; homemade sausage, muffins, and breads. In Victorian dining room.
Plus: Fireplaced living room with VCR, classic old movies, game board, books. Welcoming beverages. Picnic table area with gas grill. Bicycles (no charge).

Acorn Inn, Inc.   804/361-9357
P.O. Box 431, Nellysford, VA 22958

Hosts: Kathy Plunket Versluys and Martin Versluys
Location: Rustic, rural, peaceful. In orchard and vineyard country in Blue Ridge Mountains' foothills. On Route 634—12 miles from Wintergreen resort's ski slopes; 2½ miles to golf course, deli, restaurants; 30 miles southwest of Charlottesville.

Open: Year round. Two-night minimum on weekends in October, in ski season, and some holidays.
Rates: In barn $47 double, $39 single. In farmhouse (available seasonally) $65, $10 third person. Cottage $95 for two, $10 additional person over age 16. MC, Visa.
♥ ♨ ♣ ✗ ⌿

The original horse stall doors are still used—now for each of the guest rooms in the converted one-story barn. The hosts, two world travelers, have created a clean, warm, comfortable, and affordable European-style place to stay. It has a (1991) solar water heating system and a skylit "uncommon room" with a huge locally made wood-burning soapstone fireplace and bake-oven. (Cookies often made here on chilly weekends.)

Martin, a carpenter and conservationist, formerly did microfiche work for a Dutch publisher. A native of Holland, he has bicycled through almost 100 countries. Kathy, a photographer and wood-block printmaker, is also a court translator. (Before settling down here in 1987, the hosts lived in South America for four years.) Their own residence, a renovated 1937 farmhouse with B&B rooms in season (see below), is 100 yards from the inn.

In residence: Son Klaas, age six, rides as a stoker on parents' tandem.
Foreign languages spoken: Dutch, German, Spanish, some Portuguese.
Bed and bath: Ten carpeted rooms, each about 12 feet square, with double bed, wardrobe, chair and desk, five-foot-high screened window, individually controlled baseboard electric heat. Two baths, one for men and one for women, each with two sinks, two toilets separated by shuttered doors, and handicapped-accessible showers. Cottage with one bedroom, living room with TV, air conditioning, bath, kitchen, sleeps four or five. In January, February, May, October, and by special arrangement—two farmhouse queen-bedded rooms share a tub/shower bath.
Breakfast: Usually 8–9. Orange juice, fresh fruit, homemade whole wheat breads, sweet loaves, cream cheese, butter and jams, fruit cobbler in season. Coffee, tea. Buffet style.
Plus: Central air conditioning in barn rooms. Color TV. Sauna. Hot beverages always available. Microwave and toaster. Refrigerator space. Outdoor table and gas barbecue. Laundry facilities.

From North Carolina, New York, Maryland, Virginia, Washington, D.C.: "*Congenial innkeepers who specialize in the art of conversation. . . . Impressive collection of their own photographs and woodcuts. . . . The Acorn created our adventure. . . . A hybrid of a pension and a hostel. . . . Helped them make cider on [wooden, hand-cranked] press. . . . Treated us like family.*"

The Meander Inn

P.O. Box 443, Routes 612 and 613
Nellysford, VA 22958

804/361-1121
fax 804/361-1380

Hosts: Kathy and Rick Cornelius
Location: Secluded. On a granite knoll with spectacular panoramic views of Blue Ridge Mountains and Wintergreen. A 50-acre working farm off a dirt road, just across a trestle bridge. Half a mile off Highway 151. Within 10 minutes of wineries, Wintergreen Ski Resort, championship golf courses, tennis, horseback riding, and Appalachian Trail. Thirty minutes

south of Charlottesville.
Open: Year round. Two-night minimum on most weekends and holidays.
Rates: Per room. Monday–Wednesday $75 private bath, $70 private hall bath. Thursday–Sunday $95 private bath, $85 private hall bath. Weekend rates apply during holidays and in October. MC, Visa.
♥ ♣ ♦ ✕ ⌇

"Many of our guests, who come to focus on Monticello and other historic sites, stay in the country. They visit the small wineries, hike to Crabtree Falls, go horseback riding, attend crafts or antiques shows, or visit the new Walton's Museum. Or they stay right here, rock on the porch, watch the horses in the pastures, and allow Waylon to escort them to the river to fish or to swim in our swimming hole. After skiing, they sip wine in the outdoor hot tub and then enjoy a gourmet meal at the nearby Veranda Restaurant."

This B&B sort of started with the player piano that the Corneliuses restored when they were living in Washington, D.C. Rick was the U.S. Navy's environmental attorney, and Kathy, an avid tennis player, was in sales with AT&T. Subsequently they spent all of 1987 restoring this 1913 Victorian farmhouse—"perfect for the piano and people too"—and filled it with comfortable antiques and reproductions. Here they keep chickens, raise hay, and board 10 horses (not for public riding). Kathy is full-time innkeeper. Rick is president of an environmental consulting firm.

In residence: "Waylon, our rottweiler, loves to play tug-of-war with his rope and guests." Four outdoor cats. "Oscar is the great blue heron who lives on our stretch of the Rockfish River."
Foreign languages spoken: French and some Spanish.
Bed and bath: Five second-floor rooms accessed by front and back stairs. All private baths. Four with queen beds (two are four-posters), full baths; one queen room with hall shower bath. Rollaway available.
Breakfast: Until 10. Eggs (gather your own, if you'd like) served in vegetable frittata, sausage-and-grits casserole, or pear pancakes. Blueberry or raspberry (freshly picked) strudel, muffins, or sweet breads. Breakfast meats, fresh or baked fruits, coffee, and juice. In dining room or on deck overlooking the river.
Plus: Central air conditioning on first level; separate units and ceiling fans in bedrooms. Ornate wood stove in living room. Refreshments. Robes for outdoor hot tub, open until 11 p.m. (River) swimming hole right here.

From Delaware: *"Rick and Kathy will feed your body in the morning while the Meander Inn (if you let it) nourishes your soul."*

A Touch of Country

540/740-8030

9329 Congress Street, New Market, VA 22844

Hosts: Dawn Kasow and Jean Schoellig
Location: On main street (Route 11) in a small town (population: 1,400), ¼ mile off I-81. Two hours from Washington, D.C. Thirty minutes to Skyline Drive, 15 to Luray Caverns. Across from two churches. Within walking distance of restaurants and shops.

Open: Year round. Two-night minimum on holiday and October weekends.
Rates: Hallway bath $60. En-suite bath $65 double bed, $75 queen. Singles $10 less. Ten percent discount for entire house. MC, Discover, Visa.
🖊 ⁂ ♦ ✈ ✄

> From Washington, D.C.: *"Comfortably furnished . . . everything is immaculate . . . floor plan and arrangement of house enables maximum privacy . . . breakfast is a high point . . . generous and attractive portions of healthy fare . . . a wealth of information on local points of interest and history . . . a friendly and warm setting."*

The 1870s frame house was, except during its 1920s days as a tourist house, a private residence. In 1988 Jean and Dawn restored it and furnished with collectibles and some antiques. In Washington, D.C., Jean was a registered nurse and educator; Dawn was in pharmaceutical sales and education. Here they host guests who come for hiking (several special overlooks and mountain paths recommended), bicycling (routes suggested), the Skyline Drive, antiquing, and caverns. Jean dovetails hosting with nursing; Dawn cooks at a local restaurant.

In residence: Four dogs—two Labradors and two cocker spaniels—live in their own outdoor houses.
Bed and bath: Six air-conditioned rooms; all private shower baths. In main house—four rooms with ceiling fan and adjoining baths. Three with queen bed; one room with a double and a twin bed, paneling from old church parsonage. Carriage house has two double-bedded rooms, en-suite baths. Rollaway available.
Breakfast: 8–9:30. Fruits, eggs, breakfast meats, pancakes, French toast, breads, muffins. In dining room at three tables set for four.
Plus: Wood stove in family and living rooms. Air-conditioned family room with TV, VCR, CD, tape player. Tea and sodas. Use of refrigerator. Alpenglo sparkling cider in bedrooms. Porch swings.

---

*T*hink of bed and breakfast as a people-to-people concept.

Page House Inn

323 Fairfax Avenue, Norfolk, VA 23507-2215
804/625-5033
fax 804/623-9451

Hosts: Stephanie and Ezio DiBelardino
Location: "In Norfolk's secret garden, the old-fashioned tree-lined Ghent Historic District, a neighborhood filled with history and culture." A block from Chrysler Museum with renowned glass collection. Short walk to financial district, Waterside, Sentara Norfolk General Hospital, Eastern Virginia Medical School, and Nauticus—The National Maritime Center.
Open: Year round. Two-night minimum for Harborfest (first week in June) and some holiday weekends.
Rates: $75–$95 twin, double bed, or European king. $105 queen canopy with fireplace and whirlpool; $120 with fireplace, whirlpool for two. $130–$145 suites with wet bar. Singles $5 less. Corporate rates, Sunday–Thursday. MC, Visa.
♥ ⁂ ♦ ✗ ⚡

From New Jersey: *"Breathtaking . . . crisp, white linens that make you feel as though you were the first person to use them . . . Stephanie is warm, friendly, charming, helpful . . . have stayed at 38 Mid-Atlantic B&Bs . . . this is the best."*

Some other guests speak of the "drawing room atmosphere created by the Perle Mesta of Norfolk" in this Georgian Revival built in 1898 with Flemish bond–pattern brickwork and a colonnaded front porch. It was scheduled for demolition in 1990 before being rebuilt by contractor Ezio DiBelardino, a Renaissance man who, like the original builder, Herman Page, immigrated to this country. Following an intense series of zoning hearings (a saga in itself), the DiBelardinos opened as a B&B in 1991. Today the elegant, comfortable, award-winning house symbolizes the impact that B&Bs have had on historic preservation and the hospitality industry. It is filled with wonderful artwork; 19th- and early 20th-century antiques and reproductions; Staffordshire china; 51 new handmade solid oak paneled doors; a monumental three-storied staircase; handmade oak Venetian blinds; and Page family mementos, including the family Bible and an 1863 lineage chart that dates back to A.D. 1237.

And there's effervescent Stephanie. A former chemical corporation executive, she, together with craftsman Ezio, is hailed by major media; by business guests who appreciate power breakfasts at separate tables; by romantics; by in-vitro patients who were B&B guests in the previous Norfolk DiBelardino home; Herman Page descendants; and by 1,000-plus local residents who toured the house for the benefit of the Children's Hospital.

In residence: Tootsie and Charlie, two Boston terriers.
Foreign languages spoken: "Fluent Italian, limited Spanish."
Bed and bath: Six rooms—two are suites with living room and wet bar; all private baths. On second floor, queen-bedded rooms with working fireplaces; two have canopied bed, whirlpool bath. On third floor, skylit rooms. Room with European king (antique twins now a king), oversized shower in bath. Double sleigh bed, claw-footed tub and hand-held shower. Large twin-bedded room with deep soaking tub in bath. Each floor has a common sitting area with views of the turn-of-the-century row houses.
Breakfast: Flexible; usually 7–9. Fresh fruits. Freshly baked bread, muffins, or scones. Yogurt, granola, cereals. Cheeses. "Best cappuccino in town!" In

(Please turn page.)

formal dining room at table set with starched linens, fine china, crystal. (Continental menu for room service.)

Plus: Private phones in rooms. Free fax. Central air conditioning. Fireplaced living room. Tea or cappuccino. Soft drinks and juices in guest refrigerator. Fresh fruit and flowers. Hospitality baskets. Same-day laundry service.

The Spinning Wheel Bed and Breakfast

31 North Street, Onancock, VA 23417   **804/787-7311**
Winter contact: (winter) **540/684-0067**
509 South Fairfax Street, Alexandria, VA 22314

Hosts: David and Karen Tweedie
Location: On residential block on main street in historic 1680 waterfront town. Steps to Tweedies' own gallery and antiques shop. One block to town hall, bakery, four restaurants, gazebo in old town square, and historic museum open to public. Short walk to wharf in deep-water harbor (come by boat) or to ferry to Tangier Island. Near ocean beach and boat rentals. One mile from Route 13; 30 minutes to Chincoteague.

Open: May-October (weekends only in spring and fall).
Rates: $85 per room; $95 Friday or Saturday only. $15 rollaway. MC, Visa.
♥ ❀ ♦ ✈

"Yes, bid on tandems! Some day we're going to have a B&B." The Tweedies' "some day" happened in 1993, when they opened the first B&B, an overnight success story, in this "charming nonresort-like" National Register town they fell in love with during "an adventure—a trip where we stay at B&Bs and explore unfamiliar areas."

David thinks Onancock looks the way Long Island did when he grew up there. For Karen it is reminiscent of New England, where she learned how to spin on an antique wheel. Now she has a collection—some are 250 years old—displayed throughout this 1890s folk Victorian. Over a five-year period the house was impeccably restored by Karen, a teacher of the deaf, and David, a speech pathologist and audiologist who teaches graduate courses at Gallaudet University in Washington, D.C. The Tweedies—"we're auction hounds!"—also restored their extensive and still-growing antiques collection. All the pine floors are refinished. Baths are new. Old hardware and fixtures are on the third-floor custom-made reproduction doors. The quilts, made by Karen, are modeled after traditional patterns in her collection.

In residence: A big hit with guests—"Frequently photographed Nelly, our national champion Old English sheepdog."
Foreign language spoken: Karen and David know American Sign Language.
Bed and bath: Five air-conditioned rooms, each with a spinning wheel, antique brass or iron queen bed, attached private shower bath, plush robes. The three third-floor rooms have cathedral ceilings and share a deck. Rollaway available.
Breakfast: At 9. Crepes with seasonal fruit, eggs a la moutarde, country casseroles, French toast a l'orange. Homemade scones and muffins. Or "a continental picnic left at your door."

Plus: Bedroom ceiling fans on first and second floors. Ornate 1880s parlor stove for chilly evenings. Welcoming refreshments. Turndown service. Tandem and 10-speed bikes. Arrangements made for golf, tennis, and swimming at a private club nearby. And if you tell them that you are from Scotland, the Scottish flag will be hung for your arrival.

Hidden Inn   540/672-3625
249 Caroline Street, Orange, VA 22960   fax 540/672-5029

Hosts: Barbara and Ray Lonick
Location: A surprise. At the intersection of Routes 15 and 20, turn into the unpaved drive to a pocket of seven acres of lawn and trees. Four miles from Montpelier; 25 to Monticello and Charlottesville. Within 15 miles of three wineries and two battlefields; 90 minutes from Washington, D.C.

Open: Year round. Two-night minimum on weekends.
Rates: $79–$129 double, $59–$79 single. $139–$159 whirlpool tub rooms. $20 third person. Dinner option $29 per person. Winery, wedding, and honeymoon packages available. Amex, MC, Visa.
♥ ❖ ♦ ✈ ✄

An amazing transformation. My husband and I stayed here when it was decorated in country style. When the Lonicks bought the Victorian farmhouse in 1986, they redecorated the spacious public areas with beautiful reproduction Victorian gas chandeliers, Oriental rugs, and formal swags. The dining room is picture perfect. (*Forbes* magazine thought so too—when they covered a cycling group that stayed here.) The large fireplaced living room has comfortable seating. A guest house, carriage house, and cottage have been renovated. Jacuzzis and fireplaces are added features. And by popular demand, Barbara has written a 50-page cookbook.

Before becoming fun-loving hosts—seen on the Learning Channel's "Great Country Inns"—the Lonicks lived in Washington, D.C., and San Francisco while Ray was a Xerox sales executive. Their four-year search for a new career and place brought them to this area, which they knew from driving their daughter to Sweet Briar College. Now they host many who come for romantic getaways, many returnees, and many who like good food.

In residence: Outdoor cats patrol the grounds.
Foreign language spoken: Spanish.
Bed and bath: Ten rooms. Five in main house (first and second floors). Total of five—two with working fireplace—in three other buildings; one with screened porch, one with private deck, one with private veranda. All private baths; oversized Jacuzzi tubs, tub/shower units, or shower only. King/twins, queen, or double beds; some four-posters, some canopied or brass; handmade quilts (some by Barbara). Cottage has skylights, double-sized Jacuzzi tubs, color TV.
Breakfast: 8–10; other times for business travelers. Juice, cereal (oatmeal in winter), homemade muffins and biscuits, fresh fruit with yogurt and granola, cheese eggs, maple-flavored sausage, pumpkin pancakes. "Our own special coffee."
Plus: Air conditioners in all bedrooms, ceiling fans in some. Electronic piano in main living room. Tea (included in rate) at 4 p.m. with cookies or

(Please turn page.)

homemade breads. Wicker-furnished wraparound porch. Guest refrigerators. Bath sheets. For late arrivals, candlelight picnic basket ($39) with champagne or wine. With advance notice, dinner option Tuesday–Saturday.

The Holladay House

155 West Main Street
Orange, VA 22960-1528

540/672-4893
800/358-4422
fax 540/672-3028

Hosts: Pete and Phebe Holladay
Location: On a block of older homes—next door to Pete's Uncle Billy's house—with lovely gardens and treed yards in this friendly historic town. Minutes' walk to popular new restaurant, James Madison Museum, church where General Robert E. Lee worshiped, historical society, cafe and market in an old firehouse. Four miles east of Montpelier. "Our countryside has rich farmlands, pick-your-own orchards, interesting little shops, and vineyards to tour." Ninety minutes from Washington, D.C., and Richmond, Virginia; 30 from Charlottesville.
Open: Year round except Thanksgiving and Christmas. Two-night minimum on October weekends.
Rates: $75 semiprivate bath. $95–$120 private bath. $25 rollaway. $185 two-room suite with kitchenette. Midweek ski rates available. MC, Visa.

♥ ♨ ◄ ⁂ ◆ ⇥ ✗

If your idea of B&B is "a sense of place," you have come to the right place. Doctor Holladay, Pete's grandfather, bought this 1830 Federal house in 1899 and added to it as the family grew. In 1989, after Phebe and Pete restored the brick house—and, still, they make changes—they received a beautification award. Phebe, an elementary school art teacher, selected all the wonderful room tones of peach, blue, rose, and green. For all to see, at the top of the stairs, she has placed a magnificent silk and velvet quilt made with intricate patches, each signed by friends and relatives of Pete's great-grandmother. Pete, a born innkeeper (complete with beard), "placed other family heirlooms where Phebe told me to." Formerly a college business manager, now he is also a part-time real estate agent—and president of the superb state association of bed and breakfasts.

In residence: Zachery Lee Taylor and Tigger Two, "yellow tabbies kept in hosts' quarters, although some guests encourage them to break the rules."
Bed and bath: On three levels, five large rooms and two suites, each suite with sitting area. Largest room has queen bed, three windows, adjoining large full bath. Room with queen four-poster shares large full hall bath with smaller (but popular) room with double rope bed (chamber pot and washstand are part of decor). Victorian queen-bedded room, adjoining large full bath. Another queen-bedded room has adjoining private shower bath. Ground-level suite (great for families or two couples traveling together)—room with a double and a single bed, sitting area, kitchenette; large full bath connects to room with double bed. New in 1995—suite with queen bed, separate sitting room, bath with whirlpool and shower. Rollaway available.
Breakfast: Any time before 10. "Different menu every day of your stay." Pete's almost-famous biscuits, award-winning muffins, and scones. Juice, fresh fruit, fried apples, eggs. Usually brought to your room; if you prefer, served in dining room.

Plus: Guest rooms have air conditioners (some have ceiling or window fans, TV upon request, phone jack, refrigerator too). Mints. Robes. Fresh garden flowers. Side porch. Back deck with swing.

Sleepy Hollow Farm B&B

540/832-5555
800/215-4804
fax 540/832-2515

16280 Blue Ridge Turnpike
Gordonsville, VA 22942

Hosts: Beverley Allison and Dorsey Allison Comer
Location: In historic rural district, on U.S. Route 231. Three miles north of Gordonsville; 9 miles southwest of Orange; 6 to Montpelier; 25 to Skyline Drive; 60 from Richmond; 90 from Washington, D.C. Near horseback riding, golf, wineries, antiquing, fishing, crafts, hiking, bicyling, gardens, old Indian digs.

Open: Year round. Two-night minimum most weekends in April, May, June, October, and November.
Rates: Main house $60–$95 double, $50–$75 single; $125 quad suite, $15 fifth person. Cottage $95 double, $75 single; $120–$130 two couples; $225 four couples. MC, Visa.
♥ ♯ ⁂ ◆

Set in a peaceful hollow, the (constantly) added-on-to 18th-century house (bricked over in the 1940s) is surrounded by a pond used for swimming and fishing; gazebo; barn; croquet lawn and playing field; stream; and herb gardens used for cooking and garnishing. The Blue Ridge Mountains form the backdrop for cattle on a neighbor's pasture.

Since Beverley began hosting in 1984, she has made some interesting changes with the help of her builder son. Now adjoining the gracious antiques-filled beamed and fireplaced dining room is a glass-enclosed terrace filled with light, plants, and an enchanting dollhouse too. The cottage, finished in antique pine and old chestnut wood, has country charm. A former ABC news journalist and missionary in Central and South America, Beverley is a writer, a graphic designer, the chairman of a missionary organization for Honduras, and a fabulous cook who sets a very attractive table. In addition, as parents will tell you, she has a special way with kids. Guests—including many who come for retreats—also receive a warm welcome from daughter Dorsey, one of five siblings who grew up here.

In residence: Two dogs: "Sheila is a good Aussie. Bartles, a Border terrier, suffers from terminal cuteness." Two cats. "And one grandchild is on the payroll."
Foreign languages spoken: Spanish and French.
Bed and bath: Six rooms, each quite different; all private baths. In main house on first floor, room with antique double four-poster canopied bed (pictured in *New York Times*), dressing room, private tub/shower bath; another with antique queen bed, working fireplace, whirlpool bath. On second floor, smallish double-bedded room with private hall tub/shower bath. Suite of two connecting rooms (one beyond the other); one with a double and a single, other with two twin beds; tub bath tucked under eaves. In cottage—one two-storied suite has kitchen, great room with wood stove and queen sofa bed, upstairs double-bedded room and shower bath. Other suite has fire-

(Please turn page.)

placed sitting room, double sofa bed, upstairs double-bedded room, shower bath. Rollaway and crib available.

Breakfast: Usually 7:30–9:30. Farm-fresh eggs (Dorsey raises chickens), local bacon and sausage. Fried apples. Home-baked breads and biscuits. Hot and cold cereals. Fruit cobbler, sausage/cheese/herb pies, or cheese grits.

Plus: Central air conditioning. Welcoming refreshments. Fresh fruit and flowers. Turndown service. Mints. Phone jacks. TV in some rooms. Guest refrigerator. Swings. Sandbox. Babysitting.

> From Virginia: *"Beverley Allison is genuinely interested in people. The house and grounds say 'welcome!' . . . full of beautiful old furniture and pictures . . . could easily be Grandmother's house."*

The Count Pulaski
Bed and Breakfast and Gardens

540/980-1163
800/980-1163

821 N. Jefferson Avenue, Pulaski, VA 24301-3609

Host: Florence Byrd Stevenson
Location: In historic district, four blocks from downtown business area, two miles from I-81. On hilltop—"every inch of this town is up or down"—with view of town below.

Near "interesting restaurants," lake, antiques shops, universities.
Open: Year round.
Rates: $75 per room. $20 third person. MC, Visa.
♥ 🛄 ❖ ◆ ✈ ✄

For her sixty-third address, Flo traveled I-81, looking for an old house with a big dining room in a small mountain area town. As daughter and wife of an army officer, she has traveled extensively and lived in 15 states, in Europe, and in Asia. Her careers include academic life (counselor, administrator, dean of women), the Red Cross, and innkeeping. Avocationally, she has been a self-taught painter since 1988, and a gardener (the extensive rear grounds are in process) since buying this Colonial Revival house in 1993. The entire house is carpeted. Furnishings include family treasures, some reproductions, her paintings, and, in the sunroom, collections—flags, military patches, match folders—each with a story.

Bed and bath: Three large second-floor rooms; all private full baths. American Room has canopied king four-poster, gas fireplace, across-hall clawfooted tub bath. French Room has queen bed; single sofa bed in small glassed-in adjoining room. Polish Room with king/twins option; new bath.

Breakfast: "At guests' convenience. Ring the Vietnamese temple bell to let me know you're in the dining room." Juice. Fruit, hot in winter. Main dish includes meats. (Special diets accommodated.) Sweet breads and muffins. In candlelit dining room with a different place setting every day.

Plus: Steinway baby grand piano (Flo's since she was 12). Living room fireplace. Welcoming beverage. Picnic baskets available.

> From Ohio: *"Breakfast is a treat. Large, comfortable, tastefully furnished rooms."* From Tennessee: *"Feel as if you are visiting a friend."* From France: *" . . . a little bit of the old world nestled in the mountains of Virginia, which also recall a similar European setting."*

The Emmanuel Hutzler House

804/355-4885
804/353-6900

2036 Monument Avenue, Richmond, VA 23220

Hosts: Lyn M. Benson and John Richardson
Location: In middle of 1⅓-mile-long historic district of boulevard with grassy median in middle, imposing bronze statues of Confederate heroes, and architecturally diverse mansions on both sides. Ten minutes to downtown financial district or West End. Within walking distance of restaurants. One and a half miles from I-64 and I-95.
Open: Year round.
Rates: Rooms $89–$105. Suites $110–$135. Rollaway $10. Corporate midweek discounts. Amex, Discover, MC, Visa.

♥ ❖ ♦ ✖ ✄

The grand Italian Renaissance home was totally restored in two phases—in the late 1980s and then in 1993—by Lyn, a former social worker and volunteer coordinator for the state of Virginia (she now works in the mortgage industry), and John, her partner, who manages corporate apartments. The result is a warm, welcoming "old Richmond" ambiance with the original mahogany and oak paneling, marble fireplace, interior columns, and coffered beamed ceiling on the first floor. Upstairs, rebuilt rooms feature added architectural details such as old moldings and fireplace mantels. Throughout, there are antiques and reproductions and Lyn's collections of miniature antique furniture and oil-on-board folk art paintings by a Virginia artist. The hosts are well versed in the history of the house. And about the famous boulevard and its other houses too.

In residence: TC, "a handsome 22-pound gray striped tabby cat."
Bed and bath: Four second-floor rooms; two are very large (suites). All with queen four-poster beds, coordinated fabrics and wallcoverings, adjoining private tiled shower and tub baths; one has standard Jacuzzi; another with separate dressing area, double sinks, 4-by-6-foot Jacuzzi tub, separate shower.
Breakfast: Usually 8–9:30. (Earlier weekdays for business guests.) Juice, fresh fruit, baked breads, cereals, hot beverages. With hot entree on weekends. Served in formal dining room.
Plus: Central air conditioning. In-room telephone and cable television. Lighted off-street parking.

> From England: *"A wonderful combination of comfort, antiques, and hospitality."*
> From Pennsylvania: *"What a great place to fall in love!"*

The Mary Bladon House

540/344-5361

381 Washington Avenue, SW, Roanoke, VA 24016-4303

Hosts: Bill and Sheri Bestpitch
Location: On a corner in a National Register historic district with other Victorian homes. Just outside and within walking distance of downtown business district. Twelve blocks from restored Farmers' Market and "Center in the Square" arts and entertainment complex. Five minutes from Blue Ridge Parkway, 10 minutes south of I-81.
Open: Year round.
Rates: $62.50 single. $80 double. $110 suite for one or two; $10 each additional person. For business travelers and for five or more consecutive nights, 20 percent less. MC, Visa.

♥ ♠ ❖ ♦ ✖ ✄

(Please turn page.)

From Virginia: *"For personality, warmth ,and informative directions, it sure beats a chain hotel. A wonderful, clean, comfortable place to stay while on business. . . . Went beyond the call of duty when my husband discovered he didn't bring enough shirts . . . washed, dried, and ironed it for him."* From California: *"Delicious breakfast . . . charming atmosphere."* From Scotland: *"Very attractive . . . friendly, welcoming proprietors."*

Bill was a state agency administrator (now he coordinates a children's residential program) and Sheri an accountant when, in 1990, they changed careers by buying this established Victorian B&B. It is furnished with a blend of fanciful Victorian and simpler Eastlake pieces.

Foreign language spoken: German.

Bed and bath: Two rooms plus a two-room suite; all private baths. Rockers and easy chairs in all bedrooms. One upstairs room and one downstairs with access to wraparound front porch each have a double bed and shower bath. Second-floor suite (good for families) has private balcony, full bath, eat-in kitchen, three-quarter rollaway bed, a double bed in two bedrooms, each with ceiling fan. Crib available.

Breakfast: Any time until 9:30. Cook's choice of pancakes, waffles, French toast, or eggs; bacon, ham, or sausage; home fries or grits; fresh fruit, juice, coffee, tea. Hot and cold cereals available.

Plus: Window air conditioners throughout. Victorian-furnished parlor with Victorian playing cards on writing table. Late-afternoon refreshments. Refrigerator privileges. Fresh flowers. Transportation from local airport.

The Manor at Taylor's Store

Route 1, Box 533
Smith Mountain Lake, VA 24184

540/721-3951
fax 540/721-5243
800/248-6267

Hosts: Lee and Mary Lynn Tucker
Location: On 120 Piedmont region acres with magnificent mountain views, six private spring-fed ponds, trails. Five minutes from restaurants and recreational facilities of Smith Mountain Lake; 20 minutes to Blue Ridge Parkway and Roanoke.

Open: Year round. April–October, two-night minimum with Saturday night stay.
Rates: Per room. Private bath $80, $95, $105, and $125. Semiprivate bath $95. Ten percent less for business travelers and innkeepers. MC, Visa.
♥ ♨ ✿ ♦ ✄ ⚷

It's romantic. And historic. And the perfect setting for frequent hot-air balloon launchings. (All featured in *Southern Living* and *Mid-Atlantic Country*.) This is a place to get away from it all. Or find plenty to do.

The easy-to-be-with Tuckers added a sun room, a lattice-enclosed hot tub, an exercise room, and a slate-floored great room with billiard table and large-screen TV to the circa 1820 Federal-style Colonial mansion that they, as newlyweds in the mid-1980s, restored and furnished with lovely antiques. Mary Lynn, a former registered nurse specializing in nutrition, thinks of renovating as "having a three-dimensional canvas to paint on." (Subsequently, she became the first president of the Bed & Breakfast Association of

Virginia, a model organization.) Lee is a pathologist, a vintager (chardonnay and gewurztraminer grapes are maturing in the vineyard), and, at times, a bricklayer too.

In residence: Outdoors—Saint George and Basil, Newfoundlands; three cats; two Arabian horses and one quarter horse. Ducks and geese at the ponds.
Foreign language spoken: A little German.
Bed and bath: Six rooms (plus three-bedroom cottage for families or groups). On garden level with private exterior entrance—double bed, shower bath, private indoor wicker-furnished sitting porch. Main-level room has two canopied double beds, working fireplace, tub and shower bath. On second floor—queen canopied bed, bath, and dressing room with sunken bath for two. Victorian room with double bed, shower bath. Colonial room with queen canopied bed and French doors to balcony shares large tub and shower bath with queen canopied bed that has French doors to (same) balcony.
Breakfast: Time arranged with guests. Heart-healthy full menu. Fresh fruit. Low-fat baked pancakes, waffles, muffins, quiches, souffles. In formal fire-placed dining room with picture window overlooking mountains (and, sometimes, a hot-air balloon launch) or in plant-filled sun room.
Plus: Central air conditioning. Beverages and cookies. Guest kitchen. Five working fireplaces in common rooms. Baby grand piano and Stanford White tall clock in parlor. Library. Movies. Newly planted Colonial herb and flower garden with Lee's brick walks. Right here—canoeing, fishing, hiking, swimming, cross-country skiing, ice skating. And—someday—an archaeological dig on site.

From North Carolina: *"Elegant charm. . . . Having stayed in inns and B&B in North America and Europe, we would give this outstanding B&B and its hosts the highest rating."*

Four Square Plantation   804/365-0749
13357 Four Square Road, Smithfield, VA 23430

Hosts: Roger and Amelia Healey
Location: In a town known for "history, hams, and hospitality." On a 700-acre farm with acres of lawn, pecans, dogwoods, cedar, beech and maples. Surrounded by peanut, corn, soybean, and wheat straw farms. Seventeen miles from Scotland for 20-minute ferry ride to Jamestown. Across river from Williamsburg, Newport News, Norfolk.
Open: Year round. Two-night minimum preferred on holiday weekends.
Rates: $75 per room.
🖋 ♣ ✈ ⊬

"It's a marvelous place that needed redecorating only. It has big rooms, 11-foot ceilings, wainscoting, fireplaces in every bedroom, and many out-buildings (dependencies). Yes, I still iron all those antique table linens. And we love introducing guests to this historic area."

In 1994 Amelia transferred her exuberance from their Pennsylvania B&B to this National Register 1807 plantation farm home, which is now filled with family antiques "from both sides." Some come from Roger's grandfather, who was an antiques dealer in New York City from 1895 until 1936. Roger was an army officer on several continents for 22 years. Following 10 years in the

(Please turn page.)

defense industry, he became a restoration contractor. Amelia is a former English teacher who has owned a needlework shop.

In residence: Six cats; two are indoors.
Foreign languages spoken: Portuguese, Spanish, and some French.
Bed and bath: Three large fireplaced second-floor rooms with ceiling fans. All private baths. Empire furnishings in queen-bedded room with tub/shower bath. One room with king four-poster, hall tub/shower bath; one queen four-poster, attached tub/shower bath.
Breakfast: Flexible hours. Ham biscuits, pancakes, Southwestern eggs, egg-nog French toast, or broccoli-cheese casserole. Juice, fresh fruit, homemade sweet bread, breakfast meat, "tons of coffee and tea." Family style at eight-foot-long 1500s Spanish table set with china, crystal, sterling silver.
Plus: Central air conditioning. Welcoming refreshments. Turndown service. Feather beds. Fresh flowers. Books. Games. Porch rockers. Grounds appreciated by fund-raising groups too.

Ashton Country House

540/885-7819
1205 Middlebrook Avenue, Staunton, VA 24401-4546   800/296-7819

Hosts: Sheila Kennedy and Stan Polanski
Location: Peaceful. Set way back from secondary road on 24 acres with lots of trees and Lewis Creek in front. In back—a bank barn, pastureland, and a hill from which there's a great view of mountains (Alleghenies and Blue Ridge) and spires of Staunton.

Open: Year round. Two-night minimum July 4, Memorial Day, late-September weekends, and all October weekends.
Rates: $90 master room; $20 adjacent room with single sleigh bed. Other rooms $75 double, $70 single.
♥ ⬧ ⁎ ◆ ✂

> From Florida: *"Great food, a lovely house, and, best of all, super people."* From New York: *"Truly a gem. Comfortable yet grand at the same time. . . . Gourmet breakfast served with fine china and silver. When Stan played the piano [on weekends, with Porter, Gershwin, and Ellington selections] during coffee, we felt as if we were in a movie."* From North Carolina: *"Exactly what we had pictured a B&B to be . . . attention to detail in each room. . . . First evening ended up in the kitchen while Sheila was cooking . . . one by one other guests joined us—probably drawn by the aroma."*

That's just the B&B style Sheila, a fifth-grade teacher and graduate of the New York Restaurant School, dreamed about "all through my thirties—with a vow to open by age 40!" When she and husband Stan, a professional musician and a computer programmer, "discovered" Staunton in 1987, they bought this spacious pillared 1860 Greek Revival with brick walls inside and out (privacy ensured) and four porches (hear birds, cows, the creek). Since they opened in 1990, they have been part of a *Bon Appétit* Shenandoah Valley feature. Background decor is in yellow, rose, and creamy green tones, with pattern-on-pattern concepts. Furnishings are a blend of antiques, many oil lamps "for an old-timey smell," and lots of rocking chairs.

In residence: All outdoors—Joey, the goat, who takes walks with guests; Jasper Angus White (Jaws), a West Highland white terrier; Winston, a Pekingese; 11 cats, all named.

Bed and bath: Four air-conditioned second-floor rooms (one has adjoining single) with nonworking fireplaces. Private baths with shower stalls for two (little seat in each corner) and heat lamps. Beds are queen or double; some canopied.

Breakfast: Flexible timing. Usually one serving. Orange juice, spiced coffee, teas, freshly baked muffins, fresh fruit, or compote. Baked egg dish with bacon or sausage, home fries, or pancakes. In fireplaced dining room with rose-colored ceiling. (Can last for a very long time on winter Sundays!) On fall–spring weekdays, juice, muffins, yogurt, coffee, tea.

Plus: Fireplaced living room with 1930 Knabe grand piano. Ceiling fans in bedrooms (on 11-foot ceilings). Screened gazebo. Wicker-furnished porch. Refreshments. Recipes shared. Maps for hiking, biking, antiquing, dining.

Frederick House   540/885-4220

Frederick and New Streets, P.O. Box 1387   (U.S./Canada) **800/334-5575**
Staunton, VA 24402-1387

Hosts: Joe and Evy Harman
Location: In downtown historic Staunton, across from Mary Baldwin College. Within walking distance of Woodrow Wilson Birthplace and refurbished Amtrak train station. Near Skyline Drive, Blue Ridge Parkway, and Museum of American Frontier Culture.
Open: Year round.
Rates: $95 suite, $85 large room, $65 small rooms, $20 extra person. Amex, Diners, Discover, MC, Visa.
♥ ♫ ⁂ ♦ ✶ ⚹

From New York: *"Akin to staying at the home of a good friend or doting relative! . . . More reasonable than places with half the amenities or hospitality."* From Maine: *"The combination of Joe Harman, a super-accommodating innkeeper, and the warm and immaculate, relaxing and luxurious accommodations really helped me unwind."* From Virginia: *"Drew a map with unusual places . . . never would have found on our own . . . suggested good restaurants and bookstores."* From Pennsylvania: *"A delight. Antique furnishings, hardwood floors, Oriental rugs. . . . Breakfast was stupendous."*

The feeling is mutual: Joe Harman loves doing what he does here in the town where he grew up. In Washington, D.C., he was a banker, Evy an auditor. In 1983 they became award-winning restorers after supervising a crew that converted three adjoining houses, built in 1810, 1850, and 1910, into the inn. In time they bought one neighboring building and then another. So now there are five on the same block. Between two there's a courtyard with a fragrant garden that brings a lavender aroma to the inn, a lovely place furnished with antiques and period pieces.

The hosts also have a jewelry store (Evy's work). Joe is the full-time innkeeper who tells guests about restaurants, a walking tour (right here) of the historic area, mountain hiking trails, or back roads for cycling or driving.

(Please turn page.)

Bed and bath: Fourteen rooms—six suites (three with fireplace) and eight rooms, each with private bath and entrance. King, queen, double, and twin-sized beds. Cots and crib available.

Breakfast: Usually 8–10:30. Choose from long menu including apple raisin quiche, ham-and-cheese pie, granola with yogurt and fruit, homemade waffles. Special diets accommodated. Juice, fresh fruit, homemade bread, coffee and tea. Evy is chef. Classical or mountain (dulcimer) music plays. Guests tend to linger here in the just-for-guests Chumley's Tearoom.

Plus: Each room has TV, AM/FM radio, phone, air conditioning, ceiling fan, terry robes. Extra charge for exercise facilities and indoor swimming pool (both at athletic club next door), and for laundry facilities or babysitting.

The Sampson Eagon Inn   540/886-8200
238 East Beverly Street, Staunton, VA 24401   800/597-9722

Hosts: Frank and Laura Mattingly
Location: Bordered by wrought iron fence in a neighborhood of beautifully preserved mid- to late 19th-century residences. One block from Woodrow Wilson Birthplace and Mary Baldwin College; two from downtown shops and restaurants.

Four miles from I-81/I-64. Forty minutes west of Charlottesville.
Open: Year round. Two-day minimum on May and October weekends.
Rates: $80–$89. Suites $95–$99. Daybed in suites $15.
♥ ♦ ✗ ⊁

From Virginia: *"Everything exquisitely attended to—from the restoration, furnishings, and landscaping to the elegant but very relaxed and delicious breakfast."* From California: *"Have thought of everything . . . extremely helpful and friendly."*

The Mattinglys, Renaissance folks indeed, combined all their interests and B&B experiences when they spent 18 months restoring their elegant in-town residence. "Pick a period," Laura says of the restoration. "This Greek Revival (circa 1840) mansion has Italianate, Victorian, and Colonial Revival elements in its five later remodelings and additions." The gracious setting is enhanced by antique furnishings—mostly Federal and Empire—from the Mattinglys' personal collection. In 1992, a year after opening, they received the Historic Staunton Foundation Preservation Award. And after being featured in *Country Inns*, they were designated as one of the magazine's "Best Inn Buys for 1993."

For 20 years Frank was a hospital administrator in the Washington, D.C., area. Then he started a company to preserve old buildings. "His specialties of paint finishes and plaster came in handy when he decided to become an innkeeper." Laura was an art college administrator with the Corcoran Gallery in Washington. And together, the avid gardeners had a part-time antiques business. Now Frank has a part-time business in old-house restoration including log houses.

Bed and bath: Five large air-conditioned rooms, each with canopied queen bed, private attached modern bath, TV with VCR (and movies). One large first-floor bedroom with sitting area and sit-down shower (with hand-held shower head). On second floor—four rooms (two are suites with sitting room and daybed) with tub/shower bath.

Breakfast: Usually 8–9. (Early coffee on porch or in library.) Fresh fruit, fresh orange juice, homemade breads, hot beverages. Main-course favorites include Grand Marnier souffleé pancakes; Kahlua/pecan waffles with strawberry sauce or real maple syrup; omelets with fresh mushrooms, cheese, and herbs from garden. Bacon or sausage. Low-cholesterol diets accommodated. In formal dining room with English bone china, sterling, and cut crystal.

Plus: Formal living room. Beverages. Bedside Belgian chocolates. Basket of personal items. Guest refrigerator. On-site parking.

Thornrose House at Gypsy Hill

531 Thornrose Avenue, Staunton, VA 24401   540/885-7026
                                                 800/861-4338

Hosts: Suzanne and Otis Huston
Location: On a landscaped acre directly across from Gypsy Hill Park's lighted tennis courts and Victorian band shell (summer concerts). Also in park: swimming pool, 18-hole golf course ($12), jogging paths. Six blocks to Staunton's walking tour.

Open: Year round. Two-day minimum on May and October weekends.
Rates: $55 double bed, $65 queen bed, $75 king bed. Singles $10 less. Rollaway $10.
♥ ♨ ♣ ✈ ⌇

From Maryland: "Picked for proximity to golf course, not knowing what to expect . . . decorated beautifully . . . white-glove clean . . . fell so in love with one of the wallpaper borders that we are putting it in our home . . . a five-star breakfast . . . all the special touches are reflective of its innkeepers . . . provide restaurant menus, give suggestions from own dining experiences, sightseeing tips complete with directions . . . everything we hoped it would be and more."

"After our own B&B trips in New England, we talked about doing this in Virginia; so when Otis took early retirement from DuPont, we drove 2,200 miles all over this state looking at many wonderful properties. We fell in love with Staunton, small-town America with wonderful Victorian architecture—very different from other places we have lived in. Everyone—from neighbors to tradespeople—was so helpful and welcoming! Guests, too, get a good sense of this warm community when they take the self-guided tour and have chance conversations with 80-year-olds who talk about the old days. There's a lot to see and do in this area, yet some guests just want to sit on the porch and unwind."

In 1992, when the Hustons bought this B&B, a two-storied modified Georgian brick house, they redecorated with light colors, establishing a rose theme throughout the house "to create a homey Victorian feeling."

Suzanne has worked in newspaper production, as a teacher, and as a historic-site docent "all over." The Hustons' own travels have taken them to Canada, Mexico, Europe, and Japan.

In residence: Two cats reside in hosts' quarters, sometimes visit cat lovers.
Bed and bath: Five second-floor rooms with antique or period pieces. King, queen, or double bed. All private baths with tub and/or shower.

(Please turn page.)

Breakfast: 8–9:30. House specialty is Otis's birchemuesli—oats, raisins, fresh fruit, whipped cream, and nuts. Heart-healthy hot entree. In fireplaced dining room or on veranda.

Plus: All bedrooms are air conditioned; three have ceiling fans. Fireplaced parlor with grand piano and TV. Tea or lemonade with homemade snacks at 4 p.m. Turndown service. Wicker-furnished veranda. Gardens (booked for weddings too) with brick walkways and two pergolas.

The Burton House/Hart's Harbor House

9 and 11 Brooklyn Street, Wachapreague, VA 23480   804/787-4560
804/787-4848

Hosts: Pat and Tom Hart
Location: One block to waterfront with rental and fishing boats and restaurant. On an undeveloped peninsula that overlooks barrier islands. On a corner adjoining grounds of Volunteer Firemen's Carnival (held two weeks in July) with ferris wheel and merry-go-round. Forty-five-minute drive to Chincoteague Island.
Open: Year round. Two-night minimum weekends May–September.
Rates: Private half bath $55 single, $65 double. Private full bath $65 single, $75 double. MC, Visa.
♥ 🖋 ♣ ♦ ✈ ✁

"Tom's wonderful breakfasts—and, in summer, the marvelous breeze off the water. That's what everyone remembers! There are 300 year-round residents in this town, where we have lived 'forever.' Tom and I love fishing, outdoor life, and antiques. From B&B articles in magazines, we got 'the bug' in 1986 and completely restored the century-old place that's always been called 'The Burton House.' We repaired and refinished locally found furniture—brass beds, rockers, china cabinets, you name it.

"Tom is a carpenter whose pride and joy is the screened gazebo made with posts and trim from a 1902 hotel. It provided a great background for a cover photo of us used on an AT&T promotion piece. In 1991 we bought the next-door house, which had not been lived in for 27 years. Now it's Hart's Harbor House, our home with four uncovered and working fireplaces (especially appreciated by winter guests) and with enormous guest rooms. The yard extends to some rental cabins and a 14-boat-slip marina. And we have extensive vegetable and perennial gardens."

Townspeople and guests alike are amazed and pleased.

Bed and bath: Ten rooms. On three floors in Burton House are seven rooms with queen, double, two twins, or a double and a daybed. Private full bath for first-floor double-bedded room. Six rooms, each with a private half bath, each share a shower bath or a shower/tub bath with one other room. (Exception: three third-floor rooms share one shower bath.) Hart's Harbor House has three second-floor rooms. Private skylit baths with tub and shower for the two queen-bedded rooms. Private shower bath for room with double bed and "best view."

Breakfast: Until 10. Juice. Fruit (homegrown in season). Bacon, sausage, or ham. Eggs. Muffins or biscuits. Sometimes waffles, Latvian or buttermilk blueberry pancakes, or French toast. Or squash/potato/onion dish made with freshly picked vegetables. Served family style in the Burton House dining room or on gazebo porch.

Plus: Beverages. Central air conditioning in common rooms and Hart's Harbor House; individual units in Burton House guest rooms. Ceiling fans, too, in bedrooms. Large deck next to gazebo. Fruit and vegetable garden. Bicycles (no charge).

Anderson Cottage Bed & Breakfast

Old Germantown Road   540/839-2975
Warm Springs, VA 24484-0176   fax 540/839-3058

Host: Jean Randolph Bruns
Location: In a mountain valley village, west of Shenandoah Valley. On two acres (one is lawn) with gardens and mature plantings. With stream from (96°F) Warm Spring Pools, half a mile away, flowing through property. Two excellent restaurants nearby. Five miles to Hot Springs and renowned Homestead Hotel.
Open: Main house, March–November. Cottage, year round.
Rates: Main house $60 or $65 per room, $75 or $80 suite. Cottage $110 single or double occupancy.
◖ ⁂ ◆ ⅄

From England: *"A living museum . . . if you encourage her to talk about the house, you have a privileged view back in time, through the eyes and memories of a witty, articulate chronicler and protector of a lost American tradition. We had meant to stay a night, stayed for three, and would have moved in permanently if life had allowed!"* From Virginia: *"Gives you space to be alone and be yourself, yet your needs are always met quietly and quickly. This is a place to come if you enjoy peace and quiet and genuineness. If you want frilly lace, Godiva on your pillow, and television in your room, go elsewhere. But if the old summer places intrigue you, explore here."* Also from Virginia: *"I love the little hallways and old wood floors, the pretty wildflowers in front of the house, breakfast near the fireplace on a chilly morning."*

Jean usually describes it as "a quiet place with plenty to do." What began in the 18th century as a four-room log tavern "rambles without one right angle or straight line." An inn for 80 years until the 1950s, it has been in Jean's family for over 100 years, and her permanent residence since 1981. She is a former journalist/medical center public relations director/Realtor who is active as a library trustee, as a Meals-on-Wheels driver, and with Amnesty International. She reads (extensive library right here), gardens, refinishes furniture—and spends winters in Thailand with her son and his family. When Homestead Hotel guests tour the small museum room here, Jean is official guide. Her guests poke around this old house, read on the porch, wade in the creek, take the warm baths, hike, explore—and write lyrical letters to me. This B&B makes me feel good all over.

Bed and bath: Four rooms plus a family-friendly cottage. First-floor suite has private entrance, queen-bedded room, fireplaced parlor, tub/shower bath. On second floor—suite with queen-bedded room, parlor with twin bed, old-fashioned tub in bath. One large queen-bedded room with claw-footed tub bath. Very large room with a double and a twin bed, beamed ceiling, working fireplace, shared bath. In cottage—one queen-bedded room, another with two twins, one tub/shower bath and one with shower only, living room with windows on three sides, fireplaced dining room/kitchen.

(Please turn page.)

Breakfast: About 9. Cheese strata and apples; buttermilk pancakes with maple syrup and sausage or bacon; or turkey hash, basil tomatoes, wheat rolls, peach preserves. Juice, fruit, coffee, tea.
Plus: Fireplaced parlor and dining room. Extensive library. Upright piano. Croquet. Badminton. Suggestions for one day; other days; eating out; driving tours with hand-drawn maps and stops at old family cemeteries, hiking trails. "Creek shoes" for wading. "Forgot a sweater? I have a collection of old ones in assorted sizes and colors."

The Foster-Harris House

540/675-3757
800/666-0153
Main Street, P.O. Box 333, Washington, VA 22747

Host: Phyllis Marriott
Location: With mountain views from 40 acres to one side and behind; private home on other side. In a town (population: 250) that is six blocks long and two blocks wide, with two art galleries and three crafts shops in old houses and a bookstore in an old cabin. Three blocks from the Inn at Little Washington and minutes from three other fine restaurants. Near antiquing, hiking, horseback riding. Fifteen minutes from Skyline Drive; 12 from Shenandoah National Park; 65 miles west of Washington, D.C.
Open: Year round.
Rates: Queen bed $135 with wood stove, sun room, and whirlpool; $115 with minisunroom. Double bed $95. Discover, MC, Visa.
♥ ❖ ♦ ✗ ✗

"You must have a lot of hobbies," said one guest who was delighted with the peace and quiet here. Others ask if the morning mooing from "over the hill" is a recording. In 1993, with experience in food (Washington, D.C., Capitol Hill gourmet deli owner and caterer) and real estate, Phyllis pursued her B&B idea and found this turn-of-the-century house, which had been opened as the area's first B&B (1983) by an owner who left a legacy of perennial flower beds. Phyllis decorated in country style.

In residence: Lulu, a friendly mixed breed, part Lab, "loved by everyone."
Bed and bath: Four second-floor rooms, all private full tub and shower baths. Suite with queen bed, ceiling fan, wood-burning stove, sun room "with spectacular mountain views," oval whirlpool tub. Two rooms with queen bed; one has ceiling fan and minisunroom. Smaller double-bedded room.
Breakfast: At 9 or 9:30. Juice, fruit, breads or muffins, an egg dish or baked French toast, breakfast meat, hot beverages. Served (rave reviews) in dining room by fireplace wood stove.
Plus: Central air conditioning. Late-afternoon beverages and cookies. Popular front porch with swing. Picnic table under plum tree. Fireplaced parlor. Restaurant reservations made. Hiking trail suggestions. For small business meetings, inquire about use of historic town hall.

From Virginia: *"Wonderful creative breakfasts . . . great hostess who helped us make reservations and discover the scenery."*

Gay Street Inn   540/675-3288

P.O. Box 237, Gay Street, Washington, VA 22747

Hosts: Donna and Robin Kevis
Location: "Wake up to the birds" setting with mountain views. On "morning side" of dead-end street in town of 187 people. Across from 250-year-old cabin, a fruit broker's office that looks like a residence. Next to private home—also a log cabin—on one side; on other side, an 1877 church with chiming bell and, in summer, the sound of choirs. Five-minute walk to Inn at Little Washington. Near canoeing, hiking, horseback riding, vineyards.
Open: Year round.
Rates: $110 first floor, $95 second-floor room. $25 extra bed. $5 portacrib.

♥ ⚓ ✿ ◆ ✄

From New York: *"It's a find. A pretty house. Stayed at beginning of trip. When we stayed again on the return, we were treated like old friends, and even taken by Mrs. Kevis on a walking tour of Little Washington."*

In 1987 the Kevises moved from Nantucket Island—"where everyone does everything"—and bought this restored 1860 farmhouse, an established B&B decorated with Shelburne Museum wallcoverings. They furnished with Shaker and country pine pieces. Robin, a contractor, "is always changing and rejuvenating." To innkeeping Donna brings various experiences; she has been a winter scalloper ("best facial you'll ever get"), a chef (she's a graduate of Johnson & Wales University's College of Culinary Arts), and a real estate agent.

In residence: Daughter Kate, age five. "Kitty, a friendly 21-pound Maine Coon cat, and Digit, a part Lab, part lap dog who loves company, have limited access to guest areas."
Foreign languages spoken: Some French and Spanish.
Bed and bath: Three rooms; all private en-suite full baths with hair dryers. First-floor handicapped-accessible room with double canopied bed, wood-burning fireplace. On second floor, one room with double sleigh bed, one with double four-poster.
Breakfast: Usually 9–10:30. Souffled egg, quiche, or breakfast enchiladas. Home-baked buttermilk muffins. Juice, fruit in season, hot beverages. Served buffet style in living room.
Plus: Individual air conditioning and heat control. No TV. Picnic baskets, $5. Pets allowed with prior notice.

Can't find a listing for the community you are going to? Check with a reservation service described at the beginning of this chapter. Through the service, you may be placed (matched) with a welcoming B&B that is near your destination.

Sycamore Hill House & Gardens

Route 1, Box 978, Washington, VA 22747   540/675-3046

Hosts: Kerri and Stephen Wagner
Location: Spectacular. On top of Menefee Mountain, on 52 undeveloped acres of woodlands and meadows. "At end of mile-long, romantic winding road." Twelve miles from Skyline Drive and Shenandoah National Park. Sixty-six miles west of Washington, D.C.

Open: Year round. Two-day minimum May and October weekends and holidays.
Rates: Per room. $100 full bath. $120 shower bath. $140 full bath with double sinks. MC, Visa.
♥ ⬤ ⁂ ✗ ⚲

"How did you ever find this place?" ask first-timers as they arrive. The mountain's only structure, this contemporary (1967) stone home features a round glass center with a 65-foot veranda. Here, at seemingly the top of the world, is the mesmerizing panoramic view filled with layers of other mountaintops that prompted Kerri to leave her 15-year position as an agricultural lobbyist in Washington, D.C. What a setting for Stephen, a freelance commercial illustrator, to create works seen in major publications such as *National Geographic* and Time-Life books. And all because two people followed their curiosity when chancing upon a "For Sale" sign during a drive in the countryside.

Since buying the house in 1987 from the original owners, the Wagners have refurbished inside and out—and been designated a *Washingtonian* "Great Getaway." Decor includes Oriental rugs, traditional and modern furnishings, originals of Stephen's works, window treatments framing views, and—everywhere—plants, trees, and flowers. On the property, which has become a certified National Wildlife habitat, are Kerri's organic herb and vegetable gardens, appreciated by local restaurants; annual and perennial flower beds; thousands of spring bulbs and hundreds of dogwoods and redbuds; and hummingbirds, bluebirds, white-tailed deer, maybe red fox or wild turkey. And more views.

In residence: Mollie Bean, a 40-pound fluffy white miniature sheep dog. The cat is named Miss Kitty.
Bed and bath: Three rooms, each with queen bed, private bath. Master Bedroom has pine four-poster, dressing room, full bath with double sink. Peach Room has brass bed, shower bath. White Wicker Room has full bath just across the hall.
Breakfast: At 9; flexible when house is not full. Repertoire includes home-baked cranberry braided bread; baked apples; cinnamon apple puff; yeast breads; rolls, coffee cake. French toast; omelets; souffles; shrimp-and-cheese strata. Breakfast meats, fresh fruits, local cider, freshly squeezed orange juice. Fresh trout on occasion. In formal dining room with classical music and floor-to-ceiling view of mountains.
Plus: Central air conditioning. Ceiling fans. Stereo and piano in living room, which has tiled fireplace flanked by bentwood chairs. Home-baked cookies and brandy in bedrooms. Special occasions acknowledged. Turndown service. Bird books. Binoculars. List of birds and seasonal flowers.

Caledonia Farm—1812

540/675-3693

Route 1, Box 2080
Flint Hill, VA 22627

(for reservations) 800/BNB-1812

Host: Phil Irwin
Location: Four miles north of Washington and "the number one-rated restaurant in North America and four for more affordable great evening dining options." On a "never-to-be-divided" 52-acre cattle farm bordered by stone fences. On Route 628, near Skyline Drive. Sixty-eight miles southwest of Washington, D.C.

Open: Year round. Two-night minimum on holiday weekends and the entire month of October.
Rates: $80 main-house room, semi-private bath. $140 suite. Fifty percent surcharge for Saturday one-night stays. Discover, MC, Visa.
♥ ⬛ ⁂ ◆ ✈ ⊬

Phil, a retired Voice of America broadcaster who has visited hundreds of B&Bs throughout North America and Europe, raises beef cattle. His Federal-style manor house, built in 1812 and restored in 1965, is on the National Register of Historic Places. It has two-foot-thick stone walls, individual heat and air conditioning, heart pine floors, working fireplaces in each room—and all that acreage with views. Take a house tour and you'll hear about its history and about the family cemetery. Phil offers the treat of a hayride into Shenandoah National Park. He has suggestions for walking here or mountain climbing (nearby) to 3,300 feet. He sometimes hosts small conferences, and he participates in movable feasts with other area B&Bs.

In residence: "One gregarious outside cat." Beef cattle herd.
Foreign languages spoken: (Minimal) German and Danish.
Bed and bath: Two suites and/or two rooms, all with working fireplaces, individual heat control, air conditioning. On main-house second floor, two double-bedded rooms share a full bath. Converted 1807 summer kitchen (connected by portico to main house) has double-bedded room and full bath upstairs, and a living room with huge original cooking fireplace on the first floor. Handicapped-accessible room available by reservation.
Breakfast: On the hour (arranged night before), 7–11. Choose from menu that includes fruit, eggs, smoked salmon, omelets, grits, and eggs Benedict. Served by candlelight and with "unannounced extras."
Plus: Antiques-filled gathering room. Patio and three porches with spectacular views. Cycling routes (bicycles provided). Directions to nearby stables, wineries, caves, antiquing, scenic drives. Hayride ($10/person) with refreshments. Reservations made for horse-drawn carriage rides, balloon ascensions, special photography, conferencing, battlefield tours.

Many B&Bs that allow smoking restrict it to certain rooms and/or public areas. Although some of those B&Bs that have the ⊬ symbol allow smoking on the porch and/or patio, others do not allow smoking anywhere on the property.

Apple Hill Farm Bed & Breakfast

Route 1, Box 285-D, Sperryville, VA 22740 540/987-9454

Hosts: Wayne and Dorothy Waller
Location: Rural. "Without lights of neighboring houses except in winter; with sound of bullfrogs and bordering river." On 20 acres with woods, ponds, pastures, and a working springhouse. Four miles from Inn at Little Washington. Close to Shenandoah National Park for hiking. Near horseback riding; canoeing; golfing; antiquing; and cycling on Old Hollow Road, which follows river for "about a five-mile loop."

Open: Year round. Minimum stay required for some holidays.
Rates: Double bed $95 year round, except New Year's Eve. Queen $110, $120, or $125 (with fireplace and private balcony) January–March; $5–$10 more April–December. New Year's Eve $125–$150. Extra person $25. MC, Visa.
♥ ❖ ♦ ✈

"When visiting an area B&B, we found and fell in love with then-unoccupied Apple Hill, realized it would be a perfect B&B, and purchased it that weekend. It's a decision we have never regretted. Guests—some who threaten not to leave!—enjoy the peace, the birds at the feeders, a walk in the woods or down by the river, the geese in the ponds, the deer in the pasture, even an occasional bear."

In California Wayne was a flight test engineer/senior scientist for Hughes Aircraft. From here, he does some consulting. Dot is an intensive care nurse. And together they own and operate a small country store and deli. Their transformed Victorian farmhouse has fresh paper and paint, prints and crystal from European travel, family treasures, and photographs.

In residence: Bear, a protective Akita who, after introductions, enjoys walks. "You have no choice!" Candy, a canine senior citizen who loves everyone. Paul Newcat, an outdoor blue-eyed Siamese.
Bed and bath: Four rooms; all private en-suite shower baths. First floor—queen bed, wood-burning fireplace, access to front veranda. Second floor—queen four-poster, wood-burning fireplace, private balcony. Queen bed, private balcony. Double bed, antique glassed-front wood stove, access to sun porch.
Breakfast: 8–10. Eggs Benedict over croissant with Smithfield ham; egg/avocado/crabmeat with lemon hollandaise; or quiche with feta cheese, Smithfield sausage, sour cream. Spiced apples in cider and brown sugar. Lemon or peach scones. Served in dining room or under a huge red maple tree.
Plus: Central air conditioning. Late-afternoon or evening cider or lemonade. Picnic baskets, $12–$19. Dinner by request, $25–$35/person.

According to many: "Guests come with plans and discover the joys of hammock sitting."

Colonial Capital Bed & Breakfast   804/229-0233

501 Richmond Road   (U.S./Canada) **800/776-0570**
Williamsburg, VA 23185   fax **804/253-7667**

Hosts: Barbara and Phil Craig
Location: Residential. Across the street from stadium of College of William and Mary and its Alumni House. Three blocks from historic area. Five-minute drive to Colonial Parkway entrance.
Open: Year round. Two-night minimum on Easter, Valentine's Day, and Presidents' Day weekends and on April–December weekends.

Rates: March 15–December: $75 single, $95 double, $135 triple in suite ($20 additional person), $105 king bed. January–March except Easter weekend: $60 single, $76 double, $108 triple in suite ($16 additional person), $84 king. Honeymoon packages available. Amex, Discover, MC, Visa.
♥ ♨ ◀ ♣ ♦ ✈

> From Illinois: *"Twelve of us who enjoyed a family reunion feel we've found our home away from home . . . hosts epitomize warm hospitality, thoughtfulness, and graciousness . . . charming coordinated early American decor . . . complimentary toiletries . . . excellent restaurant suggestions. . . . As the wife of a former resort innkeeper, I am keenly aware of comforts and amenities provided and, of greater importance, of the personality of a place. This B&B is outstanding."* From Florida: *"Prepared a separate breakfast to accommodate my wife, who is a vegetarian."* From Pennsylvania: *"Even met our plane."*

Williamsburg accents combined with antiques acquired over a 30-year period are throughout this Colonial Revival house, which was built in 1926 and served as a tourist home. When Phil and Barbara, native Virginians, bought it in 1988, they returned from North Carolina to redo the entire place as a B&B. "Our inspiration came from trips to England and Scotland," says Barbara, former associate director of admissions at Meredith College. Phil was vice president of a securities corporation. Because of their 1994 vacation in Australia, "Down Under" may be well represented among guests who come to find out what the hosts mean when they say, "We're here to spoil you."

In residence: Well-trained Ginny (Virginia Lee), a golden retriever, does not enter the parlor, dining room, or sleeping areas.
Bed and bath: Five rooms, all canopied beds; private baths, some with sink in room. On second floor—one with antique double bed with en-suite shower and claw-footed tub. Two with queen bed; one has full 1920s tub/shower bath in hall (robes provided), and one has en-suite shower bath. Room with four-poster twin/king option with en-suite shower bath. Narrow steep steps to third floor, which has room with windows on three sides (two are dormered, with love seats), a double bed, private tub/shower bath; if coupled with room (with TV/VCR) across the hall, this becomes a suite that sleeps five with a bath and a half (robes provided). Rollaway available.
Breakfast: Usually 8:30. Baked French toast with caramelized topping, strawberries, and sour cream; Virginia ham-and-cheese souffle; or three-cheese stuffed French toast. Fresh fruits, specialty teas and coffees, juices. In dining room or adjoining solarium.

(Please turn page.)

Plus: Bikes (no charge). Zoned central air conditioning. Fireplaced living room with Oriental rugs. Welcoming refreshments. Turndown service. Screened porch and patio overlooking fenced yard. Off-street parking. Central ticketing service for Colonial Williamsburg, Busch Gardens, Jamestown.

Legacy of Williamsburg Inn

930 Jamestown Road, Williamsburg, VA 23185

804/220-0524
800/962-4722
fax 804/220-2211

Hosts: Mary Ann and Ed Lutkewich
Location: On a heavily wooded lot with English gardens in front; wonderful view of pine, holly, and dogwood trees from back deck. Across the street from wooded acreage owned by the College of William and Mary. Four blocks from historic area.
Open: Year round.
Rates: Per room, $85. Suite $130. MC, Visa.

♥ ⚬ ✻ ✖ ✗

Eighteenth-century ambiance everywhere. With authentic colors and fabrics. A fireplaced library with many books on antiques and Colonial Williamsburg. Eighteenth-century games in a fireplaced tavern/game room modeled after the Weatherburn Tavern in Colonial Williamsburg. A billiards room with a billiards table made in England and an English dart board. A keeping room where candlelit breakfasts are served by the fireplace. One trip to Colonial Williamsburg in 1985 convinced the Lutkewiches, dealers in 18th-century furnishings, that they should go back to Ohio, sell the farm, and move to Virginia. Earlier, Mary Ann and Ed had designed, built, and managed a restaurant; they also raised race horses. Here they bought a many-dormered clapboard house that was built in 1976 and remodeled it into this B&B. Mary Ann is a full-time innkeeper "still very much in love with people and 18th-century decor." Ed is vice president of sales for a commercial refrigeration company. Together they enjoy "sharing our antiques, favorite eating places, biking routes, wonderful walks, and our travel experiences."

Bed and bath: Four rooms; each with canopied and curtained queen or double bed, private bath. Two are suites with working fireplaces. Suites have shower/tub baths and other rooms have showers only.
Breakfast: At 8. (Coffee at 7:45.) House specialty—hotcakes. Or Belgian waffles, omelets, quiche, homemade peach cobblers, biscuits and gravy. By fire or in gazebo. Can last for two hours; some call it an "all-day breakfast."
Plus: Central air conditioning. Turndown service. Chocolates. TV/VCR with Colonial Williamsburg tapes. "Treetop (high) gazebo in middle of bird sanctuary with deer too."

> From Georgia: *"Authentic in every detail save the very fine and modern bath.... Mary Ann had book lights for reading, plush bathrobes, umbrellas, iron ... every extra imaginable."* From Maryland: *"Friendly and open hosts.... Elaborate and delicious breakfasts.... Enthusiasm for their beautifully decorated home is evident.*

Liberty Rose B&B

804/253-1260

1022 Jamestown Road, Williamsburg, VA 23185 · 800/545-1825

Hosts: Brad and Sandra Hirz
Location: One mile from restored area. On a hilltop acre of old trees.
Open: Year round. Two-night minimum on major event weekends.

Rates: $105 "Savannah Lace." $135 "Magnolias Peach"; $40 third person. $165 "Rose Victoria." $165 "Suite Williamsburg."
♥ ♦ ✈ ⚡

Intentionally romantic. With yards and yards of custom-colored vintage reproduction fabrics—silks, jacquards, and cut velvets; lovely wallcoverings; seven trees at Christmas; and—everywhere—collectibles, quilts, and refinished antiques. (All are pictured in a detailed brochure.)

The enthusiastic hosts do everything themselves and are happy to share decorating ideas, resources, and bargains. (A catalog is planned.) The Hirzes do such a good job of hosting that 6 out of 10 of their guests leave with the dream of opening a B&B. While they lived on the West Coast, Brad was in farming, Sandi in interior design. In 1986 they both came to Williamsburg and fell in love while doing the first restoration on this 1922 dormered clapboard house. Since, they've added architectural accents, exquisite bed coverings, reporcelained claw-footed tubs, and the ultimate touch of a take-home long-stemmed silk rose.

In residence: Mister Goose, "our gorgeous outdoor kitty."
Bed and bath: Four queen-bedded rooms, one with adjoining twin room. All private baths. Savannah Lace has tub bath, TV. Magnolias Peach—lace-canopied bed, TV/VCR in armoire, black marble shower bath; adjoining room with antique twin feather bed. Rose Victoria with French canopied bed, elaborate bed curtains, TV/VCR, long down sofa, full bath with Victorian wall from turn-of-century house, floor from 1740s plantation. Suite Williamsburg—huge carved four-poster with elaborate coverings, working fireplace, six windows, TV/VCR in dollhouse, French sofa, chandeliered bath with black Italian tile shower, claw-footed tub.
Breakfast: 8:30. Waffles, hotcakes, or stuffed French toast. Bacon, sausage, or Virginia baked ham. Homemade croissants filled with eggs, bacon, cheese, tomato, spices. Coffee, tea, juice, fresh fruit, homemade muffins, scones. Served on glass-enclosed parlor porch.
Plus: Central air conditioning. Baby grand piano in the fireplaced living room. Chocolate-chip cookies. Soft drinks always available. Refrigerator space. Gold flashlights by the bed. Bubble bath. Robes. "Finishing Touches," their "tiny but irresistible gift shop."

The tradition of paying to stay in a private home—with breakfast included in the overnight lodging rate—was revived in time to save wonderful old houses, schools, churches, and barns all over the country from the wrecking ball or commercial development.

Newport House   804/229-1775

710 South Henry Street, Williamsburg, VA 23185-4113

Hosts: John and Cathy Millar
Location: In residential neighborhood. Set back about 50 feet from Route 132. A five-minute walk to historic area and Colonial Williamsburg.

Open: Year round. Two-night weekend minimum.
Rates: Per room, $115–$120 first night, $105–$110 each additional night. $20 third person in room.
♥ ♯ ♣ ♦ ✸ ⅄

> From Virginia: *"A treasure in every sense of the word. . . . The result is delightful visit with old friends. . . . Close to restored area but far from the madding crowd."* From Maryland: *"Combines 20th-century comfort with 18th-century elegance and taste."*

Historical stories at breakfast. Colonial country dancing in the ballroom (beginners and observers welcome) on Tuesday evenings. Eighteenth-century recipes. A hammock between two pecan trees. Hints about a quiet saltwater beach, historic plantations, a ferry ride. Antiques for sale. A rabbit that captivates guests. Even Colonial clothing to rent for dinner at a tavern!

In 1988 the Millars, descendants of 18th-century Williamsburg area residents, built this authentic reproduction of a Newport, Rhode Island, house designed in 1756 by Peter Harrison, "an architect who is primarily responsible for our speaking English rather than French today." (Ask them to tell you the story.) Siding is wood carved to resemble stone.

John, a college teacher/former museum director/former captain of an historic full-rigged ship, has written a dozen books on historical topics. Cathy, a practicing registered nurse when the Millars lived in Rhode Island, is an innkeeper/mom/beekeeper/gardener who sews 18th-century clothing. Their entire home is furnished in English and American period antiques and reproductions.

In residence: Son Ian, age five. Sassafras, a house-trained Dutch rabbit.
Foreign language spoken: French.
Bed and bath: Two second-floor rooms (overlooking gardens), each with one extra-long queen four-poster canopy bed plus one single four-poster canopy bed, attached private shower bath. Rollaway and crib available.
Breakfast: Usually 8–9. Johnnycakes, muffins, waffles, eggs, casseroles. Fruit compote or baked apples. Coffee. Tea made from their own herbs. Honey from garden. In formal dining room.
Plus: Central air conditioning. Individual thermostats. Fireplaced living room. Harpsichord (guests may play) in ballroom. Babysitting. Rides to/from transportation points. Nonallergenic comforters. Off-street parking. Some Thursdays, Scottish country dancing.

---

*G*uests *arrive as strangers, leave as friends.*

Williamsburg Manor Bed and Breakfast

600 Richmond Road, Williamsburg, VA 23185   804/220-8011
800/422-8011
fax 804/220-0245

Hosts: Laura and Michael Macknight
Location: Between a church and Alumni House of College of William and Mary. Three blocks to historic area.

Open: Year round. Two-night minimum on weekends.
Rates: $90 per room. Less in winter.
♥ ⊯ ♣ ♦ ✄ ⚗

Your place at the breakfast table is always set and waiting—with 15-inch Villeroy and Boch plates, stemmed goblets for juice, and poufed and pressed napkins too. It's at the 12-foot-long table in the fireplaced dining room that was "switched" with the living room when newlyweds Laura and Michael redid the entire brick Colonial house. Originally built for professors, it became a guest house in the 1930s and was most recently a rooming house for students. Friends of the still-in-their-twenties Macknights took care of new ceilings. Laura's mom (from Williamsburg Sampler, page 376) made new crown moldings and frames for pictures and helped with decorating—with hunter greens, deep burgundys, swags and jabots, Oriental rugs, and Waverly prints. Dad, too, "helped a lot" with what he calls "a wonderful big dollhouse." Auction finds and family treasures are throughout. Since opening in the fall of 1992, Laura is no longer working as a catering director. She and Michael, a graduate of Johnson & Wales University's College of Culinary Arts, cater together. And a cookbook is in the works.

In residence: Zeus, an outdoor golden retriever.
Bed and bath: Five rooms, all private en-suite baths. One on first floor with queen four-poster, shower bath. Second floor—two queen four-posters, tub/shower bath; one canopied double, shower bath; one queen-bedded room shares (with same party only) connecting bath with room with two twin beds.
Breakfast: At 8:30. Eggs in pastry with roasted tomatoes, chives, and Swiss cheese; Surry sausage hash; or malted waffles with homemade syrups and preserves. Fresh fruit; freshly baked muffins, breads, or rolls. Special diets accommodated.
Plus: Central air conditioning. Bedroom ceiling fans. Guest refrigerator. Cable TV in each room. Off-street parking. Dinner by reservation; $35 per person.

Six weeks *after* one B&B opened, a neighbor inquired: "I need lodging for visiting relatives. When are you going to open?" This was the same neighbor who, during a zoning hearing, had expressed great concern about traffic and noise that a B&B would create!

Williamsburg Sampler Bed and Breakfast

922 Jamestown Road, Williamsburg, VA 23185-3917   804/253-0398
800/722-1169
fax 804/220-0245

Hosts: Helen and Ike Sisane
Location: Across from the College of William and Mary. Less than a mile to Colonial Williamsburg. Three miles from I-64, two to business district, one to restaurants.

Open: Year round. Two-night minimum on weekends.
Rates: Per room $90–$95; two persons maximum per room. Suite $140; $25 third person.
♥ ⬤ ❖ ◆ ✕ ✀

The sampler collection began when Dag Hammarskjold, then secretary general of the United Nations, gave a sampler to the Sisanes as a wedding gift. After Helen left her UNICEF position as postal administrator, she became a Realtor and interior designer and continued collecting samplers, pewter, antiques, and reproductions. Now she is an accomplished woodworker who makes furniture and, occasionally, a picket fence. As Ike says, "She can do all those things so well!"

In 1984 Ike, a federal government administrator, and Helen bought this Colonial-style brick mansion within just 15 minutes of viewing it. Built in 1975 (ask Ike about the fascinating site research/archaeological process), it was designed inside and out to replicate a colonial plantation house with early 18th-century architectural authenticity, with crown and dentil moldings and pegged hardwood planked floors. In 1988 Ike's opportunity to be a policy administrator in Europe prompted the idea of B&B with Helen as hostess—as a way to keep this unusual property. He returned in 18 months to innkeeping, "a job I really love." In 1990 the Sisanes built a replica of Colonial Williamsburg's 18th-century Coke-Garrett Carriage House as a woodworking studio for Helen. And in 1994 guests joined the Sisanes on the inn's front steps to sing "Oh What a Beautiful Morning" on "CBS This Morning."

In residence: In hosts' quarters—Toby, a friendly Yorkshire terrier.
Bed and bath: Four second-floor rooms (two can be suites), each with king or queen rice-carved four-poster bed. All with private shower baths, wing chairs, concealed TV. Suites have adjoining room (new in 1995) with fireplace, sofa, wing chairs, wet bar, porch.
Breakfast: At 8:30. The "skip lunch" kind. Juice, coffee, sweet cake, muffins, fruit cup. Waffles, French toast, quiche, or Western eggs with potatoes, sausage. Served in dining room that has an 1887 pump organ, one of those acquired treasures that comes complete with a story collectors love to hear.
Plus: Central air conditioning. Bedroom ceiling fans. Fireplaced great room. Back porch overlooking wooded grounds. "A little tour of the carriage house workshop." Special occasions acknowledged. Off-street parking. Transportation to/from airport, train, or bus station.

From Iowa: *"We enjoyed our stay at Williamsburg Sampler as much as we enjoyed the city itself."* From New Jersey: *"Homey, friendly, and accommodating."*

Edgewood Plantation

804/829-2962

4800 John Tyler Memorial Highway, Charles City, VA 23030   **800/296-3343**

Hosts: Julian and Dot Boulware

Location: Set back from Route 5 (which has a cycling path) with its 3 miles of plantations, including Shirley, Evelynton, Berkely, and Sherwood Forest, open to the public. Adjoining fish hatchery has walking trails and lake for fishing. Short drive to "three fantastic restaurants." One and a half miles from James River, 28 west of Williamsburg, 24 east of Richmond.

Open: Year round. Two-night minimum on major holidays and Valentine's weekend.

Rates: $138, $148, $158, depending on bed size and fireplace. Third floor $148 for one room, private bath; $120 per room for four people. Honeymoon cottage suite $168. Less January–March. MC, Visa.

♥ ⌖ ⁂ ♦ ✈

Canopied beds, armoires, settees, marble-topped tables, an 1840 square piano, Persian rugs, vintage clothing, ruffles, hatboxes filled with antebellum millinery, books, jewelry, dolls, china, folk art, huge gold leaf–framed mirrors . . . a formal parlor and dining room, a country kitchen with baskets and folk art. The 30-year collection—featured in *Country Home, Early American Life, Country Victoria,* and *Country Inns*—is arranged throughout the Gothic Revival house on property that was once part of Berkely Plantation. Restoration began when the Boulwares bought the place in 1978. That's when Julian removed a plaster wall and found a kitchen fireplace just where Dot wanted one. Neighbors stopped by to advise and to reminisce about the plantation's history and earlier appearance. By 1982 Dot, in Victorian dress, began conducting tours of the 11 rooms and the three-story freestanding winding staircase that brides love. Elaborate Christmas decor, with 17 trees, became a tradition. The Boulwares also added a swimming pool and a gazebo. As for B&B, begun in 1984, Julian, who retired from Philip Morris in 1993, is one of those won-over husbands "who also shares a passion for antiques!"

Bed and bath: Eight rooms, all private baths. In main house, second floor—four rooms with working fireplaces. One with canopied king bed, love-story-based window etching, small shower bath. One with canopied queen bed, small shower bath. Two rooms, one with canopied queen (claw-footed tub, no shower in private hall bath) and one with Victorian high-headboard queen bed. Third floor, "perfect for two couples or a group"—two large rooms, each with two double beds and a sofa, separated by a sitting room; one full bath. In cottage with country decor, first floor—1820 walnut queen four-poster, sitting area, TV hidden in a dollhouse, full bath. Second floor—rose-covered vine-canopied queen bed, sitting room, kitchen area, full bath. Trundle available.

Breakfast: 8–9:30. Fruit. French toast and bacon, biscuit and eggs, or sausage and gravy over biscuit and fresh apples. Bacon and home-fried potatoes. Coffee and tea. By country kitchen fireplace, in formal dining room by candlelight, or on wicker-furnished veranda.

(Please turn page.)

Plus: Central air conditioning. Welcoming refreshments. Turndown service with rose and sachet. Hiking trails. Creek for fishing. Antiques and gift shops here. Golf and tennis at nearby country club.

North Bend Plantation B&B   804/829-5176
12200 Weyanoke Road, Charles City, VA 23030-0128

Hosts: George and Ridgely Copland
Location: Quiet. Thirty minutes west of Colonial Williamsburg, in Virginia plantation country. Three miles off Route 5, overlooking George's 250 acres of corn, wheat, soybean, and barley fields, part of

850-acre property that has 28 acres along the river.
Open: Year round.
Rates: Double bed $95. Queen four-posters $105 or $115. Great-great-grandfather's high bed $120.
♥ ⬤ ⁂ ◆ ✗ ⅙

"George has lived all his life in this Greek Revival house built in 1819 [and enlarged in 1853] for his great-great-aunt Sarah Harrison, sister of the ninth president. Many of the antiques in the large open rooms are original to this Virginia historic landmark, which is named for its location on the James River. It is two miles by foot, on our tandem bicycle, or by car along a colonial road with much wildlife and Civil War trenches. Many guests enjoy the billiard table bought by George's grandmother in 1916. Some play the piano and others gather round to sing! They appreciate the rare book library. And from our sun porch there's a magnificent vista with deer, geese, and wild turkeys in season. Benches are under the magnolia tree. It really is beautiful here. Our pool, too, is enjoyed by guests, even those who come with a heavy agenda. Many come back for the peacefulness, to 'do' this wonderful plantation area, or to witness the pageantry of the fox hunts that take place at North Bend in November, December, or January. And to think that, in 1984, a friend had to talk us into hosting! B&B brings the world to us."

Ridgely, a registered nurse who is a nurse practitioner, has lived here for 36 years.

Foreign languages spoken: "A little French and German."
Bed and bath: Four second-floor rooms; all with private baths, armoires, Laura Ashley linens, and Waverly prints. Three (two are 20 by 20 feet) with queen beds and shower baths; one has a connecting double-bedded room. One room with double sleigh bed; bath features original deep long tub put in by George's grandfather in 1916.
Breakfast: Country style. All you can eat. "Until 9:30. If you come down at that hour, ring the old farm bell and George will come up from the barn." Fruit. Orange juice. Bacon, ham, or sausage. Eggs to order. Biscuits, home-made jelly. George's acclaimed waffles. Served on family china in dining room.
Plus: Air conditioning in bedrooms and family room. (All bedrooms also have ceiling fans.) TV in each room. Beverages. Robes. Turndown service offered. Use of refrigerator. Croquet. Volleyball. Horseshoes. Badminton. The pool. Golf nearby.

From Washington: *"To be able to write at the desk used by General Sheridan— what a thrill."* From several Virginians: *"A real home. A real working farm with very hospitable folks. . . . Far from traffic. . . . Made history come alive. . . . Made our honeymoon special . . . perfect way to heighten our experience with the grandeur of Colonial Williamsburg . . . like staying with old friends."*

Innkeeping may be America's most envied profession. As one host mused, "Where else can you get a job where, every day, someone tells you how wonderful you are?"

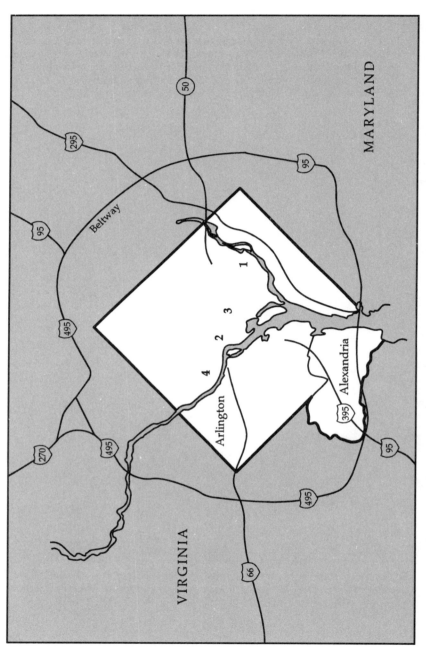

The numbers on this map indicate the locations of B&Bs described in detail in this chapter.

WASHINGTON, D.C.

1 **Capitol Hill**
  Bed & Breakfast
    Accommodations, Ltd.
    Host #133, *384*
  Bed & Breakfast
    Accommodations, Ltd.
    Host #137, *385*
  Bed & Breakfast
    Accommodations, Ltd.
    Host #170, *385*
  Bed & Breakfast
    Accommodations, Ltd.
    Host #175, *386*
2 **Dupont Circle**
  Bed & Breakfast
    Accommodations, Ltd.
    Host #111, *387*
  Bed & Breakfast
    Accommodations, Ltd.
    (unhosted) #138, *387*

  The Bed & Breakfast
    League/Sweet Dreams &
    Toast Host #1, *388*
3 **Logan Circle**
  Bed & Breakfast
    Accommodations, Ltd.
    Host #100, *388*
4 **Northwest**
  Bed & Breakfast
    Accommodations, Ltd.
    Host #126, *389*
  The Bed & Breakfast
    League/Sweet Dreams &
    Toast Host #3, *390*
  The Bed & Breakfast
    League/Sweet Dreams &
    Toast Host #4, *390*
  Kalorama Guest House at
    Woodley Park, *391*

KEY TO SYMBOLS
♥ Lots of honeymooners come here.
♣ Families with children are very welcome. (Please see page xii.)
♠ "Please emphasize that we are a private home, not an inn."
♣ Groups or private parties sometimes book the entire B&B.
♦ Travel agents' commission paid. (Please see page xii.)
✶ Sorry, no guests' pets are allowed.
✦ No smoking inside *or* no smoking at all, even on porches.

Washington, D.C.,
_____ Reservation Services _____

Bed & Breakfast Accommodations, Ltd.

P.O. Box 12011, Washington, DC 20005

Phone: 202/328-3510, Monday–Friday 10–5, Saturday 10–1.

Fax: 202/332-3885.

Listings: 85 including private homes, guesthouses, apartments (three-night minimum), and inns (six have a restaurant). Most are in and around Washington; a few are in nearby suburbs such as Alexandria, Fairfax, and Crystal City in Virginia, and Takoma Park and College Park in Maryland. All Washington accommodations are accessible to public transportation; many are in historic homes decorated with antiques. All are air conditioned.

Reservations: One month's advance notice recommended. Two-night minimum for advance private home reservations; one night available in inns or on a last-minute basis in private homes.

Rates: $45–$150 single; $55–$250 double. Family and seasonal rates available. Apartments recommended for families; $15 each additional person. $50 deposit required; balance due two weeks prior to arrival. $10 one-night surcharge. If cancellation is received with three full business days' notice (seven for holiday reservations), there is a $15 charge; less notice, two nights' charge. $10 booking fee. Amex, Diners, MC, Visa. ♦

By demand, this well-established and well-run service has grown to include more than bed and breakfasts. The staff books travelers in accommodations—many but not all are in historic properties—that range in style from budget to luxurious, and in size from 2 to 129 rooms.

The Bed & Breakfast League/
Sweet Dreams & Toast

P.O. Box 9490, Washington, DC 20016-9490

Phone: 202/363-7767, Monday–Thursday 9–5; Friday 9–1. Closed for two weeks at Christmas, and all federal holidays.

Listings: 85. Mostly hosted private residences. Ten unhosted apartments. All are in Washington, D.C. Many are in historic districts; all are within walking distance of public transportation. All are air conditioned. Many have private baths. All serve at least a continental breakfast. Short-term (more than three weeks) hosted and unhosted housing available.

Reservations: Two-day minimum stay. At least 24 hours' notice required; two weeks preferred.

Rates: $40–$125 single. $50–$140 double. $10 one-night surcharge. $10 booking fee per reservation. $25 deposit per room. Deposit is not refundable;

balance paid is refunded if cancellation is telephoned to the office more than eight days in advance of arrival; if later, rate for one night plus booking fee charged. Amex, MC, Visa; 5 percent service charge.

Founded in 1976 and directed by Millie Groobey since 1985, this is one of the oldest B&B reservation services in the country. The philosophy behind host selection is that location must be in a safe and convenient area, within walking distance of public transportation, and that all hosts are gracious and welcoming to travelers. (It is true! I have used the service several times.)

Both Virginia and Maryland offer B&B accommodations with interesting hosts who live very close to Washington, D.C., and good public transportation.

In nearby Maryland:

Chevy Chase, Chevy Chase Bed & Breakfast, page 30.
Olney, The Thoroughbred Bed & Breakfast, page 40.
Silver Spring, Bed and Breakfast of Maryland Host #185, page 44.

In Alexandria, Virginia, many hosts are represented by:

Princely Bed & Breakfast, Ltd. page 315.

Washington, D.C., B&Bs

Many bed and breakfasts in the nation's capital, a city of great diversity, are located within walking distance of interesting sites. B&Bs are in well-established residential neighborhoods, in historic neighborhoods that have been or are being restored, and in areas where there is a blend of homes, apartments, condominiums, and businesses. Some are also in suburbia. Most hosts work in the city. They are all happy to share their knowledge and appreciation of cultural activities, restaurants, transportation, sightseeing, and the urban environment.

Bed & Breakfast Accommodations, Ltd. Host #133

Washington, DC

Location: Capitol Hill. Overlooking Pennsylvania Avenue with its many restaurants and shops. Three blocks to Eastern Market Metro stop, 10 from Capitol and House office buildings.
Reservations: Year round (two-night minimum) through Bed & Breakfast Accommodations, Ltd., page 382.
Rates: Per room. $85 double bed. $100 queen.
♥ ❀ ♦ ✗ ✂

From Florida: *"Charming, informative, delightful hostess. We plan to return."*

Travelers from all over the world—including state department officials, well-known names, and tourists too—enjoy this 25th Anniversary Restoration Society "Best of the Hill" house-tour house, an antiques-filled 1859 Victorian. And they enjoy the hostess, who has "a passion for gardening." Spring through fall guests gather under the gazebo-type umbrella with table and chairs. Several weddings have been held in the private rear garden, which features a bridge that leads to a 2,100-pound koi pond with fountain and some fish that are 17 years old. (Koi fish, we learned, are the fastest-growing hobby in the country.) Many of the subtropical plants—citrus fruit trees, gardenia, and oleander—are brought into the solarium in winter.

Bed and bath: Two second-floor rooms, private baths. One with white iron–and–brass queen bed, antique armoire, ceiling fan, dressing room, en-suite bath with large walk-in shower with Corian walls and a shower head at each end. Other room has large Victorian double bed, Laura Ashley wallcoverings and linens, private en-suite tub/shower bath.
Breakfast: Usually 8–9. Freshly squeezed orange juice, croissants or sweet roll, coffee or tea. Served in dining room. "Often, conversation is very animated."
Plus: Central air conditioning. An invitation to tea in one of two sitting rooms—"usually the red room with shiny brass that reflects from the fire in the fireplace."

Bed & Breakfast Accommodations, Ltd. Host #137

Washington, DC

Location: On Capitol Hill, seven blocks behind the Capitol. Within walking distance of Supreme Court and Library of Congress. Three blocks to buses. Ten-minute walk to Eastern Market subway stop and Union Station (shops, cinemas, restaurants, Amtrak, subway).

Reservations: Year round through Bed & Breakfast Accommodations, Ltd., page 382.
Rates: $60–$65 single, $70–$75 double. $10 one-night surcharge.
♨ ♦ ✈ ⊬

Featured on several house tours as well as in the *Washington Post*, this 1902 house was restored by the host, a fashion designer who came to Washington from New York and Boston.

You enter through ántique leaded glass double doors to a property noted for its chestnut paneling and decorative moldings. The dining room is hexagonal; one bedroom, octagonal. Two of the five original gas fireplaces have been converted to burn wood.

Bed and bath: On second floor, two rooms, each with double bed, share a full bath.
Breakfast: At 8:30. Continental; sometimes with homemade bread.
Plus: Central air conditioning. Private phone and color TV in each room. Double porches overlooking a brick patio surrounded by greenery and flowers.

> From California: *"Extremely gracious host who made me feel very comfortable . . . allowed me to 'fit' into the city."*

Bed & Breakfast Accommodations, Ltd. Host #170

Washington, DC

Location: On Capitol Hill, facing Pennsylvania Avenue. Five blocks from the Capitol, Library of Congress, botanical gardens, Mall. Bus stop in front of house; one block to subway. Close to shops, restaurants, Sunday flea and farmers' markets.

Reservations: Year round through Bed & Breakfast Accommodations, Ltd., page 382.
Rates: $60–$70 single, $70–$80 double. $10 one-night surcharge.
♨ ♦ ✈ ⊬

There's a Florida room (where breakfast is served), a more formal Florentine room, and a garden. The guest room that faces the park on Washington's major avenue is decorated with rococo Victorian antiques. The New England guest room has the original tin ceiling, chestnut wood paneling, and country and Shaker antiques. Most of the original architectural details have been preserved in this carefully restored, air-conditioned Victorian townhouse.

(Please turn page.)

One of the well-traveled hosts, a hotel reservation manager, is a native Washingtonian; the other, a multilingual court reporter, was born and raised in Pennsylvania Dutch country.

Foreign languages spoken: Spanish, Italian, Russian, and a little German.
Bed and bath: One large (Victorian) double-bedded room and one (New England) with a queen bed share a full bath.
Breakfast: 7:30–9:30. Fresh fruit, juice, specialty breads, croissants, muffins, coffee and tea.

> From Massachusetts: *"We loved it. Great breakfast. . . . Offered great recommendations on sites and restaurants."* From California: *"A beautiful environment . . . hospitable surroundings."*

Bed & Breakfast Accommodations, Ltd. Host #175

Washington, DC

Location: In southeast Capitol Hill. Just off Pennsylvania Avenue. Around corner from farmers' market. Two blocks to Eastern Market Metro stop, three to Capitol South stop. Six blocks to U.S. Capitol, Library of Congress, and the Mall.
Reservations: Year round (two-night minimum) through Bed & Breakfast Accommodations, Ltd., page 382.
Rates: Shared bath $55 single, $65 double. Private bath $70 single, $80 double.
♣ ♦ ✕ ⊱

> From New Zealand: *"Wonderful. Beyond all expectations."* From California: *". . . knows how to share his city and his lovely home . . . very convenient, close to transportation, restaurants and shops . . . room was bright, tastefully decorated, comfortable, and very clean . . . fresh flowers . . . had done a house history and could tell delightful stories about his home and neighborhood."*

This 1885 Federal-style row house is furnished with pieces from the 1930s and '40s. The host, originally from New Orleans, is in charge of accounts payable for a Capitol Hill–based property management company.

Bed and bath: Three rooms, all with TV and phone. Second floor—room with double four-poster, private en-suite tub/shower bath. Room with twin beds, small seating area, private hall bath. English basement—room with double brass bed (dated April 1915), desk; shared (with host) tub/shower bath.
Breakfast: At 8, Monday–Friday; 9 on weekends. Continental menu.
Plus: Central air conditioning plus ceiling fans. Fireplaced living room. Patio with fountains and fish pond.

---

*H*ospitality is the keynote of B&B.

Bed & Breakfast Accommodations, Ltd. Host #111

Washington, DC

Location: Three blocks to Dupont Circle Metro, restaurants, shops, theaters. Ten blocks north of White House, 12 from Mall.
Reservations: Year round (two-night minimum) through Bed & Breakfast Accommodations, Ltd., page 382.
Rates: Shared bath $55 single, $65 double. Private bath $60 single, $70 double.
✦ ✦ ✦ ✦ ✦

> From Boston: *"Nutritious and delicious breakfast."* From California: *"A homey atmosphere. . . . A delightful host who made our first visit to Washington more special!"* From Florida: *" . . . felt as if I were staying at a friend's house."*

The multifaceted "friend" is an artist with a master's degree from the University of Alabama. A former caterer and picture framer, she has also served on the board of a local experimental theater. And she knows how to organize sizable fund-raising events. Currently she is attending health psychology classes at the University of Maryland and is involved with the D.C. Habitat for Humanity. As a B&B host she has been welcoming guests since the early 1980s. Her house is one of those given to Union generals in lieu of pensions after the Civil War.

In residence: Two cats.
Foreign languages spoken: A little French, less Spanish.
Bed and bath: Four rooms. Second floor—double bed, private tub/shower bath. Third floor—one room with twin beds and two, each with a double bed, share a tub/shower bath.
Breakfast: 8–8:30. Continental menu. Served in comfortable country kitchen, "the hub of the house."
Plus: Back garden patio. Window air conditioning units throughout. Off-street parking (fee charged) may be reserved in advance.

Bed & Breakfast Accommodations, Ltd. (Unhosted) #138

Washington, DC

Location: Dupont Circle. Two blocks (to the left) for Metro, Connecticut Avenue shops, restaurants, and theaters. One block (to the right) for coffee shops, more restaurants, dry cleaners, hardware store, and supermarket.
Reservations: Year round (two-day minimum) through Bed & Breakfast Accommodations, Ltd., page 382.
Rates: $60 single, $70 double.
✦ ✦ ✦ ✦

This popular air-conditioned first-floor efficiency unit is in a turn-of-the-century bay-windowed building that has been restored into four apartments. It has a fully equipped kitchen, Murphy bed, linens, a sofa, desk, television, and telephone. It is professionally decorated, using the Turkish prints and Korean and Thai baskets collected by the owner, a former Peace Corps member, who lives in the building.

(Please turn page.)

Bed and bath: A double-sized Murphy bed (pulls down from armoire), private tiled tub/shower bath.

> From Netherlands: *"Spotless."* From California: *"We were very pleased with all the arrangements. . . . Owner couldn't have been nicer."*

The Bed & Breakfast League/ Sweet Dreams & Toast Host #1
Washington, DC

Location: Dupont Circle. Near downtown Washington. Within walking distance of Dupont Circle subway stop, art galleries, several small museums, Washington Hilton Hotel, "and more restaurants than you could eat in if you stayed for two months."

Reservations: Year round, two-night minimum, through The Bed & Breakfast League/Sweet Dreams & Toast, page 382.
Rates: $40–$55 single, $50–$60 double.
◀ ✖ ✄

This location appeals to many conventiongoers and business travelers who appreciate the hospitality of the host, a former antiques dealer who is associated with an antique-lighting shop. The Victorian townhouse is filled with many wonderful Victorian and Chinese pieces.

Bed and bath: Three rooms share two tub/shower baths. On second floor, one room with double bed. Third floor has one room with double bed, one with twin.
Breakfast: A cooked breakfast is served in the kitchen or dining room.
Plus: Central air conditioning.

> From Connecticut: *"Beautifully decorated . . . clean and comfortable . . . lovely, quiet, aesthetically pleasing neighborhood."* From South Carolina: *"Overwhelmingly kind and witty host."*

Bed & Breakfast Accommodations, Ltd. Host #100
Washington, DC

Location: In Logan Circle Historic District. Ten blocks from the White House; 12 north of American History Museum, 6 east of Dupont Circle. Bus at corner to the mall; 10-minute walk to subway.
Reservations: Year round through

Bed & Breakfast Accommodations, Ltd., page 382.
Rates: $60–$70 single, $70–$80 double. $5 crib. $10 surcharge for one-night stay. Apartment $75 single, $85 double.
◀ ◀ ✿ ◆ ✖ ✄

A house-tour favorite, most recently part of "Christmas at the Smithsonian," this restored century-old Victorian has for 19 years (18 months for the woodwork) been an avocation for the hosts. Furnished with many antiques, the house provides a wonderful setting for weddings and local theater group cast parties too. The latticed porch was pictured in Manhattan's Bloomingdale's photo essay based on this book.

The host, a lawyer, is a partner in a real estate development and syndication firm. The hostess has studied interior design and for the last decade has been very involved with the bed and breakfast movement in Washington.

Bed and bath: Six rooms share three baths. On second floor, room with canopied queen plus smaller room with double bed. On third floor, two queen-bedded rooms; also one with queen bed and queen sleep sofa, and one with a queen and a double bed. Apartment with queen bed and sleep sofa, laundry facilities.

Breakfast: At 8 on weekdays, 9 on weekends. Juice, coffee or tea, and a choice of two items—muffins, croissants, raisin toast, bagels. Sometimes, German pancakes or homemade waffles. Served in dining room under Victorian chandelier.

Plus: Central air conditioning. Area-controlled heating. Private phone and color TV in guest rooms. Parking ($5) if reserved in advance. Player piano. A Barbie-doll collection for young guests to play with. Old-fashioned swing under arbor.

From England: *"A stunning home, but the hospitality is what endears this B&B to us."* From North Carolina: *"Accommodating to the extent of lending me a bike lock so I could travel by bike."* From Alabama: *"Greeted me with a cup of tea. Made me feel like a welcome friend."*

Bed & Breakfast Accommodations, Ltd. Host #126

Washington, DC

Location: Residential. On a wide tree-lined avenue. In Tenley Circle (Northwest Washington), between Georgetown and Chevy Chase, Maryland. One block from Metro (subway) and major bus routes. One mile to American University and Washington Cathedral. Two blocks to business district, tennis courts, indoor swimming pool.

Reservations: Year round (two-day minimum) through Bed & Breakfast Accommodations, Ltd., page 382.

Rates: $75 single, $80 double. $10 third person.
♦ ✖ ⊁

The Georgian-style brick Colonial is home to hosts who often stay at B&Bs during their own travels. The host, a New Englander who has lived in London, is a coordinator for a suburban school system. The hostess is a native of Washington, where her family has owned an art gallery for many years.

From Pennsylvania: *"Deserves a four-star rating . . . great."* From New York: *"Been here twice . . . clean . . . comfortable . . . hospitable . . . delicious homemade bread."*

In residence: Two school-aged daughters. One small dog.
Foreign languages spoken: French and a little Sweedish.
Bed and bath: Two large carpeted rooms, each with private en-suite tile shower bath. First floor—room with canopied double four-poster, queen sofa

bed, access to patio and garden. Second floor—master bedroom with queen bed, private balcony overlooking garden.
Breakfast: At 8. Continental menu.
Plus: Central air conditioning.

The Bed & Breakfast League/ Sweet Dreams & Toast Host #3
Washington, DC

Location: Cleveland Park. A quiet "close-in" section of Northwest Washington. Six blocks north of the Washington National Cathedral. Ten-minute walk to Cleveland Park Metro stop. One block to crosstown bus.

Reservations: Year round, two-night minimum, through The Bed & Breakfast League/Sweet Dreams & Toast, page 382.
Rates: $45–$65 single, $65–$75 double.
🛏 ✖ ⊁

The welcoming host, a native New Englander who has lived in Washington for 25 years, had a career in public health nursing before becoming immersed in tourism. Some guests follow suggestions for a walking tour of this neighborhood, which was designed in the 1880s to be an out-of-town summer resort. Others may be given a night driving tour of the lighted federal buildings and monuments. Throughout the large Cape Cod–style home, there are family antiques including rocking chairs and a rope bed.

Bed and bath: Three rooms. Master bedroom has double bed and private attached bath with tub and shower. Second bedroom has one twin bed, desk, and private or shared hall bath with tub and shower. Third bedroom has one twin bed and private or shared hall bath.
Breakfast: Flexible hour. Continental. In formal dining room with flower-filled bay window overlooking the spacious yard.

The Bed & Breakfast League/ Sweet Dreams & Toast Host #4
Washington, DC

Location: North Cleveland Park. In a quiet "close-in" section of Northwest Washington. Near the Washington National Cathedral, American University, the new embassy district, and Metro.
Reservations: Year round, two-night minimum, through The Bed & Breakfast League/Sweet Dreams & Toast, page 382.
Rates: $40–$70 single, $60–$80 double.
🛏 ✖ ⊁

From Ontario, Canada: *"Beautiful furnishings. Clean, quiet, safe location. Great breakfast with lots of coffee, fruit, and a variety of breads. Especially liked the strawberry muffins and homemade preserves. Firm beds. Very considerate and informative host."*

Antique furnishings, prints, and Oriental rugs give this home a warm ambiance. The host worked for several government agencies before owning and operating a small people-oriented business.

In residence: Two memorable and popular dogs—a standard poodle and a "zany but beautiful and well-behaved" six-year-old that came from the animal shelter.

Bed and bath: Three second-floor rooms. One with two twin beds and private attached bath with shower. Two other rooms have one double bed each and may share (or one may have as private) a private tub/shower bath.

Plus: Air conditioning throughout. Off-street parking for guests' cars. TV and phone in guest rooms.

Kalorama Guest House at Woodley Park

2700 Cathedral Avenue, NW   202/328-0860
Washington, DC 20008   fax 202/319-1262

Host: Richard L. Fenstemaker; assistants: Mike Gallagher and Mary Ann Eitler

Location: Residential. Quiet. Downtown in embassy district. At corner of 27th Street, one block off Connecticut Avenue with its many ethnic restaurants. A few blocks from National Zoo and Woodley Park subway station.

Open: Year round. Two-night minimum on most weekends March–June, September, and October.

Rates: Shared bath $45 single, $50 double. Private bath $50–$90 single, $55–$95 double. (Varies according to size and location of room.) Suite $95 single, $10 each additional person. Amex, MC, Visa.

♨ ❖ ◆ ✈

"Grandparents' house style" and noncorporate life were the main attractions of B&B for Richard, a former assistant manager of a 500-room Sheraton Hotel who sometimes gives innkeeping seminars. Here, guests appreciate the neighborhood setting and the relaxing (not elaborate) environment. Furnishings include antiques, artwork, and photographs.

Richard explains: "The area was developed in 1912 for government workers' single-family homes. This corner house was a rooming house when I redid it in 1984. In addition to many business travelers, conference attendees, and tourists [some return annually], we host friends and relatives of neighbors."

Bed and bath: Eleven rooms. Private baths for rooms on second and third floors with queen, double, or twin beds. One suite has queen bed and a double sofa bed. Three lower-level (very popular) fairly spartan double-bedded rooms share one unglamorous bath.

Breakfast: 7:30–10:30 weekdays. 8–11 weekends. Freshly baked croissants (delivered daily by a local baker), English muffins, toast, coffee, tea, butter and jam. In sun-filled breakfast room.

Plus: Sherry (5–9 p.m.). Air conditioning in bedrooms and parlor. Coffee is always on. Laundry facilities. Parking ($6 per night). Free local phone calls. Suggestions for favorite restaurants and relatively unknown walking tours of historic buildings.

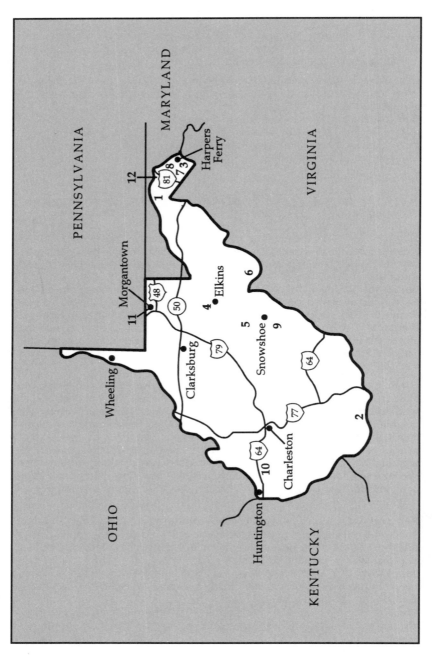

The numbers on this map indicate the locations of B&Bs described in
detail in this chapter.

WEST VIRGINIA

KEY TO SYMBOLS
♥ Lots of honeymooners come here.
♠ Families with children are very welcome. (Please see page xii.)
♠ "Please emphasize that we are a private home, not an inn."
♣ Groups or private parties sometimes book the entire B&B.
♦ Travel agents' commission paid. (Please see page xii.)
✷ Sorry, no guests' pets are allowed.
✛ No smoking inside *or* no smoking at all, even on porches.

West Virginia B&Bs

Highlawn Inn
304/258-5700
304 Market Street, Berkeley Springs, WV 25411

Hosts: Sandra Kauffman and Timothy Miller
Location: On a quiet side street. At the top of a steep hill, three blocks from low-key town center with mineral baths, 99-cent 1930s Star Theatre, antiques malls, Tari's Cafe (performances too). Near 18-hole championship golf course. Two hours from Washington, D.C.
Open: Year round. Two-night minimum on most weekends.

Rates: Highlawn: $70–$85; suite $98. Aunt Pearl's: $90 large room, ridge view; $95 with lattice-enclosed porch; $98 with sitting area, private exterior entrance; $98 huge first-floor room. Six-course candlelit dinners (May through October): $35/person includes complimentary bottle of award-winning West Virginia wine.
❤ ⚬⚬ ✳

From Virginia: "Truly a gem. . . . Delightful renovation . . . hard to believe the dining room tin ceiling came from Dallas . . . felt pampered. . . . Ms. Kauffman can make low-fat food taste divine . . . no-fat cheesecake is to die for!" From Maryland: *"Warm hospitality, privacy, sense of caring . . . handsome wicker-furnished porch with hand-cranked ice cream on Fourth of July!"*

On her way to becoming an innkeeper known for her culinary talents, Sandy was an urban law firm legal administrator (manager of 60 staff members), president of the Association of Legal Administrators, and an antiques dealer. After restoring the 1890s Highlawn, she and Tim, the conference and wedding specialist, restored an adjacent turn-of-the-century house. They named it Aunt Pearl's and decorated with Victorian wallpapers and white iron–and–brass beds. Breakfasts as well as the popular silver service dinner parties feature local ingredients; homegrown herbs; and reduced salt, fat, and sugar recipes.

In residence: "Jackie, a special kitty who adopted our inn and loves hallway naps. Several friendly porch cats for petting."
Bed and bath: Ten rooms. In Highlawn, five second-floor rooms plus a first-floor suite with private entrance and porch. All private baths, all but one with claw-footed tub and shower. King or double beds. In Aunt Pearl's, four queen-bedded rooms, private en-suite baths—two tub and shower, two shower only.
Breakfast: 8:30–10. "Unforgettable." Could be freshly squeezed orange juice, egg-and-cheese casserole, locally produced country sausage and bacon, grits, homemade jams to top "mile high" biscuits, hot glazed cinnamon rolls, honey orange pastry made with local wildflower honey, prizewinning locally made apple butter. Fresh seasonal herb dishes; always a vegetarian dish. Sandy's own coffee blend. Served in garden-like fireplaced dining room.
Plus: Air conditioning and color TV in rooms. Rockers and swing on verandas. Large lawn. English soaps. Mineral water. Coffees, teas.

Three Oaks and A Quilt   304/248-8316

Duhring Avenue, P.O. Box 84, Bramwell, WV 24715

Host: "B.J." Kahle
Location: Off the beaten path. In a town of about 1,000 people. Eight miles north of Bluefield, West Virginia. In a residential section atop a hill across from the Thomas Mansion "Carriage House."

Open: Year round.
Rates: $55 double. $5 less for single occupancy. Discounts for stays of more than three nights.
♥ ⬤ ✕ ✘

"Most people come here to see the coal operators' mansions in this town, which is on the National Register of Historic Places. They fall in love with the area and want to return. One is quickly renewed in the restful, relaxing atmosphere. My grandfather bought this house in 1904, and it has remained in the family ever since. I restored it, using and reusing everything possible. The oaks are to keep you cool; the quilts are to keep you warm."

A magnificent "Whig Rose" appliqued quilt, one of B.J.'s collection (of four dozen), is hanging on the front porch wall. Other quilts, all handmade, all in traditional patterns, are on every bed and throughout the freshly painted and papered homestead. B.J., mother of three grown children, has taught in five states.

Bed and bath: Three second-floor rooms. Two shared baths, one with tub, the other with shower. Two rooms with double beds (one is grandparents' cherry bed, the other a Henry Ford four-poster pencil bed). One room with twin beds.
Breakfast: Weekdays at 7; flexible on weekends. Juice, casseroles, cinnamon rolls, Christmas Eve Plum Pudding Bread, quick breads, glazed apples, hot beverages. Menu varies according to guests' tastes and B.J.'s schedule. Served in the dining room amidst a quilt collection.
Plus: Late-afternoon beverages. Bedroom fans. Mints. Fresh flowers. When time permits, tour of area.

From Florida: *"A return to genteel hospitality . . . in a 19th-century town so well preserved that it lacks a gas station on Main Street . . . everything in apple-pie order . . . intangible comforts of a welcoming front porch with a swing, a formal 19th-century dining room, and kitchen conversations."* From Mississippi: *"Special insight into the town's past and present . . . it's not just a comfortable place to stay at a great price; it's an experience."*

Many B&Bs that allow smoking restrict it to certain rooms and/or public areas. Although some of those B&Bs that have the ✘ symbol allow smoking on the porch and/or patio, others do not allow smoking anywhere on the property.

The Carriage Inn

304/728-8003

417 East Washington Street
Charles Town, WV 25414

fax (call first) **304/725-3810**

Hosts: Bob and Virginia Kaetzel; Karen Crum, assistant
Location: On half a city block. With many shade trees, including two massive copper beeches flanking the front entrance. On Route 51, two blocks from Route 340 and two blocks west of Charles Rown Races. Five-minute walk to restaurants or Civil War Museum. Five miles to Harpers Ferry. Close to Martinsburg outlets; Antietam Battlefield in Sharpsburg, Maryland; and Shenandoah River raft trips.
Open: Year round. "Please check in by 6 p.m."
Rates: $65 weekdays. $95 Friday, Saturday, and holidays. Birthday, anniversary and getaway packages. MC, Visa.
♥ ♣ ✼

The breakfast, history, and quiet—"a real step back in time" guests often say—are major attractions of this 1836 Colonial restored in 1985 by Bob, a builder/restorer/ excavator. Virginia, the official gardener, has decorated with a blend of Victorian and country—with antiques, Oriental rugs, and original crystal chandeliers. The beds were built with walnut wood from West Virginia trees. A flag carried by General Stonewall Jackson was once hidden in a hollowed-out space beneath one fireplace hearth. In the West Parlor there are prints of the original drawings depicting General Ulysses S. Grant and General Philip Sheridan when they met here in 1861 to plan Civil War strategy. And outside there's Bob's 1956 red and white Buick Century with just 17,000 original miles on it! Karen greets guests during the day. Enthusiastic Bob—"this is a great town to live in"—is the late-afternoon and evening host.

In residence: Jack (for Stonewall Jackson), a playful dog, a favorite of many guests.
Bed and bath: Five lace-curtained rooms, all with private full baths, on three levels. All queen beds (four are canopied). Four rooms have wood-burning fireplace. One has its own glass-enclosed porch, TV, and refrigerator.
Breakfast: 8:30–9. Fruit dish—maybe baked grapefruit. Carribean French toast made with French bread, bananas, whipped cream, kiwi, pineapple, and fresh strawberries. Or buttermilk pancakes. All served with bacon and eggs.
Plus: Central air conditioning. Fireplaces in living and dining rooms. Parlor Victrola with 78-rpm records. Guest refrigerator. Passes to Charles Town races.

---

*U*nless otherwise stated, rates in this book are per room for two and include breakfast in addition to all the amenities in "Plus."

Gilbert House B&B of Middleway

P.O. Box 1104, Charles Town, WV 25414   304/725-0637

Host: Bernie Heiler
Location: In the National Register village of Middleway, with 18th-century architecture, footbridge by mill, gazebo, old cemeteries. Surrounded by churchyards and fronted by old flagstone sidewalk. Five minutes to Charles Town and I-81, 15 to Harpers Ferry, 30 to Antietam Battlefield.

Open: Year round. Two-night minimum preferred September–November weekends. Reservations required.
Rates: $100 third-floor room. $120 or $140 second-floor suites. Amex, MC, Visa.
♥ ✿ ⁂ ◆ ✈ ✄

Thanks to the Heilers' restoration, the village has a historic B&B with 20th-century comforts. The early Georgian stone Colonial is furnished with Oriental rugs, master artworks, fine antiques, and interesting pieces collected during the worldwide travels of Bernie, a petroleum engineer who works in Washington, and his late wife, Jean, who was an artist and financial analyst. They were Boston based for 20 years before moving here for a new lifestyle with much participation in historic preservation, and in arts organizations and Washington's Shakespeare Theater. Bernie's latest project is the addition of two more rooms on top of the 1760 part of the house.

Foreign languages spoken: Spanish and German.
Bed and bath: Three rooms; soon to be five. On third floor (with sound of rain on tin roof): queen bed; sitting area, en-suite shower/tub bath. On second floor: one large room, queen bed plus a single bed, working fireplace, two sitting areas, tub/shower bath. Champagne in bridal suite with huge living room, 18th-century bed (adapted to queen size) with curtains, working fireplace, en-suite bath with claw-footed tub, hand-held shower.
Breakfast: At 9. (Coffee ready earlier.) Freshly squeezed orange juice, fresh fruit. Pastries. Quiche with asparagus, spinach, or salmon, or French toast. Homemade jelly or Jamaican marmalade. Maybe steak and eggs. Cake or pie. Special diets accommodated. In main room or on porch.
Plus: Air-conditioned bedrooms. Candy. Fresh fruit. Chinese sandalwood and English Pears soaps. Fireplaces. Piano. Library.

From Maryland: *"Made for a romantic getaway . . . breakfasts were feasts . . . good advice on restaurants and sightseeing."*

All the B&Bs with the ✿ symbol want you to know that they are a private home set up for paying guests, not an inn. Although definitions vary, these private home B&Bs tend to have one to three guest rooms. For the owners—people who enjoy meeting people—B&B is usually a part-time occupation.

Hillbrook Inn   304/725-4223

Route 2, Box 152, Charles Town, WV 25414-9635

Host: Gretchen Carroll
Location: It's there, "farther down the drive than you think possible," five miles west of town, an hour from D.C. Beltway, off a winding country road, on 17 acres. Surrounded by miles of peach orchards, a thorough-bred farm, and hundreds of acres of Angus. In the crook of Bullskin Run, with "wildly angled roofs" reflected in the duck pond.

Open: Year round (except Christmas eve and day).
Rates: Per couple, $240 Sunday–Thursday, $330–$380 Friday-Saturday; includes breakfast and seven-course dinner with wine. $99 "procrastination B&B rate" available only for same-day bookings; dinner optional. Specials January–March. Discover, MC, Visa.
♥ ❖ ◆ ✶

This award-winning inn is noted for its setting, its decor, its cuisine—and Gretchen, the innkeeper, who still remembers when the property was just her Sunday-drive destination inspired by a *Washington Post* photograph. That was in 1984, when she was Georgetown University's director of study abroad and the founding director of the International Student Exchange Program—following a Foreign Service–oriented life with her father and her husband. Gretchen fell in love with the one-room-wide, half-timbered Tudor manor house that cascades down 15 levels (no two rooms are on the same level) and transformed it into "a feast for the senses." It has an English country house ambiance with collections of antiques—"all are used; we're not a museum"—and polished floors, lots of old wood and brass, Oriental rugs, and more than 2,000 window panes. There are no secrets: personally and in a printed guide Gretchen directs guests to auctions and shops, the source of many of the inn's furnishings. She is also an avid hiker who shares hints about trails.

Foreign language spoken: French.
Bed and bath: Only six rooms, each with queen or antique double bed and feather bed, sitting area, air conditioning, ceiling fan, views. Each unique (working fireplace, wood stove, whirlpool tub, porch, or location); fully described when you call. All private baths; one with tub and shower, some with hand-held shower.
Breakfast: 9–10. Chef Christine's menus include French toast with warm cranberry orange syrup; pecan pancakes with apricot-ginger butter, apple brandy syrup, sour cream dollop; eggs with fresh herbs, meat, grilled tomato. Served on glassed-in porch.
Plus: Fireplace at each end of 20-foot-high living room. Library. Beribboned chocolates. "Lots of places to just be." Small tables and chairs on Bridge of Sighs over stream. Hammock. Terrace with fountain. Perennial gardens. Picnic baskets. Fresh Bullskin Run springwater from original springhouse on property.

The Retreat at Buffalo Run   304/636-2960

214 Harpertown Road, Elkins, WV 26241-9662

Hosts: Bertha and Earl Rhoad (year round); Kathleen Rhoad (summers and holidays)
Location: On five acres of wooded grounds. Three blocks from Davis and Elkins College. One mile from downtown Elkins. Between Canaan Valley/Timberline and Snowshoe/Silver Creek ski areas. Near a cranberry wilderness; white-water outfitters; caves and caverns for spelunking; the Augusta Heritage Arts Workshops. Four hours west of Washington, D.C.
Open: Year round.
Rates: Tax included. $54 single. $64 double. $10 under age 10; $15 age 10 and over.
♥ ♨ ☕ ♣ ✈ ✂

The wraparound porch has swing and rocking chairs. Hummingbirds are at the feeders. Tall shade trees, evergreens, rhododendron groves, and a hammock are on the grounds of the turn-of-the-century house that Kathleen "just knew" would be the right place (and new career) for her parents. Within half an hour of the Realtor's showing, the Rhoads made an offer. They redecorated and furnished with homey antiques, art, and contemporary pieces.

Kathleen has been a college career counselor in Chicago, in Washington, D.C., and now at a Florida community college. In Florida, Kathleen is a member of the Rare Fruit and Vegetable Council. Here she skis, hikes, goes antiquing, floats down Cheat River on inner tubes—and hosts! Her parents, avid bird-watchers and gardeners, met as teenagers in Hershey, Pennsylvania. Cook and seamstress Bert is a member of a local hiking club. Earl, most recently a Sweetheart Cups training director, was a printer and small-town newspaper publisher. They all concur: "For us, B&B in this wonderful old house was meant to be."

Bed and bath: Six rooms on second and third floors share three tub/shower baths plus a half bath. Queen or double beds; one room has two double beds, two have extra-long queen beds. Rollaways available.
Breakfast: At guests' convenience. Fresh fruit. Homemade muffins. Entree possibilities: Dutch babies, Swedish pancakes, blackberry custard, overnight French toast with calamondin marmalade, or something "new." Selected from Kathleen's cookbook collection or from Bertha's recipes inspired by home territory, Pennsylvania's Lancaster County.
Plus: Afternoon beverages. Piano. Living room ceiling fan. Guest refrigerator. TV. Games. Coloring books for children.

From Michigan: *"Superior because of personal care and attention to detail . . . I would go back for the breakfasts alone. . . . The most important element of the Retreat's charm is human. The combination of two generations of hosts who take an interest in their guests, without intruding on their privacy."* From Virginia: *"All sorts of information was computerized and available as a handout. . . . My son called them Grandma and Grandpa by the time we left."*

Hutton House Bed & Breakfast   304/335-6701
Route 219/250, Huttonsville, WV 26273   800/234-6701

Hosts: Dean Ahren and Loretta Murray
Location: High on a hill, overlooking "tiny Huttonsville" (population: 250), Tygart Valley, Laurel Mountains. Within 45 minutes of Snowshoe ski resort, Cass Scenic Railroad, National Radio Observatory; 17 miles south of Elkins. "Near great home cooking as well as four-star dining."

Open: Year round. Two-night minimum on holiday weekends and October Forest Festival.
Rates: $60–$65 detached bath; $65–$70 en-suite bath; $70–$75 whirlpool bath. Singles $10 less. $10 extra adult in room, $5 ages 5–9. Ten percent less for senior citizens. MC, Visa.

♥ ♫ ♨ ♣ ♦ ✗ ⚚

From Ohio: *"We never wanted to leave."* From Virginia: *"Spacious enough to offer complete privacy, but also a warm, homey atmosphere."* From Pennsylvania: *"Wonderful, creative cook . . . incredible array of baked goods . . . lacy curtains . . . rich woods that glow . . . knickknacks . . . huge soft towels . . . hints for our four days . . . most of all, sitting on that glorious porch and reading, looking at the sunset, talking, even singing old folk songs . . . left feeling pampered, rested and full."* And from a guest as she was leaving: *"I don't get it. No TV, no Nintendo, and my 11-year-old wants to know why we can't stay longer."*

"Unscheduled highlights" is what Loretta refers to. Spontaneity and laughter are bywords here. You are welcome to help yourself to coffee in the kitchen, "hang out" at the bar-type counter while breakfast is being prepared, have muffins in the dining room and move on to the wraparound porch for the main course. Play badminton, croquet—or jacks! Bring up some subject and later, maybe, find a book about it on your pillow. Be prepared for flexible, happy, sharing hosts—who, while on their honeymoon in 1988, followed a garage sale sign and came upon this turreted National Register Queen Anne Victorian, vacant then, with winding staircase that inspired the next-day deposit. They opened as a summer B&B for three years, while Loretta continued in Philadelphia as a physical education teacher ("some qualifications for this!") and Dean as a contractor. In 1991 the community activists became full-time innkeepers (and Dean, a real estate developer).

In residence: Three outdoor cats—Mica, Yip, and Stinky.
Bed and bath: Six rooms; all private baths. Three on second floor, three on third. King/twins, queen, queen and one or two twins, double bed with Jacuzzi bath. Turret room has cathedral ceiling, shower bath. Crib available.
Breakfast: Flexible hours. Repertoire includes creme brulee with raspberries, zucchini frittata, stuffed Italian sausage, pineapple sorbet with kiwi, lemon pancakes, stuffed French toast, whole-grain pancakes with maple syrup made right here. Special diets accommodated.
Plus: Hints for walking trails. Trips—sometimes with the hosts—to Augusta Heritage Arts Festival, to eat ramps, or to area convenience store that has six pool tables.

McCoy's Mill B&B   304/358-7893

Thorn Creek Road, Box 610, Franklin, WV 26807

Hosts: Iris and Glen Hofecker
Location: Peaceful. At the foot of mountains, where Thorn Creek rushes into the headwaters of the south branch of the Potomac River. Just off Route 220; waterwheel visible. Three miles south of Franklin.

Open: Year round. Two-night minimum on September and October weekends.
Rates: $50 single, $60 double. Less for three or more nights.
♥ ◀ ♣ ✗

Guests wrote: *"A fantastic experience. . . . A combination of a step back into history, into a mill that is being restored; a memorable evening and morning visiting with fascinating folks; a stick-to-the-ribs breakfast with the best homemade apple butter we've ever had. . . . Sleeping next to the sound of a rushing stream. Waking up to one of the most picturesque scenes in West Virginia. What more could one ask for?"*

And all because of the great flood of 1985. Glen, a sought-after cabinetmaker who reproduces clocks and Chippendale furniture—mostly Newport style—had restored a 1756 mill in Virginia. While working with the West Virginia flood disaster relief, he found McCoy's Mill, the state's oldest (1757) landmark, and felt it would be a great place to share with others via B&B. What the Hofeckers have created is "an escape, a place where guests never seem to be in a hurry," a friendly, comfortable B&B with a bedroom that has been pictured in *Mid-Atlantic Country*.

The present mill of post-and-beam construction was built in 1848. The adjoining miller's house was built in 1909. Glen has created a small hydro-electric plant that uses the mill and mill wheel to produce electricity for heat and lighting in the B&B and shop. And he has built a wonderful log cabin workshop with the stone fireplace that remained, all by itself, from miller's original house.

In residence: Daughter Jane and her husband Joerg Shrierer (from Germany) are planning to share innkeeping roles—and lead hiking and biking trips. A Yorkie, Tinker, "terribly bright, terribly human" (the Yarmouth Port, Mass., *Register*); "adorable . . . goodwill ambassador" (Maryland guests).
Bed and bath: With view of creek, dam, or river—three large second-floor rooms (several horizontally paneled walls) with private tub/shower baths. Two with queen-size beds. One with two double four-poster beds.
Breakfast: 7–9. Full country breakfast could include sausage, biscuits, and gravy; pancakes; or French toast with cinnamon apples. Juice. Fruit. Homemade breads. Glen and Iris join guests on deck overlooking waterwheel or in country kitchen.
Plus: Fully equipped guest kitchen ($30 charge for cooking). Tour of house, mill, workshop—with lots of shared expertise. Barbecue. Picnic tables. Fishing on premises; some fishing equipment available.

Gerrardstown's Prospect Hill Bed & Breakfast

304/229-3346

P.O. Box 135, Gerrardstown, WV 25420

Hosts: Hazel and Charles Hudock
Location: Secluded. On a 225-acre working farm. At the foot of North Mountain. Four miles from I-81. About a 90-minute drive from Washington, D.C. Near Harpers Ferry, Antietam, Gettysburg, and Winchester.
Open: Year round. Two-night minimum on holidays—and generally preferred. Arrival time 3–10; departure by 11.
Rates: Per room, $85; $95 Saturday night only. Cottage, $95 for two; $20 each additional person. MC, Visa.
♥ ♦ ♦ ♣ ✈

"A discovery," say first-time guests, who drive between the stone pillars, cross over the stone bridge, and pass ducks and geese before arriving at the Georgian mansion. The grand main hall has a graceful open stairway with a three-storied mural of early colonial life. Built between 1789 and 1802 by a businessman who outfitted wagon trains going west, the elegant residence was restored in 1978 when the Hudocks decided to come for what B&B guests seek: peace and quiet. With five children grown—now visiting grandchildren come—"B&B just sort of happened."

The house is on the Register of Historic Places and is filled with antiques collected through the Hudocks' 28 years of traveling when Charlie was a meteorologist with the U.S. Navy. (He delights in seeing guests guess the origin of some items.) It's the kind of place where you can be very private or "wander into the kitchen for tea and talk." Or spend time with Charlie, who loves to share his extensive collection of books and photographs. Or go for long walks through the woods. Discover herb, vegetable, and fruit gardens. Enjoy the scene of cows and calves.

In residence: Charlie smokes a pipe. Elmo, a "Morris-like" outdoor cat. Horses in summer.
Bed and bath: Two large mansion rooms, each with a private full bath, working fireplace, and sofa and comfortable chairs. One with a double bed; the other, a queen. In a Flemish brick cottage, former servants' quarters, down the hill where stream can be heard—one second-floor room with double bed plus a queen foldout sofa in the keeping room, shower bath, kitchenette, living room, working fireplace, and dining area.
Breakfast: At 9. Juice, fruit, baked omelet or apple pancakes with sour cream and maple syrup, homemade biscuits, jams and syrups. In formal dining room with china, silver, and crystal. Cottage guests, too, eat breakfast in main house.
Plus: Tea or wine. Tour of house. Ponds for fishing (release catch) and ice skating. Country roads for cycling.

From Missouri: *"Homemade cookies . . . beds turned down . . . a historic and lovely house with great people."* From Maryland: *"Photographed beautiful stream, bridge, farm grounds, everything! . . . Incredible breakfast . . . quiet, private cottage—nicely restored, with enough of a rustic country look so you know you're away from the big city . . . delightful."*

Fillmore Street Bed & Breakfast   304/535-2619

Fillmore Street, Box 34   (answering service) 410/321-5634
Harpers Ferry, WV 25425-0034

Hosts: Alden and James Addy
Location: On a quiet side street in the historic area. Within walking distance of all historic attractions.
Open: Year round. Closed Thanks-

giving, Christmas, and New Year's. Advance reservations requested.
Rates: Per room. $75 full bath, $70 shower bath. "Sorry, no credit cards."
♥ ✗

From Connecticut: "It's like staying at my grandmother's—warm and very comforting." From D.C.: "Everything from the wicker furniture on the porch to the matching bed and dresser makes you feel at home." From Maryland: "Superb host and hostess. I especially loved breakfast—served by the most charming butler, waiter, PhD!"

No longer a well-kept secret, the antiques-filled Victorian with white picket fence has been home to two educators for 19 years. "We do B&B—as we have for 12 years—for fun and to make practical use of our house, which is in a wonderful area. Although most guests come to visit the Harpers Ferry National Historic Park, many come, particularly in winter, for a getaway from urban areas."

The Addys often share their interest in history, antiques, art, theater, and gardening. Fillmore Street is definitely a B&B where the hospitality is remembered at least as much as the country Victorian decor.

Bed and bath: On second floor, two air-conditioned rooms. Each has a queen bed, private adjoining bath. Larger room has bath with tub and shower; the other bath, shower only.

Breakfast: Continental (brought to guests' rooms) 8:30–10:30. Full at 9 in dining room. Juice. Fresh fruit. Sausages, herbed scrambled eggs with mushroom and/or tomato garnish, buttered rosemary potatoes, spiced applesauce, muffins and homemade preserves; or baked stuffed eggs, omelets, or baked eggs au gratin; muffin, cheese and bread souffle, steamed buttered apples, apple-rum cake or pie, or orange-cinnamon French toast. Vegetarian diets accommodated. Everything prepared without salt and with natural ingredients. Served in fireplaced dining room.

Plus: As a Pennsylvania guest wrote, "The finest details to the letter." Fresh flowers. Chocolates. Beverages. Turndown service. In-room television. Guests' upstairs sitting room/library. "Guests are free to tour the house." Garden. Will meet guests at Harpers Ferry train station.

The place to stay has become the reason to go.

The Current   304/653-4722

HC 64, Box 135, Hillsboro, WV 24946

Hosts: Leslee McCarty and John Walkup
Location: In the Allegheny Mountains, within sight of the Greenbrier River. Five miles from the Pearl S. Buck Birthplace. Near cross-country skiing and hiking in Cranberry Wilderness, Droop Mountain, and Watoga state parks.
Open: Year round. Two-night minimum on holiday weekends.
Rates: $40 single, $50 double. $15 extra person.
♥ ⬤ ⚘ ⚹

After pedaling along the incredibly beautiful Greenbrier River Trail on our first mountain-bike B&B-to-B&B trip, we approached The Current to find a hot tub on the near side, a Morgan horse farm across the way, and beyond, the spire of a white church against a mountain backdrop.

Since, Leslee and John have bought that church—"maybe for meetings or more guest rooms." Their 1905 farmhouse, owned by one family until 1985, has refinished woodwork. The furnishings and collections, arranged with flair, include John's great-grandfather's walnut and cherry bed with six-foot headboard; Leslee's grandmother's quilts; Raggedy Ann and Andy dolls; and West Virginia crafts and photographs.

The easy-to-be-with hosts met while organizing a local festival for world hunger. Since their marriage they have continued to work on benefit events, a land trust for the Greenbrier River Trail, and individual people-to-people projects too. John, a native who can trace his family's arrival in Greenbrier Valley back to about 1760, is a photographer and guitar player and runs a cattle farm that you are likely to pass "15 miles down the river." Leslee, a community activist, is a substitute teacher. (She was a hit in a Woodward & Lothrop cooking demonstration, representing B&Bs in this book.)

We left—well fed—with "don't miss" suggestions and fond memories.

In residence: Leslee's parents, retired teachers and avid golfers, are first-floor-suite summer residents. Squeaky, a German shepherd. Ross Perot, a beagle hound. Ashley, a mixed shepherd. Four outdoor cats, all named "Kitty."
Foreign languages spoken: Spanish fluently. German haltingly.
Bed and bath: Four spacious double-bedded rooms. First-floor suite has TV, private tub/shower bath. Three second-floor rooms share upstairs half bath and a first-floor tub/shower bath. Enclosed porch has two "especially nice for kids" daybeds. Rollaway bed.
Breakfast: 8–9. Omelet, quiche, or cottage cheese pancakes with strawberries. Freshly baked bread, homemade jelly, cereal, juice, fruit. Served in dining room with wood stove or in large fireplaced country kitchen.
Plus: Beverages. Wood stove makes for skiers' "hangout" dining room. Canoe and bicycle rentals arranged. Dinner (semivegetarian available) for guests ($12 per person) traveling the Greenbrier River Trail. Kitchen and laundry privileges.

Wine Cellar Bed and Breakfast

2300 Dry Creek, P.O. Box 213　(daytime answering machine) **304/743-5665**
Milton, WV 25541　　　　　　　(many evenings) **304/743-5257**

Hosts: Susan and Bob Maslowski
Location: Real country. No city lights—and not another building for a quarter of a mile. On 140 acres at the end of a state-maintained gravel road. Two miles to fast-food restaurants and to Blenko Glass Company, one of the country's few handblown glass production plants. A center-point for Midwest–to–East Coast travelers. Three miles off I-64; 30 minutes to Huntington or Charleston.

Open: Year round. Advance reservations required.

Rates: Room with half bath, $50. Other rooms, $40. MC, Visa.
♠ ♣ ♥ ♦

Yet a new version of B&B. The first floor is a showroom for Susan's wheel-thrown stoneware pottery; *pisanki* (Polish egg decorating); West Virginia crafts and wines; and Bob's wine- and beer-making supplies. On the second floor, a commercial kitchen (for special events) and the bedrooms, too, open into a big L-shaped space with dining area. It's all new construction—completed in 1993—with unfinished furniture now finished in oak or fruitwood stain.

After Bob and/or Susan welcome you, they usually sleep at home (a short distance away) and return in the morning for a breakfast "that can last for two hours!" And it's no wonder. Bob, an archaeologist with the U.S. Army Corps of Engineers, is working at a site that dates back 8,000 years. Earlier, he participated in excavations in Israel and Cyprus and did predoctoral work with the Smithsonian. Susan, one of the state's best-known potters, has worked with museums and schools and as Pumpkin Festival chairman. The native West Virginians bought "this whole head of hollow"—the very top of the hollow—in 1989, and developed the one existing structure into this modern multi-purpose building. When we last spoke, Bob declared, "At the moment we're entering our homemade wine in the state fair, and we hope to win a whole lot of prizes!" (They won five ribbons; the elderberry melomel received a blue one.)

Foreign languages spoken: Polish understood.
Bed and bath: Three second-floor rooms. Three booked only by same party; otherwise two rooms maximum. All share one shower bath. One large room with queen bed and half bath. One large room with double bed. Smaller room has single bed.
Breakfast: Until 9; continental thereafter. West Virginia sausage, biscuits and gravy, fried apples; shiitake mushroom omelet, home-cured bacon, grits; or French toast with homemade maple syrup. Sorghum coffee cake. Homemade jams, jellies, granola, hot cross buns. Served in dining area facing atrium door that leads onto porch.
Plus: Central air conditioning. Living room TV/VCR. Well water (no chlorine). Hiking trails. Quiet country roads for walking or biking. Blenko Glass Company (weekday) tour schedule.

Maxwell Bed & Breakfast   304/594-3041

Route 12, Box 197, Morgantown, WV 26505-8615

Host: Pat Keith
Location: At Ridge Way Farm, surrounded by woods and fields overlooking Cheat Lake. Two miles from U.S. 68, exit 10. Eight miles east of Morgantown and West Virginia University. Two miles to Lakeview Resort and restaurants.

Open: Year round. "Best to call in evening."
Rates: "How much? Not much!" First-floor bed/sitting room $50; disabled person 10 percent less; additional person $10. Upstairs $40 double, $30 single; suite (both rooms) $80.
♦ ♠ ✗ ⅍

If meeting people is what B&B is all about, you've come to the right place, an organic farm where Pat, a former social worker and retired rural mail carrier, raises Highland cattle and tends the garden and orchard. (It is worth staying here just to be on her annual newsletter mailing list.)

Sometimes white-tailed deer and wild turkeys wander by the "no-longer-looks-old 1895 house with down-home decor." It became a B&B—with added solar room—after Pat's mother, in her seventies then, returned from a solo worldwide trip.

In residence: Two dogs, Kate and Allie, "trained staff members who greet guests politely." One cat, Miss Pansy, "the hostess with the mostest."
Bed and bath: Three rooms. First floor—wheelchair-accessible room with queen bed, sitting area, private bath with tub, hand-held shower. Second (B&B only) floor—two cozy rooms, each with king bed, two chairs, and desk, share bath with wall-hung, hand-held shower, and a common room.
Breakfast: 6–9. Full farm breakfast varies. Juice, cereal, warm muffins. French toast; pancakes; potatoes, bacon or sausage, eggs. In season, figs, raspberries, or strawberries from the garden. Homemade applesauce, jams, and jellies. Herbal teas. Freshly ground coffees. Special diets accommodated.
Plus: Many ceiling fans. In winter snows, four-wheel-drive ride provided up the hill.

From West Virginia: *"Friendly and funny . . . a small farm that leans toward self-suffiency . . . a raised vegetable garden that any gardener would drool over. . . . Relished fireside conversation. . . . Could solve all the country's problems if given a chance. Spectacular scenery eclipsed only by the sumptuous breakfasts."* From New Jersey: *"French toast in the shape of a daisy!"* From Georgia: *"A little bit of heaven shared."*

---

*B*ed and breakfast gives a sense of place.

Thomas Shepherd Inn   304/876-3715

300 West German Street, P.O. Box 1162, Shepherdstown, WV 25443

Host: Margaret Perry
Location: Residential. At crossroads of Routes 45, 230, and 34. Minutes' walk to shops and restaurants. With landscaped yard—in the state's oldest community, which has a college-town aura, a 1738 gristmill, and not a single stoplight. Within walking distance of Chesapeake and Ohio Canal towpath (halfway mark for cyclists from Georgetown to Cumberland). Eight miles to Harpers Ferry, four to Antietam Battlefield. Ninety minutes from Washington, D.C., and Baltimore. Near antiquing, rafting, tubing.
Open: Year round. Two-night minimum on weekends and holidays.
Rates: $85 weekday, $95–$125 weekend. $10 surcharge for one-night weekend stay. $20 extra person. Business rates Sunday–Thursdays except holidays. Five percent discount for AARP members and senior citizens. Amex, Discover, MC, Visa (plus 5 percent surcharge).
♥ ♨ ⚘ ✈ ✁

"Sour cream pancakes with blueberries or maybe strawberry sauce. Nectarines poached in white wine and ginger with creme fraiche. Stuffed French toast with apricot-raisin sauce. Omelets with garden nasturtium and chive fillings. Blueberry orange soup from a guest's recipe. Sausage ricotta pancake. Austrian plum cake. Poppyseed muffins. My own peach preserves. . . . "

In the morning Margaret decides what she'll make for your breakfast, the feature of her inn. Innkeeping followed years of restoring and selling houses. When Margaret moved from Connecticut to Washington, she became a full-time culinary student at L'Academie de Cuisine, worked with caterers, and then decided to "create her own internship." In 1989 she bought this stately 1868 Federal (painted) brick house, which had been meticulously restored as a B&B by a former Foreign Service officer and his wife. They filled it with antiques and items collected from around the world. Margaret added many indoor plants and a garden of herbs and edible flowers.

In residence: Walter and Veronica, Lhasa apsos "who stay in their apartment unless asked to visit."
Bed and bath: Six rooms, all private baths. Double, queen, or a double and a twin bed; some canopied, four-posters, and sleighs. Four shower baths en suite; one hall tub/shower bath; one claw-footed tub bath. Rollaway.
Breakfast: Usually at 9. A daily creation. Served family style in two dining rooms.
Plus: Fireplaced living room. Central air conditioning. Guest phone and TV in library. Complimentary beverages. Sometimes, spontaneous treats. Treetop porch. Margaret's own potpourri. Picnic baskets ($12) or dinner with advance notice.

American white-on-white quilted coverlet, ca. 1800. A detail of this quilt appears on the cover. Photo by E. Irving Blomstrann. Courtesy Wadsworth Atheneum, Hartford, Connecticut; gift of Mrs. Frederic J. Agate.

INDEX

NORTH CAROLINA

PENNSYLVANIA

WASHINGTON, D.C.

ABOUT THE AUTHOR

Bernice Chesler, "America's bed and breakfast ambassador," has appeared on dozens of television and radio programs, including "CBS This Morning," CNN, and NPR's "Morning Edition." She is known for her personalized approach and attention to detail. Guests from all over the world write to her about their B&B experiences. She shares their impressions—and her own, gathered through hundreds of stays and extensive interviews—in her books; in Meet-the-Hosts programs conducted at such retailers as Bloomingdale's, L.L. Bean, Filene's, and Macy's; in workshops; and in lectures at universities and at bed and breakfast conferences from Maine to California.

Recipient of the nation's first B&B Achievement Award and the first B&B Reservation Service Award, the author has served on the Advisory Board of the Professional Association of Innkeepers International. She has written for 'GBH, Yankee, Country Almanac, Family Circle, and Innsider magazines and for the Boston Globe and the Washington Post.

Ms. Chesler and her husband have bicycled "slowly" from B&B to B&B in fourteen states and six countries.

BBB—Before Bed and Breakfast—Ms. Chesler conducted thousands of interviews throughout the country for documentary films seen on national public television. As publications coordinator for the Emmy Award–winning television program "ZOOM," produced at WGBH, Boston, she edited twelve books emanating from the series. She is also the author of the classic guide In and Out of Boston with (or without) Children.